SPORTS RULES ENCYCLOPEDIA

Second Edition

Jess R. White, PED
Arkansas State University

Leisure Press
Champaign, Illinois

Library of Congress Cataloging-in-Publication Data

Sports rules encyclopedia / edited by Jess R. White. -- 2nd ed.
    p.   cm.
   ISBN 0-88011-363-4
    1. Sports--Rules.   I. White, Jess R., 1929-
  GV731.S75 1989
  796--dc19   89-2280
                                        CIP

ISBN: 0-88011-363-4

Developmental Editor: June I. Decker, PhD
Production Director: Ernie Noa
Copyeditor: Laurie McGee
Assistant Editors: Robert King and Holly Gilly
Proofreader: Pamela S. Johnson
Typesetter: Angela K. Snyder
Text Design: Keith Blomberg
Text Layout: Kimberlie Henris
Cover Design: Jack Davis
Printer: Braun-Brumfield

Printed in the United States of America

10 9 8 7 6 5 4 3 2 1

Leisure Press
A Division of Human Kinetics Publishers, Inc.
Box 5076, Champaign, IL 61825-5076
1-800-342-5457
1-800-334-3665 (in Illinois)

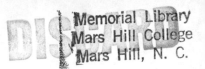

To my wife, Dorothy,
and daughters
Cynthia, Martha, and Nancy

CONTENTS

PREFACE

□

The primary purpose of this book is to provide a comprehensive source of sports rules for those who must administer programs involving multiple sports activities. Although any sport enthusiast will find the book interesting and helpful, the directors, managers, and supervisors of organized sports programs will find it invaluable in fulfilling their professional responsibilities.

All sports program directors have suffered the frustration of not having a set of rules available when they needed it and, often, not even knowing where the rules could be obtained. I realized the need for a comprehensive rules publication while I was a teacher, attempting to help professional physical education and recreation students learn various sport rules so they could conduct well-rounded programs. The best efforts of the students, even with assistance from librarians and sport professionals, produced meager results. This experience, coupled with the comments of a number of sports program directors and nationally recognized sports authorities led me to believe that probably the greatest void in the voluminous sport literature is the official rules of play. Although it might seem that such basic information would be readily available, numerous obstacles exist.

Supporting the tens of millions of Americans participating in sports activities are hundreds of national organizations concerned in some way with sports. Although all of these organizations have some code of regulations for their functions, only a few consider the development of rules of play to be a primary concern. This latter type of organization, formed for the expressed purpose of promoting a particular sport and standardizing its rules of play, has been identified here as the governing body for each sport. One or more national organizations of this nature exist for all established competitive sports, and thus this book can serve as a directory for these governing bodies, listing their names, addresses, and functions. Since some sports have more than one national organization, the official rules must be identified in regard to which organization is being recognized. Typically, a recognized governing body has earned its recognition by demonstrating credibility over years of dedicated service to the promotion of the sport. Most sports governing bodies provide services in addition to the development of the rules. Readers interested in a particular sport should contact the governing body to learn about other services.

The sizes of sports governing bodies vary, from those with permanent national headquarters and a full-time staff to those whose "headquarters" is the home address of a current elected officer. Although a few of the large governing bodies have established national networks capable of extensively distributing their rules, most organizations find this an impossible task. It has rarely been economically feasible to make single-sport rules available through regular publishing channels. As a result, sports rules have been available only directly from each governing body.

Most sport participants learn the rules of play from practical experience and word of mouth. Few of the millions who play a sport have ever seen its official rules. Although brief summaries of rules are included in various publications, they are frequently inadequate, especially for sports program directors.

The sports included in this book are widely played or traditionally recognized competitive physical activities for which standardized rules are available. Although most of the rules included here are the complete official rules, abridgement and summarizing was necessary for some sports; where modifications have been made, they are indicated clearly.

Relatively simple games that require few rules or are frequently modified by local preferences have not been included. Activities that involve animals or mechanical devices as primary elements in the performance were intentionally omitted.

The rules are arranged alphabetically by sport title. Each title contains three elements: the rules for the sport, a description of the governing body, and names and addresses of selected magazines that cover the sport. Format and style are inconsistent among sports because the rules are, for the most part, official, published rules and have not been edited. The length of the entries varies greatly according to the nature and complexity of the sports.

The closing of the gender gap reflected in many aspects of society is also present in sports rules. Separate rules for men and women have become the exception rather than the expected (although rules written in language referring exclusively to men have, again, not been edited). The occasional differences that occur are noted.

The *Sports Rules Encyclopedia* is intended to be the most comprehensive and authoritative sports rules source in print. Readers who would care to suggest improvements for the overall publication are encouraged to direct their observations to the author.

J.R.W.

ACKNOWLEDGMENTS

☐

Acknowledgment is made to the following sport governing bodies, without whose coopera-
tion this book would not be possible. A brief description and the address of each governing body follows the rules developed for each sport, beginning on the page indicated.

Amateur Athletic Union (p. 726)
Amateur Hockey Association of the United States (p. 362)
Amateur Skating Union of the United States (p. 498)
Amateur Trapshooting Association (p. 629)
American Amateur Racquetball Association (p. 432)
American Bowling Congress (p. 62)
American Canoe Association (p. 106)
American Casting Association (p. 114)
American Darts Organization (p. 197)
American Lawn Bowls Association (p. 381)
American Taekwondo Association (p. 559)
Hockey Rules Board (p. 283)
International Badminton Federation (p. 25)
Marylebone Cricket Club (p. 147)
National Archery Association of the United States (p. 15)
National Field Archery Association (p. 263)
National Horseshoe Pitchers' Association of America (p. 340)
National Intramural-Recreational Sports Association (p. 296)
National Paddleball Association (p. 405)
National Shuffleboard Association (p. 440)
The National Crossbowmen of the United States (p. 165)
United States Acrogymnastics Federation (p. 612, 638)
United States of America Amateur Boxing Federation (p. 86)
United States Croquet Association (p. 159)
United States Curling Association (p. 171)
United States Cycling Federation (p. 189)
United States Diving, Inc. (p. 213)
United States Fencing Association (p. 243)
United States Handball Association (p. 334)
United States Orienteering Federation (p. 399)
United States Paddle Tennis Association (p. 408)
United States Powerlifting Federation (p. 416)
United States Ski Association (p. 458)
United States Soccer Federation (p. 469)
United States Squash Racquets Association (p. 511)
United States Swimming, Inc. (p. 542)
United States Table Tennis Association (p. 552)
United States Team Handball Federation (p. 565)
United States Tennis Association (p. 585)
United States Volleyball Association (p. 657)
United States Water Polo, Inc. (p. 676)
United States Weightlifting Federation (p. 692)

It is not possible to acknowledge individually the many people who have contributed to the completion of this book or the previous edition, but special debts of gratitude are due to Dr. John Hosinski for summarizing the rules of baseball, basketball, football and softball; to Dr. Thomas Adams for assistance with the computer technology required for processing the manuscript; and to Teresa Brun for her dedication in keyboarding the manuscript.

I am especially indebted to Dr. George F. Cousins, professor emeritus, Indiana University, and the late Dr. Elmer D. Mitchell, University of Michigan, for their encouragement and helpful suggestions in developing the original edition of this volume.

Finally, such an undertaking would never have been possible without the support, patience, understanding, and assistance of my wife, Dorothy.

Jess R. White

• ARCHERY •

OFFICIAL NATIONAL ARCHERY ASSOCIATION TARGET RULES OF SHOOTING

(Reproduced by permission of National Archery Association*)

☐

FOREWORD

The rules contained herein govern conduct in the National Archery Association Annual Tournament, and any Federation of International Target Archery (F.I.T.A.) Star Tournament, or Tryout Tournaments, Qualifying Tournaments, as well as all Six-Gold Tournaments, officially recognized by the National Archery Association of the United States. In the event of a conflict between N.A.A. rules and F.I.T.A. rules, the F.I.T.A. rules shall prevail in all N.A.A. sanctioned tournaments.

Because local conditions may prevent elaborate field arrangements, properties, or personal usage, minimum rules are stated and allowable tolerances indicated. In the interest of uniformity, local clubs and associations are urged to adopt these rules to govern local archery competition.

Such local clubs or associations may adopt special regulations, or additional rules, providing that such additions do not conflict with, or in any way alter, any of the rules contained herein.

Decisions not regulated by the Official N.A.A. Target Archery Rules of Shooting, or by specific regulations of local clubs and associations, shall fall under the authority of the tournament officials involved.

PRIMARY RULES

SAFETY & COURTESY

Every precaution must be taken to ensure that the highest possible safety standards have precedence over all other considerations or rules. Any practices, attitudes, equipment, or conditions, which are in the least degree unsafe, are prohibited. It shall be the responsibility of every N.A.A. member to insist upon strict maintenance of safety standards at all times.

Official practice shall be from a common shooting line (for each division) and shall be controlled by whistle signals. To ensure fair enjoyment of archery competition by all contestants, a high standard of personal courtesy and sportsmanship is enjoined upon all. Discourteous and unsportsmanlike conduct is an unwarranted offense against other archers and an affront to the heritage, dignity, and tradition which is an integral part of the sport

---

*See page 15 for additional information.

of archery. Persistence in discourteous or unsportsmanlike conduct, after one warning by a tournament official, shall be considered grounds for expulsion from the tournament without a refund.

1.0 RANGE LAYOUT

1.1 The target field shall be laid out so that the shooting is from South to North. A maximum deviation of 45 degrees is allowed for N.A.A. Annual Tournaments. Local tournament deviation from this rule is allowed if required by local terrain.

1.2 The range shall be squared off and each distance accurately measured from a point vertically beneath the Gold on each target to the shooting line.

1.3 Points on the shooting line directly opposite each buttress shall be marked and numbered correspondingly.

1.4 At right angles to the shooting line (and extending from the shooting line to the target line), lines may be laid down to create lanes containing one, two, or three buttresses; *or* center lines or center point markers from the shooting line to each buttress may be used.

1.5 Each two-target lane is a minimum of 5 m wide *or* if center lines or markers are used, the minimum distance between centers is 2.5 m (see Conversion Table, page 3).

1.6 For a Star F.I.T.A., or any regional or national tournament, the shooting line shall remain stationary and the targets shall be brought forward from the longer to the lesser distances. For local tournaments the target line may remain stationary and the shooting line moved up at each distance.

1.7. Four (4) archers shall be the maximum number assigned to each target. Local, school, and club tournaments may exceed this number if absolutely necessary. The minimum number on a target shall be three (3).

1.8 A waiting line shall be indicated at least 5 m behind the shooting line.

1.9 Each target shall be set up at an angle of 15 degrees plus or minus 3 degrees.

1.10 Buttresses shall be pegged securely to the ground, to prevent their being blown over by wind. Any portion of a buttress likely to damage an arrow shall be covered.

1.11 Each target shall be numbered. The numbers (30 cm sq.) shall be clearly visible from 90 m and shall be attached either above or below the center of each buttress so as to be clear of the target face. At local tournaments, target numbers may be attached to the right leg of the target stand.

1.12 The center of the gold shall be 130 cm plus or minus 5 cm (or 51″ plus or minus 2″), above the ground.

1.13 At least every third target shall have wind flag of a color easily visible from 90 m and mounted at least 40 cm above the top of the target. The size of the flag shall be from 25 to 30 cm square. Local tournaments may deviate from this rule. However, at a Star F.I.T.A. or a Qualifier, there shall be a wind flag on every target.

1.14 Suitable barriers shall be erected around the field to keep spectators off the shooting area. Such barriers should be at least 10 m behind the waiting line, at least 10 m away from each side of the field, as far beyond the target base line as necessary to prevent members of the public from moving into the archer's line of vision or shooting.

1.15 The organizing committee shall provide lights, plates, or flags to be used for time control. Sufficient numbers of these items shall be provided so that they are clearly visible to the shooters.

1.16 Recommended—a raised platform for the Director of Shooting.

1.17 Recommended—a loudspeaker system for use of the Director of Shooting.

1.18 Recommended—sufficient chairs or benches behind the waiting line for all competitors, Team Captains, and other officials.

Conversion Table

Centimeters-Meters	Yards	Feet	Inches
1 centimeter			0.3937
80 centimeters			31.50
122 centimeters			48.00
1 meter		3	3.37
5 meters	5	1	4.85
30 meters	32	2	5.10
50 meters	54	2	0.50
60 meters	65	1	10.20
70 meters	76	1	7.90
90 meters	98	1	3.30

2.0 TARGET FACES

(a) Description:

There are two standard circular target faces: 122 cm and 80 cm diameters. Both these faces are divided into 5 concentric color zones arranged from the center outwards as follows: Gold (yellow), Red, Light Blue, Black, and White. Each color is in turn divided by a thin line into 2 zones of equal width, thus making in all 10 scoring zones of equal width measured from the center of the Gold:

6.1 cm on the 122 cm target face

4 cm on the 80 cm target face

Such dividing lines, and any dividing lines which may be used between colors, shall be made entirely within the higher scoring zone in each case.

Any line marking the outermost edge of the White shall be made entirely within the scoring zone.

The width of the thin dividing lines as well as the outermost line shall not exceed 2 mm on both the 122 cm and the 80 cm target faces.

The center of the target face is termed the "pinhole" and shall be indicated by a small "x" (cross), the lines of which shall not exceed 2 mm.

(b) Scoring Values and Color Specifications:

Scoring Values Zone	Colors	Munsell Color Scale Notations
Inner 10	GOLD/YELLOW	5Y 8/12
Outer 9		
Inner 8	RED	8.3R 3.9/13.5
Outer 7		
Inner 6	LIGHT BLUE	5B 6/8
Outer 5		
Inner 4	BLACK	N2
Outer 3		
Inner 2	WHITE	N9
Outer 1		

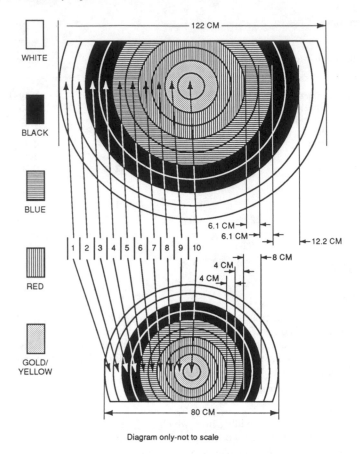

Diagram only-not to scale

(c) Tolerance of Measurements

The permissible variations in dimensions of the target face in each of the 10 zones shall be measured by the diameters of each separate circle enclosing each of the 10 zones. The tolerance of each such diameter shall not exceed plus/minus 3 mm on the 122 cm target face and plus/minus 2 mm on the 80 cm target face; i.e., measured through the center outwards:

Zone	Diameters 122 cm face	Tolerance plus/minus	Diameters 80 cm face	Tolerance plus/minus
10	12.2 cm	3 mm	8 cm	2 mm
9	24.4	3	16	2
8	36.6	3	24	2
7	48.8	3	32	2
6	61.0	3	40	2
5	73.2	3	48	2
4	85.4	3	56	2
3	97.6	3	64	2
2	109.8	3	72	2
1	122	3	80	2

(d) Size of Target Faces at Different Distances

For distances of 90, 70, and 60 meters, the Target Face of 122 cm shall be used.

For distances of 50 and 30 meters, the Target Face of 80 cm shall be used. The size of the buttress, whether round or square, must not be less than 124 cm in any direction to ensure that any arrow hitting the buttress and touching the outermost edge of the target face remain in the buttress.

3.0 ARCHER'S EQUIPMENT

This article lays down the type of equipment archers may use when shooting either F.I.T.A. or N.A.A. events. Items of equipment not mentioned in this article are not allowed without prior approval of the N.A.A. Board of Governors.

3.1 A *bow* of any type may be used provided it subscribes to the accepted principle and meaning of the word "bow" as used in target archery; e.g., an instrument consisting of a handle (grip), riser, and 2 flexible limbs each ending in a tip with a string nock.

The bow is braced for use by a single bowstring attached directly and in operation is held in 1 hand by its handle (grip), while the fingers of the other hand draw, hold back, and release the string.

3.2 A *bow string* may be made by any number of strands of the material chosen for the purpose, with a center serving to accommodate the drawing fingers, a nocking point to which may be added serving(s) to fit the arrow nock as necessary, and to locate this point *1 or 2 nock locaters may be positioned*. In each of the 2 ends of the bow string, a loop may be made to be placed in the string nocks of the bow when braced. In addition, 1 attachment, which may not exceed a diameter of *1 centimeter* in any direction, is permitted on the string to serve as a lip or nose mark.

The serving on the string must not end within the archer's vision at full draw.

A bow string must not in any way offer aid in aiming through peephole marking or any other means.

3.3 An arrowrest, which can be adjustable, any movable *Pressure Button*, *Pressure Point*, or *Arrowplate* and *Draw Check Indicator* may be used on the bow provided they are not electric or electronic and do not offer any additional aid in aiming.

3.4 A *bow sight*, a bowmark, or a point of aiming are permitted, but at no time may more than 1 such device be used.

(a) A bow sight as attached to the bow for the purpose of aiming may allow for windage adjustment as well as elevation setting for aiming, but it is subject to the following provisions:

1. It shall *not* incorporate a prism or lens or other magnifying, leveling or electric devices, nor shall it provide more than one (1) sighting point.

2. For Star F.I.T.A. and Qualifying Tournaments the length of any sight (ring, barrel, conical, hood, etc.) shall not exceed the minimum inside diameter of the aperture. A hood is not to exceed a length of 1 cm, irrespective of shape.

3. An attachment to which the bow sight is fixed is permitted.

(b) A bowmark is a single mark made on the bow for the purpose of aiming. Such mark may be made in pencil, tape, or any other suitable marking material.

A plate or tape with distance marking may be mounted on the bow as a guide for marking, but must not in any way offer any additional aid.

(c) A point of aim on the ground is a marker placed on the shooting line and the target. Such marker may not exceed a diameter of 7.5 cm and must not protrude above the ground more than 15 cm.

3.5 *Stabilizers* on the bow are permitted provided they do not:

serve as a string guide;

touch anything but the bow;

represent any obstacle to other archers as far as place on the shooting line is concerned.

(The term "stabilizer" shall also include counterbalancing weights.)

3.6 *Arrows* of any type may be used provided they subscribe to the accepted principle and meaning of the word "arrow" and as used in target archery, and that arrows do not cause undue damage to target faces and buttresses.

An arrow consists of nock, shaft, and arrow head (point) with fletching and, if desired, cresting.

Each archer's arrows shall be marked *with the archer's name, initials, or insignia*, and shall have the same color(s) of fletching, nock, and cresting.

3.7 *Finger protection* in the form of finger stalls on tips, gloves, shooting tab, or tape (plaster) to draw, hold back and release the string are permitted, provided they are smooth with no device to help hold and/or release the string.

A separator between the fingers to prevent pinching the arrow may be used.

On the bow hand, an ordinary glove, mitten, or similar item may be worn.

Shooting tabs may be built up of several layers of suitable material (such as leather, plastic, metal a.o.) to stiffen the part of the tab behind that used for drawing the string. Note: No shapes have been specified and no limitations stated with respect to size.

3.8. *Field glasses,* telescopes and other visual aids may be used for spotting arrows.

However, ordinary spectacles as necessary or shooting spectacles provided they are fitted with the same lenses normally used by the archer, and sun glasses may be worn. None must be fitted with microhole lenses, glasses or similar, nor marked in any way to assist in aiming.

3.9 *Accessories* are permitted such as bracers, dress shield, bowsling, belt or ground quiver, tassel; foot markers not protruding more than 1 centimeter.

3.10 *Changing Equipment*—If it becomes necessary for an archer to use tackle which has not been inspected by the Field Officials, the responsibility is on the archer to show such tackle to a Field Official before using it. Any competitor contravening this rule may be disqualified.

4.0 RANGE CONTROL & SAFETY

4.1 *Field Officials* shall be appointed by the Tournament Committee.

(a) A Director of Shooting (D.O.S.) shall be appointed for all tournaments (for tournaments of fewer than ten targets, he may act also as a Judge). His duties shall include:

1. Control of shooting with a whistle;

2. Ensuring the 2-1/2 minute time allowance for 3 arrows is enforced;

3. Exercising control over use of the loudspeaker;

4. Exercising control over newsmen and photographers so that the comfort and concentration of the competitors is not disturbed;

5. Seeing that spectators stay behind the restraining line at all times;

6. Seeing that Team Coaches and Managers remain behind the waiting line;

7. Being responsible for all safety precautions;

8. Act as Head Official and, in conjunction with the appointed Judges, controlling the tournament.

(b) *Judges* sufficient in number to cover the targets being used. These Judges work under the direction of the D.O.S. and their responsibilities will include:

1. Checking all distances and field set up;

2. Inspecting archer's equipment before the tournament begins and at any time thereafter during the tournament: (At the N.A.A. National Tournament this inspection shall take place the day before official scoring starts.)

3. Checking the conduct of shooting and scoring which includes making decisions on questionable arrows. The decision of the Judge on a questionable arrow shall be final;

4. Resolving disputes and queries in connection with the shooting, scoring and field equipment (targets, bows, etc.);

5. In liaison with the D.O.S., interrupting shooting if necessary, because of weather conditions, a serious accident, or like occurrence, but to ensure if at all possible, that each day's program is completed on the scheduled day.

4.2 *Whistle Signals* to be used in conjunction with light or flags as follows:

2 blasts on the whistle—archers move from waiting line to the shooting line

1 blast—signal to shoot

3 blasts—signal to score arrows

4 or more blasts—stop all shooting—emergency

4.3 Under the control of the Director of Shooting, two ends of three (3) sighter arrows are permitted preceding the commencement of shooting each day. No other trial shots in any directions are allowed on the shooting field during the days of competition. (If the rounds used in the competition are N.A.A. rounds, practice on the field may be permitted prior to and after the official round—at the option of the Tournament Committee.)

4.4 No archer may draw his bow, with or without an arrow except when standing on the shooting line.

If an arrow is used, the archer shall aim toward the target, but only after being satisfied that the field is clear both in front of and behind the targets. If, while drawing his bow with an arrow before the shooting starts or during breaks between distances, an archer looses an arrow, intentionally or otherwise, such an arrow shall count as part of the next end to be shot.

The scorer shall make a note to this effect on the archer's scoresheet and enter the values of all hits for that end (3, 5, or 6 arrows as the case may be), but the highest scoring arrow will be forfeited.

This also applies to sighter arrows shot before or after the signal indicating the 2-1/2 minute allowed to shoot an end of three arrows. Such action must be initialled by the D.O.S. or one of the Judges *and* the archer concerned.

4.5. While shooting is in progress, only those archers whose turn it is to shoot may be on the shooting line. All other archers shall remain behind the waiting line with their tackle. After an archer has shot his arrows, he shall retire behind the waiting line immediately. (He may not spot his last arrow before leaving the line.)

4.6 No archer or official may touch the tackle of any archer without the latter's consent.

4.7 An archer who arrives after the shooting has started shall forfeit the number of arrows already shot, unless the D.O.S. is satisfied that he was delayed by circumstances beyond his control, in which case he may be allowed to make up the arrows lost after the distance then being shot has been completed.

4.8 The Director of Shooting has the authority to extend the 2-1/2 minute time limit in exceptional circumstances. The most common occurrences and procedures are listed below.

In any other unforeseen instance, the D.O.S., in conjunction with the Judges, shall make and announce their decision to the competitors. This decision is final.

Bounce-Outs—When a bounce-out occurs, the archer shooting the bounce-out will tell the archer shooting with him. The other archer will stop shooting, but remain on the shooting line, while the archer who had the bounce-out finishes his end. Both will then raise their bows overhead. An official will respond to the signal, and will signal the D.O.S. who then announces the problem and the number of arrows to be shot by the archer who did not complete the end.

After the official and the archer who shot the bounce-out have scored the arrow and returned behind the shooting line, the archer with arrows to shoot will be signalled by the D.O.S. to go to the line and shoot when the signal is given. A time limit of 50 seconds will be given for each arrow to be shot.

Equipment Failure—An archer with equipment failure will step back from the shooting line and raise his bow overhead. The other archer will continue shooting the end. At the completion of the end (3 arrows), the official responding to the signal will signal the D.O.S., who will make an announcement and the numbers of arrows to be shot. Upon completion of repairs, the D.O.S. will signal the archer to complete the end, allowing 50 seconds for each arrow. No other archer may occupy the line at this time.

Repairs must be completed within 5 minutes of completion of the end in progress when the failure occurred. The timing of this interval will be the responsibility of the Director of Shooting.

The Hanging Arrow—The archer who shot a hanging arrow will advise the other archer on his target and both will step back from the shooting line with bows held overhead. An official will respond and stop the shoot. The D.O.S. will make an announcement. The official and the archer who shot the hanger will advance to the target, score the arrow and remove it, following the same procedure as with a bounce-out. Fifty (50) seconds will be allowed for each remaining arrow to be shot.

Pass-Through—If noted from the shooting line, it is handled the same way as a bounce-out.

Trouble at the Target, such as loose target face, fallen flag, etc.—Both archers will stop shooting, step back from the shooting line and signal official by raising bows overhead. The official will stop the shoot. The D.O.S. will make an announcement. Shooting will resume when officials have corrected the problem.

4.9 When time control is used, archers may not raise the bow arm until the signal for shooting to begin is given; i.e., when the light changes to green and/or the whistle is blown.

5.0 SHOOTING

5.1 Initial target assignments may be made according to any system designated by the Tournament Officials. Normal procedure is in the order of registration. There shall not be less than 3 or more than 4 archers assigned to each target in use. Four (4) is the optimum number. (Schools, club and local tournaments may increase the maximum to 6 if necessary.)

5.2 Archers shall be reassigned targets after each round on the basis of their total score for the rounds completed. At Olympic Tryouts, there is no target reassignment.

5.3 The Director of Shooting shall control shooting and ensure the observance of the 2-1/2 minute time allowance for an end of 3 arrows. Any arrow shot either before the signal or after the signal indicating the time limit will forfeit the highest scoring arrow for that end of 3, 5, or 6 as the case may be.

5.4 The Director of Shooting shall control shooting with a whistle. (See Art. 4.2 and 4.3) If shooting is suspended during an end for any reason, 1 blast on the whistle will be the signal for shooting to recommence.

5.5 Except for persons who are permanently disabled, archers shall shoot from a standing position and without support, with 1 foot on each side of the shooting line, or marker.

5.6 Whenever 2 archers are shooting together, neither shall stand closer than 18 inches (46 cm) from either the center marker nor the side boundary markers.

5.7 An arrow shall not be deemed to have been shot if: the archer can touch it with his bow without moving his feet from their position in relation to the shooting line; or the target face or butt blows over (in spite of having been fixed and pegged down to the satisfaction of the Field Officials).

The Field Officials will take whatever measures they deem necessary to compensate the adequate time for shooting the relevant number of arrows.

5.8 While an archer is on the shooting line, he shall receive no assistance nor information, by work or otherwise, from anyone, other than for the purpose of making essential changes in equipment.

6.0 SCORING

6.1 Two (2) archers on each target shall act as scorekeepers and shall verify that scores agree after each end.

6.2 At 90, 70, and 60 meters, scoring may take place after every end of 3 arrows or every second end (6 arrows). At 50 and 30 meters, scoring shall always take place after each end of 3 arrows. (Local or club shoots may modify this rule.)

For rounds other than F.I.T.A., scoring shall take place after either 5 or 6 arrows have been shot.

6.3 Scorers shall enter the value of each arrow on the scoresheets as called out by the archer to whom the arrows belong. Other archers on that target shall check the value of each arrow called out.

6.4 Neither the arrows nor the face shall be touched until all the arrows on that target have been recorded.

6.5 An arrow shall be scored according to the position of the shaft in the target face.

6.6 If more than 3 arrows (5 or 6 as the case may be), belonging to the same archer, should be found in the target or on the ground in the shooting lanes, only the 3 lowest (5 or 6 as the case may be), in value shall be scored. Should an archer be found to repeat this, he/she may be disqualified.

6.7 Should the shaft of an arrow touch 2 colors, or touch any dividing line between scoring zones, that arrow shall score the higher value of the zones affected.

Should a fragment of a target face be missing (including a dividing line, or where 2 colors meet), then an imaginary line shall be used for judging the value on any arrow that may hit such a part.

6.8 Unless all arrow holes are suitably marked on each occasion when arrows are scored and drawn from the target, arrows rebounding from the target face shall not be scored. (Local clubs or schools may elect to count rebounds from the scoring face as 7 points if holes have not been marked, providing the rebound has been witnessed.)

6.9 An arrow hitting:

(a) the target and rebounding, shall score according to its impact on the target. (See 6.8 above)

(b) another arrow and remaining embedded therein, shall score according to the value of the arrow struck.

(c) another arrow, and then hitting the target face after deflection, shall score as it lies in the target.

(d) another arrow, and then rebounding from the target, shall score the value of the struck arrow, provided the damaged arrow can be identified.

(e) the target face after rebounding off the ground, shall not score.

(f) a target other than the archer's own target, shall not score.

(g) and passing through the target shall score according to the value of the unmarked hole. (See 6.8 above)

6.10 The Director of Shooting will ensure that, after scoring, no arrows are left in the target before any signal is given to recommence. If this inadvertently happens, the shooting shall not be interrupted.

An archer may shoot that end with other arrows, or make up the arrows lost, after shooting over that distance has been completed. In such circumstances, one of the Judges shall participate in the scoring after that end, making sure that the arrows which remained in the target are checked back to the archer's score sheet before any arrows are withdrawn from the target.

6.11 In the event of an archer leaving arrows; e.g., on the ground in the target area, he may use others provided he informs the D.O.S. before shooting. The D.O.S. shall exercise such checks as he deems fit in such circumstances.

6.12 An archer may delegate authority to score and collect arrows to his Team Captain or to another archer on his own target. (In the case of a handicapped archer, he may request that someone be appointed by the D.O.S. to score and collect his arrows.)

6.13 A scoring board or some such device with the competitor's name and/or target number is permitted for displaying progressive total scores after each end. When such a device is used, it shall be placed below each buttress *or* behind the waiting area. It must be pegged to the ground so that it will not move from the wind. It shall be changed by the scorer appointed and aided by the archers on that target after the arrows have been scored and drawn.

6.14 Score sheets shall be signed by the scorer and the archer, denoting that the archer agrees with the score, and thereafter no claim may be made to alter the score. If the scorer is participating in the shooting, his score sheet shall be signed by some other archer on the same target.

6.15 In the event of a tie in score, the results shall be determined as follows:

(a) For individuals:

Of those tying, the archer with greatest number of scoring hits.

If this is also a tie, then the archer of those tying with the greatest number of 10s. If this is also a tie, then the archer with the greatest number of 9s. Should this be tied, then the archers shall be declared equal.

(b) For teams:

Of those tying, the team with the archer having the highest individual score. If this is also a tie, then the team (of those tying) with the archer having the highest second score. If this is also a tie, then the teams shall be declared equal.

7.0 APPEALS AND DISPUTES

7.1 In the case of questionable arrows, either the scorers or the participants shall refer any question about the value of an arrow in the target to a Judge before the arrows are drawn. (See Art. 4.1b)

7.2 A mistake on a score sheet, discovered before the arrows are drawn, may be corrected, but the correction must be witnessed and initialed by one of the Judges and the archer concerned before the arrows are drawn. Any other disputes concerning entries on a score sheet shall be referred to a Judge by the archer.

7.3 Should a target face become unreasonably worn or otherwise disfigured, or should there be any complaint about field equipment, an archer may appeal to a Field Official to have the defective item repaired or replaced.

7.4 Questions concerning the conduct of the shooting or the conduct of a competitor shall be lodged with the Director of Shooting the same day.

7.5 In the event of a competitor not being satisfied with a ruling given by a Field Official, he may, except as provided in 7.1, appeal in writing to the Tournament Committee.

8.0 ELIGIBILITY AND CLASSIFICATION

8.1 Archers shall be classed in the following groups:

Men	18 years old or over
Ladies	18 years old or over
Intermediate Boys	15 to 18 years old
Intermediate Girls	15 to 18 years old
Junior Boys	12 to 15 years old
Junior Girls	12 to 15 years old
Cadet Boys and Girls	less than 12 years old

8.2 An archer must shoot in the highest class if the official start of the tournament shall be on or after the birthday which places him in the higher class.

8.3 An archer may by choice compete in a higher class and may also by choice return to his established class provided the choice is made before scoring begins. However, an archer may not shoot in a lower class.

8.4 No archer shall be barred from a tournament because of a physical handicap unless his or her shooting requires mechanical aids which, in the judgment of the Field Officials, would give him undue advantage over other archers, or if his or her participation makes it impossible for archers sharing the target to operate under the time sequence.

9.0 TARGET ARCHERY CHAMPIONSHIP ROUNDS

All N.A.A. Approved Championship rounds will use the 10-ring face and be scored from the center out: 10, 9, 8, 7, 6, 5, 4, 3, 2, 1.

Shooting shall be in one direction only and will commence at the longest distance and finish at the shortest distance. If a F.I.T.A. Round is included in the program, it shall be shot first and may be shot in one day or over two consecutive days. If the F.I.T.A. Round is shot over two days, the two longer distances shall be shot the first day and the two shorter distances on the second day.

When a tournament includes more than 1 round, archers shall be reassigned to targets in the order of their scores after the first round is completed. (See Art. 5.2)

9.1 Men and Intermediate Boys *F.I.T.A. Round*

36 arrows @ 90 m   122 cm face
36 arrows @ 70 m   122 cm face
36 arrows @ 50 m   80 cm face
36 arrows @ 30 m   80 cm face

Ladies and Intermediate Girls *F.I.T.A. Round*

36 arrows @ 70 m   122 cm face
36 arrows @ 60 m   122 cm face
36 arrows @ 50 m   80 cm face
36 arrows @ 30 m   80 cm face

Junior Metric Round (Boys and Girls under 15 years)

36 arrows @ 60 m   122 cm face
36 arrows @ 50 m   122 cm face
36 arrows @ 40 m   80 cm face
36 arrows @ 30 m   80 cm face

Cadet Metric Round (Boys and Girls under 12 years)

36 arrows @ 45 m   122 cm face
36 arrows @ 35 m   122 cm face
36 arrows @ 25 m   80 cm face
36 arrows @ 15 m   80 cm face

9.2 900 Metric Round

30 arrows @ 60 m   122 cm face
30 arrows @ 50 m   122 cm face
30 arrows @ 40 m   122 cm face

Junior 900 Round (under 15 years)

30 arrows @ 50 m   122 cm face
30 arrows @ 40 m   122 cm face
30 arrows @ 30 m   122 cm face

Cadet 900 Round (under 12 years)

30 arrows @ 40 m   122 cm face
30 arrows @ 30 m   122 cm face
30 arrows @ 20 m   122 cm face

9.3 James D. Easton (600) Round*

20 arrows @ 60 m   122 cm face
20 arrows @ 50 m   122 cm face
20 arrows @ 40 m   122 cm face

9.4 Collegiate (720) Round

24 arrows @ 50 m   80 cm face
24 arrows @ 40 m   80 cm face
24 arrows @ 30 m   80 cm face

9.5 Collegiate (600) Round*

20 arrows @ 50 m   122 cm face
20 arrows @ 40 m   122 cm face
20 arrows @ 30 m   122 cm face

*Both these rounds have 5-arrow ends at each distance.

9.6 Indoor F.I.T.A. Round I

30 arrows @ 18 m   40 cm face

Perfect Score—300 points

9.7 Indoor F.I.T.A. Round II

30 arrows @ 25 m   60 cm face

Perfect Score—300 points

9.8 Clout Round—36 arrows

165 m—men and intermediate boys

125 m—ladies and intermediate girls

110 m—junior and cadet boys and girls

10.0 CLOUT RULES OF SHOOTING

10.1 The Clout Round consists of

36 arrows @ 165m—men and intermediate boys

36 arrows @ 125m—ladies and intermediate girls

36 arrows @ 110m—junior and cadet boys and girls

10.2 Two (2) sighter ends of 3 arrows each are permitted preceding the commencement of shooting. These shall be shot under the control of the Field Captain and shall not be scored.

10.3 The Clout target shall be circular, 15 m in diameter and shall be divided into 5 concentric scoring zones each measuring 1.5 m in width. Each dividing line shall be entirely within the higher scoring zone.

The Clout target may be marked on the ground *or* the scoring lines may be determined by a steel tape or non-stretch cord marked off at the dividing lines.

10.4 The center of the Clout Target shall be marked by a brightly colored distinctive triangular flag, the CLOUT. This flag shall not measure more than 80 cm in length and 30 cm in width. The flag is to be affixed to a round pole of soft wood, firmly fixed vertically in the ground, so that the lower edge of the flag shall not be more than 50 cm from the ground.

10.5 Scoring values of each scoring zone starting from the center outward are: 5, 4, 3, 2, 1.

10.6 Equipment (See Article 3.0)

10.7 Range Control and Safety (See Article 4.0)

10.8 Shooting (See Article 5.0)

10.9 Scoring

(a) Scoring shall take place after every second end of 3 arrows.

(b) The Field Captain shall appoint one person to hold the Clout rope, and one person for each scoring ring to collect the arrows in that ring. After all arrows are collected, they are sorted according to the archer's individual markings, and the arrows shall remain in that scoring ring until scored.

(c) Each competitor shall then call the value of his arrows, commencing with those of the highest value. The Field Captain shall check that all arrows are correctly called. Arrows must remain in or on the ground untouched until withdrawn or removed; otherwise, the arrows shall not be scored.

(d) The value of the arrows that do not stick in the ground shall be determined by the position of their points as they lie.

(e) Arrows sticking in the Clout Flag shall score 5.

(f) No archer, except the appointed arrow gatherers, shall enter the Clout Target until his name has been called to record the value of his arrows.

(g) Ties in the Clout events shall be decided as follows: First—by the least number of misses; if the tie is still undecided, then the least number of ones, and so on. Should all the arrows be the same, the archers so tying shall be declared equal.

11.0 TEAM ROUNDS

11.1 The recommended round to be used for the Team Round is the James D. Easton Round. (See Article 9.3)

11.2 An Official Team shall consist of not more than 8 archers who are active fellow members of at least 1 month's standing of an Archery Club affiliated with the N.A.A.

The scores for the 4 highest scoring archers from a team shall be used to arrive at a team total. If less than 4 archers wish to compete as a team, their scores must count as a complete team. An Official Team must be so located geographically that members may meet reasonably often for practice.

11.3 Team Shoot entries, including names, must be registered with the Secretary, or his designate, by the time announced in the program.

11.4 Groups of 4 archers who cannot qualify as an Official Team may register to compete as above, but shall not be eligible for Team Awards.

11.5 The Official Team making the highest aggregate score shall be the winner of the Team Award. The Highest Scoring Archer, whether of an Official Team or an unofficial team, shall be the individual winner.

11.6 Shooting and scoring and all rules shall be in accordance with the rules for regular target rounds, except that 1 of the 2 scorers for each target shall be from an adjacent target.

11.7 At the N.A.A. National Tournament, *State Teams* shall be recognized in the following manner. The scores of the top 4 individuals from each state in each class shall make up the State Teams. Men's and Ladies' State Teams shall be recognized at every N.A.A. National Tournament. Recognition of State Teams in other classifications shall be left to the discretion of the Tournament Committee.

12.0 ADDITIONAL REGULATIONS

12.1 The 2 F.I.T.A. Indoor Rounds are:

Round I   30 arrows @ 18 m   40 cm face

Round II   30 arrows @ 25 m   60 cm face

12.2 Target set up:

(a) The center of the Gold shall be 130 cm above the ground. If the 40 cm faces are in 2 lines—1 above the other—the center of the Gold shall be 100 cm and 160 cm, respectively, above the ground.

(b) The targets may be set up at any angle between vertical and 15 degrees, but a line of targets shall be set up at the same angle.

12.3 Shooting and scoring:

(a) Each archer shall shoot his arrows in ends of 3 arrows each.

(b) Scoring shall take place after each end of 3 arrows.

(c) A Scoring Board is permitted. (See Article 6.13 for details.)

12.4 Other rules and regulations:

(a) Target Archery Rules of Shooting shall apply *except* the 2-1/2 minute time limit may not be extended.

(b) If space does not permit, the Waiting Line requirement may be waived.

13.0 (Crossbow rules, omitted here, are covered under separate listing—Crossbow Archery.)

14.0 (Appendix, omitted here, deals with dress regulations for N.A.A. championships and recommended target archery field layout.)

GOVERNING BODY

National Archery Association of the United States, 1750 East Boulder St., Colorado Springs, CO 80909.

The National Archery Association (N.A.A.) is a Group A member of the U.S. Olympic Committee (USOC). The Association is recognized by the Federation of International Target Archery (F.I.T.A.) and the USOC for the purpose of selecting and training men's and women's archery teams to represent the USA in the Olympic Games, Pan American Games, World Championships, and other international meets. It also sponsors an annual National Championship for males and females of all ages, Junior Olympic development programs, and a College Division, including an annual Intercollegiate Championship. Local, state, and regional associations and clubs make up the N.A.A. network. Educational materials, awards programs, clinics, and consultant assistance are available through the Association.

MAGAZINES

Archery World, Winter Sports Publishing, Inc., 11812 Wayzata Blvd. No. 100, Minnetonka, MN 55343-5323

Bow and Arrow, Gallant Publishing Co., Box HH, Capistrano Beach, CA 92624

U.S. Archer, N.A.A., 1750 E. Boulder St., Colorado Springs, CO 80909

• BADMINTON •

THE LAWS OF BADMINTON
AS REVISED IN THE YEAR 1939
AND ADOPTED BY
THE INTERNATIONAL BADMINTON FEDERATION
INCORPORATING ALL AMENDMENTS
SUBSEQUENTLY ADOPTED

(Reprinted with the permission of The International Badminton Federation*)

☐

Note: Imperial measurements, some of which vary slightly from the metric measurements, are quoted in brackets and comply with the Laws.

COURT

1. (a) The court shall be laid out as in the following diagram "A" (except in the case provided for in paragraph (b) of this Law) and to the measurements there shown, and shall be defined preferably by white or yellow lines, or, if this is not possible, by other easily distinguishable lines, 40mm. (1-1/2 inches) wide.

In marking the court, the width 40mm. (1-1/2 inches) of the centre lines shall be equally divided between the right and left service courts; the width 40mm. each (1-1/2 inches each) of the short service line and the long service line shall fall within the 3.96 metre (13 feet) measurement given as the length of the service court; and the width 40mm. each (1-1/2 inches each) all other boundary lines shall fall within the measurements given.

(b) Where space does not permit of the marking out of a court for doubles, a court may be marked out for singles only as shown in diagram "B." The back boundary lines become also the long service lines, and the posts, or the strips of materials representing them as referred to in Law 2, shall be placed on the side lines.

POSTS

2. The posts shall be 1.55 metres (5 feet 1 inch) in height from the surface of the court. They shall be sufficiently firm to keep the net strained as provided in Law 3, and shall be placed on the side boundary lines of the court. Where this is not practicable, some method must be employed for indicating the position of the side boundary line where it passes under the net, e.g., by the use of a thin post or strips of material, not less than 40mm. (1-1/2 inches) in width, fixed to the side boundary line and rising vertically to the net cord. Where this is in use on a court marked for doubles it shall be placed on the side boundary line of the doubles court irrespective of whether singles or doubles are being played.

---

*See page 25 for additional information.

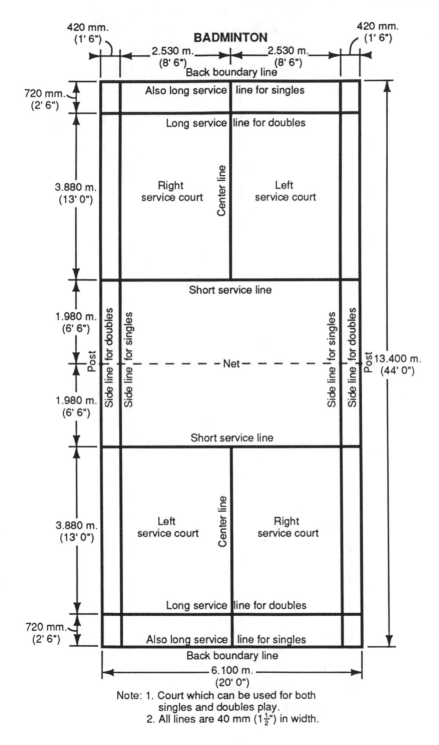

BADMINTON

420 mm. (1' 6")

420 mm. (1' 6")

2.530 m. (8' 6")   2.530 m. (8' 6")

Back boundary line

720 mm. (2' 6")

Also long service | line for singles

Long service | line for doubles

3.880 m. (13' 0")

Right service court

Center line

Left service court

Short service line

1.980 m. (6' 6")

Post

Side line for doubles

Side line for singles

Side line for singles

Side line for doubles

Post

13.400 m. (44' 0")

- - - - - - Net - - - - - -

1.980 m. (6' 6")

Short service line

3.880 m. (13' 0")

Left service court

Center line

Right service court

Long service | line for doubles

720 mm. (2' 6")

Also long service | line for singles

Back boundary line

6.100 m. (20' 0")

Note: 1. Court which can be used for both singles and doubles play.
2. All lines are 40 mm (1½") in width.

BADMINTON

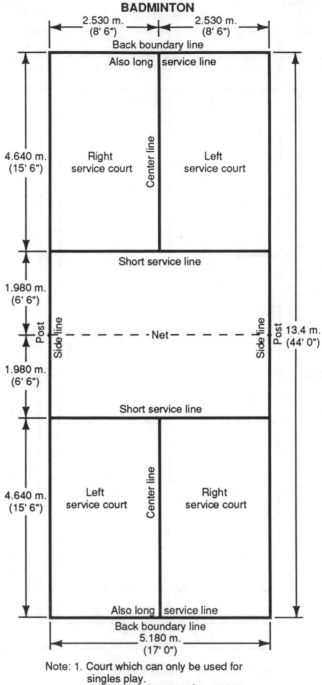

Note: 1. Court which can only be used for
      singles play.
   2. All lines are 40 mm (1½") in width.

NET

3. The net shall be made of fine natural cord or artificial fibre of a dark colour and an even thickness not less than 15mm. (5/8 inch) and not more than 20mm. (3/4 inch) mesh. It shall be firmly stretched from post to post, and shall be 760mm. (2 feet 6 inches) in depth. The top of the net shall be 1.524 metres (5 feet) in height from the floor at the centre, and 1.55 metres (5 feet 1 inch) at the posts, and shall be edged with a 75mm. (3 inches) white tape doubled and supported by a cord or cable run through the tape and strained over and flush with the top of the posts.

THE SHUTTLE

Principles

The shuttle may be made from natural, synthetic or other manufactured product or any of those combinations. The feel on the racket and the flight characteristics, generally, should be similar to those produced by the natural feathered shuttle, which has a cork base covered by a thin layer of leather.

Having regard to the principles:

4. (a) General Design

(i) The shuttle shall have 14 to 16 feathers fixed in the base.

(ii) The feathers can have a variable length from 64mm. to 70mm. (2-1/2 to 2-3/4 inches), but in each shuttle they shall be the same length when measured from the tip to the top of the base.

(iii) The tips of the feathers shall form a circle with a diameter within the range of 58mm. to 68mm. (2-1/4 to 2-5/8 inches).

(iv) The feathers shall be fastened firmly with thread or other suitable material.

(v) The base shall be

—25mm. to 28mm. (1 inch to 1-1/8 inches) in diameter

—rounded on the bottom.

(b) Weight

The shuttle shall weigh from 4.74 to 5.50 grammes (73 to 85 grains).

(c) Non-Feathered Shuttles

(i) The skirt, or simulation of feathers in synthetic or other manufactured materials, replaces natural feathers.

(ii) The base is described in paragraph 4 (a) (v).

(iii) Measurements shall be the same as in paragraph 4 (a) (i)-(iv). However, because of the difference in the specific gravity and behaviour of synthetic and manufactured materials in comparison with feathers, a variation of up to ten percent in the stated measurements is acceptable.

(d) Pace and Flight

A shuttle shall be deemed to be of correct pace when it is hit by a player with a full underhand stroke from a spot immediately above one back boundary line in a direction parallel to the sidelines and at an upward angle, to fall not less than 530mm. (1 foot 9 inches) and not more than 930mm. (3 feet 3 inches) short of the other back boundary line.

(e) Modifications

Subject to there being no variation in the general design, pace and flight of the shuttle, modifications in the above specifications may be made, with the approval of the national organization concerned:

(i) in places where atmospheric conditions due either to altitude or climate make the standard shuttle unsuitable; or

(ii) if specific circumstances exist which make it otherwise necessary in the interests of the game.

THE RACKET

4. (f) (i) The hitting surface of the racket shall be flat and consist of a pattern of crossed strings connected to a frame and alternatively interlaced or bonded where they cross—and the stringing pattern shall be generally uniform and, in particular, not less dense in the centre than in any other area.

(ii) The frame of the racket, including the handle, shall not exceed 680mm. in overall length and 230mm. in overall width.

(iii) The overall length of the head shall not exceed 290mm.

(iv) The strung surface shall not exceed 280mm. in overall length and 220mm. in overall width.

(v) The frame, including the handle, and the strings

—shall be free of attached objects and protrusions, other than those utilized solely and specifically to limit or prevent wear and tear, or vibration, or to distribute weight, or to secure the handle by cord to the player's hand, and which are reasonable in size and placement for such purposes; and

—shall be free of any device which makes it possible for a player to change materially the shape of the racket.

PLAYERS

5. (a) The word "Player" applies to all those taking part in a game.

(b) The game shall be played, in the case of the doubles game, by two players a side, and in the case of the singles game, by one player a side.

(c) The side for the time being having the right to serve shall be called the "In" side, and the opposing side shall be called the "Out" side.

THE TOSS

6. Before commencing play the opposing sides shall toss, and the side winning the toss shall have the option of:

(a) Serving first; or

(b) Not serving first; or

(c) Choosing ends.

The side losing the toss shall then have choice of any alternative remaining.

SCORING

7. (a) The doubles and men's singles game consists of 15 points provided that, when the score is 13-all, the side which first reached 13 has the option of "setting" the game to

5, and that when the score is 14-all, the side which first reached 14 has the option of 'setting' the game to 3. After a game has been 'set' the score is called 'love all', and the side which first scores 5 or 3 points, according as the game has been 'set' at 13-all or 14-all, wins the game. In either case the claim to 'set' the game must be made before the next service is delivered after the score has reached 13-all or 14-all.

(b) The ladies' singles game consists of 11 points. Provided that when the score is "9 all" the player who first reached 9 has the option of "setting" the game to 3, and when the score is "10 all" the player who first reached 10 has the option of "setting" the game to 2.

(c) A side rejecting the option of "setting" at the first opportunity shall not thereby be debarred from "setting" if a second opportunity arises.

(d) Notwithstanding paragraph (a) above, it is permissible by prior arrangement for only one game to be played and also for this to consist of 21 points, in which case "setting" shall be as for the game of 15 points with scores of 19 and 20 being substituted for 13 and 14 points, respectively.

(e) In handicap games "setting" is not permitted.

8. The opposing sides shall contest the best of three games, unless otherwise agreed. The players shall change ends at the commencement of the second game and also of the third game (if any). In the third game the players shall change ends when the leading score reaches:

(a) 8 in a game of 15 points;

(b) 6 in a game of 11 points;

or, in handicap events, when one of the sides has scored half the total number of points required to win the game (the next highest number being taken in case of fractions). When it has been agreed to play only one game the players shall change ends as provided above for the third game. In a game of 21 points, the players shall change ends when the leading score reaches 11 or in handicap games as indicated above.

If, inadvertently, the players omit to change ends as provided in this Law at the score indicated, the ends shall be changed immediately the mistake is discovered, and the existing score shall stand.

DOUBLES PLAY

9. (a) It having been decided which side is to have the first service, the player in the right-hand service court of that side commences the game by serving to the player in the service court diagonally opposite. If the latter player returns the shuttle before it touches the ground, it is to be returned by one of the "In" side, and then returned by one of the "Out" side, and so on, till a fault is made or the shuttle ceases to be "in play" (vide paragraph (b)). If a fault is made by the "In" side its right to continue serving is lost, as only one player on the side beginning a game is entitled to do so (vide Law 11), and the opponent in the right-hand service court then becomes the server; but if the service is not returned, or the fault is made by the "Out" side, the "In" side scores a point. The "In" side players then change from one service court to the other, the service now being from the left-hand service court to the player in the service court diagonally opposite. So long as a side remains "in," service is delivered alternately from each service court into the one diagonally opposite, the change being made by the "In" side when, and only when, a point is added to its score.

(b) The first service of a side in each innings shall be made from the right-hand service court. A "Service" is delivered as soon as the shuttle is struck by the server's racket. The shuttle is thereafter "in play" until it touches the ground, or until a fault or "let" occurs, or except as provided in Law 19. After the service is delivered the server and the player served to may take up any positions they choose on their side of the net, irrespective of any boundary lines.

10. The player served to may alone receive the service, but should the shuttle touch, or be struck by, his partner the "In" side scores a point. No player may receive two consecutive services in the same game, except as provided in Law 12.

11. Only one player of the side beginning a game shall be entitled to serve in its first innings. In all subsequent innings each partner shall have the right, and they shall serve consecutively. The side winning the game shall always serve first in the next game, but either of the winners may serve and either of the losers may receive the service.

12. If a player serves out of turn, or from the wrong service court (owing to a mistake as to the service court from which service is at the time being in order), and his side wins the rally, it shall be a "Let," provided that such "Let" be claimed and allowed, or ordered by the umpire, before the next succeeding service is delivered.

If a player of the "Out" side standing in the wrong service court is prepared to receive the service when it is delivered, and his side wins the rally, it shall be a "Let," provided that such "Let" be claimed and allowed, or ordered by the umpire, before the next succeeding service is delivered.

If in either of the above cases the side at fault loses the rally, the mistake shall stand and the players' positions shall not be corrected.

Should a player inadvertently change sides when he should not do so, and the mistake not be discovered until after the next succeeding service has been delivered, the mistake shall stand, and a "Let" cannot be claimed or allowed, and the players' position shall not be corrected.

SINGLES PLAY

13. In singles Laws 9 to 12 hold good except that:

(a) The players shall serve from and receive service in their respective right-hand service courts only when the server's score is 0 or an even number of points in the game, the service being delivered from and received in their respective left-hand service courts when the server's score is an odd number of points. Setting does not affect this sequence.

(b) Both players shall change service courts after each point has been scored.

FAULTS

14. A fault made by a player of the side which is "In," puts the server out; if made by a player whose side is "Out," it counts a point to the "In" side.

It is a fault:

(a) If in serving, (i) the initial point of contact with the shuttle is not on the base of the shuttle, or (ii) any part of the shuttle at the instant of being struck be higher than the server's waist, or (iii) if at the instant of the shuttle being struck the shaft of the racket be not pointing in a downward direction to such an extent that the whole of the head of the racket is discernible below the whole of the server's hand holding the racket.

(b) If, in serving, the shuttle does not pass over the net, or falls into the wrong service court (i.e., into the one not diagonally opposite to the server), or falls short of the short service line or beyond the long service line, or outside the side boundary lines of the service court into which service is in order.

(c) If the server's feet are not in the service court from which service is at the time being in order, or if the feet of the player receiving the service are not in the service court diagonally opposite until the service is delivered. (Vide Law 16).

(d) If, once the service has started, any player makes preliminary feints or otherwise intentionally baulks his opponent, or if any player deliberately delays serving the shuttle or in getting ready to receive it so as to obtain an unfair advantage. (When the server and receiver have taken up their respective positions to serve and to receive, the first forward movement of the server's racket constitutes the start of the service and such must be continuous thereafter.)

(e) If, either in service or play, the shuttle falls outside the boundaries of the court, or passes through or under the net, or fails to pass the net, or touches the roof or side walls, or the person or dress of a player. (A shuttle falling on a line shall be deemed to have fallen in the court or service court of which such line is a boundary.)

(f) If, when in play, the initial point of contact with the shuttle is not on the striker's side of the net. (The striker may, however, follow the shuttle over the net with his racket in the course of stroke.)

(g) If, when the shuttle is "in play," a player touches the net or its supports with racket, person, or dress.

(h) If the shuttle be caught and held on the racket and then slung during the execution of a stroke; or if the shuttle be hit twice in succession by the same player with two strokes; or if the shuttle be hit by a player and his partner successively.

(i) If, in play, a player strikes the shuttle (unless he thereby makes a good return) or is struck by it, whether he is standing within or outside the boundaries of the court.

(j) If a player obstructs an opponent.

(k) If Law 16 be transgressed.

(l) If a player is guilty of flagrant repeated or persistent offences under Law 22.

GENERAL

15. The server may not serve till his opponent is ready, but the opponent shall be deemed to be ready if a return of the service be attempted.

16. The server and the player served to must stand within the limits of their respective service courts (as bounded by the short and long service, the centre, and side lines), and some part of both feet of these players must remain in contact with the surface of the court in a stationary position until the service is delivered. A foot on or touching a line in the case of either the server or the receiver shall be held to be outside his service court (vide Law 14 (c)). The respective partners may take up any position, provided they do not unsight or otherwise obstruct an opponent.

17. (a) If, in the course of service or rally, the shuttle touches and passes over the net, the stroke is not invalidated thereby. It is a good return if the shuttle having passed outside either post drops on or within the boundary lines of the opposite court. A "Let" may be given by the umpire for any unforeseen or accidental hindrance.

(b) If, in service, or during a rally, a shuttle, after passing over the net, is caught in or on the net, it is a "Let."

(c) If the receiver is faulted for moving before the service is delivered, or for not being within the correct service court, in accordance with Laws 14 (c) or 16, and at the same time the server is also faulted for a service infringement, it shall be a let.

(d) When a "Let" occurs, the play since the last service shall not count, and the player who served shall serve again, except when Law 12 is applicable.

18. If the server, in attempting to serve, misses the shuttle, it is not a fault; but if the shuttle be touched by the racket, a service is thereby delivered.

19. If, when in play, the shuttle strikes the net and remains suspended there, or strikes the net and falls towards the surface of the court on the striker's side of the net, or hits

the surface outside the court and an opponent then touches the net or shuttle with his racket or person, there is no penalty, as the shuttle is not then in play.

20. If a player has a chance of striking the shuttle in a downward direction when quite near the net, his opponent must not put up his racket near the net on the chance of the shuttle rebounding from it. This is obstruction within the meaning of Law 14 (j). A player may, however, hold up his racket to protect his face from being hit if he does not thereby baulk his opponent.

21. It shall be the duty of the umpire to call "fault" or "let" should either occur, without appeal being made by the players, and to give his decision on any appeal regarding a point in dispute, if made before the next service; and also to appoint linesmen and service judge at his discretion. The umpire's decision shall be final, but he shall uphold the decision of a linesman or service judge. This shall not preclude the umpire also from faulting the server or receiver. Where, however, a referee is appointed, an appeal shall lie to him from the decision of an umpire on questions of law only.

22. Continuous Play, Misconduct and Penalties

(a) Play shall be continuous from the first service until the match be concluded except that:

(i) in international competitive events, there shall be allowed an interval not exceeding five minutes between the second and third games of all matches;

(ii) in countries where conditions render it desirable, there shall be allowed, subject to the previously published approval of the national organization concerned, an interval not exceeding five minutes between the second and third games of a match, either singles or doubles or both;

(iii) when necessitated by circumstances not within the control of the players, the umpire may suspend play for such a period as he may consider necessary. If play be suspended, the existing score shall stand and play be resumed from that point.

(b) Under no circumstances shall play be suspended to enable a player to recover his strength or wind, or to receive instruction or advice.

(c) Except in an interval provided above, no player shall be permitted to receive advice during a match or, without the umpire's consent, to leave the court until the match be concluded.

(d) The umpire shall be the sole judge of any suspension of play.

(e) A player shall not:

(i) deliberately cause suspension of play, or

(ii) deliberately interfere with the speed of the shuttle, or

(iii) behave in an offensive manner, or

(iv) be guilty of misconduct not otherwise covered by the Laws of Badminton.

(f) The umpire shall administer any breach of (e) by:

(i) issuing a warning to the offending side;

(ii) faulting the offending side, if previously warned;

(iii) in case of flagrant offence or persistent offences, faulting the offending side and reporting the offending side immediately to the Referee, who shall have the power to disqualify.

(g) Where a Referee has not been appointed, the responsible tournament official shall have the power to disqualify.

NOTE

INTERVALS IN PLAY AS SANCTIONED BY THE I.B.F.

The international competitive events referred to in (a)(i) above are:

(1) The Thomas Cup and Uber Cup;

(2) The World Championships;

(3) All official international matches;

(4) International Open Championships and other international events of a higher status as sanctioned by the I.B.F.

INTERPRETATIONS

1. Any movement or conduct by the server that has the effect of breaking the continuity of service after the server and receiver have taken their position to serve and to receive the service is a preliminary feint. For example, a server who, after having taken up his position to serve, delays hitting the shuttle for so long as to be unfair to the receiver, is guilty of such conduct. (Vide Law 14 (d)).

2. It is obstruction if a player invades an opponent's court with racket or person in any degree except as permitted in Law 14 (f). (Vide Law 14 (j)).

3. Where necessary on account of the structure of a building, the local Badminton authority may, subject to the right of veto of its national organisation, make bye-laws dealing with cases in which a shuttle touches an obstruction.

GOVERNING BODY

United States Badminton Association, 501 West Sixth St., Papillion, NE 68046

The U.S. Badminton Association (USBA) is the official governing body for the game of badminton within the United States and is a member of the International Badminton Federation. The U.S. Olympic Committee has recognized the USBA as a Class A member and thereby extended to it the authority to select U.S. participants for international competition. Badminton was an Exhibition Sport at the Seoul games in 1988 and will become a Medal Sport in the 1992 Olympics. The primary objectives of the Association are (a) to promote and develop the game of badminton, (b) to assist in the development of clubs and associations, (c) to establish and uphold rules of play and amateur status, (d) to conduct and manage all national tournaments, (e) to sanction all sectional and state championship tournaments, and (f) to act as the United States authority in all international competition.

MAGAZINES

Badminton U.S.A., USBA, 501 W. Sixth St., Papillion, NE 68046

World Badminton, International Badminton Federation, 24 Winchcombe House, Winchcombe St., Cheltenham, Glos., England, GL52 2NA

• BASEBALL •

(Rule summary by author)

□

Note: In view of the many levels of organized baseball competition and the resulting rules modifications by the various recognized governing bodies,* the basic rules of the game are summarized here.

RULE I. THE GAME, FIELD, PLAYERS AND EQUIPMENT

A. THE GAME

1. Baseball is a game involving pitching, batting, catching and throwing a ball, and running a series of bases. The game is played on a large open field between two teams of nine players each. The object of the game is to score more runs than the opponents during nine innings of play. (The number of innings is modified at various levels of play.) An inning consists of each team having the opportunity to bat and score runs before three of its batters or base runners are put out. The team at bat is referred to as the offensive team while the team in the field is referred to as the defensive team. The designated pitcher of the defensive team throws (pitches) the ball to the batter who attempts to hit the ball into the field of play, become a base runner, and advance around the bases in sequence to score a run. There are a number of ways in which the defensive team may put the batter out; the most common being: a) pitching the ball in such a manner that the batter cannot hit it; b) catching a batted ball before it strikes the ground; or c) fielding a batted ball off the ground, and throwing it to first base before the batter can run and touch the base.

B. THE FIELD

1. As illustrated in Diagram A, the overall field consists of the infield area (90 feet square with a base at each corner) and the outfield area (the large area beyond the infield and between the two foul lines). The dimensions and markings for the infield are indicated in Diagrams A and B. The distances from home plate to the outfield fence vary greatly from one ball park to another. A distance of 325 feet or more down the foul lines to the fence and rounding out to 400 feet or more in straightaway center field is recommended. A distance of 250 feet to the nearest fence is the minimum acceptable distance. All measurements are made from the back point of home plate. Field dimensions are modified for different levels of competition.

2. The dimensions for the home plate area (including batter's box, catcher's box and home plate) and pitcher's plate (mound) are illustrated in Diagram B.

3. The field should be level except that the pitcher's plate (rubber) should be 10 inches above the level of home plate with the area around the pitcher's plate uniformly sloping 1 inch per 1 foot until blending into the level surface of the field.

---

*See page 36 for additional information.

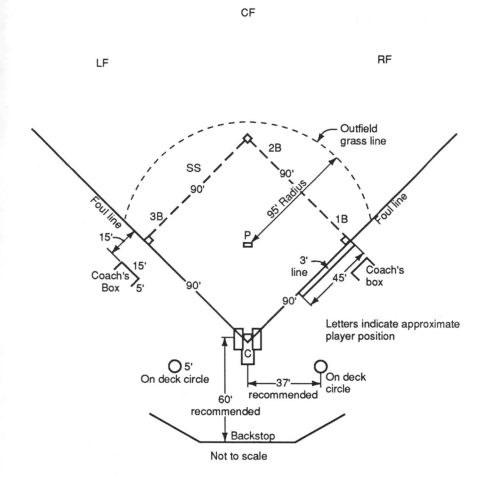

CF

LF

RF

Not to scale

4. If possible, the field should be oriented in an east-northeast direction as determined by a straight line from home plate through second base.

5. It is recommended that the backstop be 60 feet behind home plate and all bleachers, fences or other obstructions along the baselines be 60 feet away from the lines. (These dimensions are frequently modified due to space limitations.)

C. THE PLAYERS

1. The name of each player starting the game must be listed in the official scorebook in the order in which they will take their turn at bat.

2. Players are primarily identified by the position they play defensively. The customary position on the field for each of the defensive players is indicated in Diagram A. Actually, only the pitcher and catcher are restricted to a given location when the ball is put in play. The other players need only to be in fair territory.

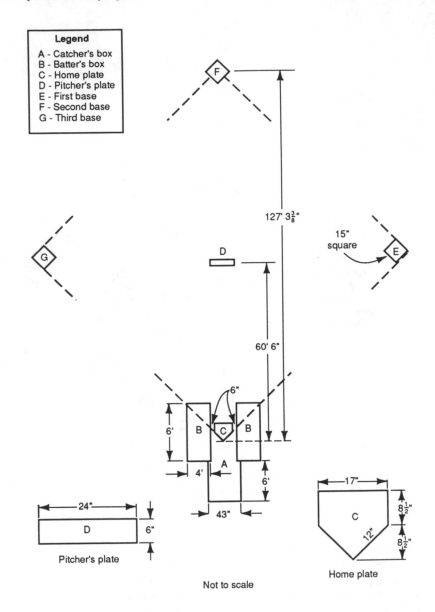

Legend
A - Catcher's box
B - Batter's box
C - Home plate
D - Pitcher's plate
E - First base
F - Second base
G - Third base

127' 3⅜"

15"
square

60' 6"

6"

6'

B   C   B

A

4'

43'

6'

24"

D

6"

Pitcher's plate

17"

C

8½"

12"

8½"

Home plate

Not to scale

3. Substitutions may be made at any time during the game when the ball is dead.

a. A substitute's place in the batting order will be the same as that of the player replaced.

b. A player who has been removed from the game may not re-enter the game. (This rule is modified in some youth league play.)

c. A player designated as the pitcher must pitch until at least one batter is put out or reaches first base.

D. EQUIPMENT

1. The official ball is a sphere not less than 9 nor more than 9-1/4 inches in circumference. The weight of the ball should not be less than 5 nor more than 5-1/4 ounces. The outer surface is covered with two panels of tightly stitched cowhide or horsehide. The stitching between the panels slightly protrudes allowing for gripping the ball tightly with the fingers.

2. The bat must be a smooth, rounded piece of wood (metal is acceptable in some competition) not more than 2-3/4 inches in diameter at the thickest part and no longer than 42 inches. As much as 18 inches of the handle may be covered with any type of material to improve the grip.

3. All fielders, other than the catcher and the first baseman, are restricted to the use of the recognized fielder's type glove. The fielder's glove shall not be more than 12 inches in length from the tip of any of the four fingers to the back edge of the glove. The width of the glove may not be more than 7-3/4 inches measured across the base of the fingers. The space between the thumb and the first finger may be closed with leather webbing.

4. The catcher may use a glove (mitt) measuring not more than 15-1/2 inches from top to bottom and not more than 38 inches in circumference.

5. The first baseman may use a glove (mitt) measuring not more than 12 inches in length and not more than 8 inches in width measured across the palm. The web between the thumb and the finger section may not be more than 4 inches wide at the top of the mitt nor more than 3-1/2 inches wide at the base of the thumb.

6. A protective helmet shall be worn by all players while batting.

7. No loose equipment (gloves, helmets, bats, etc.) shall be left anywhere (fair or foul territory) on the playing field.

8. The catcher must wear a head protector, face mask, throat protector, body protector, protective cup and shin guards.

9. All players and coaches of a team must wear the same color and style of uniform with 6 inches high or larger numbers on the back of the shirt.

RULE II. DEFINITIONS

Appeal. A claim by a player or coach that a violation or misinterpretation of the rules has occurred.

Balk. A violation of the legal pitching motion if one or more runners are on base. A called balk results in all runners advancing to the next base. (See Rule V.)

Ball. A pitch that does not pass through the defined strike zone or any illegal pitch.

Base Coach. A player or coach positioned in the designated coach's boxes for the purpose of directing the base runners.

Base on Balls. The batter is permitted to advance to first base when four pitches are judged by the umpire to be balls.

Base Path. The area bounded by an imaginary line three feet on each side of a straight line between the bases.

Batter's Box. The designated area within which the batter must stand while batting.

Bench or Dugout. The area provided for all team personnel engaged in the game, including participants, substitutes and coaches.

Bullpen. The area provided for substitute pitcher and other players to warm up while the game is in progress.

Bunt. A ball not swung at, but intentionally met with the bat to tap it slowly within the infield.

Dead Ball. A ball that is no longer in play and play is temporarily suspended.

Defense. The player or team that is in the field.

Designated Hitter. A player who is designated to bat for the pitcher. (An optional league rule.)

Double Play. A continuous play by the defense resulting in two offensive players being legally put out.

Fair Ball. A batted ball into or over fair territory which: a) settles or is touched between home and first or third bases: b) bounces past first or third base on or over fair territory; c) initially falls on fair territory beyond first or third base; d) passes out of the playing field, beyond the outfield fence, while over fair territory.

Fair Territory. The area within and including the first and third base foul lines from home plate to the outfield fence. The foul lines are in fair territory, and extend perpendicularly upward in an imaginary line.

Fielder's Choice. The decision of a fielder, when playing a ground ball to put out another base runner other than the batter.

Fly Ball. A batted ball that goes high in the air.

Force Play. The circumstance in which a ground ball play requires a runner to advance to the next base. A runner at first base must advance to second base since the batter is entitled to occupy first base. Runners at second and third bases are also required to advance if a runner from the previous base is forced to advance to the base they occupy. Fielders need only to secure the ball while touching the base with any part of their body in order for the advancing runner to be called out. Base runners are not required to advance if a fly ball is caught.

Foul Ball. A batted ball that: a) settles or is first touched by a defensive player on or over foul territory between home plate and first base or third base; b) goes past first or third base over foul territory; c) first falls on foul territory beyond first or third base; d) touches the batter, umpire or any object not part of the playing field while over foul territory; e) hits the batter while he is in the batter's box. The hitter is out if a foul fly ball is caught before touching the ground.

Foul Territory. The area of the playing field outside the first and third base foul lines and extending to the outfield fence.

Foul Tip. A batted ball that goes directly from the bat to the catcher's hands and is legally caught. It shall be called a strike and the ball is in play. It is not a foul tip unless caught.

Ground Ball. A batted fair ball that rolls along the ground.

Ground Rules. Any local rules adopted to make unusual conditions more equitable.

Illegal Pitch. The pitcher delivering a pitch to the batter without the pivot foot being properly in contact with the pitcher's plate or the pitcher making a quick return pitch before the batter is ready. (See Rule V.)

Infielder. The fielders who normally play along the base paths and around the bases.

Infield Fly. A fair fly ball hit within the fielding range of infielders when there are base runners at first and second, or first, second and third bases and less than two outs. The umpire will immediately declare an infield fly as soon as it is apparent, and the batter is automatically out. Should the ball go foul, it is played as any foul ball.

Inning. A segment of the game consisting of each team having the opportunity to bat and score runs before three of its batters or base runners are put out. Each team's time at bat is termed a half-inning.

Interference. Any obstruction of play, intentional or unintentional, that alters the course of play by impeding, hindering or confusing a player attempting to make a play.

Leading Off. Movement by a base runner in stepping from the base before the pitcher delivers the ball to the batter. (The term is also used to indicate the first batter to bat in each half-inning.)

Out. (See Rule IV-C-3.)

Outfielder. A player playing a position which is outside and beyond the baselines of the infield.

Overslide. A base runner losing contact with a base as a result of sliding past the base.

Overthrow. A thrown ball by a fielder which goes into foul territory beyond the boundary lines of the playing field.

Pick Off. An attempt to throw a runner out by throwing the ball to a fielder who must tag the runner while he is off the base. (Usually attempted by the pitcher when a runner is leading off the base.)

Pitch. The delivery (throw) of the ball by the pitcher to the batter.

Run. A score made by an offensive player who as a batter becomes a base runner and advances touching first, second, third and home bases in that order before being put out.

Run Down. A circumstance in which the defense attempts to put out a runner who is caught between bases.

Runner. An offensive player who is advancing toward, or touching, or returning to any base.

Safe. A declaration by the umpire to indicate that a runner has legally occupied the base for which he is trying.

Stretch. A legal movement by the pitcher in which, from the set position, both arms are extended approximately head high and then returned to the set position.

Strike. A legal pitch that meets any of the following conditions:

a. Is struck at by the batter and is missed.

b. Enters the strike zone in flight and is not struck at.

c. A foul not caught on the fly when there is less than two strikes. (After two strikes have been called succeeding foul balls are merely dead balls, unless the ball is caught in flight.)

d. An attempt to bunt that results in a foul.

e. Touches the batter when he swings and misses.

f. A foul tip.

Strike Out. An out made by batter who either swings and misses or foul tips a third strike, bunts a third strike foul or does not swing at a pitch which is declared a third strike by the umpire.

Strike Zone. The area over home plate between the batter's armpits and the top of his knees when he assumes his natural stance. The umpire will determine the appropriate strike zone according to the batter's customary stance.

Tag. The action of a fielder in touching a base with any part of his body while holding the ball in his hand or glove or touching a runner with the ball or with glove while holding the ball in that hand or glove.

Tag Play. During any play in which the runner is not forced to run to the base, he must be touched with the ball or the hand (glove) holding the ball to be put out.

Time (Time Out). A term used by the umpire to declare suspension of play. (See Rule IV-B-3.)

Walk. (See Base on Balls.)

RULE III. STARTING AND ENDING THE GAME

A. The team managers shall give the batting order (in duplicate) for their team to the umpire. The duplicate is given to the opposing manager.

B. To begin the game the home team is the defensive team (fielding) while the visiting team is the offensive (batting) team.

C. Play begins upon the declaration of the umpire, "Play".

D. The batting order must be followed throughout the game except that any substitute players entering the game will bat in place of the player they replaced.

E. Other than the pitcher and catcher, the fielders may take a position anywhere in fair territory. The pitcher must have one foot in contact with the pitcher's plate during the pitching motion. The catcher must be in the confines of the catcher's box until the ball is pitched.

F. The offensive team will continue to bat until three of its players are put out. When three offensive players are put out the offensive team becomes the fielding (defensive) team while the team in the field becomes the batting (offensive) team.

G. The regulation game is normally nine innings but may be shortened to seven innings by mutual consent. Should the score be tied at the end of regulation play, extra innings are played until one team has scored more runs than the other in an equal number of innings.

H. Should the umpire deem it necessary to call a game due to inclement weather, darkness, or other reasons, the game will be considered a regulation game if five innings of play have been completed. If less than five innings are played the umpire will declare the game no contest. It is not necessary for the second team at bat to bat in the fifth inning if they have already scored more runs than the opponents.

RULE IV. CONTINUING PLAY

A. BALL IN PLAY (LIVE BALL)

1. When the umpire indicates the beginning of play, the ball is considered alive and in play and remains alive and in play until it becomes dead under the rules or the umpire calls "time". While the ball is dead, no action may be taken to put a player out, no bases may be run and no runs may be scored.

2. The ball is alive and in play after the catch of a fly ball whether fair or foul.

3. A thrown ball that strikes an umpire or a coach is alive and in play.

4. Base runners may advance at their own risk at any time while the ball is in play.

B. BALL OUT OF PLAY (DEAD BALL)

1. The ball is dead and base runners must return to the base previously occupied when:

a. A foul ball is hit that is not caught.

b. An offensive player, coach, or umpire interferes with a defensive player's attempt to make a throw.

c. A runner or umpire is struck by a fair hit ball before the ball passes all infielders who have a reasonable chance to make a play other than the pitcher. If a batted ball strikes a runner or umpire after it has passed a fielder, other than the pitcher, the runner is not out and the ball continues in play.

2. The ball is dead and base runners are permitted to advance one base when:

a. There is any interference with a thrown ball or the catcher interferes with the batter.

b. The pitcher commits a balk.

c. A batter is hit (including his clothing) by a pitched ball while in batting position. Base runners also advance, if forced.

d. A fielder interferes with a runner.

3. The ball is dead and base runners are permitted to advance two bases when:

a. A fair ball bounces or is deflected into the stands along the first or third base foul lines.

b. A wild throw goes into the stands, through a fence, or lodges in some obstruction. (Local ground rules for this rule are normally agreed upon before the game begins.)

4. The ball is dead and base runners are permitted to advance three bases when:

a. A fielder throws and touches a thrown ball with his cap, glove, or other object.

5. The umpire may suspend play when:

a. In his opinion the weather, ground condition or light conditions become unsuitable for play.

b. Play is disrupted by spectators or other unusual occurrences.

c. He desires to examine equipment or give instructions in carrying out his duties.

d. Time is requested for a substitution, a conference with the pitcher, or other legitimate causes.

C. BATTING

1. Each player of the side at bat will bat in the order that his name appears in the designated batting order. Note: A designated hitter, as permitted in some league play, is a player designated to bat for the starting pitcher and all subsequent pitchers and may be placed in any position in the batting order.

2. A batter continues to bat until he either hits the ball and becomes a base runner, strikes out, or is awarded a base on balls. (See definitions of terminology.)

3. A batter is out when:

a. He fails to bat in the proper order. (Must be appealed by the opponents before the wrong batter completes the turn at bat.)

b. After hitting a fair ground ball, he or first base is tagged before he reaches that base.

c. He hits a fly ball fair or foul, and it is caught by a fielder.

d. A third strike is caught by the catcher or, if not caught, first base is occupied with less than two out.

e. On a third strike which is not caught, the runner does not reach first base before he or the base is tagged with the ball. He will also be called out if no attempt is made to run.

f. The ball is bunted foul on the third strike.

g. An infield fly is called.

h. A fair ball touches him before touching a fielder.

i. He interferes with a hit or bunted ball or with a fielder attempting to make a play.

j. Running to first base he runs outside the three-foot restraining line or inside the foul line and, in so doing interferes with the fielder taking the throw at first base. (It is permissible to go outside these lines to avoid a collision with a fielder attempting to field a batted ball.)

4. The batter becomes a base runner when:

a. He hits the ball into fair territory.

b. Four balls are called by the umpire.

c. A third strike is dropped unless there is a runner on first and less than two outs.

d. He is hit by a pitched ball at which he is not attempting to strike. (The batter must make an effort to avoid being hit.)

e. The catcher interferes with the batter's swing.

f. A fielder interferes with a batted fair ball by throwing his glove, cap, or other objects at the ball.

5. The base runner:

a. Must touch each base in order (first, second, third, and home) and must retouch the bases in reverse order when it is necessary to return to a base while the ball is in play.

b. Is entitled to an unoccupied base if he touches it before being put out. The runner continues to be entitled to a base until he is put out or advances one or more bases under the following conditions:

(1) Forced to vacate a base because the following runner must move to that base.

(2) The pitcher commits a balk.

(3) A fielder interferes with the progress of the runner.

(4) Is awarded one base if the pitcher makes a wild throw which goes into the stands, or over or through a fence.

(5) Is entitled to two bases if a fair ball bounces over or passes through a fence (unless local ground rules stipulate otherwise) or if a fair ball bounces into foul territory outside the playing field and goes out of the field of play.

(6) Is entitled to two bases if a thrown ball goes into a dugout or out of the field of play.

6. A base runner is out when:

a. He runs out of the base paths, more than three feet from a direct line between bases, to avoid being tagged. (Running out of the base path to avoid collision with a fielder is not a violation.)

b. He is tagged with the ball while he is off the base. He may run past first base without jeopardy if no move is made to continue to second base.

c. He interferes with a throw or thrown ball or hinders a fielder who is attempting to field a batted ball. (Contact is allowable (as in sliding into a base) if the runner is on the ground at the time, however actions such as a cross-body block or kicking the fielder is not permitted. The raised leg during a slide must be no higher than the fielder's knee when the fielder is in a standing position.) The interpretation of this rule varies with league play.

d. He is given any physical assistance by a coach or teammate.

e. There is any interference with the play by coaches or teammates of the runner.

f. He passes a preceding runner.

g. He fails to touch a base or home plate and makes no attempt to return to the base, and a fielder touches the base while holding the ball and appeals to the umpire.

h. An appeal is made to the umpire that the runner did not retouch a base before advancing, after a fair or foul fly ball is caught.

i. He fails to return to a base, after a fair or foul ball is caught and a defensive player in possession of the ball either touches him or the base.

RULE V. PITCHING

A. PITCHING POSITIONS

1. The pitch may be made from one of two legal pitching positions ("windup" and "set"). Either position may be used at any time.

a. In the windup position, the pitcher shall stand facing the batter with his pivot foot touching the rubber and the other foot free. The pitch must be made in a continuous uninterrupted fashion once an obvious movement to begin the pitch is made. Neither foot shall be raised from the ground, except that in the actual delivery of the ball to the batter, one step backward and one step forward may be taken with the free foot. Before actually beginning the pitching motion, the pitcher may remove the pivot foot from the rubber with a backward step. With pivot foot removed from the rubber he may make movements toward any base.

b. In the set position, the pitcher stands facing the batter, with his pivot foot touching the pitcher's rubber and the free foot in front of the pitcher's rubber while holding the ball in both hands in front of his body no higher than the chin. In the "set" motion, the pitcher must come to a complete stop before the ball may be delivered to the batter. From this position the pitcher may either: a) deliver the ball to the batter; b) step toward and throw the ball to first base if occupied by a runner or step toward and throw (or feint a throw) to second or third bases if occupied; or c) remove the pivot foot from the rubber with a backward step. After assuming the set position, any motion indicating intent to deliver the ball to the batter must be completed without interruption.

B. PITCHING VIOLATIONS

1. The pitcher may not:

a. Make an illegal pitch or quick pitch.

b. Apply any substance to the ball or in any way deface the ball. (This rule is not designed to prohibit the pitcher from touching his mouth, however, he must wipe his hand off prior to touching the ball.)

c. Intentionally pitch at the batter.

d. Wear any garment or attach anything to his uniform or glove which may in any way be distracting to the batter.

C. BALKS

1. A balk may be called on the pitcher for any of the following violations:

a. Pitching the ball when not in contact with the rubber.

b. Any feinting or false motion (without completing the throw) from the pitching position toward the batter or toward first base when it is occupied by a runner.

c. Dropping the ball when in contact with the pitching rubber.

d. Making a quick pitch.

e. Throwing to any base from the set position in an attempt to retire a runner without first stepping directly toward that base.

f. Pitching from the set position without coming to a complete stop.

g. Making a feinting motion as if to pitch the ball when actually not holding the ball.

h. Pitching the ball when the catcher is not legally in the catcher's box.

i. Throwing to an unoccupied base.

j. Attempting to deceive a base runner by being on or near the mound without the ball.

RULE VI. SCORING

A detailed system scoring (recording) the progress of a baseball game has been standardized and is included as part of the official rules. The system provides for a detailed accounting of each put out, hits, advancement of base runners and runs scored.

It is the responsibility of the home team to provide an Official Scorer for the game. The Official Scorer should sit in the press box or stands (if necessary) and not near or in a dugout. The Scorer shall keep the necessary batting, fielding, pitching and other game statistics that are vital for game continuity and record keeping. The Scorer will provide information as requested from the umpire.

GOVERNING BODIES

All American Amateur Baseball Association, 1481 Franklin St., Johnstown, PA 15905

American Amateur Baseball Congress, 215 East Green St., Marshall, MI 49068

(DIVISIONS: Stan Musial, Connie Mack, Mickey Mantle, Sandy Koufax, Pee Wee Reese, Willie Mays)

American Legion Baseball, P.O. Box 1055, 700 N. Pennsylvania St., Indianapolis, IN 46206

Babe Ruth Baseball, P.O. Box 5000, 1770 Brunswick Ave., Trenton, NJ 08638

Little League Baseball, P.O. Box 3485, Williamsport, PA 17701

National Association of Intercollegiate Athletics, 1221 Baltimore St., Kansas City, MO 64105

National Baseball Congress, P.O. Box 1420, Wichita, KS 67201

National Collegiate Athletic Association, P.O. Box 1906, Nall Ave. at 63rd St., Mission, KS 66201

National Federation of State High School Associations, P.O. Box 20626, 11724 Plaza Circle, Kansas City, MO 64195

Pony Baseball, P.O. Box 225, Washington, PA 15301

(Mustang, Bronco, Pony, Colt)

United States Baseball Federation, 4 Gregory Drive, Hamilton Square, NJ 08690

(Recognized by the United States Olympic Committee [USOC] as the governing body for amateur baseball in the United States.)

MAGAZINES

Athletic Journal, Athletic Journal Publishing Co., 1719 Howard St., Evanston, IL 60202

Scholastic Coach, Scholastic Coach, Inc., 730 Broadway, New York, NY 10003

• BASKETBALL •

(Rules summary by author)

☐

Note: In view of the many levels of organized basketball competition and the resulting rules modifications by the various recognized governing bodies,* the basic rules of the game are summarized here.

RULE I. GAME, COURT AND EQUIPMENT

A. THE GAME

1. The game is played between two teams of 5 players each on a rectangular court with a goal at each end. Free substituting is permitted anytime the ball is dead and the clock is stopped.

2. The object of each team is to score points by shooting (throwing) the ball into its own goal (basket) and in turn, to prevent the opponents from scoring goals. The ball may be passed, thrown, tapped, rolled or dribbled (subject to the provisions of the rules) as a team advances the ball for a shot at the basket.

3. The game begins with a jump ball at the center court circle. The Referee tosses the ball into the air between the two opposing centers who attempt to tap the ball to a teammate.

4. The team in possession (control) of the ball advances the ball toward its own goal and, at an opportune time, attempts to score a basket. If the basket is scored, the opposing team is given possession of the ball out of bounds behind the end line. If the shot at the basket is missed, the rebound off the goal and/or backboard is a free ball and possession may be obtained by either team. The offensive team may lose possession of the ball as a result of mishandling the ball or committing violations of the rules. The offensive team is permitted to retain possession of the ball and/or shoot free throws (unmolested opportunity to score) when fouled (illegally obstructed) by the defensive team.

B. THE COURT

1. See Diagram A for playing court markings and dimensions.

C. BACKBOARDS AND BASKETS

1. See Diagram B for dimensions of backboards and baskets.

D. THE BALL

1. The ball is spherical with an outer surface of leather, rubber or synthetic material. The circumference of the ball is 29-1/2″ minimum to 30″ maximum. The weight should not exceed 22 ounces or be less than 20 ounces. The ball is inflated to a pressure which

---

*See page 48 for additional information.

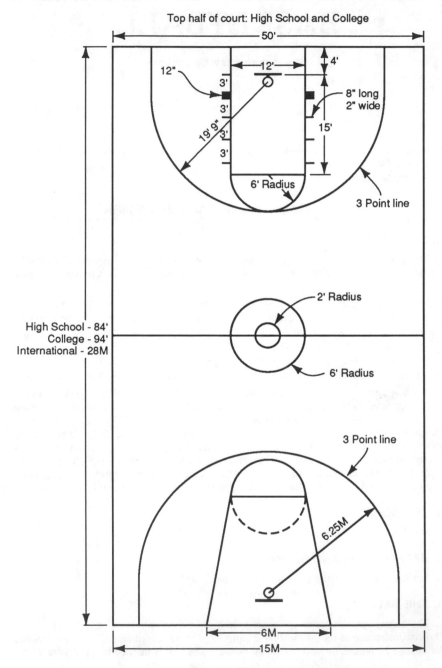

Top half of court: High School and College

Bottom half of court: International

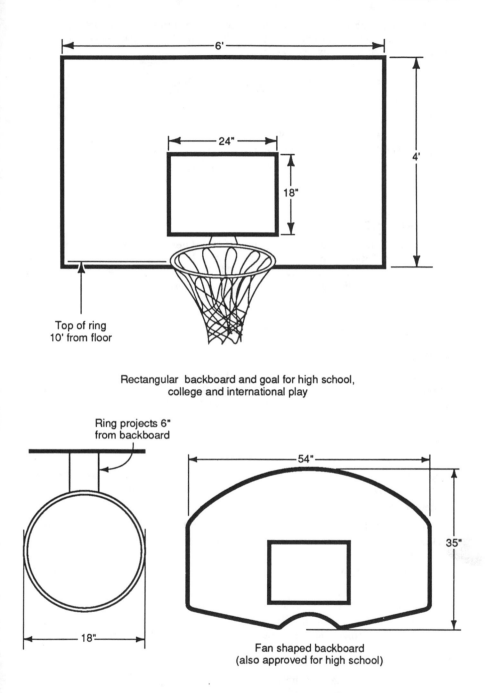

6'

24"

4'

18"

Top of ring
10' from floor

Rectangular backboard and goal for high school,
college and international play

Ring projects 6"
from backboard

54"

35"

18"

Fan shaped backboard
(also approved for high school)

Not to scale

will result in a bounce of 49 to 54 inches when dropped to the playing surface from a height of 6 feet measured to the top of the ball. Channels or seams between panels on the outer cover shall not exceed 1/4 inch.

RULE II. DEFINITIONS

A. BASKET

The ring with attached net into which players attempt to throw the ball.

1. The basket for each team is the one into which its players attempt to throw the ball.

2. The visiting team has the choice of which of the two baskets it prefers as its basket for the first half of play.

3. The teams change baskets for the second half.

B. BASKET INTERFERENCE

A violation which results in awarding points (if by the defense) or the ball out of bounds to the opponents (if by the offense). It occurs if the ball is touched while it is on or within the basket ring or above the basket cylinder. The basket (including the net) may not be touched while the ball is on the ring or within the cylinder.

C. BLOCKING

Illegal contact which interferes with the movement of an opponent.

D. BONUS FREE THROW

A second free throw awarded to a player who has been fouled in a nonshooting situation after the opponents exceed the limit of common fouls permitted for a half. (Four in interscholastic play; six in intercollegiate play.) The first free throw must be made to qualify for a second free throw.

E. CONTACT

To hold, push, trip or charge into an opponent is illegal contact. This must be tempered with the fact that fast movement in a restricted area will result in some physical contact. When no advantage is gained from contact it is to be overlooked.

1. Responsibility:

a. The first player to establish a position on the court without contact has priority.

b. The player moving into the path of another player when contact occurs is generally responsible for the contact.

c. Extending a portion of the body into the path of the opponent carries responsibility for contact.

d. No player may move into the path of an airborne opponent.

e. A player has the right to all space within his vertical base. (Principle of verticality.) The player who intrudes into this space causes the contact if contact occurs.

F. CONTROL

1. Player: when holding or dribbling a live ball.

2. Team: when the ball is in player control, or being passed between teammates.

a. Team control ceases when a player shoots, the defense secures possession, or the ball becomes dead.

3. There is no control during a jump ball, or a throw-in.

4. After the ball is shot there is no control until a rebound is firmly secured by any player.

G. COURTS

1. A team's front court extends from the inner edge of the midcourt to the end line. It includes all inbounds parts of the basket and backboard.

2. The front court is divided by an imaginary line parallel to the end line and 28 feet from it. The area nearer the midcourt is the midcourt area and the larger area the forecourt area.

3. The backcourt is all remaining parts of the court including the entire division line and all inbounds parts of the opponent's basket and backboard.

4. For purposes of control, the ball is in backcourt when either the ball or a player controlling the ball is touching the backcourt. To be in front court all parts of the player and ball must be totally in the front court.

5. On a throw-in from out of bounds the position of the ball is established when a player gains control of the ball inbounds.

H. DISQUALIFIED PLAYER

A disqualified player is one who has committed a 5th personal foul or a flagrant foul.

I. DRIBBLING

1. Legal: tapping the ball to the floor in a legal manner with one hand.

2. Illegal:

a. tapping the ball to the floor after having ceased a previous legal dribble.

b. tapping the ball with both hands or allowing it to touch both hands before the ball returns to the floor.

3. The dribble ends when the dribbler catches the ball. A dribble may continue and/or a dribbler may dribble a second time if the opponent interrupts the dribble by touching the ball or by batting it from the possession of a dribbler who has ceased to dribble.

J. DUNKING

Attempting to push the ball through the basket from above the rim.

K. EXTRA PERIOD

A shortened period played to break a tie score following regulation time. The length of the extra period varies at different levels of play.

L. FOUL

A rule infraction for which the offender is charged with a foul and the player offended is awarded either a throw-in, a free throw, or two free throws. In some instances the offended team may be given the ball for a throw-in in addition to the free throws.

1. A common foul is any personal foul, other than a flagrant or intentional foul or a foul committed against a player who is attempting a field goal.

2. A double foul is a circumstance in which two opponents are called for personal fouls against each other at approximately the same time. Both fouls are charged and play is resumed by a throw-in at midcourt using the alternate possession method.

3. A flagrant foul may be a personal or technical foul of a violent nature, or a technical non-contact foul which involves vulgar or abusive conduct. It may or may not be intentional. The player is ejected from the game.

4. An intentional foul is a personal or technical foul which in the judgment of the official appears designed or premeditated. Severity of the act is not a factor.

5. A personal foul is a player foul which involves illegal contact with an opponent while the ball is alive or after the ball is in possession of a player for a throw-in.

6. A player control foul is a common foul committed by a player while in control of the ball.

7. A technical foul is a foul by a player or non-player which does not involve contact with an opponent or a player foul which involves intentional or flagrant contact with an opponent while the ball is dead.

M. FREE THROW

An unobstructed try to score a basket (1 point) from the free throw line.

N. GOAL OR BASKET

A legal goal is made when a live ball enters the basket from above and passes through the net. Passage of the ball in the opposite direction is a violation. A goal counts: (a) 1 point for each free throw; (b) 2 points for each goal from within the 3 point line; and (c) 3 points for each goal scored from beyond the 3 point line.

O. GOALTENDING

A violation for touching a shot or a tap while it is in its downward path and above the ring level or touching a free throw before it touches the basket ring.

1. Violation results in award of the appropriate points or award out of bounds to the defense if the offensive team violates. (Also see Basket Interference.)

P. JUMP BALL

A method of putting the ball in play to start the game and each extra period. The Referee tosses the ball between any two opponents in the center circle of the court.

1. In numerous other situations a jump ball is indicated by the officials but the teams alternate taking the ball out of bounds for a throw-in instead of actually jumping the ball. These situations are as follows:

a. The ball is held steady between two opponents

b. The ball goes out of bounds and uncertainty exists as to which player last touched the ball

c. The ball settles on a basket support

d. A double foul is charged

e. A simultaneous free throw violation by opposing players.

Q. PENALTIES

1. For a foul: the offender is charged with the foul. The player offended is given one or two free throws depending on the circumstances of the foul. In some cases the offended team is given the ball for a throw-in.

2. For a violation: the opponents of the violating team are given the ball for a throw-in. In some instances points are awarded or a substitute free throw is permitted.

R. PIVOTING

Movement by a player holding a live ball in which one foot (pivot foot) remains in contact with the floor at a point. The free foot may be moved in any direction.

S. PROGRESS WITH THE BALL

Progress with the ball in any direction is made by passing from one player to another or by dribbling the ball.

1. Various restrictions related to foot movement are placed on the player who secures the ball and either a) begins progress, b) continues progress, or c) stops his/her progress.

2. Basically movement is related to whether one or both feet are in the air or off the ground when the ball is secured.

3. As a general rule of thumb the ball must be released before a second step is completed.

T. SCREENING

Action in an attempt to interfere with the movement of an opponent without causing excessive contact. This is done by a player securing a position on the floor before the opponent reaches the same position. A player who has the ball must anticipate the screener. A screen set for an opponent without the ball and outside his visual field must allow the opponent space to change direction of movement.

U. SUBSTITUTIONS

A substitute reports to the scorer before entering the court. Such player must wait until the ball is dead and the clock is stopped before entering the game. The official timer signals the floor officials who beckon the substitute.

V. TRAVELING

A violation involving moving the feet in excess of the prescribed limitations. Generally involves moving the pivot foot or taking more than one step without dribbling.

RULE III. OFFICIALS AND THEIR FUNCTIONS

A. FLOOR AND BENCH OFFICIALS

1. The Referee and Umpire(s) (2 Umpires may be used) are the floor officials.

2. The bench officials include the official Timer, the Scorer, and a Shot Clock Operator (if needed).

B. RESPONSIBILITIES

1. The Referee approves the Timer, Scorer and Shot Clock Operator. These persons are usually provided by the home management.

2. The Referee approves all equipment used, tosses the ball to start the game and each extra period, settles any disagreements that arise, and approves the score at the end of each period and the game.

3. Both officials have equal responsibility to put the ball in play and administer penalties and violations of all the rules. Uncertainties are decided by consultation with each other.

4. The floor officials may correct errors in any of the following circumstances should they occur:

a. An earned free throw was not awarded.

b. An unearned free throw was awarded.

c. The wrong player attempted a free throw.

d. A score was incorrectly counted or cancelled.

Note: These corrections must be acknowledged by the official before the ball becomes alive for a second time following the starting of the clock after the error occurs. If recognized corrections are made; i.e. awarding, cancelling, reshooting or counting/cancelling a score, any action which occurred in the interim period played before the error was recognized stands. The game is resumed from the point it was stopped when the error was recognized.

5. The following infractions are appropriately penalized if discovered at the time of violations. They include:

a. More than 5 participants on the floor at one time while the ball is alive.

b. Player participation after having been disqualified.

c. Wearing a number identical to a teammate's.

d. Playing after changing a number and not reporting it to the scorer.

C. THE SCORER RECORDS

1. A running account of all scoring.

2. The names and numbers of all players.

3. All fouls (The floor officials are notified when either a 5th personal or 3rd technical foul is charged to any player).

4. All time outs (Number varies with level of play).

5. All jump balls (For alternating possessions).

D. THE TIMER(S) RESPONSIBILITIES

The timer(s) are responsible for controlling and sounding the timing device as follows:

1. Three minutes before the start of each half.

2. At the end of each official time out.

3. At the expiration of time for each period.

4. To allow for substitutions when the ball is dead.

5. Sounding an auxiliary device (shot clock) if one is specified at the particular level of play.

RULE IV. GAME CLOCK OPERATIONS

A. THE GAME CLOCK IS STARTED

1. When the ball is tapped during a jump ball.

2. If a free throw is not successful and the ball is to continue in play, when the ball touches a player on the court.

3. If the game is resumed by a throw-in from out-of-bounds, when the ball touches a player on the court.

B. THE GAME CLOCK IS STOPPED

At the end of each period, and when an official blows his whistle for:

1. A violation.
2. A foul.
3. A held ball.
4. Unusual delay in re-starting the game following a dead ball.
5. Suspension of play for injury, or for removal of a player.
6. Suspension of play for any reason, ordered by the officials.
7. When the shot clock is sounded.
8. A player requests time out if the ball is dead or his team has control.

C. DIVISION OF PLAYING TIME

Playing time may be divided into 4 quarters or 2 halves. The length of the game varies at different levels of play. (6-minute quarter to 12-minute quarters, 20-minute halves.)

D. EXTRA PERIOD

An extra period is played when the regulation game ends in a tie score. The length of each possible extra period also varies at different levels of play (2 minutes to 5 minutes.)

E. LEGAL CHARGED TIME OUTS

Teams may request a time out when they have possession of a live ball, or when the ball is dead. Time outs are of 1 minute duration. The number varies at different levels of play and they may be called consecutively.

F. MAJOR TIMING RULES

1. Shot clock rule. At some levels of play the team gaining possession of a live ball when the clock is running is given a specific amount of time to try for a goal. (Time varies from 24 to 45 seconds.) Failure to try for a goal is a violation. Ball is given out of bounds to opponents. The clock is reset for the total amount of time for nonshooting and technical fouls by the defense and defensive violations other than deflecting the ball out of bounds. If the ball goes out of bounds and belongs to the offense with less than 5 seconds on the clock it is reset to 5 seconds.

2. Three second rule. No player may remain within the free throw lane nearest his team basket for more than 3 seconds while he or his team is in control of the ball. Failure to completely vacate the area is a violation.

3. Five second rule. It is a violation to hold or dribble the ball in the front court while closely guarded (within 6 feet) for longer than 5 seconds.

4. Ten second rule. A team gaining possession of the ball in its backcourt must progress into the front court with the ball before 10 seconds expires. Failure to do so is a violation.

5. Once a team gains control of the ball in its front court a violation will be charged if the team causes the ball to go back into its backcourt and then resecures the ball.

6. The game clock is stopped at the end of each period and when any of the following occur: a) a violation; b) a foul; c) a held ball; d) a charged or official time out; and e) when the ball is caused to be out of bounds through misplay.

RULE V. CONTINUING PLAY

A. ALTERNATING JUMP BALL

When a jump ball occurs, play continues by giving the ball to one of the teams out of bounds for a throw-in near the position on the floor where the jump ball situation occurred. The jump ball to begin the game determines initial possession followed by the teams alternating subsequent (jump ball) throw-in possessions instead of executing the jump ball.

B. THROW-IN AFTER CLOCK STOPPAGE

Play is resumed by a throw-in after a:

1. Time out.
2. Foul for which free throws are not prescribed.
3. Held ball or end of a period.
4. Violation.
5. Successful free throw which is not followed by another free throw.
6. Ball is out of bounds due to misplay by a player.

C. CLOCK STARTS

1. When the ball is legally tapped on a jump ball.
2. When the ball is touched by a player on the floor during a throw-in.
3. After an unsuccessful free throw, if play continues, when the ball is touched by any player in retrieving the missed shot.

D. THROW-IN REGULATIONS

1. Following a violation or nonshooting foul the ball is given to the opponent by the official for a throw-in at an out-of-bounds spot near where the violation occurred. The inbounding player must:

a. Release the ball without in any way breaking the plane of the playing court.
b. Release the ball (by throwing) within 5 seconds.
c. Not move from the designated throw-in spot.

2. After a score other than for a technical or intentional foul, an opponent of the scoring team secures the ball from anywhere behind the end line and throws the ball to a player on the court. (The provisions in D-1-a. and b. above also apply.)

3. After a technical or intentional foul, the offended team retains possession of the ball after the free throws are awarded. The official gives the offended team the ball for a throw-in (a) at midcourt for a technical foul or (b) at an out-of-bounds spot near where the intentional foul occurred.

4. In 1, 2, or 3 above the defensive player may not break the plane of the out-of-bounds line and touch the ball during the throw-in attempt. Such an act by the defense is a technical foul.

E. FREE THROW PROVISIONS

1. The shooter must:

a. shoot from beyond the free throw line and within the free throw circle within 10 seconds;
b. make a single continuous movement once he begins the actual shooting motion;

c. remain behind the free throw line until the ball touches the basket.

2. The opponents of the shooter:

a. are assigned the first space from the basket on either side;

b. must remain in designated positions along the free throw lane until the ball leaves the shooter's hand;

c. must not disturb the free thrower in any way.

3. Teammates of the shooter:

a. are assigned alternate spaces from those of the opponents;

b. must remain in positions along the free throw lane until the ball leaves the shooter's hand.

4. General provisions:

a. Opponents and teammates may not touch the ball until the free throw has touched the rim and is outside the cylinder of the basket.

b. Players from either team may choose not to fill lane spaces. If this is the choice, such players must remain beyond the three point line until the free throw touches the basket rim.

RULE VI. TECHNICAL FOULS AND PENALTIES

A. TECHNICAL FOULS

Technical fouls generally are fouls committed by players, substitutes, or team officials while the ball is dead. These fouls are for the most part non-contact although in some cases violent contact occurs. Technical fouls include the following:

1. Disrespectfully addressing or contacting an official.

2. Unsportsmanlike language, gestures or conduct toward anyone officially involved in the game.

3. Delaying tactics; after a score, before a throw-in, by substitutes.

4. Failing to report properly, or participating with an illegal jersey number.

5. Illegally grasping the basket or hitting the backboard.

6. More than 5 participants on the floor.

B. PENALTIES (FREE THROWS) FOR ALL TYPES OF FOULS

1. One free throw for a shooter whose goal is successful and is fouled while shooting.

2. Two free throws for a shooter whose attempted goal is unsuccessful or any intentional foul or flagrant foul.

3. One free throw plus an additional free throw (one and one) for a common foul after the bonus rule goes into effect. (Rule varies at different levels of play.)

a. If the first shot is successful the second throw is allowed.

b. If the first free throw is missed play continues.

4. No free throws for:

a. Common fouls committed before the bonus rule goes into effect.

b. All double fouls. (No matter the type of foul.)

c. Player control fouls.

5. Intentional fouls are two shot fouls.

MAJOR DIFFERENCES IN
INTERNATIONAL (OLYMPIC) AND USA RULES

1. The three point goal line is slightly farther from the basket.

2. A team is given 30 seconds to shoot after gaining control.

3. Three free throws for a foul on a missed three point try for goal.

4. Personal and technical fouls count toward the total of 5 allowed each player.

5. No free throws are awarded for team control fouls.

6. Once a shot has touched the ring on a goal try, either team may touch the ball no matter its position. The basket itself may not be touched in tapping a rebound.

7. No offensive player may receive a pass or touch a shot above ring level in the three second area.

8. Offended team has the option to take the ball out of bounds at mid-court following a foul.

9. A team is allowed three seconds to throw a ball in bounds.

10. A free thrower has five seconds to release the ball after given control at the free throw line.

11. Officials need not handle the ball after violations in the backcourt.

12. A ball may not deliberately be thrown off the body of an opponent causing it to go out of bounds.

13. The free throw violation of stepping into the lane is only called on the free thrower. Violations by others are ignored if the basket is made.

14. Substitutions are allowed only for the team who has possession on a throw-in. However, if the team with the ball makes a substitution the opponent is also allowed to replace players.

a. The same basic rule applies specifically to the free thrower after a successful throw. The opponent may then substitute one player.

15. On the throw-in the ball may not be thrown to a teammate in backcourt if the throw-in comes from a front court position.

16. All jump balls are thrown up by officials. No alternate possession rule.

17. Aggressive defensive position is identified as being within 3 feet.

18. The ball is in front court when any part of player or ball is touching that court.

19. The free throw lane is wider at the base line.

GOVERNING BODIES

Amateur Basketball Association of the United States, 1750 East Boulder St., Colorado Springs, CO 80909

(Recognized by the United States Olympic Committee (USOC) as the governing body for amateur basketball in the United States.)

National Association of Intercollegiate Athletics, 1221 Baltimore St., Kansas City, MO 64105

National Collegiate Athletic Association, P.O. Box 1906, Nall Ave. at 63rd St., Mission, KS 66201

National Federation of State High School Associations, P.O. Box 20626, 11724 Plaza Circle, Kansas City, MO 64195

MAGAZINES

Athletic Journal, Athletic Journal Publishing Co., 1719 Howard St., Evanston, IL 60202

Scholastic Coach, Scholastic Coach, Inc., 730 Broadway, New York, NY 10003

• BILLIARDS •

POCKET BILLIARDS—POOL

(Rules summary by author)

☐

NATURE OF THE GAME

Although originally the term *billiards* referred to a particular game, it is now used in a generic fashion to refer to a number of games which employ the common elements of playing surface, equipment, object, and basic rules. Billiard games are played on rectangular tables, twice as long as wide, with rubber cushioned side rails and vary in size from 4 feet by 8 feet to 6 feet by 12 feet. The 4-1/2 by 9 feet and the 5 by 10 feet tables are most commonly used in the United States. The two basic forms of billiards are pocket billiards (commonly referred to as pool) played on a table with 6 pockets and carom billiards played on a table without pockets. The various games require a different number of balls ranging from 3 balls in carom billiards to 22 balls in American snooker. A tapered wooden stick (cue), 53 to 57 inches in length, and weighing 12 to 22 ounces is used to stroke the cue ball. Most balls are made of a hard plastic composition but ivory balls are still used in some championship play. Pocket billiard balls measure 2-1/4 inches in diameter, while carom billiard balls are slightly larger with a 2-3/4 inches diameter. Snooker balls are 2-1/8 inches in diameter. The object of play in pocket billiards is to stroke (punch) the cue ball (white ball) against the colored-numbered balls (object balls) to knock them into the pockets.

In addition to the numerous widely recognized American and English games of billiards there are many variations found in different regions of the country as well as in local communities. The rules for the three most popular American games (14.1 continuous pocket billiards, rotation, and 8-ball) are presented here. It should be noted that modifications of these rules to make the play more/less difficult are not uncommon.

Note: There are a number of basic rules that apply to all pocket billiard games. To avoid unnecessary duplication, the common rules for the three games included here are covered in the basic rules section as follows.

BASIC RULES COMMON TO POCKET BILLIARD GAMES

A. BEGINNING THE GAME

1. The players may lag or flip a coin to determine who will shoot first (to make the break). The lag is executed by each player shooting a cue ball from behind the head string (see diagram) to the foot rail attempting to rebound the ball back closest to the head rail. The winner of the lag has the option of shooting first (making the break) or delegating the break to the opponent.

2. The 15 balls to be pocketed (object balls) are placed in position (racked) at the foot of the table on the foot spot (see diagram). The balls are racked in a triangle with the apex on the foot spot.

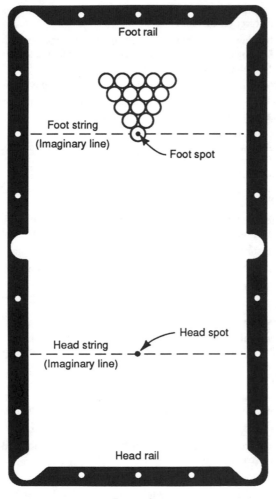

Pool table

3. The first shooter attempts to scatter (break) the object balls by stroking the cue ball forcibly against the racked object balls. A legal break requires that either an object ball be pocketed or two balls must be bounced off a cushion. If the break is not legal, the opponent may play the balls as positioned or require that the break be repeated until break requirements are met.

B. CONTINUING PLAY

1. Play is conducted in innings with each player's turn being termed an inning. The inning continues as long as a player legally pockets a ball on each stroke. When the shooter fails to legally pocket a ball or fouls, the inning ends and the opponent becomes the shooter.

2. The shooter must call the number of the ball he intends to pocket. If the called ball is pocketed, the shooter is also credited with any other balls that are pocketed on the same stroke. If the called ball is not pocketed, other balls pocketed on same stroke do not count and must be spotted.

3. A ball which bounces from inside a pocket back onto the table does not score and is played as the ball rests on the table.

4. If the called ball jumps the table it is an error and ends the inning. A jumped ball is spotted. If the called object ball is made but another object ball jumps the table, the pocketed ball counts and the jumped ball is spotted.

5. A ball that rolls up on a rail but returns to the table remains in play as ball rests.

6. Should the balls be disturbed by persons other than the player at the table, they should be returned as near as possible to their original position.

7. When the cue ball is "in hand" (must be placed on table by hand to continue play) and the object ball is within the head string (between head string and top rail), the object ball is spotted. If more than one object ball is within the head string, the ball nearest the head string is spotted.

C. PENALTIES

1. The penalty for the following fouls is forfeiture of one point (in straight pool) in addition to loss of turn, and forfeiture of any pocketed points on the stroke:

a. Touching or disturbing the cue ball or any object ball, accidental or otherwise.

b. Striking the cue ball or an object ball while the ball is in motion.

c. Jumping cue ball off table.

d. One foot must be on floor while executing stroke.

e. Cue ball goes into a pocket (scratch).

f. Striking the cue ball below center of ball causing the ball to jump off the surface of the table. It is not a foul if the cue ball is struck in the center or above center.

D. SPOTTING

1. Balls which are pocketed in an illegal manner or are knocked from the table are to be returned to play by placing (spotting) them on the table. Balls are spotted when:

a. The ball(s) is made on a stroke in which the cue ball is also pocketed.

b. The ball(s) is made on a stroke in which the cue ball does not strike the designated object ball before striking other balls.

c. The ball(s) is knocked from the table.

2. Balls to be spotted are placed on the foot spot unless a ball already occupies the spot. In this event or when more than one ball is to be spotted, the balls are placed (touching) behind one another on a straight line. An imaginary straight line running from the foot spot to the bottom rail is called the long-string. When multiple spotting of balls is required, they are placed in line on the long-string. Non-spotted balls which may be positioned along the long-string line are not to be moved.

14.1 CONTINUOUS POCKET BILLIARDS (STRAIGHT POOL)

Note: The basic rules common to pocket billiard games apply except as follows.

A. OBJECT OF THE GAME

1. The players attempt to be first to score an arbitrarily set number of points; i.e., 50, 75, 100, etc. Championship games are usually played to 150 points. One point is scored for each ball legally pocketed.

B. BEGINNING THE GAME

1. The 15 numbered-object balls are racked in a triangle at the foot of the table with the 15-ball placed at the apex and on the foot spot. The 1-ball is placed on the rear left-hand corner of the triangle and the 5-ball is placed on the rear right-hand corner. The remaining higher numbered balls are placed in the top of the triangle while the lower numbered balls are placed at the bottom of the triangle.

C. CONTINUING PLAY

1. The shooter must call the ball being played and the pocket in which it is intended to drop.

2. On each shot the shooter must either (1) pocket the called ball, (2) strike the called ball and another object ball knocking the second ball into a cushion or pocket, or (3) strike the called ball and then a rail with the cue ball.

a. Failure to meet requirement (1) above results in loss of turn.

b. Failure to meet either requirement (2) or (3) above results in loss of one turn and a one point penalty.

3. After 14 balls have been pocketed the 15th ball and cue ball are left in place on the table and the remaining 14 pocketed balls are racked for play to continue. The shooter who made the 14th ball continues to play and may shoot at the remaining object ball or at the racked balls.

D. PENALTIES

1. A scratch results in loss of turn and a one point penalty is assessed.

2. Three succeeding scratches by a player, including table scratches (failure to meet the requirements for a legal shot), results in an additional 15 point penalty.

3. If a player has no points at the time a penalty point is assessed, his score is −1 or the penalty point is deducted after the player does score.

8-BALL

The basic rules common to pocket billiard games apply except as follows.

A. OBJECT OF THE GAME

1. Each player or side attempts to be first to pocket the 8-ball. The balls numbered 1 through 7 are the object balls for one player or side while the balls numbered 9 through 15 are the object balls for the opponent(s). The 8-ball cannot be pocketed, except on the break, until the designated object balls have been pocketed.

B. BEGINNING THE GAME

1. The balls are racked with the 8-ball placed in the center of the third row from the front apex of the rack.

2. If ball(s) is pocketed on the break the shooter has the choice of the high or low numbered balls as his object balls. If the first shooter does not pocket a ball on the break, the opponent plays the balls as they are positioned and has the option of playing either the high or low numbered balls. The final designation of the object balls assigned is not made until a ball is pocketed.

3. At least one object ball must be driven to a rail on the break or the break must be repeated.

4. The shooter wins the game if the 8-ball is pocketed on the break.

C. CONTINUING PLAY

1. A legal shot requires that the shooter contact his own object ball first. Combination shots involving any balls are permissible.

2. Opponent's balls pocketed by shooter are credited to opponent.

3. All designated object balls must be pocketed before the 8-ball is pocketed.

4. A legal shot at the 8-ball requires that the shooter call the pocket into which the ball is to fall and the 8-ball must be the first ball struck.

D. PENALTIES

1. The following errors result in loss of the game:

a. In failing to make the 8-ball, neither the 8-ball or cue ball contact a rail.

b. The 8-ball is pocketed before it becomes the object ball.

c. Failure to strike the 8-ball when it is the object ball.

d. A scratch occurs when the 8-ball is pocketed.

e. Eight-ball is pocketed in pocket other than that called by shooter.

ROTATION

The basic rules common to pocket billiard games apply except as follows.

A. OBJECT OF THE GAME

1. The balls are pocketed in numerical order—1 through 15. Players receive points equal to the numerical designation of the numbered balls. The player or side first to score 61 points wins the game.

B. BEGINNING THE GAME

1. The 1-ball is placed at the apex of the triangular rack with the 2-ball placed on the left-hand corner (from shooter perspective) and the 3-ball placed on the right-hand corner. The remaining balls are dispersed at random within the rack.

2. The 1-ball is the object ball on the break and must be struck first for pocketed balls to count.

C. CONTINUING PLAY

1. The object ball for each shot is established by the requirement that the balls must be played in numerical order. The cue ball must strike the lowest numbered ball on the table before striking any other balls.

2. All balls pocketed on a legal stroke are counted even if the object ball was not pocketed.

3. Any ball pocketed on an illegal stroke is spotted.

D. PENALTIES

(See penalties under Basic Rules Common to Pocket Billiard Games.)

MAGAZINES

Billiards Digest, National Bowlers Journal, 875 N. Michigan Ave., #1801, Chicago, IL 60911

National Billiard News, Puhka-Publishing Co., Box 487, Birmingham, MI 48012

• BOWLING •

ABC BOWLING RULES

(Reproduced by permission of the American Bowling Congress*)

□

Note: Only the rules and playing regulations pertaining to the actual play of the game are included here. Rules and regulations relating to constitutions, equipment specifications, tournaments and leagues, as sanctioned by the American Bowling Congress (ABC), are fully covered in the official rules publication. The Women's International Bowling Congress (WIBC)* has adopted the general playing rules of the ABC.

GENERAL PLAYING RULES

SCORING THE GAME

Rule 1a. A game of American Tenpins shall consist of ten frames. Each player shall bowl two balls in each of the first nine frames except when he shall make a strike. A player who scores a strike or spare in the tenth frame shall deliver three balls.

LEGAL DELIVERY

Rule 1b. A ball is legally delivered when it leaves the bowler's possession and crosses the foul line into playing territory. A bowling ball must be delivered entirely by manual means and shall not incorporate any device either in the ball or affixed to it which is either detached at time of delivery or is a moving part in the ball during delivery except that any person who has had his hand or major portion thereof amputated may use special equipment to aid in grasping and delivering the ball providing the special equipment is in lieu of the amputee's hand.

MECHANICAL AIDS

Rule 1c. Where an artificial or medical aid is necessary for grasping and delivering the ball because of any other disability of the hand or arm, permission to use the aid in sanctioned competition may be granted by the ABC Executive Secretary-Treasurer's office under the following conditions:

(1) The aid does not incorporate a mechanical device with moving parts which would impart a force or impetus to the ball.

(2) A description or drawing and model of the aid is furnished ABC.

(3) A doctor's certificate describing the disability together with his recommendation that the aid should be used is furnished ABC.

If permission is not granted, the claimant shall have the right of appeal to the ABC Legal Committee.

---

*See page 62 for additional information.

Should permission be granted for the use of an artificial or medical aid, a special identification card (not an ABC membership card) will be issued the applicant indicating that the aid may be used in sanctioned competition providing the bowler has a current membership card and the use of the aid is specially authorized by the league or tournament management.

Permission to use the device may be withdrawn for cause.

SPECIAL CONSIDERATIONS

Rule 1d. Those individuals unable to execute a legal delivery as defined in Rule 1b may bowl in sanctioned competition provided:

1. The league's board of directors or tournament management authorize such participation.

2. The league's board of directors or tournament management establish specific provisions to govern such participation.

Averages established by such participants shall not be acceptable for entry purposes in subsequent league or tournament competition unless authorized by league or tournament rules.

Such bowlers will be eligible for all ABC awards except that ABC will provide special awards for the following accomplishments:

Games of 300, 299 or 298

11 strikes in a row where the score is 297 or less

Three game series totaling 700 to 799

Three game series in excess of 799

1	2	3	4	5	6	7	8	9	10
X	X	X	7 2	ⓞ /	F 9	X	7 /	9 –	X X 8
30	57	76	85	95	104	124	143	152	180

STRIKE

Rule 2. A strike is recorded when the player completes a legal delivery and bowls down the full setup of ten pins on the first ball. It is designated by an (x) in the small square in the upper right-hand corner of the frame in which the complete set of ten pins is bowled down with the first ball. The count in each frame where a strike is bowled shall be left open until the player has completed two more deliveries. The maximum count on one strike when followed by a spare is 20.

DOUBLE

Rule 3. When a player bowls two strikes in succession legally delivered, he shall have scored a double. The count in the frame where the first strike was bowled shall be left open until the player has completed his next delivery. When all pins are down twice in succession the count for the first strike is 20 plus the number of pins knocked down with the first ball of the third frame following. The maximum count on a double figuring a nine pin count on the first ball following the second strike is 29.

TRIPLE OR TURKEY

Rule 4. In scoring three successive strikes, the player shall be credited with 30 pins in the frame in which the first strike was bowled. Thus, in a game of ten full frames, a player must bowl 12 strikes in succession in order to bowl a game of 300.

SPARE

Rule 5. Any player who bowls down the remaining pins with a legally delivered second ball in any frame has scored a spare. A spare is designated by a (/) in the small square in the upper right-hand corner of the frame in which it is made. The number of pins knocked down after the first delivery before the player bowls for the spare should be marked by a small figure in the upper right corner of the frame. The count in such frame proper is left open until the player shall have bowled his first ball in the next frame following, when the number of pins knocked down by the first ball shall be added to the ten pins represented by his spare, and the total shall be credited therein. When a spare is scored in the tenth frame, a third ball shall be bowled in that frame.

ERROR

Rule 6. A player shall have made an error when he fails to bowl down all ten pins after having completed two legal deliveries in a given frame provided the pins left standing after the first legal delivery do not constitute a split. When an error is made, the number of pins bowled down by the player's first legal delivery shall be marked next to the small square in the upper right-hand corner of that frame, and the number of pins bowled down by the player's second legal delivery shall be marked inside the small square. Where the player fails to bowl down at least one pin with his second delivery, a (−) shall be recorded in the small square. When an error is committed, the count in that frame shall be recorded immediately following the player's second legal delivery.

SPLIT

Rule 7. A split shall be a setup of pins remaining standing after the first ball has been legally delivered provided the headpin is down, and:

(1) At least one pin is down between two or more pins which remain standing, as for example: 7-9, or 3-10.

(2) At least one pin is down immediately ahead of two or more pins which remain standing, as for example: 5-6.

Editor's Note. If a split is designated, it is normally done with a (0) but any other symbol may be used.

PINFALL—LEGAL

Rule 8. Every ball delivered by the player shall count, unless declared a dead ball. Pins must then be respotted after the cause for declaring such dead ball has been removed.

(1) Pins which are knocked down by another pin or pins rebounding in play from the side partition, rear cushion or sweep bar when it is at rest on the pin deck prior to sweeping dead wood are counted as pins down.

(2) If when rolling at a full setup or in order to make a spare, it is discovered immediately after the ball has been delivered that one or more pins are improperly set, although not missing, the ball and resulting pinfall shall be counted. It is each player's responsibility to determine if the setup is correct. He shall insist that any pins incorrectly set be respotted before delivering his ball, otherwise he implies that the setup is satisfactory. No change

in the position of any pins which are left standing can be made after a previous delivery in order to make a spare, unless the pin setter has moved or misplaced any pin after the previous delivery and prior to the bowling of the next ball.

(3) Pins which are knocked down or displaced by a fair ball, and remain lying on the lane or in the gutters, or which lean so as to touch kickbacks or side partitions, are termed dead wood, counted as pins down, and must be removed before the next ball is bowled. If a bowler makes a legal delivery while there is dead wood on the lane or in the gutters, and his ball comes in contact with such dead wood before leaving the lane surface, then that bowler shall receive a score of zero for that delivery.

PINFALL—ILLEGAL

Rule 9. When any of the following incidents occur the ball counts as a ball rolled, but pins knocked down shall not count:

(1) When pins are knocked down or displaced by a ball which leaves the lane before reaching the pins.

(2) When a ball rebounds from the rear cushion.

(3) When pins come in contact with the body, arms or legs of a human pinsetter and rebound.

(4) A standing pin which falls when it is touched by mechanical pinsetting equipment, or when dead wood is removed, or is knocked down by a human pinsetter, shall not count and must be replaced on the pin spot inscribed on the pin deck where it originally stood before delivery of the ball.

(5) Pins which are bowled off the lane, rebound and remain standing on the lane must be counted as pins standing.

(6) If in delivering the ball a foul is committed, any pins knocked down by such delivery shall not be counted.

DEAD BALL

Rule 10. A ball shall be declared dead if any of the following occur, in which case such ball shall not count. The pins must be respotted after the cause for declaring such dead ball has been removed and player shall be required to rebowl.

a. If, after the player delivers his ball and attention is immediately called to the fact that one or more pins were missing from the setup.

b. When a human pinsetter removes or interferes with any pin or pins before they stop rolling or before the ball reaches the pins.

c. When a player bowls on the wrong lane or out of turn.

d. When a player is interfered with by a pinsetter, another bowler, spectator, or moving object as the ball is being delivered and before delivery is complete, player must then and there accept the resulting pinfall or demand that pins be respotted.

e. When any pins at which he is bowling are moved or knocked down in any manner, as the player is delivering the ball and before the ball reaches the pins.

f. When a player's ball comes in contact with any foreign obstacle.

NO PINS MAY BE CONCEDED

Rule 11. No pins may be conceded and only those actually knocked down or moved entirely off the playing surface of the lane as a result of the legal delivery of the ball by the player may be counted. Every frame must be completed at the time the player is bowling in his regular order.

REPLACEMENT OF PINS

Rule 12. Should a pin be broken or otherwise badly damaged during the game, it shall be replaced at once by another as nearly uniform in weight and condition as possible with the set in use. The league or tournament officials shall in all cases be the judges in the matter of replacement of such pins.

A broken pin does not change the score made by a bowler. The number of pins knocked down are counted, after which the broken pin is replaced.

BOWLING ON WRONG LANE

Rule 13. When only one player or one player on each team bowls on the wrong lane and the error is discovered before another player has bowled, a dead ball shall be declared and the player(s) required to rebowl on the correct lane(s).

When more than one player on the same team has bowled on the wrong lane, the game shall be completed without adjustment and the next game shall be started on the correctly scheduled lane.

In singles match play competition, where a player normally bowls two frames each time it is his turn to bowl, and a player bowls on the wrong lane for these two frames, a dead ball shall be declared and the player required to rebowl both frames on the correct lanes providing the error is discovered prior to the time the opposing player has made a legal delivery. If the error is not discovered until the opposing player has bowled, the score shall count and the player shall be required to bowl his subsequent frames on the correct lanes.

BALLS—PRIVATE OWNERSHIP

Rule 14. Bowling balls used in the game and marked by their owners are considered private and other participants in the game are prohibited from using the same, unless the owner consents to such use. (The surface hardness of bowling balls shall not be less than 72 Durometer "D".)

FOUL—DEFINITION OF

Rule 15. A foul is committed with no pinfall being credited to the player although the ball counts as a ball rolled, when a part of the bowler's person encroaches upon or goes beyond the foul line and touches any part of the lane, equipment or building during or after executing a legal delivery. A ball is in play after legal delivery has been made and until the same or another player is on the approach in position to make a succeeding delivery.

If the player commits a foul which is apparent to both captains or one or more members of each of the opposing teams competing in a league or tournament on the same pair of lanes where the foul is committed or to the official scorer or a tournament official, and should the foul judge or umpire through negligence fail to see it committed or an ABC approved automatic foul detecting device fails to record it, a foul shall nevertheless be declared and so recorded.

DELIBERATE FOUL

Rule 16. When a player deliberately fouls to benefit by the calling of a foul, the player shall receive zero pinfall for that delivery and shall not be allowed any further deliveries in that frame.

FOUL COUNTS AS BALL BOWLED

Rule 17. A foul ball shall be recorded as a ball bowled by the player, but any pins bowled down when a foul is committed shall not count. When the player fouls upon delivering the first ball of a frame, all pins knocked down must be respotted, and only those pins knocked down by the second ball may be counted. If he bowls down all the pins with his second ball after fouling with the first, it shall be scored as a spare. When less than ten pins are bowled down on the second ball after fouling on the first, it shall be scored as an error. A player who fouls when delivering his second ball of a frame shall be credited with only those pins bowled down with his first ball, provided no foul was committed when the first ball was delivered. When a bowler fouls during the delivery of his first ball in the tenth frame and bowls down all ten pins with his second ball (making a spare) he bowls a third ball and is credited with a spare plus the pins bowled down with the third ball. When a player fouls while delivering his third ball in the tenth frame, only those pins bowled down in delivering his first two balls shall be counted.

OTHER FOUL LINE POINTS

Rule 18. Wherever it is deemed necessary to determine fouls, the officials of any local association, upon authorization by their board of directors, may require that a foul line be plainly painted on the walls, posts, division boards or any other structure in a bowling establishment at any point on a line with the regular foul line.

PROTESTS—PROVISIONAL BALL

Rule 19. When a protest involving a foul or the legality of pinfall is entered and it cannot immediately be resolved between the two team captains, a provisional ball or frame shall be bowled by the contestant.

If the protest occurs on the first delivery in a frame, the player shall complete his frame and then bowl another complete frame immediately, unless it involves a question of whether a bowler should receive credit for a strike or a lesser number of pins on his first delivery. In such event, the pin or pins which were protested as constituting illegal pinfall shall be respotted and the player required to bowl another ball.

When the protest occurs on the second delivery, the player shall bowl a provisional ball against the same setup of pins which were standing at the time except when the protest involves a foul in which case no provisional ball shall be necessary.

A record of both scores for the frame in which the provisional delivery was made shall be maintained and the protest referred to the league's board of directors or the tournament's managing committee for decision. If unable to reach a decision, the local association or the Congress can be asked for a decision upon submission of all the facts relating to the protest.

NO UNREASONABLE DELAY

Rule 20. The league or tournament officials shall allow no unreasonable delay in the progress of any game. Should any member or team participating in a league or tournament refuse to proceed with the game after being directed to do so by the proper authorities, such game or series shall be declared forfeited.

FOUL—DETECTION

Rule 21. League and tournament officials may adopt and use any ABC approved automatic foul detecting device and where none is available a foul judge must be stationed so he has an unobstructed view of the foul line.

FOUL—APPEAL

Rule 22. No appeal shall be allowed when a foul is indicated by an approved automatic foul detecting device or is called by a foul judge except when it is proved that the device is not operating properly, or there is a preponderance of evidence that the bowler did not foul. If the device becomes temporarily inoperative the following procedures shall be used in calling fouls:

(1) In tournament play tournament management shall assign a human foul judge or arrange for the official scorers to call fouls.

(2) In league play, the opposing captains shall call fouls or designate someone to act as a foul judge.

Failure to have the automatic foul detecting device in operation or provide for foul line observance when it is inoperative shall disqualify scores bowled for ABC high score consideration.

Rule 23. (No present rule.)

Rules 24-38. (These rules are basically concerned with proprietors and their employees, unfair tactics, suspensions, gambling and automatic scoring devices.)

GOVERNING BODIES

American Bowling Congress, 5301 South 76th St., Greendale WI 53129-0500 (Men)

Women's International Bowling Congress, 5301 South 76th St., Greendale, WI 53129-0500 (Women)

The American Bowling Congress (ABC) and the Women's International Bowling Congress (WIBC) are the recognized governing bodies for men's and women's tenpin bowling in the United States. Both organizations are members of the U.S. Olympic Committee— Group C. The two organizations provide the leadership and jurisdiction for the 50 states and 6 Canadian provincial associations along with approximately 2,800 local associations. The objectives of the organizations are to provide specific guidelines for bowlers to compete, whether they bowl for social or competitive reasons. The organizations promote the sport as well as its performers and serve as the watchdogs that assure bowlers they will be competing under playable conditions with standard equipment, rules, and regulations. The ABC and WIBC provide guides, forms, score sheets, and other materials for league play; sponsor national championships; sanction tournaments; provide awards; provide field service for development of programs; and provide educational materials including instructional film series, as well as numerous other services.

MAGAZINES

Bowling Magazine, ABC, 5301 South 76th St., Greendale WI 53129-0500

Woman Bowler, Women's International Bowling Congress, Inc., 5301 South 76th St., Greendale, WI 53129

• BOXING •

ABRIDGMENT OF 1987-88 USA/ABF OFFICIAL RULES

**(Reproduced by permission
of the United States of America Amateur Boxing Federation*)**

☐

Note: The rules included here are an abridgment of the USA Amateur Boxing Federation's (USA/ABF) technical rules for amateur boxing. Article I, a portion of Article VII, and all of Articles VIII through XIII (which primarily deal with the administrative aspects, national championships, Junior Olympic boxing, and international amateur boxing) are not included here. The USA/ABF Official Rules publication also includes Constitution and By-Laws, boxing history, and appendix material in addition to the technical rules.

ARTICLE II CONTESTANTS

102.1 All contestants must be registered under their own name with the USA/ABF and compete in their respective age and weight categories.

(1) Contestants must be registered with the LBC (Local Boxing Committee) in which they reside and have been passed as physically sound by the attending examining physician immediately before and after the contest.

(2) A contestant may not represent a club or an organization that is not a member of an LBC or USA/ABF. Any contestant who boxes for a club or organization which is not a registered member of the LBC must enter a contest as "unattached".

(3) Contestants must report to the clerk at the time specified on the entry blank (form) or other notice(s).

(4) No contestant shall be permitted to participate in any amateur boxing contest conducted or sanctioned by the USA/ABF on more than two days in any seven, except in regularly sanctioned tournaments requiring more than two days to complete. To the maximum extent possible, boxers will compete only once per day and in no case will a boxer compete more than twice in one day in said tournament.

(5) Boxers shall not compete more than once per day in non-tournament competitions such as club shows.

(6) Any competitor who participates in an unsanctioned boxing contest or tournament or in a tough man, wild man, barroom brawl, professional kick-boxing or any similar competition that is never sanctioned by USA/ABF automatically disqualifies himself.

102.2 Ring name or nicknames. All contestants must enter and compete in all boxing contests or tournaments under their own names. The use of a ring name or nickname is strictly prohibited.

---

*See page 86 for additional information.

102.3 Shaking of hands. As a sign of good sportsmanship, boxers may touch gloves before the beginning of the first and last rounds after the decision has been announced.

102.4 Medical aptitude.

(1) Medical certification. A competitor shall not be allowed to compete in a sanctioned competition unless he shall have been certified as fit to do so by a qualified doctor of medicine (MD) or doctor of osteopathy (DO).

(2) Medical certificate. Every boxer competing outside his own country must have in his possession a certificate signed by an authorized doctor of medicine stating that prior to leaving his own country he was in good physical condition and not suffering from any injury, infection or disability liable to affect his capacity to box in the country being visited. Such certificate may be incorporated in a record or passbook maintained by the boxer in accordance with the practice of his national association and must be produced at the medical examination before general weigh-in.

(3) Prohibited conditions.

(a) Vision. A boxer possessing the sight of only one eye is prohibited from boxing. The use of contact lenses by boxers in the ring is prohibited.

(b) Deaf and mute boxers who can pass a physical exam are eligible to compete.

(c) Cuts and abrasions. No boxer shall be allowed to take part in any contest if he wears a dressing (bandage or band-aid) on a cut, wound, abrasion, laceration or blood swelling on his scalp or face including the nose and ears. A boxer is allowed to box if an abrasion is covered with collodion. The decision should be made by the doctor examining the boxer on the day of competing.

ARTICLE III BOXER'S ATTIRE AND EQUIPMENT

103.1 All boxers must use USA/ABF-approved equipment. Said equipment must be approved by the Safety Education Committee, Sports Medicine Committees and the Board of Directors, with the approval of the Board of Governors.

(1) Hair shall be cut in such a manner as not to interfere with his vision. The first time a boxer's hair interferes with his vision, have the coach/assistant coach correct the interference and issue a caution. A second occurrence will result in another caution, and on the third interference, a warning will be issued. The next time, another warning, and on the third warning, the referee will disqualify the subject boxer.

(2) Contestants shall not wear contact lenses or eye glasses during competition.

(3) The use of any type of grease or other substance on the body is prohibited.

(a) Purpose of a prohibition against grease (vaseline)

1. grease or vaseline could interfere with medical personnel inspecting wounded tissue.

2. grease, after contact with gloves, collects dust and dirt and if the athlete comes in contact with the mat, small rock, resin, etc.

3. "tacky gloves" transmit debris to the facial area or eyes and can render potential harm—infection or a scratched cornea.

(4) All contestants must be clean, present a tidy appearance and be clean-shaven, with no goatee or beard. A thin-line mustache on the lip to the edge of the outer corners of the mouth is authorized.

(a) Purpose of a prohibition against beards/goatees

1. for some ethnic groups, facial hair is very coarse and sharp. It has the capability to cut or scratch the surface of the eye or face.

2. hair that interferes with one's vision is dangerous.

3. a strand of hair is sharp and can cut or scratch the surface of the eye.

(5) Boxers must wear a sleeveless athletic shirt (singlet or jersey), preferably a d ifferent color from the trunk's waistband.

(a) Purpose of jerseys (singlets)

1. to distinguish the amateur boxer.

2. to facilitate easier recognition of athletes for the officials.

3. to absorb body moisture and allow a contestant to wipe his own gloves.

4. to reduce/eliminate rope burns.

5. to keep gloves ''somewhat'' clean after each blow.

(6) Contestants must box in proper costume, including an approved foul-proof protection cup, which shall be firmly adjusted before the boxer leaves the dressing room. Jock strap cups are also authorized.

(7) Each contestant shall wear a pair of loose-fitting trunks made of light material that provides a contrasting color waistband and reaches at least halfway down the thigh but no lower than the knee. The wearing of tights is prohibited.

(8) The belt line of the trunks shall not extend above the waistline. The waistline is defined as an imaginary horizontal line through the navel to the top of the hips.

(a) Purpose of a discernible belt (waistline)

1. to facilitate easy recognition of legal or low blows for the officials.

(9) Socks may be of any color and may extend to within one (1) inch below the knee.

(10) No metal, straps, buckles, necklaces, jewelry of any kind or any other object which may cause injury to either opponent shall be worn.

(11) Shoes shall be of soft material, without spikes, cleats or heels.

(12) No apparel other than as specified above may be worn in the ring by a contestant, except a boxing robe and/or a clean towel which must be removed before the contest begins.

(13) Dress infractions. A referee shall exclude from competing any boxer who does not wear a cup-protector, individually fitted mouthpiece, headguard or who is not clean and properly dressed. In the event of a boxer's glove or dress becoming undone during boxing, a referee shall stop the contest to have it attended to.

(14) Contestants will face the center of the ring during the one minute interval (rest period) between rounds, either sitting or standing.

103.2 The manufacturer shall indemnify and hold USA/ABF harmless from and against any and all claims, damages, liabilities, costs and expenses, including, but not limited to, reasonable attorney's fees arising out of any lawsuits filed against said manufacturer regarding product liability.

103.3 Wearing of approved headguard.

(1) The wearing of competitive headguard is mandatory at all levels of USA/ABF competition.

(a) Only competitive headguards made to USA/ABF specifications and bearing the official USA/ABF label or stamp shall be used in contests sanctioned by the USA Amateur Boxing Federation, Inc. A $10,000 bond is required by USA/ABF from all manufacturers using this label stamp.

(b) The use of competitive headguards with cheek protectors that do not impair vision are permissible.

(c) Purpose of headguards

1. to diminish/reduce impact of a blow.

2. to reduce/eliminate cuts over the eyes, forehead, cheek, etc.

3. to eliminate cauliflower ears.

4. to eliminate perforated ear drums.

5. to absorb any fall to the head.

(2) The official USA/ABF competitive headguard is ten (10) ounces in weight.

Note: The remainder of Rule 103.3 details the precise materials and dimensions required for headguard.

103.4   Mouthpieces.

(1) A custom made, individually fitted mouthpiece must be worn by each contestant during each round. Examples of custom-made are the "dentist molded" and individually fitted are the clear plastic.

(a) Purpose of mouthpiece

1. to reduce potential knockdowns by allowing the athlete to "set" his jaw (mandible).

2. to reduce/eliminate cuts inside the mouth.

3. to reduce/eliminate potential harm/injury to the teeth and jaw.

(2) Mouthpieces must be examined by the attending physician.

(3) For rule when the mouthpiece is dislodged, unintentionally or intentionally, from the mouth, see 106.5(17)(a).

(4) If a boxer carries his mouthpiece halfway out of his mouth, he will be "cautioned" to reinsert it. A second offense will carry another caution. A third time will require an official "warning," etc.

103.5   USA/ABF-approved gloves.

(1) Authorized gloves. Competitors shall wear the gloves which the organizers of the competitions have placed at their disposal, if required. Boxers are not allowed to wear their own gloves under these conditions.

(a) Purpose of gloves

1. to diminish/reduce impact of a blow.

2. to protect the hands (metacarpal).

3. for two-tone gloves, to facilitate easier recognition of legal blows for the officials.

(2) Specifications. The boxing glove shall be 10 ounces in weight for 106-156 pounds and 12 ounces in weight for 165-201+ pounds.

Authorized gloves for each age and weight category are as follows:

Category	Weight class	8-oz.	10-oz.	12-oz.
Junior Olympic boxers	60-156		X	
	165-201+			X
Open boxers	106-156		X	
	165-201+			X
Open Junior (USA/ABF)	106-156		X	
	165-201+			X
Open Junior (AIBA)	106-147	X		
	156-201+		X	
International (AIBA)	106-147	X		
	156-201+		X	

(3) To establish uniformity and reduce confusion, an LBC may use 10 oz. gloves for all competitions other than tournaments.

(4) All competitive gloves must be thumbless or thumb-attached.

(5) The construction of the gloves shall be in accordance with the specifications approved by USA/ABF and shall have the USA/ABF label in each glove.

(6) If gloves have been used before, the gloves must be whole, clean, and in sanitary condition, subject to inspection and approval by the referee or a representative of the boxing committee. Defective gloves must be immediately replaced with gloves meeting USA/ABF requirements. No breaking, roughing or twisting of gloves shall be permitted.

(7) In U.S. championships, the sponsor must supply new gloves, with the USA/ABF label or stamp affixed. A sufficient number of sets of gloves must be on hand for the entire tournament. This regulation is intended to protect boxers from injuries due to the use of improper gloves.

(8) The glove laces shall be tied on the outside of the back of the wrist of the glove. Eyelets of the laces shall be clipped and a wrist band or 6″-8″ × 1″ of adhesive tape shall be used to cover the laces.

Note: The remainder of Rule 103.5 details glove specification requirements.

103.6 Bandages (handwraps) and tape specifications.

(1) The purpose of bandages is to protect a boxer's hands and not to add force to a blow.

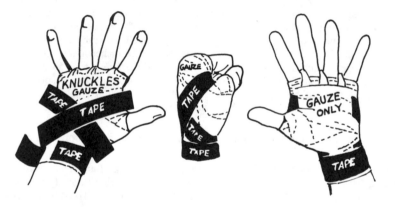

(2) Each boxer shall wear handwraps that are made of cotton gauze, soft surgical or velpeau based on the following:

(a) Weights 156 lbs. and under—2″ × 10 yards

(b) Weights 165 lbs. and over—2″ × up to 12 yards

(c) Velpeau—all weights—6′7″

(3) A strip of one inch (1″) adhesive tape by eight inches (8″) in length may secure the bandages around the wrist.

No substance other than the above prescribed may be used between the fingers or over the knuckles. For maximum protection, the tape should go around the side of the hand and not over 1/2-inch (approximately) into the palm of the hand. There must be no tape over the knuckles or across the palm of the hand. Also, the boxer's hands may have two (2) one inch (1″) pieces of tape on top of the gauze in a crisscross pattern. This shall be optional.

(4) The "A-Fist" handwrap has been approved for use in competition.

(5) Bandaging should be supervised by an official specifically assigned for this purpose. Anyone officially connected with a boxing contest may have a boxer's bandages examined upon request.

ARTICLE IV RING AND RING IMPLEMENTS

104.1 The Ring.

(1) The ring shall be not less than 16 nor more than 20 feet square within the ropes, the apron of the ring floor shall extend beyond the ropes not less than two feet. The ring shall not be more than four feet above the floor of the building or grounds of an outdoor arena, and shall be provided with three sets of suitable steps for the use of contestants, coaches, and officials, one in each contestant's corner and one in a neutral corner for use by doctors and referees.

(a) For international competition, the minimum size shall be 16 feet square and the maximum size 20 feet square, measured inside the line of the ropes. In international championships, the size of the ring shall be 20 feet square, measured inside the line of the ropes (6m.10 in metric measures), and it shall not be less than 3 feet (91cm.) or more than 4 feet (1m.22) above the ground or base.

(2) The ring shall be equipped with at least 4 ropes. A 20-foot ring will have (2) spacer ties on each side of the ring to secure the ropes. The rope shall not be less than one inch in diameter. Such ropes shall be manila rope, synthetic, plastic rope or any similar material, and shall not be made of metal of any type. All ropes shall be wrapped securely in soft material. Of the four ropes used, the lower rope shall be 18 inches above the ring floor, the second rope 30 inches, the third rope 42 inches, and the fourth rope 54 inches above the ring floor. The ring floor shall be padded with a one inch layer of ensolite AAC or AL closed cell foam rubber (or chemical equivalent). The padding shall be covered with canvas, duck or similar material tightly stretched and laced securely in place, preferably under the apron.

(a) If the ropes are colored red, white and blue, red is the top rope followed by white, blue, etc.

(3) Ring posts shall not be less than three inches or more than four inches in diameter, extending from the floor to the height of 58 inches above the ring floor. The ropes shall be connected to posts with the extension not shorter than 18 inches. The turnbuckles must be covered with a protective padding.

(4) Corner pads should be arranged in the following way: In the nearer left-side ring corner facing the announcer or president of the jury—red; the far left-side corner—white; in the far right-side corner—blue; and the near right corner—white.

(5) More than one ring can be used in competitions where there are several entries.

104.2 Ring implements—Water buckets, stools, bottles, resin, sponges, etc.

(1) Organizations conducting amateur boxing contests/tournaments shall provide a sufficient number of sanitary water buckets, sponges, and unbreakable drinking bottles for contestants. Also two stools with short legs, extra laces for gloves, and such other articles as are required in the conduct of the contests. Resin, if used, shall not be sprinkled on the ring canvas but must be placed in trays near each corner.

(2) The use of a common sponge or water bottle for all contestants is strictly prohibited. For the U.S. Championships, the local body holding the tournament shall furnish each contestant with an individual sponge and a water bottle.

104.3 Gong, bells, horn, klaxon, etc.

(1) The gong, bell, buzzer, horn or klaxon, whichever is used, must be sufficiently loud so that the officials and contestants can hear it clearly.

(2) When using more than one ring in competition/tournament, it is recommended a bell or whistle not be used as sounding devices. This creates confusion and should be used when only one ring is used.

104.4 Other equipment.

(1) Tables and chairs for officials—judges, announcers, timekeeper(s), physician(s), jury, administration, media, etc.

(2) Score cards (judges')—top portion filled out. Extra blank copies of scorecards. Extra pens and pencils and clipboards.

(3) Microphones and speakers.

(4) A portable resuscitator with oxygen equipment and a stretcher should be available at ringside.

ARTICLE V COACHES/ASSISTANT COACHES

105.1 Each competitor is entitled to one coach and one assistant who shall be governed by the following rules:

(1) Registration. See 203.1(3)(5) in the Constitution and By-laws.

(2) Only one coach and assistant coach will mount the ring apron and only one may enter the ring during the interval.

(3) A registered boxer may serve as an assistant coach in order to assist with a boxer competing for the same club.

(4) During the boxing, neither the coach nor the assistant coach shall remain on the platform of the ring. They shall, before a round begins, remove from the platform of the ring, seats, towels, buckets, bottles, etc. Coaches and assistant coaches must be seated during the duration of the round.

(5) Any coach or assistant coach or official encouraging or inciting spectators by words or signs to advise or encourage a boxer during the progress of a round shall not be permitted to continue to act as a coach or assistant coach or official at the tournament where the offense is committed.

(6) If a coach or his assistant infringes the rules, his boxer may be warned or disqualified by the referee.

(7) No coach shall attempt to render aid to a seriously injured boxer without the approval of the attending physician. Coaches shall leave the ring enclosure on the command of the timekeeper and referee five seconds before the beginning of each round.

(8) Coaches must wear clean outer apparel with no commercial advertising matter appearing on same. They will not be permitted to wear hats of any style.

(9) Every coach working in a boxer's corner should have the following equipment: first aid supplies, two clean white towels, sterile gauze pads, sterile cotton and Q tips, bottle of adrenalin chloride, ice bag with ice.

(a) Coaches must submit first aid kits and corner equipment to the attending physician, referee or committee member for inspection and/or approval if requested by same.

(b) The above-referenced items are the 'maximum' equipment a coach may have in the corner. First aid supplies do not include ammonia, ammonia inhalants or smelling salts. These items are prohibited.

(10) Violations of the foregoing provisions shall result in the removal of offenders from the ring corner and from further participation as coaches in the contest or tournament,

or forever with amateur boxing and may result in the disqualification of their contestant by the referee.

(11) A coach may retire his boxer by throwing a sponge or towel into the ring, or mounting the ring apron, except when the referee is in the course of counting.

(12) For procedure when mouthpiece is dislodged, intentionally or unintentionally, see 106.5(17)(a)(1-2).

(13) The USA/ABF shall only allow its officially-elected coaches, trainers, manager and medical staff to be responsible for the training, coaching and supervision of the Olympic, Pan American and World Championship teams, from the start of the designated training period to the end of the competition.

(14) Whenever a contestant is charged with an infraction of rules, that his coach is aware of and has not reported or is responsible for said infraction, he also shall be subject to disciplinary action.

ARTICLE VI
PHYSICIANS, SAFETY PRECAUTION, AND BOXING OFFICIALS

106.1 Safety precautions and physicians.

(1) One or more physicians (medical doctors—M.D., or doctor of osteopathy—D.O.) must be in attendance at ringside at all times during competitions, prepared to deal with any medical emergency which may arise.

(2) The physician who is operating under the Good Samaritan Rule shall determine if any injury warrants the match to be discontinued. Upon his decision, he shall advise the boxer and his coach/assistant coach, in writing, of treatment for such injury. He is not personally obligated to perform such medical treatment but must make the appropriate medical referral for such treatment.

(3) Contestants shall be thoroughly examined immediately before and after each bout. One physician must be in attendance at ringside at all boxing contests. It is preferred, if possible, that two physicians be in attendance, one to be at ringside and one in or near the boxer's dressing room. For club shows, all boxers must be examined before and after their bout.

(4) In the event of a RSCH (referee stops contest for head blows) or RSCM (referee stops contest for medical reasons) or if a boxer is seriously injured, the referee will immediately request the physician to check the boxer's condition and/or to tender aid to the injured boxer as may be necessary before the boxer is permitted to rise from the floor or leave the ring. A physician may, at his own discretion, enter the ring immediately if a bout is stopped or if it is stopped because of an injury.

(5) A referee, before officiating in any USA/ABF competition, must be examined and approved by the attending physician.

(6) No boxer shall be allowed to take part in any contest if he wears a dressing on a cut, wound, abrasion, laceration or blood swelling on his scalp or face including the nose and ears. The decision shall be made by the doctor examining the boxer on the day of his competing. Dressing is interpreted as items such as cocoon, tape bandages, gauze, etc.; material such as new skin, Collodion, and other liquid substances which solidify are permitted. The referee will inspect the boxer prior to commencement of the bout, and if the boxer is found in violation of the aforementioned requirements, he will not be allowed to compete unless the dressing can be removed and the injury or cut or wound is not of sufficient caliber to endanger the boxer.

(7) The attending physician may suspend a bout at any time by mounting the ring apron. He/she shall examine the boxer, and if in his/her opinion, a contestant is in danger of further physical injury, he/she shall notify the referee to terminate the bout. The referee will notify the jury and all judges that the bout has been stopped on RSC (referee stops contest). No restriction period will be required of the boxer. The termination of the bout is deemed in the best interest of safety and the well-being of the boxer.

(8) The attending physician shall not enter the ring between rounds for the purpose of examining an injured contestant, unless requested by the referee. He may indicate to the referee that he wants to examine the boxer and the referee shall after the bell sounds, suspend the match and bring the boxer mid-ring at the apron in front of the physician for examination. If, in the opinion of the physician, a contestant is in danger of further physical injury, he shall notify the referee to terminate the bout.

(9) In the event of any serious injury, the attending physician shall immediately render treatment and prescribe further treatment if necessary.

(10) Any boxer who has sustained a severe injury, RSCH or RSCM in a contest shall be required to follow the instructions of the attending physician.

(11) In the case of repeated stopped contests, the boxer concerned should be retired by the LBC chairman on advice from a physician.

(12) When a boxer is down as a result of a blow and is unresponsive, no individuals are to touch him except to remove his mouthpiece until the attending physician enters the ring and personally attends the fallen boxer and issues such instructions as he deems necessary to the coaches.

(13) A portable resuscitator with oxygen equipment and a stretcher should be available at the ringside.

(14) Procedure after an RSCH or RSCM.

(a) Unconscious boxer. If a boxer is rendered unconscious, then only the referee and the doctor summoned should remain in the ring, unless the doctor needs additional assistance.

(b) When an athlete represents the USA and USA/ABF in an international event, the assessment of an (H) (head blow) by an international referee and/or if a medical restriction period should apply will be determined by the designated USA/ABF team physician.

(c) Medical attention. A boxer who has been stopped in a contest as a result of head blows, or wherein the referee has stopped the contest due to a boxer receiving hard blows to the head, making him defenseless or incapable of continuing, shall be examined by a doctor immediately afterwards and accompanied to his home or suitable accommodations by one of the officials on duty at the event. The official accompanying the boxer shall give a Restrictions Affidavit to a responsible adult at the home or accommodation and explain its use clearly and thoroughly.

The referee in the bout will notify the jury and all judges that the bout was stopped due to the boxer receiving hard blows to the head. Judges must annotate their scorecards "RSCH" or "RSCM."

Note: The remainder of Rule 106.1 defines the participation restriction periods to be applied following a RSCH or RSCM.

106.2 Restrictions affidavit.

(1) For a bout ending in a RSCH or RSCM, the injured boxer should be issued a Restrictions Affidavit. If any of the following symptoms occur, contact a physician immediately: (a) Headache or dizziness lasting over two hours; (b) increasing drowsiness or loss of consciousness following the bout (arouse every two hours during the night following the

bout); (c) repeated vomiting; (d) blurred vision; (e) mental confusion or irrational behavior; (f) convulsive seizure; (g) inability to move a limb; (h) excessive restlessness; (i) oozing of blood or watery fluid from the ears or nose; (j) inability to control urine or feces.

(2) The release or permission to return to competitive boxing shall be completed on the reverse side of the Restrictions Affidavit. When signed and approved by the athlete's personal physician, who is a qualified doctor of medicine, to return, the Restrictions Affidavit will be submitted to the LBC (LBC president or registration chairman) and a copy will be forwarded to the USA/ABF Office immediately.

106.3 Administration—boxing officials.

(1) Registrations. Officials and non-athlete members who are responsible for, and/or enforce ABF policy, rules, regulations, etc., must be registered, i.e., referee, judge, timekeeper, weighmasters, physicians, inspectors, clerks, glove stewards, competition director/administrator, drawmaster, trainers, coaches, etc., and consistent with Article 203.1(b).

(2) Each USA/ABF Local Boxing Committee (LBC) is responsible for the recruitment, certification, registration and assigning of all officials, coaches and non-athlete members. Each member is required to attend an annual (re)certification program (clinic) under the direction/responsibility of the LBC.

(3) Assigning of officials is the responsibility of the LBC in the territory in which the competition is held. For Regional tournaments, the Regional Committee will determine the assigning process. For national events, such as the U.S. Championships, Eastern and Western Regional Trials, Olympic Festival, box-offs and USA/ABF international events, the USA/ABF Officials Committee will assume responsibility.

(4) Prohibited participation. Boxers, coaches, officials (judges, timers, clerks, sponsors, promoters, etc.) who participate or serve in any capacity in tough man, wild man, barroom brawl, professional kick-boxing or any similar competition that is never sanctioned by USA/ABF or its local LBC forfeits his or her right to box and/or participate in any capacity in amateur boxing competition held under sanction of USA/ABF or its local LBC.

106.4 (This rule details the certification and selection of officials for national USA/ABF tournaments/events.)

106.5 Referees

(1) Primary concern. The primary concern/duty of the referee is to ensure the safety of the boxers.

(2) Dress. Referees and male officials in all USA/ABF-sanctioned competitions shall be dressed in white shirt, white trousers and boxing shoes without heels, preferably white. Referees while officiating in USA/ABF national championships may wear the AIBA and/or USA/ABF patch on their attire. Officials working in USA/ABF group member's tournaments may wear the uniforms of that organization at its competitions.

(3) Duties. The referee shall officiate in the ring. He shall:

(a) See that the rules and fair play are strictly observed.

(b) Maintain control of the contest at all its stages.

(c) Prevent a weak boxer from receiving undue and unnecessary punishment.

(d) Check the gloves and dress.

(e) He shall use three words of command:

"Stop" when ordering the boxers to stop boxing.

"Box" when ordering them to continue.

"Break" when breaking a clinch, upon which command each boxer shall step back before continuing boxing.

(f) He shall indicate to a boxer by suitable explanatory signs or gestures any infringement of the rules.

(g) At the end of a contest collect and check the papers of the five judges; after checking he shall hand these papers to the president of the jury, or on occasions when there is no jury, to the announcer.

(h) The referee shall not indicate the winner, by raising a boxer's hand or otherwise, until the announcement has been made. When the referee has disqualified a boxer or stopped the bout, he shall first inform the president of the jury or announcer which boxer he has disqualified or the reason for which he has stopped the bout, to enable the president to instruct the announcer to make the decision correctly known to the public. When the winner of a bout is announced, the referee shall raise the hand of the winning boxer.

(4) Powers of the referee. The referee is empowered:

(a) To terminate a contest at any stage if he considers it too one-sided.

(b) To terminate a contest at any stage if one of the boxers has received an injury on account of which the referee decides he should not continue.

(c) To terminate a contest at any stage if he considers the contestants are not in earnest. In such cases he may disqualify one or both contestants.

(d) To caution a boxer or to stop the boxing during a contest and administer a warning to a boxer against fouls or for any other reason in the interests of fair play, or to ensure compliance with the rules.

(e) To disqualify a boxer who fails to comply immediately with his orders, or behaves towards him in an offensive or aggressive manner at any time.

(f) To disqualify a coach or assistant who has infringed the rules, and the boxer himself if the coach or assistant does not comply with the referee's orders.

(g) With or without previous warning, to disqualify a contestant for committing a foul.

(h) In the event of a knock-down, to suspend a count, if a boxer deliberately fails to retire to a neutral corner or delays to do so.

(i) To interpret the rules in so far as they are applicable or relevant to the actual contest or to decide and take action on any circumstance of the contest which is not covered by a rule.

(5) Warnings. If a boxer infringes the rules but does not merit disqualification for such infringement, the referee shall stop the contest and shall issue a warning to the offender. As a preliminary to a warning the referee shall order the boxers to stop. The warning shall be clearly given and in such a way that the boxer understands the reason and the purpose of the warning.

The referee shall signal with his hand to each of the judges that a special warning has been given and shall clearly indicate to them the boxer whom he has warned. After giving the warning, the referee shall order the boxers to "box." If a boxer is given three warnings in a contest, he shall be disqualified.

(6) Cautions. A referee may caution a boxer. A caution is the nature of advice or admonishment given by the referee to a boxer to check or prevent undesirable practices or the less serious infringements of the rules. To do so he will not necessarily stop the contest but may avail of a suitable safe opportunity during a round to admonish a boxer for an infringement of the rules.

(7) Dress infractions. A referee shall exclude from competing any boxer who does not wear a cup-protector and mouthpiece or who is not clean and properly dressed. In the event of a boxer's glove or dress becoming undone during boxing, a referee shall stop the contest to have it attended to.

(8) Replacing the referee during the bout. If a referee is incapacitated in the course of a bout, the timekeeper shall strike the gong to stop the bout and the next available neutral referee on the list shall be instructed to control the bout and order boxing to be resumed.

(9) Medical considerations. A referee, before officiating in any U.S. Championship or similar event, shall undergo a medical examination as to his physical fitness for carrying out his duties in the ring. His vision shall be at least six diopters in each eye. The wearing of spectacles by a referee during the progress of a bout is not permitted, but contact lenses are allowed.

(10) A referee may, at his discretion, call a doctor into the ring during the round to examine an injured boxer. Once the referee has asked the advice of a doctor, either during the round or between rounds, he must abide by the doctor's decision.

(11) The referee upon noticing any bleeding about the head shall give the command "STOP." The referee will have on his person a gauze pad to clean the injured area. If the area continues to bleed, the referee will consult the ringside physician. The physician will inform the referee whether the bout is to continue or issue an RSC (see section 106.1(6)). The referee may summon the physician as often as necessary during a bout to include between rounds.

(12) The referee, or official designated, shall inspect the bandages and gloves, and make sure no foreign substance has been applied to either the gloves or the bodies of the boxers.

(13) Down—Definition. A boxer is considered "down":

(a) if he touches the floor with any part of his body other than his feet as the result of a blow or series of blows, or

(b) if he hangs helplessly on the ropes as the result of a blow or series of blows, or

(c) if he is outside or partly outside the ropes as the result of a blow or series of blows, or

(d) if following a hard punch he has not fallen and is not lying on the ropes, but is in a semi-conscious state and cannot, in the opinion of the referee, continue the bout.

(14) The count. In the case of a knock-down, the referee shall immediately begin to count the seconds. When a boxer is "down," the referee shall count aloud from one to 10 with intervals of a second between the numbers, and shall indicate each second with his hand in such a manner that the boxer who has been knocked down may be aware of the count. Before the number "one" is counted, an interval of one second must have elapsed from the time when the boxer has fallen to the floor, and the time of announcing "one." If the opponent should not go to the neutral corner on the command of the referee, the referee shall stop counting until the opponent has done so. The counting shall be then continued where it has been interrupted.

(a) Opponent's responsibilities. If a boxer is down, his opponent must at once go to the neutral corner as designated by the referee. He may only continue against the opponent who is knocked down after the latter has gotten up and on the command "box" of the referee.

(b) Mandatory eight count. When a boxer is "down" as the result of a blow, the bout shall not be continued until the referee has reached the count of eight, even if the boxer is ready to continue before then.

After the referee has said "eight or ten," whichever is applicable, the bout ends and shall be decided as an RSC, RSCH or RSCM.

(c) Boxer down at end of round. In the event of a boxer being "down" at the end of a round, the referee shall continue to count. Should the referee count up to 10, such boxer shall be deemed to have lost the bout by an RSCH or RSCM. If the boxer is fit to resume boxing before the count of 10 is reached, the referee shall immediately use the command "box."

(d) Second time boxer down without another blow. If a boxer is "down" as the result of a blow and the bout is continued after the count of eight has been reached, but the boxer falls again without having received another blow, the referee shall continue the counting from the count of eight at which he had stopped.

(e) Both boxers down. If both boxers go down at the same time, counting will be continued as long as one of them is still down. If both boxers remain down until "10," the bout will be stopped, and the decision given in accordance with the points awarded up to the time of the knock-down.

(f) Boxer fails to resume. A boxer who fails to resume boxing immediately after the termination of the rest interval, or who, when knocked down by a blow, fails to resume within 10 seconds, shall lose the contest.

(g) Compulsory count limits. When a boxer has three compulsory counts in the same round or four times for the whole bout, the referee shall stop the contest (RSC or RSCH).

(15) RSCH. The referee will indicate to the jury and judges to annotate the scorecard "RSCH," when he has stopped the contest as a result of a boxer being unable to continue as a result of blows to the head.

(a) RSCH is a term to be used only when a boxer has received hard head blows making him defenseless and incapable of continuing. The term RSCH is not to be used when a boxer is simply outclassed and receiving too many scoring hits without scoring himself.

(16) Fouls.

(1) Cautions, warnings, disqualifications. The competitor who does not obey the instructions of the referee, acts against the boxing rules, boxes in any unsportsmanlike manner, or commits fouls, can at the discretion of the referee be cautioned, warned or disqualified in any order. A referee may, without stopping a contest, caution a boxer at some safe opportunity. If he intends to warn a boxer, he shall stop the contest, and will demonstrate the infringement. He will then point to the boxer and to each of the five judges. A referee having once administered a warning for a particular foul, e.g., holding, cannot issue a caution for the same offense. A third caution for the same type of foul will mandatorily require a warning to be issued. Only three warnings may be given to the same boxer in one contest. The third warning brings automatic disqualification.

(2) Types of fouls. The following are fouls:

(a) Hitting below the belt, holding, tripping, kicking, and butting with foot or knee.

(b) Hits or blows with head, shoulder, forearm, elbow, throttling of the opponent, pressing with arm or elbow in opponent's face, pressing the head of the opponent back over the ropes.

(c) Hitting with open glove, the inside of the glove, wrist or side of the hand.

(d) Hits landing on the back of the opponent, and especially any blow on the back of the neck or head and kidney punch.

(e) Pivot blows.

(f) Attack whilst holding the ropes or making any unfair use of the ropes.

(g) Lying on, wrestling and throwing in the clinch.

(h) An attack on an opponent who is down or who is in the act of rising.

(i) Holding.

(j) Holding and hitting or pulling and hitting.

(k) Holding, or locking, of the opponent's arm or head, or pushing an arm underneath the arm of the opponent.

(l) Ducking below the belt of the opponent in a manner dangerous to his opponent.

(m) Completely passive defense by means of double cover and intentionally falling to avoid a blow.

(n) Useless, aggressive, or offensive utterances during the round.

(o) Not stepping back when ordered to break.

(p) Attempting to strike opponent immediately after the referee has ordered "break" and before taking a step back.

(q) Assaulting or behaving in an aggressive manner towards a referee at any time.

(r) Spitting out mouthpiece.

(s) Coaching from the corner (verbal or by gesture) during the progress of the round.

(t) Pushing, shoving.

(3) Coach/assistant coach. Each boxer is responsible in the same way for his coach/assistant coach.

(17) Specific fouls—mouthpiece and low blows.

(a) Mouthpiece

(1) When a mouthpiece is knocked out of a competitor's mouth, the referee will "stop" the bout, escort the boxer and mouthpiece to his corner where the mouthpiece will be washed (rinsed). A coach will replace the mouthpiece in the boxer's mouth after such washing.

(2) If a boxer deliberately spits his mouthpiece out without receiving a blow, the referee will take the boxer to his corner, have the coach/assistant coach wash (rinse) the mouthpiece and return it to its proper position, and then the referee will issue a "warning" to the offending boxer.

(3) A boxer who loses his mouthpiece more than once (for any reason), will have it washed and returned, but will receive a "warning" for each such loss after the first time.

(4) Also see 103.4(4).

(b) Low blows

(1) Blow observed by referee

(a) If a boxer has received a low blow (a punch below the beltline) and the referee saw the foul blow delivered, the referee shall give the command "STOP," and then issue a warning to the boxer delivering the blow. In the opinion of the referee, if the blow was of such force as to incapacitate the offended boxer so he cannot continue to box, the referee shall inform the judges and the jury about his decision to disqualify the boxer who delivered the low blow.

(b) If a boxer is down as the result of a low blow, the referee will begin a count (the same as in any knockdown). At the end of eight, if the boxer is ready to continue, the referee will issue a warning to the offending boxer and give the command "BOX" to continue the bout.

(2) Blow not observed by referee

(a) If the boxer is still down at the count of eight (8) and the referee did not see the blow delivered, he shall continue to the count of ten, and the bout shall be terminated.

(i) However, if the boxer or his coach complains that the blow was low, the referee shall then give the command "STOP" and consult the judges.

(ii) In this case he will abide by the majority of the votes cast. (If a judge did not see the blow delivered, he/she shall not cast a vote.) If the majority of the judges who saw the blow indicate the blow was low, the referee will then issue the warning and inform the judge and the jury about his decision to disqualify the boxer who delivered the low blow.

(iii) If the majority of judges indicate the blow was not low, no warning is issued, and the bout is terminated.

(c) Naming a winner as a result of a deliberate low blow

(i) If in the opinion of the referee a low blow is delivered and was of such force as to seriously incapacitate the offended boxer so that he could not continue to box, the offender is disqualified.

(ii) If such is the case, upon seeing the deliberate low blow, the referee will give the command "STOP."

(1) He shall immediately assist the offended boxer and summon the ringside physician and motion the other boxer to a neutral corner.

(2) The referee then issues a warning to the boxer who delivered the deliberate blow.

(3) The referee then informs the judges and jury about his decision to disqualify the boxer who delivered the low blow. The referee collects the scorecards from the judges and delivers them over to the jury so the winner may be announced.

(18) Suitable gestures or signs

(a) In international contests, where difficulties arise concerning language, the referee in the case of cautions or warnings should first of all make sure that the boxer concerned realizes that it is he whom the referee is addressing. The referee shall then by sign or demonstration clearly indicate the offense.

(b) In order to overcome language difficulties, a referee shall use suitable gestures or signs which indicate some of the common offenses. It is desirable also, that boxers be taught this "international boxing sign language"; following are some examples:

(1) Hitting with open glove or inside the glove or prohibited part of the glove. Referee taps the palm of one hand with the fingers of the other hand.

(2) Holding in various ways. Referee imitates the nature of the hold.

(3) Dangerous use of the head. Referee taps the forehead, accompanied by appropriate movements of the head.

(4) Lying on. Referee bends the body forward.

(5) Not stepping back on the command "Break." Referee demonstrates "stepping back."

(6) Hitting below the belt. Referee points to the position below the belt, or moves the edge of the palm of the hand along the belt line and then points below it.

(7) Low ducking. Referee touches the forehead with the fingers and points below the belt line.

(8) Blows on the back of the head, neck or the kidneys. Referee touches the back of his head, neck or kidneys.

Additionally, even when there is no language difficulty, the referee should officiate all boxing contests in a similar manner wherever possible, refraining from using any vocal language other than the commands, "stop," "break," "box."

Note: Knowledge of this "sign language" will help U.S. boxers who compete in international boxing contests.

(19) Referee consults judges. If a referee has any reason to believe that a foul has been committed which he himself has not seen, he may consult the judges.

(20) Interpretation. The interpretation of any of these rules, or any questions not answered in these rules, insofar as they concern the bout and the occurrences connected with same, shall be decided by the referee.

(21) Hints for referees. *Note:* The official rules publication includes a list of 51 comments to serve as a guide for referees to hone skills and improve their ring mechanics.

106.6 Judges.

(1) Dress. The judges shall officiate in white clothing, similar to the referee. Female officials will be dressed in white blouses, white skirt or slacks, and preferably, white shoes.

(2) Duties.

(a) Each judge shall independently judge the merits of the two contestants and shall decide the winner according to the rules.

(b) He/she shall not speak to a contestant nor to another judge, nor to anyone else except the referee during the contest, but may, if necessary, at the end of a round, bring to the notice of the referee any incident which he (the referee) may appear not to have noticed, such as the misconduct of a coach, loose ropes, etc.

(c) The number of points awarded to each competitor shall be entered by a judge on his/her scoring card immediately after the end of each round.

(d) At the end of the bout, a judge shall total the points and nominate a winner.

(e) He/she shall not leave his/her seat until the verdict has been announced to the public.

(3) Each contest shall be marked by five USA/ABF judges who shall be seated separate from the public and immediately adjacent to the ring. Two of the judges shall be seated on the same side of the ring at a sufficient distance from one another, and each of the other three judges shall be seated at the center of one of the other three sides of the ring. When the number of officials available is insufficient, three judges instead of five may be used, but this shall not apply to the U.S. Championships or similar events.

(4) Before a contest begins, the referee and the judges should confirm the identity of each boxer, fill in the necessary preliminary entries on their scoring card, such as weight class, bout number, date, and then affix their signature to the bottom of the paper. Each official will print, in large block letters, the names of the boxers in the red and blue corners in the corresponding left and right columns on his/her scoring card.

NOTE: Competition organizers should strive to have all score cards pre-printed or typed with names, club representation, weights, etc.

(5) Advice to judges.

A judge is advised to direct his gaze on a point midway between the two boxers—this will enable him to see and note the actions of each. He should avoid any inclination to watch a particular boxer, who by reason of his style or personality may attract more attention than his opponent. Therefore, such concentration on one boxer is not advisable as a judge may fail to see some of the scoring actions of the other boxer. Judges are advised to assess the scoring value of each incident as it occurs and credit it mentally to each boxer concerned. When a boxer has obtained a lead in points, further gains made by him shall be added to his score. Judges are to use a system of three blows for one point to determine the winner of a round. It is important that there be a uniform method to be applied to eliminate the situation of each boxer having the same number of points at the end of a bout.

106.7 Awarding of points.

(1) Directives. In awarding points, the following directives shall be observed:

(a) Concerning blows.

(i) Scoring blows. During each round, a judge shall assess the respective scores of each boxer according to the number of blows obtained by each. Each blow to have scoring value must, without being blocked or guarded, land directly with the knuckle part of the closed glove of either hand on any part of the front or sides of the head or body above the belt. Swings landing as above described are scoring hits. The value of blows scored in a rally of infighting shall be assessed at the end of such rally and shall be credited to the boxer who has had the better of the exchanges according to the degree of his superiority.

(ii) Non-scoring blows. Non-scoring blows are blows which are struck by a boxer:

(aa) while infringing any of the rules, or

(bb) with the side, the heel, the inside of the glove or with the open glove or any part other than the knuckle part of the closed glove, or

(cc) which land on the arms, or

(dd) which merely connect, without the weight of the body or shoulder.

(b) Concerning fouls—W, X, and J.

(i) There are three symbols the Judge uses to annotate fouls on the scorecard—W, X, and J.

W—Referee's Warning. If the referee issues a "warning" against one (or both) of the boxers, the judge will indicate a "W" on his/her scorecard in the column of the offending boxer. The judge will also note the reason for the warning, i.e., "W—Holding."

X—Judge disagrees with referee's warning. If the judge concludes "unequivocally" the warning was inappropriate or in error, the judge will annotate an "X" in the appropriate column and indicate the reason for the warning, i.e., "X—Low Blow." In this case, there will be no loss of a point. It must be noted, if the judge did not see the foul or was unsure if it was a foul, the judge "will" accept the advice of the referee and issue a "W" for the warning.

J—Judge's Warning. If the judge detects a foul, apparently unnoticed by the referee, the judge may impose a warning by writing a "J" on his/her scorecard in the column of the offending boxer. The judge will also note the reason for the judge's warning, i.e., "J—Ducking." A "J" foul carries the same penalty as a "W" warning.

(c) How to administer the penalty (foul) deductions.

(i) There are four (4) rules the judge must remember in dealing with fouls (W or J).

Rule #1. The judge must compute the boxing score first. Example: during a round, the boxer in the Red Corner commits a foul, and a warning is issued by the referee. The judge will "mentally" note the violation and continue counting blows until the end of the round.

Rule #2. If the winner of the round fouled, credit his opponent with one (1) point. Referring to Rule #1 above, Red Corner was "warned," and the boxing score was Red-20, Blue-19. The score that the judge will write on his/her scorecard will be Red-20, Blue-20.

Rule #3. If the loser of the round fouled, subtract from the loser. Again, refer to Rule #1, Red-20, Blue-19. This time, Blue Corner was issued a warning, so subtract from him. Correct score, Red-20, Blue-18.

Rule #4. If the round is tied, subtract from the boxer who committed the foul. If the boxing score is Red-20, Blue-20 (Rule #1), and Blue Corner fouled, subtract from him. Correct score, Red-20, Blue-19.

(ii) How to administer "offsetting" fouls in a round. Red Corner and Blue Corner both foul. At the end of the round, the judge must compute the boxing score (Rule #1). Because both contestants fouled, they offset each other and would not change the score.

(iii) How to administer "multiple" fouls in a round. Red Corner fouls twice during a round. At the end of the round, the boxing score is Red-20, Blue-18 (Rule #1). Deal with each foul individually. For the first violation, Rule #2 is applied, and the "new" score is now Red-20, Blue-19. The second violation also comes under Rule #2 because the winner fouled. The round score is Red-20, Blue-20. Red Corner fouls twice during a round. At the end of the round, the boxing score is Red-20, Blue-19 (Rule #1). Deal with each foul individually. For the first violation, Rule #2 is applied and the "new" score is now Red-20,

Blue-20. The second violation is addressed by using Rule #3 (score is tied). The round score is now Red-19, Blue-20.

(d) Concerning the awarding of points.

(i) End of each round. Twenty points shall be awarded for each round. No fraction of points may be given. At the end of each round, the better (more skillful) boxer shall receive twenty points and his opponent proportionately less. When boxers are equal in merit, each shall receive twenty points.

(ii) Points determination. The awarding of points shall follow the principles: one point for three correct hits; one point for a warning by the referee or judge; if the number of hits differs from 3, 6, 9, 12, etc., the attached table is to be used:

Number of hits: 1 2 3 4 5 6 7 8 9 10 11 12 13 14 . . .

Points awarded: 0 1 1 1 2 2 2 3 3 3 4 4 4 5 . . .

(iii) End of contest. If, at the end of a contest and having marked each round in accordance with directive (i) and (ii), a judge shall find that the boxers are equal in points, he/she shall award the decision to the boxer:

(aa) Who has done most of the leading off or was the aggressor, or if equal in that respect;

(bb) Who has shown the better defense (blocking, parrying, ducking, side-stepping, etc.) by which the opponent's attacks have been made to miss;

(cc) If still equal, who boxed cleaner and had the better style?

(dd) A winner must be nominated in all USA/ABF competitions. (In International Amateur Boxing Association [AIBA] dual matches, a draw decision may be awarded.)

(iv) Knock-downs. No extra points shall be awarded for a knock-down.

106.8 Method of scoring.

(1) Each boxer automatically starts each round with 20 points.

(2) Consistent use of 20-20 rounds usually indicates the judge is weak and scores impressionistically.

(3) A judge is advised to fixate in between the two boxers; do not develop a tendency to study or follow just one of the competitors.

(4) Never rely on past performances, reputations or titles earned by a particular athlete.

(5) Amateur boxing is scored on a point system, not on a round basis.

(6) The winner is decided on the majority of judges, i.e., 5-0, 4-1 or 3-2.

(7) Computing a boxing score employs simple mathematics, counting legal blows.

(i) Round one: Red Corner hits Blue with three legal blows. Blue responds with two legal blows. Red returns four more legal blows. Blue continues with two legal blows. End of round: Red Corner is ahead by three legal blows and therefore the round score is Red-20, Blue-19.

(ii) Round two: Blue Corner scores four solid left jabs. Red retaliates with one hard knock-down blow. After the count, Red continues and connects with three legal blows. Blue responds with two jabs that don't connect. End of round: score is tied 20-20. Remember, knock-down blows only score 1/3 of a point. The two left jabs didn't count.

(iii) Round three: Red Corner is tired and backpedals. Red scores six legal blows with his jabs while backpedaling. Blue Corner rushes Red and tries for the "bombs" and connects with three. End of round: the score is Red-20, Blue-19. Remember, being aggressive per se, or retreating is immaterial; the criteria for scoring is "legal blows."

(8) Decisions.

(a) Types. Decisions shall be as follows:

(i) Win on points. At the end of a contest the boxer who has been awarded the decision by a majority of the judges shall be declared the winner. If both boxers are injured or are knocked out simultaneously and cannot continue the contest, the judges shall record the points gained by each boxer up to its termination, and the boxer who was leading on points up to the actual end of the contest shall be declared the winner. RSC is a term used to stop a bout when a boxer is outclassed or unfit to continue.

(ii) Win by retirement. If a boxer retires voluntarily owing to injury or other causes, or if he fails to resume boxing immediately after the rest between rounds, his opponent shall be declared the winner.

(iii) Win by referee stopping contest:

(aa) Outclassed. If a boxer, in the opinion of the referee, is being outclassed or is receiving excessive punishment, the bout shall be stopped and his opponent declared the winner. RSC is a term used to stop a bout when a boxer is outclassed or unfit to continue.

(bb) Injury.

(1) If a boxer, in the opinion of the referee, is unfit to continue because of injury or other physical reasons, the bout shall be stopped and his opponent declared the winner. The right to make this decision rests with the referee, who may consult the doctor. Having consulted the doctor, the referee must follow his advice.

(2) When a referee calls a doctor into the ring to examine a boxer, only these two officials should be present. No coaches should be allowed into the ring, nor on the apron.

(3) The ringside physician has the right to request the bout be suspended if he/she thinks, for medical reasons, the bout should not be allowed to continue.

(cc) Compulsory count limits. When a boxer has three compulsory counts in the same round or four counts during the same bout, the match must be stopped.

(dd) RSCH/RSCM. If a boxer is down and fails to box within eight to ten seconds, whichever applicable, his opponent shall be declared the winner by RSCH or RSCM. For more information on awarding RSCH and RSCM, see Section 106.1(14).

(iv) Win by disqualification. If a boxer is disqualified, his opponent shall be declared the winner. If both boxers are disqualified, the decision shall be announced accordingly.

A disqualified boxer shall not be entitled to any prize, medal, trophy, honorable award, or grading, relating to any stage of the competition in which he has been disqualified.

(v) No contest. A bout may be terminated by the referee inside the scheduled distance owing to a material happening outside the responsibility of the boxers, or the control of the referee, such as the ring becoming damaged, the failure of the lighting supply, exceptional weather conditions, etc. In such circumstances the bout shall be declared "no contest," and in the case of championships, the jury shall decide the necessary further action.

(vi) Win by walkover. Where a boxer presents himself in the ring fully attired for boxing and his opponent fails to appear after his name has been called out by the public address system, the bell sounded and a maximum period of three minutes has elapsed, the referee shall declare the first boxer to be the winner by a walkover. He shall first inform the judges to mark their papers accordingly, collect them and then summons the boxer to the center of the ring and after the decision is announced raises his hand as winner.

(aa) Medical disqualifications determined by a medical doctor and administrative disqualifications, such as a contestant not making weight, the winning boxer may enter the ring for the announcement of the verdict, but shall not be required to be in proper boxing attire. The official in charge or tournament administrator should endeavor to inform the affected contestant as soon as possible.

(vii) A draw (AIBA dual matches only). Two clubs or two nations in a friendly dual match may agree to a draw decision when the majority of the judges scored the competition equally. Likewise, an accidental injury in the first round may result in a draw in dual matches.

106.9 Score cards.

(1) Score cards from each competition will be submitted to the LBCs', designated officer within ten (10) days following the event and will be kept on file for one (1) year.

(2) *Note:* Sample scorecard is shown in official rulebook.

106.10 Hints for judges. Note: The official rules include comments regarding judges' duties and conduct.

106.11 The timekeeper.

(1) Position. He/she shall be seated directly at the ringside.

(2) Duties.

(a) The main duty of the timekeeper is to regulate the number and duration of the rounds and the intervals between rounds. The intervals between rounds shall be of a full minute's duration.

(b) Five seconds before the start of each round, the timekeeper shall signal "seconds out" by use of a whistle or similar device.

(c) The timekeeper shall commence and end each round by striking the gong, bell, ringing the buzzer, or blowing the horn.

(d) Stops of the contest for warnings, cautions, bringing the dress or equipment into order or for any other reason, are not included in the three (3) minutes.

(e) In the event of a knockdown, the timekeeper shall immediately start his count loud enough to be heard by the referee, who, after waving the opponent to a neutral corner, shall pick up the count from the timekeeper and proceed from there.

(f) The timekeeper must monitor the clock in the event of a boxer being "unresponsive" for under or over two (2) minutes if the bout is terminated due to head blows. The physician must be notified in that event in order to render a decision on medical suspension. (See 106.1(14c).)

(g) In the event of a "standing knock-down," the timekeeper will commence counting simultaneously with the referee. The signal by the referee will be a start of the count in loud vocal tones, accompanied by a hand signal, ONE FINGER.

(h) The timekeeper shall count "1-2-3-4-5-6-7-8-9-10" (total ten seconds) with intervals of one second.

(i) In the event of a boxer being "down" from a head blow at the end of a round, the referee shall continue the count. Should the referee count to "10," the downed boxer will have lost the contest by RSCH or RSCM. If a boxer rises and is fit to resume before the count of 10 is reached, the referee shall immediately give the command "box" and the timekeeper will then sound the bell, gong, horn, or buzzer, as applicable.

(j) A competitor failing to resume boxing at once after the rest between rounds, or after an interval of 10 seconds if he has been down, shall lose the bout.

(k) Replacing the referee during the bout. If a referee is incapacitated in the course of a bout, the timekeeper shall strike the gong to stop the bout and the next available neutral referee on the list shall be instructed to control the bout and order boxing to be resumed.

106.12 The announcer.

(1) The announcer will announce the names of all contestants, the weight of the class in which they are competing and the club they represent.

(2) The announcer shall announce the names of the referee, judges and timekeeper when competitions are about to begin and also all changes made either in the referee, judges or timekeeper as the tournament progresses so that the audience knows who the officials are for each bout.

(3) He/she will receive the score sheets from the referee if a jury has not been appointed; however, if a jury has been appointed, the referee will deliver the sheets to the jury who will then announce the decision.

(4) The announcer should not indicate whether or not there is a split decision, simply the winner.

(5) In each case, no decision is announced until the referee has the boxers in the center of the ring and is ready.

106.13 Clerks and inspectors.

(1) The Clerks shall conduct the drawing as specified in the rules.

(2) They shall examine bandages of all contestants to see that they comply with the rules.

(3) They shall also examine the gloves put on each contestant, which must conform with the rules.

(4) They shall notify the contestants when to get ready for their bout.

(5) Inspectors shall be assigned to perform the above duties of the clerk if he/she is unable to do so.

106.14 Weigh-ins, Weighmasters and Scales

(1) Weigh-ins.

(a) Weigh-ins must be conducted for all USA/ABF tournaments.

(b) All contestants must weigh-in at least stripped to the shorts.

(c) All contestants must weigh-in on the day they box.

(d) All contestants must report to the scales at the starting time as announced or printed on the entry information.

(e) For one day events, such as club shows, contestants must weigh-in within four (4) hours of competition.

(f) For USA/ABF regional and national championships, the weigh-in shall begin at 8 a.m. Contestants over weight as per 106.14 (1)(j) must make their weight no later than 10:00 a.m. when the scales close.

(g) For U.S. Championships, Olympic Trials and Box-off, domestic and international competitions, etc., boxers shall not be required to make weight officially until the day of the competition.

(h) No contestant may compete in a weight class unless he weighs more than the maximum limit for the class below and no more than the maximum limit for the class in which he desires to compete.

For example: To compete in the 139 lb. class, a contestant must weigh more than 132 lbs. but not more than 139 lbs.

(i) No contestant shall be allowed to compete in more than one weight class in a tournament.

(j) A competitor will present himself at the official weigh-in. Upon being weighed, if he is within two (2) pounds of his weight classification, he will be given whatever time remains to reduce to his weight limit. His next weigh-in will be deemed final. If he fails to make his weight limit, he is disqualified. A competitor who is over two (2) pounds of his weight limit is disqualified without further recourse.

(k) If a weigh-in is scheduled to establish a tournament weight category, the weight recorded at that official weigh-in will decide the weight class of the contestant. But, the boxer will still need to weigh in on each day he competes.

(2) Weighmasters.

(a) At least two weighmasters must be appointed for all USA/ABF tournaments.

(b) Weighmasters will not weigh in athletes from their own LBC or region at regional or national championships.

(c) Weighmasters must read and record "exact" weight. They are not allowed to "give" weight.

(d) The decision of the weighers as to weight of each contestant shall be final and without appeal.

(3) Scales.

(a) Scales for LBC, regional and national championships will be doctor's scales, dead-weight, digital or balance beam type, in avoirdupois weight.

(b) For tournaments or contests where more than one scale is used, contestants in various weight categories must be weighed on the same scale, i.e., all 106-lb. boxers must weigh on the same scale; 139-lb. athletes can be weighed on a different scale, but all 139-lb. boxers must be weighed on that scale.

ARTICLE VII TOURNAMENTS AND TOURNAMENT ORGANIZATION

107.1 Weight classes for tournaments.

	Avoirdupois system	Metric system
(1) Light flyweight	106 lbs	48 kgs
Flyweight	112 lbs	51 kgs
Bantamweight	119 lbs	54 kgs
Featherweight	125 lbs	57 kgs
Lightweight	132 lbs	60 kgs
Light welterweight	139 lbs	63.5 kgs
Welterweight	147 lbs	67 kgs
Light middleweight	156 lbs	71 kgs
Middleweight	165 lbs	75 kgs
Light heavyweight	178 lbs	81 kgs
Heavyweight	201 lbs	91 kgs
Super heavyweight	Over 201 lbs	91+ kgs

(2) Weights for all international competitions.

	lbs	oz	dr		lbs	oz	dr
Light flyweight and not exceeding 48 kgs.					105	13	2
Flyweight over 48 kgs. and not exceeding 51 kgs.	105	13	2	to	112	6	15
Bantamweight over 51 kgs. and not exceeding 54 kgs.	112	6	15	to	119	0	12
Featherweight over 54 kgs. and not exceeding 57 kgs.	119	0	12	to	125	10	9

Equivalent in poundage

| | | Equivalent in poundage | | | | | |
	lbs	oz	dr		lbs	oz	dr
Lightweight over 57 kgs. and not exceeding 60 kgs.	125	10	9	to	132	4	7
Light welterweight over 60 kgs. and not exceeding 63.5 kgs.	132	4	7	to	139	15	14
Welterweight over 63.5 kgs. and not exceeding 67 kgs.	139	15	14	to	147	11	5
Light middleweight over 67 kgs. and not exceeding 71 kgs.	147	11	5	to	156	8	7
Middleweight over 71 kgs. and not exceeding 75 kgs.	156	8	7	to	165	5	8
Light heavyweight over 75 kgs. and not exceeding 81 kgs.	165	5	8	to	178	9	3
Heavyweight over 81 kgs. and not exceeding 91 kgs.	178	9	3	to	200	9	15
Super heavyweight over 91 kgs.	200	9	15	up			

107.2 The draw.

(1) Immediately before the contest a competitor who has weighed in, or his representative, shall draw numbers to determine the bouts in which he will participate. The drawing shall be as follows: The proper number of byes shall be drawn in the first preliminary round to reduce the number of competitors to 2, 4, 8, 16, and so on.

(2) Competitors drawing a bye on the first drawing on each day shall receive the lowest numbers on the second drawing. Thus, if there be one bye drawn, such competitors shall receive numbers 1 and 2 for the second drawings; and if there are three byes, such competitors shall receive numbers 1, 2, and 3 in the second drawing. In all drawings where numbers 1, 2, 3, 4, and so on are drawn, number 1 competes with number 2, 3 with 4, and so on. When the class is brought to multiple of 2, 4, 8, 16, the contest proceeds regularly to the final bout. Where the competition is not concluded in one day, there shall be a new drawing for each subsequent round of bouts started on the following day. The winner of the final bout receives first prize and the loser receives second prize.

(3) Table of Bouts and Byes, applying to Para (1): NOTE: Table not shown here indicates the number of bouts and byes that would be required in the first round for 1 to 40 participants, following the directions in (1) and (2) above.

(4) No contestant shall receive more than one bye in a tournament.

(5) One drawing may be made for the entire tournament using brackets, at the request of the tournament director. In national championships, this decision shall be subject to the approval of the USA/ABF Board of Directors present at the national championships.

(6) USA/ABF Board of Directors shall authorize the use of a computerized draw to be conducted whenever it is available and feasible.

(7) No competitor may receive a bye in the first series and a "walk-over" in the second series or two consecutive "walk-overs." Should such a possibility arise, a fresh draw shall be made of the other boxers remaining in the series who have not received a bye or a "walk-over" in the preceding series. The first boxer to be drawn will meet the boxer who has benefited from a bye or "walk-over" in the preceding series, and the new draw shall then proceed in the normal way.

(8) For a sample copy on "How to Conduct a Draw," call or write the National Office.

107.3 Length and number of rounds.

(1) Sanctions may be granted for contests not to exceed three rounds of three minutes duration with one minute intervals between each round.

(2) All USA/ABF-sanctioned competitions shall consist of no more than three rounds of three minutes duration each round for open class and no more than three rounds of two minutes duration each round for novice and sub-novice classes.

(3) Stops of the contest for warnings, cautions, bringing the dress or equipment into order or for any other reason, are not included in the three (3) minutes. A full one (1) minute of rest shall be given between the rounds.

GOVERNING BODY

United States of America Amateur Boxing Federation, Inc. (USA/ABF), 1750 E. Boulder St., Colorado Springs, CO 80909

Under the auspices of the U.S. Olympic Committee and the Association Internationale de Boxe Amateur (AIBA), the USA/ABF administers, develops, and promotes Olympic-style boxing through its 58 local boxing committees nationwide. The USA/ABF was established in 1980 through the joint efforts of the AAU (Amateur Athletic Union), Golden Gloves, U.S. Armed Forces, and the Police Athletic League. In fulfilling its primary objective of fostering, developing, promoting, and coordinating both recreational and competitive amateur boxing opportunities, the Federation sponsors a host of programs—from developing the sport and its athletes at local, regional, and national levels, to sponsoring national and international meets, to selecting teams for international events, including the Olympics, World Championships, and Pan American Games. The Federation also conducts national training camps for top boxers and sponsors clinics and seminars for coaches, officials, and physicians.

MAGAZINES

Amateur Boxing, Box 249, Cobalt, CT 06414

Boxing USA, c/o USA/ABF, 1750 E. Boulder St., Colorado Springs, CO 80909

International Boxing, T.V. Sports, Inc., Box 48, Rockville Centre, NY 11571

• CANOEING •

RACING RULES FOR
OLYMPIC FLATWATER CANOES AND KAYAKS

(Reproduced by permission of the American Canoe Association*)

□

Note: In addition to the Olympic Flatwater Canoe and Kayak Rules presented here, the American Canoe Association establishes and distributes the rules for Canoe Poling Competition, Canoe Sailing Regulations, Marathon Racing, Whitewater Open Canoe Slalom and Downriver Racing, and Whitewater Slalom Racing.

AUTHORITY

The National Paddling Committee, as constituted under Article VII, Sec. 1, of the Constitution of the American Canoe Association (ACA) and as empowered under Chapter V, Sec. 8, of the Bylaws hereby promulgates the following Racing Rules to govern paddling competition.

RULE 1. SANCTIONS

Sec. 1 All Olympic flatwater paddling competitions held within the limits of the U.S.A. in order to be recognized as "Official" shall be held only under sanction from the National Paddling Committee (NPC) as the official representative of the American Canoe Association.

RULE 2. AUTHORITIES

Sec. 1 The annual National Championship Regatta, the Long Distance Nationals and all National and International Regattas shall be held only under direct assignment and sanction from the NPC.

Sec. 2 Final qualification competitions to determine the U.S. Olympic Canoeing team shall be sanctioned by the NPC through the National Olympic Canoeing and Kayaking Committee which is responsible for organizing and conducting these competitions.

Sec. 3 Competitions to qualify ACA members for participation in International Flatwater Championship competitions sanctioned by the International Canoe Federation (ICF) and in the Pan American Canoe Racing Championships governed by the Pan American Canoe Racing Council shall be held only under sanction of the National Paddling Committee.

Sec. 4 Any person wishing to compete in an International Regatta must have his/her entry sanctioned by the NPC.

---

*See page 106 for additional information.

Sec. 5 The annual Divisional Championship Regattas and all State Championship Regattas shall be held only under direct sanction from the respective Divisional Paddling Committee.

Sec. 6 Local paddling competitions wherein more than two ACA clubs participate shall be held only under the sanction of a Divisional Paddling Chairman.

RULE 3. ELIGIBILITY

Sec. 1 Paddling competitions sanctioned by the NPC shall be open only to amateur canoeists, as defined by the Amateur Rules of the ACA, who are ACA members. They must hold a swimming certificate issued by an organization regularly conducting instruction in swimming or must be able to, upon request from the regatta committee, demonstrate ability to swim fifty (50) yards in reasonable good form.

Sec. 2 All competitors must be bona fide members of the club they represent or must race unattached. Any competitor who changes clubs may not compete for the new club within 30 days after he/she has joined the new club *and* has notified the NPC Registrar of the change.

Sec. 3 The National Paddling Committee requires all racing paddling competitors to be properly registered with the NPC in accordance with current registration procedures prior to competing in any NPC sanctioned competition.

RULE 4. INTERNATIONAL COMPETITIONS

Sec. 1 International competitions:

a. All competitions announced as international shall be held in accordance with the regulations of the ICF. Competitions arranged by the national federations or their clubs are considered international if competitors of a foreign country are invited to participate.

b. Competitions between two clubs of only two countries are not regarded as international.

c. These competitions must be controlled by at least one accredited official in possession of a valid International Official card.

Sec. 2 Competitors:

a. Only members of clubs affiliated to a national federation, which is a member of the ICF, have the right to take part in an international competition, except that unattached athletes may take part in a competition representing the NPC (ACA).

b. All competitors must comply with the amateur regulations in accordance with Art. 39 of the Statutes of the ICF.

c. If a competitor is a member of the federation of a foreign country in which he is domiciled he is, moreover, allowed to take part in a competition on behalf of that foreign association, but must in each individual case obtain special permission from the national federation of his country of origin. If a competitor has been domiciled in one and the same foreign country for two years or more, it is unnecessary for him to obtain permission from the federation of his country of origin. This rule does not apply to competitors who leave their country of origin and acquire by marriage the nationality of the country in which they reside. In this case, they can compete for the federation of this country without the delay of two years.

RULE 5. CLASSES AND BUILDING RULES

Sec. 1 Limitations:

a. Olympic Hulls:

		K-1	K-2	K-4	C-1	C-2
Maximum Length	cm	520	650	1100	520	650
	in.	204.72	255.90	433.07	204.72	255.90
Minimum Beam	cm	51	55	60	75	75
	in.	20.08	21.65	23.62	29.53	29.53
Minimum Weight	kg	12	18	30	16	20
	lb	26.46	39.69	66.15	35.28	44.10

b. Boats, accessories or clothing may carry trademark symbols and words. In all cases, these symbols should not exceed 20 x 5 cm. on boats and 10 x 3 cm. on paddles and, in the latter case, only once on each face. Any boat or accessory which does not comply with the above mentioned conditions will not be acceptable. Advertising symbols are to be in order with the amateur regulations.

c. Teams are responsible for their own equipment.

Sec. 2 Limitations Special Design Classes:

a. C-4 Javelin:
Length 24′0″ Maximum
Beam 30″ Maximum
Weight 65 lbs. Minimum
Minimum opening—not less than 1/2 the length.

Sec. 3 Construction:

a. Kayaks:

All kinds of building materials are permitted. Sections and Longitudinal lines of the hull of the kayak shall be convex and not interrupted. Steering rudders are allowed. The maximum thickness of the rudderblade must not exceed 10 mm. in the case of K-1 and K-2, or 12 mm. in the case of K-4, in cases where the rudder forms an extension to the length of the kayak.

b. Canoes:

All kinds of building materials are permitted. Sections and longitudinal lines of the hull of the canoe shall be convex and not interrupted. The canoe must be built symmetrically upon the axis of its length. Steering rudders or any guiding apparatus directing the course of the canoe are not allowed. A keel, if any, must be straight, shall extend over the whole length of the canoe and not project more than 30 mm. below the hull. The C-1 canoe may be entirely open and shall not be covered more than 150 cm. from the stem and 75 cm. from the stern, reckoned from the outer edge of the deck for the fore and aft decks, respectively. The C-2 canoe may be entirely open, the minimum length of the opening shall be 295 cm.

Sec. 4 Measuring:

The length of a kayak or a canoe shall be measured between the extremes of the stem and the stern. Stembands or other protection of the stem or stern, if any, are to be included. Any rudder forming a continuation of the length of a kayak is not to be included in the measurement. The beam of a kayak or a canoe shall be measured at the widest part. Rubbing strake, if any, is not to be included in the measurement.

Sec. 5 Weighing:

a. No alterations in canoes and kayaks are permitted after the measuring and weighing and before the competition has taken place.

b. All loose outfit shall be removed. Permanent knee rests attached to the floorboard and buoyancy attachments consisting of water-absorbing material must be absolutely dry at the first weighing prior to the race. The first four boats in the final as well as all boats which have qualified for a higher round shall immediately after the race be measured and weighed again.

RULE 6. ORGANIZATION OF THE COMPETITIONS

Sec. 1 Officials:

a. Competitions shall be held under the supervision of the following officials:

Chief Official
Competition Organizer
Competition Secretary
Starter(s)
Aligner
Course Umpire(s)
Turning Point Umpire(s)
Finishing Line Judge(s)
Timekeeper(s)
Measurer(s)
Announcer
Press Official

b. If circumstances permit, one person may function in two of the above offices. The top management of the competition shall be in the hands of a Competition Committee which shall consist of:

Chief Official
Competition Organizer

One additional person who may be one of the other officials, provided that his function allows him to be near the finishing line at all times. This person is appointed by the Competition Organizer. Unauthorized persons must not enter any official's area unless the Competition Committee sends for persons in order to solve problems.

c. The Competition Committee must:

1. organize the competition and supervise its arrangement;

2. in the event of inclement weather or other unforeseen circumstances which make it impossible to carry out the competition, postpone the competition and decide on another time when it may be held;

3. hear any protests that may be made and settle any disputes that may arise;

4. decide matters concerning disqualification in cases where the regulations are broken during a competition. Should a competitor be injured during a heat, the Committee may allow him to participate in another heat or in the final. The decision of the Committee shall be based on the NPC racing rules. Penalties in accordance with the NPC rules may

also be imposed—i.e., disqualification for a longer period than the duration of the competition in question;

5. before any decision is made regarding an alleged infraction of the rules, hear the opinion of the Umpire who controlled the race in which the infraction was said to have occurred. The Committee shall also seek the opinions of other officials in the race, if it is felt to be of importance in clearing up the alleged infraction;

6. if a member of the Competition Committee belongs to a club which is connected with a decision of a disqualification, his function will be suspended during this case;

7. publish at least 5 weeks in advance of the date set for the competition an invitation per Rule 8;

8. provide team captains and competitors with printed or posted information as to heats, repechages, semifinals and finals on a timely basis, i.e., at least 1 hour before the specific competition;

9. if the Competition Committee has doubt as to the eligibility of any entry, it shall notify the NPC which shall immediately investigate the same and, if the circumstances justify, empower the Competition Committee to refuse the entry;

10. within one week after the conclusion of the regatta provide to the sanctioning body a complete report covering the finances; a list of the events contested; and for each event (heats, repechages, semifinals and finals), the name, club, and the position of each paddler finishing. Such report shall contain a statement of any protest lodged with the committee and the decision rendered.

11. the Regatta Committee shall see that proper provisions are made for the presentation of the awards to the contestants. An area shall be provided preferably at the finish area, where the ceremony for awarding the medals can be conducted and suitable pictures taken.

RULE 7. DUTIES OF THE OFFICIALS

Sec. 1. Championship Officials:

In National Championships, Pan American Canoe Championships, National Regattas, and Divisional Championships, the Chief Official, Competition Organizer, Starter, Finish Line Judges, Umpires, Turning Point Controls, and the Chief Timekeeper must all be recognized NPC Regatta Officials. Such recognition is given by the National Paddling Committee to persons who have passed an examination. The examination will be based on the knowledge of the NPC Paddling Racing Rules and practical regatta experience.

Sec. 2. The CHIEF OFFICIAL, who is also the Chairman of the Competition Committee, shall decide all matters arising during the actual contest, which are not dealt with in these rules. The Chief Official may disqualify any competitor who behaves improperly or who by his conduct or speech shows contempt toward the competition officials, other competitors or onlookers.

Sec. 3. The COMPETITION ORGANIZER shall supervise the races and be responsible for seeing that they take place according to the program and without unnecessary delay. He shall inform the officials concerned in good time, before a fresh race is started. With the assistance of the Measurer he must ensure that regulations concerning measurements are complied with by all boats taking part in the contest. He shall make certain that the Announcer gives the onlookers all necessary information about the races, such as the order of starting, the name of any competitor failing to start, and the result. The Competition Organizer shall supervise the laying out and buoying of the race course and certify to the sanctioning body the accuracy of the course. He shall ensure that all physical equipment necessary for the competition is available.

Sec. 4 The COMPETITION SECRETARY shall be responsible for preparing the heat sheets, recording and posting results, and preparing the list of prize winners. He/she shall keep the minutes of the proceedings of any protest. He/she shall provide the Announcer and Press Officials with all necessary information regarding the running of the races and the results.

Sec. 5 The STARTER decides all questions concerning the start of the races, and is alone responsible for decisions as to false starts. His decision is final. He shall see that the starting gun or pistol is in good working order. By means of a signal, he shall communicate to the officials at the finishing line, and after having received a signal from there that all is ready, he shall order the competitors to their places and carry out the start according to the racing rules.

Sec. 6 The ALIGNER brings the boats to the starting line with least possible delay to check the competitor's attire and the competition number on the back. When all boats are level he shall notify the starter.

Sec. 7 The COURSE UMPIRE shall see to it that during a race the rules are complied with. The Course Umpire may give directions to the competitors during the race. If the rules are broken, the Course Umpire shall report the infraction to the Chief Official, who in turn, shall refer it to the Competition Committee. The Competition Committee shall decide whether any of the competitors concerned shall be disqualified or not. If the Course Umpire has to report an infraction of the rules he shall show a red flag after the race and shall make a report before the next race takes place. In such a case, the Competition Committee shall make known its decision immediately and before the result of the race is announced. If there is no infraction to report, the Course Umpire shall show a white flag. In races of 500 to 1000 meters, the Course Umpire shall follow the race in a boat. He shall be completely unhampered during the race. No one except the Course Umpire and his secretary shall be admitted to the boat reserved for him. In long distance races with many competitors more than one Course Umpire may be nominated. One of the Course Umpires shall, if possible, follow the leading group in the race, but without disturbing the other competitors. In case of a broken paddle in the defined area or in case of hindrances, the Course Umpire must stop the competition, passing all boats in the race and waving the red flag or using a sound signal until all boats have stopped paddling. After this all boats shall return to the start.

Sec. 8 TURNING POINT UMPIRES:

When a race is run along a course with one or more turning points, one or more umpires and one secretary must be stationed at every turning point where they gain the best view of the turn. The Turning Point Umpire shall see that the competitors turn according to the rules and shall give directions and specify the right-of-way as he deems necessary. The secretary shall make a list of all who pass the turning point. Immediately after the race, the Turning Point Umpire shall report to the Chief Official as to who has turned and if any infraction of the rules has taken place. The authority and duties of the Turning Point Umpires correspond with those of the Course Umpire.

Sec. 9 FINISH LINE JUDGES decide the order in which the competitors have passed the finishing line. The judges shall be placed at the finishing post. If the judges differ regarding the placing of two or more competitors, the dispute, in the absence of photo finish, shall be decided by the Chief Judge based on his consultation with the Finish Line Judges. When the photo finish is used the final decision should be coordinated with the results of the photo finish. The decision of the judges is final.

Sec. 10 The TIMEKEEPERS are responsible for recording the time. This shall be done by means of stop watches. Before each individual race, the Chief Timekeeper shall see that the watches have been wound and tested and shall divide the work among the Timekeepers. At the end of each race, he shall compare the official times with the other

Timekeepers and immediately inform the Competition Secretary of them. Each race shall be timed by at least two watches. When the watches have not recorded the same time, the longest (worst) time shall be taken as correct. The stop watches are to be started by the first indication of the agreed upon signal. Timekeepers may also be employed as Finish Line Judges.

Sec. 11 The MEASURER shall assist the Competition Organizer to test the craft taking part in the race. Should any of them not fulfill the NPC requirements concerning classification, they shall be excluded from the competition.

Sec. 12 The ANNOUNCER shall, on the instructions of the Competition Organizer, announce the start of each race, the order of starting and the position of the competitors during the race. After the race is finished, he will announce the results.

Sec. 13 The PRESS OFFICIAL must supply all necessary information to the representatives of the press, radio and television about the race and its progress. He is authorized therefore to ask information from the different officials who must also procure for him, as soon as possible, the copies from the officials' results.

RULE 8. INVITATIONS

An invitation to a competition shall contain the following information:

a. Time and place of the competition and directions thereto.

b. Classes and distances of races.

c. Sequence and starting times of races.

d. Whether the races are to be held on still or running water, up or downstream, and minimum depth of water.

e. Amount of entrance fee.

f. Address to which entries should be sent.

g. Last date for receiving entries. This date shall not be earlier than 14 days prior to the first day of the competition.

h. Name of sponsor.

i. Name of sanctioning body.

j. Name of regatta committee.

RULE 9. ENTRIES

Sec. 1 An entry shall always contain the following:

a. The name of the club to which the competitor(s) belongs or designation of unattached.

b. The classes and distances in which the competitor proposes to compete.

c. First and last name of each competitor, together with the date and year of his birth and eligibility classification, NPC registration number, and ACA number.

d. Paddlers must conform to their proper eligibility classifications as stated in Rule No. 21.

e. In addition to named crews, substitutes are allowed to be entered in every race as follows:

> K-2 and C-2 1 person
> K-4 and C-4 2 persons

f. An entry may be telegraphed if it is dispatched before midnight on the last day for receiving entries. Entry by telegram must be confirmed immediately by letter.

Sec. 2 Contestants may not compete for two clubs within a thirty-day period. Contestants may not compete unattached and for a club during the same regatta (see Rule 3, Section 2).

Sec. 3 Except for designated mixed competitions, male and female competitors shall not compete with or against each other.

RULE 10. ALTERATIONS IN ENTRIES AND WITHDRAWALS

Only those substitutes named in the entry are allowed to replace the named competitors. Notifications of such alterations must be given in written form to the Competition Secretary at least one hour before the first race of the day. The withdrawal of an entry is considered final, and no renewed entry of the same crew is allowed. Entrance fees cannot be refunded. If a competitor does not start an assigned heat, and has no valid reason approved by the Competition Committee, the competitor shall be disqualified for the duration of that day of competition.

RULE 11. ENTRY FEES AND SANCTIONING FEES

Sec. 1 When entry fees are a condition for participation in a regatta, no competitor may start in any race unless his entry fee has been paid.

Sec. 2 Sanction fees shall be payable upon granting of a sanction. A sanction fee only shall be returnable in whole, if and when for just and adequate cause the sponsoring body, with the agreement of the sanctioning body, effects cancellation of the proposed regatta or competition.

Sec. 3 Sanction fees shall be paid into the Paddling Fund administered by the sanctioning body.

Sec. 4 The amount of a sanction fee shall be a matter for agreement between the sanctioning body and the applicant for a regatta or competition.

RULE 12. ALTERATION IN THE SEQUENCE OF EVENTS

The sequence of races given in the invitation and the intervals between the races as given in the racing program are binding on the organizers. Alterations cannot be made unless a majority of the respective team managers or representatives at the competition give their consent.

RULE 13. COURSE

Sec. 1 Criteria:

a. At least 5 hours before the start of the races the racing course shall be measured and marked by means of clearly visible flags mounted on buoys. The course at the start shall permit a clear width of at least 5 meters for each boat.

b. The starting and finishing lines shall lie at right angles to the course. The finishing line shall be at least 45 meters long and be marked by two flags. The finishing line judges must be placed as near the finishing line as possible.

c. For races up to 1,000 meters, the course shall be straight and in one direction.

d. For races exceeding 1,000 meters, turning points are permitted. In this case the following conditions shall be fulfilled, if possible:

1. The distance between the starting line and the first flag of the first turning point shall be straight and at least 1,000 meters.

2. The distance between the last flag at the last turning point and the finishing line shall be straight and at least 1,000 meters.

3. The distance between the centers of the turns shall be at least 1,000 meters. The radius of each turn shall be at least 40 meters.

Sec. 2 Marking Signs:

The turning points shall be marked by at least four flags. The flags shall be diagonally divided with one half in red and the other yellow. Both the start and finishing lines shall be marked with red flags at the points where these lines intersect the outer limits of the course. The 15 meters distance from the starting line from where the competitors can be called back according to Rule 17, Sec. 4 (broken paddle) must be marked by flags or by other means.

RULE 14. CANOE NUMBERS

All kayaks and canoes shall carry a vertical plate marked with black numbers on a yellow ground indicating the lane. The plates shall be placed on the centerline on the aft-deck (Canadian canoes foredeck). Size of number 7 in. high x 8 in. wide. The rules require that each individual paddler have attached to his boat a lane number holder and that each individual paddler or club provide its own set of lane numbers (1 through 9).

RULE 15. INSTRUCTIONS FOR COMPETITORS

Each competitor shall receive printed or written instructions at least 5 hours before the beginning of the regatta, concerning the following information:

a. Detailed information of the course and the markings.

b. Starting time.

c. Starting line.

d. Finishing line.

e. Time and place where competition information as to heats, repechages, semifinals and finals may be obtained or will be posted.

RULE 16. CLOTHING

No competitor shall be allowed to start in a race unless he is properly clad in his organization's, club's or personal racing shirt and trunks.

RULE 17. RACING REGULATIONS

Sec. 1 Disqualifications:

a. Any competitor who attempts to win a race by any other than honorable means, breaks the racing regulations, or disregards the honorable nature of the racing regulations shall be disqualified from the race concerned.

b. Should a competitor have completed a race in a kayak or canoe which is shown upon inspection not to fulfill the ICF classifications, he shall be disqualified from the race in question.

c. It is forbidden to receive, during a race, outside help or to be accompanied by other boats along the course—even outside the lanes—or by throwing objects into the course. All such acts shall entail the disqualification of the competitor(s) concerned.

d. All disqualifications by the Competition Committee have to be confirmed in writing immediately with the reasons. The team leader has to acknowledge the receipt on a copy with exact time, which is the start of the protest time.

Sec. 2 Means of Propulsion:

Kayaks shall be propelled solely by means of double-bladed paddles. Canadian canoes shall be propelled solely by means of single-bladed paddles. The paddles may not be fixed on the boats in any way. If a paddle is broken (except at the start: see Sec. 4) a competitor may not be provided with a new one by a supporter.

Sec. 3 Heats and Finals:

a. At least three kayaks or canoes must be entered before a race can be held.

b. If the number of entries in races up to and including 1,000 meters is so great that heats are necessary, the number of kayaks or canoes in each heat and in the final must not exceed nine. The division of the competitors into heats shall be determined by drawing lots. Eight or nine kayaks or canoes shall participate in the final. If more than this number have been entered in the entire race, the race shall be conducted as follows:

3 to 9 entries   direct final

10 to 11 entries   two heats and four from each to the final

12 to 27 entries   three heats and three from each to the final

over 27 entries   required number of heats and three intermediate heats with six competi-
                    tors in each. Three from each of the intermediate heats to the final.

The division into heats must be made in such a way that at least three competitors proceed to the final (or the intermediate heats) from each proceeding heat.

c. When making the draw, the difference between the number of competitors in the heats of a race shall not exceed one. If the number of competitors in the heat varies, the earlier heats shall have the larger number.

d. Any crew which has not taken part in a heat as instructed shall not be allowed to compete in the final. The composition of a crew which has qualified for intermediate heats or for the final must not be changed.

e. Heats and finals shall be run on the same stretch of water.

f. Participation in the final must not depend upon times attained in the heats.

g. For races of more than 1,000 meters, heats shall not be held, and all canoes/kayaks taking part shall start simultaneously. Should the width of water not permit a simultaneous start, starts at regular intervals shall be permitted.

Sec. 4 Start:

a. Lots shall be drawn to determine the stations of boats at the start. Number one shall be placed to the left, then number two and so on. In competitions where heats are required, lots must be drawn for each heat separately.

b. Competitors shall be at the start at the time specified in the racing program. The start shall be given without reference to any absentees.

c. The position of the boats at the start shall be such that the bows of the competing boats are on the starting line.

d. Boats must be stationary.

e. The starter shall give the starting signal by the word "Ready" to be followed by a shot. The shot can be replaced by the word "Go." The interval between the word "Ready" and the shot or the word "Go" shall not exceed two (2) seconds. If the competitor starts paddling after the word "Ready" and before the shot has been fired, he/she has made a false start. The Starter must immediately warn the offending competitor(s) and if two false starts are made by the same competitor(s), the Starter must exclude him/her (them) from the race. All crews making a false start, and not only the competitor(s) who caused the false start, shall be subject to the same penalties.

f. Any competitor who disregards the second warning of the Starter to take up the correct position at the start or who keeps ahead of the other competitors shall be excluded from the race in question.

g. Should any competitor break his paddle within 15 meters from the start, the Starter shall immediately call back all competitors and a new start shall be made after the broken paddle has been replaced. The team managers of the competing teams are responsible for having reserve paddles available at the start for their respective teams.

h. The recall shall be made by means of a second shot.

Sec. 5 Interruptions:

The Umpire has the right to interrupt a correctly started short distance race if unforeseen hindrances arise. Such an interruption may be effected in the same way as is prescribed for recall in Sec. 4 h. The competitors must immediately stop paddling and await further instructions. If a race is declared null and void, no change of the composition of a crew is permitted at the new start. In the event of a capsize the competitor or crew is eliminated from the race if he or they are not able to get in again without outside help.

Sec. 6 Taking Pace and Hanging:

a. Taking pace or receiving assistance from boats not in the race or by any other means is not permitted. When a race is in progress crews not taking part in the race are strictly forbidden to proceed over any part of the race area, inside or outside the marking buoys.

b. In races up to 1,000 meters, competitors must keep their lane from the start to the finish of the course. It is forbidden to hang, and no competitor must come nearer than five meters in any direction to another competitor or derive benefit from his wake.

c. In races over the distances of more than 1,000 meters, competitors may deviate from their lane, providing they do not impede other competitors.

d. In long distance races every competitor shall be warned by a sound signal (e.g., a bell), when he passes a point 1,000 meters from the finishing line.

Sec. 7 Turns:

a. When a race is run on a course with turning points these shall be passed to port (i.e., in a counterclockwise direction).

b. When going around a turning point, the competitor on the outer course must leave room for the competitor on the inner course if that competitor has the bow of his boat at least level with the front edge of the cockpit of the boat on the outer course. With respect to K-2 and K-1 this refers to the fore cockpit. With respect to C-1, it refers to the level of the competitor's body, and for C-2, it refers to the level of the body of the foremost member of the crew.

c. A competitor will not be disqualified for touching a turning point buoy, unless, in the opinion of the Turning Point Umpires, an advantage has been gained therefrom.

d. In making a turn, the boat shall follow as closely as possible the course as marked by the buoys at the turning points.

Sec. 8 Overtaking:

When a canoe or kayak is overtaking another canoe or kayak in a race, it is the duty of the overtaking craft to keep clear at all times of the boat being overtaken. On the other hand, the craft being overtaken is not allowed to alter its course to make difficulties for the overtaking craft.

Sec. 9 Collision or Damage:

Any competitor who collides with another, or who damages the canoe or kayak or paddle of another can be disqualified not only from the race but from the regatta at the discretion of the Chief Official.

Sec. 10 Finish:

a. The finishing line is reached when the bow of the canoe or kayak with the/all competitor(s) in it has passed the line between the red flags.

b. If two or more boats reach the finishing line at the same time they get the same classification.

RULE 18. PROTEST

Sec. 1 A protest against the right of a crew to take part in a race shall be referred to the Chief Official not later than one hour before the start of the race. A protest made later—within 30 days from the date when the race in question was held—is only permitted if the person making the protest can prove that the facts on which the protest is based came to their knowledge later than one hour before the start of the race. A late protest shall be referred to the Sanctioning Body accompanied by the prescribed fee (see Sec. 3).

Sec. 2 A protest made during a competition must be addressed to the Competition Committee and handed to the Chief Official not later than 20 minutes after the team leader/representative has been informed of the decision against his competitor or team and has signed the receipt.

Sec. 3 All protests concerning a race must be made to the Competition Committee within 20 minutes after the race results have been announced.

Sec. 4 All protests shall be made in writing and be accompanied by a fee of ten dollars. The fee will be refunded if the protest is upheld.

Sec. 5 Competitors have the right of appeal to the NPC against a decision of the Competition Committee within 30 days from the date when the race was held. The NPC shall pronounce the final decision. A fee of ten dollars shall accompany such appeals and will be refunded if the appeal is upheld.

RULE 19. POINT SCORING

Sec. 1 Team championships in the annual National Championships shall be based on points scored as follows:

Senior National Championship	points scored in Senior, Intermediate, Master and Mixed events.
Junior National Championship	points scored in Junior, Juvenile and Bantam events.
Overall National Championship	sum of all points scored in Senior and Junior Championships.

Sec. 2 For National Championships and other competitions where team scores are recorded points shall be awarded as follows:

Points are scored on the basis of ten (10) for first place, six (6) for second, three (3) for third, two (2) for fourth, and one (1) for fifth place in each race.

Sec. 3 If ties occur, points shall be divided equally and duplicate awards will be given.

Sec. 4 Points won by team boats shall be divided equally among the team members and credited to the club that they represent.

RULE 20. PRIZES

Prizes shall conform with amateur rules of the ACA.

RULE 21. ELIGIBILITY CLASSIFICATIONS

Sec. 1 A BANTAM is one who has not reached his or her 14th birthday as of January 1st of the current year.

Sec. 2 A JUVENILE is one who has not reached his or her 16th birthday as of January 1st of the current year.

Sec. 3 A JUNIOR is one who has reached his or her 15th birthday as of January 1st of the current year and has not reached his or her 18th birthday on January 1st of the current year.

Sec. 4 An INTERMEDIATE is one who meets the following qualifications:

a. Must have reached his or her 18th birthday as of January 1st of that year.

b. Shall NOT have won an Intermediate National Championship in that event in which he or she desires to enter.

c. Shall not have placed 1st, 2nd, or 3rd in a Senior National Championship in that event and distance in which he/she desires to enter.

d. Shall not have been a competing member of a World Championship or Olympic team.

e. Shall not be in the Bantam, Juvenile, Junior or Senior class.

f. Any change in classification will be effective after the end of the current season.

Sec. 5 A SENIOR is anyone who does not meet the requirements of any other class. Seniors may paddle only in Senior or Open events.

Sec. 6 A MASTER is one who has reached his or her 40th birthday as of January 1st of that year.

Sec. 7 In addition to their own class:

a. A Bantam may paddle in the Juvenile class.

b. A Juvenile may paddle in the Junior class.

c. A Junior may paddle in the Senior Open class.

d. An Intermediate may paddle in the Senior Open class.

e. A Master may paddle in the Intermediate and Senior Open class.

RULE 22. SPECIAL RULES
FOR THE NATIONAL CANOEING CHAMPIONSHIPS

Sec. 1 Regatta Committee:

A Regatta Committee shall be appointed immediately after the place of holding the National Championship Regatta has been selected by the National Paddling Committee. This committee shall have entire charge of the regatta and all matters pertaining thereto, subject to the rules of the Association. This committee shall be appointed by the Chairman of the National Paddling Committee. The Regatta Committee shall hold a meeting on the day immediately preceding the first day of the regatta. The time and place of this meeting shall be made known to all interested organizations, their coaches and athletic directors. This is:

a. to allow the coaches, athletic directors, or captains of the participating organizations to inform the Committee of any information pertaining to the conduct of the regatta.

b. to allow the Regatta Committee an opportunity to explain procedures essential to the conduct of the regatta and announce any changes.

c. to allow the local committees to assist the visiting crews, to receive any protests, and make judgments pertaining to the conduct of the regatta. The Regatta Committee should be available during the course of the regatta to receive any protests, and make judgments pertaining to the conduct of the regatta.

Sec. 2 Program of Events:

The program for the annual National Canoe and Kayak Championship Regatta shall be comprised of the following Championships hereafter named:

Senior Events

Single Kayaks Men Senior	500 meters	(K 1M Sr.	500 m)
Single Kayaks Men Senior	1,000 meters	(K 1M Sr.	1,000 m)
Single Kayaks Men Senior	10,000 meters	(K 1M Sr.	10,000 m)
Single Canoes Men Senior	500 meters	(C 1M Sr.	500 m)
Single Canoes Men Senior	1,000 meters	(C 1M Sr.	1,000 m)
Single Canoes Men Senior	10,000 meters	(C 1M Sr.	10,000 m)
Single Kayaks Women Senior	500 meters	(K 1W Sr.	500 m)
Single Kayaks Women Senior	5,000 meters	(K 1W Sr.	5,000 m)
Tandem Kayaks Men Senior	500 meters	(K 2M Sr.	500 m)
Tandem Kayaks Men Senior	1,000 meters	(K 2M Sr.	1,000 m)
Tandem Kayaks Men Senior	10,000 meters	(K 2M Sr.	10,000 m)
Tandem Canoes Men Senior	500 meters	(C 2M Sr.	500 m)
Tandem Canoes Men Senior	1,000 meters	(C 2M Sr.	1,000 m)
Tandem Canoes Men Senior	10,000 meters	(C 2M Sr.	10,000 m)
Tandem Kayaks Women Senior	500 meters	(K 2W Sr.	500 m)
Tandem Kayaks Women Senior	5,000 meters	(K 2W Sr.	5,000 m)
Kayaks Four Men Senior	500 meters	(K 4M Sr.	500 m)
Kayaks Four Men Senior	1,000 meters	(K 4M Sr.	1,000 m)
Kayaks Four Men Senior	10,000 meters	(K 4M Sr.	10,000 m)
Kayaks Four Women Senior	500 meters	(K 4W Sr.	500 m)
Kayaks Four Women Senior	5,000 meters	(K 4W Sr.	5,000 m)
Canoes Four Men Senior	1,000 meters	(C 4M Sr.	1,000 m)
Canoes Four Men Senior	500 meters	(C 4M Sr.	500 m)

Intermediate Events

Single Kayaks Men Intermediate	1,000 meters	(K 1M Int.	1,000 m)
Single Canoes Men Intermediate	1,000 meters	(C 1M Int.	1,000 m)
Single Kayaks Women Intermediate	500 meters	(K 1W Int.	500 m)
Tandem Kayaks Men Intermediate	1,000 meters	(K 2M Int.	1,000 m)
Tandem Canoes Men Intermediate	1,000 meters	(C 2M Int.	1,000 m)
Tandem Kayaks Women Intermediate	500 meters	(K 2W Int.	500 m)
Kayaks Four Women Intermediate	500 meters	(K 4W Int.	500 m)
Kayaks Four Men Intermediate	1,000 meters	(K 4M Int.	1,000 m)

Junior Events

Single Kayaks Men Junior	500 meters	(K 1M Jr.	500 m)
Single Kayaks Men Junior	1,000 meters	(K 1M Jr.	1,000 m)
Single Kayaks Men Junior	5,000 meters	(K 1M Jr.	5,000 m)

Single Canoes Men Junior	500 meters	(C 1M Jr.	500 m)
Single Canoes Men Junior	1,000 meters	(C 1M Jr.	1,000 m)
Single Canoes Men Junior	5,000 meters	(C 1M Jr.	5,000 m)
Single Kayaks Women Junior	500 meters	(K 1W Jr.	500 m)
Single Kayaks Women Junior	5,000 meters	(K 1W Jr.	5,000 m)
Tandem Kayaks Men Junior	500 meters	(K 2M Jr.	500 m)
Tandem Kayaks Men Junior	1,000 meters	(K 2M Jr.	1,000 m)
Tandem Kayaks Men Junior	5,000 meters	(K 2M Jr.	5,000 m)
Tandem Canoes Men Junior	500 meters	(C 2M Jr.	500 m)
Tandem Canoes Men Junior	1,000 meters	(C 2M Jr.	1,000 m)
Tandem Canoes Men Junior	5,000 meters	(C 2M Jr.	5,000 m)
Tandem Kayaks Women Junior	500 meters	(K 2W Jr.	500 m)
Tandem Kayaks Women Junior	5,000 meters	(K 2W Jr.	5,000 m)
Kayaks Four Men Junior	500 meters	(K 4M Jr.	500 m)
Kayaks Four Men Junior	5,000 meters	(K 4M Jr.	5,000 m)
Kayaks Four Women Junior	500 meters	(K 4W Jr.	500 m)
Kayaks Four Women Junior	5,000 meters	(K 4W Jr.	5,000 m)
Canoes Four Men Junior	500 meters	(C 4M Jr.	500 m)

Juvenile Events

Single Kayaks Men Juvenile	500 meters	(K 1M Juv.	500 m)
Single Kayaks Women Juvenile	500 meters	(K 1W Juv.	500 m)
Single Canoes Men Juvenile	500 meters	(C 1M Juv.	500 m)
Tandem Kayaks Men Juvenile	500 meters	(K 2M Juv.	500 m)
Tandem Canoes Men Juvenile	500 meters	(C 2M Juv.	500 m)
Tandem Kayaks Women Juvenile	500 meters	(K 2W Juv.	500 m)
Kayaks Four Men Juvenile	500 meters	(K 4M Juv.	500 m)
Kayaks Four Women Juvenile	500 meters	(K 4W Juv.	500 m)
Canoes Four Men Juvenile	500 meters	(C 4M Juv.	500 m)

Bantam Events

Single Kayaks Men Bantam	250 meters	(K 1M Ban.	250 m)
Single Kayaks Women Bantam	250 meters	(K 1W Ban.	250 m)
Tandem Kayaks Men Bantam	250 meters	(K 2M Ban.	250 m)
Tandem Kayaks Women Bantam	250 meters	(K 2W Ban.	250 m)
Single Canoes Men Bantam	250 meters	(C 1M Ban.	250 m)
Canoes Four Men Bantam	250 meters	(C 4M Ban.	250 m)
Kayaks Four Men Bantam	250 meters	(K 4M Ban.	250 m)
Kayaks Four Women Bantam	250 meters	(K 4W Ban.	250 m)

Special Events

Tandem Kayaks Mixed (1 man/1 woman)	500 meters	(K 2 mixed	500 m)
Single Kayaks Men 40 & Over	500 meters	(K 1M 40 & over	500 m)
Single Canoes Men 40 & Over	500 meters	(C 1M 40 & over	500 m)

Sec. 3 Schedule of Events:

PROGRAM OF EVENTS

The order of events shall be as follows with heats to be held as required before start of the program.

1st Day		2nd Day		3rd Day		4th Day	
K-2 M Int	1000	K-1 M Int	1000	C-1 M Jr	500	K-1 M Jr	500
C-2 M Int	1000	C-1 M Int	1000	K-4 W Sr	500	K-1 M Sr	500
K-1 M Jr	1000	K-2 M Jr	1000	K-2 M Sr	500	C-1 M Sr	500
C-1 M Jr	1000	C-2 M Jr	1000	C-2 M Sr	500	K-1 W Sr	500
K-4 M Int	1000	K-4 W Int	500	C-4 M Jr	500	C-2 M Jr	500
K-2 W Juv	500	C-2 M Juv	500	K-1 W Int	500	K-2 M Jr	500
K-1 M Juv	500	K-4 M Sr	500	K-1 M Mas	500	K-4 W Jr	500
K-1 W Jr	500	K-2 M Juv	500	K-2 W Jr	500	K-2 W Int	500
K-2 Mixed	500	K-2 W Sr	500	K-4 M Jr	500	C-4 M Sr	1000
C-1 M Juv	500	C-4 M Juv	500	K-1 M Sr	1000	K-4 M Sr	1000
K-1 W Juv	500	K-4 W Juv	500	C-1 M Sr	1000	C-2 M Ban	250
K-4 M Juv	500	C-2 M Sr	1000	C-4 M Ban	250		
K-1 M Ban	250	K-2 M Sr	1000				
K-2 W Ban	250	K-2 M Ban	250				
		K-1 W Ban	250				
K-2 W Sr	5000	K-4 M Jr	5000	K-4 W Sr	5000		
K-4 W Jr	5000	K-1 W Sr	5000	K-2 M Jr	5000		
K-1 M Jr	5000	K-2 W Jr	5000				
C-2 M Jr	5000	C-1 M Jr	5000	K-1 W Jr	5000		
		K-4 M Sr	10000	K-2 M Sr	10000	K-1 M Sr	10000
				C-2 M Sr	10000	C-1 M Sr	10000

Sec. 4 Entries:

a. The NPC will develop, publish and distribute, (such as in its *News Bulletin*), qualification standards for the National Championship regatta. Changes to the standards previously established by the NPC must be distributed by April 15th to be effective for that paddling season. Performance meeting time standards must be certified in accordance with NPC established requirements. The NPC may determine the National Championship regatta to be open to all competitors with valid registrations.

b. Entries must be made in accordance with the official entry form published for the current year's championships and mixed K-2.

c. The following events are exempt from NPC qualifying standards: C-1 Men 40 & over, K-1 Men over 40.

d. All boats raced in the National Championships shall be weighed and measured.

Sec. 5 Awards:

The present ACA die (the Indian) shall be used for awards in the Bantam, Juvenile, Junior and Intermediate events. For the Senior, Master and Mixed events a separate medal shall be used; said medal shall be 1-1/2 to 2-1/2 inches in diameter, with neck ribbon of red, white and blue in gold, silver and bronze finishes. The symbol or design to be approved by the National Paddling Committee. Only the National Paddling Committee may approve trophies for awards in the National Championship Regatta.

Sec. 6 Requirements and Specifications:

In consideration of being awarded the National Canoeing Championships of the American Canoe Association, it is understood and agreed that the Local Organization or Division under whose auspices the Regatta is to be held agrees in all good faith to assume full responsibility for carrying out to the letter all provisions which are absolutely essential to insure proper conduct of the National Championships.

a. Sanctioning fee—pay a $300.00 Sanctioning Fee to the National Paddling Committee.

b. Lodging Arrangements and Race Headquarters:

Arrange in advance at motels and campgrounds for a special rate for the accommodation of visiting canoeists and members of canoeing clubs attending this regatta. Designate a place which is readily accessible at all times, as race headquarters. This information should be communicated to the Secretary of the National Paddling Committee as soon as possible in order that it may be incorporated in all literature and notices of the regatta sent out to the Divisions and member organizations of the Association.

Sec. 7 Laying Out of Course:

a. The regatta shall be held on sheltered water of sufficient depth to insure even current and fair canoeing conditions. The canoeing course is to be surveyed by a civil engineer, with certified copies available to officials and crews.

b. The depth of the water over the entire course shall be at least 2 meters if possible. If this is not possible, the depth must be uniform over the entire width of the course.

c. The width of the lanes for races up to 1,000 meters shall be 9 meters wide and the width of the course shall be sufficient to allow 9 lanes.

d. The 10,000 meter course shall meet the following conditions:

1. Distance between the center of the turns at least 1000 meters and straight.

2. Radius of the turns at least 40 meters.

3. All races shall be refereed by at least two Turn Umpires in two separate boats.

Sec. 8 Marking of Course:

In the 500 and 1,000 meters races the lanes shall be marked with buoys. The distance between the buoys along the length of the course shall not exceed 100 meters. The last buoys must be 2 meters after the finishing line. All buoys are to be made of a supple material that will not damage equipment.

Sec. 9 Starting Facilities:

a. Where possible, all races shall start from a pontoon or dock. An assistant holds the stern of the boat and releases it on the word "GO" (shot).

b. The starter must be located as close to the starting line as possible on a fixed platform with adequate protection from wind, sun and rain.

c. The start line must be marked so that the starter can maintain an accurate starting line at all times.

Sec. 10 Finish Line Facilities:

a. Except for two easily visible and well anchored red buoys topped by flags marking the outside edges of the course no other buoys shall be installed on the finish line.

b. The finish line must have fixed markers so that the judges and timers will have a steady sight line to accurately indicate the finish.

c. An adequate finish line stand must be available for the judges and timers. The stand must be constructed so as to provide an unobstructed view of the finish line for at least one judge and one timer for each lane, plus a chief judge, chief timer, video camera person, and a recording secretary.

d. The finish line stand must provide adequate protection from the wind, sun and rain for the officials.

e. The finish line stand must be isolated (roped or fenced off, or on water) from the competitors and spectators.

Sec. 11 Judging and Timing:

a. Photo-Finish:

The organization arranging the Championships must see that a photo-finish is taken of each race (heats, repechages, semifinals and finals). A line coinciding with the finishing line of the course shall show in each picture. In heats, repechages and semifinals, the photo-finish must show all participants in the race who qualify to go further in the competition. In finals, the photo-finish must record the finish of all participants. The photo-finish shall be at the disposal of the Finishing Line Judges, the Chief Official and the Jury. Prior to the announcement of the results no person shall, without the specific authorization of the Chief Official, have access to the film. The Finishing Line Judges must compare their decisions with the photo-finish in all instances in which errors of judgment might possibly be committed. The Judges should compare their decisions with the results of photo-finish which are considered decisive. If several boats come to finish simultaneously, which is proved by the photo-finish, the placing is defined identically for all the boats according to the best place. Two and more first, second and third places may be taken. (A video camera-tape with instant replay in slow motion is a must.)

b. The Chief Judge and Chief Timer shall appoint at least one person each to separately judge and to time each lane. Sufficient qualified officials shall be provided to meet this requirement.

c. Times must be taken and recorded down through the last place in every heat, repechage, semifinal and final. Digital stopwatches should be used.

d. Patrol boats shall insure that no craft of any kind, excepting a judges' stand, shall loiter on the finish line or sweep past the finish line for the purpose of watching or photographing the finish of any race. The intent of this requirement is to prevent any obstruction of the line-of-sight which might affect the judging of the order and time of finish.

Sec. 12 Advancement to Finals:

a. The division into heats shall be made in accordance with the racing rules, except that in all Senior and Junior class races requiring heats, all competitors not advancing to a higher round will have a second chance (repechage) to advance to the finals. The ICF plans may be used for the Senior and Junior class races. The Competition Committee shall be responsible for establishing the system for advancement to the finals which meets this requirement. The ICF system for advancement (Plans A through F) are incorporated in these rules for consideration by the Competition Committee or for use in international regattas.

b. All line assignments will be made by the drawing of lots.

c. In 1,000 meter races the interval between heats (heats, reps, semifinals and finals) must not be less than 1-1/2 hours; for 500 meter races not less than one (1) hour.

Sec. 13 Safety:

a. In order to insure that all manner of craft shall be kept off the course during the regatta and to act as rescue boats, there must be at least two motorboats for patrol service, each boat containing not more than two occupants, one of which should have police authority in order to maintain an absolutely clear course under all conditions.

b. A First Aid center should be established.

Sec. 14 Official Boats:

Two good reliable motorboats, each with an experienced operator must be provided for the umpires and officials. Each boat must be capable of carrying at least three persons in addition to the operator and both boats must be able to show a speed of at least eighteen miles per hour.

Sec. 15 Communications:

a. A communication system is required to provide reliable and direct communication between the starter, finish line and administration area (competition organizer/secretary).

b. Three megaphones shall be provided for the use of the Competition Committee.

c. A public address system is required to announce race times, results, page people, communicate with officials and to provide results.

d. A large bulletin board is necessary to post race information, i.e., to post time and lanes for heats, reps, semifinals and finals; all results, other race information, meeting and other notices and announcements.

e. Typewriters and a copy machine as well as people to operate them are a necessary part of organizing the championships.

f. The local organizing group is responsible for providing a printed program for the championships which will include schedule and time of events, clubs and competitors competing, officials and other pertinent information as desired. These programs may be sold or distributed free as the local committee may decide.

Sec. 16 Equipment Storage and Security:

The local organizing group is responsible for providing racks to store all boats or an area where the possibility of damage to the equipment will be minimized. Security for the equipment will be provided day and night.

Sec. 17 News Media Arrangements:

Satisfactory arrangements must be made to facilitate the proper reporting of the championships by the news media (newspapers, TV and radio). Adequate pre-race publicity and build-up should also be arranged.

Sec. 18 Convenience:

a. Adequate toilet facilities must be available or provided for males and females.

b. Shelter for the athletes for protection from sun and rain should be available or provided convenient to the course along with adequate, pure drinking water.

c. Showers should be made available if possible.

Sec. 19 Pennants:

All clubs or divisions in National Championships shall provide a club or divisional pennant for use at awards stand. Pennants to be returned at end of regatta. Size of pennants to be 24″ high and 30″ wide.

Sec. 20 Any other conditions not covered in the above shall be handled by the local organizing group as the Competition Committee shall direct and their expenses shall be borne by the local organization.

RULE 23. AMENDMENTS

These Paddling Rules and Regulations may be amended only by a majority vote of the National Paddling Committee, after the complete proposed amendment has been submitted to the chairman of each Divisional Paddling Committee, and further, that the proposed amendment has been published in the National Paddling Committee *News Bulletin* and/or an official organ of the American Canoe Association, at least four weeks prior to the date on which the National Paddling Committee will take a final vote thereon. The proposed amendment may be modified by the NPC in accordance with Roberts Rules of Order without being republished.

RULE 24. DISCIPLINARY MEASURES

Sec. 1 The disciplinary measures of the National Paddling Committee are:

a. Caution;

b. Reprimand;

c. Exclusion of some or all members of a club from participation in NPC sanctioned competitions and international competitions;

d. Suspension;

e. Expulsion.

These disciplinary measures can be taken against individual members for breach of the ACA Constitution, NPC By-Laws, Racing Rules for Olympic Flatwater Canoes and Kayaks, or for having harmed the interest of the NPC. Suspension bars the individual from participation in all NPC competitions (national, regional, international) until the suspension is lifted. In case of expulsion, membership in NPC ceases.

Sec. 2 Disciplinary actions a-c are taken by the NPC Board on a majority vote. Disciplinary actions d and e are taken by the NPC Board on a two-thirds majority vote of all voting NPC Board members.

Sec. 3 Appeals against a decision of the NPC Board can be made according to the provisions for appeal included in the ACA Constitution and the NPC By-Laws.

APPENDIXES

Appendix 1 (deleted here) Amateur Rules of the American Canoe Association

Appendix 2 (deleted here) ICF Plans for Advancement to Finals

---

GOVERNING BODY

American Canoe Association, 7217 Lockport Place, P.O. Box 248, Lorton, VA 22079

Flatwater canoe and kayak racing is governed by the National Paddling Committee of the American Canoe Association (ACA) and the National Olympic Canoe & Kayak Committee. The ACA, as a member of both the U.S. Olympic Committee and the International Canoe Federation, serves as the governing body for national and international competition. It is the purpose of the ACA to unite all persons interested in canoeing. The Association provides educational, informational, and training services to increase the enjoyment, safety, and skills of all canoeists at every skill level. Books dealing with all aspects of canoeing, guides to specific rivers and regions, films, and videotapes are available through the ACA.

MAGAZINES

Canoe Magazine, Canoe America Associates, P.O. Box 3146, Kirkland, WA 98033

River Runner, P.O. Box 697, Fallbrook, CA 92028

• CASTING •

RULES GOVERNING EVENTS

(Reproduced by permission of the American Casting Association*)

□

Note: The rules for seven of the twelve recognized casting events of the Association are presented here. The five events not included (Trout Fly Accuracy, Bass Bug Accuracy, Angler's Fly Distance, Fly Distance Singlehanded and Fly Distance Doublehanded) along with the complete by-laws, rules, and regulations of the Association will be found in the ACA handbook.

DRY FLY ACCURACY

I. EQUIPMENT

A. Rod.

1. Length—Shall not exceed 9-1/2 feet overall.

2. Weight—Unrestricted.

B. Reel—Unrestricted.

C. Line—Unrestricted, but shall not be marked in any way that would indicate distance, nor fastened to the reel at less than fifty (50) feet.

D. Leader—Shall consist of a single leader of natural or artificial gut or gut substitute not less than six (6) feet in length.

E. Fly.

1. Description—Official Dry Fly adopted by the ACA. The hackle shall not be less than 3/4 inch nor more than one inch in diameter. The fly shall not be oiled or treated in any way.

2. Application—Only one fly may be attached to the leader at the tip end. The fly may be changed at any time, or lost fly replaced with a fly approved by the Judge.

II. TARGET COURSE

A. Targets—Five (5) targets shall constitute the course. Each target shall be anchored so that the total movement for any reason will not exceed one foot in any direction. At no time shall the distance be less than the minimum distance specified in Section II B 1 nor exceed the maximum distance specified in II B 2.

B. Distances.

1. Near Target—The near target shall be placed from 20 to 25 feet, as measured from the center of the target to the center of the front edge of the casting box.

---

*See page 114 for additional information.

2. Far Target—The far target shall be placed from 45 to 50 feet as measured from the center of the target to the center of the front edge of the casting box.

3. Other Targets—The three remaining targets shall be placed randomly in the intervening space, and not in a straight line perpendicular to the casting box.

III. TIME

A. General—Time starts when the caster steps into casting box. Caster shall be allowed eight (8) minutes to complete the casting program without penalty.

B. Time Out—There shall be no time out for any reason, except for outside interference as determined by the Judge. The loss of a fly, unless that loss is caused by external contact such as a tree or a snag on a target, shall not be considered outside interference. The loss of a fly caused by striking any part of the casting platform shall not be considered outside interference.

C. Penalty—A penalty of three (3) demerits shall be assessed for each minute or fraction of a minute overtime.

IV. METHOD OF CASTING

A. Casting Program.

1. General—The casting program shall consist of ten (10) final forward casts, two (2) at each of the five targets in the target course, in the order and as directed by the Tournament Captain. All five targets must be cast before any target may be cast again. Consecutive casts shall not be made on any target. All casters shall cast the same order of targets. Caster must enter casting box before beginning the casting program.

2. Responsibility—After stepping into the casting box the caster shall be responsible for the results and shall accept the score and penalties assessed by the Judge.

B. Casting Style—Singlehanded.

C. Procedure.

1. Initial—Caster shall start with fly in hand and no more than leader plus two feet of line extending beyond rod tip.

2. False Cast—The false cast, in which the line, leader and fly are moved through the air without intentionally striking the surface in front of the casting box is the mechanism for letting line out, pulling line in and measuring distance to the next target. The rod must be in motion in the act of making a false cast to strip line from the reel. Caster shall not measure line by stripping along the rod. Caster has the option of holding any loose line in either hand, or of letting it drop. Caster shall not allow fly to dangle or be blown over a target in spite of wind conditions.

3. Final Forward Cast—Whenever the intact line, leader and fly settles on the surface in front of the caster on a final forward cast, it shall be scored for accuracy (see Section V). The fly shall float and be left floating a few seconds. After the Judge has ascertained whether or not the fly is floating, he shall call "Score" and the caster shall proceed to the next target.

D. Penalties.

1. Improper Strip—Should the caster strip line from the reel or pull line in through the guides while the fly is on the surface in front of the casting box and the rod is not in motion in the act of making a cast, or attempt to measure the line by stripping along the rod, it shall be scored an improper strip. A penalty of three (3) demerits shall be assessed for each such strip.

2. Tick—Should the line, leader or fly extended beyond the rod tip strike the surface in front of the casting box during a false cast it shall be scored a tick. Penalty for a tick shall count during casting time whether caster is in or out of casting box and whether or not the fly is on. A penalty of three (3) demerits shall be assessed for each tick.

3. Sunken Fly—Should the fly fail to float, or sink and rise to the surface, on a final forward cast, it shall be scored a sunken fly and a penalty of three (3) demerits shall be assessed. It is the intent of this rule to require that the final forward cast be laid delicately. The Judge must be cognizant of extreme water surface conditions that would not permit the untreated fly to float no matter how delicately the delivery cast is laid. The Judge also must be alert that small ripples caused when the fly lands on the water do not, for that reason alone, constitute a sunken fly.

4. Improper Retrieve—Should the caster lift the fly from the water after a final forward cast before the Judge calls "Score" it shall be scored an improper retrieve. A penalty of three (3) demerits shall be assessed for each such improper retrieve.

5. Improper Cast—Should the caster allow the fly to dangle or to be blown over a target, it shall be scored an improper cast. A penalty of three (3) demerits shall be assessed for each such improper cast.

E. Interruption of Casting Program.

1. Outside Interference—In the event the caster is interrupted during the Dry Fly round due to outside interference, as determined by the Judge, the caster, if he desires, may make a final forward cast to the last target scored. When the Judge is satisfied that the caster has the approximate line length required to reach the last scored target, he shall then notify the caster the time has started and the caster shall lift the line from the water and proceed to the remaining targets. If the caster does not wish to cast to the last target scored, he may proceed as in Section E 2. except that time will start with the first false cast.

2. Other Interruptions—If the caster is interrupted during the Dry Fly round for reasons other than outside interference, the caster shall begin false casting and proceed to the remaining targets.

V. METHOD OF SCORING

A. General.

1. No final forward cast shall be scored unless the line leader and fly are intact. The Judge shall notify the caster whenever he notices that the fly is off.

2. Each cast shall be scored where the fly first strikes the water regardless of where the fly may ultimately settle.

3. If the line or leader strikes the water in front of the casting box on a final forward cast when the fly is not intact, it shall be scored a tick whether or not the Judge has notified the Caster that the fly is off, unless the fly is lost during that final forward cast. In that eventuality, no penalty shall be assessed.

B. Demerits for Accuracy.

1. A fly falling within or on any portion of the target on a final forward cast shall be scored a perfect and shall be assessed zero (0) demerits.

2. For each foot or fraction thereof the fly misses the extreme edge of the target on a final forward cast, a demerit of one (1) shall be assessed.

3. Maximum demerits for any single final forward cast shall be ten (10).

C. Demerits for Penalties—Penalty demerits shall be in addition to accuracy demerits.

D. Caster's Score—One hundred (100) points less the total number of demerits for accuracy and for penalties shall constitute a caster's score.

ACCURACY PLUG

1/4 oz.; 3/8 oz.; 5/8 oz.

The rules for three accuracy plug events are similar except for Equipment. The equipment is described by event. The Target Course, Method of Casting and Method of Scoring are described collectively.

I. EQUIPMENT

1/4 oz. Plug Accuracy (Fixed Spool Reel)

A. Rod—Unrestricted.

B. Reel—Fixed Spool.

C. Line—Unrestricted.

D. Plug—Any official 1/4 oz. accuracy plug adopted by the Association.

3/8 oz. Plug Accuracy (Unrestricted Reel)

A. Rod—Unrestricted.

B. Reel—Unrestricted.

C. Line—Unrestricted.

D. Plug—Any official 3/8 oz. accuracy plug adopted by the Association.

5/8 oz. Plug Accuracy (Unrestricted Reel)

A. Rod—Unrestricted.

B. Reel—Unrestricted.

C. Line—Unrestricted.

D. Plug—Any official 5/8 oz. accuracy plug adopted by the Association.

II. TARGET COURSE

A. Targets—The following options are permitted in the target course:

OPTION 1: One (1) station with five (5) targets. One near target shall be placed as specified in Section II B 1. and one far target shall be placed as specified in Section II B 2. The remaining targets shall be placed at intervening distances and not in a straight line perpendicular to the casting box.

OPTION 2: Two (2) stations with five (5) targets at each station. Each station shall be as indicated in Option 1.

OPTION 3: Five (5) stations with two (2) targets at each station. Two near targets shall be placed as specified in Section II B 1. and two far targets shall be placed as specified in Section II B 2. The other targets shall be placed at intervening distances. In general, at any station the target distances shall be no more than approximately twenty-five (25) feet apart.

OPTION 4: Ten (10) stations with one (1) target at each station. Two near targets shall be placed as specified in Section II B 1. and two far targets shall be placed as specified in Section II B 2. The remaining targets shall be placed at intervening distances.

OPTION 5: More than two (2) stations but less than five (5) stations so that the total number of targets is ten (10). Two near targets shall be placed as specified in Section II B 1. and two far targets shall be placed as specified in Section II B 2. The other targets shall be placed at intervening distances. Distribution of targets among the stations shall be determined by the Tournament Captain. In general, at any station the target distance shall be no more than approximately twenty-five (25) feet apart.

The purpose of Options 2, 3, 4, and 5 is to effect a continuous flow of casters through the target course. The option selected will depend upon the physical facilities of the location and the number of entries.

B. Distances.

1. Near Target—The near target shall be placed from 40 to 45 feet as measured from the center of the target to the center of the front edge of the casting box.

2. Far Target—The far target shall be placed from 75 to 80 feet as measured from the center of the target to the center of the front edge of the casting box.

III. METHOD OF CASTING

A. Casting Program.

1. General—The casting program shall consist of a total of ten (10) scoring casts using one of the target course options of Section II B. in the order and as directed by the Tournament Captain. All casters shall cast the same order of targets.

2. Scoring Cast—A scoring cast is a cast made from the casting box.

3. Responsibility—After stepping into the casting box, the caster shall be responsible for the results and accept the score and penalties assessed by the Judge.

B. Casting Style—Singlehanded.

C. Procedure.

1. General—The procedure for the accuracy plug events will depend upon the selected target course option in Section II A.

Option 1 uses one station and five targets. There should be no more than five casters in a group. The first caster steps into the box, makes a scoring cast at the first target, and steps out of the box. Then the first caster retrieves the plug while the second caster steps into the box and makes a scoring cast at the same target. This procedure shall be repeated until all casters have made scoring casts at the first target and in a similar manner until all five targets have been cast. The procedure is repeated until all casters have made ten scoring casts. All five targets at the station must be cast before any target may be cast again and successive casts at any one target are not permitted.

Option 2 uses five targets at each of two stations. There should be no more than five casters in a group. The procedure is similar to Option 1 except that when the last caster in the group completes a scoring cast on the fifth target of the first station, the entire group moves to the second station and a new group of five casters moves to the first station.

Option 3 uses five stations and two targets at each station. Two casters should cast in a group. The first caster steps into the box, makes a scoring cast at the first target, and steps out of the box. Then the first caster retrieves the plug while the second caster steps into the box and makes a scoring cast at the same target. The procedure is then repeated for the second target. The first group of casters then moves to the second station and the procedure is repeated while a second group of two casters begins on the first station. This procedure is repeated until all casters have made ten scoring casts.

Option 4 uses ten stations with one target at each station. Each caster casts individually stopping at each of the ten stations in turn.

Option 5 uses more than two stations but less than five. The procedure is similar to Option 3.

D. Authorized False Cast—Regardless of the Option used for the target course, each caster shall be permitted three (3) authorized false casts. An authorized false cast is a cast executed only when it is the caster's turn to cast and made only after the approval of the Judge. The caster shall step outside the casting box and cast reasonably away from any target which constitutes any part of the target course. If the caster does not conform to the above, any such cast shall be considered an unauthorized cast, except that any cast made from the casting box shall be considered to be a scoring cast regardless of the approval granted by the Judge. For each unauthorized cast, or for each false cast in excess of three (3) authorized false casts, a penalty of five (5) demerits shall be assessed.

IV. METHOD OF SCORING

A. General—Each scoring cast shall be scored where the plug falls whether in front of or behind the forward edge of the casting box, whether or not the line is intact. If a scoring cast is arrested so as to abort the cast, a penalty of ten (10) demerits shall be assessed regardless of whether or not the plug strikes a fixed object or is caught by a caster.

B. Demerits for Accuracy.

1. A plug falling within or on any portion of the target above the water line shall be scored a perfect and shall be assessed zero (0) demerits.

2. For each foot or fraction thereof the plug misses the extreme edge of the target a demerit of one (1) shall be assessed.

3. The maximum demerits for accuracy for any cast shall be ten (10).

C. Demerits for Penalties—Penalty demerits shall be in addition to accuracy demerits.

D. Caster's Score—One hundred (100) points less the total number of demerits for accuracy and for penalties shall constitute a caster's score.

PLUG DISTANCE

1/4 oz. Singlehanded; 5/8 oz. Singlehanded; 5/8 oz. Doublehanded

The rules for the three plug distance events are similar except for equipment. The equipment is described by event. The Distance Course, Method of Casting and Method of Scoring are described collectively.

I. EQUIPMENT

1/4 oz. Plug Distance, Singlehanded

A. Rod—The complete rod shall not exceed eight feet, two inches (8'2").

B. Reel—Fixed Spool.

C. Line—Unrestricted, except that the same diameter must be used throughout the length.

D. Plug—Any official 1/4 oz. distance plug adopted by the Association.

5/8 oz. Plug Distance, Singlehanded

A. Rod—Unrestricted.

B. Reel—Revolving Spool.

C. Line—Unrestricted.

D. Plug—Any official 5/8 oz. distance plug adopted by the Association.

5/8 oz. Plug Distance, Doublehanded

A. Rod—Unrestricted.

B. Reel—Fixed Spool.

C. Line—The minimum diameter of the line shall not be less than 0.010 inches with a tolerance such that the minimum diameter is 0.25 millimeters.

D. Plug—Any official 5/8 oz. distance plug adopted by the Association.

II. DISTANCE COURSE

The Distance Course shall be of sufficient length and shall consist of a court that is a maximum of 180 degrees wide.

III. TIME

The caster shall have one (1) minute to release a cast after the Judge has declared the box open.

IV. METHOD OF CASTING

A. Casting Program.

1. General—The casting program shall consist of three (3) casts.

2. Scoring Cast—A scoring cast is a completed cast with no line breakage made from the casting box in which the plug strikes the surface within the distance court.

3. Responsibility—After stepping into the casting box the caster shall be responsible for the results and shall accept the distance measurement and penalties assessed by the Judge.

B. Casting Style—Singlehanded or Doublehanded, as specified in Section I.

C. Procedure.

1. General—Following the casting order, a caster shall be prepared to cast when the Judge declares the box open.

2. Delivery of Cast—The caster shall deliver and complete the cast with all parts of the caster's body and all attached clothing contacting only the surface of the casting box. However, any windup motion prior to releasing the cast may begin from outside the box.

3. Equipment Check—After completing a cast, the caster shall remain in the casting box until released by the Judge. After the Judge has performed all appropriate equipment checks, and has verified that the line had not broken, the caster may break and retie the line before retrieving the cast.

4. Retrieve—After having been released by the Judge, the caster shall retrieve the line while walking to the location where the plug rests.

5. Open Box—When the previous caster has safely cleared the box, the Judge shall declare the box open.

6. Equipment Problems—In case of bona fide equipment problems the Judge shall allow a caster to drop to a more convenient place in the casting order only one (1) time during the event.

V. METHOD OF SCORING

A. General—Only scoring casts shall be measured.

B. Measurement—The length of a scoring cast shall be the distance measured to the nearest foot from the center of the leading edge of the casting box to the location where the plug has come to rest within the boundaries of the court.

C. Penalties.

1. Overstep—If any part of the caster's body or any attached clothing touches any part of the surface outside of the casting box from the time of the cast's release until the Judge completes the equipment check, the cast shall be scored zero (0).

2. Early Movement from Box—If the caster moves from the box for any reason before being released by the Judge, the cast shall be scored zero (0).

3. Broken Line—If the caster's line breaks during the cast at any time after beginning any windup motion and before the caster is released from the box by the Judge, the cast shall be scored zero (0).

4. Failure to Retrieve—After having been released from the box by the Judge, if the caster fails to retrieve the line by walking to the location where the plug rests, the cast shall be scored zero (0), unless there is evidence to indicate that a line break occurred due to outside interference.

5. Overtime—If a caster is not prepared to cast when called to the open box, except as outlined in Section IV C 6., or if the caster does not release his cast within one (1) minute, the cast shall be scored zero (0).

D. Caster's Score—The caster's longest scoring cast shall constitute the caster's score. The second longest scoring cast shall be recorded, but shall be used only to break ties.

GOVERNING BODY

American Casting Association, 786 Hyatts Road, Delaware, OH 43015

The American Casting Association (ACA) is the control organization for the sport of casting in North America. The ACA in turn belongs to the International Casting Federation, which, through the World Casting Association, governs the sport worldwide. The sport of casting is a charter activity in the World Games. Membership in the ACA is made up of clubs, some of which are entirely devoted to casting, others of which are rod and gun clubs, fishing clubs, conservation clubs, industrial clubs, and physical education departments of schools and colleges. It is also possible for individuals to join the Association. For further information, write Mr. Zack Willson, Executive Secretary, American Casting Association at the above address.

MAGAZINES

The Creel, American Casting Association, 786 Hyatts Road, Delaware, OH 43015

Field & Stream, CBS Magazines, Consumer Publishing Group, 1515 Broadway, New York, NY 10036

THE LAWS
• OF CRICKET •

(1980 CODE)

**(Printed by permission of Marylebone Cricket Club.*
Copies of the current edition of the Laws of Cricket
with full notes and interpretations can be obtained
from M.C.C. at Lord's Cricket Ground, London NW8;
price 50p excluding postage.)**

☐

LAW 1 THE PLAYERS

1. NUMBER OF PLAYERS AND CAPTAIN

A match is played between two sides each of eleven Players, one of whom shall be Captain.
In the event of the Captain not being available at any time a Deputy shall act for him.

2. NOMINATION OF PLAYERS

Before the toss for innings, the Captain shall nominate his Players who may not thereafter
be changed without the consent of the opposing Captain.

Notes

(a) More or Less than Eleven Players a Side

A match may be played by agreement between sides of more or less than eleven players
but not more than eleven players may field.

LAW 2 SUBSTITUTES AND RUNNERS:
BATSMAN OR FIELDSMAN LEAVING THE FIELD,
BATSMAN RETIRING,
BATSMAN COMMENCING INNINGS

1. SUBSTITUTES

Substitutes shall be allowed by right to field for any player who during the match is
incapacitated by illness or injury. The consent of the opposing Captain must be obtained
for the use of a Substitute if any player is prevented from fielding for any other reason.

---

*See pages 147 and 148 for additional information.

2. OBJECTION TO SUBSTITUTES

The opposing Captain shall have no right of objection to any player acting as Substitute in the field, nor as to where he shall field, although he may object to the Substitute acting as Wicket-Keeper.

3. SUBSTITUTE NOT TO BAT OR BOWL

A Substitute shall not be allowed to bat or bowl.

4. A PLAYER FOR WHOM A SUBSTITUTE HAS ACTED

A player may bat, bowl or field even though a Substitute has acted for him.

5. RUNNER

A Runner shall be allowed for a Batsman who during the match is incapacitated by illness or injury. The player acting as Runner shall be a member of the batting side and shall, if possible, have already batted in that innings.

6. RUNNER'S EQUIPMENT

The player acting as Runner for an injured Batsman shall wear batting gloves and pads if the injured Batsman is so equipped.

7. TRANSGRESSION OF THE LAWS BY AN INJURED BATSMAN OR RUNNER

An injured Batsman may be out should his Runner break any one of Laws 33. (Handled the Ball), 37. (Obstructing the Field) or 38. (Run Out). As Striker he remains himself subject to the Laws. Furthermore, should he be out of his ground for any purpose and the wicket at the Wicket-Keeper's end be put down he shall be out under Law 38. (Run Out) or Law 39. (Stumped) irrespective of the position of the other Batsman or the Runner and no runs shall be scored.

When not the Striker, the injured Batsman is out of the game and shall stand where he does not interfere with the play. Should he bring himself into the game in any way then he shall suffer the penalties that any transgression of the Laws demands.

8. FIELDSMAN LEAVING THE FIELD

No Fieldsman shall leave the field or return during a session of play without the consent of the Umpire at the Bowler's end. The Umpire's consent is also necessary if a Substitute is required for a Fieldsman, when his side returns to the field after an interval. If a member of the fielding side leaves the field or fails to return after an interval and is absent from the field for longer than 15 minutes, he shall not be permitted to bowl after his return until he has been on the field for at least that length of playing time for which he was absent. This restriction shall not apply at the start of a new day's play.

9. BATSMAN LEAVING THE FIELD OR RETIRING

A Batsman may leave the field or retire at any time owing to illness, injury or other unavoidable cause, having previously notified the Umpire at the Bowler's end. He may resume his innings at the fall of a wicket, which for the purposes of this Law shall include the retirement of another Batsman.

If he leaves the field or retires for any other reason he may only resume his innings with the consent of the opposing Captain. When a Batsman has left the field or retired and is unable to return owing to illness, injury or other unavoidable cause, his innings is to be recorded as "retired, not out". Otherwise it is to be recorded as "retired, out".

10. COMMENCEMENT OF A BATSMAN'S INNINGS

A Batsman shall be considered to have commenced his innings once he has stepped on to the field of play.

Notes

(a) Substitutes and Runners
For the purpose of these Laws allowable illnesses or injuries are those which occur at any time after the nomination by the Captains of their teams.

LAW 3 THE UMPIRES

1. APPOINTMENT

Before the toss for innings two Umpires shall be appointed, one for each end, to control the game with absolute impartiality as required by the Laws.

2. CHANGE OF UMPIRE

No Umpire shall be changed during a match without the consent of both Captains.

3. SPECIAL CONDITIONS

Before the toss for innings, the Umpires shall agree with both Captains on any special conditions affecting the conduct of the match.

4. THE WICKETS

The Umpires shall satisfy themselves before the start of the match that the wickets are properly pitched.

5. CLOCK OR WATCH

The Umpires shall agree between themselves and inform both Captains before the start of the match on the watch or clock to be followed during the match.

6. CONDUCT AND IMPLEMENTS

Before and during a match the Umpires shall ensure that the conduct of the game and the implements used are strictly in accordance with the Laws.

7. FAIR AND UNFAIR PLAY

The Umpires shall be the sole judges of fair and unfair play.

8. FITNESS OF GROUND, WEATHER AND LIGHT

(a) The Umpires shall be the sole judges of the fitness of the ground, weather and light for play.

(i) However, before deciding to suspend play or not to start play or not to resume play after an interval or stoppage, the Umpires shall establish whether both Captains (the Batsmen at the wicket may deputise for their Captain) wish to commence or to continue in the prevailing conditions; if so, their wishes shall be met.

(ii) In addition, if during play, the Umpires decide that the light is unfit, only the batting side shall have the option of continuing play. After agreeing to continue to play in unfit light conditions, the Captain of the batting side (or a Batsman at the wicket) may appeal against the light to the Umpires, who shall uphold the appeal only if, in their opinion, the light has deteriorated since the agreement to continue was made.

(b) After any suspension of play, the Umpires, unaccompanied by any of the Players or Officials shall, on their own initiative, carry out an inspection immediately the conditions improve and shall continue to inspect at intervals. Immediately the Umpires decide that play is possible they shall call upon the Players to resume the game.

9. EXCEPTIONAL CIRCUMSTANCES

In exceptional circumstances, other than those of weather, ground or light, the Umpires may decide to suspend or abandon play. Before making such a decision the Umpires shall establish, if the circumstances allow, whether both Captains (the Batsmen at the wicket may deputise for their Captain) wish to continue in the prevailing conditions; if so, their wishes shall be met.

10. POSITION OF UMPIRES

The Umpires shall stand where they can best see any act upon which their decision may be required.

Subject to this over-riding consideration the Umpire at the Bowler's end shall stand where he does not interfere with either the Bowler's run up or the Striker's view.

The Umpire at the Striker's end may elect to stand on the off instead of the leg side of the pitch, provided he informs the Captain of the fielding side and the Striker of his intention to do so.

11. UMPIRES CHANGING ENDS

The Umpires shall change ends after each side has had one innings.

12. DISPUTES

All disputes shall be determined by the Umpires and if they disagree the actual state of things shall continue.

13. SIGNALS

The following code of signals shall be used by Umpires who will wait until a signal has been answered by a Scorer before allowing the game to proceed.

Boundary—by waving the arm from side to side.

Boundary 6—by raising both arms above the head.

Bye—by raising an open hand above the head.

Dead Ball—by crossing and re-crossing the wrists below the waist.

Leg Bye—by touching a raised knee with the hand.

No Ball—by extending one arm horizontally.

Out—by raising the index finger above the head. If not out the Umpire shall call "not out".

Short Run—by bending the arm upwards and by touching the nearer shoulder with the tips of the fingers.

Wide—by extending both arms horizontally.

14. CORRECTNESS OF SCORES

The Umpires shall be responsible for satisfying themselves on the correctness of the scores throughout and at the conclusion of the match. See Law 21.6. (Correctness of Result).

Notes

(a) Attendance of Umpires

The Umpires should be present on the ground and report to the Ground Executive or the equivalent at least 30 minutes before the start of a day's play.

(b) Consultation Between Umpires and Scorers

Consultation between Umpires and Scorers over doubtful points is essential.

(c) Fitness of Ground

The Umpires shall consider the ground as unfit for play when it is so wet or slippery as to deprive the Bowlers of a reasonable foothold, the Fieldsmen, other than the deep-fielders, of the power of free movement, or the Batsmen the ability to play their strokes or to run between the wickets. Play should not be suspended merely because the grass and the ball are wet and slippery.

(d) Fitness of Weather and Light

The Umpires should only suspend play when they consider that the conditions are so bad that it is unreasonable or dangerous to continue.

LAW 4 THE SCORERS

1. RECORDING RUNS

All runs scored shall be recorded by Scorers appointed for the purpose. Where there are two Scorers they shall frequently check to ensure that the score sheets agree.

2. ACKNOWLEDGING SIGNALS

The Scorers shall accept and immediately acknowledge all instructions and signals given to them by the Umpires.

LAW 5 THE BALL

1. WEIGHT AND SIZE

The ball, when new, shall weigh not less than 5-1/2 ounces/155.9 g., nor more than 5-3/4 ounces/163 g.: and shall measure not less than 8-13/16 inches/22.4 cm., nor more than 9 inches/22.9 cm. in circumference.

2. APPROVAL OF BALLS

All balls used in matches shall be approved by the Umpires and Captains before the start of the match.

3. NEW BALL

Subject to agreement to the contrary, having been made before the toss, either Captain may demand a new ball at the start of each innings.

4. NEW BALL IN MATCH OF 3 OR MORE DAYS DURATION

In a match of 3 or more days duration, the Captain of the fielding side may demand a new ball after the prescribed number of overs has been bowled with the old one. The Governing Body for cricket in the country concerned shall decide the number of overs applicable in that country which shall be not less than 75 six-ball overs (55 eight-ball overs).

5. BALL LOST OR BECOMING UNFIT FOR PLAY

In the event of a ball during play being lost or, in the opinion of the Umpires, becoming unfit for play, the Umpires shall allow it to be replaced by one that in their opinion has had a similar amount of wear. If a ball is to be replaced, the Umpires shall inform the Batsmen.

Notes

(a) Specifications
The specifications, as described in 1. above shall apply to top-grade balls only. The following degrees of tolerance will be acceptable for other grades of ball.

(i) *Men's Grades 2-4.* Weight: 5.5/16 ounces/150 g. to 5.13/16 ounces/165 g.

Size: 8.11/16 inches/22.0 cm. to 9.1/16 inches/23.0 cm.

(ii) *Women's.* Weight: 4.15/16 ounces/140 g. to 5.5/16 ounces/150 g.

Size: 8.1/4 inches/21.0 cm. to 8.7/8 inches/22.5 cm.

(iii) *Junior.* Weight: 4.5/16 ounces/133 g. to 5.1/16 ounces/143 g.

Size: 8.1/16 inches/20.5 cm. to 8.11/16 inches/22.0 cm.

LAW 6 THE BAT

1. WIDTH AND LENGTH

The bat overall shall not be more than 38 inches/96.5 cm. in length; the blade of the bat shall be made of wood and shall not exceed 4-1/4 inches/10.8 cm. at the widest part.

Notes

(a)
The blade of the bat may be covered with material for protection, strengthening or repair. Such material shall not exceed 1/16 inches/1.56 mm. in thickness.

LAW 7 THE PITCH

1. AREA OF PITCH

The pitch is the area between the bowling creases—see Law 9. (The Bowling, Popping and Return Creases). It shall measure 5 ft./1.52 m. in width on either side of a line joining the centre of the middle stumps of the wickets—see Law 8. (The Wickets).

2. SELECTION AND PREPARATION

Before the toss for innings, the Executive of the Ground shall be responsible for the selection and preparation of the pitch; thereafter the Umpires shall control its use and maintenance.

3. CHANGING PITCH

The pitch shall not be changed during a match unless it becomes unfit for play, and then only with the consent of both Captains.

4. NON-TURF PITCHES

In the event of a non-turf pitch being used, the following shall apply:

(a) LENGTH: That of the playing surface to a minimum of 58 ft. (17.68 m.)

(b) WIDTH: That of the playing surface to a minimum of 6 ft. (1.83 m.)

See Law 10. (Rolling, Sweeping, Mowing, Watering the Pitch and Re-marking of Creases) Note (a).

LAW 8 THE WICKETS

1. WIDTH AND PITCHING

Two sets of wickets, each 9 inches/22.86 cm. wide, and consisting of three wooden stumps with two wooden bails upon the top, shall be pitched opposite and parallel to each other at a distance of 22 yards/20.12 m. between the centres of the two middle stumps.

2. SIZE OF STUMPS

The stumps shall be of equal and sufficient size to prevent the ball from passing between them. Their tops shall be 28 inches/71.1 cm. above the ground, and shall be dome-shaped except for the bail grooves.

3. SIZE OF BAILS

The bails shall be each 4-3/8 inches/11.1 cm. in length and when in position on the top of the stumps shall not project more than 1/2 inch/1.3 cm. above them.

Notes

(a) Dispensing with Bails

In a high wind the Umpires may decide to dispense with the use of bails.

(b) Junior Cricket

For Junior Cricket, as defined by the local Governing Body, the following measurements for the Wickets shall apply:

Width—8 inches/20.32 cm.

Pitched—21 yards/19.20 m.

Height—27 inches/68.58 cm.

Bails—each 3-7/8 inches/9.84 cm. in length and should not project more than 1/2 inch/ 1.3 cm. above them.

LAW 9 THE BOWLING, POPPING AND RETURN CREASES

1. THE BOWLING CREASE

The bowling crease shall be marked in line with the stumps at each end and shall be 8 ft. 8 inches/2.64 m. in length, with the stumps in the centre.

2. THE POPPING CREASE

The popping crease, which is the back edge of the crease marking, shall be in front of and parallel with the bowling crease. It shall have the back edge of the crease marking 4 ft./1.22 m. from the centre of the stumps and shall extend to a minimum of 6 ft./1.83 m. on either side of the line of the wicket.

The popping crease shall be considered to be unlimited in length.

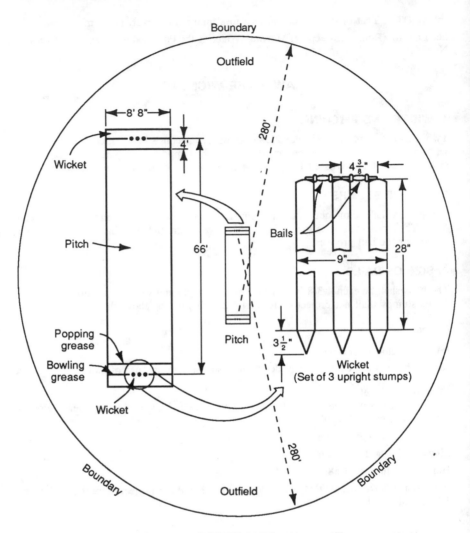

Cricket ground
The field may vary in size and shape, but most official
fields are roughly circular with diameter of 450 to 550 ft.

3. THE RETURN CREASE

The return crease marking, of which the inside edge is the crease, shall be at each end of the bowling crease and at right angles to it. The return crease shall be marked to a minimum of 4 ft./1.22 m. behind the wicket and shall be considered to be unlimited in length. A forward extension shall be marked to the popping crease.

LAW 10 ROLLING, SWEEPING, MOWING, WATERING THE PITCH AND RE-MARKING OF CREASES

1. ROLLING

During the match the pitch may be rolled at the request of the Captain of the batting side, for a period of not more than 7 minutes before the start of each innings, other than the first innings of the match, and before the start of each day's play. In addition, if, after the toss and before the first innings of the match, the start is delayed, the Captain of the batting side shall have the right to have the pitch rolled for not more than 7 minutes.

The pitch shall not otherwise be rolled during the match. The 7 minutes rolling permitted before the start of a day's play shall take place not earlier than half an hour before the start of play and the Captain of the batting side may delay such rolling until 10 minutes before the start of play should he so desire.

If a Captain declares an innings closed less than 15 minutes before the resumption of play, and the other Captain is thereby prevented from exercising his option of 7 minutes rolling or if he is so prevented for any other reason the time for rolling shall be taken out of the normal playing time.

2. SWEEPING

Such sweeping of the pitch as is necessary during the match shall be done so that the 7 minutes allowed for rolling the pitch provided for in 1. above is not affected.

3. MOWING

(a) Responsibilities of Ground Authority and of Umpires

All mowings which are carried out before the toss for innings shall be the responsibility of the Ground Authority. Thereafter they shall be carried out under the supervision of the Umpires, see Law 7.2. (Selection and Preparation).

(b) Initial Mowing

The pitch shall be mown before play begins on the day the match is scheduled to start or in the case of a delayed start on the day the match is expected to start. See 3(a) above. (Responsibilities of Ground Authority and of Umpires.)

(c) Subsequent Mowings in a Match of 2 or More Days' Duration

In a match of two or more days' duration, the pitch shall be mown daily before play begins. Should this mowing not take place because of weather conditions, rest days or other reasons the pitch shall be mown on the first day on which the match is resumed.

(d) Mowing of the Outfield in a Match of 2 or More Days' Duration

In order to ensure that conditions are as similar as possible for both sides, the outfield shall normally be mown before the commencement of play on each day of the match, if ground and weather conditions allow. See Note (b) to this Law.

4. WATERING

The pitch shall not be watered during a match.

5. RE-MARKING CREASES

Whenever possible the creases shall be re-marked.

6. MAINTENANCE OF FOOT HOLES

In wet weather, the Umpires shall ensure that the holes made by the Bowlers and Batsmen are cleaned out and dried whenever necessary to facilitate play. In matches of 2 or more days' duration, the Umpires shall allow, if necessary, the re-turfing of foot holes made by the Bowler in his delivery stride, or the use of quick-setting fillings for the same purpose, before the start of each day's play.

7. SECURING OF FOOTHOLDS AND MAINTENANCE OF PITCH

During play, the Umpires shall allow either Batsman to beat the pitch with his bat and players to secure their footholds by the use of sawdust, provided that no damage to the pitch is so caused, and Law 42. (Unfair Play) is not contravened.

Notes

(a) Non-Turf Pitches
The above Law 10 applies to turf pitches.

The game is played on non-turf pitches in many countries at various levels. Whilst the conduct of the game on these surfaces should always be in accordance with the Laws of Cricket, it is recognized that it may sometimes be necessary for Governing Bodies to lay down special playing conditions to suit the type of non-turf pitch used in their country. In matches played against Touring Teams, any special playing conditions should be agreed in advance by both parties.

(b) Mowing of the Outfield in a Match of 2 or More Days' Duration
If, for reasons other than ground and weather conditions, daily and complete mowing is not possible, the Ground Authority shall notify the Captains and Umpires, before the toss for innings, of the procedure to be adopted for such mowing during the match.

(c) Choice of Roller
If there is more than one roller available the Captain of the batting side shall have a choice.

LAW 11 COVERING THE PITCH

1. BEFORE THE START OF A MATCH

Before the start of a match complete covering of the pitch shall be allowed.

2. DURING A MATCH

The pitch shall not be completely covered during a match unless prior arrangement or regulations so provide.

3. COVERING BOWLERS' RUN-UP

Whenever possible, the Bowlers' run-up shall be covered, but the covers so used shall not extend further than 4 ft./1.22 m. in front of the popping crease.

Notes

(a) Removal of Covers
The covers should be removed as promptly as possible whenever the weather permits.

LAW 12 INNINGS

1. NUMBER OF INNINGS

A match shall be of one or two innings of each side according to agreement reached before the start of play.

2. ALTERNATE INNINGS

In a two innings match each side shall take their innings alternately except in the case provided for in Law 13. (The Follow-On).

3. THE TOSS

The Captains shall toss for the choice of innings on the field of play not later than 15 minutes before the time scheduled for the match to start, or before the time agreed upon for play to start.

4. CHOICE OF INNINGS

The winner of the toss shall notify his decision to bat or to field to the opposing Captain not later than 10 minutes before the time scheduled for the match to start, or before the time agreed upon for play to start. The decision shall not thereafter be altered.

5. CONTINUATION AFTER ONE INNINGS OF EACH SIDE

Despite the terms of 1. above, in a one innings match, when a result has been reached on the first innings the Captains may agree to the continuation of play if, in their opinion, there is a prospect of carrying the game to a further issue in the time left. See Law 21. (Result).

Notes

(a) Limited Innings—One Innings Match
In a one innings match, each innings may, by agreement, be limited by a number of overs or by a period of time.

(b) Limited Innings—Two Innings Match
In a two innings match, the first innings of each side may, by agreement, be limited to a number of overs or by a period of time.

LAW 13 THE FOLLOW-ON

1. LEAD ON FIRST INNINGS

In a two innings match the side which bats first and leads by 200 runs in a match of five days or more, by 150 runs in a three or four-day match, by 100 runs in a two-day match, or by 75 runs in a one-day match, shall have the option of requiring the other side to follow their innings.

2. DAY'S PLAY LOST

If no play takes place on the first day of a match of 2 or more days' duration, 1. above shall apply in accordance with the number of days' play remaining from the actual start of the match.

LAW 14 DECLARATIONS

1. TIME OF DECLARATION

The Captain of the batting side may declare an innings closed at any time during a match irrespective of its duration.

2. FORFEITURE OF SECOND INNINGS

A Captain may forfeit his second innings, provided his decision to do so is notified to the opposing Captain and Umpires in sufficient time to allow 7 minutes rolling of the pitch. See Law 10. (Rolling, Sweeping, Mowing, Watering the Pitch and Re-Marking of Creases). The normal 10 minute interval between innings shall be applied.

LAW 15 START OF PLAY

1. CALL OF PLAY

At the start of each innings and of each day's play and on the resumption of play after any interval or interruption the Umpire at the Bowlers' end shall call "play".

2. PRACTICE ON THE FIELD

At no time on any day of the match shall there be any bowling or batting practice on the pitch.

No practice may take place on the field if, in the opinion of the Umpires, it could result in a waste of time.

3. TRIAL RUN-UP

No Bowler shall have a trial run-up after "play" has been called in any session of play, except at the fall of a wicket when an Umpire may allow such a trial run-up if he is satisfied that it will not cause any waste of time.

LAW 16 INTERVALS

1. LENGTH

The Umpire shall allow such intervals as have been agreed upon for meals, and 10 minutes between each innings.

2. LUNCHEON INTERVAL—INNINGS ENDING OR STOPPAGE WITHIN 10 MINUTES OF INTERVAL

If an innings ends or there is a stoppage caused by weather or bad light within 10 minutes of the agreed time for the luncheon interval, the interval shall be taken immediately. The time remaining in the session of play shall be added to the agreed length of the interval but no extra allowance shall be made for the 10 minutes interval between innings.

3. TEA INTERVAL—INNINGS ENDING OR STOPPAGE WITHIN 30 MINUTES OF INTERVAL

If an innings ends or there is a stoppage caused by weather or bad light within 30 minutes of the agreed time for the tea interval, the interval shall be taken immediately. The interval shall be of the agreed length and, if applicable, shall include the 10 minute interval between innings.

4. TEA INTERVAL—CONTINUATION OF PLAY

If at the agreed time for the tea interval, nine wickets are down, play shall continue for a period not exceeding 30 minutes or until the innings is concluded.

5. TEA INTERVAL—AGREEMENT TO FOREGO

At any time during the match, the Captains may agree to forego a tea interval.

6. INTERVAL FOR DRINKS

If both Captains agree before the start of a match that intervals for drinks may be taken, the option to take such intervals shall be available to either side. These intervals shall be restricted to one per session, shall be kept as short as possible, shall not be taken in the last hour of the match and in any case shall not exceed 5 minutes.

The agreed times for these intervals shall be strictly adhered to except that if a wicket falls within 5 minutes of the agreed time then drinks shall be taken out immediately. If an innings ends or there is a stoppage caused by weather or bad light within 30 minutes of the agreed time for a drinks interval, there will be no interval for drinks in that session.

At any time during the match the Captains may agree to forego any such drinks interval.

Notes

(a) Tea Interval—One-Day Match
In a one-day match, a specific time for the tea interval need not necessarily be arranged, and it may be agreed to take this interval between the innings of a one innings match.

(b) Changing the Agreed Time of Intervals
In the event of the ground, weather or light conditions causing a suspension of play, the Umpires, after consultation with the Captains, may decide in the interests of time-saving, to bring forward the time of the luncheon or tea interval.

LAW 17 CESSATION OF PLAY

1. CALL OF TIME

The Umpire at the Bowler's end shall call "time" on the cessation of play before any interval or interruption of play, at the end of each day's play, and at the conclusion of the match. See Law 27. (Appeals).

2. REMOVAL OF BAILS

After the call of "time", the Umpires shall remove the bails from both wickets.

3. STARTING A LAST OVER

The last over before an interval or the close of play shall be started provided the Umpire, after walking at his normal pace, has arrived at his position behind the stumps at the Bowler's end before time has been reached.

4. COMPLETION OF THE LAST OVER OF A SESSION

The last over before an interval or the close of play shall be completed unless a Batsman is out or retires during that over within 2 minutes of the interval or the close of play or unless the Players have occasion to leave the field.

5. COMPLETION OF THE LAST OVER OF A MATCH

An over in progress at the close of play on the final day of a match shall be completed at the request of either Captain even if a wicket falls after time has been reached. If during the last over the Players have occasion to leave the field the Umpires shall call "time" and there shall be no resumption of play and the match shall be at an end.

6. LAST HOUR OF MATCH—NUMBER OF OVERS

The Umpires shall indicate when one hour of playing time of the match remains according to the agreed hours of play. The next over after that moment shall be the first of a minimum of 20 6-ball overs, (15 8-ball overs), provided a result is not reached earlier or there is no interval or interruption of play.

7. LAST HOUR OF MATCH—
INTERVALS BETWEEN INNINGS AND INTERRUPTIONS OF PLAY

If, at the commencement of the last hour of the match, an interval or interruption of play is in progress or if, during the last hour there is an interval between innings or an interruption of play, the minimum number of overs to be bowled on the resumption of play shall be reduced in proportion to the duration, within the last hour of the match, of any such interval or interruption.

(a) In the case of an interval or interruption of play being in progress at the commencement of the last hour of the match, or in the case of a first interval or interruption a deduction shall be made from the minimum of 20 6-ball overs (or 15 8-ball overs).

(b) If there is a later interval or interruption a further deduction shall be made from the minimum number of overs which should have been bowled following the last resumption of play.

(c) These deductions shall be based on the following factors:

(i) The number of overs already bowled in the last hour of the match or, in the case of a later interval or interruption in the last session of play.

(ii) The number of overs lost as a result of the interval or interruption allowing one 6-ball over for every full three minutes (or one 8-ball over for every full four minutes) of interval or interruption.

(iii) Any over left uncompleted at the end of an innings to be excluded from these calculations.

(iv) Any over left uncompleted at the start of an interruption of play to be completed when play is resumed and to count as one over bowled.

(v) An interval to start with the end of an innings and to end 10 minutes later; an interruption to start on the call of "time" and to end on the call of "play".

(d) In the event of an innings being completed and a new innings commencing during the last hour of the match, the number of overs to be bowled in the new innings shall be calculated on the basis of one 6-ball over for every three minutes or part thereof remaining for play (or one 8-ball over for every four minutes or part thereof remaining for play); or alternatively on the basis that sufficient overs be bowled to enable the full minimum quota of overs to be completed under circumstances governed by (a), (b) and (c) above. In all such cases the alternative which allows the greater number of overs shall be employed.

8. BOWLER UNABLE TO COMPLETE AN OVER
DURING LAST HOUR OF THE MATCH

If, for any reason, a Bowler is unable to complete an over during the period of play referred to in 6. above, Law 22.7. (Bowler Incapacitated or Suspended during an Over) shall apply.

LAW 18 SCORING

1. A RUN

The score shall be reckoned by runs. A run is scored:

(a) So often as the Batsmen, after a hit or at any time while the ball is in play, shall have crossed and made good their ground from end to end.

(b) When a boundary is scored. See Law 19. (Boundaries).

(c) When penalty runs are awarded. See 6. below.

2. SHORT RUNS

(a) If either Batsman runs a short run, the Umpire shall call and signal "one short" as soon as the ball becomes dead and that run shall not be scored. A run is short if a Batsman fails to make good his ground on turning for a further run.

(b) Although a short run shortens the succeeding one, the latter, if completed shall count.

(c) If either or both Batsmen deliberately run short the Umpire shall, as soon as he sees that the fielding side have no chance of dismissing either Batsman, call and signal "dead ball" and disallow any runs attempted or previously scored. The Batsmen shall return to their original ends.

(d) If both Batsmen run short in one and the same run, only one run shall be deducted.

(e) Only if three or more runs are attempted can more than one be short and then, subject to (c) and (d) above, all runs so called shall be disallowed. If there has been more than one short run the Umpires shall instruct the Scorers as to the number of runs disallowed.

3. STRIKER CAUGHT

If the Striker is Caught, no run shall be scored.

4. BATSMAN RUN OUT

If a Batsman is Run Out, only that run which was being attempted shall not be scored. If, however, an injured Striker himself is run out no runs shall be scored. See Law 2.7. (Transgression of the Laws by an Injured Batsman or Runner).

5. BATSMAN OBSTRUCTING THE FIELD

If a Batsman is out Obstructing the Field, any runs completed before the obstruction occurs shall be scored unless such obstruction prevents a catch being made in which case no runs shall be scored.

6. RUNS SCORED FOR PENALTIES

Runs shall be scored for penalties under Laws 20. (Lost Ball), 24. (No Ball), 25. (Wide Ball), 41.1. (Fielding the Ball) and for boundary allowances under Law 19. (Boundaries).

7. BATSMAN RETURNING TO WICKET HE HAS LEFT

If, while the ball is in play, the Batsmen have crossed in running, neither shall return to the wicket he has left even though a short run has been called or no run has been scored as in the case of a catch. Batsmen, however, shall return to the wickets they originally left in the cases of a boundary and of any disallowance of runs and of an injured batsman being, himself, run out. See Law 2.7. (Transgression of the Laws by an Injured Batsman or Runner).

Notes

(a) Short Run

A Striker taking stance in front of his popping crease may run from that point without penalty.

LAW 19 BOUNDARIES

1. THE BOUNDARY OF THE PLAYING AREA

Before the toss for innings, the Umpires shall agree with both Captains on the boundary of the playing area. The boundary shall, if possible, be marked by a white line, a rope laid on the ground, or a fence. If flags or posts only are used to mark a boundary, the imaginary line joining such points shall be regarded as the boundary. An obstacle, or person, within the playing area shall not be regarded as a boundary unless so decided by the Umpires before the toss for innings. Sight-screens within, or partially within, the playing area shall be regarded as the boundary and when the ball strikes or passes within or under or directly over any part of the screen, a boundary shall be scored.

2. RUNS SCORED FOR BOUNDARIES

Before the toss for innings, the Umpires shall agree with both Captains the runs to be allowed for boundaries, and in deciding the allowance for them, the Umpires and Captains shall be guided by the prevailing custom of the ground. The allowance for a boundary shall normally be 4 runs, and 6 runs for all hits pitching over and clear of the boundary line or fence, even though the ball has been previously touched by a Fieldsman. 6 runs shall also be scored if a Fieldsman, after catching a ball, carries it over the boundary. See Law 32. (Caught) Note (a). 6 runs shall not be scored when a ball struck by the Striker hits a sight-screen full pitch if the screen is within, or partially within, the playing area, but if the ball is struck directly over a sight-screen so situated, 6 runs shall be scored.

3. A BOUNDARY

A boundary shall be scored and signalled by the Umpire at the Bowler's end whenever, in his opinion:

(a) A ball in play touches or crosses the boundary, however marked.

(b) A Fieldsman with ball in hand touches or grounds any part of his person on or over a boundary line.

(c) A Fieldsman with ball in hand grounds any part of his person over a boundary fence or board. This allows the Fieldsman to touch or lean on or over a boundary fence or board in preventing a boundary.

4. RUNS EXCEEDING BOUNDARY ALLOWANCE

The runs completed at the instant the ball reaches the boundary shall count if they exceed the boundary allowance.

5. OVERTHROWS OR WILFUL ACT OF A FIELDSMAN

If the boundary results from an overthrow or from the wilful act of a Fieldsman, any runs already completed and the allowance shall be added to the score. The run in progress shall count provided that the Batsmen have crossed at the instant of the throw or act.

Notes

(a) Position of Sight-Screens

Sight-screens should, if possible, be positioned wholly outside the playing area, as near as possible to the boundary line.

LAW 20 LOST BALL

1. RUNS SCORED

If a ball in play cannot be found or recovered any Fieldsman may call "lost ball" when 6 runs shall be added to the score; but if more than 6 have been run before "lost ball" is called, as many runs as have been completed shall be scored. The run in progress shall count provided that the Batsmen have crossed at the instant of the call of "lost ball".

2. HOW SCORED

The runs shall be added to the score of the Striker if the ball has been struck, but otherwise to the score of byes, leg-byes, no-balls or wides as the case may be.

LAW 21 THE RESULT

1. A WIN—TWO INNINGS MATCHES

The side which has scored a total of runs in excess of that scored by the opposing side in its two completed innings shall be the winners.

2. A WIN—ONE INNINGS MATCHES

(a) One innings matches, unless played out as in 1. above, shall be decided on the first innings, but see Law 12.5. (Continuation After One Innings of Each Side).

(b) If the Captains agree to continue play after the completion of one innings of each side in accordance with Law 12.5. (Continuation After One Innings of Each Side) and a result is not achieved on the second innings, the first innings result shall stand.

3. UMPIRES AWARDING A MATCH

(a) A match shall be lost by a side which, during the match,

(i) refuses to play, or

(ii) concedes defeat,

and the Umpires shall award the match to the other side.

(b) Should both Batsmen at the wickets or the fielding side leave the field at any time without the agreement of the Umpires, this shall constitute a refusal to play and, on appeal, the Umpires shall award the match to the other side in accordance with (a) above.

4. A TIE

The result of a match shall be a tie when the scores are equal at the conclusion of play, but only if the side batting last has completed its innings. If the scores of the completed first innings of a one-day match are equal, it shall be a tie but only if the match has not been played out to a further conclusion.

5. A DRAW

A match not determined in any of the ways as in 1, 2, 3 and 4 above shall count as a draw.

6. CORRECTNESS OF RESULT

Any decision as to the correctness of the scores shall be the responsibility of the Umpires. See Law 3.14. (Correctness of Scores).

If, after the Umpires and Players have left the field, in the belief that the match has been concluded, the Umpires decide that a mistake in scoring has occurred, which affects the result, and provided time has not been reached, they shall order play to resume and to continue until the agreed finishing time unless a result is reached earlier.

If the Umpires decide that a mistake has occurred and time has been reached, the Umpires shall immediately inform both Captains of the necessary corrections to the scores and, if applicable, to the result.

7. ACCEPTANCE OF RESULT

In accepting the scores as notified by the scorers and agreed by the Umpires, the Captains of both sides thereby accept the result.

Notes

(a) Statement of Results

The result of a finished match is stated as a win by runs, except in the case of a win by the side batting last when it is by the number of wickets still then to fall.

(b) Winning Hit or Extras

As soon as the side has won, see 1. and 2. above, the Umpire shall call "time", the match is finished, and nothing that happens thereafter other than as a result of a mistake in scoring, see 6. above, shall be regarded as part of the match.

However, if a boundary constitutes the winning hit—or extras—and the boundary allowance exceeds the number of runs required to win the match, such runs scored shall be credited to the side's total and, in the case of a hit to the Striker's score.

LAW 22 THE OVER

1. NUMBER OF BALLS

The ball shall be bowled from each wicket alternately in overs of either 6 or 8 balls according to agreement before the match.

2. CALL OF "OVER"

When the agreed number of balls has been bowled, and as the ball becomes dead or when it becomes clear to the Umpire at the Bowler's end that both the fielding side and the Batsmen at the wicket have ceased to regard the ball as in play, the Umpire shall call "over" before leaving the wicket.

3. NO BALL OR WIDE BALL

Neither a no ball nor a wide ball shall be reckoned as one of the over.

4. UMPIRE MISCOUNTING

If an Umpire miscounts the number of balls, the over as counted by the Umpire shall stand.

5. BOWLER CHANGING ENDS

A Bowler shall be allowed to change ends as often as desired provided only that he does not bowl overs consecutively in an innings.

6. THE BOWLER FINISHING AN OVER

A Bowler shall finish an over in progress unless he be incapacitated or be suspended under Law 42.8. (The Bowling of Fast Short Pitched Balls), 42.9. (The Bowling of Fast High Full Pitches), 42.10. (Time Wasting) and 42.11. (Players Damaging the Pitch). If an over is left incomplete for any reason at the start of an interval or interruption of play, it shall be finished on the resumption of play.

7. BOWLER INCAPACITATED OR SUSPENDED DURING AN OVER

If, for any reason, a Bowler is incapacitated while running up to bowl the first ball of an over, or is incapacitated or suspended during an over, the Umpire shall call and signal "dead ball" and another Bowler shall be allowed to bowl or complete the over from the same end, provided only that he shall not bowl two overs, or part thereof, consecutively in one innings.

8. POSITION OF NON-STRIKER

The Batsman at the Bowler's end shall normally stand on the opposite side of the wicket to that from which the ball is being delivered, unless a request to do otherwise is granted by the Umpire.

LAW 23 DEAD BALL

1. THE BALL BECOMES DEAD, WHEN:

(a) It is finally settled in the hands of the Wicket-Keeper of the Bowler.

(b) It reaches or pitches over the boundary.

(c) A Batsman is out.

(d) Whether played or not, it lodges in the clothing or equipment of a Batsman or the clothing of an Umpire.

(e) A ball lodges in a protective helmet worn by a member of the fielding side.

(f) A penalty is awarded under Law 20. (Lost Ball) or Law 41.1. (Fielding the Ball).

(g) The Umpire calls "over" or "time".

2. EITHER UMPIRE SHALL CALL AND SIGNAL "DEAD BALL" WHEN:

(a) He intervenes in a case of unfair play.

(b) A serious injury to a Player or Umpire occurs.

(c) He is satisfied that, for an adequate reason, the Striker is not ready to receive the ball and makes no attempt to play it.

(d) The Bowler drops the ball accidentally before delivery, or the ball does not leave his hand for any reason.

(e) One or both bails fall from the Striker's wicket before he receives delivery.

(f) He leaves his normal position for consultation.

(g) He is required to do so under Laws 26.3. (Disallowance of Leg-Byes), etc.

3. THE BALL CEASES TO BE DEAD, WHEN:

(a) The Bowler starts his run-up or bowling action.

4. THE BALL IS NOT DEAD, WHEN:

(a) It strikes an Umpire (unless it lodges in his dress).

(b) The wicket is broken or struck down (unless a Batsman is out thereby).

(c) An unsuccessful appeal is made.

(d) The wicket is broken accidentally either by the Bowler during his delivery or by a Batsman in running.

(e) The Umpire has called "no ball" or "wide".

Notes

(a) Ball Finally Settled
Whether the ball is finally settled or not—see 1(a) above—must be a question for the Umpires alone to decide.

(b) Action on Call of "Dead Ball"
(i) If "dead ball" is called prior to the Striker receiving a delivery the Bowler shall be allowed an additional ball.

(ii) If "dead ball" is called after the Striker receives a delivery the Bowler shall not be allowed an additional ball, unless a "no ball" or "wide" has been called.

LAW 24 NO BALL

1. MODE OF DELIVERY
The Umpire shall indicate to the Striker whether the Bowler intends to bowl over or round the wicket, overarm or underarm, or right or left-handed. Failure on the part of the Bowler to indicate in advance a change in his mode of delivery is unfair and the Umpire shall call and signal "no ball".

2. FAIR DELIVERY—THE ARM
For a delivery to be fair the ball must be bowled not thrown—see Note (a) below. If either Umpire is not entirely satisfied with the absolute fairness of a delivery in this respect he shall call and signal "no ball" instantly upon delivery.

3. FAIR DELIVERY—THE FEET
The Umpire at the bowler's wicket shall call and signal "no ball" if he is not satisfied that in the delivery stride:

(a) the Bowler's back foot has landed within and not touching the return crease or its forward extension

OR

(b) some part of the front foot whether grounded or raised was behind the popping crease.

4. BOWLER THROWING AT STRIKER'S WICKET BEFORE DELIVERY
If the Bowler, before delivering the ball, throws it at the Striker's wicket in an attempt to run him out, the Umpire shall call and signal "no ball". See Law 42.12. (Batsman Unfairly Stealing a Run) and Law 38. (Run Out).

5. BOWLER ATTEMPTING TO RUN OUT NON-STRIKER BEFORE DELIVERY
If the Bowler, before delivering the ball, attempts to run out the non-Striker, any runs which result shall be allowed and shall be scored as no balls. Such an attempt shall not

count as a ball in the over. The Umpire shall not call "no ball". See Law 42.12. (Batsman Unfairly Stealing a Run).

6. INFRINGEMENT OF LAWS BY A WICKET-KEEPER OR A FIELDSMAN

The Umpire shall call and signal "no ball" in the event of the Wicket-Keeper infringing Law 40.1. (Position of Wicket-Keeper) or a Fieldsman infringing Law 41.2 (Limitation of On-side Fieldsmen) or Law 41.3. (Position of Fieldsmen).

7. REVOKING A CALL

An Umpire shall revoke the call "no ball" if the ball does not leave the Bowler's hand for any reason. See Law 23.2. (Either Umpire Shall Call and Signal "Dead Ball").

8. PENALTY

A penalty of one run for a no ball shall be scored if no runs are made otherwise.

9. RUNS FROM A NO BALL

The Striker may hit a no ball and whatever runs result shall be added to his score. Runs made otherwise from a no ball shall be scored no balls.

10. OUT FROM A NO BALL

The Striker shall be out from a no ball if he breaks Law 34. (Hit the Ball Twice) and either Batsman may be Run Out or shall be given out if either breaks Law 33. (Handled the Ball) or Law 37. (Obstructing the Field).

11. BATSMAN GIVEN OUT OFF A NO BALL

Should a Batsman be given out off a no ball the penalty for bowling it shall stand unless runs are otherwise scored.

Notes

(a) Definition of a Throw
A ball shall be deemed to have been thrown if, in the opinion of either Umpire, the process of straightening the bowling arm, whether it be partial or complete, takes place during that part of the delivery swing which directly precedes the ball leaving the hand. This definition shall not debar a Bowler from the use of the wrist in the delivery swing.

(b) No Ball Not Counting in Over
A no ball shall not be reckoned as one of the over. See Law 22.3. (No Ball or Wide Ball).

LAW 25 WIDE BALL

1. JUDGING A WIDE

If the Bowler bowls the ball so high over or so wide of the wicket that, in the opinion of the Umpire is passes out of the reach of the Striker, standing in a normal guard position, the Umpire shall call and signal "wide ball" as soon as it has passed the line of the Striker's wicket. The Umpire shall not adjudge a ball as being wide if:

(a) The Striker, by moving from his guard position, causes the ball to pass out of his reach.

(b) The Striker moves and thus brings the ball within his reach.

2. PENALTY

A penalty of one run for a wide shall be scored if no runs are made otherwise.

3. BALL COMING TO REST IN FRONT OF THE STRIKER

If a ball which the Umpire considers to have been delivered comes to rest in front of the line of the Striker's wicket, "wide" shall not be called. The Striker has a right, without interference from the fielding side, to make one attempt to hit the ball. If the fielding side interfere, the Umpire shall replace the ball where it came to rest and shall order the Fieldsmen to resume the places they occupied in the field before the ball was delivered.

The Umpire shall call and signal "dead ball" as soon as it is clear that the Striker does not intend to hit the ball, or after the Striker has made one unsuccessful attempt to hit the ball.

4. REVOKING A CALL

The Umpire shall revoke the call if the Striker hits a ball which has been called "wide".

5. BALL NOT DEAD

The ball does not become dead on the call of "wide ball"—see Law 23.4. (The Ball is Not Dead).

6. RUNS RESULT FROM A WIDE

All runs which are run or result from a wide ball which is not a no ball shall be scored wide balls, or if no runs are made one shall be scored.

7. OUT FROM A WIDE

The Striker shall be out from a wide ball if he breaks Law 35. (Hit Wicket) or Law 39. (Stumped). Either Batsman may be Run Out and shall be out if he breaks Law 33. (Handled the Ball) or Law 37. (Obstructing the Field).

8. BATSMAN GIVEN OUT OFF A WIDE

Should a Batsman be given out off a wide, the penalty for bowling it shall stand unless runs are otherwise made.

Notes

(a) Wide Ball Not Counting in Over
A wide ball shall not be reckoned as one of the over—see Law 22.3. (No Ball or Wide Ball).

LAW 26 BYE AND LEG-BYE

1. BYES

If the ball, not having been called "wide" or "no ball" passes the Striker without touching his bat or person, and any runs are obtained, the Umpire shall signal "bye" and the run or runs shall be credited as such to the batting side.

2. LEG-BYES

If the ball, not having been called "wide" or "no ball" is unintentionally deflected by the Striker's dress or person, except a hand holding the bat, and any runs are obtained the Umpire shall signal "leg-bye" and the run or runs so scored shall be credited as such to the batting side.

Such leg-byes shall only be scored if, in the opinion of the Umpire, the Striker has:

(a) Attempted to play the ball with his bat, or

(b) Tried to avoid being hit by the ball.

3. DISALLOWANCE OF LEG-BYES

In the case of a deflection by the Striker's person, other than in 2(a) and (b) above, the Umpire shall call and signal "dead ball" as soon as one run has been completed or when it is clear that a run is not being attempted or the ball has reached the boundary.

On the call and signal of "dead ball" the Batsmen shall return to their original ends and no runs shall be allowed.

LAW 27 APPEALS

1. TIME OF APPEALS

The Umpires shall not give a Batsman out unless appealed to by the other side which shall be done prior to the Bowler beginning his run-up or bowling action to deliver the next ball. Under Law 23.1.(g) (The Ball Becomes Dead) the ball is dead on "over" being called; this does not, however, invalidate an appeal made prior to the first ball of the following over provided "time" has not been called. See Law 17.1. (Call of Time).

2. AN APPEAL "HOW'S THAT?"

An appeal "How's That?" shall cover all ways of being out.

3. ANSWERING APPEALS

The Umpire at the Bowler's wicket shall answer before the other Umpire in all cases except those arising out of Law 35. (Hit Wicket) or Law 39. (Stumped) or Law 38. (Run Out) when this occurs at the Striker's wicket.

When either Umpire has given a Batsman not out, the other Umpire shall, within his jurisdiction, answer the appeal or a further appeal, provided it is made in time in accordance with 1. above (Time of Appeals).

4. CONSULTATION BY UMPIRES

An Umpire may consult with the other Umpire on a point of fact which the latter may have been in a better position to see and shall then give his decision. If, after consultation, there is still doubt remaining the decision shall be in favour of the Batsman.

5. BATSMAN LEAVING HIS WICKET UNDER A MISAPPREHENSION

The Umpires shall intervene if satisfied that a Batsman, not having been given out, has left his wicket under a misapprehension that he has been dismissed.

6. UMPIRE'S DECISION

The Umpire's decision is final. He may alter his decision, provided that such alteration is made promptly.

7. WITHDRAWAL OF AN APPEAL

In exceptional circumstances the Captain of the fielding side may seek permission of the Umpire to withdraw an appeal providing the outgoing Batsman has not left the playing area. If this is allowed, the Umpire shall cancel his decision.

LAW 28 THE WICKET IS DOWN

1. WICKET DOWN

The wicket is down if:

(a) Either the ball or the Striker's bat or person completely removes either bail from the top of the stumps. A disturbance of a bail, whether temporary or not, shall not constitute a complete removal, but the wicket is down if a bail in falling lodges between two of the stumps.

(b) Any player completely removes with his hand or arm a bail from the top of the stumps, providing that the ball is held in that hand or in the hand of the arm so used.

(c) When both bails are off, a stump is struck out of the ground by the ball, or a player strikes or pulls a stump out of the ground, providing that the ball is held in the hand(s) or in the hand of the arm so used.

2. ONE BAIL OFF

If one bail is off, it shall be sufficient for the purpose of putting the wicket down to remove the remaining bail, or to strike or pull any of the three stumps out of the ground in any of the ways stated in 1. above.

3. ALL THE STUMPS OUT OF THE GROUND

If all the stumps are out of the ground, the fielding side shall be allowed to put back one or more stumps in order to have an opportunity of putting the wicket down.

4. DISPENSING WITH BAILS

If owing to the strength of the wind, it has been agreed to dispense with the bails in accordance with Law 8. Note (a) (Dispensing with Bails) the decision as to when the wicket is down is one for the Umpires to decide on the facts before them. In such circumstances and if the Umpires so decide the wicket shall be held to be down even though a stump has not been struck out of the ground.

Notes

(a) Remaking the Wicket
If the wicket is broken while the ball is in play, it is not the Umpire's duty to remake the wicket until the ball has become dead—see Law 23. (Dead Ball). A member of the fielding side, however, may remake the wicket in such circumstances.

LAW 29 BATSMAN OUT OF HIS GROUND

1. WHEN OUT OF HIS GROUND

A Batsman shall be considered to be out of his ground unless some part of his bat in his hand or of his person is grounded behind the line of the popping crease.

LAW 30 BOWLED

1. OUT BOWLED

The Striker shall be out Bowled if:

(a) His wicket is bowled down, even if the ball first touches his bat or person.

(b) He breaks his wicket by hitting or kicking the ball on to it before the completion of a stroke, or as a result of attempting to guard his wicket. See Law 34.1. (Out—Hit the Ball Twice).

Notes

(a) Out Bowled—Not L.B.W.
The Striker is out Bowled if the ball is deflected on to his wicket even though a decision against him would be justified under Law 36 (Leg Before Wicket).

LAW 31 TIMED OUT

1. OUT TIMED OUT

An incoming Batsman shall be out Timed Out if he wilfully takes more than two minutes to come in—the two minutes being timed from the moment a wicket falls until the new batsman steps on to the field of play.

If this is not complied with and if the Umpire is satisfied that the delay was wilful and if an appeal is made, the new Batsman shall be given out by the Umpire at the Bowler's end.

2. TIME TO BE ADDED

The time taken by the Umpires to investigate the cause of the delay shall be added at the normal close of play.

Notes

(a) Entry in Score Book
The correct entry in the score book when a Batsman is given out under this Law is "timed out", and the Bowler does not get credit for the wicket.

(b) Batsmen Crossing on the Field of Play
It is an essential duty of the captains to ensure that the in-going Batsman passes the out-going one before the latter leaves the field of play.

LAW 32 CAUGHT

1. OUT CAUGHT

The Striker shall be out Caught if the ball touches his bat or if it touches below the wrist his hand or glove, holding the bat, and is subsequently held by a Fieldsman before it touches the ground.

2. A FAIR CATCH

A catch shall be considered to have been fairly made if:

(a) The Fieldsman is within the field of play throughout the act of making the catch.

(i) The act of making the catch shall start from the time when the Fieldsman first handles the ball and shall end when he both retains complete control over the further disposal of the ball and remains within the field of play.

(ii) In order to be within the field of play, the Fieldsman may not touch or ground any part of his person on or over a boundary line. When the boundary is marked by a fence or board the Fieldsman may not ground any part of his person over the boundary fence or board, but may touch or lean over the boundary fence or board in completing the catch.

(b) The ball is hugged to the body of the catcher or accidentally lodges in his dress or, in the case of the Wicket-Keeper, in his pads. However, a Striker may not be caught if a ball lodges in a protective helmet worn by a Fieldsman, in which case the Umpire shall call and signal "dead ball". See Law 23. (Dead Ball).

(c) The ball does not touch the ground even though a hand holding it does so in effecting the catch.

(d) A Fieldsman catches the ball, after it has been lawfully played a second time by the Striker, but only if the ball has not touched the ground since being first struck.

(e) A Fieldsman catches the ball after it has touched an Umpire, another Fieldsman or the other Batsman. However a Striker may not be caught if a ball has touched a protective helmet worn by a Fieldsman.

(f) The ball is caught off an obstruction within the boundary provided it has not previously been agreed to regard the obstruction as a boundary.

3. SCORING OF RUNS

If a Striker is caught, no runs shall be scored.

Notes

(a) Scoring From an Attempted Catch
When a Fieldsman carrying the ball touches or grounds any part of his person on or over a boundary marked by a line, 6 runs shall be scored.

(b) Ball Still in Play
If a Fieldsman releases the ball before he crosses the boundary, the ball will be considered to be still in play and it may be caught by another Fieldsman. However, if the original Fieldsman returns to the field of play and handles the ball, a catch may not be made.

LAW 33 HANDLED THE BALL

1. OUT HANDLED THE BALL

Either Batsman on appeal shall be out Handled the Ball if he wilfully touches the ball while in play with the hand not holding the bat unless he does so with the consent of the opposite side.

Notes

(a) Entry in Score Book
The correct entry in the score book when a Batsman is given out under this Law is "handled the ball", and the Bowler does not get credit for the wicket.

LAW 34 HIT THE BALL TWICE

1. OUT HIT THE BALL TWICE

The Striker, on appeal, shall be out Hit the Ball Twice if, after the ball is struck or is stopped by any part of his person, he wilfully strikes it again with his bat or person except for the sole purpose of guarding his wicket: this he may do with his bat or any part of his person other than his hands, but see Law 37.2. (Obstructing a Ball From Being Caught).

For the purpose of this Law, a hand holding the bat shall be regarded as part of the bat.

2. RETURNING THE BALL TO A FIELDSMAN

The Striker, on appeal, shall be out under this Law, if, without the consent of the opposite side, he uses his bat or person to return the ball to any of the fielding side.

3. RUNS FROM BALL LAWFULLY STRUCK TWICE

No runs except those which result from an overthrow or penalty, see Law 41. (The Fieldsman), shall be scored from a ball lawfully struck twice.

Notes

(a) Entry in Score Book
The correct entry in the score book when the Striker is given out under this Law is "hit the ball twice", and the Bowler does not get credit for the wicket.

(b) Runs Credited to the Batsman
Any runs awarded under 3. above as a result of an overthrow or penalty shall be credited to the Striker, provided the ball in the first instance has touched the ball, or, if otherwise as extras.

LAW 35 HIT WICKET

1. OUT HIT WICKET

The Striker shall be out Hit Wicket if, while the ball is in play:

(a) His wicket is broken with any part of his person, dress, or equipment as a result of any action taken by him in preparing to receive or in receiving a delivery, or in setting off for his first run, immediately after playing, or playing at, the ball.

(b) His hits down his wicket whilst lawfully making a second stroke for the purpose of guarding his wicket within the provisions of Law 34.1. (Out Hit the Ball Twice).

Notes

(a) Not Out Hit Wicket
A batsman is not out under this Law should his wicket be broken in any of the ways referred to in 1(a) above if:

(i) It occurs while he is in the act of running, other than in setting off for his first run immediately after playing at the ball, or while he is avoiding being run out or stumped.

(ii) The Bowler after starting his run-up or bowling action does not deliver the ball; in which case the Umpire shall immediately call and signal "dead ball".

(iii) It occurs whilst he is avoiding a throw-in at any time.

LAW 36 LEG BEFORE WICKET

1. OUT L.B.W.

The Striker shall be out L.B.W. in the circumstances set out below:

(a) Striker Attempting to Play the Ball

The Striker shall be out L.B.W. if he first intercepts with any part of his person, dress or equipment a fair ball which would have hit the wicket and which has not previously touched his bat or a hand holding the bat, provided that:

(i) the ball pitched, in a straight line between wicket and wicket or on the off side of the Striker's wicket, or in the case of a ball intercepted full pitch would have pitched in a straight line between wicket and wicket, and

(ii) the point of impact is in a straight line between wicket and wicket, even if above the level of the bails.

(b) Striker Making No Attempt to Play the Ball

The Striker shall be out L.B.W. even if the ball is intercepted outside the line of the off-stump, if, in the opinion of the Umpire, he has made no genuine attempt to play the ball with his bat, but has intercepted the ball with some part of his person and if the circumstances set out in (a) above apply.

LAW 37 OBSTRUCTING THE FIELD

1. WILLFUL OBSTRUCTION

Either Batsman, on appeal, shall be out Obstructing the Field if he wilfully obstructs the opposite side by word or action.

2. OBSTRUCTING A BALL FROM BEING CAUGHT

The Striker, on appeal, shall be out should wilful obstruction by either Batsman prevent a catch being made. This shall apply even though the Striker causes the obstruction in lawfully guarding his wicket under the provisions of Law 34. See Law 34.1. (Out Hit the Ball Twice).

Notes

(a) Accidental Obstruction
The Umpire must decide whether the obstruction was wilful or not. The accidental interception of a throw-in by a Batsman while running does not break this Law.

(b) Entry in Score Book
The correct entry in the score book when a Batsman is given out under this Law is "obstructing the field", and the bowler does not get credit for the wicket.

LAW 38 RUN OUT

1. OUT RUN OUT

Either Batsman shall be out Run Out if in running or at any time while the ball is in play—except in the circumstances described in Law 39. (Stumped)—he is out of his ground and his wicket is put down by the opposite side. If, however, a Batsman in running makes good his ground he shall not be out Run Out, if he subsequently leaves his ground, in order to avoid injury, and the wicket is put down.

2. "NO BALL" CALLED

If a no ball has been called, the Striker shall not be given Run Out unless he attempts to run.

3. WHICH BATSMAN IS OUT

If the Batsmen have crossed in running, he who runs for the wicket which is put down shall be out; if they have not crossed, he who has left the wicket which is put down shall be out. If a Batsman remains in his ground or returns to his ground and the other Batsman joins him there, the latter shall be out if his wicket is put down.

4. SCORING OF RUNS

If a Batsman is run out, only that run which is being attempted shall not be scored. If however an injured Striker himself is Run Out, no runs shall be scored. See Law 2.7. (Transgression of the Laws by an Injured Batsman or Runner).

Notes

(a) Ball Played on to Opposite Wicket
If the ball is played on to the opposite wicket neither Batsman is liable to be Run Out unless the ball has been touched by a Fieldsman before the wicket is broken.

(b) Entry in Score Book
The correct entry in the score book when the Striker is given out under this Law is "run out", and the Bowler does not get credit for the wicket.

LAW 39 STUMPED

1. OUT STUMPED

The Striker shall be out Stumped if, in receiving a ball, not being a no ball, he is out of his ground otherwise than in attempting a run and the wicket is put down by the Wicket-Keeper without the intervention of another Fieldsman.

2. ACTION BY THE WICKET-KEEPER

The Wicket-Keeper may take the ball in front of the wicket in an attempt to Stump the Striker only if the ball has touched the bat or person of the Striker.

Notes

(a) Ball Rebounding From Wicket-Keeper's Person
The Striker may be out Stumped if in the circumstances stated in 1. above, the wicket is broken by a ball rebounding from the Wicket-Keeper's person or equipment or is kicked or thrown by the Wicket-Keeper onto the wicket.

LAW 40 THE WICKET-KEEPER

1. POSITION OF WICKET-KEEPER

The Wicket-Keeper shall remain wholly behind the wicket until a ball delivered by the Bowler touches the bat or person of the Striker, or passes the wicket, or until the Striker attempts a run.

In the event of the Wicket-Keeper contravening this law, the Umpire at the Striker's end shall call and signal "no ball" at the instant of delivery or as soon as possible thereafter.

2. RESTRICTION ON ACTIONS OF THE WICKET-KEEPER

If the Wicket-Keeper interferes with the Striker's right to play the ball and to guard his wicket, the Striker shall not be out, except under Laws 33. (Handled the Ball), 34. (Hit the Ball Twice), 37. (Obstructing the Field) and 38. (Run Out).

3. INTERFERENCE WITH THE WICKET-KEEPER BY THE STRIKER

If in the legitimate defence of his wicket, the Striker interferes with the Wicket-Keeper, he shall not be out, except as provided for in Law 37.2. (Obstructing a Ball From Being Caught).

LAW 41 THE FIELDSMAN

1. FIELDING THE BALL

The Fieldsman may stop the ball with any part of his person, but if he wilfully stops it otherwise, 5 runs shall be added to the run or runs already scored; if no run has been scored 5 penalty runs shall be awarded. The run in progress shall count provided that the Batsmen have crossed at the instant of the act. If the ball has been struck, the penalty shall be added to the score of the Striker, but otherwise to the score of byes, leg-byes, no balls or wides as the case may be.

2. LIMITATION OF ON-SIDE FIELDSMEN

The number of on-side Fieldsmen behind the popping crease at the instant of the Bowler's delivery shall not exceed two. In the event of infringement by the fielding side the Umpire at the Striker's end shall call and signal "no ball" at the instant of delivery or as soon as possible thereafter.

3. POSITION OF FIELDSMEN

Whilst the ball is in play and until the ball has made contact with the bat or the Striker's person or has passed his bat, no Fieldsman, other than the Bowler, may stand on or have any part of his person extended over the pitch (measuring 22 yards/20.12 m. x 10 ft./3.05 m.). In the event of a Fieldsman contravening this Law, the Umpire at the Bowler's end shall call and signal "no ball" at the instant of delivery or as soon as possible thereafter. See Law 40.1. (Position of Wicket-Keeper).

Notes

(a) Batsmen Changing Ends

The 5 runs referred to in 1. above are a penalty and the Batsmen do not change ends solely by reason of this penalty.

LAW 42 UNFAIR PLAY

1. RESPONSIBILITY OF CAPTAINS

The Captains are responsible at all times for ensuring that play is conducted within the spirit of the game as well as within the Laws.

2. RESPONSIBILITY OF UMPIRES

The Umpires are the sole judges of fair and unfair play.

3. INTERVENTION BY THE UMPIRE

The Umpires shall intervene without appeal by calling and signalling "dead ball" in the case of unfair play, but should not otherwise interfere with the progress of the game except as required to do so by the Laws.

4. LIFTING THE SEAM

A Player shall not lift the seam of the ball for any reason. Should this be done, the Umpires shall change the ball for one of similar condition to that in use prior to the contravention. See Note (a).

5. CHANGING THE CONDITION OF THE BALL

Any member of the fielding side may polish the ball provided that such polishing wastes no time and that no artificial substance is used. No one shall rub the ball on the ground or use any artificial substance or take any other action to alter the condition of the ball.

In the event of a contravention of this Law, the Umpires, after consultation, shall change the ball for one of similar condition to that in use prior to the contravention.

This Law does not prevent a member of the fielding side from drying a wet ball, or removing mud from the ball. See Note (b).

6. INCOMMODING THE STRIKER

An Umpire is justified in intervening under this Law and shall call and signal "dead ball" if, in his opinion, any Player of the fielding side incommodes the Striker by any noise or action while he is receiving a ball.

7. OBSTRUCTION OF A BATSMAN IN RUNNING

It shall be considered unfair if any Fieldsman wilfully obstructs a Batsman in running. In these circumstances the Umpire shall call and signal "dead ball" and allow any completed runs and the run in progress or alternatively any boundary scored.

8. THE BOWLING OF FAST SHORT PITCHED BALLS

The bowling of fast short pitched balls is unfair if, in the opinion of the Umpire at the Bowler's end, it constitutes an attempt to intimidate the Striker. See Note (d). Umpires shall consider intimidation to be the deliberate bowling of fast short pitched balls which by their length, height and direction are intended or likely to inflict physical injury on the Striker. The relative skill of the Striker shall also be taken into consideration. In the event of such unfair bowling, the Umpire at the Bowler's end shall adopt the following procedure:

(a) In the first instance the Umpire shall call and signal "no ball", caution the Bowler and inform the other Umpire, the Captain of the fielding side and the Batsmen of what has occurred.

(b) If this caution is ineffective, he shall repeat the above procedure and indicate to the Bowler that this is a final warning.

(c) Both the above caution and final warning shall continue to apply even though the Bowler may later change ends.

(d) Should the above warnings prove ineffective the Umpire at the Bowler's end shall:

(i) At the first repetition call and signal "no ball" and when the ball is dead direct the Captain to take the Bowler off forthwith and to complete the over with another Bowler, provided that the Bowler does not bowl two overs or part thereof consecutively. See Law 22.7. (Bowler Incapacitated or Suspended during an Over).

(ii) Not allow the Bowler, thus taken off, to bowl again in the same innings.

(iii) Report the occurrence to the Captain of the batting side as soon as the Players leave the field for an interval.

(iv) Report the occurrence to the Executive of the fielding side and to any governing body responsible for the match who shall take any further action which is considered to be appropriate against the Bowler concerned.

9. THE BOWLING OF FAST HIGH FULL PITCHES

The bowling of fast high full pitches is unfair. See Note (e). In the event of such unfair bowling the Umpire at the Bowler's end shall adopt the procedures of caution, final warning, action against the Bowler and reporting as set out in 8. above.

10. TIME WASTING

Any form of time wasting is unfair.

(a) In the event of the Captain of the fielding side wasting time or allowing any member of his side to waste time, the Umpire at the Bowler's end shall adopt the following procedure:

(i) In the first instance he shall caution the Captain of the fielding side and inform the other Umpire of what has occurred.

(ii) If this caution is ineffective he shall repeat the above procedure and indicate to the Captain that this is a final warning.

(iii) The Umpire shall report the occurrence to the Captain of the batting side as soon as the Players leave the field for an interval.

(iv) Should the above procedure prove ineffective the Umpire shall report the occurrence to the Executive of the fielding side and to any governing body responsible for that match who shall take appropriate action against the Captain and the Players concerned.

(b) In the event of a Bowler taking unnecessarily long to bowl an over the Umpire at the Bowler's end shall adopt the procedures, other than the calling of "no ball", of caution, final warning, action against the Bowler and reporting.

(c) In the event of a Batsman wasting time (See Note (f)) other than in the manner described in Law 31. (Timed Out), the Umpire at the Bowler's end shall adopt the following procedure:

(i) In the first instance he shall caution the Batsman and inform the other Umpire at once, and the Captain of the batting side, as soon as the Players leave the field for an interval, of what has occurred.

(ii) If this proves ineffective, he shall repeat the caution, indicate to the Batsman that this is a final warning and inform the other Umpire.

(iii) The Umpire shall report the occurrence to both Captains as soon as the Players leave the field for an interval.

(iv) Should the above procedure prove ineffective, the Umpire shall report the occurrence to the Executive of the batting side and to any governing body responsible for that match who shall take appropriate action against the Player concerned.

11. PLAYERS DAMAGING THE PITCH

The Umpires shall intervene and prevent Players from causing damage to the pitch which may assist the Bowlers of either side. See Note (c).

(a) In the event of any member of the fielding side damaging the pitch the Umpire shall follow the procedure of caution, final warning and reporting as set out in 10(a) above.

(b) In the event of a Bowler contravening this Law by running down the pitch after delivering the ball, the Umpire at the Bowler's end shall first caution the Bowler. If this caution is ineffective the Umpire shall adopt the procedures, other than the calling of "no ball", of final warning, action against the Bowler and reporting.

(c) In the event of a Batsman damaging the pitch the Umpire at the Bowler's end shall follow the procedures of caution, final warning and reporting as set out in 10(c) above.

12. BATSMAN UNFAIRLY STEALING A RUN

Any attempt by the Batsman to steal a run during the Bowler's run-up is unfair. Unless the Bowler attempts to run out either Batsman—see Law 24.4. (Bowler Throwing at Striker's

Wicket Before Delivery) and Law 24.5. (Bowler Attempting to Run Out Non-Striker Before Delivery)—the Umpire shall call and signal "dead ball" as soon as the Batsmen cross in any such attempt to run. The Batsmen shall then return to their original wickets.

13. PLAYERS' CONDUCT

In the event of a player failing to comply with the instructions of an Umpire, criticising his decisions by word or action, or showing dissent, or generally behaving in a manner which might bring the game into disrepute, the Umpire concerned shall, in the first place report the matter to the other Umpire and to the Player's Captain requesting the latter to take action. If this proves ineffective, the Umpire shall report the incident as soon as possible to the Executive of the Player's team and to any governing body responsible for the match, who shall take any further action which is considered appropriate against the Player or Players concerned.

Notes

(a) The Condition of the Ball
Umpires shall make frequent and irregular inspections of the condition of the ball.

(b) Drying of a Wet Ball
A wet ball may be dried on a towel or with sawdust.

(c) Danger Area
The danger area on the pitch, which must be protected from damage by a Bowler, shall be regarded by the Umpires as the area contained by an imaginary line 4 ft./1.22 m. from the popping crease, and parallel to it, and within two imaginary and parallel lines drawn down the pitch from points on that line 1 ft./30.48 cm. on either side of the middle stump.

(d) Fast Short Pitched Balls
As a guide, a fast short pitched ball is one which pitches short and passes, or would have passed, above the shoulder height of the Striker standing in a normal batting stance at the crease.

(e) The Bowling of Fast Full Pitches
The bowling of one fast, high full pitch shall be considered to be unfair if, in the opinion of the Umpire, it is deliberate, bowled at the Striker, and if it passes or would have passed above the shoulder height of the Striker when standing in a normal batting stance at the crease.

(f) Time Wasting by Batsmen
Other than in exceptional circumstances, the Batsman should always be ready to take strike when the Bowler is ready to start his run-up.

GOVERNING BODY

Marylebone Cricket Club, Lord's Cricket Ground, London, NW8, England

Since its formation in 1787, the Marylebone Cricket Club (MCC) has been recognized as the sole authority for drawing up the Laws of Cricket and for all subsequent alterations. The Laws apply equally to women's and men's cricket. The Laws refer to the male person only, for convenience and brevity. The MCC is available to answer queries on the Laws and give interpretations under the following conditions:

1. In the case of league or competition cricket, the inquiry must come from the committee responsible for organizing the league or competition. In other cases, inquiries

should be initiated by a representative officer of a club, an Umpire Association on behalf of his or her committee, or by a master or mistress in charge of school cricket.

2. The incident on which a ruling is required must not be merely invented for disputation, but must have actually occurred in play.

3. The inquiry must not be connected in any way with a bet or wager.

MAGAZINES

The Cricketer International, Beech Hanger, Ashurst, Tunbridge Wells, Kent TN3 95T, England

• CROQUET •

THE UNITED STATES CROQUET ASSOCIATION
STANDARD AMERICAN SIX-WICKET GAME

(Reproduced by permission of the United States Croquet Association*)

☐

Note: Since the turn of the century, countless variations of the game of croquet have evolved in America while the rest of the English-speaking world has refined the games under the British Croquet Association laws. The formation of the USCA recognizes two basic games: 1) the six-wicket, one-stake game which balances the rules most Americans have played with the court setting most widely played in the world and 2) the nine-wicket, two-stake variation (court setting familiar to most Americans). The six-wicket version is considered the most challenging, strategically stimulating and skill-developing, and is the version that is played in all major USCA tournaments. In addition to the rules for the six-wicket game presented here, the USCA rule book includes the rules for the nine-wicket game and golf croquet, as well as, court standards, equipment specifications, accessories, customs and etiquette, and standards of conduct.

THE COURT AND SETTING

THE STANDARD COURT

The standard court is a rectangle, measuring 35 by 28 yards (105 by 84 feet). Its boundaries shall be marked clearly, the INSIDE edge of the definitive border being the actual boundary. Nylon string (#18) stapled or otherwise affixed to the ground is recommended to be used for the boundary lines.

COURT REFERENCES

The four corners of the court are known respectively as Corners 1, 2, 3 and 4. The four boundaries are known as South, West, North and East boundaries—regardless of the orientation of the court (refer to diagram).

The North baulk line is a line measured one mallet's head (9 inches) in from the North boundary and extends from the third corner to midway between the second and third corners. The South baulk line is a line measured one mallet's head (9 inches) in from the South boundary and extends from the first corner to midway between the first and fourth corners.

THE STANDARD SETTING

The stake shall be set in the center of the court. The wickets shall be set parallel to the North and South boundaries; the centers of the two inner wickets, 21 feet to the north

---

*See pages 159 and 160 for additional information.

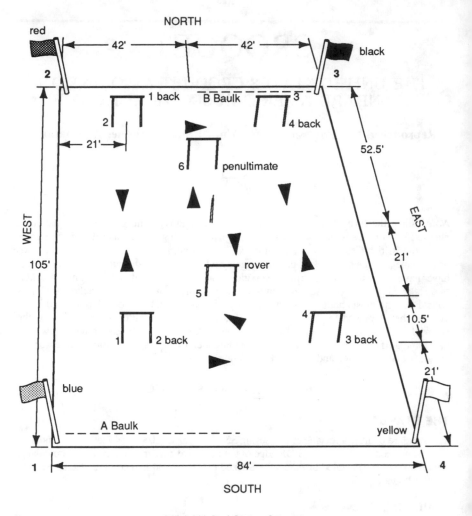

Official United States Croquet
Association 6-wicket layout

and south of the stake; the centers of the four outer wickets, 21 feet from their adjacent boundaries. This is the preferred court size and should be the official setting for major tournaments.

MODIFIED COURT SIZE AND SETTING

Should the area be too small to accommodate a standard court, a modified court may be laid out in accordance with the above by maintaining the same proportions of five length units long by four length units wide or by using a smaller modified length unit. EXAMPLE: Units of ten feet could be used to set the court dimensions. Thus 40 feet wide by 50 feet long with the stake in the middle at the intersection of the two diagonals is a possible setup.

The corner wickets are 1 unit (10 feet) from their adjacent boundaries. The center wickets are 1 unit (10 feet) in each direction from the stake. Local conditions may require other layouts, but the size above is generally considered the minimum for this game.

PART 1. USE OF MALLET

1. A player must hit his ball with either striking face of his mallet. A mallet head is usually nine inches in length (when it is not, a nine inch designation should be marked somewhere on the mallet for measurement purposes). He may hold any part of the mallet shaft but cannot touch the head of the mallet nor rest the shaft on the ground during the stroke. See Part 9, Penalties, Rule 55 a).

2. a) The striker may not push his ball. NOTE: A push means maintaining contact between mallet and ball for an appreciable period or any acceleration following a check of the mallet head after its initial contact with the ball. See Part 9, Penalties, Rule 55 a).

b) The striker shall not strike his ball audibly or distinctly twice in the same stroke (double tap) or maintain contact between mallet and ball after his ball has hit another ball, except that no fault can be committed under this rule if the cause of the second hit is the result of a roquet. See Part 9, Penalties, Rule 55 a).

3. a) It shall be counted as a stroke if, with the intent of striking his ball, the player's mallet hits a wicket and not the ball, or if he drives his mallet into the ground without contacting the ball, or misses the ball entirely.

b) A player may waive or pass his turn. He must audibly so declare by stating the color of the ball playing and the intention to waive the turn. Once the announcement has been made, the turn has finished and may not be replayed. A player who has waived out of turn is subject to Rule 47.

4. a) If a ball lies so that a player cannot strike it squarely, he may not place another mallet against the ball and hit that mallet with his own.

b) The striker may not move or shake a ball at rest by hitting a wicket or the stake with the mallet.

c) The striker may not strike his ball so as to cause it to touch an upright or the stake while still in contact with the mallet (crush shot).

d) The striker may not strike his ball when lying in contact with an upright or the stake other than in the direction away from the upright or the stake (crush shot). For a), b), c) and d) above, see Part 9, Penalties, rule 55 a).

5. In the course of the stroke the player may strike only his own ball without touching another ball with his mallet. See Part 9, Penalties, Rule 55 a).

PART 2. STARTING THE GAME AND WICKET #1

6. The toss of a coin determines the starting order of play. The side winning the toss has the choice of playing first and third with blue and black or second and fourth with red and yellow.

7. All balls must start from the starting area which is a space 12-5/8 inches wide, three feet (one average mallet's length) south of the first wicket parallel to the South Boundary so that a ball could be placed at either end of a mallet's head (nine inches) or anywhere within that area and be three feet from the wicket. Balls must start in order of colors shown descending on the center stake (Blue, Red, Black and Yellow) and they will play in that rotation until the end of the game or being put out of play by completing the course.

8. Any ball that has not made the #1 wicket cannot receive more than one stroke per turn.

9. A player who has not made wicket #1 may drive his ball and hit any other ball which has likewise not made that wicket, so as to put it into position, out of position, or through the wicket. This ends his turn unless his ball also makes a clear passage through the wicket, which entitles his ball to one continuation stroke. The other ball which has thus been put through the wicket shall be considered to have made the wicket but is not entitled to a continuation stroke.

10. A player who makes the #1 wicket is entitled to one continuation stroke [exception, Rule 21 a] but is nevertheless dead on all balls that have not made #1 wicket. See Part 9, Penalties, Rule 55 a).

11. A player who drives through the #1 wicket and in the same stroke hits a ball that has not made the #1 wicket is not penalized and is entitled to a continuation stroke [exception, Rule 21 a)] with the other ball remaining where it lies.

12. Any ball that has made #1 wicket may not block or impede the stroke of any ball that has not made the #1 wicket. If it does, the offending ball is marked and becomes ball in hand immediately preceding the turn of the ball not in the game and is replaced immediately after that shot. If the marked space becomes occupied by another ball the lifted ball is then placed three feet directly north of the #1 wicket (which is also the #2 back wicket).

PART 3. MAKING A WICKET

13. To score a wicket point, a ball must make a complete passage through a wicket and in the proper direction. This shall be visually observed by seeing whether any part of the ball breaks the plane of the playing side of the wicket. This shall not be tested by placing a mallet against the approach side of the wicket. If a striker or his partner uses a mallet to test the position, the ball will be deemed not through the wicket.

14. A ball stopping in the wicket, or one which goes through but rolls back into it, has not made the wicket.

15. a) If a ball is for a wicket but on the wrong side, it may be played through the wicket but must have completely cleared the non-playing side before it can be played back through in the proper direction on a subsequent shot.

b) A ball may take croquet from another ball located in the jaws of a wicket and run that wicket, provided that no part of the striker's ball breaks the plane of the non-playing side and is running the wicket in the proper direction.

16. A ball that is dead on another ball resting in the jaws of its wicket (as determined by encroachment into either the playing or non-playing side) may not hit that ball in trying to make the wicket [see Part 9, Penalties, Rule 55 a)]. A player may use the jump shot to make a blocked wicket or blocked stake but must not hit the blocking ball at any time during the shot (except after hitting the stake when staking out).

17. A ball that is dead on another ball lying beyond (not intruding into) a wicket may hit that ball while attempting to run the wicket but must make a complete passage through the wicket in order to be clear and receive a continuation stroke. Should the striker fail to completely clear the wicket, see Rule 33. Part 9, Penalties, Rule 55 a) applies.

18. A ball running a wicket other than the one in the proper sequence or direction shall not receive credit for that wicket nor receive an extra stroke, except if it is a rover. See Part 7, Rule 39.

19. A side (either ball) may block (stymie) a wicket once with a ball (or balls) upon which the opponent is dead. The side must leave the opponent a clear shot at the wicket by the beginning of the blocked ball's second turn. If the side does not do so, the stymied ball

will be deemed alive on the blocking ball (or balls) provided that the blocking side is responsible for the stymie. In order to be blocked, a player must have a possible shot at making the wicket until a ball encroaches on that direct path.

20. At the beginning of the game all clips shall be placed on the first wicket and upon making a wicket the player shall remove his clip and place it on his next wicket at the conclusion of his turn. For the first six wickets the clip is placed on the top or crown of the wicket and for the back six wickets the clip is placed on either side of the wicket. As clips serve as an aid to the players and do not necessarily denote the official status of the game, each player, referee or official scorer shall call attention to a misplaced clip, giving the correct wicket placement if requested by the player in question and the clip shall then be properly placed. Notice of a misplaced clip shall be mentioned as soon as it is observed.

PART 4. WICKET POINTS, ROQUET, CROQUET AND ADDITIONAL STROKES

21. Wicket Points: a) When the striker's ball has scored a wicket point the striker shall be entitled to play one continuation stroke. If the striker's ball or any other ball it hits in running the wicket goes out of bounds, his turn ends and each ball off the court is replaced one mallet's head (nine inches) in from where it crossed the boundary line. ·

b) When a ball other than the striker's is caused to score a wicket point, it is said to have been peeled through that wicket but does not receive a continuation stroke.

22. a) During a turn the striker is entitled to roquet any ball he is alive on and receive two extra strokes (exception, Rule 47). Upon making his proper wicket the striker becomes alive on all balls and receives one extra stroke [exception, Rule 21 a)].

b) The striker makes a roquet when his ball hits another ball it is alive on either directly or by glancing off of a wicket or stake.

c) When hitting two or more balls upon which he is alive in the same stroke, the roquet will be deemed to have been made on the first ball hit with the second ball being replaced. If two balls are roqueted simultaneously, the striker has the choice of which one to play from.

d) A ball that has made a roquet cannot thereafter in the same stroke make or score a wicket point for itself.

23. A striker who makes his wicket and then roquets another ball in the same stroke is deemed to have made the wicket but must roquet that or another ball in the continuation stroke in order to receive two additional strokes. The ball hit after clearing the wicket is not replaced. [Exception, Rule 21 a).]

24. The Croquet Stroke: a) When a roquet is made the striker's ball becomes a ball in hand and shall be brought to and placed in contact with the roqueted ball. (Exception, Rule 32.)

b) To take croquet, the striker must place his ball in contact with the roqueted ball however he chooses, but may not have his ball touching any other ball except the roqueted ball.

c) Before playing his stroke, the striker may touch or steady the roqueted ball and may further apply such pressure by hand or foot, but not by mallet, as is reasonably necessary to make it hold its position. He may not move any ball except his own intentionally, but if he does so unintentionally, he shall replace it without penalty.

d) The ball hitherto known as the roqueted ball is in the croquet stroke known as the croqueted ball.

e) The striker now takes the croquet stroke with the balls placed as in (b) above and by hitting into the croqueted ball must move or shake the croqueted ball.

f) If a player feels an opponent has repeatedly committed faults in the croquet stroke, such as failing to move the croqueted ball on his take-off shots, he may summon the referee to watch subsequent croquet strokes. The referee shall so notify the player he is watching. See Part 9, Penalties, Rule 55 a).

g) After the croquet stroke, the striker shall be entitled to play an additional stroke unless his turn has ended under Rule 46 or he has made another legal roquet, whereafter he takes croquet from that ball.

h) The striker may not place his foot or hand on his ball during the croquet stroke.

i) After each stroke any ball, except the striker's, less than a mallet's head off the boundary is replaced that length from the line. If that ball cannot be replaced directly in from the line from where it rests due to the presence of another ball, it may at the discretion of the striker be placed one mallet's head in from the line and up to a mallet's head in either direction from, but not in contact with, the ball.

Should two balls be sent over the boundary the first ball out is replaced first. If two balls come to rest within nine inches from the boundary at the same place, the closest to the boundary is replaced first.

j) A ball may be placed in bounds by an adversary only if the adversary has the consent of the striker to do so.

25. Any player may handle any ball which is replaceable after contact, or may return any ball which has made a roquet to its player without penalty. A player may place a ball for his partner's croquet stroke to save time, and may give a temporary mark which must be removed before the stroke is taken. A player may lift his ball to clean it at any time during the game, but must advise his opponent before doing so. Any ball accidentally moved shall be replaced without penalty. [Exception: Rule 51 a).]

PART 5. BISQUES

26. A bisque is a handicap wherein the striker is allowed to replay a shot from its original position on the court. A bisque may be taken only if the ball can be replaced accurately. The intention of taking a bisque need not be announced before the original shot is made, however, care shall be taken to mark the ball accurately when in a critical position.

27. A bisque may be taken only for the immediately preceding stroke.

28. A bisque may be taken on any infringement or fault except for a ball played out of turn. See Rule 47.

29. A player may take more than one bisque per turn.

30. a) In doubles matches, the averaging method will be used. This is done by averaging the partners' handicaps to determine the average strength of the partnership. For example, a 2 and a 4 will average 3. A 5 and a 7 will average 6. The difference between each team's average handicap team will receive bisques equivalent to this difference. In the example above, the difference would be 3 bisques. Where the difference between the average handicaps results in a 1/2 bisque this is moved up to the next full number (for example 2-1/2 bisques becomes 3 bisques).

b) Only the higher handicap player in the team receiving a bisque(s) may use the bisques. When both players on the side receiving a bisque(s) have the same handicap then either player may use the bisque(s). For example, a side receiving three bisques may decide that one player uses all three bisques or that one player uses two bisques and the other player one bisque, at their discretion.

31. In singles matches, a player may use his handicap quota between both balls. The two opponents will net out the difference in handicaps and where the handicaps are the same

no bisques will be given. Where the handicaps differ, the lower handicap plays at zero while the higher handicap player receives the difference between the handicaps (example: player A had 2 bisques, player B has 4 bisques therefore, player A plays at zero and player B plays at 2).

PART 6. DEAD BALL

32. When a striker's ball roquets another upon which it is alive, it is immediately ball in hand and dead on that ball until the player has made his next wicket in order, but he must play off it as in Rule 24 b). EXCEPTION: When the striker's ball roquets a ball out of bounds, his turn ends, but he remains alive on that ball, which is replaced one mallet's head from where it went out.

33. If a striker's ball hits a ball on which it is dead (except after a roquet), the striker's turn ends and all balls shall be replaced. EXCEPTION: During a croquet stroke, the ball being croqueted may be hit by the striker's ball more than once without penalty.

34. If the striker's ball roquets one it is alive on and thereafter during the same stroke hits another ball, whether alive or dead on it, the latter shall be replaced without penalty (i.e., no penalty if out of bounds, or credit for wicket or stake). The player must play off the first ball hit and is not dead on the second ball if originally alive on it.

35. If during a croquet stroke the striker's ball hits another ball upon which it is dead, the turn ends, and the ball just roqueted and the striker's ball are replaced with the croqueted ball remaining where it lies after the stroke and given credit for any wicket or stake point made. If, however, in croquet stroke, the striker's ball hits a ball on which it is alive, it has then made a roquet on the ball and must play off it as in Rule 24 b).

36. a) Any third or fourth ball struck (cannoned) by a roqueted or croqueted ball will be treated as having been played directly, with all balls remaining where they lie at the end of the stroke. The struck ball is given credit for wicket or stake points if made and no deadness is credited between the roqueted or croqueted ball and the cannoned ball. If no fault has occurred, the striker may then take his next stroke. If any ball (except the striker's on the roquet stroke) goes out of bounds, the striker's turn ends, all balls remain where they lie, and any out of bounds ball is replaced 9 inches in from the boundary where it went out.

b) Special relief from deadness: When each ball of both sides passes through the 1-back wicket, the opposing side may (or may choose not to) clear the deadness from one of its balls. The side eligible to receive this relief must declare which ball it chooses to clear before playing the first shot of its next turn or no relief is given. The side whose ball has just made 1-back may request that the opposing side declare which ball they choose to clear, at which point that side must declare or lose its right to do so.

c) Should the striker peel his opponent through the 1-back hoop, the striker will have an option to clear either his or his partner's ball. If the peel is accomplished on the roquet stroke, the striker may clear himself but must place his ball in contact with the roqueted ball and play his croquet stroke and is considered dead on the croqueted ball. If the peel is accomplished on the croquet stroke, the striker may clear himself on all balls and play his continuation stroke as if he had just scored a wicket. When a striker peels the opponent through the 1-back wicket he must clear one of his balls, if he so chooses, before the next stroke of his turn.

d) A rover ball may be cleared of deadness on 1, 2 or 3 balls when an opponent scores 1-back but may not be cleared of last deadness.

37. A ball becomes alive on all balls upon being driven through its next wicket in order and in the proper direction.

PART 7. ROVER AND FINISHING THE GAME

38. A ball that has made all the wickets in the proper sequence becomes a rover and is considered alive on all balls upon making the rover wicket (red crown).

39. To become alive from a 2- or a 3-ball deadness, a rover may go through any wicket in any direction, receiving a continuation stroke. If the ball does not clear the wicket, it must, unless knocked out, continue through in the same direction in order to be considered clear.

A rover may receive a continuation stroke for having made a wicket only if he was 2- or 3-balls dead.

40. a) A rover may roquet any other ball only once per turn. [See Part 9, Penalties, Rule 55 a).] Before clearing himself he must be dead on at least 2 balls, but nevertheless he remains dead on the ball last hit (last dead) until he hits another ball whereupon his temporary deadness disappears.

b) A rover that runs a wicket in clearing its deadness and in the same stroke hits a ball upon which it was last dead incurs no penalty, and unless either ball is driven out of bounds, both balls remain where they lie and the striker is entitled to take his continuation stroke.

41. a) A rover ball may hit the stake itself or be driven into the stake by another rover, whereupon it will be considered to have finished the game provided no fault occurred.

42. When one ball of a side has staked out of the game it is removed from the court immediately and play continues in proper rotation, without the staked out ball.

43. If in a roquet shot a striker's rover ball drives another rover ball into the stake, the roqueted ball is removed from play and the striker receives two strokes, the first taken nine inches in any direction from the stake.

44. The game is won by the side that finishes the game with both balls first, or in a time limit game by the side scoring the highest total of wicket and stake points.

PART 8. FAULTS AND PENALTIES FOR OUT OF BOUNDS, PLAYING OUT OF TURN, PLAYING THE WRONG BALL, ILLEGAL SHOTS AND CONDONED PLAY

45. A ball is out of bounds when its vertical axis crosses the boundary line (more than halfway over). It shall be replaced one mallet's head (nine inches) from where it first crossed the line, or, if in a corner, one mallet's head from both boundaries.

46. If the striker sends any ball out of bounds, his turn ends. [See Part 9, Penalties, Rule 55 b).] (Exception: if, after a roquet, the striker's ball either goes out of bounds or caroms another ball out. See Rule 32.)

47. If a ball plays out of turn, all balls are replaced with no deadness incurred and proper play is resumed with the offending side losing its turn (example: if black plays when it was blue's turn, the balls are replaced and blue loses its turn; if black plays when it is the opponent's turn, the balls are replaced, the proper opponent plays and the next player for the blue/black side loses its turn).

48. If the striker plays a foot or hand shot his turn ends. [See Part 9, Penalties, Rule 55 a).]

49. If an opponent observes the striker playing a stroke with any ball (except the striker's, in his continuation or croquet stroke), not placed nine inches in from the boundary line, he may request that the shot be replayed from the proper position providing he does so before the next stroke of the turn. If he does not so request the replay, the shot will be deemed condoned.

50. If a player plays a ball other than the ball he started the game with, his turn ends. See Part 9, Penalties, Rule 55 a). In a singles game, a striker playing the wrong partner ball shall be considered to have played out of turn with the penalty as in Rule 47.

51. a). If a player, in attempting to strike his own ball, touches (with his foot or mallet) another ball, his turn ends and both balls are replaced.

b) If, after striking his ball, the striker interferes with his ball in any way, his ball and all other balls affected by the stroke shall be replaced and the turn shall end.

c) If a ball is interfered with by an outside agent, except weather, or accidentally by an opponent, in any way that materially affects the outcome of the stroke, that stroke shall be replayed. Otherwise, the ball shall be placed, as nearly as can be judged, where it would have come to rest, provided that no point or roquet can thereby be made.

52. If the striker plays his ball from a misplaced position, all balls are replaced to their correct position and the striker replays that stroke without penalty. Misplaced position refers to a striker taking croquet when not entitled to, taking croquet from a wrong ball, or lifting to an incorrect position.

LIMIT OF CLAIMS

53. a) A fault or misplay shall be called by the striker or opponent as soon as it is discovered but must be called before the opponent plays the first stroke of his next turn or the error is automatically condoned.

b) Any player, referee, or official shall bring attention to any misplacement error as soon as it is noticed. The limit of claims [see Rule 53 a)] is in effect for unnoticed errors.

c) If an out-of-turn fault is discovered by either side after two or more turns have been played (and condoned), play shall continue in the new sequence with all wicket points, deadness, or faults incurred during any turn up to that turn in which the fault is discovered being deemed valid.

54. If a player makes any stroke or strokes as the result of any incorrect information concerning the state of the game supplied by the adversary or referee, he shall have the right to replay. This shall apply to the deadness board accuracy as well as accuracy of the placement of the clips provided the opponent or referee has confirmed this incorrect information beforehand.

PART 9. PENALTIES

55. The following penalties shall apply as noted in the preceding rules:

a) All balls are replaced and the turn is over.

b) All balls shall remain where they lie (balls out of bounds or less than nine inches in bounds being placed nine inches in from the boundary) and the turn is over.

PART 10. REFEREES

56. The role of the referee is to resolve disputes between players by referring to the Rule Book. Any situation that does not appear to be covered by these rules shall be decided by the best judgement of the referee.

57. A referee shall not intervene unless asked by the players except that the referee may correct clip placement, deadness board, misplacement of balls, and may make time announcements.

58. In the absence of an appointed referee, the players will act as their own joint referees, but there is an obligation on the adversary to watch the game, and if he fails to do so, the striker is, during such period, the sole referee. In doubles, all players share the rights and duties of a referee, and a reference to the striker includes his partner.

59. If, during a tournament match, a player fails to request that an adversary call a referee to observe a questionable stroke before it is taken, he may not appeal. Otherwise he may appeal as in Rule 66.

PART 11. TOURNAMENT PLAY

60. For each tournament there shall be a tournament director selected who shall be empowered to: administrate, interpret and enforce the Rules of the Game; appoint a committee to assist and provide referees, timekeepers and deadness board attendants; arrange the draw; assign handicaps; schedule matches; assign courts and otherwise direct all aspects of the competition, including the disposition of any appeal by players or teams not resolved by a referee.

61. In tournaments, game and shot time limits may be set by a tournament committee before the start of the first tournament game. These time limits may be increased or decreased by the committee at the conclusion of each full round (e.g., first, quarter, or semifinal rounds) as overall time and weather conditions dictate.

62. Until 15 minutes to the end of a time-limit game each player will be allowed no more than 60 seconds (45 in advanced game) to strike his ball following the completion of the last stroke by either side. A stroke will be deemed completed when the ball comes to a complete stop or crosses the boundary line.

The timekeeper will announce when 15 seconds remain in the time allotted for the next stroke and will call "Time" when the 15 seconds has elapsed. Should the player not have struck his ball his turn ends and play resumes with the next player, after replacing balls displaced by the striker after time was called.

Each side is entitled to receive two (2) one-minute time-out periods to be taken only during that side's turn.

63. The timekeeper shall announce when fifteen minutes remain in the game, and thereafter each player will be allowed no more than 45 seconds to strike his ball. The timekeeper will announce when one minute is remaining and declare "Match Time" when that minute has elapsed, taking particular care to note whether the striker's ball was in play when match time was called.

64. a) When "Match Time" is called, the player in play shall complete his turn (which is his last), and each remaining ball shall have one turn in rotation. The side that has scored the greatest number of wickets and stake points is declared the winner, but if there is a tie, play shall continue in full rounds until the tie is broken or both balls of one side stake out.

b) When "Match Time" has been called and the player then playing has finished his turn, a one-minute official's time-out may be called by any player to determine and announce the wicket score at that point. After that time-out, play shall resume under the 45 second per stroke limit until the tie is broken and the game has ended as in (a) above.

65. In doubles tournaments, where one player is absent at the beginning of play, that player's partner may place the absent player's ball in the starting area and waive that and any subsequent turn or, may wait for the shot time limit to expire.

66. a) If, during the course of a tournament, either the players or the referee are unable to resolve a question of fact or rule, they may appeal to the tournament director, who

shall decide accordingly. If he by coincidence happens to have been a witness and is satisfied that he knows the answer, he shall inform the players that he is deciding the subject matter of appeal by observation, and give his decision accordingly. If he is not so satisfied, he should decide the dispute by investigation. He should hear what the parties have to say; at his discretion he may hear witnesses. He shall then give a decision to the best of his ability. If he is in doubt, he may, in the last resort, give a compromise decision, which may involve adjusting the clips arbitrarily and directing where the balls shall be placed. This includes the right to decide that the players shall replay the disputed play or begin the game again.

b) A referee or tournament official may call for a time-out or stop play at any time during a match to adjudicate any dispute, delay or postpone completion of a match due to inclement weather or court conditions. The time taken by these official actions will be added to the time left in the match when play resumes.

PART 12. WIRING

67. A ball is said to be wired from another ball if:

a) any part of an upright of a wicket or the stake or another ball on which the striker is dead would impede the direct course of any part of the striker's ball toward any part of another ball upon which it is alive.

b) any part of a wicket, stake or third ball so interferes with any part of the swing of the mallet prior to impact between mallet and ball that the striker, with his usual style of play, cannot, in order to make a roquet, drive his ball freely toward any part of another ball he is alive on when striking the center of his ball with any part of the face of his mallet.

c) any part of the striker's ball is within the jaws of a wicket.

The mere interference of a wicket or stake or third ball with the stance of the striker does not constitute wiring.

68. If, at the beginning of a turn, the striker's ball (in rotation) is wired from all balls on which it is alive, and if the adversary is responsible for its position, then the striker may lift his ball and place it in contact with any ball on which it is alive and then play his croquet stroke. But if instead of lifting, the striker waives his turn then, unless the striker has lost a turn as a result of having played out of turn, he is deemed to be responsible for that ball's position.

69. If the next ball to play is dead on all three other balls, it may be left in any position on the court without being considered wired under this rule.

GOVERNING BODY

United States Croquet Association, 500 Avenue of Champions, Palm Beach Gardens, FL 33418-9990

The U.S. Croquet Association (USCA) is the national not-for-profit organization for the development, coordination, and promotion of the game of croquet. Twenty years from conception to fruition, the USCA was formally launched in 1976 when its longtime goal of codifying the rules of the American version of the game was fulfilled. The USCA sponsors national, regional, and district championships and sanctions club championships and other croquet events. The Association is also responsible for the selection and sponsorship of the U.S. National Team, which competes with other croquet-playing nations. The basic types of croquet clubs that make up the Association are (a) family size clubs; (b) private croquet clubs; (c) country, tennis, and sports clubs; (d) hotels and resorts; (e) schools and colleges; (f) retirement groups and communities; and (g) municipal parks and recreation departments. Assistance with the formation of clubs, court construction, purchasing equipment, conducting tournaments, instructional materials, and videotapes is provided by the Association.

MAGAZINES

Croquet News, USCA, 500 Avenue of Champions, Palm Beach Gardens, FL 33418

U.S. Croquet Gazette, USCA, 500 Avenue of Champions, Palm Beach Gardens, FL 33418

CROSSBOW
• ARCHERY •

OFFICIAL T.N.C. TOURNAMENT RULES

(Reproduced by permission of the National Crossbowmen of the U.S.A.*)

☐

PRIMARY RULES

SAFETY AND COURTESY

A. Every precaution must be taken to insure the highest possible safety standards have precedence over all other considerations or rules. Any practice, attitudes, equipment, or conditions, either mentioned herein, or not mentioned herein, which are in the least degree unsafe, are prohibited. Repetition, after one warning by a tournament official, shall require the offending participant, or participants, to be expelled from the tournament without refund. It shall be the responsibility of every T.N.C. member to insist upon strict maintenance of safety standards at all times.

B. To insure a fair enjoyment of crossbow competition by all contestants, a high standard of personal courtesy and sportsmanship is enjoined upon all. Discourteous unsportsmanlike conduct is an unwarranted offense against other participants and an affront to the heritage of dignity and tradition which is an integral part of the sport of the crossbow. Persistence in discourteous or unsportsmanlike conduct shall, after one warning by a tournament official, be considered grounds for expulsion from the tournament, without refund, of the offending participants.

C. Crossbowmen will keep their bows when drawn, whether loaded or not, pointed in the direction of the target.

D. During the act of loading, and while being adjusted to aiming position, the crossbow barrel should be directed downward.

E. The Crossbow Field Captain may, at his discretion, reprimand or even bar from further competition a shooter who exhibits carelessness in handling his weapon. The Field Captain may also bar from competition a crossbow he considers dangerous to other shooters or spectators.

1. OFFICIAL RULES

1.1 T.N.C. tournament rules are the same as the N.A.A. tournament rules for longbowmen except where in conflict with the rules given herein.

---

*See page 165 for additional information.

2. TARGET FACES

2.1 Target faces for the crossbow championship round shall be the standard 80 cm. F.I.T.A. target face.

2.2 For crossbow events which have no counterpart in the longbow division, such as the King's and Queen's rounds, the appropriate target faces shall be used.

2.3 Crossbow archers use the same size target as do longbow archers for Clout, F.I.T.A.—I and F.I.T.A.—II Rounds.

3. CROSSBOW TACKLE

3.1 The crossbow and parts may be made of any safe material.

3.2 Arrows (or bolts) may be made of any material, but must not be of such design that they will unreasonably damage the target face or bast. They should be plainly marked for ease in scoring.

3.3 Telescopic or magnifying sights, compound prods, and slings are not permitted. Prismatic sights or other optical nonmagnifying sights are allowed.

3.4 Crossbows shall be drawn by hand. No mechanical aids for spanning the bow shall be permitted. Foot stirrups attached to the stock or foot plates on the ground will be allowed.

3.5 Binoculars or spotting scopes may be used at any time to locate hits.

4. CLASSIFICATION

4.1 Crossbow archers shall be classed in the following groups:

a) Men

b) Women

c) Open

4.2 Crossbow archers competing in the open class will not be eligible for the championship awards but will compete with each other for a special award for that class.

4.3 Crossbow archers competing in the open class will not be subject to the tackle restrictions of the championship divisions and will be allowed to use equipment such as compound prods, telescopic sights, slings, etc.

5. FIELD OFFICIALS

5.1 The Field Captain shall have the responsibility and authority to organize, supervise and regulate all practice, shooting and competition in accordance with regulations and customs; to interpret and to decide questions of rules; to maintain safety conditions; to enforce sportsmanlike behavior; to score doubtful arrows; to signify the start, interruptions, delays, postponements and finish of competition.

6. SHOOTING, SCORING, AND CONDUCT OF PARTICIPANTS

6.1 Crossbowmen do not compete with longbowmen. They compete with and against each other for awards within their own division.

6.2 Two to four crossbowmen shall be assigned per target until all are filled.

6.3 Archers shall be reassigned targets after each round, at the discretion of the field captain, on the basis of their total score for rounds completed.

6.4 There shall be one practice end, limited to six optional sighter arrows, prior to shooting each distance.

6.5 There shall be no practice permitted after a postponement or delay, unless such postponement or delay exceeds 30 minutes. In such cases, one practice end shall be permitted.

6.6 The field captain shall control the shooting with a whistle.

6.7 An archer shall stand so that one foot is on each side of the shooting line.

6.8 If an archer shoots less than the appropriate number of arrows in one end, he may shoot the remaining arrows if the omission is discovered before the end is officially completed; otherwise, they shall score as misses.

6.9 If an archer shoots more than the appropriate number of arrows in one end, only the lowest proper number of arrows shall score.

6.10 If an arrow in the target touches a dividing line between two colors, the higher color shall count. Doubtful arrows must be determined for each end before the arrows in the target face have been touched; otherwise, the lower value must be taken.

6.11 An arrow that has passed through the scoring face so that it is not visible from the front may be pushed back and scored according to the position of the arrow in the face.

6.12 Unless all arrow holes are marked on each occasion when arrows are scored and drawn from the target faces, arrows rebounding or passing through the target face when witnessed by another competitor or a tournament official shall count 7 points when scoring is 10, 9, 8, 7, 6, 5, 4, 3, 2, and 1; and 4 points when the scoring is 5, 4, 3, 2, and 1.

6.13 Hits on the wrong target shall score as misses.

6.14 Any archer may retire from the shooting line to avoid proximity to tackle or a shooting practice that he considers unsafe and may resume shooting when safe conditions prevail.

6.15 Crossbowmen stand to shoot and shall shoot "offhand". No rests or straps of any description shall be permitted. The field captain may permit a physically incapacitated contestant to shoot while seated.

6.16 Having completed the shooting of an end, a crossbowman shall step back with his crossbow, several feet behind the shooting line.

6.17 Coaching an archer on the shooting line by means of inaudible and inconspicuous signs or symbols is permitted, provided that such coaching is not distracting to other contestants. If a contestant on the same target, or adjacent targets, complains that such activity is personally distracting, such coaching must be terminated immediately. Audible coaching of archers on the shooting line is not permitted.

6.18 Bow racks, tackle boxes or other objects which protrude above the ground shall not be allowed within six feet of the shooting line.

7. ROUNDS

7.1 T.N.C. championships for both men and women shall be determined by the highest total scores shot in the Quadruple International Crossbow Round. The tournament officials may at their discretion, add such other events as they consider desirable, such as the Clout, Pistol, American 900, novelty rounds, etc., but the scores made in such events shall not count toward determining the Championships.

(7.1a) International Crossbow Round: Official F.I.T.A. 80 cm. (31.5″) diameter, 10-ring target face. Scoring is 10, 9, 8, 7, 6, 5, 4, 3, 2, 1.

30 arrows at 65 meters (71.1 yards)
30 arrows at 50 meters (54.7 yards)

30 arrows at 35 meters (38.3 yards)
90 arrows, possible score 900

(7.1b) American 900 Round: Official F.I.T.A. 60 cm. (23.6″) diameter. 10-ring target face. Scoring is 10, 9, 8, 7, 6, 5, 4, 3, 2, 1.

30 arrows at 60 meters (65.6 yards)
30 arrows at 50 meters (54.7 yards)
30 arrows at 40 meters (43.8 yards)
90 arrows, possible score 900

(7.1c) Clout Round: Six ends of six arrows shot from 165 meters (180.5 yards) at a 48 foot diameter target on the ground, scored 9, 7, 5, 3, 1.

36 arrows, possible score 324

(7.1d) Indoor F.I.T.A. Round I: Official FITA 40 cm. (15.7″) diameter. 10-ring target face. Scoring is 10, 9, 8, 7, 6, 5, 4, 3, 2, 1.

30 arrows at 18 meters (19 yards, 1 foot, 9 inches), possible score 300.

(7.1e) Indoor F.I.T.A. Round II: Official F.I.T.A. 60 cm. (23.6″) diameter. 10-ring target face. Scoring is 10, 9, 8, 7, 6, 5, 4, 3, 2, 1.

30 arrows at 25 meters (27 yards, 1 foot, 0.029 inches), possible score 300.

(7.1f) Indoor Pistol Round: Indoor F.I.T.A. I Round.

(7.1g) Outdoor Pistol Round: Indoor F.I.T.A. II Round.

7.2 In the event of a tie, the tie shall be broken based upon the following criteria: at the conclusion of a tournament in which crossbow archers are tied on score, the higher placed crossbow archer will be the one with the higher number of scoring hits. If this number is equal, then the crossbow archer with the higher number of 10's not touching the scoring line dividing the 10 and 9 rings will be the higher placed crossbow archer. If this number is the same, then the crossbow archer with the higher number of 10's touching the scoring line between the 10 and 9 rings will be higher placed. If this number is the same then the higher number of 9's, then 8's, then 7's, 6's, 5's, 4's, 3's, 2's, 1's etc., will break the tie until the tie is broken.

7.3. King's and Queen's Rounds: The three men having shot the highest single International Round scores while participating in the N.A.A.-T.N.C. championship event may shoot the King's Round. The three women similarly qualifying may shoot the Queen's Round.

Distance: The contest shall be staged at 35 meters.

Target Faces: Each target will be a special 48″ face which shall contain six standard 4-3/4″ golds clocked on an 18″ radius at 12, 2, 4, 6, 8, and 10 o'clock, respectively. Within each gold there is to be centered a black 1″ bull's-eye.

Shooting: One contestant shall shoot at a time, shooting one bolt and then stepping back from the shooting line. The persons having the highest individual International Round score shall shoot first, the next highest second, etc. All shall shoot in turn, first at 12 o'clock, then 2 o'clock, etc. Each contestant shall shoot one end only of 6 arrows. There shall be no preliminary practice on the King's or Queen's Round faces.

Scoring: Arrows must cut the gold to score. Each hit in the gold counts 9 points while a hit in the 1″ black spot counts 10.

Awards: The contestants having the highest scores shall be known as the King and Queen and shall be awarded the King's Dagger and the Queen's Scepter, respectively, which may be held for the tournament year. The two runners-up shall be known as the King's men and the Queen's Ladies. The contestants may place on their pennors (or gonfalons) small crowns of either yellow (gold) or white (silver) to denote their participation and standing in a National King's and Queen's Round contest.

GOVERNING BODY

The National Crossbowmen of the USA, 2020 Hackett Ave., Easton, PA 18042

The National Crossbowmen is a member organization of the National Archery Association and the International Armbrust Union, the world governing body for crossbow shooting. The primary purpose of TNC is to perpetuate and promote the sport of crossbow target archery. Information on the availability of equipment, publications, and the construction of bows is available from the TNC. The TNC sponsors annual National Indoor and Outdoor Tournaments. The organization also makes the selection of teams to represent the United States in international crossbow competition.

MAGAZINES

International Field Crossbow Shooting News, Crossbow Archery Development Association, Frost Street, Wolverhampton WV46UD, England

The Crossbow Chit Chat, The National Crossbowmen, 2020 Hackett Ave., Easton, PA 18042

• CURLING •

ICF/USCA RULES OF PLAY

(Reproduced by permission of United States Curling Association*)

☐

1. INTERPRETATION.

In these rules, umpires' rulings, and other official documents of the Federation and its officers:

(a) "competition" means a playdown by any number of teams playing games to determine a winner;

(b) "end" means that part of a game in which the two opposing teams each deliver eight stones alternatively and then determine the score;

(c) "The Federation" means the International Curling Federation;

(d) "game" means play between two teams to determine a winner;

(e) "house" means the area within the outside circle at each end of the rink;

(f) "match" means play between two or more teams on one side against an equal number of teams on the other side to determine a winning side by the total number of shots or games;

(g) "rink" means an area of ice marked in accordance with Rule 3.

2. APPLICATION.

These rules apply to games:

(a) within the jurisdiction of the Federation; or

(b) to which they have been made applicable by the curling body having jurisdiction.

3. RINK.

(1) Where possible, the rink shall be drawn on the ice in accordance with the diagram below.

(2) Two rubber hacks of a style and size approved by the Federation shall be placed on the foot line with the inside edge of each hack 7.62 cm (3 inches) from the centre line and on opposite sides of the centre line. The length of the hack shall not exceed 20.32 cm (8 inches). The rubber of the hack shall be attached firmly to wood or other suitable material and the hack shall be recessed into the ice as much as is practical, but no more than 5.04 cm (2 inches) in depth. There shall be no obstruction behind the hack structure.

---

*See page 171 for additional information.

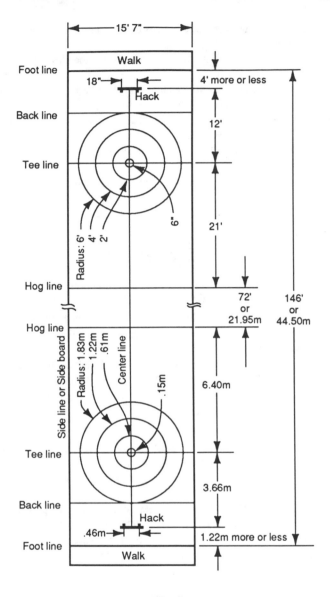

4. STONES.

(1) Curling stones shall be of circular shape.

(2) No stone, including handle and bolt, shall be of greater weight than 19.96 kilograms (44 lbs.) or of greater circumference than 91.44 centimetres (36 inches) or of less height than 11.43 centimetres (4.5 inches).

(3) If a stone is broken in play, the largest fragment shall be counted in that end, the player using another stone thereafter.

(4) A stone that rolls over in its course or comes to rest on its side or top shall be removed immediately from play.

(5) Where the handle of a stone quits the stone in delivery, the player is entitled to replay the shot.

(6) A stone that does not clear the farther hog line shall be removed immediately from play, except where it has struck another stone lying in play.

(7) A stone that passes the back line and lies clear of it shall be removed immediately from play.

(8) A stone that hits a side board or comes to rest biting a side line shall be removed immediately from play.

(9) A stone that touches or crosses a side line and finishes within the rink remains in play.

(10) No stones shall be measured by instrument until the last stone of the end has come to rest except by the umpire, when requested by a skip, to decide whether or not a stone is in play.

5. TEAMS.

(1) At the start of a competition, every team shall be composed of four players and each player shall deliver two stones in each end alternately with his opponent.

(2) No player shall use footwear or equipment that may damage the surface of the ice.

(3) The rotation of play established by a team during the first end of a game shall be observed throughout the game.

(4) The teams opposing each other in a game shall settle by lot the team that will lead at the first end, after which the winner of the preceding end shall lead.

(5) Where a player because of illness or accident or for any other valid reason is unable:

(a) to continue to play in a game; or

(b) to play at the start of a game, his skip may

(c) finish the game then in progress and start any subsequent game with the remaining players, in which case the first two players shall play three stones each; or

(d) bring in a qualified substitute for the game then in progress or at the start of any subsequent game.

(6) A player who was unable to continue to play in a game or to play at the start of a game may not resume play until the start of a subsequent game.

(7) No team shall play more than two substitutes in a competition.

(8) A team shall not play under any circumstances with fewer than three players.

6. SKIPS.

(1) The skip has the exclusive direction of the game for his team.

(2) Subject to Rule 5(3), the skip may play any position in his team that he chooses.

(3) When it is the skip's turn to play, he shall select one of his players to act as skip in his place who shall remain in that capacity throughout the course of that game. The skip may, however, return to the house for brief consultation.

7. POSITION OF PLAYERS.

(1) Only the skips or acting skips in charge of the house for the time being may stand within the house and the skip of the playing team has the choice of place and shall not

be obstructed by the other skip, but behind the tee line the privileges of both in regard to sweeping are equal.

(2) The players, other than the skip and acting skip, shall not stand behind the house, but shall place themselves along the sides of the rink between the hog lines, except when sweeping or about to deliver a stone.

8. DELIVERY.

(1) Right-handed players shall play from the hack on the left of the centre line, and left-handed players from the hack on the right of the centre line.

(2) In the delivery of the stone, the stone shall be clearly released from the hand before the stone reaches the nearer hog line. If the player fails to so release the stone, it shall be removed from play immediately by the playing team.

If the stone has struck another stone, the played stone shall be removed from play by the playing team and any displaced stone shall be placed as nearly as possible where it originally lay to the satisfaction of the opposing skip.

(3) A stone that has not been released from the player's hand and that has not reached the nearer tee line may be returned to the hack and re-delivered.

(4) Each player shall be ready to deliver his stone when his turn comes, and shall not take an unreasonable time to play. Where the chief umpire considers that play is unnecessarily slow, he shall notify the skip of the team at fault that if their next stone is not delivered within 30 seconds from the time he gives a signal, he will order the stone to be removed from play immediately.

(5) Where a player delivers a stone belonging to the opposing team, a stone belonging to his team shall be put in its place.

(6) Where a player delivers a stone out of proper rotation it shall be removed from play immediately by the playing team and returned to the player to be delivered in proper rotation, but where the mistake is not discovered until after the stone has come to rest or struck another stone, the end shall be continued as if the mistake had not occurred, and the missed stone shall be delivered by the player missing his turn as the last stone for his team in that end.

(7) Where the skips agree that a stone has been missed but are unable to agree as to which player missed his turn, the lead of the team that made the mistake shall play the last stone for his team in that end.

(8) Where two stones of a team are delivered in succession in the same end, the opposing skip shall remove the stone played by mistake, replace to his satisfaction any stone displaced by the stone played by mistake, and continue the end as if the mistake had not occurred, and the player who delivered the stone played by mistake shall re-deliver it as the last stone for his team in that end.

(9) Where a player delivers three stones in one end, the end shall be continued as if the mistake had not occurred and the fourth player of the team that made the mistake shall deliver one stone only in that end.

9. SWEEPING.

(1) Between the tee lines, a running stone, or a stone set in motion by a running stone, may be swept by any one or more of the team to which it belongs.

(2) Behind the tee line the skip or acting skip of each team is entitled to sweep any stone but neither of them shall start to sweep an approaching stone until it reaches the tee line.

(3) The sweeping motion shall be from side to side across the entire running surface in front of the stone and clearly finish to either side of the stone, and no sweepings or other debris shall be left in front of a running stone.

(4) When sweeping with a brush no part of its handle shall be over the stone.

10. TOUCHED RUNNING STONES.

(1) If a running stone is touched by any of the playing team or by his equipment, the burned stone shall be removed from play immediately by that team. However, if in the opinion of the opposing skip, removal of the stone would be beneficial to the offending team, then he may place the stone as nearly as possible to the position where he considers it would have come to rest had it not been touched. He may also reposition any stone or stones that would have been displaced had the running stone not been touched and been allowed to continue.

(2) If a running stone is touched by any of the opposing team or by his equipment, the stone shall be placed where the skip of the team to which it belongs considers it would have come to rest if it had not been touched.

(3) If the position of any stone is altered by a burned stone, the skip opposed to the team at fault may elect:

(a) to remove the burned stone and replace all other altered stones to the position where he considers they originally lay; or

(b) to leave the burned stone and all altered stones where they came to rest.

11. DISPLACED STATIONARY STONES.

(1) If a stone which would have altered the course of a running stone is displaced by the playing team, the running stone shall be allowed to come to rest and may be left there or removed from play immediately at the discretion of the opposing skip.

(2) If the running stone is removed from play then all displaced stones shall be placed where the opposing skip considers they originally lay.

(3) If the running stone is left where it came to rest, then displaced stones must remain where they came to rest.

12. SCORING.

(1) Games shall be decided by a majority of shots and a team scores one shot for each stone that is nearer the tee than any stone of the opposing team.

(2) Every stone that is within 1.83 metres (6 feet) of the tee is eligible to be counted.

(3) Measurements shall be taken from the tee to the nearest part of the stone.

(4) An end shall be considered as decided when the skips or acting skips in charge of the house at the time agree upon the score for that end.

(5) If two or more stones are so close to the tee that it is impossible to use a measuring device to determine the scoring stone, the end shall be scored as a blank end.

13. UMPIRE.

(1) The umpire has the general superintendence of, and shall govern, any game to which he is assigned.

(2) The umpire shall determine any matter in dispute between opposing skips, whether or not the matter is covered in the rules.

(3) The umpire shall not intervene in any game or determine any matter in dispute unless requested to do so by one of the opposing skips.

14. CHIEF UMPIRE.

(1) The chief umpire shall hear and determine appeals from decisions of umpires. His decision is final.

(2) Where the chief umpire has been so authorized, he may intervene at any time in any game and give such directions concerning the conduct of the game as he considers proper.

GOVERNING BODY

United States Curling Association, 100 Center Point Drive, Box 971, Stevens Point, WI 54481

The U.S. Curling Association (USCA) is affiliated with the International Curling Federation (ICF) and has adopted the ICF rules of play. Curling was a demonstration sport at the 1988 Winter Olympic Games. The USCA is concerned with the development and promotion of curling at all levels from local recreational league play to the World Championship Tournament. The local clubs that form the membership of some 23 state associations serve as the strength of the USCA. State and national championship tournaments are held annually for the various classes of competition. Information concerning the organization of clubs, instructional materials, supplies, and related matters is available through the USCA.

MAGAZINES

North America Curling News, Summit Publishing, Inc., 214 Summit St., Portage, WI 53901

• CYCLING •

ABRIDGMENT OF USCF OFFICIAL RULES
OF CYCLING

(Reproduced by permission of the United States Cycling Federation*)

☐

Note: Due to the lengthiness of the official rules, only selected portions are reproduced here. It should also be noted that the USCF Rule Book contains complete information regarding the structure and function of the Federation and the requirements for USCF sanctioned races.

RACING RULES

1. GENERAL RACING RULES

1A. Definitions

The following special terms are used.

1A1. A bicycle race is a competition among persons using bicycles where awards are given on the basis of relative performance.

1A6. Licensees are persons holding Federation licenses, such as riders, officials, coaches, trainers, and mechanics.

1A10. A session is a sequence of races with no major time breaks. Most championships are held with two or possibly three sessions per day.

1A11. A mishap is a crash, a tire puncture, or a mechanical accident. However, a puncture caused by the tire coming off due to inadequate gluing is not a mishap.

1A12. A mechanical accident is the breakage of an essential part of the bicycle. A malfunction due to insufficient tightening of any component is not a mechanical accident.

1A13. Relegation is a penalty consisting of a loss of finish position, points, or time, depending on the type of race. It may be assessed against a rider, a team or both.

1F. Mixing of Classes and Categories

1F1. Senior riders may compete in any race for their age group or younger, but not including junior races. Junior riders may compete in any race for their age group or older, up to and including general (not age-graded) senior races, subject to distance limitations specified elsewhere in these rules. No riders may race in a category other than that which is stated on their license.

---

*See pages 189 and 190 for additional information.

1F3. Juniors may not race over distances greater than the following:

Junior	Distance
9-11	40 km
12-13	80
14-15	100
16-17	120

1G. Officials

(The duties of officials are outlined in the official rules publication.)

1H. Bicycles

1H1. Bicycles used in competition must be propelled solely by human force, and shall have the following characteristics:

(a) Bicycles may be no more than 2 meters long and 75 cm. wide. For use in National Championships, an international race, a world record attempt, or for recognition of a national record, a rider's bicycle must conform to these additional dimensions:

The distance between the center of the chainwheel axle and the ground must be no less than 24 cm.;

The distance between a vertical line passing touching the frontmost point of the saddle and a vertical line through the center of the chainwheel axle must be 15 cm. or less;

The distance between a vertical line passing through the center of the chainwheel axle and a vertical line through the center of the front wheel axle must be no less than 54 and no more than 60 cm.

(b) There may be no protective shield, fairing, or other device on any part of the bicycle (including the frame, wheels, handlebars, chainwheel or accessories) which has the effect of reducing air resistance;

(c) Any propulsive action brought about by means of the hands is prohibited;

(d) The front wheel may be of a different diameter than the rear; each may be made with spokes or solid construction; the only advertising that may appear on a wheel is the name or trademark of its manufacturer, and no wheel may contain any mechanism which is able to accelerate the wheel.

(e) The handlebars and stem must be fashioned in such a way as to present no danger. Their ends shall be solidly plugged to lessen the chance of injury. "Bull horn" or "Up-turned" handlebars are permitted only in individual and team pursuit, timed individual track events, and in team or individual road time trials.

1H3. For track races, only a bicycle with a single cog fixed wheel and without a brake, freewheel, derailleur, or wing-nuts shall be used except for an event organized as an individual record attempt, where the rider is alone on the track, a bicycle equipped with a freewheel and gears may be used (but without a brake or wing-nuts). For road races, only a bicycle with a freewheel and one working brake on each wheel shall be used, except as allowed elsewhere in these rules.

1H4. Tubular (i.e., sewup) tires may not be used in road races that are exclusively for riders with racing ages of 13 or less. However, riders in this age group may use tubular tires when competing with older riders.

1H5. In all cases where gear restrictions are specified, the only determining factor of a bicycle meeting the restriction shall be its development as measured by the roll-out test—the distance traveled by the bicycle in one revolution of the cranks with the tires inflated to racing pressure. The gear restriction in a given race shall be that of the least restricted class in the race. Maximum permissible developments are as follows, in meters and feet-inches:

Junior	Road		Track	
9-11	5.91 m.	19'5"	5.91 m.	19'5"
12-13	6.50	21'4"	6.40	21'0"
14-15	7.00	23'0"	6.80	22'4"
16-17	7.47	24'6"	7.07	23'2"

Gear restrictions for junior riders shall not apply at the Junior World Trials.

1H6. In roller races, either road or track bicycles may be used. All classes are restricted to a development of 7.69 meters (25 feet 3 inches) and cranks must be at least 165 mm. long.

1I. Competitors' Uniform

1I1. Every rider starting a race shall wear a protective, securely fastened helmet which meets or exceeds the safety standards of American National Standards Institute (ANSI) Standard Z90.4 (Protective Headgear for Bicycle Users) and/or Snell Memorial Foundation standards and which is clearly labeled by the manufacturer of such helmet with a label, approved by ANSI and/or Snell Memorial foundation, establishing that such helmet meets such standards. No form or part of a transmitting or receiving device may be fitted on or under the helmet.

1I2. The rider and uniform must be neat and clean at least at the beginning of a race. Helmets, shoes, or clothes that are torn, discolored, or in disrepair may not be used.

1I3. Racing jerseys shall cover the shoulders. Cycling shorts shall be black and shall reach to approximately mid-thigh. Cycling shorts may contain vertical colored panels on each side in domestic amateur races. One piece uniforms conforming to this color scheme may also be used. White socks or no socks may be worn.

1J. Start of a Race

1J3. Starts or the resumption of racing shall be signaled by a single gunshot or whistle. The starter alone judges the validity of the start. Stopping or neutralization of the race because of a false start or other conditions specified in the rules shall be signaled by a double gunshot or double whistle.

1J4. All competition shall be started in the same manner, either all with holders, all with one foot on the ground, or all with a rolling start. Holders may not step over the starting line at the start of a race.

1J5. Where a massed rolling start is used on the track, there shall be one or more neutral laps to ensure that the riders are sufficiently together to provide a fair start in the judgment of the starter.

1J6. If more than one massed start race is to be on the course simultaneously, starting intervals should be chosen so as to insure that different groups will not overlap.

1J7. Unless prevented by unavoidable circumstances, any riders qualifying for a reride or for any of the final rounds of a race shall start the reride or the next round. When qualification for the second round is based on time, if qualified riders are unable to start, they may be replaced by riders who had the next best times. No replacements are allowed after the second round.

1K. Finish of a Race

1K1. The finish of a race shall be judged when the front tire first penetrates the imaginary vertical plane passing through the leading edge of the finish line.

1K2. The beginning of the last lap of a race will be announced by ringing a bell and display of the lap card "1." In a road race, if the finish line is off the immediate course, the bell shall be sounded at the point of departure on the preceding lap.

1K3. Should the bell be rung by error at the wrong lap, the judges shall record the order of the finish at the end of that lap. The chief referee shall decide whether to declare these results final or to rerun some or all of the race. The chief referee may bar from the rerun any rider who appeared to have no chance to win a prize had the bell rung on the proper lap.

1K4. Dead Heats

(a) Should two or more riders make a dead heat for a qualifying place in a trial heat, they shall all be allowed to enter the final.

(b) In track races, should two or more riders make a dead heat for a place for which there is a prize, they may again ride the distance to decide the race or a shorter distance considered sufficient by the chief referee to allow for a fair settlement.

(c) In road races, should two or more riders make a dead heat for first place only, they shall reride the final sprint for 1,000 meters on road bicycles to determine the winner. If the dead heat is for any other place, the riders concerned shall be declared equal and the prizes for those places shall be added and equally divided or duplicated at the discretion of the promoter.

1K5. After the first competitor has finished, the chief referee may excuse one or more riders from completing the distance in order to secure a place which would clearly have been won by finishing. The chief referee may also excuse from completing the distance a rider who, by accident or withdrawal of others, is the only competitor left in the race.

1K6. At the end of the race, the chief judge will inform the riders of the time and place where the results will be posted or announced and the chief judge shall be available there to resolve any protests. Prizes may not be distributed until any protests have been answered and at least 15 minutes have passed since the results were announced.

1K7. In races consisting ordinarily of qualification, semifinal, and final rounds, the disqualification of a rider or team after the finals shall not change the placings of other riders. In other races, when a rider or team is removed from the placings by disqualification, any lower placed riders will be advanced to their next higher finishing place.

1L. Conduct of Licensees

1L1. No licensee shall benefit from his or her own misconduct, nor shall any team benefit from the misconduct of one of its members or support personnel.

1L2. A rider who has not covered the full course may not cross the finish line as a competitor for prize honors (disqualification and 30 days suspension).

1L3. Riders must follow a referee's order to withdraw from the race immediately (ten days suspension).

1L4. No licensee may use foul or abusive language or conduct during a race meet (15 days suspension).

1L5. No rider may make an abrupt motion so as to interfere with the forward progress of another rider, either intentionally or by accident (relegation or disqualification; possible 20 days suspension if a crash results).

1L6. Competitors may dismount at their pleasure, but must not interfere with other riders in so doing (disqualification and possibly ten days suspension).

1L7. Any rider who appears to present a danger to the other competitors may be disqualified by the chief referee either before or during a race.

1L8. Pushing or pulling among riders is prohibited in all races except the madison (relegation or disqualification).

1L9. Competitors may make no progress unaccompanied by a bicycle (relegation or disqualification). In case of a crash, they may run with their bicycles to the finish line, staying on the course.

1L10. A licensee may be penalized for causing a crash or spill through inadequate tightening or adjustment of a bicycle component, including gluing of tires (disqualification and ten days suspension).

1L11. A rider may not be on the track or course during a race in which he or she is not competing (relegation or disqualification).

2. ROAD RACING RULES

2A. Road Course

2A1. A road course may be from place to place, around a circuit, out and back, or any combination of these. The course shall not cross itself—there must be no chance that riders may have to cut through other groups of riders.

2A2. The start and finish of a road race shall be situated so as to cause the least possible inconvenience to other users of the road. The promoter shall insure that the arrangements for the race respect the law of the land and that proper notification of law enforcement agencies is accomplished.

2A3. Feeding stations and repair pits shall be located at points wide enough to allow passage of riders with one clear lane at all times. If possible, they should be situated on an uphill stretch with a wide shoulder. Feeding stations should be along the right side of the roadway unless the course is closed to traffic and it is not practical to use the right side.

2A4. A conspicuous marker shall denote the final kilometer. A white flag shall mark the point 200 meters from the finish.

2A5. The finishing area should be at least 8 meters wide and be adequately protected so as to prevent spectators from running into the street. The last 200 meters should be free of turns and curves.

2A6. The finish line shall be perpendicular to the race course. For any championship event it shall be a black line of uniform width between 4 and 6 cm. painted in the middle of a 72 cm. wide white stripe. Photofinish equipment must be aimed along the leading edge of the black line.

2A7. The promoter shall insure that feeding stations are correctly located, that police and marshal facilities have been established to insure the safety of the riders, and that preparations have been made for crowd control at the finish. If these conditions are not met, the chief referee may cancel the race.

2B. Riding Conduct

2B1. If a course is not closed to traffic, all competitors must keep to the right of the center line or enforcement line, but may pass on either side of another rider (warning for accidental crossing of the center line with no advance in position; relegation or disqualification for advancing position; ten days suspension for a flagrantly dangerous attack).

2B2. Riders shall of their own responsibility conform to all traffic regulations in force in the area where the race is held (relegation or disqualification and possibly ten days suspension).

2B3. It is forbidden to cross a closed railroad crossing or any other road closure (disqualification). Should the lead rider(s) be stopped by a temporary road closure, the chief referee shall neutralize the race and allow the riders to restart at the same time intervals as their arrival at the closure. Should the lead rider(s) get through before the closure or should circumstances not permit neutralization, the closure shall be considered an unforeseeable incident and no compensation shall be allowed.

2B4. The responsibility of keeping on the prescribed course rests with the rider. A rider may not leave the prescribed course unless ordered to do so by public authorities or a race official (disqualification).

2B5. Acceptance of pace or assistance from any outside means is forbidden, including taking pace from riders in a different race that is concurrently on the same course (relegation or disqualification).

2B6. Competitors who suffer a mishap may be assisted in remounting and may be pushed up to 10 meters (relegation or disqualification for excessive pushing).

2B7. Riders are permitted to start with feeding bottles or such refreshments as they wish to carry, but glass containers are strictly prohibited (disqualification).

2B8. When not otherwise prohibited, competitors may exchange food, drink, tires, tools, pumps, wheels, and bicycles among themselves. Such items may also be handed from a person on foot, but not directly from a moving vehicle (relegation or disqualification).

2B9. The passing of food or refreshments to competitors shall be at the discretion of the chief referee (relegation or disqualification for illegal feeding).

2C. Individual Road Race

2C1. If a circuit course is used for an individual road race, the distance should be at least 5 km. per lap.

2C2. Individual road races shall be massed start races, in which all riders start from the same mark, or handicap races, in which starting positions are assigned in accordance with past performance so as to give all riders an equal chance at winning.

2C3. A lapped rider or one who has fallen too far behind and is considered to be out of contention may be called off the course by the chief referee. Riders on different laps may not give or receive pace from one another. A lapped rider must not interfere in any prime sprint or finishing sprint and must ride sufficient laps at the end so as to cover the entire distance in order to qualify for a prize.

2C4. The chief referee may either permit or prohibit following vehicles.

2C5. Following vehicles are under the control of the chief referee. Failure to follow instructions or actions detrimental to the race may result in penalties against the personnel of the support vehicle, or competitors, or both.

2C6. Each vehicle associated with the race in any capacity should have on board a referee, who shall submit a written report detailing observed infractions of rules to the chief referee at the end of the race.

2D. Criterium

2D1. A criterium is a circuit race held on a small course entirely closed to traffic. The length of the course is normally 1 to 3 km.

2D2. The following are alternative methods for handling lapped riders in criteriums. The method chosen by the promoter with the chief referee must be clearly explained to the riders prior to the start of the race.

(a) A rider who has been lapped by the field or who falls so far behind as to be considered out of contention may be removed from the race by the chief referee.

(b) Alternatively, lapped riders may be permitted to remain in the race and all will finish on the same lap as the leaders. At the finish, these riders will be placed according to the number of laps they are down and then their position in the finish. It must be clearly specified whether or not lapped riders may sprint for primes. Riders on different laps may work with each other except that no rider may drop back to assist a rider who has broken away from the field (disqualification for accepting such assistance).

(c) In stage races, all riders finish on the same lap as the winner and each lapped rider will be given a time penalty which is that rider's average lap time multiplied by the number of laps the rider is down at the finish.

2D3. Free lap rule

Riders shall normally cover the distance of the race regardless of mishaps and must make up any distance lost on their own ability unless a free lap is granted for mishaps. When stipulated in the official race announcement ("Free lap rule applies"), a free lap may be granted for mishaps subject to the following rules:

(a) Bicycle inspection and repairs must be made in an official repair pit. Either an official following vehicle shall transport riders to a single repair pit, normally near the start/finish line, or riders must proceed in the direction of the race to the next repair pit. If no following vehicle is used, there should be repair pits at intervals of 1 km. around the course.

(b) There must be a referee stationed in each repair pit to determine if the mishap was a legitimate one and if the rider is entitled to a free lap. The referee must keep track of all riders who are granted free laps and submit a written report to the chief referee at the end of the race.

(c) A rider who is granted a free lap must return to the race in the position held at the time of the mishap. A rider who was in a group shall return at the rear of the same group the next time around.

(d) There will be no free laps granted in the last 8 km. of a race and no rider may have more than one free lap in any race. A rider who is ineligible for a free lap must make up any lost ground (disqualification and ten days suspension for fraudulent use of the free lap rule).

2D4. Primes are sprints within a race. They may be for the lead riders or any group or field of riders. A bell shall be sounded on the lap preceding the prime sprint at the appropriate line for that prime sprint. The line used for prime sprints need not be the same as the start or finish line. Primes may be either predetermined for certain laps or spontaneously designated under the supervision of the chief referee. All primes won shall be awarded to riders even if they withdraw from the race.

2E. Individual Time Trial

2E1. Courses may be out and back, around a circuit, or one way. Only out and back and circuit courses may be used for record purposes. A one-time out and back course or a circuit large enough for a single lap is ideal.

2E2. Road bicycles shall be used. Bicycles with a front hand brake and fixed wheel may also be used.

2E3. Starting times shall be at equal intervals, normally one minute.

2E4. Starting order may be chosen by random selection, by numeric order, by seeding (fastest last), or in stage races by inverse order of general classification.

2E5. If a rider appears later than the appointed starting time, the start will be allowed only if it does not interfere with other riders starting on schedule. If it does interfere, the rider may be further delayed. In case of a late start, the appointed time shall be used in computing the results.

2E6. The start sheet with starting order and appointed starting times should be available for riders' perusal at least one hour before the start.

2E7. The rider shall be held by an official at the start, but shall neither be restrained nor pushed.

2E8. On an out and back course, riders must stay to the right of the center line at all times. Failure to do so will result in disqualification.

2E9. No rider shall take pace behind another rider closer than 25 meters (80 feet) ahead, or 2 meters (7 feet) to the side. A rider who is observed taking pace shall receive a time penalty as specified in Table 1.

2E10. No restarts are permitted. In a stage race, a rider who suffers a mishap and does not finish may be assigned the time of the slowest rider who finishes. Alternatively, following vehicles may be permitted at the discretion of the chief referee. Any such vehicle must contain a referee.

2F. Team Time Trial

2F1. Teams may be made up of two or more riders. The distance, timing basis, and number of riders who are required to finish must be specified in the official race announcement. Times may be based on any specified finishing position or on the sum of the times of any specified finishers.

2F2. Courses may be out and back, around a circuit, or one way. Only out and back and circuit courses may be used for record purposes. A one-time out and back course or a circuit large enough for a single lap is ideal.

2F3. Only road bicycles shall be used.

2F4. The starting interval between teams will normally be at least two minutes, but may be increased according to the course.

2F5. Starting order may be chosen by random selection, by numeric order, by seeding (fastest last), or in stage races by inverse order of team general classification.

2F6. If a team appears later than the appointed starting time, the start shall be allowed only if it does not interfere with other teams starting on schedule. If it does interfere, the team may be further delayed. In case of a late start, the appointed time shall be used in computing results.

2F7. The riders from each team shall line up side by side at the start. All riders shall be held by officials at the start and shall neither be restrained nor pushed. When there are too few holders, all riders must start with one foot on the ground. All teams must start in the same manner. No restarts shall be permitted for any reason.

2F8. In championship events, teams shall consist of four riders and the team time is the time of the third rider. Thus, at least three riders must finish.

2F9. Teammates on different laps may not work together (entire team disqualified).

2F10. All pushing of riders is forbidden, even among teammates. Such pushing will result in the entire team being disqualified.

2F11. No team shall take pace behind another team closer than 25 meters (80 feet) ahead, or 2 meters (7 feet) to the side (time penalties in Table 1).

2F12. The exchange of food, drink, minor repair items, help with repairs and exchange of wheels or bicycles shall be permitted solely among members of the same team.

2F13. Each team may be followed by a car having no more than four people aboard: a driver and a referee in the front seat and possibly a coach and a mechanic in back. The car may carry up to four bicycles ready for use in case of a mishap. This car may also carry spare wheels and repair material.

2F14. Follow cars shall not be allowed in front of the team but must remain at least 20 meters (65 feet) behind the third rider and must not pass the fourth rider until there is a 75 meter gap between the third and fourth riders, or until the referee decides that it is safe.

2G. Stage Race

2G1. A stage race is a sequence of races, usually road races, criteriums, and time trials. Normally, the individual winner is the rider with the lowest cumulative time for all stages,

Table 1   Time Penalties for Time Trials

Time penalties for taking pace in time trial events are listed below in both metric and English units. These penalties, in seconds, are based on the estimated speed and distance over which the infraction occurred.

Speed (km/h)	Distance (meters)									
	100	200	300	400	500	600	700	800	900	1000
30	1	2	2	3	4	5	6	7	7	8
31	1	2	2	3	4	5	6	7	8	9
32	1	2	3	3	4	6	7	7	9	11
33	1	2	3	3	5	6	7	8	10	12
34	1	2	3	4	5	7	8	9	11	13
35	1	2	3	4	5	7	8	9	12	14
36	1	3	4	4	6	8	9	10	13	15
37	1	3	4	5	6	8	9	11	14	17
38	1	3	4	5	7	9	10	12	15	19
39	2	3	4	5	7	9	12	14	17	21
40	2	3	4	5	7	10	13	15	19	23
41	2	4	5	6	8	11	14	16	20	25
42	2	4	5	6	8	11	15	17	22	27
43	2	4	5	7	9	12	16	19	24	29
44	2	4	6	7	9	12	17	21	28	31
45	2	4	6	8	10	13	19	23	28	34
46	2	5	6	8	11	14	19	24	30	36
47	2	5	7	9	12	15	20	25	32	38
48	2	5	7	9	12	16	21	27	34	40
49	3	5	7	9	13	17	23	29	36	43
50	3	5	7	10	14	19	25	31	39	46
51	3	5	8	10	15	20	27	33	42	49
52	3	6	8	11	16	21	29	36	45	52
53	3	6	8	12	17	23	31	39	48	56
54	3	6	9	13	18	25	33	42	51	60
55	4	6	9	14	20	27	36	45	55	64
56	4	6	9	15	21	29	38	47	58	68
57	4	6	10	16	22	31	40	49	61	72
58	4	7	10	17	24	33	42	52	65	77
59	5	7	11	18	26	35	46	56	69	82
60	5	7	12	19	28	38	49	61	75	90

Speed (mph)	Distance (yards)									
	100	200	300	400	500	600	700	800	900	1000
20	1	2	3	3	4	6	7	7	9	11
21	1	2	3	4	5	7	8	9	11	13

Speed (mph)	Distance (yards)									
	100	200	300	400	500	600	700	800	900	1000
22	1	2	4	4	5	7	8	9	12	14
23	1	3	4	5	6	8	9	11	14	17
24	1	3	4	5	7	9	10	12	15	19
25	2	3	5	5	7	10	13	15	19	23
26	2	4	5	6	8	11	15	17	22	27
27	2	4	6	7	9	12	16	19	24	29
28	2	4	6	8	10	13	18	23	28	34
29	2	5	7	8	11	14	19	24	30	36
30	2	5	7	9	12	16	21	27	34	40
31	3	5	8	10	14	19	25	31	39	46
32	3	5	8	10	15	20	27	33	42	49
33	3	6	9	12	17	23	31	38	48	56
34	3	6	9	13	18	25	33	42	51	60
35	4	6	10	15	21	29	38	46	58	68
36	4	7	11	17	24	33	42	49	65	77
37	5	7	12	18	26	35	46	52	69	82
38	5	7	14	19	28	38	49	56	75	90
39	6	8	15	20	30	42	53	61	80	95
40	6	8	16	22	32	46	58	67	84	99

including bonuses and penalties. This cumulative time is referred to as "general classification." International stage races are required to have also points competition and team general classifications.

(a) Team general classification is based on the total times of the first three or more finishing riders of a given team in each stage, to which any bonuses or penalties are added.

(b) Point winners may be calculated on cumulative points earned for places in the stages. King or Queen of the Mountains may be awarded on points earned in selected sprints to the tops of climbs along the route. A Hot Spots award may be given on the basis of points earned in special sprints along the route.

2G2. Each stage shall have winners, and riders may receive prizes in each stage according to their order of finish.

2G3. Riders shall sign a control sheet before the start of each stage. At the completion of each stage riders may be required to sign a finish control sheet.

2G4. Time for the riders will be calculated to the nearest second. Riders finishing in a group will all be credited with the same time as the lead rider of that group.

2G5. Bonus times may be awarded to the first three riders in each stage, excluding time trials. The maximum bonuses allowable are: 30 seconds for first, 20 seconds for second, and 10 seconds for third. The bonuses are subtracted from the riders' times.

2G6. Riders must normally complete all previous stages in order to start the next stage. A rider suffering a mishap during a prologue who is delayed or prevented from finishing may start the next stage, but will be given the same finishing time as the slowest finisher in the prologue. A rider suffering a mishap in the final kilometer of the remaining stages who is delayed or prevented from finishing may be given the same time as would have been attained had the mishap not occurred.

2G7. Riders who do not finish a stage within 20% of the winner's time may be eliminated from the race by the referees. In extenuating circumstances, the chief referee may extend the time limit to as much as 50%.

2G8. In a team time trial stage every member of the team must complete the distance. Team time trial times are not normally included in individual general classifications.

2G9. In the case of a tie on general classification, the riders' sum of stage placings shall count to break the tie. If still tied, the tie shall be broken on the basis of the riders' placing in the final stage.

2G10. Race rules and particulars for the entire event must be printed on the official race description and all competitors shall be made aware of these particulars. The official race description shall include stage starts, finishes, highways used, mileage, road and terrain conditions, bonus times, points, scores, stage prizes (number and value), and special awards or competitions, and a listing of time penalties for various infractions. Results on general classification and from the preceding stage should be made available to riders at least one hour before the start of the next stage.

2G11. The appropriate racing rules will apply to each stage when not covered expressly under rules for stage races.

2H. Cyclocross

2H1. The course shall be over generally rough terrain of which no more than half shall be paved. The course shall be such that approximately 75% of it can be covered on a bicycle.

2H2. The length of a lap shall be at least 1 kilometer (0.6 miles). The first stretch of the course, immediately after the start, shall be of sufficient length and width to allow the field to string out properly before reaching the narrow part of the course and the obstacles.

2H3. The course should be at least 2 meters (7 feet) wide so that riders can pass at nearly all points. The course should be marked with arrows or cords to insure that it can be followed. Ditches and brooks should be no more than 1 meter across so that they can be jumped.

2H4. No artificial barrier shall exceed 40 cm. (16 inches) in height and the sole purpose of such obstacles is to oblige the rider to cover a certain distance on foot, without performing feats of acrobatics.

2H5. The number of equipment stations and pits shall be left to the discretion of the chief referee, who shall take into consideration the specific requirements of the course. They shall be set up at the most difficult points in such a way as not to hinder the race or endanger the participants. Riders may exchange equipment or bicycles only at these stations.

2H6. Normally, bicycles may be exchanged only in case of a puncture or mechanical mishap. In case course conditions are bad, the chief referee may authorize the changing of bicycles every lap.

2H7. Rules regarding lapped riders are the same as for criteriums.

2I. Cross-Country Time Trial

2I1. A cross-country time trial is an individual or team event from point to point, possibly including intermediate check points. The route between these points is normally not prescribed.

2I2. The course and starting times should be arranged so that competitors will be able to pass each other without having to take pace.

2I3. All riders shall be started in the same way, either held or with one foot on the ground. If a rider appears later than the appointed starting time, the start will be allowed only if it does not interfere with other riders starting on schedule; if it does interfere, the rider may be further delayed. In case of a late start, the appointed time shall be used in computing the results.

2I4. Each rider or team may be followed by a support vehicle or, if specified in the official race announcement, by two vehicles. Each vehicle shall carry a driver and a referee and shall be operated in accordance with the referee's instructions. Support vehicles shall normally stay at least 20 meters behind the nearest rider.

2I5. No rider shall take pace behind another rider other than a teammate closer than 25 meters ahead or 2 meters to the side. A rider who is observed taking pace shall receive a time penalty as specified in Table 1.

2I6. Riders shall obey all traffic regulations. Stage race penalties shall be assessed where applicable, in accordance with Rule 2G12. Riders shall lose any time lost as a result of apprehension for violations and in addition shall be assessed the following time penalties whether or not they are stopped:

(a) Passing through a stop sign without coming to a complete stop or crossing against a red light (two minute penalty),

(b) Following a road that is closed to bicycles (one minute per kilometer).

2I7. Feeding may be done in accordance with road race procedures or, where conditions permit in the judgment of the chief referee, from a motorcycle with a driver and a feeder.

2J. Track Events on the Road

Track events may also be run on the road. In such events the appropriate track rules shall apply, as interpreted by the chief referee.

3. TRACK RACING RULES

3A. Track Markings

All lines on the track shall be of uniform width between 4 and 6 cm.

3A1. The following shall be placed circumferentially around the track:

(a) The measurement line shall be black or white, to contrast with the track, and shall be placed with its inner edge 20 cm. from the inner edge of the track. It shall be marked off at every 5 meters and numbered at every 10 meters going counterclockwise from the finish line. The official length of the track is to be measured on the inner edge of this line.

(b) The sprinters line shall be red and shall be placed with its inner edge 90 cm. from the inner edge of the track.

(c) A blue band at least 20 cm. wide shall be placed below the inner edge of the track all the way around.

3A2. The following lines shall be placed perpendicular to the inner edge:

(a) The finish line shall be black and placed in the middle of a 72 cm. wide white strip, for contrast.

(b) The 200 meter line shall be either black or white, to contrast with the track, and shall be placed 200 meters before the finish line. This line is used for sprint timing only.

(c) Two pursuit finish lines shall be red and located exactly in the middle of the two straights, even with each other, and shall extend from the inner edge halfway across the track.

(d) Where the starting lines for 3 km. and 4 km. pursuit events do not coincide with other markings, they shall be red and shall extend from the lower edge of the track to the sprinters line.

(e) At intervals of 10 meters back from the finish line there shall be a yellow mark and a distance label. At the intervening 5 meter points there shall be a yellow half-mark.

3B. Riding Conduct

These rules apply to massed start, handicap, miss and out, madison, and points races.

3B1. Leaders must occupy the sprinters lane unless far enough in the lead as not to interfere with competitors seeking to pass. If the leader is below the sprinters line the following riders may not pass underneath (relegation or disqualification).

3B2. A competitor overtaking another must pass on the outside unless the rider ahead is riding above the sprinters line. A rider who passes another must not in any way impede the progress of the passed rider (relegation or disqualification).

3B3. In the homestretch on the last lap, the leader(s) must ride a straight line parallel to the edge of the track (relegation or disqualification).

3B4. In all races it is permissible to ride below the measurement line, but never below the track surface on the blue bank (relegation or disqualification).

3B5. When a rider has a crash that does not present a danger to the other riders, the race will not be neutralized. In case of a crash that causes a hazard to the other riders, the race may be neutralized by the starter. While the race is neutralized, all riders must ride slowly around the top of the track, maintaining their relative positions. Resumption of racing will be signaled by the starter when it becomes safe.

3B6. Riders who suffer a mishap may be assisted in restarting.

3C. Massed Start Race

3C1. A massed start race is one in which all riders start from the same point at the same time. The race shall be run over a specified number of laps and the riders classified according to the order in which they cross the line on the final lap.

3C2. Lapped riders not in contention are normally removed. When lapped riders are not removed, they will finish on the same lap as the leaders and shall be placed according to the number of laps they are down and then their position at the finish.

3D. Handicap Race

3D1. A handicap is a race in which the stronger riders are given either a greater distance to travel or a later start so as to equalize competition.

3D2. The starting positions or the time allowances must be announced to all participants before the start of the race. The official handicapper shall decide what distance or time allowance is to be granted to each competitor. The competitor must supply accurate information to the handicapper.

3D3. Starts will be made on the track itself unless the banking is too steep for safety, in which case the competitors shall start on the blue band.

3D4. If two or more riders are to start from the same point, they may be placed one after the other or side by side, whichever is safer. The holders may be allowed to run with their riders for a short distance at the start provided this is clearly stated before the race.

3D5. The starter shall be positioned so as to see all riders and may have an assistant with a flag to assist in observing a possible false start.

3E. Miss and Out

3E1. A miss and out (sometimes called "devil take the hindmost") is a massed start race in which the last rider over the line on designated laps is eliminated from the race. Riders may be eliminated every lap, every other lap, or on whatever regular schedule is stipulated before the race.

3E2. The back edge of the rear tire determines who is the last rider over the line.

3E3. The chief judge shall notify the last rider over the line. The rider shall withdraw with due caution as soon as it is practical.

3E4. If a rider does not come out as instructed, the chief referee may call one or more free laps until the rider has retired. (A rider who blatantly disregards instructions to leave the field shall be subject to disqualification from the remaining events in the meet and possible suspension).

3E5. The miss and out may be ridden to the last person or to a specified number of survivors. In the latter case, there may be a free lap followed by a conventional sprint, judged on the order of finish by the front wheels. The format to be used must be explained to all riders before the start of the race.

3F. Sprint

3F1. Sprints involve a series of races, each with a small number of riders, leading to a final. The structure of these races is chosen by the chief referee to meet the needs of the racing program for the number of riders.

3F2. The matching of riders in the qualifying and succeeding rounds should be done in such a way that the fastest riders meet in the final race. In National Championships, riders shall be seeded by the chief referee on the basis of their national and international placings in the current and preceding years.

3F3. Sprints are run over three laps on a track of 333.33 meters or less, or over two laps on a larger track.

3F4. The starting position of each rider shall be decided by the drawing of lots. The rider drawing the inside position shall lead the entire first lap at a minimum of a walking pace, except that if another rider chooses to take the lead then he assumes this obligation. Failure of the obligated rider to maintain a walking pace on the first lap will result in the race being stopped and restarted with the rider responsible leading in the reride. Should the race be run in two heats, each rider shall lead one heat. A further draw shall be made if a third and deciding heat proves necessary.

3F5. In National Championship events, heats in the qualifying round may include two to four competitors. Riders losing in a qualifying round will be given another chance in a repechage. Upon reaching the quarterfinals, each rider will advance upon winning two out of three sprints against an opponent. A competitor must be beaten twice in a single round in order to be eliminated. The four losers from the quarterfinals shall compete in a four-up race to determine fifth through eighth positions.

3F6. Once the start has been given and adjudged valid by the starter, the race shall not be stopped without a legitimate reason. Should any rider suffer a mishap at any time during the race, a restart shall be signaled by the starter unless it is obvious that at that moment the rider concerned had no chance to place. In a reride following a mishap, the starting positions of the riders are not changed. Should a race be stopped because of an apparent mishap that turns out to be not legitimate, the race will be restarted without the rider at fault.

3F7. The starter may stop a race if during a standstill a rider backs up by more than 20 cm. (8 inches). The starter shall stop a race should any standstill occur on the blue band, which is not part of the riding surface of the track, should any rider use the blue band as part of an acceleration maneuver to reach sprint speed, or should any rider touch the track surface or the outside fence or railing before the sprint has begun. (The rider responsible will lead the reride.)

3F8. Once the sprint has begun (the riders are moving at full speed or near full speed) no rider may make an abrupt motion that impedes the forward progress of another rider. The leader must always leave room on the outside for other riders to pass. If the leader is below the sprinters line, all following riders must pass on the outside. If the leader is riding above the sprinters line, following riders may pass on either side, wherever there is room.

3F9. A rider in a two-up sprint who intentionally causes a fall or who falls while attempting an illegal maneuver shall be disqualified. The wronged party shall be declared the winner without necessarily passing the finish line.

3F10. If one rider in a two-up heat defaults, the other must put in an appearance on the starting line in order to be declared the winner, but need not cover the distance.

3F11. In a sprint with three or more contestants, a rider may be disqualified for blocking, interfering with another rider, or deliberately causing a crash. Whenever such a situation is detected the race should be stopped, if not completed, and in any case shall be rerun without the rider responsible. In the case of an accidental collision before the sprint has begun, the race will be stopped by the starter and rerun with the original participants in the same starting positions.

3F12. In the case of a dead heat, the race will be rerun with only the riders who made the dead heat.

3G. Tandem Sprint

3G1. Tandem sprints shall be run over the integral number of laps nearest to 1,500 meters for the particular track.

3G2. Tandem sprint events on the track shall be run in accordance with sprint regulations.

3G3. In no case shall more than four tandems be raced together, or three on tracks smaller than 333 meters.

3H. Time Trial

3H1. Riders are timed over a fixed distance and compete one at a time. Starts may be either flying or standing, as specified. If a session is interrupted, all competitors must ride in a subsequent session.

3H2. In flying start events, two laps are permitted before timing starts.

3H3. Standing Start Events

(a) The rider shall be held by an official at the start and shall be neither restrained nor pushed. The starter shall insure that all riders start from exactly the same point, with the leading edge of their front wheels directly over the starting line and the bicycle not pointed up or down the track.

(b) In a kilometer time trial where the start and finish are adjacent and whenever automatic electronic timing is used, the following procedure shall be used. When the rider is ready, the starter shall blow the whistle to alert the timers that the start is imminent. The rider then has up to five seconds to start. Failure to do so may result in a restart. Timing is started when the front wheel of the bicycle moves over the line.

(c) When only hand timing is used or the start and finish of the race are not adjacent, the rider and the timing shall both start immediately with the starting signal.

3H4. In case of an apparent mishap, the officials must immediately determine the cause. If the mishap is verified, the rider is automatically entitled to a restart. Any rider intentionally causing a mishap shall be disqualified.

3H5. Any restart will be made after the next five riders have gone. If there are not five riders remaining, the restart shall be after ten minutes. A rider is permitted at most two restarts (that is, three starts).

3H6. Should two or more riders make the same time, they shall be placed equal.

3H7. The blue band shall be made impractical for riding by the placement of sponges 50 cm. by 8 cm. by 8 cm. in the turns at 5 meter intervals, 20 cm. below the lower edge of the measurement line.

3I. Individual Pursuit

3I1. Pursuit is a race between competitors who are started at equal intervals around the track and is run until one rider catches the others or until a certain distance is covered, as specified in advance. A rider catches another by overtaking and drawing even.

3I2. Australian pursuit is a race between two or more riders starting simultaneously at equal intervals around the track. A rider who is passed by any other rider must immediately retire. The race is run until one rider catches all the others.

3I3. Championship individual pursuit, treated below, is a race between two riders starting on opposite sides of the track and ending either when one rider catches the other or a certain distance is covered. The distances used are 3,000 meters for senior women and juniors and 4,000 meters for seniors. The rider who catches the other or covers the distance in the shortest time is the winner.

3I4. All timing shall be to 0.1 second or better. Both riders will be timed at half-laps throughout the race.

3I5. One person only may indicate a rider's position in relation to the other rider. That person may occupy a position before or after the finish line, but shall not make any rash gestures of encouragement.

3I6. A rider may not participate in more than two pursuit matches on the same day except in unavoidable circumstance which shall be decided by the chief referee. A minimum interval of two hours must be allowed between rides.

3I7. Qualifying Round

(a) The qualifying round is a time trial rather than a pursuit. A rider who catches another must continue and complete the distance for time, while the rider who is caught is automatically eliminated.

(b) The officials shall try for close competition by matching riders of approximately equal ability. In the first round the fastest riders shall start last.

(c) Should a rider who has qualified for the second round be prevented from riding for unavoidable circumstance, the officials may permit that rider's place to be taken by the rider who made the next best time in the qualifying round. No replacements are allowed after the second round.

3I8. Quarterfinals

(a) If quarterfinals are used, the eight fastest riders from the qualifying round shall be matched on the basis of their times as follows: 1st with 8th, 2nd with 7th, 3rd with 6th, 4th with 5th. The winners advance to the semifinals. The four losers from the quarterfinals shall be classified fifth through eighth based on the times they recorded in that round.

(b) A rider who catches an adversary shall complete the specified distance to record a time for the seeding of the semifinals.

3I9. Semifinals

If semifinals are used the four riders selected in the preceding round shall be matched on the basis of their times in that round as follows: 1st with 4th, 2nd with 3rd.

3I10. Finals

(a) If a semifinal is used, the winners of that round race for first and second and the losers race for third and fourth.

(b) If no semifinal is used, then the two fastest riders from the qualifying round race for first and second and the next two fastest race for third and fourth.

3I11. Equipment

(a) There shall be separate lap cards and a bell for each rider.

(b) A green disc shall be placed in the homestraight and a red disc in the backstraight exactly at the starting points of each rider. There shall be conspicuous markers 30 meters ahead of the starting point of each rider.

(c) A single green flag and a single red flag shall mark the first kilometer of each rider, respectively. A double green flag and a double red flag shall mark the last kilometer of each rider, respectively. These discs and flags permit the starter to determine the location of the rider for the purpose of calling restarts.

(d) The blue band shall be made impractical for riding by the placement of sponges 50 cm. by 8 cm. by 8 cm. in the turns at 5 meter intervals, 20 cm. below the lower edge of the measurement line.

3I12. Starts

(a) The two riders shall be positioned to start on the inside of the track diametrically opposite each other. If the track has an integral number of half-laps to the kilometer, this will be at the red lines in the center of the straights.

(b) The start shall be by gunshot. The starter and assistant starter shall be in the center of the track. The riders shall be held by officials and neither restrained nor pushed. The same two officials shall hold all riders except in the case of unavoidable circumstance. The referees located at each starting point shall insure that all riders start in exactly the same manner, with the front part of their front wheel directly over the starting line and the bicycle not pointed up or down the track. They put up a flag when the rider is ready.

(c) A false start shall be called by the starter within the first 30 meters should either rider move forward before the gun is fired or if either rider is pushed.

(d) Each rider is allowed two rerides only for false starts or mishaps. Therefore, a rider is entitled to three starts only.

3I13. Mishaps

(a) The officials must immediately determine the cause for stoppage and whether or not a legitimate mishap has occurred.

(b) Qualifying round: If either rider has a mishap the other rider shall continue the time trial. The rider suffering the mishap shall ride at the end of the qualifying round, either alone or against another rider who has suffered a mishap.

(c) Quarterfinal, semifinal, or final: If either rider has a mishap in the first kilometer, the race will be stopped and entirely rerun.

If a mishap occurs after the first kilometer but before the last, the race will be stopped and restarted with both riders positioned relative to the last half-lap lines they crossed; the race leader will be on the line and the other rider a distance back of the line equivalent to the gap in seconds, given by

$B = G \times D/S$ where

B = Distance back of the half-lap line for the slower rider,

G = Gap in seconds between the time of the faster and slower rider at the last completed half-lap,

D = Distance completed up to the last half-lap,

S = Time of the slower rider at the last half-lap.

If either rider suffers a mishap in the last kilometer, the starter shall stop the race and the times at the preceding half-lap shall be used to decide the winner. Should the lead rider have a mishap in the last kilometer of the quarterfinals, this rider's average speed will be used to calculate a time to allow a fair placement in the semifinal, where the formula for the corrected time is:

$C = L \times R/D$ where

C = Corrected time for the lead rider,

L = Time of the lead rider up to the last completed half-lap,

R = Total distance of the race,

D = Completed distance up to the last half-lap.

3I14. Finish

(a) Quarterfinal: A rider who catches the other must complete the distance to record a time so as to be properly placed in the semifinal. The rider who was caught is eliminated.

(b) Semifinal or final: If one rider passes the other the starter shall signal the end of the race.

(c) In all rounds, if neither rider catches the other, then a single gunshot shall be fired when the first rider finishes and another fired when the second rider finishes.

(d) If both riders have the same time at the finish, the riders shall be placed according to the better time at the end of the next-to-last lap, followed by the previous lap, etc.

3J. Team Pursuit

(The official rules include the rules for pursuit teams, made up of two or more riders.)

3K. Points Race

3K1. A points race is a massed rolling start race in which sprints for points are held on certain laps as designated by the promotor, usually every five laps. (The official rules include the rules for points races.)

3L. Madison

A madison is a points race between teams of two or three riders who relay each other for a specified distance or time. (The official rules include the rules for madison races.)

3M. Omnium

3M1. An omnium is a set of races in which riders compete for points in each event and final placings are determined by total points in all events. Different numbers of points may be given in different events. The scoring scheme shall be specified in the official race announcement. In National Championship Omniums, the points awarded in each event shall be 7-5-3-2-1 for first through fifth places.

3M2. In case of a tie on total points, the tie will be broken in favor of the rider who has:

(a) The most finishes at the highest placing among the tied riders, or if still tied,

(b) The highest placing in the last race, or the race nearest the last race of the omnium in which at least one of the tied riders placed.

GOVERNING BODY

United States Cycling Federation, Inc., 1750 E. Boulder St., Colorado Springs, CO 80909

The U.S. Cycling Federation (USCF) is a member of the U.S. Olympic Committee and is an official member of the International Amateur Cycling Federation (FIAC), which is the amateur arm of the International Cycling Union (UIC). The USCF is also allied with the International Human Powered Vehicle Association (IHPVA) and the National Off-Road Bicycle Association (NORBA). The primary purpose of the Federation is the preservation, development, and administration of the sport of bicycle racing within the United States. Major functions of the Federation include (a) conducting or coordinating programs for all aspects of amateur and professional bicycle racing competition, (b) establishing rules to govern the conduct of bicycle racing, (c) conducting programs to assist riders in the development of their competitive skills, (d) conducting national championships and selecting teams to represent the United States in international and Olympic competition; and (e) representing bicycle racing in the USA to other national, international, and Olympic sports organizations.

MAGAZINES

Bicycling, Rodale Press, Inc., 33 E. Minor St., Emmaus, PA 18049

Cycle, Box 2776, Boulder, CO 80323

• DARTS •

AMERICAN DARTS ORGANIZATION
TOURNAMENT RULES

(Reproduced by permission of American Darts Organization*)

☐

GLOSSARY OF TERMS

The following terms/meanings shall apply when used in the body of these Tournament Rules.

ADO: American Darts Organization
Match: The total number of Legs being competed for between two players/teams
Leg/Game: That element of a Match recognized as a fixed odd number, i.e., 301/501/1001
Scorer: Scorekeeper, Marker or Chalker
Cork: Bullseye or Bull
Masculine: Masculine gender nouns or pronouns shall include female
Singular: Singular terms shall, where necessary, include the plural

PLAYING RULES

All darts events played under the exclusive supervision of and/or sanctioned by the ADO, shall be played in accordance with the following rules.

GENERAL

1. All players/teams shall play by these Tournament Rules and, where necessary, any supplemental Rules stipulated by local Tournament Organizers.

2. Any player/team who, during the course of any event, fails to comply with any of these Tournament Rules, shall be subject to disqualification from that event.

3. The interpretation of these Tournament Rules, in relation to a specific darts event, shall rest with the local Tournament Organizers, whose decisions shall be final and binding. Protests after the fact shall not be considered.

4. Good sportsmanship shall be the prevailing attitude throughout the tournament.

5. Gambling is neither permitted nor sanctioned by the ADO.

6. The ADO will, in the course of Tournament Sanctioning, ensure, to the best of its ability, that the host/sponsor organization for a darts event has the funding and/or sponsorship necessary to support the advertised cash prize structure for same. The manner and matter of tournament prize payments shall be the responsibility of the respective host/sponsor organization and not that of the ADO.

7. The ADO assumes no responsibility for accident or injury on the premises.

---

*See page 197 for additional information.

8. The ADO reserves the right to add to or amend, any, or all, of the ADO Tournament Rules, at any time for any purpose deemed necessary at that time.

PROCEDURAL

9. Decisions regarding the prize structure and event schedule, the method of player registration, and the choice of the match pairing system, shall be left to the discretion of the local Tournament Organizers.

10. Nine darts warm-up is the maximum allowance per player.

11. Tournament boards are reserved for assigned match pairings only. Boards are not to be used for practice, unless so designated by the Tournament Organizers.

12. Match pairings will be called 3 times only (minimum of 5 minutes between calls). Should a player/team fail to report to the assigned board within 15 minute allotted time, a Forfeit will be called.

13. Players and Scorers ONLY are allowed inside the playing area.

14. Opposing players must stand at least 2 feet behind the player at the Hockey.

THROW

15. All darts must be thrown by, and from, the hand.

16. A Throw shall consist of three darts, unless a Leg/Match is completed in a lesser amount.

17. Any dart bouncing off, or falling out of the dartboard, shall not be rethrown.

STARTING AND FINISHING

ALL EVENTS

18. All Matches will be begun by THROWING THE CORK. The player throwing the Cork 1st will be decided by a coin flip, with the winner having the option of throwing 1st or 2nd. The player throwing closest to the Cork shall throw first in the 1st Leg. The Loser of the 1st Leg has the option of throwing the Cork first in the 2nd Leg. If a 3rd Leg is necessary, the Cork will again be thrown, with the loser of the original coin flip having the option of throwing first for the Cork.

19. The second thrower may acknowledge the first dart as an inner or outer Bull (Cork) and ask for that dart to be removed prior to his throw. The dart must remain in the board in order to count. Additional throws may be made when throwing the Cork, until such time as the player's dart remains in the board. Should the 2nd thrower dislodge the dart of the 1st, a rethrow will be made with the 2nd thrower now throwing first. Rethrows shall be called if the scorer cannot decide which dart is closest to the Cork, or if both darts are anywhere in the outer bull. Decision of the scorer is final. Should a rethrow be necessary, the person who shot 2nd will now shoot 1st.

20. In all events, each Leg shall be played with a Straight Start (no double required), and a double will be required to finish, unless otherwise stated by the local Tournament Organizers.

21. For the purpose of starting and finishing a Leg/Match, the INNER BULL is considered a double 25.

22. The 'BUST RULE' shall apply. (If the player scores one less, equal, or more points than needed to reach zero, he has "busted." His score reverts back to the score required prior to the beginning of his throw.)

23. Fast finishes such as 3 in a bed, 222, 111, shanghai, etc., do not apply.

24. A Leg/Match is concluded at such time as a player/team hits the 'double' required to reduce their remaining score to zero. Any and all darts thrown subsequently, shall not count for score.

DOUBLES/TEAM EVENTS

25. It is permissible for the Doubles/Team player finishing a Leg, to throw the Cork and start the subsequent Leg. It is also permissible for one member of a Doubles or Team to throw the Cork 1st, and have his partner or teammate shoot first.

26. It is permissible for a Doubles or Team to participate with fewer than the required number of players, provided that team forfeits a turn(s) in each rotation, equal to the number of missing players. The missing player(s) may NOT join a Leg in progress, but is allowed to participate in subsequent Leg(s) of that Match.

27. No player may participate on more than one Doubles or Team, in any respective darts event. There shall be NO recycling of players (either male or female) under any circumstances.

28. No substitutes shall be allowed after the first round of Doubles/Team play.

SCORING

29. For a dart to score, it must remain in the board 5 seconds after the 3rd or final dart has been thrown by that player. The tip of the dart point must be touching the bristle portion of the board, in order for that dart to be counted as score.

30. No dart may be touched by the thrower, another player, scorer, or spectator, prior to the decision of the scorer.

31. A dart's score shall be determined from the side of the wire at which the point of the dart enters the board.

32. It is the responsibility of the player to verify his score before removing his darts from the board. The score remains as written if one or more darts has been removed from the board. Errors in arithmetic must stand as written, unless corrected prior to the beginning of that player's next throw. In case of Doubles/Team matches, such errors must be rectified prior to the next turn of any partner/player on that team.

33. In Doubles/Team events, no player may throw (during a Leg) until each of his teammates has completed his throw. The FIRST player throwing out of turn shall receive a score of ZERO points for that round and his Team shall FORFEIT such turn.

34. The Scorer shall mark the board so that scores made are listed in the outer columns of the scoreboard, and the totals remaining are listed in the two middle columns.

35. The scoreboard/sheet must be clearly visible in front of the player at the Hockey.

36. The Scorer may inform the thrower what he has scored and/or what he has left. He MAY NOT inform the thrower what he has left in terms of number combinations. It IS permissible for a partner, teammate, or spectator to advise the thrower during the course of a Match.

EQUIPMENT

DARTS

37. Darts used in tournament play shall not exceed an overall maximum length of 30.5 cm (12 in.), nor weigh more than 50 gm per dart. Each dart shall consist of a recognizable point, barrel, and flight.

DARTBOARD

38. The dartboard shall be a standard 18'' bristle board, of the type approved by the ADO (Sportcraft/Nodor), and shall be of the standard 1–20 clock pattern.

International Dartboard

Double score
(Twice the number)

Single score
(Face value)

Triple score
(triple the score)

Inner bull
(Double 25 or
50 points)

Outer bull
(25 points)

Out of play area
(no score)

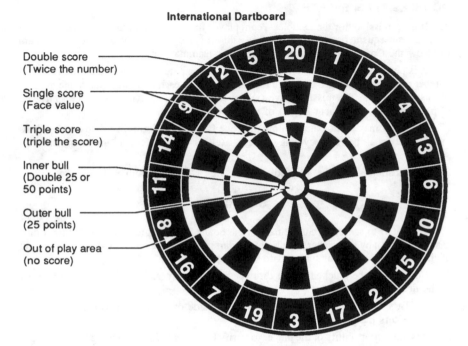

STANDARD DIMENSIONS

Double and triple rings inside width measurement	= 8 mm. (0.3125 ins)
Inner bull inside diameter	= 12.7 mm. (0.5 ins)
Outer bull inside diameter	= 31 mm. (1.25 ins)
Outside edge of double wire to center bull	= 170 mm. (6.75 ins)
Outside edge of triple wire to center bull	= 117 mm. (4.25 ins)
Outside edge of double wire to outside edge of double wire	= 342 mm. (13.5 ins)
Overall dartboard diameter	= 457 mm. (18.0 ins)
Spider wire gauge (maximum standard wire guage)	= 16 SWG.

39. The scoring wedge indicated by 20 shall be the darker of the two wedge colors and must be the top center wedge.

40. No alterations/accessories may be added to the board setups.

41. The inner narrow band shall score 'Triple' the segment number and the outer narrow band shall score 'Double' the segment number.

42. The outer center ring shall score '25' and inner center ring shall score '50' and shall be called the 'Bull.'

43. The minimum throwing distance shall be 7'9 1/4". The board height shall be 5'8" (floor to center bull; 9'7 1/2" measured diagonally from the center bull to the back of the raised hockey at floor level).

LIGHTING

44. Lights must be affixed in such a way as to brightly illuminate the board, reduce to a minimum the shadows cast by the darts, and not physically impede the flight of a dart.

HOCKEY

45. Whenever possible, a raised hockey, at least 1 1/2" high and 2' long, shall be placed in position at the minimum throwing distance, and shall measure from the back of the raised hockey 7'9 1/4" along the floor to a plumb line at the face of the dartboard.

46. Should a player have any portion of his feet or shoes over the hockey line during a throw, all darts so thrown shall be counted as part of his throw, but any score made by said darts shall be invalid and not counted. One warning by the official shall be considered sufficient before invoking this rule.

47. A player wishing to throw a dart, or darts, from a point either side of the hockey line, must keep his feet behind an imaginary straight line extending from either side of the hockey line.

SCOREBOARD

48. A scoreboard must be mounted within 4' laterally from the dartboard and at not more than a 45 degree angle from the dartboard.

ADO AMERICAN CRICKET RULES

All darts events played under the exclusive supervision of and/or sanctioned by the ADO, shall be played in accordance with established ADO Tournament Rules. In addition, the following rules shall apply for ADO Sanctioned Cricket events, effective January 1, 1984.

1. The objective shall be to 'own'/'close' certain numbers on the board, and to achieve the highest point score. The player/team to do so first, shall be the winner.

2. Cricket shall be played using the numbers 20, 19, 18, 17, 16, 15 and both the inner and outer bull (cork).

3. Each player/team shall take turns in throwing. (Three darts in succession shall constitute a 'turn'/'inning.')

4. To close an inning, the player/team must score three of a number. This can be accomplished with three singles, a single and a double, or a triple.

5. Once a player/team scores three of a number, it is 'owned' by that player/team. Once both players/teams have scored three of a number, it is 'closed,' and no further scoring can be accomplished on that number by either player/team.

6. To close the bullseye, the outer bull counts as a single, and the inner bull counts as a double.

7. Once a player/team closes an inning, he/they may score points on that number until the opponent also closes that inning. All numerical scores shall be added to the previous balance.

8. Numbers can be 'owned' or 'closed' in any order desired by the individual player/team. Calling your shot is not required.

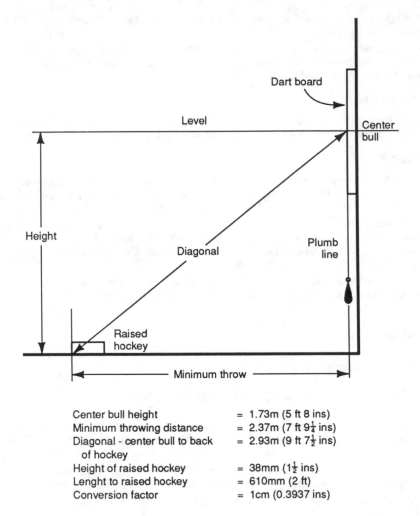

Center bull height	= 1.73m (5 ft 8 ins)
Minimum throwing distance	= 2.37m (7 ft 9¼ ins)
Diagonal - center bull to back of hockey	= 2.93m (9 ft 7½ ins)
Height of raised hockey	= 38mm (1½ ins)
Lenght to raised hockey	= 610mm (2 ft)
Conversion factor	= 1cm (0.3937 ins)

9. For the purpose of 'owning' a number, the double and triple ring shall count as 2 or 3, respectively. Three marks will close an inning.

10. After a number is 'owned' by a team, the double and triple ring shall count as 2 or 3 times the numerical values, respectively.

11. Winning the game:

a. The player/team that closes all innings first and has the most points, shall be declared the winner.

b. If both sides are tied on points, or have no points, the first player/team to close all innings shall be the winner.

c. If a player/team closes all innings first, and is behind in points, he/they must continue to score on any innings not closed until either the point deficit is made up, or the opponent has closed all innings.

12. It shall be the responsibility of the player to verify his score before removing his darts from the board. The score remains as written if one or more darts has been removed from the board. In accordance with the inherent "strategy" involved in the Cricket game, no alterations in score shall be allowed, after the fact.

AMERICAN DARTS ORGANIZATION
APPROVED 8/19/83
REVISED 8/14/86

GOVERNING BODY

American Darts Organization, 13841 Eastbrook Ave., Bellflower, CA 90706

The American Darts Organization, Inc. (ADO) is a member of the World Darts Federation and, as such, is recognized as the official darts body of the USA. In addition to standardizing tournament rules and equipment, the functions of the ADO include (a) coordination of tournaments and functions of its affiliated associations, leagues, and dart clubs on a national basis; (b) maintaining a national darts tournament calendar; (c) sanctioning tournaments; (d) promoting international competition and representing America; (e) providing advice and counseling to sponsoring firms of local, regional, and national darts tournaments; (f) developing a national youth movement in darts competition; and (g) providing awards programs. ADO membership provides for individual as well as organizational membership. The by-laws of the ADO dealing with its organizational structure and functions are available through the organization.

MAGAZINES

Double Eagle, ADO, 13841 Eastbrook Ave., Bellflower, CA 90706

• DIVING •

OFFICIAL DIVING RULES AND REGULATIONS
OF UNITED STATES DIVING, INC.
1985-86

(Reproduced by permission of United States Diving, Inc.*)

☐

Note: The United States Diving Rules and Regulations consist of four parts including: (1) Technical Rules of Competition, (2) Code of Regulations of the Organization, (3) Athletes and Athletic Events, (4) Disciplinary Proceedings and Athletes' Rights. Due to the lengthiness of the rules, selected portions are included here.

COMPETITIVE AND TECHNICAL RULES

The following rules shall govern United States Diving Championships and all other diving competitions held under the sanction of United States Diving and the various Local Diving Committees. These rules likewise have been adopted generally, as the diving rules of the National Collegiate Athletic Association, the National Association for Girls and Women in Sport and the National Association of Intercollegiate Athletics. These rules with some amendments are practically the same as the Federation Internationale de Natation Amateur (FINA) diving rules.

ARTICLE 1: THE DIVING POOL

101.1. Facility Requirements

(a) For the United States Diving Championships, including Preliminary Meets, the springboard diving equipment shall consist of not less than two (2) one meter and two (2) three meter springboards. The height of the high platform must be 10 meters. The intermediate platforms may be from 5 to 7-1/2 meters.

For all other classifications of diving competition (e.g., Regional, Association, Invitational, etc.) it is not necessary to have more than one one meter and one three meter springboard.

(b) The United States Diving Site Selection Committee must approve the diving facilities and equipment before acceptance of a bid for a United States Diving Championship. A written report of the nature of the diving facilities and equipment shall be delivered to the National Office by certified mail 120 days before the day the bid is to be presented at the Annual Meeting. In the event that there are not more than two site applications, the committee has the prerogative to use an alternative procedure to secure additional applications.

---

*See page 213 for additional information.

(c) All Diving equipment so approved by the Committee chairman shall be inspected one week before the United States Diving Championships by the Meet Director or his appointed representative. The facilities shall not be changed or altered after inspection except when a springboard is broken or should repair be necessary.

(d) Diving facility requirements for other Diving competitions are the same except as to the specific number of springboards and need of platform. Whenever there are more than 125 competitors entered in a diving meet, it is recommended that two or more one meter and three meter springboards be available.

101.2. Equipment Regulations for Springboard

(a) The springboards shall be one meter and three meters above the water level. Variations not exceeding five percent on the one meter springboard and two percent on the three meter springboard are permissible. The springboard shall be 20 inches wide and 16 feet long, and shall be covered along the whole length with an adequate nonskid material.

(b) The front edge of the board shall project at least five feet, and preferably six feet beyond the edge of the pool.

(c) It is recommended that all diving boards be set up and maintained according to requirements, especially with regard to elevation and pitch. Diving boards approved by United States Diving shall be used in all springboard competitions. A mechanically adjustable fulcrum of a type readily adjustable between dives shall be required for both the one meter and three meter standards. Manufacturers' specifications should be followed for all springboards and fulcrum location of dimension of fulcrum to anchor should comply with the usable dimensions of the diving board to allow proper function of the board. No two types of diving boards will use the same fulcrum minimums. It is recommended by United States Diving that the diving boards should be approximately level at the tip (over the water) when the fulcrum is at a midpoint along the track.

(d) It is recommended that three meter springboard stands be equipped with safe guardrails that extend at least to the pool edge and will prevent divers from falling off the board onto the deck at the sides.

(e) The depths of water shall be in accordance with Recommended Dimensions of Diving Facilities.

(f) Mechanical surface agitation is recommended under the diving boards to aid the divers in their visual perception of the pool.

101.3. Equipment Regulation for Platform

(a) The platform must not move, shall be at least 20 feet long and 6 1/2 feet wide, and covered with cocoa matting or other non-slip surface material as approved by United States Diving. Platform dimensions, heights and clearances shall be in accordance with the Recommended Dimensions of Diving Facility of these rules. The back and the sides of each platform level must be surrounded by safe guardrails that will prevent divers from falling off the platform onto the deck. Each level shall be accessible from the ground by suitable stairs. It is necessary that the surface of the water be agitated so that it may be distinguished easily by the diver.

(b) The height of the high platform must be 10 meters. The intermediate platforms may be from 5 meters to 7 1/2 meters. (*Note*: The degrees of difficulties for platforms of 5 to 6 meters will be the same and degrees of difficulties for platforms of 6 1/2 to 7 1/2 meters will be the same.)

(c) The depths of the water shall comply with or exceed the dimensions listed in the table and as shown in the diagram.

RECOMMENDED DIMENSIONS FOR DIVING FACILITIES

Measurements listed in meters.

Revised to 1 Jan. 1981

		Dimension	SPRINGBOARD 1 Meter Horz.	1 Meter Vert.	3 Meters Horz.	3 Meters Vert.	PLATFORM 1 Meter Horz.	1 Meter Vert.	3 Meters Horz.	3 Meters Vert.	5 Meters Horz.	5 Meters Vert.	7.5 Meters Horz.	7.5 Meters Vert.	10 Meters Horz.	10 Meters Vert.
		Length	4.80		4.80		4.50		5.00		6.00		6.00		6.00	
		Width	0.50		0.50		0.60		1.50		1.50		1.50		2.00	
		Height	1.00		3.00		0.60-1.00		2.60-3.00		5.00		7.50		10.00	
A	From plummet BACK TO POOL WALL	Designation / Minimum / Preferred	A-1 / 1.50 / 1.80		A-3 / 1.50 / 1.80		A-1 pl / 0.75		A-3 pl / 1.25		A-5 / 1.25		A-7.5 / 1.50		A-10 / 1.50	
AA	From plummet BACK TO PLATFORM plummet directly below	Designation / Minimum / Preferred									AA 5/1 / 0.75 / 1.50		AA 7.5/3/1 / 0.75 / 1.50		AA 10/5/3/1 / 0.75 / 1.50	
B	From plummet to POOL WALL AT SIDE	Designation / Minimum / Preferred	B-1 / 2.50		B-3 / 3.50		B-1 pl / 2.30		B-3 pl / 2.90		B-5 / 4.25		B-7.5 / 4.50		B-10 / 5.25	
C	From plummet to ADJACENT PLUMMET	Designation / Minimum / Preferred	C-1/1 / 2.40		C-3/3/1 / 2.60		C-1/1 pl / 1.65; 1/3 pl / 2.10		C-3/1 pl/3 pl / 2.10		C-5/3/1 / 2.50		C-7.5/5/3/1 / 2.50		C-10/7.5/5/3/1 / 2.75	
D	From plummet to POOL WALL AHEAD	Designation / Minimum / Preferred	D-1 / 9.00		D-3 / 10.25		D-1 pl / 8.00		D-3 pl / 9.50		D-5 / 10.25		D-7.5 / 11.00		D-10 / 13.50	
E	On plummet to BOARD TO CEILING	Designation / Minimum / Preferred		E-1 / 5.00		E-3 / 5.00		E-1 pl / 3.50		E-3 pl / 3.50		E-5 / 3.50		E-7.5 / 3.50		E-10 / 3.50 / 5.00
F	CLEAR OVERHEAD behind and each side of plummet	Designation / Minimum / Preferred		F-1 / 2.50		F-3 / 2.50		F-1 pl / 2.75		F-3 pl / 2.75		F-5 / 2.75		F-7.5 / 2.75		F-10 / 2.75
G	CLEAR OVERHEAD ahead of plummet	Designation / Minimum / Preferred		G-1 / 5.00		G-3 / 5.00		G-1 pl / 5.00		G-3 pl / 5.00		G-5 / 5.00		G-7.5 / 5.00		G-10 / 6.00
H	DEPTH OF WATER at plummet	Designation / Minimum / Preferred		H-1 / 3.60 / 3.80		H-3 / 3.80 / 4.00		H-1 pl / 3.40 / 3.60		H-3 pl / 3.60 / 3.80		H-5 / 3.80 / 4.00		H-7.5 / 4.10 / 4.50		H-10 / 4.50 / 5.00
J-K	DISTANCE and DEPTH ahead of plummet	Designation / Minimum / Preferred	J-1 / 5.00	K-1 / 3.50 / 3.70	J-3 / 6.00	K-3 / 3.70 / 3.90	J-1 pl / 5.00	K-1 pl / 3.30 / 3.50	J-3 pl / 6.00	K-3 pl / 3.50 / 3.70	J-5 / 6.00	K-5 / 3.70 / 3.90	J-7.5 / 8.00	K-7.5 / 4.00 / 4.40	J-10 / 11.00	K-10 / 4.25 / 4.75
L-M	DISTANCE and DEPTH each side of plummet	Designation / Minimum / Preferred	L-1 / 2.50	M-1 / 3.50 / 3.70	L-3 / 3.25	M-3 / 3.70 / 3.90	L-1 pl / 2.05	M-1 pl / 3.30 / 3.50	L-3 pl / 2.65	M-3 pl / 3.50 / 3.70	L-5 / 4.25	M-5 / 3.70 / 3.90	L-7.5 / 4.50	M-7.5 / 4.00 / 4.40	L-10 / 5.25	M-10 / 4.25 / 4.75
N	MAXIMUM SLOPE TO REDUCE DIMENSIONS beyond full requirements	Pool depth — 30 degrees; Ceiling Ht. — 30 degrees														

NOTE: Minimum dimensions "C" (plummet to adjacent plummet) apply for Platforms of minimum widths. For wider Platforms increase "C" by half the additional width(s).***

The dimensions and measurements set forth are provided by FINA and are intended for informational purposes only. USD does not warrant the accuracy or safety of these dimensions. Potential users of this information should consult qualified engineers to determine safe dimensions for intended uses of aquatic facilities.

Diving 201

DIAGRAMS OF A DIVING FACILITY

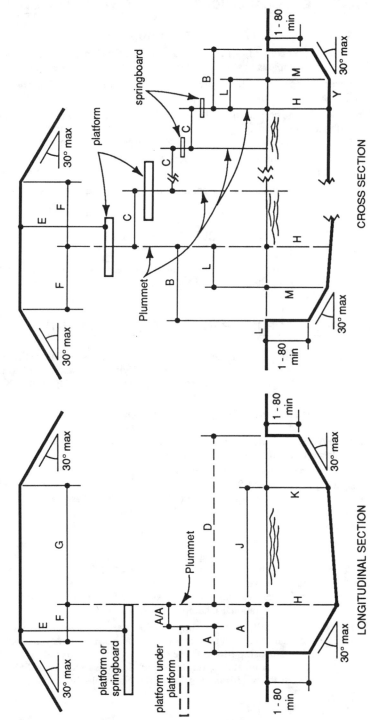

CROSS SECTION

LONGITUDINAL SECTION

ARTICLE 2: CLASSIFICATIONS OF DIVING COMPETITION

102.1. Senior Competitions are for All Registered Athletes:

(a) International Competition, (b) United States Championships, (c) Preliminary Meets, (d) Association Championships, (e) Invitational Meets, (f) Dual Meets.

102.2. Junior Olympic Competitions are for All Registered Athletes Seventeen (17) (sometimes 18) Years of Age and Under:

(a) International Competition, (b) United States Junior Olympic Championships, (c) Zone Championships, (d) Regional Championships, (e) Association Championships, (f) Invitational Meets, (g) Dual Meets, (h) Novice Meets (Ages 18 and Under).

102.3. Masters Competitions are for All Registered Athletes Twenty-one (21) Years of Age and Over:

(a) National Championships, (b) Regional Meets, (c) Association Meets, (d) Invitational Meets.

ARTICLE 3: SEASONS

103.1. Unless otherwise determined by United States Diving, June 1 to September 30 shall be considered as the Outdoor season and all the other months of the year as the Indoor season for all classifications of Diving.

ARTICLE 4: SPECIAL REQUIREMENTS FOR PARTICIPATION

104.1. In order to participate in any diving competition sanctioned by United States Diving, Inc., a diver must present a current United States Diving registration card to the Meet Director or proof of registration by letter or telegram from the Registration Chairman of their Local Diving Committee or Association if requested.

104.2. Divers who are citizens of foreign countries living in the United States and permitted by their FINA governing body to hold a United States Diving registration card, are eligible to compete in Association, Regional and Invitational Meets but must as United States Diving members adhere to all United States Diving rules.

104.3. Divers who are resident citizens of foreign countries, or who are citizens of foreign countries living in the United States registered as amateurs with the governing body of the country they represent as per FINA rules may compete in Association, Regional and Invitational meets so long as they have a valid International travel permit from their FINA governing body.

104.4. One man and one woman in each event who are registered and training in the state of Alaska or Hawaii are eligible to compete in the Semi-finals of the Senior United States Diving Championships without attending a Preliminary meet. These divers must be designated by the General Chairman of their respective state's Local Diving Committee (LDC) and must submit their qualifications for approval to the Diving Rules Chairman not less than 30 days prior to the National Championships.

104.5. For National Junior Olympic Championships, one male and one female diver per age group registered and training in the states of Alaska and Hawaii may compete without attending a Zone Championship Meet. These divers must be designated by the President of their respective Association and submit their qualifications to the Rules Subcommittee Chairman no less than thirty (30) days prior to the National Championships.

ARTICLE 5: DIVING LIST

105.1. Only those dives listed in the Official Diving Table may be performed in competition.

105.2. No dive, whether it be a required dive, a voluntary dive with limit or an optional dive, may be repeated. All dives of the same number, whether straight, pike, or tuck are to be considered as the same dive.

105.3. Each competitor at the United States Diving Championships must deposit in a designated entry box at pool side by 12:00 noon on the day prior to the competition, a complete and final list of the dives the competitor plans to perform in the contest. These dives are to be listed on an official form as distributed by the Meet Director and filled out in pen. Changes will be accepted up until one hour prior to the scheduled diving contest time. This final list of dives must be signed by the competitor. Each competitor in all diving competitions is entirely responsible for the correctness of the statements of the list. The signed portion of the score sheet shall be considered the competitor's official list of dives. For Preliminary Meets of Senior Championships and Junior Olympic Zone Championships the entry deposit deadline should be 6:00 p.m. on the day prior to the competition.

The Meet Director or his representative shall check the designated entry box at 12:00 noon to determine that all diving lists have been submitted. A grace period of 30 minutes will be given for entered divers to turn in completed diving sheets. Any time after 12:30 p.m., the drawing can be made. Entries submitted after the drawing will be considered late entries. The diver may still compete by paying a $5 fine and will dive first in the diving order. The fee should be made payable to United States Diving, Inc. (*Note*: A diving list score form listing dives and signed by the competitor may be mailed by certified mail (return receipt as proof) with the entry form or separately to the Meet Director who will deposit it into the designated entry box if the mailing meets with the deadline requirements.)

105.4. The appropriate Vice President or a representative shall inspect all diving lists and should the statement in the list be incorrect or not in accordance with the rules, shall publicly announce all the diving sheets that are in error. Competitors will be allowed up to one hour before the official starting time of the event to correct the error(s). However, any errors not detected are the responsibility of the diver. (*Note*: In Diving meets other than the U.S. Championships, the Meet Directors at their own discretion may arrange for a time different than stated for turning in the diving list for the convenience of meet procedure and/or of the meet secretary, but the deadline should not be less than one hour before the particular event and in all cases this information must be clearly stated on the entry information form.)

105.5. The Meet Director shall have someone available by the end of the first scheduled workout the first four days of the U.S. Championship to allow the divers the opportunity to check and/or change their diving sheets.

105.6. Score Sheet Errors. The purpose of a diving meet is to compare physical performance and not clerical skills. Nevertheless, a certain amount of responsibility for the accuracy of the diving sheet must be accepted by the diver or his coach.

(a) Each diver must execute the dive as listed on the score sheet, with the exception of position (refer to 109.2), or have that dive declared failed. If the announced dive is not performed and the dive performed is properly listed on the diver's sheet, it will be considered an announcer's error and the dive judged as performed. If the diver executes a dive as announced and it is determined that the announcer was in error, the diver will be permitted to immediately perform the correct dive.

(b) Dive order errors. If a dive is listed out of order as defined in Article 13, 22, 23, 24, or 30 for that particular contest, and the error is discovered prior to the execution of the dive, the referee will instruct the secretary to correct the list as directed by the diver. If the error is discovered after the execution of the "out of order" dive, then the dive that should have been performed shall be declared a failed dive and the referee will instruct the secretary to correct the balance of the list. The performed dive shall be listed in its proper place on the diving list as directed by the diver and must be performed a second time and judged and scored at its proper time.

(c) In other than U.S. Senior Championship and Preliminary Meets, if the diver makes an error in the number, description or position of a dive, the error shall be corrected if discovered and protested by the diver before execution of the dive. In such cases the diver shall perform the dive as corrected. If the error is not discovered and protested by the diver before execution, the dive performed shall be judged as described, with penalties for improper position and incorrect dives to be made as provided for elsewhere in these rules.

(d) Dive description errors. In the U.S. Senior Championship and Preliminary Meets, diving sheets must provide a space for the dive number and position (e.g., 101A). The dive number and position are the official description of the dive and take precedence over written description and the degree of difficulty. No changes can be made after the deadline of one hour prior to the contest. If the dive number and position listed on the score sheet are not found in the official diving table, it shall be declared a failed dive. If the diver listed a proper dive, but not the one he/she wanted to perform, the diver may:

(1) Perform the dive as listed, or

(2) Perform the dive in a different position and receive not more than 2 points per judge, or

(3) Perform an incorrect dive and receive zero points.

(e) At Association Championships, Invitational Meets and other local meets, greater latitude in the interpretation of this rule can be used.

105.7. At the Senior National and Junior Olympic National Championships, divers must list the name(s) of their coaches on their diving form.

ARTICLE 6: COMPETITION PROCEDURES

106.1. When the majority of the officials and coaches present declare that a diving contest cannot be completed due to the adverse weather or an act of God, the diving contest shall be postponed and held at a later time during the meet. If conditions still prevail whereby the contest cannot be conducted during the meet, then the diving event will be declared "no contest" and no champion will be named.

106.2. For the semi-finals the diving order shall be decided by lot, drawn publicly under the supervision of the Meet Director and/or the referee. The order for the finals shall be in reverse order of their respective qualifying positions. (*Note*: A redraw shall be made only in contests in which the finals are made up of a full list of dives. In dual meets, the visiting team shall have the choice of the alternate positions.)

106.3. A written or printed list of the diving order shall be posted by the Meet Secretary before the event starts in a place convenient for the divers' observation.

106.4. For U.S. Senior Diving Championships only (not including Preliminary Meets):

(a) The dive shall be executed after a signal given by the referee, preferably by whistle in the finals only.

(b) After the competition is started, a diver may not bounce the springboard except in the finals when the diver may bounce the board after scores of the previous dive have been announced.

(c) The dive number and position shall be displayed to the diver before the dive is executed in the semi-finals and finals. If an electronic device is not available a blackboard or some other visual aid is acceptable.

106.5. Before each dive, the announcer shall announce the name of the competitor, the number and position of the dive, a description of the dive, and its degree of difficulty. During the contest, the announcer shall not announce any affiliation or individual titles (i.e., Mr., Mrs., Captain, Dr., etc.) relating to the contestant. In the event the diver has a hearing loss, the dive number and position shall be displayed to the diver after the announcer has stated the dive to be executed. The visual aid shall be provided by the diver if not otherwise available.

106.6. A diver may elect to take a zero on any dive, without prejudice, and remain in the contest. (This will provide a contest for all skill levels of competition. It will eliminate the danger of trying dives without preparation and will create a desire and need for young divers to learn a full list of dives.) This applies to all competitions except the United States Championships.

106.7. Once a section of the diving competition (i.e., prelims, semi-finals or finals) has commenced, no practice springing of the board will be permitted during that section. The use of the boards and practice dives between sections or competition will be up to the referee. If the divers in the contest have been advised of this rule by the announcer or referee, a violation will result in a two point deduction from each judge's score on the competitor's next dive. If no announcement of the rule has been made, a warning will be given upon the first violation by any diver and the two point deduction made upon repeat violation by any diver.

106.8. If a diver is not present to perform the dive when announced and it is ascertained that the diver is not in the pool area, after three minutes the diver will be scratched from the event and no other diver will take the diver's place.

106.9. During the contest it is the responsibility of the diver to immediately correct the announcer if the dive or position is announced incorrectly. If a wrong dive is performed, it shall be considered a failed dive. If a dive is executed other than that which was announced, and is properly listed on the score sheet, it will be judged as a correct dive and considered an announcer error. If the diver executes a dive as announced and it is determined that the announcer was in error, then the diver will be allowed to immediately perform the correct dive.

106.10. All dives must be executed by the competitor, without assistance from any other person, after the announcer has announced the name of the competitor and the dive which the diver is to execute. Penalty for obvious assistance shall result in a failed dive for that diver on that dive, to be determined by the referee. Assistance between dives is permitted.

106.11. Under normal circumstances, divers should not unduly delay a contest. If, in the opinion of the referee, a diver is unduly delaying a contest, the referee shall instruct the diver that he/she will have one minute in which to complete his/her dive. In the event the diver does not proceed within the one minute time limit, the referee shall declare a failed dive.

106.12. In the event that a diver has qualified in the preliminary or semi-final round and then is injured and officially declared by the referee and/or Meet Physician as unable to continue, the diver in the next highest place will move up to the semi-finals or finals.

106.13. In the event that the diver is injured during the finals of any competition and is unable to continue, the diver shall not be disqualified but shall be placed in the final standing according to the sum total of points he or she has established.

106.14. Once an event has begun, if it is discovered that a diver does not meet the degree of difficulty requirement for that contest, the diver shall be disqualified from that event.

106.15. In contests where all divers perform a full list of dives, the referee shall determine and announce the time for a five (5) minute break during the contest. There shall be no more than one break in any contest.

106.16. At all meets, except the Senior and Junior Olympic National Championships, the one and three meter events may be run simultaneously.

ARTICLE 7: METHODS OF MARKING
AND DUTIES OF REFEREE, JUDGES AND SECRETARY

107.1. In each diving contest there shall be a referee, not more than ten judges, a secretary, two or more scoring table clerks and an announcer.

107.2. During the United States Championships, Junior Olympic Championships, Senior Preliminary Meets and J.O. Zone Championships no official (referee, judge, secretary, table official, etc.), coach or diver will be permitted to smoke or use tobacco in any other way or consume any intoxicant while on the pool deck.

107.3. In the United States Championships it is necessary to have two sets of scoring panels plus a recorder of scores assisting the announcer. In National Championships the referee shall not act as the announcer. (*Note*: It is recommended that in all diving competition, wherever possible, two sets of scoring panels be used for accuracy.)

107.4. It is recommended that three judges be used for dual meet competition and five judges be used for Association and Regional meets.

107.5. There will be nine judges in each event at the United States Diving Championships. In the Preliminary Meets, Junior Olympic Championships and Zone Championships there shall be two panels of five judges for each event. If not possible, one panel of five or seven judges shall be used.

107.6. The selection of judges at the United States Senior Diving Championships shall be as follows:

(a) The Judges Certification Committee shall meet the evening prior to the start of the United States Diving Championships and prior to the general meeting for selection of judges, to examine the list of certified judges and make changes as deemed necessary. Certified judges present at each U.S. Championships shall, prior to the above meeting, inform the Chairman as to which events they are willing to judge and those they prefer not to judge. The Judges Certification Committee may select up to but not more than 49% of the judges for each contest, with the remainder to be drawn at the general meeting.

(b) At an open meeting, a slate of not less than nine nor more than fifteen certified persons attending the meet shall be selected to serve as judges. Additional judges from the certification list nominated by members of the Senior section of the Board of Governors in attendance at the meeting.

(c) The names of each of the judges submitted shall have been qualified by certification determined by at least a written examination and other criteria as determined by the Judges Selection and Certification Committee.

(d) The necessary number of judges shall be drawn consecutively from three containers representing the three areas. Not more than one judge from a State and/or Local Diving Committee may judge the same event, whenever possible. The remaining names shall be drawn to serve as alternates. Replacement by alternates shall be by areas whenever possible. The same procedure shall be used for each event.

(e) Parents will not be permitted to judge in an event in which an offspring competes. Two members of the same family will not be permitted to judge in the same event.

107.7. The referee shall manage the competition and insure that all regulations are observed. The referee should meet with the judges before the contest begins to review all rules.

107.8. The judges shall be placed by the referee close together and preferably divided evenly on both sides of the diving boards. They must maintain their respective places throughout the entire contest. If it is not possible to separate the judges, they shall be placed together on one side.

107.9. At diving meets having multiple board facilities where the boards are located in such a way that the judges may have to change their seating position to view the dives from all boards, the referee may divide the divers into groups according to the divers' previously expressed preference for the diving boards. One group shall perform on the other board for each round of dives. Within each group, the order of the divers shall be determined by lot and the order of the groups shall also be determined by lot.

107.10. Judges who are selected for a contest are responsible for judging that entire contest, unless, due to unavoidable circumstances, a judge must be replaced. This action must have a majority vote of the Diving Rules committee members present. If no members are present the referee shall have the power to make the change.

107.11. In judging diving events, a scoring device that shows the judges' scores to the public but not the other judges is desired.

107.12. After each dive, on a signal from the referee, each of the judges, without communicating with any other judge or judges, shall immediately and simultaneously flash their award.

107.13. The referee shall have the individual awards placed one by one in the same consecutive order on a score sheet, cancel the highest and lowest awards, and pass the score sheet to the secretary. If two or more awards of those of which are to be cancelled are equal, either of them can be cancelled. When three judges are used, there shall be no cancellation of awards. When nine judges are used, the two highest and two lowest awards will be cancelled. When five or seven judges are used only the highest and lowest awards will be cancelled.

107.14. After cancellation of the necessary high and low awards, the secretary shall announce the sum total of the remaining awards and the degree of difficulty to the calculator clerk, who shall compute the total points for that dive and shall announce same to the secretary. The secretary will then enter the points thus established on the score sheet. When seven or nine judges' awards are used, it is recommended that a 3/5 calculator be used. If one is not available then the sum of the middle five awards is multiplied by the degree of difficulty and then by .6 to obtain the equivalent of a three judge score.

107.15. At the end of the contest the referee shall supervise the score sheets and the list of results in collaboration with the secretary, and confirm the final result by his signature in the main minutes.

107.16. The winner shall be the competitor who has obtained the greatest sum of points. If two or more competitors obtain the same number of points, it is a tie.

107.17. Awards Presentation: The Meet Director shall be responsible for the Awards Presentations.

(a) Within 10 minutes after completion of a contest the awards will be presented.

(b) The finalists who are to receive awards will gather at a site designated by the Meet Director.

(c) The Meet Director will make certain that divers eligible for an award appear on the stand properly attired. Proper attire may consist of swim suits and/or warm-ups. Divers wearing jackets of affiliations other than their own or street clothes or improper attire in the opinion of the Meet Director will not appear on the award stand.

ARTICLE 8: STARTING POSITION
AND BALK RULE FOR SPRINGBOARD AND PLATFORM

108.1. The starting position of a forward approach shall be assumed when the diver is ready to take the first step.

108.2. The starting position of standing dives shall be assumed when the diver stands on the front end of the springboard or the front end of the platform. The body shall be straight, head erect with the arms straight and in a position of the diver's choice. After assuming the starting position for standing or running dives, if the diver makes an obvious attempt to start the approach or press and stops, a balk will be declared. In standing dives the diver has the option of moving the arms to various preparatory positions without a balk being declared, so long as there is no obvious attempt to start the press.

108.3. In the event the diver balks, the diving referee, upon completion of the second attempt, shall instruct the announcer to reduce each judge's award by two points. If the diver balks twice, it is a "failed" dive. No further attempt shall be permitted. In cases of questionable circumstances, benefit always goes to the diver. (NOTE: In the case of strong winds, T.V. cameras, bright sun or lights, it is the responsibility of the diver to determine when the time is best to assume the starting position. The limit of time is three minutes. The diving referee at the beginning of the competition may give special instructions to the divers in regard to the balk rule on forward and back take-off if the wind conditions are extreme.)

108.4. It shall be considered a failed dive if the diver falls into the water from the board prior to assuming the starting position.

108.5. For Armstand Dives, it shall be assumed that the diver has reached a starting position when both of the diver's feet leave the platform. If, in an armstand dive, a steady balance in the straight position is not shown the judges should deduct from one to three points. If a diver loses his/her balance and his/her feet touch the platform, it is a balk.

ARTICLE 9: SCORING THE EXECUTION OF THE DIVE

109.1. Points or half points shall be awarded from 0-10 according to the opinion of the judges and the following table:

Very Good..................................	8 1/2 to 10 points
Good.......................................	6 1/2 to 8 points
Satisfactory..................................	5 to 6 points
Deficient....................................	2 1/2 to 4 1/2 points
Unsatisfactory	1/2 to 2 points
Completely Failed...........................	0 points

109.2. If the dive is performed clearly in a position other than as written, the referee shall instruct the judges that it shall be awarded not more than two points. In any other circumstances in which the dive shall be considered deficient, the judges shall award not more than four and one-half points.

109.3. The diving referee is authorized to have a spoiled dive repeated, when in his opinion the execution of the dive was influenced by exceptional circumstances. The request for such repetition must be made by the diver immediately after the execution of the spoiled dive. (*Note*: Exceptional circumstances include only the most unusual happenings.)

ARTICLE 10: JUDGING THE EXECUTION OF THE DIVE

110.1. When judging a dive, only the dive is to be considered, without regard to the approach to the starting position. The points to be considered are the approach, the take-off, the technique and grace of the dive during the passage through the air and the entry into the water. Judges shall not consider or score a diver's actions beneath the surface of the water.

110.2. Dives should be executed and judged on the following principles:

(a) The approach to the starting position shall not be taken into consideration; the starting position shall be free and unaffected.

(b) The forward approach shall be smooth, straight and forceful, and shall comprise not less than three steps before the hurdle. If a diver takes less than three steps before the hurdle, the referee shall deduct two points from the award of each judge.

(c) The hurdle is described as the jump to the end of the springboard following the approach. The take-off for the hurdle shall be from one foot only. Both feet shall contact the end of the springboard simultaneously following the hurdle. A take-off for the hurdle from both feet shall constitute a balk.

(d) The take-off shall be forceful, reasonably confident and shall proceed without undue delay. In running dives the take-off from the springboard must be from both feet simultaneously immediately following the hurdle. A diver is entitled to his own method of armswing on back and standing front take-offs, but must not lift his feet from the board before the take-off. When executing a backward or standing front dive, the diver must not bounce on the board or rock the board excessively before the take-off. For a violation of the above, the Judges (not the referee) shall deduct not more than two points from their award according to their individual opinions. If in any dive the diver touches the end of the board or dives to the side of the direct line of flight, this indicates, no matter how well the dive may have been executed, that he was too close to the board for proper execution, and each judge must exercise his own opinion regarding the deduction to be made.

(e) During the passage through the air the body can be carried straight, with a pike, or with a tuck. In the straight position, the body shall be held straight without bending at either the knees or the hips, with the feet together and toes pointed. In a dive in the straight position, if the knees are bent, the dive is to be judged on its overall performance and the judges (not the referee) shall deduct their awards according to their individual opinion. In Head First Dives, if the feet enter the water before the hands, the referee shall declare the dive to be a failed dive.

In the pike position, the body shall be bent at the hips, but the legs must be kept straight at the knees, toes pointed. The pike should be as compact as possible. In the tuck position, the body shall be bent at the knees and hips with the feet together and toes pointed. The tuck should be as compact as possible. If the diver opens his knees in a tuck, the judges shall deduct from one to two points.

The free position (a combination of straight, pike or tuck) may be used in twisting dives only as listed in the tables. The tuck position may be used as part of the free position only in the following dives: 5152, 5154, 5221, 5231, 5251, 5321, 5331, 5351. The use of the tuck position in any other twisting dives which permit the use of the free position shall result in a judge's award of no more than four and one-half points.

The diving illustrations serve as guides only and it is to be noted that the positions of the arms shall be the choice of the diver, except in the case of the front dive in straight position, where the arms must be stretched out sideways in line with the shoulders during the flight through the air. The arms must be kept still until just before entry into the water, when they must be brought rapidly together and extended beyond the head in a line with the body. (This refers to the execution of only the forward dive in straight position.)

(f) In dives with twists, the twisting must not manifestly be done directly from the board. In somersault dives with twists, the twist may be performed at any time during the dive at the option of the diver, unless otherwise specified. It is a failed dive if the amount of the twist is greater or less than that announced by 90 degrees or more.

(g) In somersaults in the tuck position (other than flying somersaults) the turn must commence as soon as the diver leaves the board. In flying somersault dives there must be a well defined straight position for approximately half a somersault (body inverted), with the somersault made as rapidly as possible.

(h) The entry into the water must in all cases be vertical, or nearly so, with the body straight and toes pointed. All head first entries shall be executed with the arms stretched beyond the head in a line with the body, with the hands close together. All feet first entries shall be performed with the arms held close to the body, and without bending the arms at the elbows. If the arms are not in the correct prescribed position on entry into the water, each judge shall deduct from one to three points from the award according to circumstances.

(i) All springboard dives with a forward take-off may be performed either standing or with an approach at the option of the diver. A prior declaration of the manner of take-off is not required. The judge shall award points for a standing dive bearing in mind the height and standards of execution which might be expected from a dive with an approach.

(j) In platform dives the position of the arms shall be at the choice of the diver, except in the case of the front dive in straight position, where the arms must be stretched out sideways in line with the shoulders during flight. The arms must be kept still until just before the entry into the water when they must be brought together rapidly and extended beyond the head in a line with the body.

(k) In all running platform dives, the diver must take no less than three steps and a hop for two feet take-offs and no less than four steps for one foot take-offs. For a violation of this rule, the referee shall instruct the announcer to deduct two points from the award of each judge.

ARTICLE 13: SENIOR COMPETITIONS

113.1. International. All International Diving competition, including the World Swimming Championships, Pan American and Olympic Games, is governed and conducted under FINA Rules.

113.2. United States Diving Championships. Annually, United States Diving, Inc. will conduct an Indoor and an Outdoor National Diving Championship. To compete in any of these events, including the Preliminary Meets, the registered athlete must be a citizen of the United States of America.

113.3. Competition Requirements for Springboard Events

(a) Men's One Meter: Competition requirements for the Men's One Meter Springboard event shall consist of five voluntary dives, in any order, one from each group, with a total degree of difficulty not to exceed 9.5; followed by six optional dives, in any order, one from each group, with a minimum degree of difficulty of 14.0. The contest shall consist of finals only. The places shall be determined by the score of the finals.

(b) Men's Three Meter: Competition requirements for the Men's Three Meter Springboard event shall consist of five voluntary dives, one from each group, with a total degree of difficulty not to exceed 9.5 and six optional dives, at least one from each group, with a minimum degree of difficulty of 16.1. The contest shall consist of semi-finals and finals. In the semi-finals all contestants shall perform five voluntary dives with limit in any order followed by six optional dives in any order.

The eight contestants having the highest scores after the semi-finals shall compete in the finals which shall consist of five voluntary dives, one from each group, done in any order, with a total degree of difficulty not to exceed 9.5 followed by six optional dives, at least one from each group, in any order, with a minimum degree of difficulty of 16.1. The places will be determined by the score of the finals only.

(c) Women's One Meter: Competition requirements for the Women's One Meter Springboard event shall consist of five voluntary dives, in any order, one from each group, with a total degree of difficulty not to exceed 9.5; followed by five optional dives, in any order one from each group, with a minimum degree of difficulty of 10.5. The contest shall consist of finals only. The places shall be determined by the score of the finals.

(d) Women's Three Meter: Competition requirements for the Women's Three Meter Springboard event shall consist of five voluntary dives, one from each group, with a total degree of difficulty not to exceed 9.5 and five optional dives, one from each group, with a minimum degree of difficulty of 11.1. The contest shall consist of semi-finals and finals. In the semi-finals all contestants shall perform five voluntary dives with limit in any order followed by five optional dives in any order.

The eight contestants having the highest scores after the semi-finals shall compete in the finals which shall consist of five voluntary dives, one from each group, done in any order, with a total degree of difficulty not to exceed 9.5 followed by five optional dives, one from each group, in any order, with a minimum degree of difficulty of 11.1. The places will be determined by the score of the finals only.

113.4. Competition Requirements for Platform Events

(a) The Men's Platform event shall consist of ten dives, four voluntary dives from different groups with a total degree of difficulty not to exceed 7.6 and six voluntary dives from different groups with no degree of difficulty limit.

All dives must be performed from the 10 meter platform.

The contest shall consist of semi-finals and finals. In the semi-finals, all contestants shall perform all ten dives, beginning with the four voluntary dives with limit, followed by the six voluntary dives without limit.

The eight contestants having the highest scores shall compete in the finals, which shall consist of the four voluntary dives, from different groups, with limit, followed by the six voluntary dives, one from each group, without limit. The places will be determined by the score of the finals only.

(b) The Women's Platform event shall consist of eight dives, four dives from different groups with a total degree of difficulty not to exceed 7.6 and four voluntary dives from different groups with no degree of difficulty limit. All dives must be performed from the 10 meter platform. The contest shall consist of semi-finals and finals. In the semi-finals, all contestants shall perform eight dives, beginning with the four voluntary dives with limit, followed by the four voluntary dives without limit.

The eight contestants having the highest scores shall compete in the finals, which shall consist of the four voluntary dives, from different groups, with limit, followed by the four voluntary dives, each from a different group, without limit. The places will be determined by the score of the finals only.

113.5. Diving List. The deadline for depositing the list of dives shall be 12:00 noon on the day prior to the competition.

113.6. Any diver listing one or more coaches at the Junior Olympic National Championships must list the same one or more coaches at the Senior Outdoor National Championship and any coaches' points shall be equally divided between the listed coaches.

113.7. Individual and Team Scoring. Points shall be awarded to the top 16 places in each event. Points will be awarded as follows: 24-20-19-18-17-16-15-14-8-7-6-5-4-3-2-1. There will be individual High Point Awards given for Men and Women. There will be First, Second and Third place Championship Team Awards for Men and Women. There will be a combined Men's and Women's Championship Team Award.

113.8. Preliminary Meets for United States Diving Championships

(a) Competition Requirements for Springboard Events

(1) Men's One Meter: The preliminaries shall consist of all contestants doing six optional dives, at least one from each group, in any order with a minimum degree of difficulty of 14.0. The 16 highest finishers shall complete the contest, which shall consist of the

five voluntary dives, one from each group, in any order, with a degree of difficulty not to exceed 9.5.

(2) Men's Three Meter: The preliminaries shall consist of all contestants doing six optional dives, at least one from each group in any order, with a minimum degree of difficulty of 16.1. The 16 highest finishers shall compete in the finals, which shall consist of five voluntary dives, one from each group, in any order, with a degree of difficulty not to exceed 9.5.

(3) Women's One Meter: The preliminaries shall consist of all contestants doing five optional dives, one from each group, in any order, with a minimum degree of difficulty of 10.5. The 16 highest finishers shall complete the contest, which shall consist of five voluntary dives, one from each group, in any order, with a degree of difficulty not to exceed 9.5.

(4) Women's Three Meter: The preliminaries shall consist of all contestants doing five optional dives, one from each group, in any order, with a minimum degree of difficulty of 11.1. The 16 highest finishers shall complete the contest, which shall consist of five voluntary dives, one from each group, in any order, with a degree of difficulty not to exceed 9.5.

(b) Competition Requirements for Platform Events

(1) Indoor Platform Preliminary Meet

The contest shall consist of all divers performing a full list of dives. The Men shall perform four voluntary dives from different groups with a total degree of difficulty not to exceed 7.6 and six voluntary dives, one from each group, with no degree of difficulty limit. The Women shall perform four voluntary dives from different groups with a total degree of difficulty not to exceed 7.6 and four voluntary dives each from a different group with no degree of difficulty limit.

(2) Outdoor Platform Preliminary Meet

The Men shall perform four voluntary dives from different groups with a total degree of difficulty not to exceed 7.6 and three voluntary dives from different groups with no degree of difficulty limit. The Women shall perform four voluntary dives from different groups with a total degree of difficulty not to exceed 7.6 and one voluntary dive with no degree of difficulty limit. The 12 highest finishers shall complete the contest, which consists of three remaining voluntary dives with no degree of difficulty limit for Men and Women.

(c) Once an event has begun, a diver participating in a Preliminary Meet of U.S. Diving Championships who exceeds the maximum degree of difficulty for the voluntary dives with limit for Platform or Springboard shall be disqualified from the event. Similarly, once an event has begun, a diver participating in a Preliminary Meet of U.S. Diving Championships who does not meet the minimum degree of difficulty shall be disqualified from the event.

113.9. Association Championships

(a) Competition requirements for the Women's Association One and Three Meter Springboard Championships shall consist of five voluntary dives, one from each group, with a total degree of difficulty not to exceed 9.5 and five optional dives, one from each group. The contest shall consist of preliminaries and finals. In the preliminaries, all contestants shall perform, in any order the five voluntary dives and three optional dives from different groups. The 16 highest finishers shall compete in the finals, which shall consist of the remaining two optional dives.

(b) Competition requirements for the Men's Association One and Three Meter Springboard Championships shall consist of five voluntary dives, one from each group, with a degree of difficulty not to exceed 9.5 and six optional dives, at least one from each group. The contest shall consist of preliminaries and finals. In the preliminaries all contestants shall perform, in any order, the five voluntary dives and three optional dives from different groups. The 16 highest finishers shall compete in the finals, which shall consist of the remaining three optional dives.

113.10. Invitational Meets

(a) Such meets may be held because of local conditions, preferences, limited facilities and personnel.

(b) Eligibility for participation is open to all registered amateur athletes in accordance with Parts III and IV of these regulations.

(c) It is recommended that invitational meets be conducted as closely as possible to all the rules governing the United States Championships.

(d) In invitational meets, any difference in the rules such as the number of dives to be performed, the order of dives, the delivery of the diving list or the number of finalists must be clearly stated on the entry blanks.

ARTICLE 33: DEGREE
OF DIFFICULTY TABLES, FORMULA AND NEW DIVES

133.1. A Degree of Difficulty table has been adopted by United States Diving effective January 1, 1981 (see pp. 214-218).

133.2. All degrees of difficulty are based on a formula taking into account the various component elements of a dive (Somersault Rotation, Flight Position, Twist Rotation, Type of Entry, and Approach) and based on a logical incremental progression for each of the elements.

133.3. Application for the addition of new dives to be included in the Official Diving Tables shall be made to the Chairman of the Diving Rules Committee on or before the date for the submissions of entries for either the United States Indoor or Outdoor Championships. The application must include the following information: date, full name of coach, name of the new dive, description of the new dive, height of the board from which the dive is to be performed, name of the diver(s) who will demonstrate the dive for the Diving Rules Committee, and signature of the coach and diver submitting the dive. The degree of difficulty for the new dive will be derived from the accepted formula.

GOVERNING BODY

United States Diving, Inc., 901 W. New York Street, Indianapolis, IN 46202

United States Diving, Inc., is the national governing body of diving. United States Diving is a member of United States Aquatic Sports, Inc., the United States member of FINA (the International Swimming Federation).

The primary goal of United States Diving is to conduct and promote the sport of diving in such manner as to appeal to the broadest possible number of participants. United States Diving conducts a Junior Olympic Program (ages 12 to 17), Senior Program (national and international caliber divers), International Program (world class competition), and Masters Program (diving enthusiasts no longer competing in the Senior Program).

MAGAZINES

The Diver, P.O. Box 249, Cobalt, CT 06414

SPRINGBOARD								FINA DIVING DEGREES OF DIFFICULTY	PLATFORM											
1 METER				3 METERS					10 METERS				7.5 METERS				5 METERS			
strt.	pike	tuck	free	strt.	pike	tuck	free		strt.	pike	tuck	free	strt.	pike	tuck	free	strt.	pike	tuck	free
A	B	C	D	A	B	C	D		A	B	C	D	A	B	C	D	A	B	C	D
								FORWARD GROUP												
1.4	1.3	1.2		1.6	1.5	1.4		101 Forward Dive	1.6	1.5	1.4		1.6	1.5	1.4		1.4	1.3	1.2	
1.6	1.5	1.4		1.7	1.6	1.5		102 Forward Somersault	1.8	1.7	1.6		1.7	1.6	1.5		1.6	1.5	1.4	
	1.7	1.6		1.9	1.6	1.5		103 Forward 1-1/2 Somersault	1.9	1.6	1.5		1.9	1.6	1.5		2.0	1.7	1.6	
	2.3	2.2			2.1	2.0		104 Forward Double Somersault	2.5	2.2	2.1			2.1	2.0			2.3	2.2	
	2.6	2.4			2.4	2.2		105 Forward 2-1/2 Somersault		2.3	2.1			2.4	2.2			2.6	2.4	
		2.9				2.5		106 Forward Triple Somersault												
		3.0			3.1	2.8		107 Forward 3-1/2 Somersault		3.0	2.7				2.8				3.0	
						3.5		109 Forward 4-1/2 Somersault			3.5									
	1.7	1.6			1.8	1.7		112 Forward Flying Somersault		1.9	1.8			1.8	1.7			1.7	1.6	
	1.9	1.8			1.8	1.7		113 Forward Flying 1-1/2 Som.		1.8	1.7			1.8	1.7			1.9	1.8	
								114 Forward Flying Double Som.			2.3				2.2					
						2.5		115 Forward Flying 2-1/2 Som.		2.6	2.4				2.5					
						2.5		1051 Fwd. Som. with Fly 1-1/2 Som.			2.4				2.5					
								BACK GROUP												
1.7	1.6	1.5		1.9	1.8	1.7		201 Back Dive	1.9	1.8	1.7		1.9	1.8	1.7		1.7	1.6	1.5	
1.7	1.6	1.5		1.8	1.7	1.6		202 Back Somersault	1.9	1.8	1.7		1.8	1.7	1.6		1.7	1.6	1.5	
2.5	2.4	2.0		2.4	2.2	1.9		203 Back 1-1/2 Somersault	2.4	2.2	1.9		2.4	2.2	1.9		2.5	2.4	2.0	
	2.5	2.2		2.5	2.3	2.0		204 Back Double Somersault	2.6	2.4	2.1		2.5	2.3	2.0			2.5	2.2	
		3.0			3.0	2.8		205 Back 2-1/2 Somersault	3.3	2.9	2.7			3.0	2.8				3.0	
						3.4		207 Back 3-1/2 Somersault			3.3				3.4					
	1.7	1.6			1.8	1.7		212 Back Flying Somersault		1.9	1.8			1.8	1.7			1.7	1.6	
		2.1				2.1		213 Back Flying 1-1/2 Som.			2.1				2.1					

	A	B	C	D	A	B	C	D	A	B	C	D	A	B	C	D	A	B	C	D
REVERSE GROUP																				
3 0 1 Reverse Dive	1.8	1.7	1.6		2.0	1.9	1.8		2.0	1.9	1.8		2.0	1.9	1.8		1.8	1.7	1.6	
3 0 2 Reverse Somersault	1.8	1.7	1.6		2.0	1.9	1.8		2.0	1.9	1.8		1.9	1.8	1.7		1.8	1.7	1.6	
3 0 3 Reverse 1-1/2 Somersault	2.7	2.4	2.1		2.6	2.3	2.0		2.6	2.3	2.0		2.6	2.3	2.0		2.7	2.4	2.1	
3 0 4 Reverse Double Somersault		2.6	2.3			2.4	2.1			2.5	2.2			2.4	2.1			2.6	2.3	
3 0 5 Reverse 2-1/2 Somersault			3.0			3.0	2.8			2.9	2.7			3.0	2.8				3.0	
3 0 7 Reverse 3-1/2 Somersault			3.5				3.4				3.4				3.4					
3 1 2 Reverse Flying Somersault		1.8	1.7				1.9				1.9				1.8			1.8	1.7	
3 1 3 Reverse Flying 1-1/2 Som.			2.1				2.2				2.2				2.2					
INWARD GROUP																				
4 0 1 Inward Dive	1.8	1.5	1.4		1.7	1.4	1.3		1.7	1.4	1.3		1.7	1.4	1.3		1.8	1.5	1.4	
4 0 2 Inward Somersault		1.7	1.6			1.5	1.4			1.6	1.5			1.5	1.4			1.7	1.6	
4 0 3 Inward 1-1/2 Somersault		2.4	2.2			2.1	1.9			2.0	1.8			2.1	1.9			2.4	2.2	
4 0 4 Inward Double Somersault			2.6			2.6	2.4			2.6	2.4			2.6	2.4				2.6	
4 0 5 Inward 2-1/2 Somersault			3.0			3.0	2.7			2.8	2.5			3.0	2.7				3.0	
4 0 7 Inward 3-1/2 Somersault			3.4				3.4				3.2				3.4					
4 1 2 Inward Flying Somersault		2.1	2.0			1.9	1.8			2.0	1.9			1.9	1.8				2.0	
4 1 3 Inward Flying 1-1/2 Som.			2.7				2.4			2.5	2.3				2.4					

FINA DIVING — DEGREES OF DIFFICULTY

TWIST GROUP

#	Twist Group	SPRINGBOARD — 1 METER strt.(A)	pike(B)	tuck(C)	free(D)	3 METERS strt.(A)	pike(B)	tuck(C)	free(D)	PLATFORM — 5 METERS strt.(A)	pike(B)	tuck(C)	free(D)	7.5 METERS strt.(A)	pike(B)	tuck(C)	free(D)	10 METERS strt.(A)	pike(B)	tuck(C)	free(D)
5 1 1 1	Forward Dive, 1/2 Twist	1.8	1.7			2.0	1.9			1.8	1.7			2.0	1.9			2.0	1.9		
5 1 1 2	Forward Dive 1 Twist	2.0	1.9			2.2	2.1			2.0	1.9			2.2	2.1			2.2	2.1		
5 1 2 1	Forward Som. 1/2 Twist	1.9	1.8			2.0	1.9			1.9	1.8		1.7	2.0	1.9						
5 1 2 2	Forward Som. 1 Twist				2.0				2.0				1.9								
5 1 2 4	Forward Som. 2 Twists				2.3				2.3				2.3								
5 1 2 6	Forward Som. 3 Twists				2.7				2.7												
5 1 3 1	Forward 1-1/2 Som. 1/2 Twist	2.1	2.0	1.9		2.0	1.9	1.9			2.1	2.0									
5 1 3 2	Forward 1-1/2 Som. 1 Twist				2.2				2.1				2.2				2.1				2.1
5 1 3 4	Forward 1-1/2 Som. 2 Twists				2.6				2.5				2.6				2.5				2.5
5 1 3 6	Forward 1-1/2 Som. 3 Twists				3.0				2.9								2.9				2.9
5 1 3 8	Forward 1-1/2 Som. 4 Twists								3.3												3.3
5 1 5 2	Forward 2-1/2 Som. 1 Twist				3.0				2.8								2.8				2.7
5 1 5 4	Forward 2/1/2 Som. 2 Twists								3.2								3.2				3.1
5 2 1 1	Back Dive 1/2 Twist	1.8				2.0				1.8				2.0				2.0			
5 2 1 2	Back Dive 1 Twist	2.0				2.2				2.0				2.2				2.2			
5 2 2 1	Back Somersault 1/2 Twist				1.7				1.7				1.7								
5 2 2 2	Back Somersault 1 Twist				1.9				1.9				1.9								
5 2 2 3	Back Somersault 1-1/2 Twists				2.3				2.3				2.3								
5 2 2 5	Back Somersault 2-1/2 Twists				2.7				2.7				2.7								
5 2 3 1	Back 1-1/2 Som. 1/2 Twist				2.1				2.1				2.1				2.0				2.1
5 2 3 3	Back 1-1/2 Som. 1-1/2 Twists				2.5				2.5				2.5				2.4				2.4
5 2 3 5	Back 1-1/2 Som. 2-1/2 Twists				2.9				2.9								2.8				2.8
5 2 3 7	Back 1-1/2 Som. 3-1/2 Twists				3.2				3.2												3.2
5 2 5 1	Back 2-1/2 Som. 1/2 Twist				2.5				2.5												2.4

A	B	C	D	Dive	A	B	C	D	A	B	C	D	A	B	C	D
				TWIST GROUP												
1.9				5311 Reverse Dive, 1/2 Twist	2.0				2.0				1.9			
2.1				5312 Reverse Dive 1 Twist	2.2				2.2				2.1			
			1.8	5321 Reverse Somersault 1/2 Twist												1.8
			2.0	5322 Reverse Som. 1 Twist												2.0
			2.4	5323 Reverse Som. 1-1/2 Twists												2.4
			2.8	5325 Reverse Som. 2-1/2 Twists												2.8
			2.2	5331 Reverse 1-1/2 Som. 1/2 Twist				2.1				2.1				2.2
			2.6	5333 Reverse 1-1/2 Som. 1-1/2 Twists				2.5				2.5				2.6
			3.0	5335 Reverse 1-1/2 Som. 2-1/2 Twists				2.9				2.9				3.0
				5337 Reverse 1-1/2 Som. 3-1/2 Twists				3.3								
		2.1		5351 Reverse 2-1/2 Som. 1/2 Twist				2.5								
2.0	1.7			5411 Inward Dive 1/2 Twist	1.8	1.5			1.9	1.6			2.0	1.7		
2.2	1.9			5412 Inward Dive 1 Twist	2.0	1.7			2.1	1.8			2.2	1.9		
	1.8	1.7		5421 Inward Som. 1/2 Twist		1.7	1.6			1.6	1.5			1.8	1.7	
				5422 Inward Som. 1 Twist												
			2.4	5432 Inward 1-1/2 Som. 1 Twist				2.3				2.4				2.1
			2.8	5434 Inward 1-1/2 Som. 2 Twist				2.7								
				ARMSTAND GROUP												
				610 Armstand Dive	1.6				1.6				1.5			
				611 Armstand Back Fall	2.0				2.0				1.8			
				612 Armstand Somersault	2.0	1.9	1.7		1.9	1.8	1.6		1.8	1.7	1.5	
				614 Armstand Double Som.		2.4	2.1			2.3	2.0				2.2	
				616 Armstand Triple Som.			2.8									
				631 Armstand Fwd. Cut-through	1.9	1.8	1.6		1.9	1.8	1.6		1.6	1.6	1.4	
				632 Armstand Cut-thru-Reverse Dive		2.3	2.1			2.2	2.0				1.9	
				633 Armstand Cut-thru-Rev. Som.			2.0				2.0				2.1	
				634 Armstand Cut-thru Rev. 1-1/2 Som.			2.6				2.5				2.1	

133.2 FINA DEGREE OF DIFFICULTY FORMULA COMPONENT TABLES (D.D. = A + B + C + D + E)

A SOMERSAULTS

	0	1/2	1	1-1/2	2	2-1/2	3	3-1/2	4-1/2
1 and 5 meters	.9	1.1	1.2	1.6	2.0	2.4	2.7	3.0	—
3 and 7.5 meters	1.0	1.3	1.3	1.5	1.8	2.2	2.3	2.8	3.5
10 meters	1.0	1.3	1.4	1.5	1.9	2.1	2.5	2.7	3.5

B FLIGHT POSITION For Flying dives add Fly component (e) to either (a) or (b) comp.

	0 - 1 SOM.					1 1/2 - 2 SOM.					2 1/2 SOM.					3 - 3 1/2 SOM.					4 1/2 SOM.
	Fwd.	Back	Rev.	Inw.	Arm	Fwd.	Back	Rev.	Inw.	Arm	Fwd.	Back	Rev.	Inw.	Arm	Fwd.	Back	Rev.	Inw.	Arm	Fwd.
C-Tuck	.1	.1	.1	-.3	.1	0	0	0	.1	0	0	.1	0	.2	.1	0	—	0	.3	.1	0
B-Pike	.2	.2	.2	-.2	—	.1	.3	.3	.3	.3	.2	.3	.2	.5	—	.3	—	—	—	—	—
A-Strt.	.3	.3	.3	.1	.4	.4	.5	.6	.8	—	.6	.7	.6	—	—	—	—	—	—	—	—
D-Free	.1	.1	.1	0	—	0	-.1	-.1	.2	—	0	-.1	-.2	—	—	—	—	—	—	—	—
E-Fly	.2	.1	.1	.4	—	.2	.2	.2	.5	—	.3	.3	.3	.7	—	.4	—	—	—	—	—

C TWISTS

	1/2	1	1-1/2	2	2-1/2	3	3-1/2	4
Forward	.4	.6	—	1.0	—	1.4	—	1.8
Back Reverse Inward	.2	.4	.8	.8	1.2	—	1.6	—

D UNNATURAL ENTRY

	1/2 Som.	1 Som.	1-1/2 Som.	2 Som.	2-1/2 Som.	3 Som.	3-1/2 Som.
Forward, Inward, and Armstd. Rev.	—	.1	—	.2	—	.2	—
Back, Reverse, and Arm. Fwd.	.1	—	.2	—	.3	—	.4

E APPROACH

	Fwd.	Back	Rev.	Inward	Armstd.
1 and 5 meters	0	.2	.3	.5	.2
3 and 7.5 meters	0	.2	.3	.3	.2
10 meters	0	.2	.3	.2	.2

Note: For Armstand cut-thru dives #632, 633, and 634, only add components for Armstand and Reverse Action.

Diver does not see water until dive action is substantially completed. Component same at all levels. Component not applicable to twisting dives.

• FENCING •

RULES FOR COMPETITIONS

(Reproduced by permission of the United States Fencing Association, Inc.*)

□

Note: Due to the lengthiness of the USFA Rule Book, it is beyond the scope of this volume to include the complete seven parts: I. General Rules And Rules Applicable To All Three Weapons, II. Foil, III. Épée, IV. Sabre, V. Organization of Competitions, VI. Disciplinary Rules for Competitions, and VII. Automatic Judging Equipment. Parts I and II have been selected for inclusion here.

PART ONE:
GENERAL RULES AND RULES APPLICABLE TO ALL THREE WEAPONS

CHAPTER I—HISTORICAL NOTE

The technical rules of the Federation International d'Escrime were unanimously adopted by the International Congress of National Olympic Committees held at Paris in June 1914 for use in all events at the Olympic Games. They were first codified in 1914 by the Marquis de Chasseloup-Laubat and Monsieur Paul Anspach and issued in 1919 with the title of "Rules for Competitions."

CHAPTER II—APPLICATION OF THE RULES

1. Obligatory Use of the Rules

1 These rules are obligatory without modification for the "Official Competitions of the F.I.E." viz.:

—The World Championships,

—The fencing events at the Olympic Games,

—The World Youth Championships.

Unless "exceptions are made and announced in advance," these rules must be applied at every International Meeting of whatever nature it may be.

2. Exceptions to the Rules

2 These exceptions should be confirmed by the national association of the country to which the organizing committee belongs, and should be brought to the notice of those concerned when the announcement of the meeting is published (Cf. 1).

---

*See page 243 for additional information.

CHAPTER III—GLOSSARY

III A—President

3 Throughout these rules the word "President" means "President of the Jury" or "Director of the Bout."

III B—Competitions

1. Assaults and Bouts
4 A friendly combat between two fencers is called "an assault." When the score of such an assault is kept to determine a result it is called a "bout."

2. Match
5 The aggregate of the bouts fought between the fencers of two different teams is called a "match."

3. Competition
6 Is the aggregate of the bouts (individual competitons) or of the matches (team competitions) required to determine the winner of the event.

Competitions are distinguished by weapons, by the competitors' sex, age or occupation (military—students, etc.) and by the fact that they are for individuals or for teams.

Competitions are said to be by 'direct elimination' when the competitors are eliminated as soon as they have received their first defeat, or after their second if the Rules specify a system "with repechage."

A pool, on the other hand, is the meeting of several competitors (or of all the competitors) each of whom fence each other in order to establish their classification.

4. Championship
7 Is the name given to a competition held to determine the best fencer or the best team at each weapon for an association or for a specific region and for a specific period of time.

5. Tournament
8 The name given to a number of competitions held at the same place, at the same period and for the same reason.

III C—Explanation Of Some Technical Terms Commonly Used In Judging Fencing (1)

1. Fencing Time
9 Fencing time (Temps d'Escrime) is the time required to perform one simple fencing action.

2. Offensive and Defensive Actions
10 The different offensive actions are the attack, the riposte and the counter-riposte.

—The *attack* is the initial offensive action made by extending the arm and continuously threatening the opponent's target (Cf. 233ss, 417ss).

—The *riposte* is the offensive action made by the fencer who has parried the attack.

—The *counter-riposte* is the offensive action made by the fencer who has parried the riposte.

The different defensive actions are the parries.

—The *parry* is the defensive action made with the blade to prevent the attack arriving.

Parries are simple, direct, when they are made in the same line as the attack.

They are circular (counter-parries) when they are made in the line opposing that of the attack.

11 The different offensive actions are:

(a) The Attack or Riposte:

The action is simple when it is executed in one movement and is either direct (in the same line) or
indirect (in another line)

The action is composed when it is executed in several movements.

(b) The Riposte:

Immediate or delayed: depending on what action takes place and the speed at which it is carried out.

Examples:

1. Simple direct riposte:

Direct riposte: a riposte which hits the opponent without leaving the line in which the parry was formed.

Riposte along the blade: a riposte which hits the opponent by grazing along the blade after the parry.

2. Simple indirect ripostes:

Riposte by disengagement: a riposte which hits the opponent in the opposite line to that in which the parry was formed (by passing under the opponent's blade if the parry was formed in the high line, and over the blade if the parry was formed in the low line).

Riposte with a coupé: riposte which hits the opponent in the opposite line to that in which the parry was formed (the blade always passing over the opponent's point).

3. Composed riposte:

Riposte with a doublé: a riposte which hits the opponent in the opposite line to that in which the parry was formed, but after having described a complete circle round the opponent's blade.

Riposte with a one-two: a riposte which hits the opponent in the same line in which the parry was formed but after the blade has first been into the opposite line by passing under the opponent's blade.

3. Counter Attacks
12 Counter attacks are offensive actions or offensive-defensive actions made during the offensive action of the opponent.

(a) The stop hit:

A counter-attack made on an attack.

(b) The stop hit made with opposition (formerly called the "time-hit"):

A counter-attack made by closing the line in which the opponent's attack will be completed (Cf. 233ss, 329ss, 418ss).

(c) The stop hit made with a period of fencing time i.e., "in time" (Cf. 236, 421).

4. Varieties of Offensive Actions
13 (a) The Remise:

A simple and immediate offensive action which follows the original attack, without withdrawing the arm, after the opponent has parried or retreated when the latter has either quitted contact with the blade without riposting or has made a riposte which is delayed, indirect or composed.

222 Sports Rules Encyclopedia

(b) The Redoublement:

A new action, either simple or composed, made on an opponent who has parried without riposting or who has merely avoided the first action by retreating or displacing the target.

(c) The Reprise d'Attaque:

A new attack executed immediately after a return to the on guard position.

(d) Counter Time:

Every action made by the attacker on a stop hit made by his opponent.

CHAPTER IV—THE FIELD OF PLAY (TERRAIN).
(Cf. 201ss, 301ss, 401ss.).

14 The field of play should have an even surface. It should give neither advantage nor disadvantage to either of the two fencers concerned, especially as regards slope and light.

When announcing the particulars of a competition the organizers must always state the nature of the field of play on which the competition will be fought. In particular they should state when a competition is to be held in the open air.

15 That portion of the field of play which is used for fencing is called the piste. The piste may be made of various materials: earth, wood, linoleum, cork, rubber, plastic, metallic mesh, metal or a compound with a metal base. (Cf. 201, 304, 401).

The width of the piste must be from 1.80 metres to 2 metres. Its length varies according to the weapon used (Cf. 202, 302, 402).

In addition to the length of the piste laid down for each weapon, the piste should in practice be extended a distance of 1.50 metres to 2 metres at each end, to enable a competitor who is about to cross the limit of the piste to retire over a continuous and even surface.

If the piste is mounted on a platform the latter must not be higher than .50 metres.

If it is impractical to have a piste of regulation length the length of the piste must not be less than 13 metres including the above mentioned extensions.

CHAPTER V—THE FENCERS' EQUIPMENT
(WEAPONS—EQUIPMENT—CLOTHING)

Note: Articles 16 through 26, deleted here, deal with the technical specifications for the equipment.

5. Equipment and clothing—general condition.

27 1. The competitor must have the maximum protection compatible with the freedom of movement necessary for fencing.

2. It must not be possible for the opponent to be obstructed or injured by the equipment, nor for the opponent's weapon to be caught up in or deflected by the equipment which, in consequence, must have neither buckles nor openings in which the opponent's point may be caught up—except accidentally—and thus held or deflected. The jacket and its collars must be completely buttoned or done up.

3. All clothing must be white. It must be made of sufficiently robust material and be clean and in good condition.

In order that the judging of hits should be facilitated as far as possible; the material from which the equipment is made must not have a surface which is smooth enough to cause the pointe d'arret, the button or the opponent's hit to glance off (Cf. 313, 408).

4. At sabre and foil, for men and ladies, the lower edge of the jacket must overlap the breeches by a least 10 cm. when the fencer is in the "on guard" position (Cf. 212, 408). At épée the fencer must wear a regulation jacket covering the whole of the trunk (Cf. 315).

THE REGULATION PISTE FOR ALL THREE WEAPONS

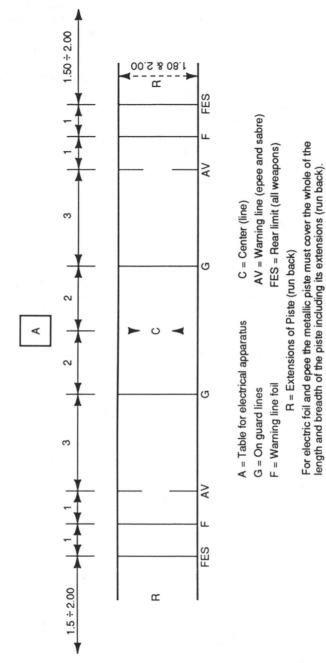

A = Table for electrical apparatus   C = Center (line)

G = On guard lines   AV = Warning line (epee and sabre)

F = Warning line foil   FES = Rear limit (all weapons)

R = Extensions of Piste (run back)

For electric foil and epee the metallic piste must cover the whole of the length and breadth of the piste including its extensions (run back).

Note: All dimensions given in meters.

The wearing of an undergarment (plastron) is obligatory at all weapons (Cf. 216, 315, 408). The jacket and collar must be completely buttoned or closed.

Ladies' equipment must include breast protectors made of metal or some other rigid material (Cf. 215).

5. The breeches must be fastened below the knees. If a fencer wears long trousers, these must be fastened or buttoned at the ankles. When breeches are worn, the fencer must wear white socks which must cover the legs right up to the breeches. These socks must be held up in such a way that they cannot fall down.

6. At all weapons, the gauntlet of the glove must, in all circumstances, fully cover approximately half the forearm of the competitor's sword arm to prevent the opponent's blade entering the sleeve of the jacket.

7. The mask must be made up with meshes (space between the wires) of maximum 2.1 mm and from wires with a minimum gauge of diameter 1 mm before tinning (which should be effected hot after the mesh has been shaped).

At foil, the mesh of the mask must be insulated inside and out. (Cf. 722/4). The bib and other trimmings must be white.

The mesh of the mask, both at the front and at the sides, must be able to withstand, without permanent deformation, the introduction into the mesh of a conical instrument, the angle of the surface of the cone being at 4 degrees to the axis and at a pressure of 7 kilos. All masks will be checked at every official championship of the F.I.E., and at the Olympic Games, using an instrument with a spring-loaded point.

However, a mask made from stainless steel mesh is permissible and need not be tinned.

CHAPTER VI—THE ASSAULT

1. Method of fencing. (Cf. 16.)

28 The competitors fence in their own ways and at their own risk with the one condition that they must observe the fundamental rules of fencing (Cf. 35).

All bouts or matches must, however, preserve the character of a courteous and frank encounter. All violent actions (flèche attack which ends by a shock jostling the opponent (Cf. 645), or disorderly fencing, irregular movements on the piste, any action which the President considers dangerous (for example, attacks made by running with loss of balance, hits delivered with undue violence) are expressly forbidden (Cf. 646 and 647).

A competitor must not remove his mask until the President has given his decision (Cf. 644).

2. Exactitude of the Hit.

29 Every thrust with the point at foil and épée must reach the target clearly and distinctly to be counted as a hit (Cf. 219 and 316).

At sabre, thrusts with the point and cuts with the edge and reverse edge must similarly reach the target clearly and distinctly to be counted as hits (Cf. 409).

3. Method of Holding the Weapon

30 With all three weapons, defence must be effected exclusively with the guard and the blade used either separately or together.

If there is no special device or attachment a fencer may hold the handle in any way he wishes and he may also alter the position of his hand on the handle during a bout. However, the weapon must not be—either permanently or temporarily, in an open or concealed manner—transformed into a throwing weapon; it must be used without the hand leaving the hilt, and without the hand being slipped along the hilt from front to back during an offensive action. The weapon must be used with one hand only; a fencer must not change hands until the end of the bout, unless the President gives special permission to the contrary because of the hand or arm being wounded. The use of the hand and arm which are not used to hold the weapon to carry out an offensive or defensive action is forbidden. The penalty for this offence is the annulment of any hit made by the fencer at fault, together with a SEVERE warning, which is valid for the bout. This offence is one of a group of six (Cf. 645) for which, in the event of a repetition in the same bout of any one of the offences, the fencer at fault will be penalised by a hit, which can cause him to lose the bout, as well as having any hit, which he may have scored, annulled. The same penalty is applied in the case of any subsequent repetition.

At foil, it is, equally, forbidden to use the non-sword arm or hand during a fight to cover or protect the target area. The penalty for breaking these rules is a MINOR warning valid for the bout. Should there be a repetition, the fencer will be penalised with a hit (Cf. 640).

During the fight, the fencer's non-sword hand must not, in any case take hold of any part of his electrical equipment. The penalty for this contravention is a MINOR warning valid for the bout. The penalty for a repetition is a hit (Cf. 641)

4. Putting on Guard.

31 The fencer whose number is called first should place himself on the right of the President, except in the case of a bout between a right and left-hander, if the left-hander is called first.

The President places each of the two competitors in such a way that the front foot of each is 2 metres from the centre line of the piste (that is behind the "on guard" lines). Competitors are always put on guard, whether at the beginning of the bout or subsequently, in the centre of the width of the piste. At sabre, when the fencers are put on guard in the centre or at any other point on the piste, the President must make absolutely sure that the fencers are a least 4 metres apart.

Competitors come on guard when the President gives the order "On Guard," after which the President asks: "Are you ready?" On receiving an affirmative reply, or in the absence of a negative reply, he gives the signal for the assault to commence with the word "Play." The fencers must come on guard correctly and remain completely still until "Play" is given by the President. (1)

If during a bout the President notices that one of the fencers is making use of his unarmed arm or hand he can call for the help of two judges (if possible neutral) who will be appointed by the Directoire Technique. These judges, one on each side of the piste, will watch one fencer each and will signal, by raising their hand or when asked by the President, if the unarmed hand or arm has been used. The President alone then decides on the penalties to impose. (Cf. 222, 640, 645).

The President may also make the fencers change places so that the fencer breaking this rule does not have his back to the President.

5. Beginning, Stopping and Restarting the Bout.

32 1. As soon as the word "Play" has been pronounced the competitors may assume the offensive. No movement made or initiated before the word "Play" is counted.

2. The bout stops on the word "Halt," except in the case of special events occurring which modify the regular and normal conditions of the bout (Cf. also 47).

Directly the order "Halt" has been given, the competitor may not commence a new action; only the movement which has been begun before the order was given remains valid. Everything which takes place afterwards is entirely invalid (But Cf. 47).

(1) At foil and at sabre no fencer may come on guard with his point in line (arm straight and point threatening the target).

If a competitor stops before the word "Halt," and is hit, the hit is valid.

The order "Halt" is also given if the play of the competitors is dangerous, confused, or contrary to the rules, if one of the competitors is disarmed or leaves the piste with one or both feet, or if, while retiring, he approaches too near the spectators or the jury (Cf. 231-7).

3. After each valid hit is scored the competitors are put on guard in the middle of the piste. If the hit is not allowed they are placed in the position which they occupied when the assault was interrupted. (However, Cf. 226, 321, 414). The competitors will change ends

—In the open air after each hit scored;

—Indoors, after each bout by direct elimination, or for bouts taking place in several hits, after one of the competitors has received half the maximum number of hits which he can receive; at sabre, if one of the competitors is a left-hander and if the President cannot cross to the other side of the piste, the competitors remain in their positions and the judges will exchange places from right to left and vice versa.

However, with the electrical judging apparatus competitors do not change ends during the bout (But Cf. 31 and 552).

4. The President cannot allow a fencer to leave the piste, save in exceptional circumstances. If a competitor does so without permission he is liable to incur the penalties enumerated in Article 646.

6. Fencing at Close Quarters.

33 Fencing at close quarters is allowed so long as the competitors can wield their weapons correctly and the President can, at foil and sabre, follow the phrase.

7. Corps a Corps.

34 The corps a corps is said to exist when the two competitors remain in contact; when this occurs the President must stop the bout (Cf. 37, 224, 318, 412). At foil and at sabre the fencer who causes corps a corps receives a MINOR warning valid for the bout. Should he repeat the offence he will be penalised by having a hit awarded against him. (Cf. 642).

At all three weapons, the fencer who causes corps a corps intentionally to avoid being hit or so that he jostles his opponent, receives a SEVERE warning valid for the bout. This offence is one of a group of six (Cf. 625) for which in the event of a repetition of any one of the offences, the fencer at fault will be penalised by a hit which can cause him to lose the bout (Cf. 645/2).

8. Displacing the Target and Passing the Opponent.

35 Displacing the target and ducking is allowed including the action of ducking during which the unarmed hand may come into contact with the piste.

However, to turn one's back on one's opponent in order to retreat is forbidden; The penalty for this offence is a MINOR warning, valid for the bout; in the event of a repetition, the penalty of a hit (Cf. 643/1).

It is also forbidden to turn one's back on one's opponent during the bout. The penalty for this offence is the annulment of any hit which the fencer at fault may have scored on his opponent (with the action in question), and a MINOR warning valid for the bout; in the event of a repetition, the annulment of any hit which the fencer at fault may have scored on his opponent and the penalty of a hit (Cf. 643/2).

When a fencer passes his opponent during a bout, the President must immediately call "Halt" and replace the competitors in the positions which they occupied before they passed one another.

When hits are made during the movement of a fencer passing his opponent, the hit made immediately is valid; a hit made after passing his opponent by the competitor who has made the passing movement is annulled, but the hit made immediately, even by turning round, by the competitor who has been subjected to the offensive action is valid (Cf. 318, 637).

When during a bout a fencer who has made a fléche attack has a hit registered against him and he continues to run beyond the extreme limit of the piste sufficiently far to cause the spool or the connecting line to the spool to be torn out, the hit which he has received will not be annulled (Cf. 625).

9. Ground Gained or Lost.

36 When the order "Halt" is given ground gained is held until a hit has been given. When competitors are replaced on guard, each fencer should retire equally in order to attain fencing distance.

However:

37 (a) When the bout has been stopped on account of a corps a corps, the fencers are replaced on guard in such a position that the competitor who has sustained the corps a corps is at the place which he previously occupied; this also applies if his opponent has subjected him to a fléche attack, even without corps a corps.

(b) The competitors may not be replaced on guard in such a way that a fencer who was in front of the warning line at the moment when the assault was stopped is placed behind this line if this competitor has not already been warned (Cf. 38).

(c) The competitors may not be replaced on guard in such a way that the fencer who was already behind the warning line, at the moment when the assault was stopped, is caused to lose ground.

10. Crossing the Limits of the Piste.

(a) Stopping a Bout

38 When a competitor crosses one of the boundaries of the piste with both feet, the President must immediately call "halt" and annul everything which has occurred after the boundary has been crossed, except a hit received by the competitor who has crossed the boundary even after he has crossed it provided that this hit is made immediately as part of the movement in the course of which he crossed the boundary.

(b) Rear Limits and Warning Lines

39 When the rear foot of a competitor reaches his warning line for the last time according to the rules laid down for each weapon, the President gives the order "halt," and advises the fencer as to how much ground remains before he will cross the extreme limit of the piste. He will repeat this warning each time the competitor, having, meanwhile, advanced until his leading foot has reached the centre line, again reaches his warning line with his rear foot. Competitors are not advised of their position at any other part of the piste (Cf. 203, 303, 403).

40 The competitor who, after being warned, crosses—i.e., crosses with both feet—the rear limit of the piste, has one hit scored against him. However, if a competitor crosses the rear limit of the piste without having been warned, he is again put on guard at the warning line.

41 Competitors must be allowed to retire on the piste as many times as is necessary in order that each should have at his disposal the regulation distance for retiring. But they are only warned when they reach the warning line for the last time (Cf. 302, 402).

42 If having crossed the rear limit of the piste, the fencer who is attacked parries and makes an immediate riposte or makes a stop hit or time hit such hit will count as valid. This rule will not apply to a fencer who crosses the rear limit of the piste for the last time (Cf. 32, 38).

(c) Lateral Boundaries
43 When one of the competitors crosses one of the lateral boundaries of the piste with one foot, he is not penalised but the President must immediately call "Halt" and replace the competitors on guard on the piste.

A competitor who crosses one of the lateral boundaries of the piste with both feet is penalised. When the competitors are replaced on guard, the opponent of the competitor who has crossed the lateral boundary will step forward from the position which he occupied when the action occurred 1 metre at foil and 2 metres at épée and sabre; the competitor who is penalised must retire an equal distance. When the infliction of this penalty places a competitor with both feet beyond the rear limit of the piste, the competitor is considered as having been hit, always provided that he had previously been warned at his warning line.

A competitor who crosses one of the boundaries of the piste with both feet—e.g., when making a fléche—to avoid being hit, will receive a SEVERE warning, valid for the bout. This offence is one of a group of six for which, in the event of a repetition of any one of the offences, the fencer at fault will be penalised by a hit which can cause him to lose the bout. (Cf. 645/5).

(d) Leaving the Piste Accidentally:
44 A competitor who crosses one of the boundaries of the piste, as the result of an "accident cause" (such as a collision or jostling) incurs no penalty whatever.

11. Duration of the Bout
45 By duration of the bout is meant the effective duration, that is the total of the intervals of time between the orders "Play" and "Halt," deduction being therefore made for the time taken for the deliberations of the jury and other interruptions.

The duration of the bout must be registered exactly by a timekeeper appointed by the organizing committee (obligatory for official competitions of the F.I.E.) (Cf. 59). For the finals of all official competitions, as well as for all bouts for which a chronometer is visible to the spectators, the chronometer must be so placed that it is visible equally to the two fencers on the piste and to the President.

The actual duration of a bout is:

—at épée for one hit—5 minutes;

—at all weapons:
　　for 4 hits—5 minutes;
　　for 5 hits—6 minutes;
　　for 8 hits—8 minutes;
　　for 10 hits—10 minutes;

46 One minute before the expiry of the time allowed for actual fencing the timekeeper must stand up and call 'one minute' (without stopping the clock). This warns the President who should stop the fight and warn the fencers that they have approximately one minute before the expiry of the time allowed for actual fencing. Any hit arriving, "coup lancé," at the moment of the President's "Halt" is valid.

During the last minute of the bout, the fencers may be told, at any interruption of the bout, how much time they have left to fence.

At the expiry of the regulation fencing time, the timekeeper must shout "Halt" (or operate a sound signal) which stops the fight; in this case even a "coup lancé" is not valid. Should there be a failure of the clock or an error by the timekeeper, the President must himself estimate how much fencing time is left.

46a One minute before the end of time allowed, the President, warned by the clock which must automatically send off a buzzer, stops the bout and warns the fencers that they have approximately one minute before the expiry of the time allowed for actual fencing. Any hit arriving, "coup lancé" at the moment the President calls "Halt" is valid.

47 For the finals of official F.I.E. competitions, the warning at one minute before the expiring of the permitted fencing time must be given automatically by the clock which must set off a sound signal. The President, alerted by the clock, must stop the fight and warn the fencers that they have approximately one minute before the expiry of effective fencing time (Cf. 46).

At the expiry of the permitted fencing time, the clock must set off automatically a powerful sound signal and automatically switch off the judging apparatus: any signals registered before the apparatus is switched off must, however, continue to be shown. As soon as the sound signal is heard, the bout is finished.

48 The President may, during the bout, after a SPECIAL warning valid for the pool, the match or the fights by direct elimination, penalise by a hit, and subsequently by exclusion from the event, the fencer who endeavours improperly to cause or to prolong interruptions in the bout (Cf. 646/4).

49 When the time limit expires before the bout is completed, the procedure to be followed is detailed in the chapters dealing with each weapon (Cf. 226, 321, 414).

12. Accidents—Indispositions—Withdrawal of a Competitor

50 If a fencer has been the victim of an accident which has been duly recognized by the doctor on duty, the President may allow him a period of rest once only, and that for a maximum of ten minutes, on the same day, in order that he may recover sufficiently to continue the bout.

(1) The rest shall be timed from the moment when the President stops the bout.

52 The President may on the advice of the doctor on duty, require the withdrawal of a competitor whose physical inability is obvious (Cf. 647).

(1) Cramp is not considered by the F.I.E. as an accident and therefore does not justify a period of rest.

CHAPTER VII—THE DIRECTION OF A BOUT AND THE JUDGING OF HITS

VII A—Officials

1. President
All bouts at fencing are directed by a President who has many duties:

53 (a) He calls the role of the competitors (Cf. 604, 615, 650);

(b) He directs the bout (Cf. 63);

(c) He controls the equipment, including the insulation of the wiring, particularly inside the guard (Cf. 18, 214, 314);

(d) He supervises his assistants (judges, ground-judges, timekeepers, scorers, etc.);

(e) He maintains order (Cf. 615);

(f) He penalises faults (Cf. 615);

(g) He awards the hits (Cf. 67, 69, 75).

2. The Jury, Judges and Ground-Judges.

54 The President fulfills his duty of Judging hits, either with the help of four judges, or with the assistance of an apparatus for the automatic registering of hits; with the latter he may be assisted by two ground-judges or two judges looking out for the use of the unarmed hand (Cf. 31). Ground judges are obligatory when there is no metallic piste.

The President and the judges (or the ground-judges) constitute the 'Jury.' For all bouts in the quarter-finals, semi-finals and final and from the quarter-finals in direct elimination, the President must be assisted by two judges each watching one of the fencers in order to draw attention to any use of the non-sword arm (Cf. 30, 31).

—at foil, either to parry the opponent's blade or to cover part of the target;

—at épée, to parry the opponent's blade; at épée they will also fulfill the functions of floor-judges (Cf. 30, 31, 71, 640).

Arm and floor-judges at foil and épée must change ends halfway through each bout so as not to judge only the same fencer.

55 By accepting a position on a jury, each of the members concerned, by so doing, pledges his honour to respect the regulations and to cause them to be respected, and to carry out his duties with the strictest impartiality and most sustained attention.

56 In an official F.I.E. competition all members of a jury must be licensed amateurs. In other international competitions they must, if they are amateurs, hold a licence.

57 They are appointed by the Directoire Technique (or in its absence by the Organizing Committee) which will select neutral juries as far as possible and will appoint the President from among the international Presidents recognized by the F.I.E. (Cf. 507).

58 For the finals of team competitions:

—If the team captains agree to accept the President proposed by the Directoire Technique and the Commission for Judging, no drawing of lots will take place.

—If the team captains do not agree, the delegates of the commission for Judging and the Directoire Technique will choose three or four presidents who seem to them suitable from among the neutral Presidents present, and lots will be drawn between these Presidents. For the finals of individual competitions comprising six fencers or more there shall be, whenever possible, two complete juries (or two Presidents when judging with an apparatus). (This is obligatory for the official competitions of the F.I.E.) (Cf. 507).

3. Auxiliary Personnel.
3.1. Scorers and Timekeepers

59 Whenever possible the organizers will appoint, on their own responsibility, scorers whose duty it will be to keep the score sheet and the scoreboards and a timekeeper whose duty it will be to keep time for the duration of the bouts (Cf. 45ss). (This is obligatory for the official competitions of the F.I.E.) For finals, the Directoire Technique will choose the timekeeper from among the President's Jury, and he shall as far as possible be neutral.

3.2. Specialist personnel.

60 When judging is done with the assistance of an apparatus for registering hits, the Organizing Committee will further appoint:

(a) A Superintendent of the Apparatus

The Organizing Committee must choose qualified persons, who should follow the working of the apparatus with careful attention in order that they may be able to advise the President as to what their apparatus has registered, and warn him, even during the course of a bout, as to any abnormal phenomena which may occur.

The superintendent of the apparatus must not touch the apparatus while fencing is in progress. When fencing ceases, he re-sets the apparatus either after the President has given his decision, or when the competitors are testing their weapons; but he must never—after a phase of the bout has caused the apparatus to signal a hit—annul this signal before the President has given his decision.

(b) One or More Experts

For each meeting, the Organizing Committee must appoint experts in matters relating to electrical judging. These experts are placed under the supervision of the Directoire Technique.

The experts may be consulted, separately or conjointly, by the President or by the Directoire Technique regarding all questions relating to the electrical apparatus. Members of the Commission for the Electrical Apparatus and Equipment of the F.I.E. who may be present are ex-officio qualified to act as experts.

(c) The Repairers

The Organizing Committee must, for any international Tournament, ensure the presence of competent repairers to remedy faults which may arise during the competition to the personal equipment of the fencers, and, if necessary, to the rest of the electrical apparatus.

VII B—Judging By A Jury

1. The Duties of the President.

61 The President will take up his position a distance from the piste which will enable him completely to follow the actions of the fencers and will follow the competitors in their movements on the piste. He must, for official F.I.E. competitions, use a microphone, preferably without a lead. He directs the bout according to the provisions of the rules (Cf. 227ss, 322ss, 415ss).

2. Position Occupied by the Judges.

62 Two judges are placed on each side of the piste on the President's right and left, respectively, and slightly behind the competitors.

The two judges placed on the President's right hand should watch the fencer who is placed on the President's left hand and especially verify the arrival of hits which this competitor may receive.

Similarly, the two judges placed on the President's left hand should watch the fencer who is placed on the President's right hand and especially verify the arrival of hits which this competitor may receive (however Cf. 69/4).

Methods of Judging.
(a) Procedure

The President, who alone is responsible for the direction of the bout, gives the orders. However, any other member of the jury may give the command "Halt," but only if he thinks that there is an accident.

Similarly the timekeeper stops the bout by calling "Halt!" when time expires.

64 As soon as a judge sees a hit (whether on a valid surface or not) arrive on the fencer whom he is watching he must raise his hand in order to advise the President.

65 All judging is carried out aloud and without the members of the jury leaving the positions which they occupy.

66 The jury is not bound to take account of the acknowledgement of a hit properly made by a competitor (Cf. 606).

67 The jury first decides as to the materiality of the hit or hits. The President then alone decides against which fencer a hit shall be scored by applying the conventional rules for each weapon.

(b) Materiality of the Hit.

68 As soon as the bout has been stopped, the President reconstructs briefly the movements which composed the last fencing phase before the order "Halt" (this formality is not obligatory at épée) and in the course of his analysis he questions the two judges watching one fencer in order to ascertain whether in their opinion any of the movements occurring in his analysis of the phrase has resulted in a hit on the competitor; he then follows the same procedure with the two other judges for the other competitor (this formality must be observed at all three weapons). When the judges are questioned they must reply in one of the following ways: "Yes," "yes but not valid," "No" or "I abstain." The President votes last.

69 The President then aggregates the votes thus made from each side, the opinion of each judge counts as one vote, the opinion of the President as one and a half votes, while abstentions are not counted at all:

1. If both judges on the same side agree in a positive opinion (either both say "yes," or both say "no," or both say "Yes but not valid") their judgment prevails.

2. If one of the judges has a definite opinion and the other abstains, the opinion of the President prevails since his vote is overriding; if he also abstains, the decision of the judge who has a definite opinion prevails.

3. If the two judges concerned are positive but contrary in their opinions or if both abstain, the President may decide according to his own observations (1); if he also abstains, the hit is regarded as doubtful (Cf. 5 below).

4. In the case of a double abstention, the President may, as an exceptional measure, ask the opinions of the two other judges if he considers that they were better placed to see the hit—for example: a riposte on the back made on a fencer who has made a fléche attack and has passed his opponent.

5. A doubtful hit is never scored against the competitor who might have received it; but, on the other hand, any hit made subsequently or simultaneously in the same phrase by the fencer who has thus been granted the benefit of the doubt must also be annulled (but Cf. 38); as regards a hit made subsequently by the fencer who originally made the doubtful hit, the following courses will apply:

I. If the new hit (remise, redoublement or riposte) is made by a fencer who made the doubtful hit without any hit having been made by his opponent, this new hit must be scored.

II. But if the doubt concerns the surface on which the hit arrived (one "Yes" and one "Yes but not valid") no other hit in this phrase can be scored.

III. This is also the case if the opponent has made a doubtful hit between the doubtful hit and the new hit made by the same competitor.

(c) Validity or Priority of the Hit.

70 After the jury has decided the materiality of a hit, the President, acting alone and by applying the conventional rules for each weapon, decides against which fencer a hit is to be awarded, whether both are hit (épée), or if there is no valid hit (Cf. 232ss, 329ss, 416ss).

VII C—Judging With A Judging Apparatus

1. Direction of the Bout.

71 1. The bout is directed by the President who should move up and down the piste in order to follow the fencing phrases while being able to see the appearance of the light signals.

Examples:

(I) Judge A says "no"; Judge B says "yes but not valid"; even if the President considers the hit valid, the judgement must be "no hit"; but in this example since one Judge and the President agree that there has been contact with the point of the opponent, after the decision "no hit" anything which occurs thereafter must be annulled.

II. Judge A says "yes; Judge B says "yes but not valid" the President abstains: he cannot therefore score the hit since there is a doubt as to whether it arrived on a valid surface or not; however, since both judges are agreed there was contact with the point on the opponent, after the decision "no hit" anything which occurs subsequently must be annulled.

2. At the beginning of each bout the President must check the weapon, clothes and equipment of each fencer. For the weapon control, which must also be carried out each time a weapon is changed, the President must check the resistance of the spring in the point of the weapon by means of the special weight, the insulation of the wires inside the guard and in the case of épée, the total travel and residual travel of the point with the 1.5mm and 0.5mm gauges (Cf. 18, 21, 719, 732).

When the apparatus is equipped with yellow lamps the President will, at foil, check that contact between the blade or guard of the foil and the same fencer's metallic lamé jacket causes the corresponding yellow lamp to light up.

If the lamp or lamps remain permanently lit without it being possible to cancel them by pressing the reset button, the bout must not be started or continued until the insulation fault in the circuit has been repaired.

If the yellow lamp of one fencer is lit by momentary contact between that fencer's foil and his jacket, and if his opponent hits him at the same moment, and if it proves possible to cancel the yellow lamp, the President may, if he considers that the fencer caused the contact deliberately while fencing, give a warning.

3. The President will superintend the proper functioning of the electrical apparatus. Either on his own initiative or when asked to do so by a team captain or competitor, he will have the necessary tests made in order to verify the apparatus and localise any faults which may be found. He will prevent the competitors complicating the tests by unplugging or untimely changing of their equipment.

4. If there are ground-judges, they will be placed on either side of the President and on opposite sides of the piste and they should observe all the actions during the bout (Cf. 54).

5. The President should consult the experts for the electrical apparatus each time he considers it necessary (Cf. 60b).

2. Method of Judging
(a) Materiality of the Hit.

72 The materiality of the hit is established according to the indications of the apparatus, when necessary after consulting the ground-judges (Cf. 74).

Only the indications of the electrical apparatus can be taken into consideration for judging hits. Under no circumstances can the President declare a competitor to be hit unless the hit has been properly registered by the apparatus (except as a penalty as laid down in the rules) (Cf. 228ss, 323ss, 626).

73 On the other hand, the President should, in the cases enumerated for each weapon, annul a hit registered by the apparatus (Cf. 230ss, 325ss).

74 Only the two ground-judges, who each have one vote, and the President, who has one and a half votes, decide if a hit has been made on the ground or not. If they cannot reach a majority decision that this is so (i.e., if there are three abstentions or the two judges of different opinions and the President abstaining) the hit must be considered doubtful (Cf. 69/5). In no circumstances may the President take account of the opinions of other persons.

(b) Validity or Priority of the Hit.

75 After reaching his decision regarding the materiality of a hit, the President, by applying the conventional rules for each weapon, decides against which fencer a hit is to be awarded, whether both are hit (épée) or if there is no valid hit (Cf. 232ss, 329ss, 416ss).

PART TWO: FOIL

CHAPTER I—HISTORICAL NOTES

The Rules for Foil were adopted on 12th June, 1914 by the Commission for Foil of the F.I.E. at a meeting in Paris under the presidency of General G. Ettore, representing the Italian Fencing Federation, who edited the proposed rules. They were basically the same as those drawn up by Monsier Camille Prévost, president of the Académie d'Armes and president of the Technical Committee for Foil of the French National Federation. They also conformed to the rules drawn up by the Marquis de Chasseloup-Laubat for "Les Armes de France," to the various earlier international regulations drawn up by the different countries affiliated to the F.I.E. and to the Franco-Italian rules.

The present rules merely define and complete those adopted in 1914.

The rules governing foil competitions judged with the electrical judging apparatus were adopted in 1957 and modified by various later congresses up to the present date.

CHAPTER II—FIELD OF PLAY (Cf. 14ss).

201 Foil competitions are held indoors on pistes made of wood, linoleum, cork, rubber, plastic, metallic mesh, etc. In competitions judged with the electrical apparatus, the piste and its extensions must be entirely covered by a metallic piste in order to neutralise hits made "on the ground" (obligatory for official competitions of the F.I.E.) (Cf. 711).

202 The width of the piste must be from 1 m 80 to 2 metres. The length of the piste must be 14 metres so that each competitor being placed at 2 metres from the centre line has at his disposal for retreating a total distance of 5 metres without it being necessary for him to cross the limit of the piste with both feet (Cf. 15, 38ss, and Pland, page 17).

203 Seven lines should be drawn very clearly on the piste parallel to its width, thus:

One centre line (which may be replaced by a central point or a special sign drawn on the edge of the piste).

Two on guard lines at 2 metres on each side of the centre line (these must be drawn across the whole width of the piste).

Two lines at the rear limits of the piste, which must be drawn across the whole width of the piste, at a distance of 7 metres when possible, from the centre line, but which may be less when sufficient space is not available but never less than 5 metres (Cf. 15).

Two warning lines drawn 1 metre in front of the rear limits of the piste (and which may be drawn only 30 cm. from each side of the piste).

When the rear foot of a competitor reaches his warning line, the president gives the order "Halt" and advises the fencer as to how much ground remains before he will cross the extreme limit of the piste (Cf. 39b).

204 The table on which the judging apparatus is placed should stand level with the centre line and at least 1 metre from the piste, and the President must ensure that its isolation is maintained by the officials, the competitors and the spectators. As a general rule the same table should not be used by the scorekeepers, timekeepers, etc.

CHAPTER III—FOIL EQUIPMENT
(WEAPONS—EQUIPMENT—CLOTHING)

III A—Weapons (Cf. 16ss, 22ss).

1. General Specification For Foils.
205 (a) Weight.

The total weight of the foil ready for use must be less than 500 grammes.

206 (b) Length.

The maximum total length of the foil is 110 cm.

(c) The Blade.

207 The blade, which must be made of steel, is rectangular in section. It is mounted with the widest face of the blade placed horizontally.

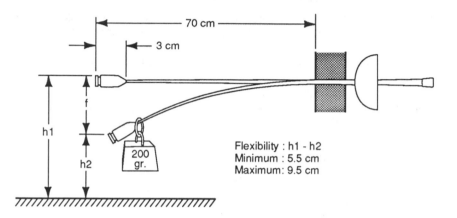

The maximum length of the blade is 90 cm.

The blade should have a flexibility equivalent to a bend of minimum 5.5 cm. and maximum 9.5 cm. measured in the following way:

1. The blade is fixed horizontally at a point 70 cm. from the extremity of the button.

2. A 200 gramme weight is suspended 3 cm. from the extremity of the button.

3. The bend of the blade is measured at the extremity of the button between the non-weighted and the weighted positions.

4. All methods of treating a blade with a view to altering its flexibility, either by grinding, filing or other methods, are forbidden. (Cf. 22).

(d) The Guard (Coquille) (Cf. 26).

208 The guard must be able to pass through a straight cylindrical gauge having a diameter of 12 cm. and length of 15 cm., the blade being parallel with the axis of the cylinder.

Eccentric mounting is forbidden, that is to say that the blade must pass through the centre of the guard. The diameter of the guard must be greater than 9.5 cm.

(e) The Martingale.

209 The martingale is obligatory when the foil is not secured to the hand by an attachment or by the body wire.

(f) Buttons and Points.

210 The point of the foil must be covered unless it is fitted with an electric point for registering hits (or one of a design previously approved), that is to say that the flattened metal button which completes the blade must be covered with waxed thread or plastic or with some other non-metallic material.

2. Specification For the Electric Foil.

211 Foil fencers' electrical equipment must conform to the following conditions, in addition to the special conditions regarding construction laid down in Part VII (Cf. 702, 712, 718).

(a) The Pointe D'arret.

The pressure which must be made on the point d'arret in order to cause the electrical apparatus to register a hit must be more than 500 grammes, that is to say that this weight must be lifted by the spring of the point (Cf. 719). The distance which the pointe d'arret must travel back in order to cause the electrical apparatus to register a hit may be infinitely short: the total stroke must be less than 1 mm.

Sharpening the edges or surface of the point is forbidden. It is absolutely forbidden during a bout for fencers intentionally to thrust or push the tip of the electric weapon into the metal piste.

Any breaking of this rule will be punished according to Article 641/d.

(b) Insulation.

The body of the tip, apart from any parts which may be insulated, and the foil blade for a length of 15 cm. from the tip, as well as the pommel or the extremity of the grip, must be entirely covered with some insulating material (insulating tape, sellotape or even varnish) (Cf. 721).

III B—Equipment and Clothing

1. General Specifications For All Foil Equipment
(a) The Jacket

212 When the jacket is cut horizontally at the waist, the lower edge must overlap the breeches by at least 10 cm. when the fencer is in the on guard position (Cf. 27). The jacket must compulsorily include a lining making a double thickness of material for the sleeve down to the elbow of the sword arm covering the flank in the region of the armpit.

In addition the wearing of a plastron (undergarment) made of hempcloth, nylon, etc. is obligatory; this must:

(1) Be of at least two thicknesses of cloth.

(2) Include a sleeve down to the elbow without sewn seam or opening in the region of the armpit.

(3) Ensure the best possible protection.

It may be fixed to, but not entirely sewn to, the jacket.

(b) The Glove.

213 The glove may be slightly padded (Cf. 27).

(c) Mask (Cf. 27, 722/4).

214 For foil, the mask must be of such a design that, when the fencer is in the on guard position, the bib is not lower than 2 cm. below the collar and in any case not below the prominences of the collar bones (clavicles).

(d) Specifications for Clothing for Ladies' Foil.

215 Ladies' clothing must include breeches closed below the knee, or the divided skirt, and inside the jacket breast-protectors of metal or other rigid material must be worn (Cf. 27).

2. Specifications for Clothing and Equipment Required to Fence With the Electrical Judging Apparatus.

(a) Metallic Plastron (Overjacket).

216 The conducting surface of the metallic plastron which is worn over the jacket must cover the valid target of the fencer entirely and without omission both when in the "on guard" position and when lunging (Cf. 220). Whatever the means of fastening used, the metallic material must cover a sufficient area to ensure that it covers the valid target in all positions of the fencer. The overlap at the closure or fastening point must always be attached on the sword arm side.

The metallic collar must have a minimum height of 3 cm. The lamé material must satisfy the conditions for its verification detailed elsewhere (Cf. 722).

The plastron must be so made that when it is laid flat there is a staight line between the point of junction of the lines of the groin and the two points corresponding to the tops of the hip bones (ilium). The band of non-metallic material passing between the legs must be at least 3 cm. wide.

(b) Body Wire and Attachment Plugs.

217 The conducting wires of the body wire (fencers' personal equipment) must be well insulated electrically from each other, twisted or joined together, and not be affected by humidity. The body wire has a connecting plug at each end. The electrical resistance of each of these conducting wires (plug to plug and plug to crocodile clip) must not exceed 1 ohm.

At the spool-end the three pronged male connection, which must satisfy the conditions of manufacture and assembly laid down in section 7 (Cf. 710, 717), will be attached to the wires in the following manner:

—the prong at 15 mm.: to the metallic plastron

—the central prong: to the wire in the weapon

—the prong at 20 mm.: to the foil blade and the metallic piste.

The wire which joins the rear connection of the body wire to the metallic plastron by a crocodile clip must be separate for at least 40 cms. This wire must be soldered to the crocodile clip and this soldering must not be covered by any insulation or any material whatever. However, any method of fixing which presents the same guarantees as soldering may be used, provided it has been accepted by the Commission de la Signalisation Electrique et de Material. The crocodile clip must be robust and ensure perfect contact with the metallic plastron. Its width at the point of contact must be at least 10 mm.; the inside of the clip must leave a free space at least 8 mm. long by 3 mm. high. It should be clipped onto the back of the metallic jacket on the sword-arm side.

At the end nearest the foil, inside the coquille, any method of attachment is allowed but the method adopted must always conform to the specification laid down in Article 712. Further, the male plugs of the connection must in no circumstances be able to touch the metal part of the guard. The wire from the point will be protected by an insulated sheath from the place where it enters the coquille to the insulated socket of the plug.

Under no circumstances may the non-insulated wire extend beyond this insulated socket (Cf. 26, 208, 712).

(c) Mask.

218 The wire mesh of the mask must be insulated internally and externally, with a plastic material which will not chip off, applied before the mask is made up (Cf. 722).

CHAPTER IV—THE CONVENTIONS OF FOIL FENCING

IV A—Method of Making a Hit

219 The foil is a thrusting weapon only. Offensive actions with this weapon must be made with the point and with the point only. Any hit with the point must arrive cleanly and openly to be counted as a hit (Cf. 29).

IV B-Target

1. Limitation of the Target.

220 At foil, only hits which arrive on the target are counted as valid.

The target at foil, for ladies as for men excludes the limbs and the head. It is confined to the trunk, the upper limit being the collar up to 6 cm. above the prominences of the collar bones; at the side to the seams of the sleeves which should cross the head of the humerus; and the lower limit following a horizontal line across the back joining the tops of the hip bones (ilium) thence following in straight lines the junction of the lines of the groin.

221 The bib of the mask is not included in the target (Cf. 214, Cf. illustration below).

2. The Possible Extension of the Valid Target

222 However, hits which arrive off the target are counted as valid whenever, by reason of an abnormal position, the fencer who is hit has substituted a part of his body which is not counted as the target for a part which is. The President may question the judges or arm-judges about this, but he alone must decide whether the hit is valid or not.

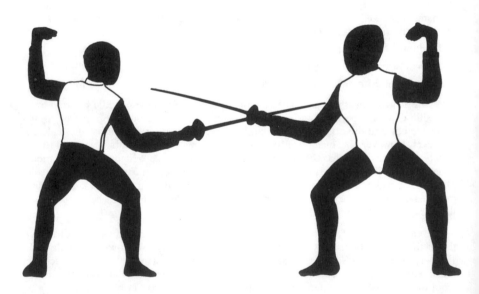

3. Hits Off the Target.

223 A hit which is made on a part of the body other than the target (whether directly or as a result of a parry) is not counted as a valid hit, but stops the phrase and annuls all hits which are scored thereafter (but Cf. 222).

IV C—Corps a Corps and Fléche Attacks

224 At foil, when a fencer causes corps a corps (even without brutality or violence) he receives a MINOR warning valid for the bout. Should the offence be repeated, he will be penalised with a hit (Cf. 642).

The fencer, who intentionally causes corps a corps either to avoid being hit or in such a way that the opponent is jostled, is given a single severe warning, valid for the bout. This offence is one of a group of six (Cf. 645) for which, in the event of a repetition of any one of the offences, the fencer at fault will be penalised by a hit which can cause him to lose the bout (Cf. 645).

IV D—Number of Hits Duration of a Bout

225 At foil, for men and for ladies, bouts are for five hits, with a time limit of six minutes in pools: in direct elimination, either two bouts for five hits, with a deciding bout if necessary, time limit six minutes per bout, or bouts for any specified number of hits (Cf. 544, 555 bis).

226 When the time limit expires before the bout has been completed:

(a) If one competitor has received more hits than his opponent, the number of hits required to bring it up to the maximum being fought for must be added to his score, and the same number of hits must be added to his opponent's score;

(b) If both competitors have received the same number of hits, they are counted as having both received the maximum number of hits being fought for less one and they fence for the last hit without time limit. They are replaced on guard in the position which they occupied when the bout was interrupted (Cf. 32).

IV E—Judging of Hits at Foil

227 Foil competitions are judged with an electrical judging apparatus. This is obligatory for the official competitions of the F.I.E. In the case of all other competitions, the organisers are obliged to make an announcement in advance if it is intended that they should be judged by a jury (Cf. Is).

IV E 1—Materiality of the Hit
1. With a Jury (Cf. 61ss).
2. With an Electrical Judging Apparatus

228 1. The indications of the electrical apparatus can alone be taken into consideration for judging the materiality of hits. Under no circumstances can the President declare a competitor to be hit unless the hit has been properly registered by the apparatus (except as a penalty as laid down in the regulations) (Cf. 72, 626).

229 When using the apparatus it should be noted that:

(a) If both signal lights (white and coloured) appear on the same side of the appratus, a non-valid hit has preceded a valid hit;

(b) The apparatus does not otherwise indicate whether there is any priority in time between two or more hits which it registers simultaneously.

230 2. The President will disregard hits which are registered as a result of actions:

—started before the word "Play" or after the word "Halt" (Cf. 32);

—which are made on the ground (when there is no metallic piste or outside it) or which are made on any object other than the opponent or his equipment (Cf. 73s).

A competitor who, intentionally, causes the apparatus to register a hit by placing his point on any surface other than that of his opponent will receive a single severe warning valid for the bout. This offence is one of a group of six (Cf. 645) for which, in the event of a repetition of any one of the offences, the fencer at fault will be penalised by a hit which can cause him to lose the bout (Cf. 645/6). The same penalty is applied in the case of any subsequent repetition.

Fencers are forbidden to place a non-insulated part of their weapon in contact with their metal jacket with the intention of jamming the electric equipment and thus avoiding being hit.

—the penalty for this offence is the annulment of any hit made by the fencer who caused the jamming; he will receive a severe warning, valid for the bout. This offence is one of a group of six for which, in the event of a repetition of any one of the offences, the fencer at fault will be penalised by a hit which can cause him to lose the bout. The same penalty is applied in the case of any subsequent repetition (Cf. 645/3).

When the judging apparatus is equipped with yellow lamps, the President may penalise a fencer only if the yellow lamp lights up and the audible signal sounds, indicating that one of the fencers placed an uninsulated part of his weapon in contact with his own metallic lamé jacket at the moment he was hit. The President alone, however, decides if the fencer concerned commits an offence or not.

231 3. The President must, on the other hand, take into account possible failures of the electrical equipment, in particular:

(a) He must annul a hit which he has just awarded as a result of a hit registered as on the valid target (coloured lamp) if he establishes, by tests made under his personal supervision, before the bout has effectively recommenced (1) and without any of the equipment in use having been changed (Cf. 71-3/5):

—either that a hit registered as "valid" against the competitor against whom the hit has been awarded can be made without there being in fact a valid hit:

(1) The fact that the President has called "Play," or even that thereafter a certain amount of time has elapsed, does not necessarily mean that "the bout has effectively recommenced" if the two fencers have maintained a passive attitude. In order that the bout should be considered to have effectively recommenced the fencers should have engaged in a fencing phrase which could have affected the equipment in use.

—or that a "non-valid" hit made by the fencer against whom the hit was awarded is not registered by the apparatus;

—or that a "valid" hit made by the fencer against whom the hit was awarded does not cause any hit either valid or non-valid to be registered;

—or that the registration of hits made by the competitor against whom the hit was awarded does not remain recorded on the apparatus.

(b) On the other hand, when the President has decided that a hit made by a competitor has priority, this hit shall not be annulled if subsequently it is found that a valid hit made by the opponent is registered a non-valid or that the weapon of the fencer against whom the hit was awarded is permanently registering a non-valid hit.

(c) If a fencer's equipment does not conform to the provisions of paras 2-4 of Article 722, a hit made off the target which is registered by the apparatus as valid will not be annulled.

4. The President must also apply the following rules:

(a) only the last hit made before the fault was established can be annulled;

(b) a competitor who makes any modification in, or changes his equipment without being asked by the President to do so, before the President has given his decision, loses all right to the annulment of the hit (Cf. 71/3);

(c) if the bout has effectively recommenced (Cf. note to Article 3 (a) above) a competitor cannot claim the annulment of a hit awarded against him before the said recommencement of the bout;

(d) the localization of a fault found in the equipment (including the equipment of the competitors) is of no importance for this possible annulment;

(e) it is not necessary that the failure found should repeat itself each time a test is made; but it is essential that the fault should be manifested to the President without the possibility of doubt at least once, during the tests made by him or under his supervision;

(f) the fact the competitor against whom a hit has been awarded has broken his blade cannot alone justify the annulment of that hit;

(g) the President must pay particular attention to hits which are not registered or which are registered abnormally. Should such defects be repeated, the President must ask a member of the Commission for the Electrical Apparatus and Equipment or an expert technician on duty to verify that the equipment conforms to the rules. The President must ensure that nothing is altered either in the competitor's equipment or in the whole of the electrical apparatus before the expert makes the control.

5. Whenever accidental causes make it impossible to carry out tests, the hit will be considered "doubtful" (Cf. 69/5).

6. If hits are registered simultaneously on both sides of the apparatus and the President cannot establish the priority with certainty, he must replace the competitors on guard.

7. In accordance with the general rules (Cf. 32) the President must stop the bout, even if no hit is registered by the apparatus, whenever play becomes confused and he is no longer able to analyse the phrase.

8. The President should also supervise the state of the metallic piste; he must not allow the bout to commence or to continue if the metallic piste has holes in it which might affect the proper registering of hits. (The organizers must make the necessary arrangements to ensure the rapid repair or replacement of the metallic piste.)

IV E II—Validity or Priority of the Hit
1. Preface

232 Whatever method a President has used to make a decision regarding the materiality of a hit (either with the assistance of a Jury or by the electrical judging apparatus), he then alone decides as to the validity or the priority of the hit by applying the following basic rules which are the conventions applicable to foil fencing.

2. Observance of the Fencing Phrase

233 (a) Every attack, that is every initial offensive action, which is correctly executed must be parried or completely avoided and the phrase must be followed through—that is to say, co-ordinated (Cf. 10).

In order to judge the correctness of an attack the following points must be considered:

1. The simple attack, direct or indirect, (Cf. 11) is correctly executed when the straightening of the arm, the point threatening the valid target, precedes the initiation of the lunge or the fléche;

2. The composed attack (Cf. 11) is correctly executed when the arm is straightened in the presentation of the first feint, with the point threatening the valid target, and the arm is not bent during the successive actions of the attack and the initiation of the lunge or of the fléche;

3. The attack with a step-forward-lunge or step-forward-fléche is correctly executed when the straightening of the arm precedes the end of the step forward and the initiation of the lunge or the fléche;

4. The attack, simple or compound, which is executed with a bent arm is an incorrectly performed attack which lays itself open to the initiation of the offensive or offensive-defensive action of the opponent (Cf. 12);

To judge the priority of an attack when analysing the fencing phrase, it should be noted that:

5. If the attack is initiated when the opponent is not "in line," that is to say with the arm extended and the point threatening the valid target, it may be executed either with a direct thrust, or by a disengage, or by a cut-over, or may even be preceded by a beat or successful feints obliging the opponent to parry.

6. If the attack is initiated when the opponent is "in line," that is to say with the arm straight and the point threatening the valid target, the attacker must, first, deflect the opponent's blade.

7. If the attacker, when attempting to deflect the opponent's blade, fails to find it (derobement), the right of attack passes to the opponent.

8. If the attack, the step or the feints are executed with the arm bent the right of way passes to the opponent.

234 (b) The parry gives the right to riposte: the simple riposte may be direct or indirect, but to annul any subsequent action by the attacker, it must be executed immediately, without indecision or delay.

235 (c) When a composed attack is made, if the opponent finds the blade during one of the feints, he has the right to riposte.

236 (d) When composed attacks are made, the opponent has the right to stop hit; but to be valid the stop hit must precede the conclusion of the attack by an interval of fencing time (temps d'escrime); that is to say that the stop hit must arrive before the attacker has begun the final movement of the attack.

3. Judging of Hits

237 In applying the basic conventions of foil fencing, the President should judge as follows:

When, during a phrase, both fencers are hit simultaneously, there is either a simultaneous action or a double hit. The first of these conditions is due to simultaneous conception and execution of an attack by both fencers; in this case the hits exchanged are annulled for both fencers even if one of them has been hit off the target.

The double hit (coup double) on the other hand, is the result of a faulty action on the part of one of the fencers. Therefore, when there is not a period of fencing time (temps d'escrime) between the hits:

1. Only the fencer who is attacked is counted as hit:

(a) If he makes a stop hit on his opponent's simple attack;

(b) If, instead of parrying, he attempts to avoid the hit and does not succeed in so doing;

(c) If, after a parry is effected, he makes a momentary pause which gives his opponent the right to re-attack (redoublement, or remise or reprise);

(d) If, during a compound attack, he makes a stop hit without being in time (temps d'escrime);

(e) If, having his "point in line" (arm straight and point threatening the target) and being subjected to a beat or a prise de fer which deflects his blade, he attacks or places his point in line again instead of parrying a direct thrust made by his opponent.

2. Only the fencer who attacks is counted as hit:

(a) If he initiates his attack when his opponent has his point in line (arm straight and point threatening the target) without deflecting the opponent's weapon*;

(b) If he attempts to find the blade, does not succeed (derobement) and continues the attack;

(c) If, during a composed attack, he allows his opponent to find the blade, and continues the attack while his opponent ripostes immediately;

(d) If, during a composed attack, he makes a momentary pause, during which time the opponent makes a stop hit, while the attacker continues his attack;

(e) If, during a composed attack, he is stop hit in the time (temps d'escrime) before he begins his final movement;

(f) If he makes a hit by a remise, redoublement or reprise on his opponent's parry, which has been followed by a riposte which is immediate, simple, and executed in one period of fencing time without withdrawing the arm.

3. When there is a double hit (coup double), each time the President is unable clearly to judge from which side the fault has come, he must replace the competitors on guard. One of the most difficult cases to judge arises when a stop hit is made and there is doubt as to whether it is made sufficiently in time in relation to the final movement of a composed attack. Generally, in such cases, the double hit occurs through the fault of both fencers concerned, which justifies the President replacing them on guard. (The fault of the attacker consists of indecision, slowness of execution or making of feints which are not sufficiently effective, the fault of the defender lies in delay or slowness in making the stop hit.)

*Presidents must ensure that a mere contact of the blades is not considered as sufficient to deflect the opponent's blade.

GOVERNING BODY

United States Fencing Association, 1750 East Boulder St., Colorado Springs, CO 80909-5774

The U.S. Fencing Association (USFA) is responsible for the promotion and organization of all national fencing events—the North American Circuit, the Junior Olympic Fencing Championships, and the National Senior Championships. It sets the rules by which all sanctioned events are held in the country. It is responsible for the selection of all international teams, for establishing national training programs for all levels, for the certification of officials, and for the promotion of the sport itself. The USFA is a member of the U.S. Olympic Committee and fields teams for the Pan American Games and the Olympics. The Association belongs to the international governing body, Federation Internationale d'Escrime (F.I.E.), and works closely with collegiate and scholastic organizations.

MAGAZINES

American Fencing, USFA, 1750 E. Boulder St., Colorado Springs, CO 80909

Escrime-Magazine, (French), 45, rue de Liege, 75008 Paris, France

• FIELD ARCHERY •

OFFICIAL RULES OF FIELD ARCHERY

(Reproduced by permission of the National Field Archery Association*)

☐

Note: Due to the lengthiness of the many rounds, games, medal qualifications, and tournaments sanctioned by the NFAA, only the most basic NFAA amateur rounds are presented here. The reader desiring complete information concerning all field archery competition and awards programs should contact the NFAA requesting a copy of the Constitution and By-Laws publication.

ARTICLE I GENERAL RULES FOR FIELD ARCHERY GAMES

A. TERMS:

1. Unit—A 14 target course, including all official shots.

2. Round—Two such units, or twice around one.

3. Double Round—Two complete rounds.

4. Out—First unit to be shot in a round.

5. In—Second unit to be shot in a round.

6. Stake—Shooting position.

7. Face—Target face.

8. Butt—Any object against which the face is placed.

9. Shot—This term in connection with the stake number, i.e., "4th shot," shall be used in referring to the different shots on any course.

10. Spot—Aiming center.

11. Timber—Warning call to other archers who may be in danger zone, announcing that you are ready to shoot.

B. DEFINITIONS:

1. Style—Refers to the type of shooting equipment used by the archer, i.e., Freestyle, Freestyle Limited, Barebow, Competitive Bowhunter, Bowhunter Freestyle or Bowhunter Freestyle Limited.

2. Division—Refers to separation of competitive archers by category, i.e., Adult, Junior or Professional.

3. Age or Sex—Refers to separation of competitive archers according to age and sex, i.e., adult, young adult, youth or cub; and male or female.

---

*See page 263 for additional information.

4. Class and/or Flight—Refers to the division of competitive archers according to skill level and based on established handicap.

5. Scratch Score—Refers to an archer's score before it has been adjusted by his handicap.

6. Net Score—Refers to an archer's score after his scratch score has been adjusted by his handicap.

7. Handicap—Refers to the number of artificial points an archer receives to adjust his scoring ability to the common level of perfect.

8. Handicap Differential—Refers to the difference between an archer's scratch score and perfect.

C. TARGETS:

1. They shall not be placed over any other larger targets nor shall there be any marks on the butt or foreground that could be used as points of aim.

2. All butts must be so placed that the full face is exposed to the shooter.

3. In all National and Sectional tournaments using official NFAA rounds, sixteen 20 cm target faces shall be used for the 20, 25, 30, 35 feet and the 11 yard shot. The butt shall be so constructed so as to encompass the targets in a 4 by 4 configuration. Where 35 cm target faces are specified four 35 cm target faces will be used. The butt shall be so constructed as to encompass the targets in a 2 by 2 configuration.

4. An archer shall not deface his/her target in any manner to include punching a hole, enhancing the X or any other portion of the target in an effort to gain sighting/aiming advantage. Any target so defaced shall be removed by the tournament chairman. Repeated offense shall be grounds for removal of the offender from the tournament. NOTE: The tournament chairman may have the archer's name placed on the target, as in indoor tournaments, however, the name will not be on or in the scoring area of the target.

D. SHOOTING POSITIONS:

1. All shooting position stakes shall be numbered, but the yardage given may be optional.

2. It shall be permissible to use two or more shooting position stakes at any or all one-position targets, provided the stakes are equidistant from the target.

3. All shooting positions shall be plainly visible. When ground level markers are used in place of traditional stakes, a sign shall be posted listing the various positions for each round.

ARTICLE II NFAA SHOOTING EQUIPMENT RULES

A. GENERAL:

1. A conventional bow of any type may be used provided it subscribes to the accepted principle and meaning of the word "bow" as used in archery competition, i.e., an instrument consisting of a handle (grip) riser and two flexible limbs, each ending in a tip with string nock. The bow is braced for use by a single bowstring attached directly between the two string nocks only. In operation it is held in one hand by the handle (grip) riser while the fingers of the other hand draw, hold back and release the string.

2. Compound bows may be used, provided:

a) Basic design includes a handle riser (grip) and two flexible limbs.

b) Total arrow propelling energy is developed from a flexing of the materials employed in limb construction.

c) Weight reduction factor is of no consequence.

d) Bows which develop any portion of arrow propelling energy from other sources such as compressed gas or liquid explosives, or mechanical springs shall not be allowed. This is not to be construed to mean that compound bows which employ other sources of arrow propelling energy, not specifically listed in this paragraph, will be allowed.

e) The cables of the compound bow shall be considered as part of the string and all applicable string rules except color requirements shall apply.

3. This Paragraph Is Applicable Only To Competition On Unmarked Distance Tournaments: The use of a rangefinder is prohibited. At no time shall any device be allowed that would in any manner be an aid in establishing the distance of any shot. No archer may refer to any written memoranda that would aid in determining the distance to the target.

4. Any device that would allow the mass weight, or the draw weight of the bow to be relieved from either or both arms, at full draw, shall be declared illegal.

B. BAREBOW:

1. Archers shooting Barebow style will use bow, arrows, strings and accessories free from any sights, marks or blemishes.

a) String will be made of one or more strands. Strands will be of one consistent color of the archer's choice. The center serving on the string will be served with one layer of any material suitable to use, but material will be of one consistent size and one consistent color. Placement of a nock locator on the serving will be permitted.

b) No written memoranda shall be allowed.

2. An adjustable arrow plate may be used to control the space between the arrow and the face of the sight window.

3. The use of stabilizers shall be permitted.

4. One consistent nocking point only is permitted.

a) Nocking point shall be held by one or two nock locators, which shall be snap on type, shrink tubing, thread or dental floss, tied or served on the serving. No material used for nocking locator shall extend more than 1/4 inch above or below the arrow nock when at full draw.

5. No mechanical device will be permitted other than one nonadjustable draw check and level mounted on the bow, neither of which may extend above the arrow.

6. Releases other than gloves, tabs, or fingers shall be deemed illegal.

7. All arrows shall be identical in length, weight, diameter and fletching, with allowance for wear and tear.

8. The ends or edges of laminated pieces appearing on the inside of the upper limb shall be considered a sighting mechanism.

9. No device of any type, including arrow rest, that may be used for sighting, may be used or attached to the archer's equipment.

10. The pylon (string clearance bar) will be allowed in this style if it is not located in the sight window.

11. Any part of the arrow rest extending more than 1/4 inch above the arrow is deemed illegal in the Barebow style.

12. An arrow plate extending more than 1/4 inch above the arrow is deemed illegal in the Barebow style.

C. FREESTYLE:

1. Any type of sight and its written memorandum may be used.

2. Any release aid may be used provided it is hand operated and supports the draw weight of the bow.

D. FREESTYLE LIMITED:

1. Any type of sight and its written memorandum may be used.

2. Release aids shall be limited to gloves, tabs and fingers.

E. COMPETITIVE BOWHUNTER:

1. This style of shooting is for those with heavy tackle equipment used during hunting activities. Junior Bowhunters shall not be recognized.

2. No device of any type (including arrow rest), that may be used for sighting, may be used or attached to the archer's equipment.

3. There shall be no device, mechanical or otherwise, in the sight window except the arrow rest.

4. Any part of the arrow rest extending more than 1/4 inch above the arrow is deemed illegal in the Competitive Bowhunter style.

5. An arrow plate extending more than 1/4 inch above the arrow is deemed illegal in the Competitive Bowhunter style.

6. No clickers, drawchecks, or levels will be allowed. No laminations, marks, or blemishes may appear in the sight window or upper limb.

7. A sight window may be altered from standard configuration providing that no lamination, blemish, protrusion, or any identifiable mark that could be used for an aiming reference is visible.

8. String shall be one color only. A center serving of one other color may be used. One consistent nocking point only is permitted. Nocking point shall be held by one or two locators, which shall be snap on type, shrink tubing, thread, or dental floss, tied or served on the serving. No material used for nocking locator shall extend more than 1/4 inch above or below the arrow nock when at full draw. Any marks, ties or string attachment to the string (except brush buttons and silencers properly located) shall invalidate its use in this division.

9. One anchor point only is permitted.

10. An archer shall touch the arrow when nocked with the index finger against the nock. Finger position may not be changed during competition. In cases of physical deformity or handicap, special dispensation shall be made.

11. Releases other than gloves, tabs, or fingers shall be deemed illegal.

12. Each time an archer shoots a round, all arrows shall be identical in length, weight, diameter and fletching with allowances for wear and tear.

13. The Field Captain, or his counterpart, shall be the final authority regarding equipment and style eligibility, and may reclassify at his discretion.

14. Brush buttons, string silencer, no less than 12 inches above or below the nocking point, and bow quiver installed on the opposite side of the sight window with no part of the quiver or attachments visible in the sight window are legal. One straight stabilizer, coupling device included if used, which cannot exceed 12 inches at any time, as measured

from the back of the bow may be used in the Competitive Bowhunter style. No forked stabilizer or any counterbalance will be legal.

15. The following broadheads are authorized for tournaments:

a) Male—7/8 inch cutting edge width (minimum).

b) Female—3/4 inch cutting edge width (minimum).

16. There shall be no restrictions on the bow draw weight. Arrows must be equipped with commercially manufactured, non-modified points, a minimum of 125 grain for men and a minimum of 100 grain for women, that can be replaced by broadheads.

17. Any device for lengthening or shortening the draw length of an archer shall be prohibited.

18. An archer will not be permitted to change the draw weight of the bow during a round.

19. The pylon (string clearance bar) will be allowed in this shooting style if it is not located in the sight window.

20. No written memoranda shall be allowed.

21. All official NFAA rounds shall be considered official rounds for the Bowhunter style of shooting, and further all classification shall be based upon the Field and Hunter rounds.

F. FREESTYLE BOWHUNTER:

1. A sight with a maximum of 5 fixed reference points that must not be moved during a round. Pin sights are to be of straight stock with only one sighting reference possible from each pin. Hooded pins or scopes cannot be used. The maximum sight extension measurement shall be 5'', measured from the back of the bow at the center of attachment to the foremost part of the sight assembly, as measured on a horizontal plane. Lighted or illuminated sights (pins) are illegal.

2. Release aids will be permitted.

3. A kisser button or string peep sight will be permitted, but not both. Whichever is installed must be secured so as not to be movable between shots of different distances.

4. It will not be mandatory in this style of shooting to provide for other than one division for men and one division for women.

5. All rules of the Competitive Bowhunter shooting style, except those excluded by this section, shall also apply to the Freestyle Bowhunter shooting style.

G. FREESTYLE LIMITED BOWHUNTER:

The requirements are the same as for Freestyle Bowhunter in F.

ARTICLE III DIVISIONS OF COMPETITION

A. DIVISIONS ARE RECOGNIZED AS FOLLOWS:

1. Adult: is provided for male and female archers. Archers who wish to retain their amateur status are responsible to comply with I.O.C. Rule 26 (refer to Addendums Article IV).

2. Junior: is provided for male and female archers in age groups of young adult, youth and cub. Junior archers are considered amateurs and it is their responsibility to comply with I.O.C. Rule 26 (refer to Addendums Article IV).

a) General:

1) No archer may compete with or against archers of another junior division in any official National or Sectional championship tournament.

2) Archers may elect to compete in any higher division, junior or adult, with written parental consent. An NFAA form in triplicate shall be provided for parental or guardian signature. One copy must be filed with NFAA Headquarters and one copy with the state association Secretary. Once this option has been exercised the archer may not revert back.

3) The youth and young adult archers only are eligible for 20 pins and other awards in the same manner as adult division.

4) Archer's date of birth must appear on his/her official membership card.

5) Freestyle, Freestyle Limited, and Barebow shall be the only recognized shooting styles for Junior Division archers.

b) Cub:

1) This classification is established for archers under 12 years of age at National and Sectional tournaments but is optional at state level and below.

2) Cub shooting positions shall be marked with black stakes.

3) The cub's handicap must be established entirely on the cub course and is not applicable to or from any other course.

4) Cub official target units shall consist of:

Yardage	Field	Hunter	Animal Group	International
20 ft	20 cm	20 cm	4	—
10	35 cm	35 cm	4	—
10	35 cm	35 cm	4	35 cm
10	35 cm	35 cm	4	35 cm
10	35 cm	35 cm	3	35 cm
15	50 cm	35 cm	3	50 cm
18	50 cm	50 cm	3	50 cm
20	50 cm	50 cm	3	50 cm
20	50 cm	50 cm	2	50 cm
20	50 cm	50 cm	2	65 cm
20	65 cm	50 cm	2	65 cm
25	65 cm	65 cm	1	65 cm
30	65 cm	65 cm	1	—
30	65 cm	65 cm	1	—

5) The cub archers shall receive distinctive 50 point progressive merit patches. They shall be awarded on official 28 target rounds for one consecutive score of one 50 point increment between 50 and 550. Applications for cub merit patches shall be made to the state association secretary. Patches are furnished free of charge by the NFAA.

c) Youth:

1) The youth classification is established for archers age 12 through 14.

2) The handicap must be established entirely on the youth (50 yard maximum) course and is not applicable to or from any other course.

3) Any and all official NFAA units or rounds shall not contain shots over 50 yards. Group 1 animal faces shall be shot from the closest walk-up animal stake only.

4) Youth official target units shall consist of and be the same as the adult rounds with the following exceptions:

Field Round	Youth Yardage	Face Centimeters
55 yards	40	65
60 yards	45	65
65 yards	50	65
80, 70, 60, 50 yards	50	65
Hunter Round		
70, 65, 61, 58 yards	50	65
64, 59, 55, 52 yards	50	65
58, 53, 48, 45 yards	45	65
53, 48, 44, 41 yards	41	50
International Round		
55 yards	50	65
60 yards	50	65
65 yards	50	65

5) The youth archers shall receive distinctive 50 point progressive merit patches. They shall be awarded on official 28 target rounds for one consecutive score of one 50 point increment between 50 and 550. Applications for youth merit patches shall be made to the state association secretary. Patches are furnished free of charge by the NFAA.

6) The shooting positions for youth archers shall be marked blue.

d) Young Adult:

1) The young adult classification is provided for archers 15 through 17 years of age and for those younger who have waived into this division.

2) The young adult must establish his handicap entirely on the 80 yard (adult length) course and it is not applicable to or from any other course.

ARTICLE IV TOURNAMENTS

A. NATIONAL TOURNAMENTS:

1. A National Outdoor championship tournament shall be provided annually, at a time and place to be determined by a 2/3 majority vote of the Board of Directors Council. All bids submitted for National tournaments will be sent to the host state Director at least 15 days before contracts are signed, and copies must be available at NFAA Headquarters for inspection.

2. The Board of Directors Council shall also establish entry fees, awards, and any or all other conditions.

3. At the National Outdoor championship tournament all flight awards will be presented at the tournament site immediately upon completion and tabulation of scores.

4. A National Indoor championship tournament may be provided annually by the same procedure.

5. All unused targets ordered by hosting clubs for National tournaments must be purchased by the host club at cost price, or returned postage paid to NFAA Headquarters.

The Chairman's report for National tournaments shall include an accounting of targets ordered, targets used, and targets unused.

B. Sectional Tournaments:

1. A Sectional Outdoor championship tournament shall be provided annually in each section, with the time, place and rounds to be determined by members of the Board of Directors within the section. All bids submitted for Sectional tournaments will be sent to the host state Director at least 15 days before contracts are signed, and copies must be available at NFAA Headquarters for inspection.

2. The entry fees, awards, and any or all other conditions for these tournaments, except late registration, shall be established by NFAA.

a) Late registration will be at the discretion of the NFAA directors of that section.

3. A Sectional Indoor championship tournament may be provided annually by the same procedure.

4. Sectional tournaments shall consist of official NFAA rounds.

5. An archer may choose to shoot in several Indoor and Outdoor Sectional tournaments of his choice, but only may compete for awards in that section of his residence.

C. STATE ASSOCIATION APPROVED TOURNAMENTS:

The NFAA-affiliated states may provide any number of outdoor and indoor tournaments, up to and including the state championship level.

D. DEFINITIONS:

1. NFAA Official Round: The NFAA recognizes as official those rounds described in By-Laws Article VI, which are: Field Round, Expert Field Round, Hunter Round, Animal Round, "300" Field Round, "300" Hunter Round, International Outdoor Round, NFAA Indoor Round, NFAA Indoor Championship Round, Freeman Round, Flint Bowmen Indoor Round.

2. NFAA Sanctioned Round: The NFAA shall grant official sanction to any of the above NFAA Official Rounds when said round is conducted by the NFAA or through its recognized state affiliate; when said round is held on an NFAA-approved facility using official NFAA targets; and when said round conforms to By-Laws Articles I, IV, and VI.

3. NFAA Handicap Round: The NFAA recognizes as official for recording on the NFAA handicap card any Field or Hunter round or 14/14 combination of same; and any "300" Field or "300" Hunter round, which fulfills the requirements of NFAA sanction.

E. SHOOTING EQUIPMENT STYLES:

The divisions of competition and styles of shooting provided at National and Sectional tournaments shall be those designated by the Board of Directors at an annual meeting. Said established styles of shooting and divisions of competition are not mandatory below the Sectional level. National and Sectional tournaments shall provide for the recognized styles of shooting in the Adult, Junior and Professional divisions.

F. NATIONAL AND SECTIONAL DIVISIONS AND COMPETITION:

1. Divisions of competition and styles of shooting to be recognized at National and Sectional tournaments:

a) Professional, Adult, Young Adult, Youth and Cub.

b) Members of other National Professional Archery Organizations must pay NFAA pro dues and compete in the NFAA Professional Division, at Sectional and National tournaments.

2. Styles of shooting to be recognized shall be:

ADULT/PRO	YOUNG ADULT (ages 15-17)	YOUTH (ages 12-14)	CUB (under 12)
Freestyle		Freestyle	
Freestyle Limited		Freestyle Limited	
Barebow		Barebow	
Bowhunter			
Bowhunter Freestyle			
Bowhunter Freestyle Limited			

3. In addition, a complimentary Senior Division for archers ages 55 and over shall be provided at National and Sectional tournaments and is optional at State level and below. Any member competing in the Senior Division will compete also in the flight in which he/she is placed with other archers in their style of shooting and will be eligible for both awards.

a) Styles of shooting for men and women shall be as listed in paragraph 2 above.

b) Awards shall be medals only.

G. DETERMINING FLIGHTS AT NATIONAL AND SECTIONAL TOURNAMENTS:

These methods shall be printed in the contracts and on the registration forms:

1. The NFAA flight system will be used at National and Sectional tournaments.

2. a) Flights will be provided in each division and shooting style as follows: 1 to 15 shooters, one flight; 16 to 30 shooters, two flights; 31 to 45 shooters, three flights; 46 to 60 shooters, four flights; 61 or more shooters, five flights; and so forth.

b) An optional alternate flight system for the sectional level tournaments with 200 shooters or less. (Located in policy section.)

3. For Outdoor Nationals and Sectionals, archers may be arranged in flights by their handicaps at the start of the tournament. Archers without established handicaps may be placed into flights at the end of the first handicap round (or at the discretion of the tournament chairman).

4. For Indoor Nationals and Sectionals, archers shall be arranged in flights according to score shot in the first round.

5. Equal division of the number of archers in each flight will be maintained, except that the last flight will record a lesser number (for two flights) or an unequal number (for three or more flights) as may be required. When two or more tie scores appear at the flight break, the archers tied will be placed at the top of the lower flight, without disturbing the remaining flights as originally established.

6. The flight system does not apply to the Professional Division.

H. AWARDS:

1. For purpose of awards individual groups listed in 'E' above shall decide individually what awards shall be given. The unit system may be used by any of the above groups. The unit rule is defined as follows: One award for one through three archers in a class. Two awards for four through six archers in a class. Three awards for seven or more archers in a class.

2. Archers awarded the temporary custody of prizes and trophies shall be responsible for their return in good order to the Executive Secretary at least two weeks before the next annual tournament.

I. USE OF HANDICAPS:

1. All handicaps as provided under "Handicapping" shall be recognized.

2. The NFAA shall issue official NFAA handicap cards.

J. TOURNAMENT OFFICIALS:

1. Tournament Chairman.

a) At all NFAA sanctioned tournaments a Tournament Chairman shall be appointed and it shall be his duty to:

1) See that the requirements of NFAA sanction are fulfilled, through the NFAA Director, NFAA Councilman, or designated NFAA administrator.

2) See that a target captain and two scorers are appointed for each group.

3) Designate the order in which groups are to shoot or assign the stakes from which each group is to start, depending on which system is used.

4) Have the option to set a time limit, either by target or by round, when such tournament must be completed.

5) Be the final authority in settling disputes which arise over rules or conduct of the tournament, unless notice of intent to protest is given and followed by submission of a written protest within one hour after leaving the range on the day of the protested incident. A $25.00 National and $15.00 Sectional protest fee must accompany the written protest at National and Sectional tournaments, which will be refunded if the protest is upheld.

6) Will inspect or designate an official of the tournament to inspect any Barebow, Bowhunter, Bowhunter Freestyle and Bowhunter Freestyle Limited equipment at any time during an NFAA sanctioned event that they feel necessary.

2. Target Captain.

a) At all NFAA sanctioned tournaments a Target Captain shall be appointed for each group and it shall be his duty to:

1) Report any archer in his group violating the rules set forth in the NFAA By-Laws.

2) Be the final judge of all disputed arrows in his group.

3) Verify equipment failure for any archer in his group.

K. SHOOTING RULES:

1. Archers shall shoot in groups of not less than 3, or more than 6; 4 shall be the preferred number. No group of less than three shall turn in an official score.

2. For shooting position at the shooting stake the foursome, by mutual agreement, shall decide which two shall shoot from which side of the shooting stake.

a) At the conclusion of each 14-target unit the archers shall change their order of shooting. Those who shot first shall shoot last and those who shot last shall shoot first.

b) Starting with the first target an archer shall shoot from the same side of the shooting stake for fourteen targets. At the conclusion of each 14 target unit those archers who have been shooting from the right side shall shoot the remainder of the course from the left side; those on the left shall shoot from the right side.

c) The archer must straddle an imaginary shooting line, which is marked by the distance stake and parallel to the target face, while shooting the required arrows, nor shall any archer advance to the target until all arrows have been shot by the group except for yardages that are 19 yards or less and when there are more than four archers in a group on 35 cm targets or smaller, archers may elect to shoot at a clean target after all previous shooters in the group have shot and had their arrows scored.

3. When shooting at butts requiring multiple target faces, the first 2 shooters will shoot the bottom target faces. When target faces are placed side by side (i.e., 50 cm) the archer on the left will shoot the left target face; the archer on the right will shoot the right target face. On fan positions the same applies, except each archer will shoot two arrows at each target. Any arrow striking the wrong target shall be considered a miss and may not be re-shot.

4. One group shall not hold up the following groups while looking for lost arrows. Enough arrows shall be carried so that each archer may continue shooting, and return later to find missing arrows. If one or more open targets in front and two or more groups back up, the delaying group shall allow backed up groups to shoot through.

5. No archer may practice on any shot of a course to be used for tournament shooting later the same day. Special practice targets should be supplied. The first target of each round may be used as practice at the discretion of the tournament chairman. The maximum number of arrows allowable will be determined by the round being shot.

6. An archer leaving the range for any reason other than an equipment failure may be privileged to return to his group and complete unfinished round or subsequent rounds. He will not be privileged to make up any missed in the interim.

7. In the case of an equipment failure verified by the target captain, the archer may have the needed time, with a maximum of 45 minutes, as granted by a tournament official for equipment repair or replacement and maximum of four (4) practice arrows. Then in the presence of the tournament official the archer may be allowed to shoot the targets missed. This occurrence of repair or replacement may not happen more than once in any tournament day.

8. No archer may shoot (compete) in any one tournament more than one time unless advertised as a multiple registration tournament.

9. In case of inclement weather, the tournament shall continue unless a prearranged signal is given by the tournament chairman. Any archer leaving the range shall be automatically disqualified.

10. No alcoholic beverages may be carried or consumed on any range or practice area during shooting hours at National or Sectional tournaments.

11. Tripods for spotting scopes and tripods for binoculars shall not be permitted during outdoor competition at National or Sectional Tournaments.

L. SCORING:

1. Arrows must remain in the target face until all arrows are scored. In all NFAA Rounds, an arrow shaft cutting two rings must cut completely through the line to be counted in the area of next higher value. They may then be withdrawn.

2. The status of doubtful arrows shall be determined before drawing any arrows from the target, and such arrows may not be touched until after being recorded.

3. The target captain shall be the final judge of all disputed arrows.

4. Off-ground skids or glances into the target shall not be counted. Arrows striking objects over the shooting lane may be re-shot.

5. Arrows passing through the face, but still in the butt, may be pushed back and scored as hits in the circles through which they went. This does not mean that they may be withdrawn and then stuck back through the target.

6. Arrows believed to have passed through the target may be re-shot with marked arrows, which will not be scored if the doubtful arrows are found in the butt.

7. Unsuspected pass throughs: in any instance where arrows are found to have obviously passed through in such a manner they cannot be properly scored and their location and the condition of the butt convince the target captain that the arrows did indeed pass through a scoring area, the archer may return and re-shoot from the obvious distances or furthest distances involved.

8. Witnessed bounce outs, believed to have hit the target in the scoring area, will be re-shot.

9. In any tournament where the method of shooting off a tie is not decided in advance, ties shall be decided by shooting the first three (3) targets. In any tournament where field faces are involved, field faces shall be used. If a tie still exists after three targets, continue from target to target until the tie is broken.

10. An archer who shoots arrows at the target in excess of the prescribed number shall lose the arrow or arrows of higher value in all NFAA rounds.

11. A dropped arrow is one which falls while being transferred from the quiver to be nocked on the string, or in preparation for a shot; or which falls from the string during a controlled letdown. (A dropped arrow may be re-shot.)

12. Scorecards must be signed as correct by scorekeeper and archer. Once submitted a scorecard cannot be retrieved for purposes of changing totals. An archer who has signed and submitted a scorecard as correct which has incorrect total(s) shall immediately be disqualified.

ARTICLE V THE NFAA HANDICAP

A. GENERAL:

1. Essence of the NFAA Handicap System: handicapping is the great equalizer among sportsmen of differing abilities. The National Field Archery Association presents this archery handicap system in the conviction that, when faithfully operated, it results in equitable handicaps no matter where archers live and play. The handicap system does not exclude the use of both handicap and/or scratch shooting in the same tournament. The national system of handicapping must meet two main requirements, which are:

a) Simple enough for operation by the small, modestly equipped club as well as the largest state association.

b) Thorough enough to produce fair, uniform handicapping the country over.

2. Handicap Name: the handicap produced by this system is termed an "NFAA Handicap." Such a handicap should be identified on a card or elsewhere as an "NFAA Handicap" or as "Computed under NFAA Handicap System."

3. Purposes:

a) Provide fair handicaps for all archers, regardless of ability.

b) Reflect the archer's inherent ability as well as his recent scoring trends.

c) Automatically adjust his handicap down or up as his game changes.

d) Disregard freak low scores that bear little relation to the archer's normal ability.

e) Make it difficult for the archer to obtain an unfairly large handicap increase at any revision period.

f) Make a handicap continuous from one shooting season to the next without need of adjustment.

g) Encourage the archer to keep his game near its peak.

h) Establish handicaps useful for all archers, from championship eligibility to informal games.

i) Make handicap work as easy as possible for the handicapper.

B. ESTABLISHING A HANDICAP:

1. An archer's handicap shall be computed on the official NFAA field and/or hunter round, and shall be computed by the following table:

Best score of 2 scores—80% of avg. differential

2 best scores of 5 scores—80% of avg. differential

3 best scores of last 7 scores—80% of avg. differential

The first and second methods shall be computed only for those archers who have not recorded the minimum of seven scores needed for a full handicap.

2. An archer's handicap shall be derived only from those scores shot within the last twelve (12) month period.

3. All handicaps must be established during a tournament held on official NFAA targets approved NFAA 2-Star Ranges or higher, and where official NFAA field or hunter rounds are shot.

4. The differential is the difference between the actual average and perfect. (Example: Last 7 scores are 430, 415, 440, 440, 450, 460 and 410. The best 3 scores are 440, 450 and 460. Average = 450. 560 minus 450 = 110. 80% of 110 equals 88, which is the handicap.)

C. HANDICAP PROCEDURE:

1. A new archer, or one who holds an expired handicap card, shall be issued a handicap card in the most expedient manner upon the payment of established fees, and must shoot two official scores to establish handicap.

2. No archer shall be permitted to compete in an NFAA registered tournament in which any official NFAA rounds are shot unless he holds a valid handicap card, or has made proper application, except as specified in Constitution Article III, Section B, paragraph 2e.

3. No archer shall be issued a handicap card unless the archer is a member in good standing of the NFAA and a state association chartered and recognized by the NFAA.

4. Each person will be responsible for keeping a current handicap in the proper place on the handicap card after each score is recorded by the tournament Chairman of each tournament.

5. If a person shoots more than one style, he must be handicapped in each style.

D. HANDICAP CARDS:

1. All official handicap cards shall be printed by the NFAA and shall be made available, free of charge, to affiliated state associations. The card shall have provisions to indicate NFAA state and club membership, all styles of shooting, and shall provide space for recording scores for all recognized styles of shooting.

2. Handicap cards shall be issued by the association which has granted membership as provided under Constitution Article III.

3. Handicap shall be concurrent with membership, i.e., expiration of membership in the NFAA shall void handicap.

4. Each person will be responsible for keeping a current handicap in the proper place on the handicap card after each score is recorded by the tournament chairman of each tournament.

5. No handicap card shall be issued by the NFAA in conjunction with direct NFAA membership applications, provided an affiliated state association exists in the area where the archer resides.

6. The handicap and membership card shall carry the full name, address and social security number of the archer.

7. Handicap and membership cards of military personnel in transit or on temporary duty shall be recognized.

8. A handicap chart for the NFAA field and hunter rounds will accompany all handicap cards.

E. SCORES TO BE RECORDED ON HANDICAP CARDS:

1. All scores recorded on the handicap cards shall be the actual scores for the field and/or hunter rounds.

2. All scores shot in tournaments using field and/or hunter rounds shall be recorded.

3. All recordings on the handicap card shall be on the basis of each 28 targets, i.e., a tournament of 28 targets field and 28 targets hunter . . . each score is to be recorded. If a 14 field and 14 hunter . . . the combined total shall be recorded. If a 28 field and 14 hunter . . . the round that is completed shall be recorded. No fractional round shall be recorded.

4. Tournament officials shall be responsible for the recording of actual scores on the handicap cards of all participants. Violation shall be cause to suspend club charter and/or recognition of the state association.

F. LOST OR MISPLACED HANDICAP CARDS:

1. An archer who has been handicapped but cannot submit a handicap card or statement from his club secretary showing his/her true handicap is required to compete without handicap for that tournament.

2. An archer may not submit club secretary evidence of handicap to the state handicap officer or NFAA board member for more than 14 consecutive days. The archer must apply for a replacement handicap and membership card. The application must be accompanied by the fees established by the NFAA and the state association. The replacement card shall run concurrent with his previous card as recorded in the records of the state association and/or records of the NFAA.

G. ADMINISTRATION OF HANDICAPS:

1. Handicap shall be administered through the state association chartered and recognized by the NFAA. If no chartered or recognized association exists, the NFAA shall administer the system.

2. The state association shall maintain a satisfactory control to insure that handicap is properly administered.

3. The state associations shall agree no archer is denied a handicap card upon proper application and payment of fees, regardless of race, creed, or color.

4. The state association shall agree that no member in good standing with the NFAA is denied a handicap card.

5. State associations may not impose additional requirements for handicap and membership in the NFAA.

6. The state association shall furnish the NFAA with a duplicate of current handicap card holders in a form satisfactory to NFAA. This information will be furnished at the same time as membership handicap cards are forwarded to the archer.

7. Non-compliance with these requirements shall be grounds for immediate suspension of recognition by the NFAA. The state association must submit within 30 days a brief, showing cause why the offending association's charter and recognition should not be revoked by the NFAA Board of Directors Council.

8. The use of non-official targets shall not be construed as a permissive to negate the provisions of the handicap article.

ARTICLE VI OFFICIAL NFAA ROUNDS

A. FIELD ROUND:

1. Standard Unit:

A standard unit shall consist of the following 14 shots:

15, 20, 25, 30 yards at a 35 cm face

40, 45, 50 yards at a 50 cm face

55, 60, 65 yards at a 65 cm face

(for these distances—4 arrows at each)

And the following four-position shots, each arrow to be shot from a different position or at a different target:

35 yards at a 50 cm target, all from the same distance, but from different positions of different targets: 45, 40, 35, 30 yards at a 50 cm target.

80, 70, 60, 50 yards at a 65 cm target.

35, 30, 25, 20 feet at a 20 cm target.

2. Targets:

Four face sizes shall be used. The outer ring diameter shall be 65 cm, 50 cm, 35 cm, and 20 cm. The spot shall be two black rings with white X in center ring, two white rings and two outside black rings. (X-ring used for tie breakers only.) The rings have the following diameters:

Target Diameter	65 cm	50 cm	35 cm	20 cm
Outer Black Ring:	65 cm	50 cm	35 cm	20 cm
Inner Black Ring:	52 cm	40 cm	28 cm	16 cm
Outer White Ring:	29 cm	30 cm	21 cm	12 cm
Inner White Ring:	25 cm	20 cm	14 cm	8 cm
Outer Black Spot:	13 cm	10 cm	7 cm	4 cm
X Ring:	6.5 cm	5 cm	3.5 cm	2 cm

3. Shooting Positions:

The prescribed distances in this section are to be adhered to without variation. Each NFAA chartered club with an approved field course shall have the option of marking the distances on the shooting stakes of the following NFAA Rounds: Field, Hunter and Animal. In laying out the course any order may be used as the official shooting order on any four position shot.

4. Shooting Rules:

Each archer shall shoot 4 arrows at each of the 14-target layouts in a unit. In 10 cases this shall mean shooting the 4 arrows from a single stake at a single face. In the other

4 it may mean either shooting 1 arrow from each of four stakes at a single face, or it may mean shooting all four arrows from a single stake but at four separate faces.

5. Scoring:

a) The scoring is 5 points for the spot, 4 for 2 white circles and 3 for outside black rings.

b) An arrow shaft cutting two rings shall be scored as being in the ring of the greater value. The outer line of the Field target is outside the scoring field. For that reason the arrow shaft must cut the line so that no color of the line can be seen between arrow shaft and scoring field before a hit may be counted. The same is true for the inner line between the 2 circles.

c) The X-Ring is used for tie breakers only.

B. NFAA EXPERT FIELD ROUND:

1. Standard Unit:

A standard unit shall consist of the following 14 shots:

15, 20, 25, 30 yards at a 35 cm face

(4 arrows at each distance)

40, 45, 50 yards at a 50 cm face

(4 arrows at each distance)

55, 60, 65 yards at a 65 cm face

(4 arrows at each distance)

And the following four-position shots, each arrow to be shot from a different position or at a different target:

35 yards at a 50 cm target, all from the same distance, but from different positions of different targets: 45, 40, 35, 30 yards at a 50 cm target.

80, 70, 60, 50 yards at a 65 cm target.

35, 30, 25, 20 feet at a 20 cm target.

2. Targets:

a) Four face sizes shall be used:

1) 65 cm face with a 6.5 cm X-ring

2) 50 cm face with a 5 cm X-ring

3) 35 cm face with a 3.5 cm X-ring

4) 20 cm face with a 2 cm X-ring

The spot shall be two black rings with white X in center ring, two white rings and two outside black rings (X-ring is used for tie breakers only).

3. Shooting Positions:

The prescribed distances in sub-section 1 of this by-law are to be adhered to without variation. Each NFAA chartered club with an approved field course shall have the option of marking the distances on the shooting stakes.

4. Shooting Rules:

Each archer shall shoot 4 arrows at each of the 14-target layouts in a unit. In 10 cases this shall mean shooting the four arrows from a single stake at a single face. In the other four it may mean either shooting one arrow from each of the four stakes at a single face, or it may mean shooting all four arrows from a single stake but at four separate faces.

5. Scoring:

a) The scoring is 5 points for the spot, 4 for 2nd circle, 3 points for the 3rd circle, 2 points for the 4th circle and 1 point for the 5th circle. The X-ring is used for tie breakers only.

b) An arrow shaft cutting two rings shall be scored as being in the ring of the greater value. The outer line of the field archery target is outside the scoring field. For that reason the arrow shaft must cut the line so that no color of the line can be seen between arrow shaft and scoring field before a hit may be counted. The same is true for the inner line between the two circles.

C. HUNTER ROUND:

1. Standard Unit:

The 14 targets form a unit. Twice around the unit makes a round, or two such units laid out make a round.

2. Targets:

The Hunter Round target has two white rings with black X in center ring, and two outside black rings. (X-ring used for tie breakers only). The rings have the following diameters:

Target Diameter	65 cm	50 cm	35 cm	20 cm
Outer Black Ring:	65 cm	50 cm	35 cm	20 cm
Inner Black Ring:	39 cm	30 cm	21 cm	12 cm
Outer White Ring:	13 cm	10 cm	7 cm	4 cm
X-Ring:	6.5 cm	5 cm	3.5 cm	2 cm

The following shows the target face size and aiming spot, with the yardage distances that are to be used.

Target Size: 65 cm target, with 13 cm white spot

70-65-61-58

64-59-55-52

58-53-48-45

Target Size: 50 cm target, with 10 cm white spot

53-48-44-41

48

44

40

36-36-36-36

Target Size: 35 cm target, with 7 cm white spot

32-32-32-32

28-28-28-28

23-20

19-17

15-14

Target Size: 20 cm target, with 4 cm white spot

11-11

3. Shooting Positions:

One feature of this round is that it takes a lot of stakes. Where one stake is used, a stake at least 18 inches above ground is recommended. On the two-stake shots use stakes that extend 12 inches above ground and stakes that are not over 6 inches above ground for the four-stake shots. Such an arrangement will help eliminate a lot of confusion.

4. Shooting Rules:

In shooting the Hunter Round the archer will observe the following shooting positions:

a) 1 stake—shoot 4 arrows from the same stake

b) 2 stakes—shoot 2 arrows from each stake

c) 4 stakes—shoot 1 arrow from each stake

5. Scoring:

Scoring is 5 points for the spot, 4 for center ring, and 3 for the outer ring. The X-ring is used for tie breakers only. An arrow shaft cutting two rings must cut completely through the line to be counted in the area of next higher value.

D. ANIMAL ROUND:

1. Standard Unit:

The 14 targets form a unit. Twice around the unit makes a round, or two such units laid out differently make a round. The one basic 14-target unit may be varied to make any number of courses that would all be different. It is simple and easy to lay out and change. Once the maximum and minimum distances are known, then the target distance can be laid out anywhere within these distances and be according to NFAA rules. This round, its animal targets and its sliding scale system of scoring is more of a measure of the hunting archer's shooting skill than the standard Field Round.

2. Targets:

a) The targets for this round are animal targets with the scoring area divided into two parts. The high scoring area is oblong while the low scoring area is the area between the high scoring area and the "hide and hair" line or "feathers," as the case may be. The area between the "hide and hair" line (including the line) to the outside of the carcass is considered a non-scoring area.

b) The high scoring area of Group No. 1 is 9 inches wide by 14 1/4" long with rounded ends. Targets in this group are the black bear, grizzly bear, deer, moose, elk and caribou.

c) The high scoring area of Group No. 2 is 7 inches wide by 10 1/2" long with rounded ends. Targets in this group are the small black bear, antelope, small deer, wolf, mountain lion.

d) The high scoring area of Group No. 3 is 4 1/2" wide by 7 inches long with rounded ends. Targets in this group are the coyote, raccoon, javelina, turkey, fox, goose, wildcat, and pheasant.

e) The high scoring area of Group No. 4 is 2 1/2" wide by 3 5/8 inches long with rounded ends. Targets in this group are the turtle, duck, grouse, crow, skunk, woodchuck, jack rabbit, and rockchuck.

f) In the above target groups the animals mentioned are for a general description and not to be construed as confined to the particular species. Any animal or bird which is legal game and consistent in size with a particular group may be used.

3. Shooting Positions:

a) The following chart gives distances and target groups:

Positions	Group	Targets	Max Yds	Min Yds	Spread Yds
3 walk-up shots	1	3	60	40	20
3 walk-up shots	2	3	45	30	15
4 one position shots	3	4	35	20	15
4 one position shots	4	4	20	10	10

b) The shooting distance shall be marked its exact distance, but in the spread defined, in paragraph a) above for the National and Sectional level tournament; and may be marked at tournaments below that level.

c) Each target in Group 1 faces is a five yard walk-up. There are three targets in the group. Select your distances between 60 and 40 yards for the first stake, move up five yards for the next stake and five more yards for the third stake.

d) Each target in Group 2 faces is a three yard walkup. There are three targets in Group 2. Select your distance between 45 and 30 yards for the first stake, move up three yards for the next stake and three more yards for last stake.

e) Each target in Group 3 faces is one distance. There are four targets in this group. Shoot all arrows from each stake as selected between 35 and 20 yards.

f) Each target in Group 4 is one distance. There are four targets in Group 4. All arrows shall be shot from each of the four stakes from distances selected between 20 yards and 10 yards. "The archer may shoot any target of his choice, including a target that has been shot by another member of the group." If the faces posted are different, the archer may shoot any face presented. In this instance the archer must declare his choice.

4. Shooting Rules:

A maximum of three marked arrows may be shot, in successive order, and the highest scoring arrow will count. In the case of walk-up targets the first arrow must be shot from the farthest stake, the second arrow from the middle stake, and the third arrow from the nearest stake, in order to be scored. No archer shall advance to the target and then return to the stake to shoot again in the event of a missed arrow.

5. Scoring:

a) 20 or 18 for the first arrow

   16 or 14 for the second arrow

   12 or 10 for the third arrow

b) The arrow shaft must cut through the line to score. If an arrow shaft touches the outside edge of an animal target it does not score. If it hits the target and cuts into, but not through, the "hair and hide" line, it does not score. It must cut through this line to score a shot of lower value. To score, an arrow shaft must cut through this line.

ADDITIONAL NFAA ROUNDS (Not included here)

1. 15 Target "300" Field Round

2. 15 Target "300" Hunter Round

3. 15 Target "300" Animal Round

4. NFAA International Round

5. NFAA Indoor Round

6. NFAA Indoor Championship Round
7. NFAA Freeman Round
8. Freeman Bowman Indoor Round
9. Freeman Bowhunter Indoor Round

GOVERNING BODY

National Field Archery Association, Route 2, Box 514, Redlands, CA 92373

The purpose of the National Field Archery Association (NFAA) is to foster, expand, and perpetuate the practice of field archery through (a) uniting the field archery associations of the various states, (b) providing a basic format of government from the local to the national level, (c) encouraging the use of the bow in the hunting of legal game, (d) adopting and enforcing uniform rules and regulations, (e) conducting tournaments to determine national championships, (f) developing programs dedicated to the conservation and preservation of game and its national habitat, (g) cooperating with other archery associations, and (h) conducting educational programs. The Association is available to lend assistance in formation of local clubs, course construction, conduct of tournaments, educational programs, securing supplies, and other matters of concern.

MAGAZINES

Archery, NFAA, Route 2, Box 514, Redlands, CA 92373

• FIELD HOCKEY •

RULES OF THE GAME OF HOCKEY
WITH GUIDANCE FOR PLAYERS AND UMPIRES

(Reproduced by permission of the Hockey Rules Board*)
George Croft, Honorary Secretary

Note: [The bracketed portions of the rules are the Guidance for Players and Umpires interpretations.] For convenience and clarity the masculine gender is used throughout the rules.

1. TEAMS AND DURATION OF PLAY.

(a) A game shall be played between two teams. Not more than 11 players of each team shall be on the field of play at the same time. Each team shall have one goal-keeper on the field or shall indicate a field player who has the privileges of a goal-keeper.

[Players and nominated substitutes, whether on or off the field of play, including any period of temporary or permanent suspension, are under the jurisdiction of the umpires during the whole match and are therefore subject to their decisions under the Rules of Hockey.]

b) Each team is permitted to substitute up to two players during the game. (This provision is not mandatory at any level.)

[It is permitted that the number of substitutes may be changed by F.I.H. Tournament Regulations.]

(c) No player once substituted shall be permitted on the field again and no substitute shall be permitted for a suspended player during his suspension.

(d) (i) Substitution of players shall only take place with the prior permission of an umpire and during any stoppage of play other than following the award of a penalty corner or penalty stroke subject to (ii) below.

(ii) After the award of a penalty corner or penalty stroke any player who is injured and has to leave the field of play can be substituted subject to Rule 1(c). Rules 9(b), 15(b)(ii), and 16(b)(i) shall apply.

Time may be added for completion of substitutions.

(e) The duration of the game shall be two periods of thirty-five minutes each, unless otherwise agreed before the game.

(f) At half-time the teams shall change ends, and the duration of the interval shall not exceed five minutes, unless otherwise agreed before the game, but in no case shall it exceed ten minutes.

(g) The game starts when the umpire blows his whistle for the opening pass-back. (See also Rule 10(a).)

---

*See pages 283 and 284 for additional information.

2. CAPTAINS.

Each team must have a captain on the field who may wear a distinctive arm-band and who shall:

(a) toss for choice of start. The winner of the toss shall have

(i) the right to choose which end his team will attack in the first half

OR

(ii) the right to have possession of the ball at the start of the game.

The winner of the toss having made his choice, the opposing side will automatically have the second option.

The team not having started the game will have possession of the ball for re-starting after half-time.

(b) before the start of play and on any change, indicate, if necessary, to each other and to the umpires, their respective goal-keepers subject to Rules 15(b)(ii) and 16(b)(i).

(c) In case he is substituted or suspended indicate to the umpires the player who will replace him as captain.

3. UMPIRES AND TIMEKEEPERS.

(a) There shall be two umpires to control the game and to administer the Rules. These umpires shall be the sole judges of fair and unfair play during the game.

(b) Unless otherwise provided, each team shall be responsible for providing one umpire.

(c) Each umpire shall be:

(i) primarily responsible for decisions in his own half of the field, for the whole of the game without changing ends.

(ii) solely responsible for decisions on the hit-in for the full length of his nearer side-line.

(iii) solely responsible for decisions on corners, penalty corners, penalty strokes and goals in his own half and free hits in his own circle.

(d) The umpires shall be responsible for keeping time for the duration of the game. It shall be permissible to have a timekeeper or timekeepers. Such timekeepers shall take over those duties of the umpires which concern the keeping of time and the indication of the end of each half.

[It is recommended that:

the time in each half should be kept by both umpires; but, by mutual agreement, one umpire should be primarily responsible for the starting and ending of each half.

to avoid any error, the umpires should exchange an agreed-upon signal before starting or re-starting play and also approximately one minute before the end of each half.

if the umpire primarily responsible appears to be over-running the time, then his colleague should stop play and consult him on the matter.

the umpires should when necessary agree upon the amount of time to be added after each penalty stroke and after any substantial stoppage for accident or otherwise. (See Rule 16 (f) and Rule 18(a).)]

(e) Umpires shall allow the full or agreed-upon time and shall keep a written record of the goals as they are scored.

(f) Time shall be allowed for all enforced stoppages and such time shall be added to that half in which the stoppage occurred.

Reasons justifying such stoppages include accidents, penalty strokes, time-wasting, repair of goals and other unforeseen incidents.

The penalty stroke signal also indicates time stopped.

The blowing of the whistle by the umpire to indicate a goal or no goal does not indicate the resumption of play. (See Rule 3(h)(iii).)]

(g) Umpires and timekeepers shall be debarred from coaching during a game and during the interval.

(h) Umpires shall only blow the whistle to:

(i) start and end each half of the game.

(ii) enforce a penalty or suspend the game for any other reason.

(iii) start and end a penalty stroke.

(iv) indicate, when necessary, that the ball has passed wholly outside the field of play.

(v) signal a goal.

(vi) re-start the game after a goal has been scored and after a suspension of play.

(i) Umpires shall satisfy themselves before the game that, as far as is practicable, Rules 4 to 9 inclusive are observed.

UMPIRES SHALL REFRAIN FROM ENFORCING A PENALTY IN CASES WHERE THEY ARE SATISFIED THAT BY ENFORCING IT AN ADVANTAGE WOULD BE GIVEN TO THE OFFENDING TEAM.

4. FIELD OF PLAY. (See plan of field of play)

(a) All lines used in the measurements of the field are to be 3 inches wide. The side-lines and back-lines including the goal-lines are part of the field of play.

(b) The field shall be rectangular, 100 yards long and 60 yards wide. Its boundaries shall be clearly marked out with lines in accordance with the Plan on page 267. The longer lines shall be called the side-lines and the shorter the back-lines including that part of the back-line between the goal-posts called the goal-line.

(c) A centre-line and two 25 yards lines shall be marked throughout their length on the field; the middle of these lines to be 50 yards and 25 yards, respectively, from the outer edge of the back-lines.

(d) To assist in the control of the hit-in, across the centre-line and each 25 yards line, parallel to and 5 yards from the outer edge of the side-lines a mark of 2 yards in length shall be made.

(e) A mark 12 inches in length shall be placed inside the field of play on each side-line and parallel to the back-line and 16 yards from its inner edge.

(f) For penalty corner hits, the field shall be marked inside the field of play on the back-lines on both sides of the goal at 5 yards and 10 yards from the outer edge of the nearer goal-post such distance being to the further edge of those lines. For corner hits the field shall be marked inside the field of play on the back-lines 5 yards from the outer edge of the side-line. All these marks to be 12 inches in length.

(g) A spot 6 inches in diameter shall be marked in front of the centre of each goal; the centre of the spot shall be 7 yards from the inner edge of the goal-line.

(h) No marks other than those shown on the Plan of field of play are permissible on the playing surface. [Goal-keepers should not be allowed to scrape any marks on the surface of the ground.]

PLAN OF FIELD OF PLAY

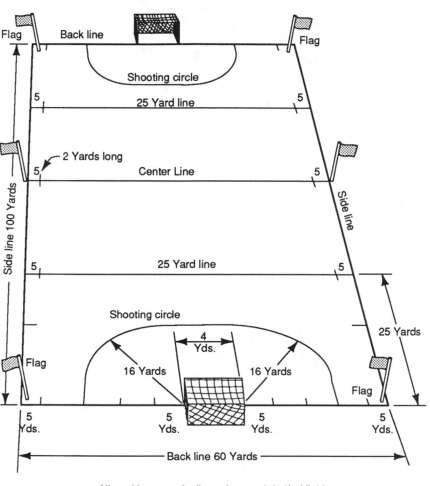

All markings are duplicated on each half of field

Not to scale

(i) Flagposts of not more than 5 feet nor less than 4 feet in height shall be placed for the whole game at each corner of the field (see Diagrams on pages 268), and at the centre; those at the centre shall be 1 yard outside the side-lines.

5. GOALS, POSTS, ETC.

[Umpires should check:

(i) that goal-posts are firmly fixed.

(ii) that the goal-posts and cross-bars are painted white.

Corner Flag

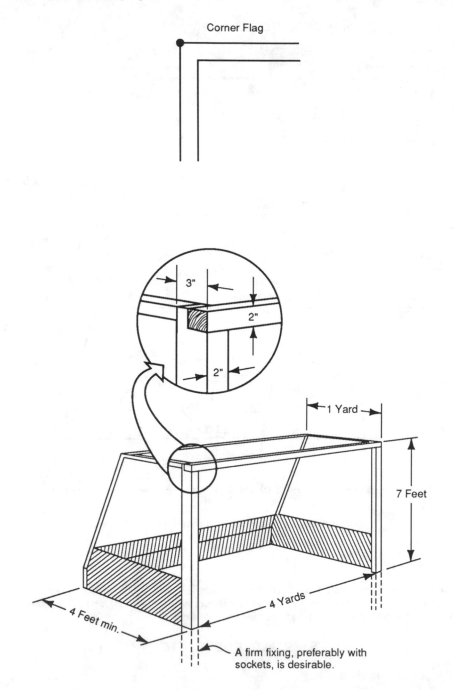

1 Yard

7 Feet

4 Yards

4 Feet min.

A firm fixing, preferably with
sockets, is desirable.

GOALS, POSTS, ETC. (Rule 5)

(iii) that the goal-posts are correctly placed in relation to the back-line.

(iv) that there are no holes or bad tears in the netting, that the goal-nets are properly attached and that goal-boards are inside the net and do not project beyond the back of the goal-posts.

Without such careful inspection there may be difficulty and even inaccuracy in making decisions of a critical nature.]

(a) There shall be a goal at the centre of each back-line, consisting of two perpendicular posts 4 yards apart, joined together by a horizontal cross-bar 7 feet from the ground (inside measurements).

The front base of the goal-posts shall touch the outer edge of the back-line.

The goal-posts shall not extend upwards beyond the cross-bar, nor shall the cross-bar extend sideways beyond the goal-posts.

(b) The goal-posts and cross-bar shall be rectangular and shall be 2 inches wide, not more than 3 inches deep and shall be painted white.

(c) Nets shall be attached firmly to the goal-post and the cross-bar, at intervals of not more than 6 inches, and shall be attached firmly to the ground behind the goal.

(d) A back-board, 18 inches in height and 4 yards in length, shall be placed at the foot of and inside the goal-nets. Side-boards 18 inches in height and a minimum 4 feet in length shall be placed at right angles to the back-lines. The side-boards shall be fixed to the back of the goal-posts, so that the width of the goal-posts is not effectively increased.

[It is recommended that the back-board/side-boards be painted in a dark color.]

(e) No chocks shall be placed inside the goal to support any of the boards.

SHOOTING CIRCLE

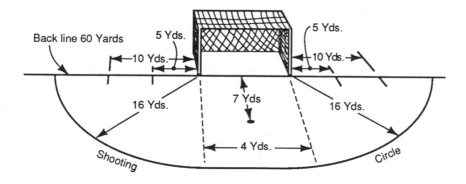

The front of the goal-posts must be touching the outer edge of the back-line. All lines are 3 in. wide. A spot 6 in. in diameter shall be marked 7 yds. in front of the center of each pool. All short indication marks must be inside the field only and shall be 12 in. in length.

Not to scale

6. SHOOTING CIRCLES. (See plan)

In front of each goal a line shall be drawn 4 yards long, parallel to and 16 yards from the back-line. The 16 yards shall be measured from the inside front corner of the goal-posts to the outer edge of that line. This line shall be continued each way to meet the back-lines by quarter circles having the inside front corner of the goal-posts as centres. The space enclosed by these lines, including the lines themselves, shall be called the shooting circle (hereinafter referred to as "the circle").

7. THE BALL.

[A ball to be used in international matches must also meet the detailed standards as laid down by the F.I.H. These will cover the hardness, balance, smoothness, surface, moisture absorbance, friction and bounce of the ball. These conditions may vary for different playing surfaces. National Associations and Clubs may, for their own competitions, tournaments and matches, set their own standards, but the specifications for this Rule must be met.]

(a) The ball shall be spherical with the specifications mentioned in this Rule.

(b) The weight of the ball shall not be more than 5 3/4 ounces (163 grammes), nor less than 5 1/2 ounces (156 grammes).

(c) The circumference of the ball shall not be more than 9 1/4 inches (23.5 centimetres) nor less than 8 13/16 inches (22.4 centimetres).

(d) (i) The ball shall be hard; it may be solid or hollow, provided it meets the other specifications in this Rule.

(ii) The ball shall have an outer surface of any natural or artificial material. The surface shall be smooth, but a seam or indentations are permitted provided they do not alter the shape of the ball.

(iii) The inner portion of a solid ball may consist of any natural or artificial material in any composition or mixture, as long as it meets the other specifications in this Rule.

(e) The traditional colour of the ball is white, but the team captains may agree upon the use of a ball of any other colour, as long as it contrasts with the colour of the field of play.

(f) Umpires shall not permit the use of a ball that in their opinion does not comply with this Rule. Should a ball during a game deteriorate in such a way that it no longer meets the specifications of this Rule, it shall be replaced immediately. See also Rule 11(a) and Rule 17.I and II.

8. THE STICK.

(a) The stick shall have a flat face on its left-hand side only. The face of the stick is the whole of the flat side and that part of the handle for the whole of the length which is above the flat side.

(b) The head of the stick (i.e., the part below the lower end of the splice) shall be curved and shall be of wood and shall not be edged with or have any insets or fittings of metal or any other substance, nor shall there be any sharp edges or dangerous splinters. The maximum length of the curved head of the stick, as measured from the lowest part of the flat face, shall not exceed 4 inches. It shall not be cut square or pointed, but shall have rounded edges.

(c) The total weight of the stick shall not exceed 28 ounces, nor be less than 12 ounces and it shall be of such a size, inclusive of any covering, that it can be passed through a ring having an interior diameter of 5.10 centimetres.

(d) Umpires shall forbid the use of any stick which in their opinion does not comply with this Rule. (See Rule 3(i).)

Penalty.

For any breach of this Rule any player concerned shall not be allowed on the field of play until such time as he has complied with this Rule.

9. PLAYERS' DRESS AND EQUIPMENT.

(a) Each player shall wear the dress approved by his Association or Club, unless varied to avoid confusion in a particular game. Goal-keepers shall wear a colour different from that of their own team and that of their opponents. Players shall not have dangerous spikes, studs or protruding nails in footwear, or wear anything that may be dangerous to other players.

[Goal-keepers are required to wear their shirt or other garments over any body protectors.]

(b) The following equipment is permitted for use by goal-keepers only: body protectors, pads, kickers, gauntlet gloves, headgear, facemasks and elbow pads.

[It is strongly recommended that goal-keepers wear protective equipment at all times. However, the wearing of such protective equipment does not permit them to conduct themselves in a manner which would not be either possible or safe without such protective equipment.]

Penalty.

For any breach of this Rule any player concerned shall not be allowed on the field of play until such time as he has complied with this Rule.

10. TO START OR RE-START THE GAME.

(a) To start the game, re-start it after half-time and after each goal scored, a "pass-back" shall be played at the centre of the field. The pass-back for the start of the game shall be made by a player of the team which did not make a choice of ends (See Rule 2(a)), after half-time by a player of the opposing team and after a goal has been scored, by a player of the team against whom the goal has been awarded. The pass-back, which may be pushed or hit, must not be directed over the centre-line.

At the moment when the pass-back is taken, no player of the opposing team shall be within 5 yards of the ball and all players of both teams other than the player making the pass-back must be in their own half of the field.

If the striker hit at but missed the ball, the pass-back still has to be taken.

After taking the pass-back, the striker shall not play the ball nor approach within playing distance until it has been touched or played by another player of either team. Time-wasting shall not be permitted.

[At the "pass-back," the ball shall not be raised intentionally. The player taking the "pass-back" shall not be penalised if the ball lifts slightly off the ground as long as the intention to play along the ground is clear.]

(b) (i) To re-start the game in accordance with Rule 12.III, Rule 12. Penalties 4(a) or Rule 18(b)(i) a bully shall be played on a spot to be chosen by the umpire in whose half of the ground the incident occurred.]

(ii) To bully, a player of each team shall stand squarely facing the side-lines, each with his own back-line on his right. The ball shall be placed on the ground between the two players. Each player shall tap with his stick, first the ground between the ball and his own back-line, and then, with the flat face of his stick, his opponent's stick, over the ball, three times alternately, after which one of these two players shall play the ball with his stick to put it into play.

[Only the flat face of the stick may be used during the bully and contact must take place over the ball. Much obstruction will be prevented if the two players are made to stand square, not moving their feet until the ball is in play.]

(iii) Until the ball is in play, all other players shall be nearer to their own back-line than is the ball and shall not stand within 5 yards of the ball.

[All players must remain on-side and 5 yards from the ball until it is in play.]

(iv) A bully in the circle shall not be played within 5 yards of the back-line or goal-line.

[The Rule requires that the bully shall not be taken 'nearer' than 5 yards from the back-line/goal-line. There is nothing to prevent it being taken at any other distance from the back-line/goal-line; no matter where in the circle the offence occurred.

(See Rule 10(b)(i)).]

Penalties.

1. For a breach of Rule 10(a) a free hit shall be awarded to the opposing team.

2. For a breach of Rule 10(b)(ii) or (b)(iii) the bully shall be played again.

3. For persistent breaches of Rule 10(b)(ii) and (b)(iii) the umpire may award a free hit to the opposing team; or, for such breaches in the circle by a defender, a penalty corner.

11. SCORING A GOAL.

[The ball must be inside the circle when hit by an attacker (although he himself may be outside). If it is hit within the circle and then touches the stick or person of a defender or defenders before crossing the goal-line, a goal is scored.

Should the ball be hit from outside the circle by an attacker and be diverted between the posts by a defender who is in or outside the circle within the 25 yards area, a corner should be given.

Note:

(i) the lines are part of the circle.

(ii) the whole ball must cross the goal-line before a goal is scored.

After a stoppage of play inside the circle the ball must again be hit from inside the circle by the stick of an attacker, before a goal can be scored.]

(a) A goal is scored when the whole ball, having been hit or deflected by the stick of an attacker whilst in the circle and not having gone outside the circle, passes completely over the goal-line between the goal-posts and under the crossbar—except in circumstances detailed in Rules 15(g) and 16. It is immaterial if the ball subsequently touch, or be played by one or more defenders. If, during the game, the goal-posts and/or the cross-bar become displaced, and the ball passes completely over the goal-line at a point which, in the umpire's opinion, be between where the goal-post and/or under where the cross-bar, respectively, should have been, a goal shall be awarded.

(b) The team scoring the greater number of goals shall be the winner.

12. CONDUCT OF PLAY.

I A PLAYER SHALL NOT:

(a) play the ball with the rounded side of the stick.

[If the ball hits the back of the stick and no advantage results, no offence has taken place.]

(b) take part in or interfere with the game unless he has his own stick in his hand, nor change his stick for the purpose of taking part in the game under Rules 14, 15, 16, and 17.

"Own stick" means the stick with which the player began to play, or any stick that he legitimately substitutes for it.

(c) raise his stick in a manner that is dangerous, intimidating or hampering to another player when approaching, attempting to play, playing or stopping the ball. A ball above the height of a player's shoulder shall not be played or played at by any part of the stick.

[A penalty stroke should be given when a defender (usually the goal-keeper) has saved a probable goal on his stick above his shoulder.]

[Umpires should penalise and warn any player who lifts his stick over the head of an opponent. This type of action often leads to injuries and is accordingly dangerous play.]

(d) stop the ball with his hand or catch it. (For goal-keepers see Rule 12.II(c)).

(THERE IS NOTHING IN THIS RULE WHICH PREVENTS A PLAYER USING HIS HAND TO PROTECT HIMSELF FROM A DANGEROUSLY RAISED BALL.)

(e) hit wildly into an opponent or play or kick the ball in such a way as to be dangerous in itself, or likely to lead to dangerous play or play the ball intentionally into an opponent's foot, leg or body or deliberately raise the ball so that it will fall into the circle.

[This rule is intended to prevent injury to players and umpires should be very firm in penalising dangerous play such as undercutting or raising the ball in any way. A rising ball is dangerous when it causes legitimate evasive action on the part of the players.

A player should be penalised who by raising the ball is guilty of or directly causes dangerous play. Hitting the ball whilst it is in the air is not permissible if the stroke is itself dangerous. The practice of lifting the ball from the ground and hitting it again while still in the air is prohibited.

It is not intended that the ball raised slightly over an opponent's stick should be penalised.]

(f) stop or deflect the ball on the ground or in the air with any part of the body TO HIS OR HIS TEAM'S ADVANTAGE (save as provided for in Rule 12.II(c)).

[If the ball is lifted dangerously into an oncoming player who uses his hand to protect himself, he should not be penalised. If a penalty is given it should be against the player who raised the ball.

BEFORE PENALISING A BREACH INVOLVING THE STOPPING OF THE BALL WITH SOME PART OF THE BODY THE UMPIRE MUST BE SATISFIED THAT THE PLAYER CONCERNED USED HIS BODY

(i) BY MOVING INTO THE LINE OF THE BALL.

(ii) BY SO POSITIONING HIMSELF THAT HIS INTENTION TO STOP THE BALL IN SUCH A MANNER WAS CLEAR.

(iii) BY MAKING NO EFFORT TO AVOID BEING HIT.

It is not necessarily an offence if the ball strikes the foot or body of a player.]

(g) use the foot or leg to support the stick in order to resist an opponent.

(h) kick, pick up, throw, carry or propel the ball in any manner or direction except with the stick. (But see guidance 12.I(f), 12.I(h) and Rule 12.II(c).)

[(i) The ball must not be carried forward in any way by the body.

(ii) a player should not be penalised for a rebound when the ball has been propelled straight at him from close quarters by an opponent.

(iii) Goal-keepers should not be penalised when using their hands or kicking or propelling the ball with their feet or pads unless the propelled ball is considered either dangerous or likely to lead to dangerous play. The act of touching/deflecting the ball over the cross-bar or around a goal-post by hand is permitted unless dangerous.]

(i) hit, hook, hold, strike at or interfere with an opponent's stick.

[Hooking and striking at sticks should be strictly penalised. Should a player slash wildly at the ball and hit an opponent or his stick instead, he should be penalised. A player may not throw his stick at the ball.]

(j) charge, kick, shove, trip, strike at or personally handle an opponent or his clothing.

(k) obstruct by running between an opponent and the ball nor interpose himself or his stick as an obstruction.

[Subject to the "advantage rule" umpires should be particularly strict on obstruction and other forms of interference dealt with in this Rule.

It should be noted that obstruction does not necessarily depend on the distance from the ball of the players concerned.

A player, even if in possession of the ball, may not interpose his body as an obstruction to an opponent. A change of direction by a half-turn of the body with this result may amount to obstruction. It should be noted, however, that even a complete turn does not constitute a breach unless an opponent has thereby been obstructed in an attempt to play the ball.

Obstruction occurs at hit-ins and should be watched for carefully.

A player must not interpose any part of his body or his stick as an obstruction between his opponent and the ball. Watch, too, for third party interference; i.e., player interposing himself between his opponent and the ball so that a fellow player has an opportunity to clear or play the ball.

Other names for these offences are:

shadow-obstruction, shepherding, blocking out or even as a general term "close-marking".]

II A PLAYER MAY:

(a) play the ball only with the flat side of his stick which includes that part of the handle above the flat side.

(b) tackle from the left of an opponent provided that he play the ball without previous interference with the stick or person of his opponent. (See Rule 12.I, particularly (i) (j) (k).)

(c) if he is goal-keeper, be allowed to kick the ball or stop it with any part of his body including his hand, but only when the ball is inside his circle. No penalty shall be incurred if, when stopping a shot at goal, the ball merely rebounds off any part of the goal-keeper's body. (See Guidance 12.I(h).)

[A goal-keeper is not allowed to strike at the ball with his hand, or breast it out with his body. (See Guidance 12.I(h).) Umpires are disposed to be too lenient towards breaches of the Rules by goal-keepers.

The more usual breaches are running between an opponent and the ball when it is about to go behind, opening the legs to let the ball go through when an opponent is within striking distance and making a wild stroke at the ball when clearing. The goal-keeper must not be allowed further privileges than those given by this Rule.

Goal-keepers are not permitted to kick dangerously. (See 12.I(e).)

The penalties for rough and dangerous play, misconduct, or time-wasting, should be noted carefully, and the appropriate penalty awarded.

Persistent breaches of the Rules may suitably be dealt with under this Rule. If rough or dangerous play becomes prevalent, a word of caution to the offender(s) should effectively prevent the game getting out of hand. For those breaches of the Rule inside the circle, Rule 16 should also be taken into consideration.

Nothing in these Rules prevents a suspended player joining his team during the half-time interval but he should return to the suspended players' position on resumption of the second half of play unless his suspension has been ended.]

III LODGED BALL.

(a) If the ball becomes lodged in one of the pads of a goal-keeper or in the clothing of any player or umpire, the umpire shall stop the game and re-start it by a bully on the spot where the incident occurred (subject to Rule 10(b)(iv)).

(b) If the ball strikes an umpire the game shall continue.

IV MISCONDUCT.

ROUGH OR DANGEROUS PLAY, TIME-WASTING, OR ANY OTHER BEHAVIOUR WHICH, IN THE UMPIRE'S OPINION AMOUNTS TO MISCONDUCT, SHALL NOT BE PERMITTED.

Penalties

1. Outside the circle.

A free hit shall be awarded to the opposing team. An umpire shall award a penalty corner for an offence by any defender in his own 25 yards area, when, in the umpire's opinion, the offence was deliberate.

2. Inside the circle—by an attacker.

A free hit shall be awarded to the defending team.

3. Inside the circle—by a defender.

For a breach inside the circle by a defender a penalty corner shall be awarded or a penalty stroke if, in the umpire's opinion, Rule 16(a) applies.

4. Inside and outside the circle.

For a simultaneous breach of this Rule by two opponents, the umpire shall order a bully to be played on the spot where the breach occurred (subject to Rule 10(b)(iv)).

5. Inside and outside the circle.

For rough or dangerous play or misconduct, in addition to awarding the appropriate penalty, the umpire may:

(i) warn the offending player(s) which may also be indicated by showing a green card.

(ii) suspend him temporarily for not less than five minutes which may also be indicated by showing a yellow card.

(iii) suspend him from further participation in the game which may also be indicated by showing a red card.

A temporarily suspended player shall remain behind his own goal or in such other places as designated before the game, until allowed by the umpire by whom he was suspended, to resume play; when necessary changing ends at the start of the second half of the game.

13. OFF-SIDE.

[The question of whether a player is off-side is governed by WHERE HE WAS AT THE MOMENT WHEN THE BALL WAS PLAYED BY A PLAYER OF THE SAME TEAM, not where he is when he received the ball. The umpire must always have this in mind otherwise he may easily give a wrong decision.

The act of 'playing' the ball includes when a player of the same team is dribbling the ball.

A player in an off-side position whether on or off the field SHOULD NOT BE PENALISED UNLESS he influences the play of an opponent or gains some advantage from his off-side position.

A player who is level with the ball is off-side.]

(a) AT THE MOMENT WHEN THE BALL IS PLAYED a player of the same team as the pusher or striker is in an off-side position if he be in his opponents' 25 yards area unless: he be behind the ball

OR

there be at least two opponents nearer to their own back-line or goal-line than he is.

For the purpose of this Rule, a player of either team shall be deemed to be on the field of play even though he be outside the side-line or behind the back-line or goal-line.

[A player cannot be off-side if:

he is nearer the centre-line than the ball is at the time it is played by a player of the same team.

there are at least two opponents nearer to their own back-line than he is at the moment when the ball is played by a player of the same team.

If a player is off-side, he is not automatically put on-side by returning to his own side of his opponents' 25 yards line to play the ball.

A whole line of forwards having outdistanced the defence and only having the goal-keeper in front of them could pass and re-pass to each other without being off-side as long as they keep behind the ball.]

(b) A player who is in an off-side position shall not play or attempt to play the ball or gain any advantage for his team or influence the play of an opponent.

[A player who is left off-side after making a previous shot should not be penalised if he is trying to get back on-side, unless he is obstructing or distracting any opponent.]

Penalty.

A free hit shall be awarded to the defending team.

14. FREE HIT.

[The free hit must be taken from the right place and the ball must be stationary. If a player taking a free hit gains extra advantage by taking the free hit from the wrong place, he should be penalised.

A free hit in the circle may be taken from any place within the circle.

Should there be any unnecessary delay by the players of the offending side in observing the 5-yards distance Rule, the umpire need not order the hit to be taken again.]

(a) A free hit shall be taken on the spot where the breach occurred except that:

(i) for a breach by an attacker within the circle it shall be taken:

EITHER from any spot within that circle

OR

from any spot within 16 yards of the inner edge of the defending team's back-line or goal-line on a line drawn through the place where the breach occurred and parallel to the side-line.

(ii) for a breach by an attacker outside the circle but within 16 yards of the defending team's back-line it shall be taken from any spot within 16 yards of the inner edge of the defending team's back-line on a line drawn through the place where the breach occurred and parallel to the side-line.

(b) The ball shall be stationary and the striker shall push or hit it. The ball must be moved and shall not be raised intentionally or in such a way as to be dangerous in itself, or likely to lead to dangerous play.

[At the free hit, the ball shall not be raised intentionally. The player taking the free hit shall not be penalised if the ball lifts off the ground as long as the intention to play along the ground is clear. Simply touching the ball with the stick is not considered to be a hit.]

(c) At the moment when the free hit is taken, no player of the opposing team shall remain within 5 yards of the ball. However, for a free hit to the attacking team within 5 yards of the circle, players of both teams shall be at least 5 yards from the ball. Should the umpire consider that a player is standing within 5 yards of the ball in order to gain time, the free hit shall not be delayed.

(d) If the striker hit at but missed the ball, provided that Rule 12.I(c) has not been contravened, the free hit still has to be taken.

(e) After taking the free hit, the striker shall not play the ball again nor remain or approach within playing distance until it has been touched or played by another player of either team.

Penalties.

1. Inside the circle.

A penalty corner or penalty stroke shall be awarded to the attacking team.

2. Outside the circle.

A free hit shall be awarded to the opposing team. An umpire shall award a penalty corner for an offence by any defender in his own 25 yards area, when in the umpire's opinion, the offence was deliberate.

15. PENALTY CORNER.

(a) A penalty corner shall be awarded to the opposing team if, in the umpire's opinion:

(i) there has been an INTENTIONAL breach of Rules 12, 14 or 17 inside the 25 yards area but outside the circle by a player of the defending team.

OR

(ii) an UNINTENTIONAL breach of Rules 12, 14 or 17 inside the circle by a player of the defending team

OR

(iii) for persistent breaches of Rule 10(b)(ii) or (b)(iii) in the circle by a defender.

(b) A player of the attacking team shall push or hit the ball from a spot on the back-line not less than 10 yards from the goal-post, on whichever side of the goal the attacking team prefers. The player concerned is not required to be wholly inside or outside the field of play when taking the corner.

The ball shall not be raised intentionally but the hit shall not be penalised if the ball lifts off the ground without causing danger or appearing likely to lead to dangerous play.

(c)(i) At the moment when such push or hit is made, no other player shall be within 5 yards of the ball. The rest of the attacking team shall be in the field of play with both sticks and feet outside the circle.

Not more than five of the defending team shall stand with both sticks and feet behind their own goal-line or back-line. The rest of the defending team shall be beyond the centre-line.

[Both teams should be correctly positioned.]

(ii) In the event of the defending goal-keeper being incapacitated or suspended, his team captain shall immediately nominate another goal-keeper. This goal-keeper shall be permitted to put on without undue delay, protective equipment. Under the provisions of this Rule, a goal-keeper may also remove his headgear, face mask and/or his gauntlet gloves (see Rule 9(b)).

[The returning incapacitated or temporarily suspended goal-keeper is permitted to put on, without undue delay, protective equipment.]

(d) Until the ball be pushed or hit no attacker shall enter the circle, nor shall a defender cross the goal-line, back-line or centre-line.

[The umpire has the right to order the penalty corner to be taken again if a defender crosses the goal-line, or back-line or the centre-line before the ball is hit. This power should, however, be used with discretion. It is often to the disadvantage of the attacker to stop the game when the corner has been well hit, well stopped and resulted in the attacker being in a good position to shoot.]

(e) The first HIT at goal shall not cross the goal-line at a height higher than the back-board/side-boards (18 inches) unless it has touched the stick or person of a defender. If the ball travels beyond 5 yards from the outer edge of the circle line, the penalty corner shall be finished.

(f) No shot at goal shall be made from a penalty corner until the ball be stopped on the ground or touches the stick or person of a defender.

[The ball must be stopped. The ball may be deflected or passed one or more times by the attacking players, but it must be stopped inside or outside the circle before a shot at goal is made.

If the ball has not previously been touched by a defender, or has not been stopped on the gound, a flying hit following a pass or deflection from one attacker to another should be penalised as a breach of this Rule.]

(g) The player taking the penalty corner hit or push from the back-line shall not, after striking the ball, approach or remain within playing distance of the ball until it has been touched or played by another player of either team.

(h) If the striker of the penalty corner hit at or pushed at but missed the ball, the penalty corner still has to be taken.

(i) No goal shall be scored directly by the player taking the penalty corner hit or push from the back-line.

["Directly" means before another player of the attacking team has played the ball.]

Penalties.

1. For a breach of Rule 15(c)(i) or 15(d) viz: Attacker(s) entering the circle or defender(s) crossing the goal-line, back-line or centre-line too soon or coming within 5 yards of the ball too soon—the penalty corner may, at the discretion of the umpire, be taken again.

2. For persistent breaches of Rule 15(c)(i) or 15(d) by the attackers—The umpire may award a free hit.

3. For persistent breaches of Rule 15(c)(i) or 15(d) by the defenders—The umpire may award a penalty stroke.

4. For any other breach of Rule 15—A free hit shall be awarded to the defending team.

16. PENALTY STROKE.

(a) A penalty stroke shall be awarded to the opposing team, if, in the umpire's opinion:

(i) there has been an INTENTIONAL breach of Rules 12, 14 or 17 inside the circle by a player of the defending team

OR

(ii) a goal would probably have been scored had an UNINTENTIONAL breach of Rule 12 inside the circle by a player of the defending team not occurred.

(iii) Rules 15(c)(i) and/or 15(d) are persistently breached by the defenders.

[Note the cases in which this may be awarded, and that it shall be awarded if, in the umpire's opinion, an intentional breach of Rules 12, 14 or 17 has been committed inside the circle even though it may seem to the umpire improbable that, but for the breach, a goal could have been scored. The intentional breach must be against a player who either has possession of the ball or the opportunity to gain possession of the ball.

It should be particularly noted that this penalty is intended to meet offences which may materially affect the game, when a more severe penalty than a penalty corner is necessary, and it should be applied accordingly by umpires.]

[It is not always easy for an umpire to decide whether a breach is intentional or not, but a distinction should be made between committing a breach of the Rules that is entirely forbidden, such as charging, and a breach which is the result of an attempt to do something lawful. A defender must show by his actions that he has tried to prevent fouling an attacker; e.g., charging into a player about to shoot from a favourable position should invariably be regarded as intentional for the purpose of this Rule. If a goal-keeper falls on or beside the ball in front of the goal, an award of a penalty stroke would be appropriate in most cases where the opponents thereby have no fair view of the ball or opportunity to play the ball.]

(b) (i) The penalty stroke shall be push, flick or scoop stroke taken from a spot 7 yards in front of the centre of the goal by a player of the attacking team and defended by the goal-keeper of the opposing team on the field at the time the breach occurred.

In the event of the defending goal-keeper being incapacitated or suspended, his team captain shall immediately nominate another goal-keeper. This goal-keeper shall be permitted to put on or remove, without undue delay, protective equipment. Under the provisions of this Rule, a goal-keeper may also remove his face mask, headgear and/or his gauntlet gloves (see Rule 9(b)).

[A goal-keeper may put on or take off his mask, headgear and/or his gauntlet gloves. If the attacking goal-keeper takes the stroke, he may also remove his mask, headgear and/or gauntlet gloves. Equally a substitute goal-keeper shall be permitted to put on without undue delay protective equipment.]

(ii) Whichever stroke is used, the ball may be raised to any height.

(iii) During the taking of a penalty stroke all the other players of both teams shall be beyond the nearer 25 yards line, and shall not influence or attempt to influence the conduct of the penalty stroke.

[For a breach of Rule 16(b)(iii) by an attacker when a goal is scored or by a defender when no goal is scored, the penalty stroke may be taken again.]

(c) (i) The attacking player shall not take the penalty stroke until the umpire, having satisfied himself that both defender and attacker are ready, has indicated approval by blowing his whistle.

[If the attacker takes the stroke before the umpire has blown his whistle, the game shall be re-started by a free hit to the defending team.]

(ii) When taking the stroke the attacker shall stand close to and behind the ball and shall be permitted in making the stroke to take one stride forward. Dragging or lifting the rear foot is not a breach of this Rule, provided that it does not pass the front foot before the ball is moved.

(iii) The attacker shall touch the ball once only and thereafter shall not approach either the ball or the goal-keeper.

(d) (i) The goal-keeper shall stand on the goal-line. After the player taking the stroke and the goal-keeper are in position and the umpire has blown his whistle, the goal-keeper shall not leave the goal-line or move either of his feet until the ball has been played.

(ii) The usual privileges of the goal-keeper shall be allowed to him, but he shall not be allowed to delay the taking of the stroke by making unnecessary changes or modifications of clothing. If the ball be caught and held by the goal-keeper the penalty stroke is ended. (See also clause (e) (ii).) He shall not be penalised, if, in stopping a shot at goal, the ball, in the umpire's opinion, merely rebounds off his body or his hand. He may not touch the ball with any part of his stick when the ball is above the height of his shoulder.

[The goal-keeper should be penalised only when his actions prevent a goal being scored. If he plays a ball with his stick above the height of his shoulder and it was not going into the goal, no breach of the rule has taken place. The game should be re-started in accordance with Rule 16(e)(ii).]

(iii) If any deliberate action by the striker prior to striking the ball induces the goal-keeper to move either of his feet, or, if the striker feints at striking the ball, the striker shall be penalised.

(e) If, as a result of the penalty stroke:

(i) the whole ball passes completely over the goal-line between the goal-posts and under the cross-bar, a goal is scored.

(ii) the ball should come to rest inside the circle, be lodged in the goal-keeper's pads, be caught by the goal-keeper, or pass outside the circle, in all cases, the penalty stroke is ended. Unless a goal has been scored or awarded, the game shall be re-started by a free hit to be taken by a defender from a spot in front of the centre of the goal and 16 yards from the inner edge of that line.

(f) All time taken between the award of a penalty stroke and resumption of play shall be added to the time of play.

[If there is any unreasonable delay or misconduct by either a defender or an attacker in carrying out any of the provisions of this Rule, the umpire may treat such action as misconduct (Rule 12.IV) and deal with it accordingly.

For a breach of Rules 16(c)(i) and (d)(iii), a free hit from 16 yards from the centre of the goal shall be awarded.]

Penalties.

1. For a breach of any Rule by the goal-keeper which prevents a goal from being scored, a goal shall be awarded to the opposing team. (See Penalty 3 below.)

2. For a breach of any Rule by an attacker, the game shall be re-started with a free hit to be taken by a defender from a spot in front of the centre of the goal-line and 16 yards from the inner edge of that line.

3. For a breach of clause (b)(iii) or (d)(i) the umpire may order the stroke to be taken again.

17. BALL OUTSIDE FIELD OF PLAY.

When the whole ball passes completely over the back-line and no goal is scored, or over the side-line, it is out of play and the game shall be re-started as in Rules 17.I and 17.II.

I OVER SIDE-LINE.

(a) When the whole ball passes completely over the side-line, it or another ball shall be placed on the line at the spot at which it crossed the side-line. The ball shall be pushed or hit without undue delay by a player of the team opposed to the player who last touched it in play. This player is not required to be wholly inside or outside the side-line when making his push or hit.

[When pushed or hit, the ball shall not be raised intentionally. The player taking the push or hit shall not be penalised if the ball lifts slightly off the ground as long as the intention to play along the ground is clear.]

(b) The ball shall be stationary and the striker shall push or hit it. The ball must be moved and shall not be raised intentionally or in such a way as to be dangerous in itself or likely to lead to dangerous play.

[Simply touching the ball with the stick is not considered to be a hit.]

(c) At the moment when the push or hit is taken no player of the opposing team shall be within 5 yards of the ball, the umpire may require the push or hit to be taken again. If, however, in the umpire's opinion, a player of the opposing team remains within 5 yards of the ball to gain time, the push or hit shall not be delayed.

(d) If the striker hit at but missed the ball, provided that Rule 12.I(c) has not been contravened, the push or hit still has to be taken.

(e) After taking a push or hit the player shall not play the ball again, nor remain or approach within playing distance of the ball until it has been touched or played by another player of either team.

Penalty.

For any breach of this Rule, a free hit shall be awarded to the opposing team.

[A free hit to the defending team may be brought up to 16 yards from the back-line, if the breach was nearer to the back-line.

(See Rule 14(a) (ii.)]

II OVER BACK-LINE.

(a) By an attacker.

(i) When the ball passes completely over the opponents' back-line by or off one of the attacking team and no goal is scored, it or another ball shall be placed on a spot opposite the place where it crossed the back-line and not more than 16 yards from the inner edge of that line. The ball shall be pushed or hit without undue delay by one of the defending team.

[When pushed or hit, the ball shall not be raised intentionally. The player taking the push or hit shall not be penalised if the ball lifts slightly off the ground as long as the intention to play along the ground is clear. Simply touching the ball with the stick is not considered to be a hit; the ball must move from its original position.]

(ii) The ball shall be stationary and the striker shall push or hit it. The ball must be moved and shall not be raised intentionally or in such a way as to be dangerous in itself or likely to lead to dangerous play.

(iii) Other than the striker, no player of the opposing team shall be within 5 yards of the ball when the push or hit is taken.

(iv) If the striker hit at but missed the ball, provided that Rule 12.I(c) has not been contravened, the push or hit still has to be taken.

(v) After taking the push or hit, the striker shall not play the ball again or remain or approach within playing distance of the ball until it has been touched or played by another player of either team.

[If the ball be hit by, or glance off, the stick or person of a defender over his own back-line or goal-line, note that the decision must, unless a goal is scored, be:]

(b) By a defender.

(i) When the ball, in the umpire's opinion is sent over defender's own back-line or goal-line by or off one of the defending team who is within his own 25 yards area, a push or hit shall be taken by the attacking team, unless a goal has been scored.

[A push or hit from the back-line if unintentionally from within his own 25 yards area.]

(a) The player shall push or hit the ball from a spot on the back-line within 5 yards of the corner flag nearer to the point where the ball crossed the back-line.

[Simply touching the ball with the stick is not considered to be a hit; the ball must move from its original position.]

(b) The ball shall be stationary and the striker shall push or hit it. The ball must be moved and shall not be raised intentionally or in such a way as to be dangerous in itself or likely to lead to dangerous play.

(c) Other than the striker, no player of the opposing team shall be within 5 yards of the ball when the push or hit is taken.

(d) If the striker hit at but missed the ball, provided that Rule 12.I(c) has not been contravened, the push or hit still has to be taken.

(e) After taking the push or hit, the striker shall not play the ball again nor remain or approach within playing distance of the ball until it has been touched or played by another player of either team.

(ii) When the ball, in the umpire's opinion, is sent over his own back-line or goal-line by or off one of the defending team who is more than 25 yards from the back-line, the game shall be re-started by a push or hit by one of the defending team from a spot opposite the place where it crossed the back-line or goal-line and not more than 16 yards from the inner edge of that line.

(a) The ball shall be stationary and the striker shall push or hit it. The ball must be moved and shall not be raised intentionally or in such a way as to be dangerous in itself or likely to lead to dangerous play.

(b) Other than the striker, no player of the attacking team shall be within 5 yards of the ball when the push or hit is taken.

(c) If the striker hit at but missed the ball, provided that Rule 12.I(c) has not been contravened, the push or hit still has to be taken.

(d) After taking the push or hit, the striker shall not play the ball again nor remain or approach within playing distance of the ball until it has been touched or played by another player of either team.

[In deciding whether a push or hit from the back-line or a penalty corner should be awarded, the only point at issue is whether the hit or deflection was intentional or unintentional. The fact that, in sending the ball over the back-line, a defender saves a goal must not influence an umpire in his decision.]

[The only point at issue is whether the stroke or deflection was intentional or not. The fact that, in sending the ball over the back-line, a defender saves a goal must not influence an umpire in his decision.

The conduct of the penalty corner is described at Rule 15.]

(iii) No player may deliberately play or deflect the ball over his own back-line or goal-line from an area enclosed by the 25 yards line.

Penalties.

1. For a breach of this Rule by an attacker, a free hit shall be awarded to the defending team.

2. For a ball raised dangerously from a free hit within the circle by a defender, a penalty corner shall be awarded.

3. For an unintentional breach of this Rule by a defender, a free hit shall be awarded to the attacking team.

4. For an intentional breach of this Rule by a defender within the 25 yards area but outside the circle, a penalty corner shall be awarded.

5. For an intentional breach of this Rule by a defender within the circle, a penalty stroke shall be awarded.

6. For a breach of Rule 17.II(b)(iii), a penalty corner shall be awarded to the opposing team.

18. ACCIDENTS.

The umpire should see that an injured player leaves the field of play as soon as possible, unless medical reasons prohibit this action.

(a) If a player or an umpire be incapacitated, the umpire or other umpire shall stop the game temporarily, noting the time lost. (See Rule 3(f).)

In either case, if a goal be scored before the game be stopped it shall be allowed if, in the umpire's opinion, it would have been scored had the accident not occurred.

(b) The umpire shall re-start the game as soon as possible, by:

(i) a bully (subject to Rule 10(b)(iv)) on a spot to be chosen by the umpire in whose half of the ground the accident occurred.

OR

(ii) the appropriate penalty when the accident was the result of a breach of the rules.

OR

(iii) the implementation of a decision given before the game was stopped.

(c) If the umpire concerned cannot continue, the other umpire shall re-start the game.

GOVERNING BODIES

International Governing Body: Hockey Rules Board, 26 Stompond Lane, Walton-on-Thames, Surrey, England KT121HB

United States Governing Body (Men): Field Hockey Association of America, 1750 E. Boulder St., Colorado Springs, CO 80909

United States Governing Body (Women): United States Field Hockey Association, 1750 E. Boulder St., Colorado Springs, CO 80909

Although the Hockey Rules Board (HRB) in conjunction with the International Hockey Federation is the recognized international governing body for field hockey, there are two United States Affiliate organizations (FHAA for men and USFHA for women) recognized by the United States Olympic Committee (USOC). The FHAA and USFHA seek to promote the game of field hockey for their particular gender through sponsorship of youth and adult programs, coaching and umpiring clinics, national and international competition, instructional aids, and newsletters. The two organizations are responsible for selection and management of teams to represent the United States in international competition, including the Olympic Games.

MAGAZINES

FHAA News, Field Hockey Association of America, 1750 E. Boulder St., Colorado Springs, CO 80909.

USFHA Newsletter, United States Field Hockey Association, 1750 E. Boulder St., Colorado Springs, CO 80909.

FLAG AND
• TOUCH FOOTBALL •

ABRIDGMENT OF OFFICIAL NIRSA RULES AND INTERPRETATIONS FOR COLLEGIATE FLAG/TOUCH FOOTBALL RULES

(By permission of the National Intramural-Recreational Sports Association*)

☐

Note: The rules presented here are an abridgment of the official rules developed and distributed by the NIRSA. The official rulebook is very comprehensive covering all play eventualities and includes interpretations as needed. The rules for Men's, Women's, and Corecreational Flag and Touch Football have been integrated into the rulebook.

**** The rules for Flag Football and Touch Football for Men and Women and Corecreational play are the same except for those rules identified with a star symbol.

RULE I. THE GAME, FIELD, PLAYERS AND EQUIPMENT

A. THE GAME

1. The game shall be played between two teams of seven players each on a rectangular field with an official football. Five players are required to avoid a forfeit.

**** Corecreational games are played with eight players on each team—four men and four women. Six players are required to avoid a forfeit.

2. The game proceeds with each team attempting to score the most points by advancing the ball across the opponent's goal line. The ball may be advanced by running or passing within the restrictions of the rules.

3. It is recommended that the game be played under the supervision of two to four officials.

4. Each team shall designate a team captain who is to make all decisions in regard to options posed by the officials. The captain's first choice of any option shall be irrevocable.

B. THE FIELD

1. The field shall be a rectangular area 40 yards wide and 100 yards long including a 10 yard end zone area at each end. The 80 yards field area between goal lines will be marked in 20 yard intervals as shown in the accompanying diagram. There shall be one inbounds hash mark dividing the field into halves. The hash mark shall run parallel with the sidelines. (Should it be necessary to modify the size of the field, the 20 yard zone intervals may be changed according to field dimensions.)

---

*See page 296 for additional information.

2. The lines bounding the sidelines and the end zones are out-of-bounds in their entirety. The entire width of each goal line shall be a part of the end zone.

3. Field markers should include soft, flexible pylons placed at the inside corner of each of the intersections of the sidelines with the goal lines and the end lines. A down marker used to indicate the number of the down should be maintained at the zone line-to-gain.

4. Ball Spotters. Two ball spotters (i.e., rubber disc, bean bag, towel) are required. One, which shall be orange in color, will mark the forward most point of the football. The second, which shall be gold in color, will mark the defensive scrimmage line. The ball spotters will always be one yard apart. Ball spotters should be constructed of a soft, pliable material.

DIAGRAM OF FIELD

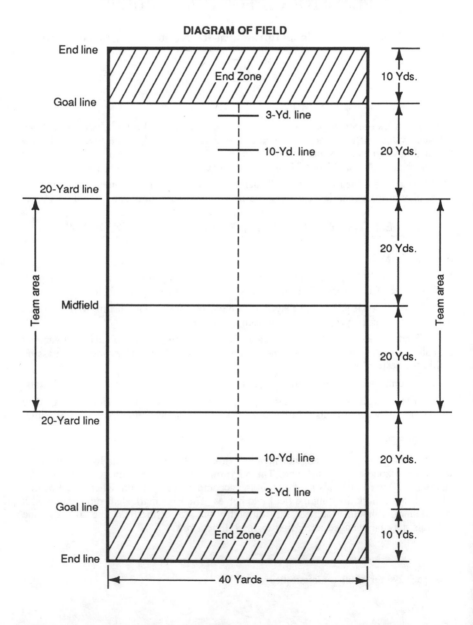

C. THE BALL

1. The ball shall be the pebble-grained leather or rubber covered ball of the size and dimensions of a regulation football.

2. Men will use the regular size while women will use the intermediate size. (The regular and intermediate size football may be used for corecreational games.)

D. PLAYER EQUIPMENT

1. Opposing teams will wear contrasting colored jerseys numbered front and back. The jersey must not in any way hinder the opponent's effort to seize a flag. The jersey must be long enough to stay tucked in the pants/shorts during play or short enough to be a minimum of 4 inches above the waist line. Pants/shorts should not have belt loops and must be of different color than that of the flags.

2. Each player must wear a one-piece belt at the waistline with three flags permanently attached, one flag on each side and one in the center of the back. The flags should be a minimum of 2 inches wide and 14 inches long.

The flags must be of a contrasting color to the opponent's flags.

3. Each player must wear shoes made of a soft, pliable upper material (canvas, leather or synthetic) which covers the foot attached to a one-piece molded composition rubber bottom.

4. A player may not wear any equipment which, in the opinion of the Referee, is dangerous or confusing. Types of equipment and substances which shall always be declared illegal include: hard/stiff headgear (includes billed hats), jewelry, pads or braces worn above the waist, shoes with cleats which are not part of a one-piece molded rubber bottom, leg and knee braces made of hard material unless covered with approximately 1/2 inch thickness of soft material.

RULE II. DEFINITIONS OF PLAYING TERMS

1. Blocking: See *screen blocking* below.

2. A *fair catch* is a catch of a free or protected scrimmage kick, which is beyond K's free kick line or K's scrimmage line and between the goal lines, by a player of the receiving team, who has signaled intention by extending one arm above his/her head and waving it from side to side more than once.

3. *Handing the ball* is a legal act of transferring player possessions from one teammate to another without throwing or kicking it.

4. A *free kick* is a kick made under restrictions which prohibit either team from advancing beyond established restraining lines until the ball is kicked.

5. A *protected scrimmage kick* is made under the restrictions which prohibit either team from advancing beyond their scrimmage line until the ball is kicked. All punts, drop kicks, and place kicks must be protected scrimmage kicks.

6. The *neutral zone* is the length of the football extended to each sideline and is established when the ball is ready for play.

7. *Removal of the flag belt* from the runner shall end the down and the ball is declared dead. A player who removes the flag belt should immediately hold the belt above his/her head to assist the official in locating the spot where the capture occurred. (If a flag belt inadvertently falls to the ground, a one hand tag between the shoulders and knees constitutes capture.) A player, who removes the flag belt, may leave his/her feet.

Contact. In an attempt to remove the flag belt from a runner, defensive players may contact the body and shoulders of an opponent with their hands, but not their face or any part of their neck or head. A defensive player may not hold, push, or knock the ball runner down in an attempt to remove the flag.

Dropped flag. The flag may be dropped at the spot of capture by the defense with no penalty.

8. *Screen blocking* is legally obstructing an opponent without contacting him/her with any part of the screen blocker's body.

9. The *scrimmage line* for Team A is the yard line and its vertical plane which passes through the point of the ball nearest its own goal line. The scrimmage line for Team B is the yard line and its vertical plane which passes one yard from the point of the ball nearest its own goal line. To be on the scrimmage line an offensive line player's head must break the plane of the line drawn through the waistline of the snapper.

Backfield line. To be legally in the backfield a player's head must not break the plane of the line drawn through the waistline of his/her nearest teammate (except snapper) on the scrimmage line.

10. *Snapping the ball* is passing it back from the position on the ground through the snapper's legs. The movement must be a quick and continuous motion of the hand or hands during which the ball actually leaves the hand or hands. The ball may not be raised more than a 45 degree angle at the snap and long axis of the ball must be at right angles to the scrimmage line.

11. *Tagging* (Touch) is placing one hand anywhere between the shoulders and knees of an opponent with the ball. The feet of the tagger may leave the ground to make the tag.

Pushing, striking, slapping, and holding are not permitted.

If the player trips the runner in his/her attempt to make a diving tag it is a penalty.

12. The *zone line-to-gain* is the next line on the playing field in the direction of and parallel to the opponent's goal line. The down marker shall be positioned on the zone line-to-gain.

RULE III. PERIODS, TIME FACTORS, SUBSTITUTIONS

A. PERIODS

1. Each of the two halves shall start with a kickoff. The Referee will toss a coin between the two opposing captains with the home team captain calling the toss. The captain winning the toss will have first choice of options for either the first or second half. The loser shall have the first choice of options for the half the winner of the toss did not select. The options for each half shall be a) to choose whether to kick or receive or b) to choose the goal his/her team will defend.

B. GAME TIME

1. Playing time shall be of 40 minute duration, divided into two halves of 20 minutes each. The intermission between halves shall be 5 minutes. When an overtime is used, there will be a 3 minute intermission.

2. Should the game end in a *tie score* the procedure for beginning the game will be repeated to begin the overtime period. If additional overtime periods are required, the opposing captains will alternate choices. Each team will be given 4 downs from the same 10 yard line. The object will be to score a touchdown. If the first team which is awarded the ball scores, the second team will still have 4 downs to attempt to win the game. Try-for-points will be attempted and scored as indicated in Rule 8. If the defense intercepts the ball and returns it for a touchdown, they will win the game. If they do not return the interception for a touchdown, the ball will be placed at the 10 yard line to begin their series of four downs. Each team is entitled to one time-out per overtime.

3. The *clock will run continuously* for the first 18 minutes unless it is stopped for a a) score, b) team time-out, c) Referee's time-out.

Approximately *two minutes before the end of each half* the Referee will stop the clock and inform both captains of the playing time remaining.

During the *final 2 minutes* of each half the clock will stop for a a) incomplete pass; b) out-of-bounds; c) any score; d) team time-out; e) first down; f) fair catch; g) penalty (except for delay of game); h) Referee time-out; i) touchback.

Each team is entitled to 2 charged time-outs during each half. The time-out period shall not exceed one minute.

4. *Delay of game* will be called and penalty assessed for a) delaying start of a half, b) consuming more than 25 seconds in putting the ball in play after it is ready for play, c) deliberately advancing the ball after it has been declared dead.

C. SUBSTITUTIONS.

Any number of substitutes may enter the game between downs provided there is no delay of game.

RULE IV. BALL IN PLAY, DEAD BALL, OUT-OF-BOUNDS

A. BALL IN PLAY—DEAD BALL

1. *Ready for play*. No player shall put the ball in play until it is declared ready for play. Penalty: 5 yards.

2. The ball shall be *put into play within 25 seconds* after it is declared ready for play. Penalty: 5 yards.

3. A live ball becomes dead when:

(a) it goes out-of-bounds.

(b) any part of runner's person other than a hand or foot touches the ground.

(c) any score or touchback is made.

(d) during a try-for-point, the defensive team obtains possession.

(e) a player of the kicking team catches a free kick or any muffed free kick or a scrimmage kick which is beyond the neutral zone.

(f) a free kick or an untouched scrimmage kick comes to rest on the ground and no player attempts to secure it.

(g) a backward pass or fumble touches the ground (this includes a snap which hits the ground before reaching the intended receiver).

(h) a forward pass is legally completed, or a loose ball is caught or recovered by a player on, above, or behind the opponent's goal line.

(i) the flag belt is legally removed from the runner.

(j) *tag*—a runner is legally tagged with one hand between the shoulders and knees, including the hand and arm.

(k) a passer is deflagged/tagged prior to releasing the ball.

(l) a free kick or scrimmage kick is muffed and strikes the ground.

(m) an inadvertent whistle is blown.

B. OUT-OF-BOUNDS

1. A player is out-of-bounds when any part of that player touches anything which is on or outside a boundary line.

2. A player *catching a forward pass* is considered out-of-bounds when any part of his/her person contacts that area declared out-of-bounds. He/she may also be considered out-of-bounds when he/she contacts a player out-of-bounds, or he/she is returning to the ground, which causes him/her then to land in the field of play.

RULE V. SERIES OF DOWNS, NUMBER OF DOWNS, AND TEAM POSSESSION AFTER PENALTY

A. A SERIES—HOW STARTED, HOW BROKEN, RENEWED

1. A team, in possession of the ball, shall have four consecutive downs to advance to the next zone by scrimmage. Any down may be repeated if provided for by the rules.

2. The *zone line-to-gain* in a series shall be the zone in advance of the ball, unless distance has been lost due to penalty or failure to gain. In such case, the original zone at the beginning of the series of downs is the zone line-to-gain. The most forward point of the ball, when declared dead shall be the determining factor.

3. A *new series of downs* shall be awarded when a team moves the ball into the next zone by legal advancement or by penalty against the opponent; and when either team gains legal possession of the ball.

B. DOWN AND POSSESSION AFTER A PENALTY

1. When a scrimmage follows the penalty for a foul committed during a free kick, the down and distance established by the penalty shall be the first down with the next zone line-to-gain.

2. After a penalty which leaves the ball in possession of a team beyond its zone line-to-gain, or when a penalty stipulates a first down, the down and distance established by that penalty shall be first down with next zone line-to-gain.

3. After a distance penalty between the goal lines incurred during a down before any change of team possession during that down, the ball belongs to the offense and the down shall be repeated unless the penalty also involves loss of a down, or leaves the ball on or beyond the zone line-to-gain. If the penalty involves loss of a down, the down shall count as one of the four in that series.

4. After a distance penalty for a foul committed during a down and after team possession has changed during that down, the ball belongs to the team in possession when the foul occurred and the down and distance established by that penalty shall be first down with zone line-to-gain.

5. If a penalty is declined the number of the next down shall be whatever it would have been if that foul had not occurred.

6. After a distance penalty incurred between downs, the number of the next down shall be the same as that established before the foul occurred unless enforcement for a foul by the defense leaves the ball on or beyond the zone line-to-gain.

7. A scrimmage following a penalty incurred after a series ends and before the next series begins shall be first down but the zone line-to-gain shall be established before the penalty is enforced.

8. If offsetting fouls occur during a down the down shall be repeated.

RULE VI. KICKING THE BALL AND FAIR CATCH

A. FREE KICKS

1. A free kick begins each half of play and begins play following a score. The kick may be a place kick or drop kick from any spot on or behind the 20-yard line. The ball may be placed on a legal tee or held or placed on the ground or holder's toe. The receiving team's free kick line shall be the yard line 20 yards beyond the kicking team's free kick line.

2. All players, except the holder and the kicker, must be behind the free kick line. At least 4 players (corecreation rules require 5 players) of the receiving team must be within 5 yards of their free kick line after the ball is ready for play and until the ball is kicked. Penalty: 5 yards from the previous spot.

3. If a member of the kicking team touches a free kick before it crosses the receiver's free kick line and before it is touched by any receiving player, it is referred to as "first touching" and the receiving team may take the ball at that spot or at a spot precipitated by a penalty.

4. There are no onside kicks. The kicking team cannot recover an onside kick.

****5. In corecreational play, only a female may advance a free kick after a catch. A male player may only move backward or perpendicular from the point of the catch for the entire down. Penalty: 5 yards.

6. If no player of either team attempts to play a free kick, the ball becomes dead and belongs to the receiving team at the dead ball spot.

7. A free kick which touches anything while the ball is on or behind the receiver's goal line is declared dead and is a touchback. The receiving team puts the ball in play at their 20-yard line.

8. A free kick which goes out-of-bounds between the goal lines untouched by the receiving team is a foul. Penalty: 5 yards from previous spot.

B. PROTECTED SCRIMMAGE KICK

1. A legal protected scrimmage kick is a punt which may be made unmolested if such a request is made of the official before the ball is made ready for play. The Referee will ask if a protected scrimmage kick is desired before all fourth down plays. The announcement of the desire to kick will be communicated to the opponent and the kick must be made.

2. Both teams must have 4 players (corecreational rules require 5 players) within one yard of their respective scrimmage line until the kick is made. Players on the line are to remain motionless.

3. The kicker must be at least 5 yards behind the scrimmage line and must kick the ball immediately in a continuous motion. Penalty: 5 yards. (The kicker may not hold the ball to allow time to run off the clock.)

4. If the kick fails to cross the scrimmage line, the ball is dead where it hits the ground or is touched. If the kicking team touches the kicked ball first or the receiving team touches the ball and it falls to the ground, the ball is declared dead and put into play by the receiving team at that spot.

5. If the kicked ball is touched by the receiving team and caught in the air by the receiving team, it may be advanced. If the ball is hit by a player on the receiving team and caught in the air by the kicking team, the ball is dead and belongs to the kicking team.

6. A protected scrimmage kick which goes out-of-bounds between the goal lines or no player attempts to secure an inbound kick, the ball becomes dead and is put in play by the receiver at the spot. A protected scrimmage kick which touches anything on or behind receiver's goal line is dead immediately and is a touchback.

C. FAIR CATCH

1. While any free kick or protected scrimmage kick is in flight beyond the kicker's scrimmage line, the kicking team shall not touch the ball nor the receiver nor obstruct the receiver's path to the ball. Penalty: 10 yards from the previous spot and replay down or an awarded fair catch after enforcement of a 10 yard penalty from the spot of the foul.

RULE VII. SNAPPING, HANDING, AND PASSING THE BALL

A. SNAPPING

1. The snapper, after assuming the position for the snap and adjusting the ball, may neither move or change the position of the ball in a manner simulating the beginning of a play until it is snapped. Penalty: 5 yards from the previous spot.

2. The snapper shall have his/her feet behind his/her scrimmage line and no part of his/her person other than a hand or hands on the ball may be beyond the foremost point of the ball. (Penalty: 5 yards from the previous spot.) The ball shall be passed back between the legs from its position on the ground with a quick and continuous motion of the hand or hands and shall leave the hand or hands in this motion.

3. No players shall interlock their legs at the scrimmage line except with the snapper. (Penalty: 5 yards.) No player shall make contact or interfere with an opponent or the ball before it is snapped. (Penalty: 5 yards.) Players may use a three or four point stance.

4. No player of the offensive team shall make a false start. A false start includes feigning a charge or a play. (Penalty: 5 yards.) All players of the offense must come to a complete stop and remain stationary without movement of feet, body, head, or arms for at least one full second before the ball is snapped. Penalty: 5 yards.

5. At least four players must be on their offensive scrimmage line. The remaining players must be either on their scrimmage line or behind their backfield line. (Penalty: 5 yards.) All players must be inbounds.

****In corecreational play, five players must be on the offensive scrimmage line.

6. One offensive player may be in motion, but not in motion toward the opponent's goal line. If such player starts from the scrimmage line, that player must be at least five yards behind that line when the ball is snapped. The offensive team must still have four players on their scrimmage line when the ball is snapped. Penalty: 5 yards.

7. No offensive player while on the scrimmage line may receive a snap. (Penalty: 5 yards.) The player who receives the snap must be at least two yards behind the offensive line. Direct snaps are not allowed on any down. Penalty: 5 yards.

8. After the ball is ready-for-play, each player on the offense must momentarily be within 15 yards of the ball before the snap. Penalty: 5 yards.

B. HANDING THE BALL

1. The ball may not be handed forward except that an offensive player behind the scrimmage line may hand the ball forward to a backfield teammate who is also behind the line to a teammate who was on the scrimmage line at the time of the snap provided that teammate left the scrimmage line, faced his/her own end line, and was at least one yard behind the scrimmage line when the player received the ball. Penalty: 5 yards and loss of down.

2. A runner may hand the ball backward at anytime.

****3. In corecreational play, a male runner cannot advance the ball beyond his scrimmage line. There are no restrictions concerning runs by a female runner. Penalty: 5 yards.

C. BACKWARD PASS AND FUMBLE

1. A runner may pass the ball backward or lose player possession by a fumble at anytime except if intentionally thrown out-of-bounds to conserve time or to avoid the deflag/tag. Penalty: 5 yards and loss of down.

2. A backward pass or fumble may be caught in flight by any player and advanced.

3. A backward pass or fumble which goes out-of-bounds between the goal lines belongs to the team last in possession at the out-of-bounds spot. If out-of-bounds behind a goal line it is a touchback or safety.

4. A backward pass or fumble which touches the ground is dead at the spot where it touches the ground and belongs to the team last in possession unless lost on downs.

D. FORWARD PASS

1. A forward pass may be thrown by the offensive team during any scrimmage down provided the ball, when it leaves the passer's hand is behind the offensive's scrimmage line. All players of either team are eligible to touch or catch a pass. Only one forward pass can be thrown per down.

2. It is illegal to intentionally throw the ball to the ground or out-of-bounds to save loss of yardage. Penalty: 5 yards from spot of foul and loss of down.

**** In corecreational play, a male passer is restricted to completing one forward pass per series of downs to a male receiver. There is no restriction on a male passer completing passes to female receivers.

3. When a legal forward pass touches the ground or goes out-of-bounds, it becomes dead, is ruled as an incomplete pass, and belongs to the passing team at the spot of the previous snap.

4. When an illegal forward pass touches the ground or goes out-of-bounds the ball becomes dead and belongs to the passing team at the spot from where the pass was thrown.

5. An offensive player who goes out-of-bounds on his/her own volition during a passing down loses eligibility until the ball has been touched by an opponent. Penalty: 10 yards.

6. A pass catcher is considered inbounds if the first part of the person to make contact with the ground, after the catch, touches inbounds.

7. A legal forward pass caught simultaneously by members of opposing teams belongs to the team that put the ball in play.

E. PASS INTERFERENCE

1. Any contact which interferes with an eligible receiver who is beyond the passing team's scrimmage line is pass interference unless it occurs when two or more eligible receivers make a simultaneous and bona fide attempt to reach, catch, or bat a pass. It is also pass interference if an eligible receiver is deflagged/tagged prior to touching the ball. The pass interference may be either offensive or defensive. Waving the arms in the face of the pass catcher is also interference. (Penalty: 10 yards.) If the interference is intentional or unsportsmanlike an additional 10-yard penalty will be assessed.

RULE VIII. SCORING PLAYS AND TOUCHBACK

A. TOUCHDOWN

1. A touchdown of 6 points is scored for the team which advances the ball to the point where any part of the ball is on, above, or behind the opponent's goal line.

2. In flag football, the player scoring the touchdown must raise his/her arms so the nearest official can deflag the player. If the official determines the flag belt has been secured illegally, the touchdown is disallowed, the player disqualified, and a 10-yard penalty from the previous spot, and loss of down are assessed.

B. TRY-FOR-POINT

1. A try-for-point opportunity to score one or two points is granted a team scoring a touchdown.

2. The scoring team has the choice of attempting to score from the 3-yard line, by running or passing, for one point or by running or passing from the 10-yard line for two points.

C. SAFETY—TOUCHBACK

1. A safety score of 2 points is scored if the defending team is responsible for the ball being out-of-bounds behind a goal line (except from an incomplete forward pass) or the ball becoming dead in possession of a player on, above, or behind the player's own goal line. If the attacking team is responsible, it is a touchback. When an accepted penalty for a foul or an illegal forward pass leaves the ball on or behind the offending team's goal line, it is a safety.

RULE IX. CONDUCT OF PLAYERS AND OTHERS

A. UNSPORTSMANLIKE CONDUCT

1. No player shall use abusive or insulting language nor commit any acts of unfair play including attempts to interfere with offensive signals or movements, kicking at opposing players, kicking at the ball other than during a legal kick, swinging arms, hand or fist at opposing player. Penalty: 10 yards.

2. When the ball becomes dead in possession of a player, he/she shall not intentionally kick the ball, spike the ball, throw the ball high in the air, fail to return the ball to huddle or toss to nearest official. Penalty: 10 yards.

3. Coaches, substitutes, or others subject to the rules shall not attempt to influence the decision of an official, address an official disrespectfully, or be on the field illegally. Penalty: 10 yards and if flagrant, the offender disqualified.

4. If play is interfered with by an obviously unfair or unsportsmanlike act not specifically covered by the rules, or if a team repeatedly commits fouls, the Referee may enforce any penalty he/she considers equitable, including awarding a score or forfeiting the game.

B. PERSONAL FOULS

1. No player shall commit personal fouls including, but not limited to, attempting to steal the ball from player in possession, tripping an opponent, throwing the runner to the ground, hurdling any other player, making any contact with an opponent which is deemed unnecessary, positioning himself/herself on the shoulders of a teammate. Penalty: 10 yards and if flagrant, the offender disqualified.

2. The defensive player must make a definite effort to avoid charging into a passer after it is clear the ball has been thrown. No defensive player shall contact the passer who is standing still or fading back as he/she is considered out of the play after the pass. Penalty: 10 yards and an automatic first down.

C. BLOCKING

1. The offensive screen block shall take place without contact. The screen blocker shall have his/her hands and arms at his/her side or behind his/her back. Any use of the arms,

elbows, or legs to initiate contact during an offensive player's screen block is illegal. A blocker may use his/her hand or arm to break a fall or to retain his/her balance. A player must be on his/her feet before, during, and after screen blocking. Penalty: 10 yards.

2. In the execution of screen blocking, a player shall not a) when behind a stationary opponent, take a position closer than a normal step from the opponent; b) when assuming a position at the side or in front of a stationary opponent, make contact with the opponent; c) take a position so close to a moving opponent that the opponent cannot avoid contact by stopping or changing directions. The speed of the players to be screened will determine where the screener may take his/her stationary position. This position will vary and be one to two normal steps or strides from the opponent; d) after assuming his/her legal screening position move to maintain it, unless he/she moves in the same direction and path of the opponent. Penalty: 10 yards.

3. Teammates of a runner or passer may interfere for him/her by screen blocking, but shall not use interlocked interference by grasping or encircling one another in any manner. Penalty: 10 yards.

4. Defensive players must go around the offensive player's screen block. The arms and hands may not be used as a wedge to contact the opponent. Penalty: 10 yards.

D. RUNNER

1. Runners may not guard their flags by blocking with arms or hands the opportunity for an opponent to pull or remove the flag belt. Penalty: 10 yards.

2. The runner is prohibited from contacting an opponent with extended hand or arm. This includes the use of a "stiff arm" extended to ward off an opponent attempting to deflag/tag. Penalty: 10 yards.

3. The runner may not grasp a teammate or be grasped, pulled or pushed by a teammate. Penalty: 5 yards.

4. The defensive player may not hold, grasp, or obstruct forward progress of a runner when in the act of removing the flag belt or making a legal tag. Penalty: 10 yards.

5. The offensive player must avoid running through a defensive player. The charge/block principles used in basketball apply. Penalty: 10 yards.

E. BATTING, KICKING, AND ILLEGAL PARTICIPATION

1. Players shall not bat a loose ball other than a pass or fumble in flight. A backward pass in flight shall not be batted forward by the passing team. Penalty: 10 yards.

2. No player shall participate by touching the ball or hindering an opponent after having been out-of-bounds during the down. This does not include being blocked or pushed out-of-bounds. Penalty: 10 yards.

3. No player shall intentionally kick a ball other than as a free kick or a scrimmage kick. Penalty: 10 yards.

F. FLAG BELT REMOVAL

The basic rules of flag football regarding legal or illegal removal of the flag belt are as follows:

1. Deflagging is allowed only under special circumstances similar to tackling in football. Offensive players must have possession of the ball before they can legally be deflagged/tagged.

2. A flag belt which becomes detached inadvertently does not cause play to stop. In all situations where a play is in progress and a runner loses the flag belt either accidentally, inadvertently, or on purpose, the deflagging reverts to a one-hand tag of the runner between the shoulders and knees.

3. In circumstances where a flag is removed illegally, play should continue with the option of the penalty or the play. Penalty: 10 yards.

4. It is illegal for a defensive player to pull or remove a flag belt from an offensive player without the ball. Penalty: 10 yards.

5. Tampering with the flag belt in any way to gain an advantage including tying, using foreign materials, or other such acts is illegal. Penalty: 10 yards from previous spot, loss of down and player disqualification.

RULE X. ENFORCEMENT OF PENALTIES

(The enforcement of penalties portion of the NIRSA Official Rules contains six sections dealing with procedure after a foul, double and multiple fouls, basic enforcement spots, administering penalties, special enforcements, and penalty enforcement philosophy.)

GOVERNING BODY

National Intramural-Recreational Sports Association, Gill Coliseum, Room 221, Oregon State University, Corvallis, OR 97331

The National Intramural-Recreational Sports Association (NIRSA) is a nonprofit professional organization of men and women dedicated to the establishment and development of quality recreational sports programs and services. The major responsibilities of the NIRSA members include informal recreational sport and fitness programming, recreation facility operations, fiscal management, sport club coordination, intramural sports programming, and administration of outdoor recreational activities. The majority of Association membership represents professionals at the collegiate level. In addition, a growing number of members are employed in the military, private industry, community, and elementary/secondary level school sectors.

The NIRSA Football Rules Committee has developed some outstanding tools to aid in the administration of flag or touch football programs.

1. Rulebook and Official's Manual—includes two, three, and four person officiating mechanics complete with diagrams depicting the basic coverages for Referee, Linesperson, Back Judge and Field Judge.

2. Videocassette tapes (1/2″ and 3/4″) entitled "Flag and Touch Football at Its Best"— this excellent 20-min videotape covers the basic rules and tough calls of the game along with various officiating mechanics. This presentation is also available as a 16-mm film.

3. "First and Twenty," a videotape covering team strategy. Utilizing game footage from the 1986 National Collegiate Flag Football Championships, the tape covers offensive/defensive strategy and sets, alignments, positions, and special drills.

4. NIRSA Clinician Kit, an excellent tool for the administrator, includes "Flag and Touch Football at Its Best" videotape, a copy of the Rulebook and Official's Manual, 8-1/2″ × 11″ overhead transparencies illustrating officials mechanics, and a 250-question test bank covering rules.

Copies of these materials may be obtained by writing the NIRSA Sports Officials Development Center, Gill Coliseum, Room 221, Corvallis, OR 97331.

• FOOTBALL •

(Rules summary by author)

☐

Note: In view of the various levels of organized football competition and the resulting rules modifications by the recognized governing bodies, the basic rules of the game are summarized here.

RULE I. FIELD, GAME, PLAYERS, EQUIPMENT, OFFICIALS

A. THE FIELD

1. The game is played on a rectangular field 160 feet wide and 360 feet long with a 10 yard end zone designated at each end of the field (See first figure). The 100 yards between the goal lines are marked in 10 yard intervals. A broken line (hash mark) running parallel to the sidelines is marked 53′4″ inside each sideline.

2. The goal posts, located on each end line of the field (equidistant from the sidelines), extend a minimum of 20 feet above ground level and are connected by a crossbar 10 feet high and 23 feet-4 inches long.

B. THE GAME

1. The game is played between two teams of 11 players each with substitutions permitted at any time the ball is not in play.

2. The object of each team is to score the most points by advancing the ball across the opponent's goal line. The ball may be advanced by running, passing or kicking in accordance with the rules of play.

3. The ball is put into play by a free kick to begin the game, to begin the second half, and after a score. Actually, most of the play is initiated from scrimmage play which permits the team in possession the opportunity to advance the ball by running a series of plays.

4. Preceding the start of the game, the referee meets with the opposing team captains for a coin toss to determine choices. The winner of the toss may choose one of the following options: a) to kick to the other team (kickoff); b) receive the kickoff; c) choose to defend either goal; or d) defer his choice until the beginning of the second half. In any case the loser of the toss has the first choice for the half the winner of the toss did not select. In each half the captain not having first choice shall exercise the remaining options.

5. The game begins with a kickoff from the kicking team's 35 yard line (College and Professional) or 40 yard line (High School). Kicks which go out of bounds are re-kicked after an assessment of a 5-yard penalty against the kicking team. Kicks into the opponents end zone may (College) or may not (High School) be run out of the end zone. If the kicked ball is declared dead in the end zone, the receiving team puts the ball in play on their own 20 yard line.

6. Each scrimmage play begins with a snap. The team in possession of the ball is given 4 scrimmage downs (plays) in which to advance the ball 10 or more yards by running or passing. If successful, a new series of 4 downs is awarded. If unsuccessful, possession

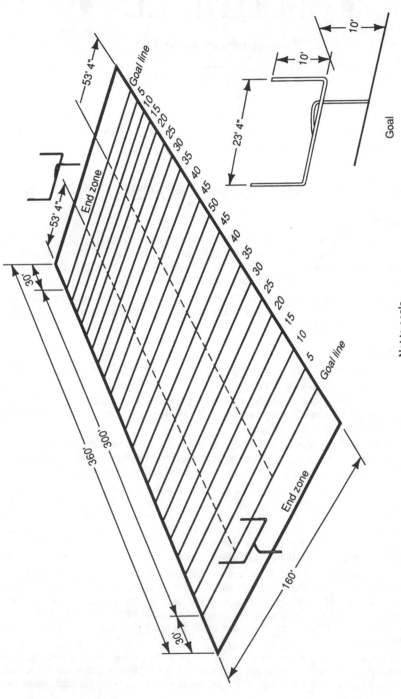

53' 4"

Goal line

5
10
15
20
25
30
35
40
45
50
45
40
35
30
25
20
15
10
5

Goal line

End zone

53' 4"

30'

300'

360'

30'

End zone

160'

23' 4"

10'

10'

Goal

Not to scale

of the ball is awarded to the opponents. Normally, if 10 yards is not gained on the first 3 downs, the team in possession will scrimmage kick (punt) the ball in order that the opponents' possession will begin at a greater distance from the goal line.

7. During the course of play, officials are charged with the responsibility of noting rules infractions. The infractions are noted by blowing a whistle if an infraction is noted before the play begins, or by throwing a yellow flag if an infraction occurs during the course of play. The official will also indicate the completion of each play by blowing his whistle. Assessment of yardage penalties is enforced after consultation with team captains.

C. THE PLAYERS

1. Players are designated by position as indicated below.

2. Required numbering of players by position for the offensive team is indicated in the next figure.

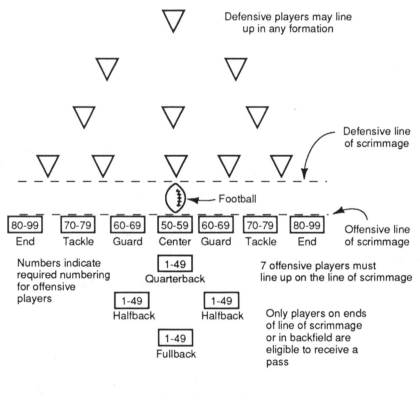

Not to scale

D. EQUIPMENT

1. Game Equipment

a. The official ball is oval shaped, approximately 11 inches long and 7 inches in diameter at the center. Normally, the ball is made of tan, pebble-grain cowhide but other approved substances such as rubber may be used. The ball should have air pressure of 12-1/2 to

13-1/2 pounds per square inch and weigh 14 to 15 ounces. The ball is constructed with leather laces along one seam to provide a good grip for passing. (The offensive team may use any legal ball during the downs they possess the ball.)

b. A ten-yard chain attached to two stakes is employed to keep accurate measurement of the point to where the ball must be advanced in order for a new series of downs to be awarded.

c. A down marker which permits display of numbers 1 through 4 is employed to indicate the number of the down being played and the yard line position from which the ball is played. The yard chain and down box are kept on one of the sidelines by sidelines helpers. The head linesman (field official) controls the movement of this equipment.

2. Player Equipment

a. Protective equipment to prevent injuries is required of all players. All players must wear a helmet with face protector, a fitted mouthpiece, shoulder pads, hip pads, thigh pads, knee pads, and shoes. Shoes may be cleated with plastic or rubber cleats. The amount of padding may vary at different levels of play.

b. No metal or other hard substances may be worn except for knee braces, which must be padded with soft material. All other padding must also be of a soft material.

c. Each team must wear standard football uniforms of a color that contrasts to that of the opponents' uniform. Large block numerals must appear on the front and back of the jersey worn by each player. Similarity of uniform colors is avoided through the practice of the home team wearing their dark colored uniforms and the visiting team wearing their white colored uniforms.

E. OFFICIALS

1. The game is supervised by 4 to 7 officials. All the officials have equal rights to call penalties although the Referee is the chief official and has general control of the game. The remaining officials (Umpire, Head Linesman, Line Judge) have various specialized duties. College and professional games also have three additional judges.

RULE II. SCORING AND TOUCHBACK

A. TYPES OF SCORES

1. Points are scored as follows: Touchdown-6 points; Field Goal-3 points; Safety-2 points; Try For Point-1 point or 2 points.

2. Touchdown

When a player who controls the ball advances from the field of play so that the ball touches the vertical plane of the opponent's goal line, it is a touchdown. It is also a touchdown if a pass (forward or backward) or fumble is caught or recovered in the opponent's end zone.

3. Try For Point

After each touchdown the team scoring is given a try for point. The ball is snapped on the defender's 3 yard line. This down is not numbered or timed. The try may either score one point by scrimmage kick or two points by pass or run. The try ends when a kick for goal is obviously good or not good, the defense secures possession, or the offense does not successfully run or pass the ball over the goal line. There are exceptions to this rule in college and professional games.

Fouls on the try play result in either a) a replay; b) declination of penalty by the offended team; or c) enforcement of the penalty on the ensuing kickoff.

4. Field Goal

A field goal is scored when a placekick or a drop kick from scrimmage, or a free kick (other than a punt) following a fair catch, is kicked over and between the uprights of the goal without touching the ground.

5. Safety

A player carrying the ball from the field into his own end zone results in a safety if such a carrier (a) has possession when tackled; or (b) loses possession out of bounds behind his goal line. It is also a safety if a player forces a live loose ball into his own end zone and it becomes dead either in his possession or out of bounds behind his goal line. (Force: The player who carries, passes, fumbles, kicks, or snaps the ball from the field of play across the goal into the end zone is responsible for the force. A muffing (touching) of a pass, or of a kick or pass in flight, is not a new force. The original force must be dissolved before a new force can be given to a grounded ball.)

B. TOUCHBACK

If a kicking team or the team on offense at the start of a down is responsible for kicking or forcing a loose ball over the opponents' goal line and the ball becomes dead in the end zone or dead by being out of bounds behind the goal line, a touchback is declared. No points are scored and the ball next put in play on the 20 yard line by the team whose goal is involved.

RULE III. TERMINOLOGY

A. *Batting*. Deliberately hitting a loose ball with the arm, hand, or leg.

B. *Blocking*. (Rules differ at various levels of play.) Blocking is obstructing an opponent with a part of the blocker's body. This must be done from the waist upward of both the blocker and the opponent. (For exception: see Free Blocking Zone.)

1. In proper blocking, the blocker uses his forearms parallel to the ground. The forearms may or may not be extended from the body. If the elbows are outside the shoulders, they cannot be swung. The hands, when extended forward may be used to push the opponent during blocking. Blocking above the opponent's shoulders is not permitted. (See Offensive and Defensive Use of Hands.)

C. *Butt Blocking*. A form of illegal blocking involving use of the helmet in making initial contact with the opponent.

D. *Catching*. The securing of player possession of a live ball in flight.

1. Catching an opponents' fumble or pass is an interception.

2. Gaining possession of a live ball (fumble or muff) after it strikes the ground is a recovery.

3. Possession of an airborne catch is not completed until such player returns to the field of play inbounds.

E. *Chop Blocking*. Illegally blocking an opponent below the waist who is already in contact with a teammate of the blocker.

F. *Clipping*. Illegally contacting the opponent from the rear. This contact is legal on a ball carrier or a pass receiver at the instant he is attempting to catch a pass. Penalty for an illegal clip is 15 yards. Doubtful cases involving the side of opponent or a turning opponent must be judged by the observing official. (See Free Blocking Zone.)

G. *Dead Ball*. The ball is declared dead and no longer in play when the play ends (e.g., the ball carrier a) is tackled or his forward progress is stopped; b) goes out of bounds; c) goes over a goal; d) a pass is incomplete; or e) the ball is kicked out of bounds).

H. *Down*. Each play is either a free kick or a scrimmage down. A free kick is used to begin each half of the game and to continue play after a score. All other plays are scrimmage downs. After a free kick down is ended, a line of scrimmage is established where the receiver of the free kick is downed.

I. *Drop Kick*. A kick by a player who drops the ball and kicks it just after it touches the ground. Such a kick can be used to score a field goal and can be used to attempt a point after a touchdown.

J. *Fair Catch*. A catch of a scrimmage kick or a free kick by a receiver who prior to the catch and while the ball is airborne waves his hand over his head. This catch is legal beyond the kicker's line of scrimmage or free kick line. The signaler forfeits the right to advance the ball in return for protection from being hit by an opponent.

K. *Foul*. A violation of a rule for which penalties are assessed.

1. Types of Fouls

a. Player foul. A foul by a player in the game.

b. Nonplayer foul. A violation by a nonplayer. It may or may not influence the play. A nonplayer interfering with play results in a 15-yard penalty for illegal participation. However, any penalty deemed equitable by the official may be assessed.

c. Double foul. Fouls committed during the same time frame by players of each team during a live ball. These fouls are generally offsetting.

d. Multiple foul. Fouls committed by the same team during a live ball. The offended team is permitted a choice of penalties. Only one is exacted. (Exception: if one foul is unsportsmanlike, it is always assessed.)

e. Unsportsmanlike conduct foul. A player or nonplayer act which is classified as unsportsmanlike and is penalized as a separate act without regard to other fouls that may occur during the same time frame.

L. *Free Blocking Zone*. On scrimmage downs this zone is an area 4 yards to either side of the snapper and 3 yards to either side of the line of scrimmage. Stationary players within the zone on the snap may make contact with each other below the waist on the initial charge. Further, offensive players on the line of scrimmage at the snap may clip an opponent who was in the zone at the snap provided the contact is within the zone. The zone disintegrates after initial line charge and the ball has left the zone.

M. *Free Kick or Kickoff*. A kick used to put the ball in play to start each half, to resume play after a field goal or extra point try, or may be used on the first scrimmage play after a fair catch (High School). During a free kick all kickers must be behind the ball when kicked except for the kicker and holder. Any form of kick (including a punt) may be used for a free kick following a safety. In all other instances (kickoffs) when a free kick is employed all forms of kicking except a punt are legal.

N. *Fumbling*. Any loss of control of the ball due to unsuccessful handling (other than kicking or passing).

O. *Illegal Contact*. (See Butt Blocking, Chop Blocking, Clipping, Spearing and Tripping.)

P. *Interference*.

1. No member of the kicking team may prevent a receiver of a kicked ball from securing possession of the kicked ball in flight. This includes making physical contact before the catch or obstructing the receiver's path to the ball. (Rule specifics vary at different levels of play.) Penalty for such interference is normally 15 yards. (See Rule VIII-D.)

2. (See Pass Interference—Rule VIII-C.)

Q. *Kicking*. Deliberately striking the ball with the leg or foot. The kicker is the player who kicks the ball. He remains the kicker (for penalty purposes) until he regains his equilibrium.

R. *Kick Off*. A kick used to put the ball in play to start each half and to resume play after a field goal or extra point try.

S. *Legal Motion*. After all offensive players are motionless, one player may be in motion at the snap provided that the motion is not forward and all other snap regulations are met.

T. *Line of Scrimmage*. When the ball is ready-for-play, the scrimmage line for each team is the line through the point of the ball nearest each team's position. (See Diagram A.)

1. An offensive player is on his line of scrimmage when he faces his opponent's goal line with his shoulders parallel to the goal line. The offensive players head must break the plane of a theoretical line through the waistline of the snapper.

2. Players may stand, crouch, or be in any legal position as prescribed above. Only the players beside the snapper of the ball may interlock legs.

3. An offensive back is in the backfield when his head does not break the plane of a theoretical line parallel to the line of scrimmage through the waistline of the next closest teammate who is on the line. This does not apply to a back taking a snap.

4. A defensive player may align himself anywhere on his side of the neutral zone. To be considered on the defensive line, defensive players must be within one yard of the defensive line of scrimmage at the snap. No specific facing is prescribed.

U. *Line to Gain*. The yard line 10 yards in advance of the leading edge of the ball when it is declared ready for scrimmage. A penalty enforcement could result in a greater distance to gain.

V. *Live Ball*. The ball becomes live when snapped or free kicked and remains live until the play ends.

W. *Loose Ball*. A loose ball is any pass, kick, or fumble, either in flight or on the ground. The ball remains loose until a) someone secures possession, or b) it becomes dead.

X. *Muffing*. Touching the ball in the air in a failed attempt to gain possession of a loose ball. (Receivers are subject to muff kickoffs, and punts.)

Y. *Neutral Zone*.

1. During any free kick the neutral zone (10 yards) is the distance between the two free kick lines.

2. During a scrimmage down the neutral zone is as wide as the length of the football and is determined when the ball is declared "ready-for-play."

Z. *Offensive and Defensive Use of Hands*.

1. An offensive player may use his hands or arms to ward off an opponent when he is a runner or may use the extended arm-open hand technique in blocking.

2. All players may push, pull or ward off an opponent when the ball is loose if the player may legally touch or possess the ball and such contact is not some form of illegal contact.

3. A defensive player may use his:

a. hand or arm to prevent an opponent from blocking him;

b. hands in an attempt to get the runner or a loose ball;

c. hands or arms only when they are in advance of the elbow at the time contact is made.

AA. *Out of Bounds*. Any area on or beyond the sidelines and end lines. (Includes the goal posts.)

1. Any player is out of bounds when he touches anything (other than another player or game official) which is out of bounds on any side of the field. This also applies to the ball if it is in player possession.

2. A loose ball is out of bounds when it touches anything or anyone that is out of bounds. (A kicked ball is not out of bounds if on a field goal or extra point try it touches a goal

post or crossbar or a defensive player in the field of play or in the end zone and goes between the uprights of the goal.)

BB. *Passing*. Passing the ball is throwing the ball from player to player. The ball may be thrown forward or backward. (Forward pass or backward pass.) A legal forward pass is one thrown forward from behind the offensive line of scrimmage. A pass is complete when any player secures possession and is on the ground or is airborne and returns to the ground inbounds. A player securing possession in the air and returning to the ground out of bounds causes the pass to be declared incomplete.

CC. *Place Kick*. A kick made while the ball is held on the ground or on a tee by a teammate.

DD. *Punt*. A kick by a player who kicks the ball after dropping it and before it reaches the ground. (Also referred to as a scrimmage kick.)

EE. *Ready for Play Signal*. A signal given by the referee that denotes the ball may be snapped or kicked. (Usual method is a short whistle blast and a downward chopping motion of the arm.) The arm motion indicates that the 25 (High School and College) or 30 (Professional) second count should begin.

FF. *Runner*. Any player who is carrying the ball.

GG. *Scrimmage*. The activity of two teams during a down which begins with the ball being snapped.

HH. *Scrimmage Down*. A down which begins with the ball being snapped by the center.

II. *Scrimmage Kick*. Any kick attempted from behind the offensive line of scrimmage during a scrimmage down. Any form of kicking may be used.

JJ. *Shift*. The movement of more than one offensive player prior to the snap. After players shift all must be still for one count before legal motion or a snap may begin. Defensive players may shift at will so long as they remain on side.

KK. *Snapping*. The legal act of the center putting the ball in play on a scrimmage down. The snap must be a rapid and uninterrupted backward motion of the hands. The ball must leave the hand(s) of the snapper and touch a backfield player or the ground before it touches any other offensive player.

LL. *Spearing (Face Tackling)*. Using the helmet as a weapon when making initial contact with the opponent in tackling.

MM. *Spotting the Ball*.

1. The inbounds spot (approximately 17 1/2 yards from either sideline). Intersection of the inbounds line and the yard line, at which point the ball became dead.

2. The previous spot. The spot where the ball was last put in play.

3. The end of the run is the spot where a run ends or where the runner loses player control. (Play continues if the ball is not declared dead.)

4. The succeeding spot. The yard line where the ball will next be put in play. After a score the succeeding spot is the 35 (College and Professional) or 40 (High School) yard line of the team which kicks off. The succeeding spot after a safety has been scored is the 20 yard line of the opponent of the team scoring the safety. The team scoring the safety is the receiving team. (Enforcement of penalties may alter the specific spot in each situation.)

NN. *Tackling*. The use of hands, arms or the body by a defensive player in an attempt to prevent forward progress of a runner or bring him to the ground. An official may declare that forward progress is stopped before the runner is brought to the ground by blowing his whistle. (The use of the helmet as a primary force in tackling the runner is illegal and a 15-yard penalty.)

OO. *Tripping*. Use of the lower leg to impede the progress of an opponent. (Legal in an attempt to bring down the ball carrier.)

PP. *Use of Hands*. (See Offensive and Defensive Use of Hands.)

QQ. *Invalid or Illegal Fair Catch Signal.* Signaling in other than the prescribed manner (Rule 35) or signaling when not allowed.

RULE IV. TIMING AND SUBSTITUTIONS

A. PLAYING TIME AND INTERMISSIONS

1. The game is divided into four periods of 15 minutes each (college), 12 minutes each (high school), or 8 minutes each (9th grade and below). One-minute intermission is taken between the first and second periods and the third and fourth periods. The intermission at half-time is 20 minutes at the college level and 15 minutes at the high school level.

2. The teams shall change goals after the 1st and 3rd periods of play. Team possession, number of the next down, the position of the ball and the line to gain remain the same with the changing of goals between the first and second periods and between the third and fourth periods.

B. ENDING A PERIOD

1. If time for any period expires during a down, play continues until the down ends.

2. A period may be extended by an untimed down if a penalty or scoring play is involved on the last play of the period.

C. THE CLOCK

1. The clock starts:

a. on a kickoff when the ball is first touched by a receiver or after the ball goes 10 yards and is touched by the kicking team.

b. on a scrimmage play when the ball is snapped or on prior signal by the Referee.

2. The clock stops when:

a. the ball goes out of bounds or over the goal line.

b. a forward pass is incomplete.

c. a fair catch is made.

d. time out is requested or a period ends.

e. a first down is declared.

f. a penalty occurs. (If during a play, the clock continues until the play ends.)

g. an injury is observed at the conclusion of a play, rule review is required, need for equipment repair, or official's application of rule mechanics (declaration of measurement for a first down.)

In a, b, c, and d above the clock resumes when the ball is next put in play by a snap or free kick. In f and g, when the situations are resolved, the clock resumes when the ball is indicated to be ready for play by the official. However, if a, b, c, or d also occurred during the previous down the clock begins when the ball is put in play (Snap or kick.) Change of ball possession will delay the starting of the clock until play actually begins at most levels of play.

3. The clock continues to run unless play dictates its stoppage.

D. CHARGED TIME OUTS

1. The number of charged time outs vary at different levels of play (Usually 3 per half).

2. A charged team time out is granted when a player's request is recognized by the official.

E. OTHER TIME OUT RULINGS

1. After one minute the official will declare the ball ready for play and begins the 25 second ready-for-play timing.

2. Successive time outs may be charged to either team.

3. Time outs may be extended for safety or discussion purposes.

4. If all permissible time outs have been used, only injury and rule review time outs may be granted. If rule review is not reversed a delay penalty is charged.

5. When a team attempts to consume time illegally the referee may start or stop the clock depending on the situation.

F. BALL READY FOR PLAY AND DELAY

1. The ball must be kicked or snapped in 25 seconds after the referee marks the ball ready for play. Failure to do so is delay of game and a 5-yard penalty.

G. SUBSTITUTIONS

1. Any number of substitutes may enter the game between downs. Replaced players must be off the field before the next live ball action begins.

2. A replaced player must leave the field on his team's side.

3. A substitute must remain in the game for one play.

RULE V. PUTTING THE BALL IN PLAY, DEAD BALL, INADVERTENT WHISTLE, OUT OF BOUNDS

A. PUTTING THE BALL IN PLAY

1. The ball is always put in play somewhere between the inbounds markers (hash marks) in center zone of the field.

B. DEAD BALL AND END OF DOWN

1. The ball is dead and the down is over:

a. when a ball carrier goes out of bounds, his forward progress is stopped, or some part of his body other than his hand or foot touch the ground.

b. when a live ball lands beyond any out-of-bounds line or touches something out of bounds.

c. when a forward pass is declared incomplete.

d. when any kick touches anything or anyone behind the receiver's goal line. (This rule varies at different levels.)

If a kick may legally score points, d. above does not apply.

e. if there is simultaneous catching or recovering by opposing players of any loose ball.

f. if the ball is motionless on the ground and no player attempts to secure possession.

g. when the kicking team catches or recovers any free kick or any scrimmage kick beyond the neutral zone.

h. when a kick is caught or recovered by the receivers after a valid or invalid fair catch signal by a member of the receiving team.

i. when a touchdown or field goal is scored.

j. when during a try for point the kick fails, the runner is stopped, or the defense secures possession. (Rule varies at different levels.)

Exception:

The ball remains alive if a placekick holder with his knee(s) on the ground and with a teammate in kicking position misplays the snap. The holder may retrieve the ball and place it on the ground for the kicker, or may rise and continue the play.

k. when an official blows his whistle for any reason.

C. INADVERTENT WHISTLE

1. If a whistle is blown inadvertently during

a. a kick, a pass, or while the ball is loose behind the scrimmage, the down is replayed.

b. a run while the ball is in player control the team in control may choose either the play or a replay of the down.

D. OUT OF BOUNDS

1. If action ends out of bounds, or in a side zone, play is resumed at the inbounds spot at the appropriate yard line.

RULE VI. SERIES OF DOWNS

A. SERIES OF DOWNS

1. At the conclusion of a scrimmage down, with the ball in the field of play or out of bounds, play continues with the next down or a new series is granted to:

a. the offensive team, if it advances beyond the line to gain during any of the four downs.

b. defensive team, if the offensive team does not advance beyond the line to gain in four downs.

c. the team in possession, if possession changes during a down.

d. the receiving team, if the kicking team during a down kicks the ball and it goes out of bounds or the ball is recovered or possessed by the receivers at the end of the down. (Kickers may retain possession if they recover the ball behind the line and the down was not fourth, or anywhere, if any receiver touches the kick beyond the line of scrimmage. Penalty enforcement may affect team possession.)

B. DOWN AFTER PENALTY

1. The down counts if a penalty is declined.

2. If there is a double foul or a penalty is accepted for a foul during a down, the down is replayed unless a penalty prescribes either loss of down or a first down.

3. When a foul occurs at the snap, or free kick, or a dead ball foul occurs, the number of the down remains as when the foul occurred. Measurement could result in a first down.

RULE VII. SNAPPING THE BALL, POSITIONS, MOTION

A. SNAPPING THE BALL

1. A snap must leave the center's hands and touch a backfield player or the ground before it touches any offensive lineman. Each scrimmage down must start with a legal snap. An illegal snap causes the ball to remain dead.

2. The snapper may not remove his hands from the ball or simulate action at the snap.

3. During any down, the ball may be handed forward behind the line of scrimmage or handed backward anywhere. After a change of possession during a down the ball may

not be handed forward. Linemen not on the end of the line may be handed the ball only if they have turned around after the snap and are 1 yard behind the line of scrimmage.

B. RESTRICTIONS FOR OFFENSIVE PLAYERS

1. After the ball is adjusted, it is encroachment for any offensive player to move into his scrimmage line. The snapper may place his hands over the ball and have his head within the vertical plane of the ball.

2. Before the snap, no offensive player may make a motion simulating action at the snap.

3. No offensive player on the line between the snapper and the end man on the line may move his hand after having placed it on or near the ground before the actual snap.

4. The offensive players on the end of the line (who are eligible receivers) may adjust their position so long as the movement does not simulate movement at the snap.

C. RESTRICTIONS FOR DEFENSIVE PLAYERS

1. No defensive player can touch the ball or an offensive player before the snap. They must be outside the neutral zone at the snap. High School and lower level play may not enter the neutral zone after the ball is ready for play.

2. No defensive player may in any way try to interfere with or cause confusion for the offensive team's attempt to snap the ball.

D. POSITIONS AND NUMBERING AT THE SNAP

1. Seven offensive players must be on the line at the snap.

2. Five offensive players must be numbered 50 through 79 (numbering does not apply on kick formation downs).

3. No restrictions apply to defensive players so long as they are on side.

4. Offensive players on the end of the line and in the backfield are eligible pass receivers. To complete their eligibility they must be numbered 1 through 49 or 80 through 99. This rule is in effect on all plays.

5. A player may not play while wearing a number identical to a teammate.

6. During the dead ball period before each play, offensive players must stand or pass within 15 yards of the ball.

E. MOTION

1. After any huddle or any shift all offensive players must come to a stop and remain still for one second, after which the ball may be snapped.

2. One offensive player may be in motion and be moving at the snap but only if such motion is not toward his opponent's goal. This motion, to be legal, must start when all offensive players are still and not in conjunction with other shift or team movement.

RULE VIII. KICKING

A. THE KICKOFF AND OTHER FREE KICKS

1. On any free kick, a free kick line is established for each team 10 yards apart. (See Rule 1-B-5 and Rule 3-M.)

2. If any kicker recovers or catches a free kick, the ball becomes dead. The kicker may not advance such a catch or recovery. (Rule varies according to level of play.)

3. If a free kick becomes dead inbounds between the goal lines while no player is in possession, the ball belongs to the receivers.

4. If any member of the kicking team touches a free kick before it crosses the receiver's free kick line it is illegal touching. The receiver may be given the ball at that spot or may choose the results of the action which follows the illegal touching.

5. A member of the receiving team may (a) touch, or (b) secure possession of and advance a kickoff anywhere in the field of play. The clock starts in both a and b above. Advancement from the end zone is legal in college and professional play. After a member of the receiving team touches a kickoff, members of the kicking team may gain possession if they recover the ball.

6. Members of the receiving team (minimum of 5 High School and College; 3 Professional) must be in receiving positions within 5 yards of their own free kick line. They may leave this area once the ball is kicked.

7. Kickoffs are repeated if the ball is kicked out of bounds or if any other penalty occurs before the receivers secure possession of the kick.

B. SCRIMMAGE KICKS

1. The offensive team may punt, drop kick, or placekick from behind its scrimmage line at any time while in possession.

2. The receiving team may catch or recover a scrimmage kick anywhere on the field and advance.

3. A kicking team member may catch and recover a scrimmage kick behind the scrimmage line and advance.

4. A kicking team member may recover and keep possession of a scrimmage kick beyond the scrimmage line if it is touched by a receiver who is beyond the neutral zone.

5. The touching of a low scrimmage kick by any player is ignored if the touching is on the kicker's side of the expanded neutral zone.

C. TOUCHBACK OF A KICK

1. Generally, if a kicked ball touches the ground behind the receiver's goal line it is a touchback. This rule varies as does the rule that allows a caught kick to be returned to the field of play if caught in the end zone. A ball touching the ground is either dead immediately or must be held down by a receiver to be ruled a touchback.

2. If a kicked ball becomes dead out of bounds in the kicker's end zone, or dead inbounds in possession of the kicking team while in the kicker's end zone, it is a safety. If the receivers gain possession of the ball under these circumstances, it is a touchdown.

D. FAIR CATCH SIGNAL

1. A receiver may signal for a fair catch by waving his hand above his head while any kick is in flight and is beyond the kicker's free kick line. The receiver is then protected from being hit by an opponent and may not advance the ball after it is caught.

2. Any receiver who has given a valid or invalid fair catch signal cannot block during this play.

3. If the catch is made by a teammate other than the player who gave the signal, it is not a fair catch but the play is ended.

4. If the kick is muffed by the receiver, it is a free ball and may be recovered, but not advanced, by either team.

RULE IX. FORWARD PASS

A. LEGAL AND ILLEGAL PASSES

1. A legal complete forward pass is a pass thrown from behind the line of scrimmage and caught:

a. by an eligible receiver;

b. by any defensive player (Intercepted);

c. simultaneously by opponents. (Ball becomes dead and belongs to the passing team.)

2. At the high school level more than one forward pass is allowed provided all passes are thrown from behind the line of scrimmage and there are no ineligible receivers beyond the neutral zone.

3. A legal incomplete forward pass is one thrown from behind the line of scrimmage which:

a. touches the ground;

b. goes out of bounds;

c. is possessed in the air by a player who first touches the ground out of bounds.

4. Illegal passes include:

a. a pass thrown from a point beyond the line of scrimmage;

b. a pass thrown after team possession changed during a down;

c. more than one forward pass if not allowed;

d. a pass thrown to an area not occupied by an eligible offensive teammate or to an ineligible teammate behind the line of scrimmage.

B. ELIGIBILITY TO RECEIVE A FORWARD PASS

1. Any offensive player who at the snap is at the end of the line of scrimmage or in the backfield and is numbered 1 through 49 or 80 through 99 is eligible to receive a forward pass.

2. All defensive players are eligible receivers at the snap.

3. If the defense touches the ball all offensive players are instantly eligible to catch the pass.

C. INTERFERENCE WITH THE PASS

1. Interference is purposely obstructing an opponent's attempt to catch a pass when it is not legally permitted.

2. No player is allowed to interfere with an eligible receiver beyond the scrimmage line during a legal forward pass play. The restriction begins at the time of the snap, for the offense, and when the ball leaves the passer's hand, for the defense.

3. It is not interference if contact occurs when eligible receivers are making a bona fide attempt to catch or deflect the pass.

D. INELIGIBLE OFFENSIVE PLAYERS

Offensive players ineligible to receive forward passes must remain in or behind the neutral zone area until the passer releases the ball. If an ineligible receiver touches a pass beyond the neutral zone it is pass interference unless the ball was previously touched by the defense. These restrictions only apply to passes which cross the line of scrimmage.

E. FORWARD PASS PENALTIES

1. Illegal forward pass. Penalty: 5 yards and loss of down—assessed from spot of the throw.

2. Forward pass interference. Penalty: 15 yards and loss of down if by the offense; 15 yards and 1st down if by the defense. The penalty is assessed from spot of the snap.

3. Ineligible receiver downfield. Penalty: loss of 5 yards assessed from spot of the snap. (These penalties vary as to interpretations and application at different levels of play.)

RULE X. PLAYER ACTIVITY

A. ILLEGAL CONTACT

1. An offensive or defensive player may not:

a. Use his hands to add impetus to the charge of a teammate.

b. Use his hands to strike a blocker's head.

c. Use his hands, arms or legs to grasp or in any way hold an opponent other than the runner.

d. Strike an opponent with his fist, forearm or elbow, nor kick or knee him.

e. Extend or swing the leg into an opponent other than the ball carrier.

f. Vigorously contact an opponent who is out of bounds, obviously out of the play, or after the ball is dead.

g. Hurdle another player who is on his feet.

h. Place himself on a teammate or opponent to gain an advantage.

i. Throw a helmet or hide the ball under the jersey.

j. Incite roughness by contacting an opponent unnecessarily.

k. Grasp an opponent's face mask.

l. Butt block, face tackle or spear any opponent.

2. Defensive players must avoid blocking, tackling or charging into a passer who has released the ball or a kicker or holder of a kick. Exceptions to this rule are 1) contact is unavoidable when it is not certain a kick will be made; 2) the defense touches the kick near the kicker and contact is unavoidable; 3) contact is slight and is partially caused by movement of the kicker; 4) contact is caused by the defensive player being blocked into the kicker.

B. UNSPORTSMANLIKE CONDUCT

1. No player nor nonplayer personnel shall act in an unsportsmanlike manner during either play or intermission. Unsportsmanlike acts include:

a. using profanity, vulgar language, or gestures;

b. baiting the opponents;

c. attempting to interfere with offensive signals;

d. intentionally kicking or swinging at any opposing player;

e. intentionally kicking at the ball when not in play;

f. disrespectfully addressing or objecting to a decision of an official;

g. use of artificial aid to direct play;

h. the use of mechanical visual-aid equipment, including computers, television and video tape for monitoring, replay, for coaching purposes during the game or intermissions;

i. being on the field except as a substitute or replaced player.

C. ILLEGAL PARTICIPATION

1. The following activities are considered illegal participation:

a. Unless blocked or pushed out of bounds, no player can participate after having been out of bounds.

b. Use a pretended substitution or sideline personnel to deceive opponents before any play begins.

c. Lie on the ground to deceive before any play begins.

d. Have more than 11 players participate during any play.

D. BATTING THE BALL

1. No player is allowed to bat a loose ball other than a pass or fumble in flight or a low scrimmage kick in an attempt to block it.

2. A backward pass in flight cannot be batted forward by the passing team.

3. Eligible receivers may bat a forward pass in any direction.

4. A player who has possession of the ball may not simulate a fumble in an attempt to gain yardage.

RULE XI. PENALTY ENFORCEMENT

A. GENERAL PRINCIPLES

1. Enforcement procedure involves the recognition of two basic factors: They are a) the type of play that occurs, and b) the "basic spot" principle.

2. There are two types of plays:

a. A loose ball play is any kick play, any legal forward pass play, and any backward pass or fumble play occurring behind the line of scrimmage.

b. A running play includes any action that is not a loose ball play and any action after a loose ball play ends.

3. The "basic spot" principle provides that fouls committed by the offense behind the basic spot are spot fouls. All other fouls are enforced from the basic spot. On loose ball plays the basic spot is the line of scrimmage. On running plays the basic spot is the spot where the run ends. Fouls occurring simultaneously with the snap of the ball are penalized from the spot of the snap. (The application of this rule varies at different levels of play.)

B. PROCEDURE WHEN A PENALTY OCCURS

1. When a foul occurs the referee explains to the captains the pertinent information with regard to the penalty(s). He then enforces the penalty as determined by the offended captain's choice.

2. If a double foul occurs, the penalties offset and the down is replayed. (Unless one is unsportsmanlike; it is always enforced.)

3. Live and dead ball fouls are administered separately in the order they occurred. They are not coupled or paired.

4. If a team commits more than one foul during a down, the offended captain may choose which penalty will be enforced.

5. Penalties may be declined.

Exception:

If during a play in which there is a change of possession, and each team commits a foul, the team last gaining possession may keep the ball provided they did not foul before gaining possession and provided they decline the opponent's penalty. They may keep the ball and the penalty against them is enforced as a single foul.

C. SPECIAL ENFORCEMENTS

1. A yardage penalty toward an opponent's goal may not take more than one-half the remaining distance to the goal.

2. If the offensive team commits a foul in its end zone and the penalty is to be measured from a point behind the goal line, it is an automatic safety.

3. A defensive foul enforced from a spot on or behind the offended team's goal line is measured from the goal line.

4. Fouls committed by the defense during a scoring play will be enforced as on any other play.

5. Non-player and unsportsmanlike fouls occurring during a touchdown, and dead-ball fouls after the score of a touchdown, will be enforced at the try-for-point spot.

6. Unsportsmanlike or non-player fouls occurring during a try for point or field goal, and dead-ball fouls after such a play are enforced on the ensuing kickoff.

7. Scores are nullified if a player on the scoring team commits a foul during the scoring down and the penalty is accepted.

8. An offended team retains the right to replay any down if a penalty is accepted, unless penalty provision cancels the down.

SUMMARY OF PENALTIES

A. LOSS OF DOWN

1. Illegal forward handing of ball
2. Any illegal forward pass
3. Pass interference by the offensive team

B. AUTOMATIC FIRST DOWN (FOR OFFENDED TEAMS)

1. Roughing of passer, kicker or kick holder
2. Defensive pass interference

C. 5-YARD PENALTIES

1. Delay of game tactics, including failure to put the ball in play
2. Participation, substitution, illegal equipment fouls
3. Snap or free kick infractions; position, motion violations
4. Illegal signals by kick receiver
5. Illegal receiver downfield

D. 10-YARD PENALTIES

1. Holding and illegal blocking techniques involving the hands and arms

E. 15-YARD PENALTIES

1. Interference or illegal contact with the pass or kick receiver (penalties vary at different levels of play)
2. Any form of illegal blocking involving parts of the body other than the techniques described as 10-yard penalties

3. Roughness and any form of illegal contact mentioned in Rule X

4. Any unsportsmanlike conduct

5. Illegal batting or kicking of the ball

No distance penalty will be enforced in a manner that exceeds more than half the distance to the offended team's goal line.

GOVERNING BODIES

National Collegiate Athletic Association, P.O. Box 1906, Nall Ave. at 63rd St., Mission, KS 66201

National Federation of State High School Associations, P.O. Box 20626, 11724 Plaza Circle, Kansas City, MO 64195

MAGAZINES

Athletic Journal, Athletic Journal Publishing Co., 1719 Howard St., Evanston, IL 60202

Referee: The Magazine of Sports Officiating, Referee Enterprises, Inc., P.O. Box 161, Franksville, WI 53126

Scholastic Coach, Scholastic Coach, Inc., 730 Broadway, New York, NY 10003

• GOLF •

(Rules summary by author)

☐

Note: The rules of golf that are basically essential to playing the game are summarized herein. These rules will be found adequate for most golf competition; however, should the reader desire a more strict and technical interpretation of the rules, the official rules of golf as distributed by the United States Golf Association* should be consulted. A familiarity with the terminology and etiquette of golf, as presented below, is essential to the understanding and proper play of the game. It is particularly important to note that in the two basic forms of the game, stroke and match play, the penalties for violations vary.

TERMINOLOGY

Addressing the ball: the position taken in preparation to stroking the ball.

Bunker: an area on the fairway usually filled with sand. Commonly called a trap.

Casual water: an unusual or temporary accumulation of water.

Divot: a piece of turf which is dug from the fairway by the club head.

Fairway: that part of the course, with the grass cut relatively short, lying between the teeing ground and the putting green. Hazards are not considered part of the fairway.

Flagstick: a circular stake about eight feet long which is placed in the hole on the putting green to show the position of the hole.

Fore: a term called out to warn players of an approaching ball.

Green: the putting surface around the hole. It is very well kept, with the grass being cropped short.

Halved hole: a hole on which each side holes out in the same number of strokes.

Hazard: see "bunker" or "water hazard."

Hole: the hole in the putting green which is 4 1/4 inches in diameter and at least 4 inches deep.

Holed ball: when the ball is within the cup and all of it below the lip of the cup.

Honor: the honor is the privilege of being first to hit from the teeing ground. On the first tee this is determined by lot, while on the remaining tees the honor goes to the individual or side which won the previous hole. Should the hole be halved, the side having the previous honor retains it.

Lost ball: a ball that cannot be located within the five minutes allowed for searching.

Match play: a form of play in which the winner is determined by the most holes won. The winner of a hole is the side holing out in the fewest strokes.

Medal play: refers to stroke play.

---

*See page 320 for additional information.

Obstruction: any artificial construction or object except for that which is an integral part of the course.

Out-of-bounds: that area lying beyond the fence, stakes, or other boundary which marks the legitimate playing area of the course.

Penalty stroke: a stroke that is added to the score of a player due to a violation of the rules.

Playing through: the situation in which one match, having been slowed by searching for a ball or some other reason, allows another match to pass them.

Rough: the longer grass and rough terrain bordering the fairway.

Stroke: the act of swinging the club with the intention of hitting the ball.

Stroke play: a form of play in which the winner is determined by the side completing the stipulated round in the fewest strokes.

Tee marker: the markers on the teeing ground that designate the area in which the ball may be teed.

Teeing ball: the artificial elevating of the ball when driving from the teeing ground. The elevation may be of soil or a peg.

Teeing ground: the starting place for each hole to be played. The most forward point from which the ball may be played is designated by the tee markers, and the farthest point back that the ball may be played is two club lengths from the marker.

Trap: see "bunker."

Unplayable lie: a lie which, in the opinion of the player, cannot be played.

Water hazard: any pond, lake, river, ditch, or other area covered with water or serving as a water bed.

Winter rules: permits the improving of the lie on the fairway. (Check local course rules.)

ETIQUETTE

Golf is a game in which a rather strict code of etiquette is employed. All real golfers are thoroughly familiar with this etiquette and they, as does the course management, expect all who go on the course to be familiar with the code and to adhere to it. The more important essentials of golf etiquette are as follows:

1. When a player is addressing the ball or making a stroke, there should be no talk or movement by others in the immediate vicinity. Nor should anyone stand close to, directly behind, or in any position which may distract the player.

2. Care should be taken that those playing ahead are out of range before a stroke is made.

3. The player who has the honor shall play first from the teeing ground, in partner play, the side with the honor shall play first.

4. On the teeing ground, care should be taken that the ball is teed in the area behind the markers.

5. The player farthest away from the hole is permitted to play first.

6. All divots should be replaced and pressed down.

7. If play is slowed while searching for a ball, players approaching from behind should be signaled to pass through. The next shot should not be taken until the passing players are out of range.

8. It is common courtesy to help other players in one's party to search for their balls.

9. The playing green should be vacated immediately upon completion of the hole.

10. Avoid stepping on that part of the green which is in line with another player's putt.

11. All holes and footprints made in bunkers should be filled before leaving.

12. Any holes or damage to the putting green, made by the ball or otherwise, should be carefully repaired before leaving. Special precaution should be taken in the removing, laying to the side, and replacing of the flagstick.

13. Play on to the putting green should be delayed until players ahead have cleared the green.

14. Call "fore" when there is any possibility that your ball may strike another player.

15. Do not take golf bag, cart, extra clubs, or other equipment onto the playing green.

16. When holding flagstick for another player, take position that will prevent your shadow from falling across the line of the putt.

17. If a group is following close behind on a par 3 hole, allow them to take tee shots before putting out.

18. Do not hold or remove flagstick for another player without first asking his permission.

19. Become thoroughly familiar with the rules and always observe them.

RULES

The first division of the rules as presented below includes those of a general nature, while the remainder of the rules are grouped into the specific categories with which they are most closely associated. Familiarity with the preceding teminology and etiquette sections will do much to clarify the rules of golf. Rules that are adequately covered in the definitions of terms are not repeated below. Local course rules should always be checked for any conditions that may be peculiar to the particular course.

The penalty for violation of the rules, unless otherwise stipulated, is stroke play, 2 strokes; match play, loss of hole.

GENERAL

1. It is the responsibility of each player to be able to identify his own ball.

2. A player who has incurred a penalty should state the fact to his opponents as soon as possible. A player is entitled at any time to ascertain from his opponent the number of strokes the latter has taken.

3. A ball coming to rest on a putting green other than one being played must be dropped off the green one club length from the nearest point of relief but not nearer the hole.

4. A player has the privilege of asking that any ball be lifted which interferes with his play.

5. Artificial devices used for measuring playing conditions or distances are not permitted.

6. The ball must be clearly struck and not pushed or scooped.

7. Should a ball be struck twice on a single stroke, the stroke is counted plus one penalty stroke.

8. Should the wrong ball be played, the standard penalty of two strokes in stroke play, or loss of hole in match play, shall apply except when the wrong ball is played from a hazard and an immediate correction is made.

9. A player may lift his ball for identification without penalty, except in a hazard, but the ball must be replaced to its exact spot.

10. The ball may not be lifted to be cleaned except from putting green, water hazard, unplayable lie, or improved ground.

11. If a player in stroke play is in doubt as to the correct procedure to follow, he may play out the hole with the ball in play and at the same time complete play of the hole

with a second ball. The player must announce his intentions of this action and make it known which ball he wishes to score if the rules permit this. (There is no privilege of a second ball in match play.)

12. All strokes must be counted. Any swing of the club with the intention of hitting the ball (whether or not it is hit) is scored as a stroke. Penalty strokes on each hole are to be added to the total strokes for the hole.

ADVICE

1. A player shall not give nor receive advice except from his partner, caddie, or partner's caddie.

2. A player may be shown the line of play at any time except on the putting green. However, it is not permissible for anyone to stand on the line during the stroke or to make any marks on the line.

DROPPED BALL

1. When a ball is dropped, an improved lie is to be expected.

2. When it is necessary to drop a ball, the correct manner is to hold it shoulder high, at arms length, while facing in any direction.

3. A ball in a hazard must be dropped in the hazard.

4. The ball may be redropped, or placed if absolutely necessary, if the contour of the surface is such as to cause the ball to roll out-of-bounds more than two club lengths away or nearer the green.

FLAGSTICK

1. The flagstick may be left in position, removed, or held up to indicate position. If the flagstick is not attended before the stroke, it shall not be attended nor removed while the ball is in motion.

2. If an authorized person is attending the flagstick and the player's ball strikes the person, flagstick, or item of equipment, a penalty is incurred. Stroke play, two strokes; match play, loss of hole.

3. If the ball strikes the flagstick, person, or equipment when an unauthorized person is attending the flag, there is no penalty and the ball is played from the lie.

4. If a ball resting against the flagstick falls into the hole when the flagstick is removed, the hole was made on the last stroke.

EQUIPMENT

1. Players must use clubs and balls that conform with USGA specifications. Penalty, disqualification.

2. A maximum of fourteen clubs are permitted. Penalty: stroke play, two strokes for each hole on which there was a violation; match play, loss of each hole on which there was a violation.

3. A player may not borrow clubs from any other player. Penalty, as in No. 2.

HAZARDS

1. Nothing shall be done to improve a lie in a hazard.

2. If a ball in a hazard is dropped due to immovable obstruction, the ball must be dropped in the hazard.

3. If the ball is lost or lies in a water hazard, it may be dropped outside the hazard, but not nearer the hole, with a one-stroke penalty, or a second ball may be played from point of lie on previous shot.

4. It is not permissible to lift a ball in a hazard unless it is to be played as an unplayable lie.

5. The club should not touch the surface in a hazard before the stroke is actually taken.

IMPROVING LIE

1. The ball must be played as it lies and shall not be touched or purposely moved, except as otherwise provided for in the rules.

2. No part of the playing surface immediately surrounding the ball shall be improved, removed, or pressed down. This includes the rough, such as long grass or bushes.

3. A player may not bend or break anything fixed or growing in order to improve his lie or line of play. However, a player is entitled to take his stance with both feet firmly on the ground.

LOOSE IMPEDIMENTS

1. Any loose material may be removed except that in a hazard.

2. Should the ball move when any loose material is removed, the player is penalized one stroke and the shot is taken from where the ball lies after movement.

LOST BALL

1. A ball is considered lost, if within the five minutes allowed for searching, it cannot be located.

2. If it appears that a stroked ball may be lost or hit out-of-bounds, a provisional ball may be played and play on this ball continued until it is known whether the original ball is lost or out-of-bounds. The original ball must be played if found, even though it may be an unplayable lie or is in a water hazard.

3. If a ball is lost or hit out-of-bounds, the next ball shall be played from the same position as the first, with a penalty of loss of distance and one penalty stroke.

OBSTRUCTIONS

1. Movable obstructions: May be removed except when a ball is in motion.

2. Immovable obstructions: If a ball comes to rest on, touching, or within two club lengths of an immovable obstruction which interferes with the player's stance or stroke, the ball may be lifted without penalty and dropped two club lengths from the original lie, but no nearer the hole.

PENALTIES

Unless otherwise stipulated, the penalty for any infraction of the rules in stroke play is two penalty strokes. In match play, unless otherwise stipulated, the penalty for infraction of the rules is loss of the hole.

PRACTICE

Practice strokes are not permitted during the play of a hole or between the play of any two holes.

PUTTING GREEN

1. The line of the putt is not to be touched. It is permissible to remove loose materials and to repair damage caused by balls, but the line of putt is not to be pressed down.

2. The ball may be lifted and cleaned while on the green.

3. The green may not be tested by taking practice shots or rolling a ball.

4. If a ball played from off the green strikes a ball on the green, there is no penalty. The ball which is moved is returned to its original position.

5. If a ball played on the green strikes another ball on the green, a two stroke penalty is incurred in stroke play. There is no penalty for this occurrence in match play.

SURFACE BLEMISHES

1. If a ball comes to rest in or touching casual water, ground that is under repair, or a hole made by burrowing animals, the ball may be dropped without penalty but not nearer the hole.

2. If a ball should be lost due to conditions as in No. 1, the ball may be dropped without penalty as near as possible to the point where it entered the area.

TEE SHOT AND TEEING GROUND

1. The tee shot must be taken from within the teeing ground.

2. A ball that falls off the tee or is knocked off while addressing the ball may be re-teed without penalty.

UNPLAYABLE LIE

1. If a ball is lifted from an unplayable lie, a stroke penalty is incurred.

2. If a second ball is played from the spot of stroke previous to an unplayable lie, a stroke penalty and loss of distance is incurred.

GOVERNING BODY

United States Golf Association, Golf House, Far Hills, NJ 07931

In addition to writing and interpreting the rules of golf, the U.S. Golf Association (USGA) conducts 12 national championships annually, provides national handicapping and course rating systems, maintains a museum and library collection, and conducts turfgrass research and course maintenance programs. It also provides data on tournament procedure, amateur status, and golf ball and implement specifications.

MAGAZINES

Golf, Times-Minor Magazines, Inc., 380 Madison Ave., New York, NY 10017

Golf Digest, Golf Digest-Tennis, Inc., 5520 Park Ave., Box 0395, Trumbull, CT 06611

Golf Journal, USGA, Golf House, Far Hills, NJ 07931

• HANDBALL •

OFFICIAL U.S.H.A. HANDBALL RULES

(Reproduced by permission of the United States Handball Association*)

☐

Note: The official rules publication includes rules interpretations to assist in clarification of certain rules as needed.

PART I. THE GAME

A. TYPES

Four-wall handball may be played by two, three or four players. When played by two it is called "singles," when played by three, "cut throat," and when played by four, "doubles."

B. DESCRIPTION

Handball, as the name implies, is a competitive game in which either hand or either fist may be used to serve and return the ball.

C. OBJECTIVE

The objective is to win each rally by serving or returning the ball so the opponent is unable to keep the ball in play. A serve or rally is won when a side is unable to return the ball to the front wall before it touches the floor twice.

D. POINTS AND OUTS

Points are scored by the serving side when it serves an ace (unreturnable serve) or wins a rally. When the serving side loses a rally it loses the serve. Losing the serve is called an "out."

E. GAME

A game is won by the side first scoring 21 points or, in the case of a tie breaker, 11 points.

F. MATCH

A match consists of two 21-point games with an 11-point tie breaker if the first two games are split. For the 11-point tie breaker, the player with the most points scored in the first two games is awarded the first serve. If the points are tied in the first two games, a flip of the coin determines the server.

---

*See page 334 for additional information.

PART II. COURT AND EQUIPMENT

A. COURT

The specifications for the standard four-wall court are:

1. Dimensions

The dimensions are: 20 feet wide, 20 feet high, and 40 feet long with back wall recommended minimum height of 14 feet.

2. Lines and Zones

Handball courts shall be divided and marked on the floors with 2-inch wide lines. Recommended colors are white or red. The lines shall be marked as follows:

a. *Short Line*

The short line is parallel to the front and back walls. Its outside measurement is 20 feet from the front wall.

b. *Service Line*

The service line is parallel with the short line and its outside measurement is 5 feet in front of the outside of the short line.

c. *Service Zone*

The service zone is the area between the outer edges of the short and service lines.

d. *Service Boxes*

A service box is located at each end of the service zone by lines whose outside measurements are 18 inches from and parallel with each side wall.

e. *Receiver's Restraining Lines*

Five feet back of the short line (outside measurement), lines should be marked on the floor extending 6 inches from the side wall. These lines are parallel to the short line. See Rule IV.B.1.

Four-Wall Handball Court

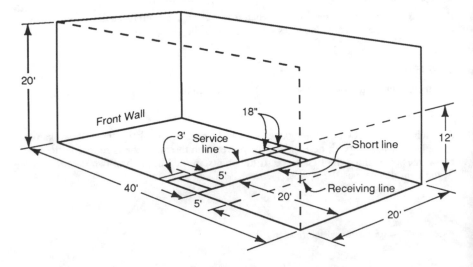

B. BALL

1. Specifications

The specifications for the standard handball are:

a. *Material* The material should be rubber or synthetic material.

b. *Color* Color is optional.

c. *Size* 1 7/8 inch diameter, with 1/32 inch variation.

d. *Weight* 2.3 ounces, with a variation of .2 ounces.

e. *Rebound* Rebound from freefall, 70-inch drop to a hardwood floor is 46 to 50 inches at a temperature of 68 degrees F.

2. Selection

A new ball must be selected by the referee for use in each match in all tournaments. During a game the referee has the authority to change balls if he deems it necessary. It is the referee's decision, not the player's.

C. GLOVES

1. General

Handball may not be played barehanded. Gloves must be worn.

2. Style

Gloves must be light in color and made of a soft material or leather, and form fitting. The fingers of the gloves may not be webbed, connected, or removed.

3. Foreign Substances

No foreign substance, tape, or rubber bands shall be used on the outside of the gloves on the fingers or on the palms. Metal or hard substances may not be worn on the hand under the glove if, in the opinion of the referee, it creates an unfair advantage.

4. Wet Gloves

Gloves must be changed when they become sufficiently wet to moisten the ball. This is the referee's decision. Gloves with large holes or tears which expose the skin of the hand may not be worn. It is the player's responsibility to have an ample supply of dry gloves for each match.

D. UNIFORM

1. General

All parts of the uniform, consisting of a shirt, shorts, socks, and shoes should be clean. Only customary handball attire, in the referee's judgment, can be worn.

Players may not play without shirts. Shirts must be full length (not a shirt cut off in the torso).

2. Color

Color is optional. Unusual patterns which affect the opposing player's view of the ball may not be worn.

3. Wet Shirts

Referee may request that a wet shirt be changed. Players should have an ample supply of dry shirts.

4. Lettering and Insignia

Lettering or insignia in poor taste is not allowed.

PART III. OFFICIALS AND OFFICIATING

A. TOURNAMENT CHAIRMAN

All tournaments shall be managed by a tournament chairman, who shall designate the officials. (The officials shall include a referee, and a scorer if available. Linesmen should be used whenever possible.)

1. Responsibilities

The chairman is responsible for overseeing the entire tournament. He, or his delegate representative, shall be present at all times.

2. Rules Briefing

Before all tournaments, all officials and players shall be briefed on rules and on local court hinders or other regulations. Referee clinics should be held prior to all USHA-sanctioned tournaments.

B. REFEREE'S CHAIRMAN

The referee's chairman is in charge of assigning referees to all tournament matches.

C. REFEREE

1. Pre-Match Duties

Before each match begins it shall be the duty of the referee to:

a. *Playability*

Check on adequacy of preparation of the handball court with respect to playability.

b. *Equipment*

Check on availability and suitability of all materials necessary for the match such as handballs, towels, scorecards, and pencils (or marking pens).

c. *Assisting Officials*

Check readiness and provide instructions to assisting officials.

d. *Court Hinders*

Explain court hinders, if any, to players. (See Rule IV.E.1.a.)

e. *Inspect Gloves and Uniforms*

Remind players to have an adequate supply of extra gloves and shirts. Inspect compliance of gloves and hands with rules.

f. *Start Game*

Introduce players, toss coin to determine order of serve, and signal start of game.

g. *Time*

The assigned referee should be present 15 minutes before match time.

h. *Two-Minute Warning*

He should give a two-minute warning before the match and before each game.

i. *Scoring*

The referee shall announce the scores before each rally. (See Rule IV.A.1.e.)

2. Decisions

During games the referee shall decide all questions that may arise in accordance with these rules. On all questions involving judgment and on all questions and situations not covered by these rules, the decision of the referee is final. This might include changing a call.

3. Appeal Calls

When linesmen are used, the server may appeal a serve called short (or a foot fault) by the referee, if he thought it was a good serve. If both linesmen disagree with the referee's call, the server is awarded the serve over. If he had one short, the call would cancel the previous short call, and he could be awarded two serves, because he was judged to have made a legal serve. If, in the opinion of the referee, the ball could not have been returned, a point should be awarded the server. If the appeal was not upheld, the call would be two shorts, a side out.

On rally-ending calls, either player may appeal on a double bounce call, kill shots called good, or kill shots called no good. The outcome may result in a point being awarded, a side out, or a replay, depending on the linesmen's opinion. If both linesmen disagree with the referee's call on a double bounce ball, the call is reversed or replayed. Other rally-ending appeals permitted are court hinders. No other hinder, or technical calls, are appealable.

The receiver, during the serve, may appeal calls on short balls, foot faults, and skip serves not called by the referee; in order to make these appeals, he must stop play before he returns the ball to the front wall. In so doing he assumes the risk of losing a point should his appeal not be upheld. If he wins the appeal, he is awarded the appropriate call. Once the ball has been legally returned to the front wall, no appeals may be made.

During the rally if a player feels his opponent did not return the ball legally (double bounce, wrist ball, or carry), he must stop play and appeal. He then accepts the consequences of the appeal.

4. Protests

Any decision not involving the judgment of the referee may be protested and then be decided by the head referee or tournament chairman.

5. Forfeitures

A match may be forfeited by the referee when:

a. *Unsportsmanlike Conduct*

Any player refuses to abide by the referee's decision or engages in flagrant unsportsmanlike conduct.

b. *Three Technicals*

A player receives three technicals in a match.

c. *Leaving the Court*

Any player leaves the court at a time not allowed by these rules without permission of the referee.

d. *Failure to Report*

 i. *No Show*

Any player for a singles match, or any team for a doubles match, fails to report to play.

ii. *Late Start Penalty*

The opponent shall be awarded one point for each minute of delay of game up to 10 minutes. The match shall then be forfeited. This applies to the start of the match, between game time outs, time outs during a game, and glove change time outs. Players should stay within earshot of the referee's call to help prevent the delay of game penalty. It is the obligation of the players to be ready to resume play on time even if the referee failed to give time warnings.

If the matches are on, or ahead of schedule, the players should be in the court warming up at least 10 minutes before the assigned match time to assure a prompt start. If running behind, the players should be dressed and ready to enter the court for a maximum 10-minute, in-court warm-up. If a player shows up five minutes late, he or she is entitled to only a five-minute warm-up, etc. The tournament chairman may permit a longer delay if circumstances warrant such a decision

6. Technical

If an argument develops, or if too frequent complaints are made against the referee's judgment calls, or if a player is guilty of unsportsmanlike conduct, the "Referee's Technical" will be invoked. A point will be deducted from the offending player's score. If, in the opinion of the referee, the appeal privileges afforded the players are being abused, the technical can be utilized. A technical warning may precede the penalty of a technical, but is not necessary.

D. LINESMEN

If possible, two linesmen will be used in all matches, positioned at the most advantageous viewpoints.

1. Appeal Responsibility

Players make appeals to the referee only. The referee then requests the opinion of the linesmen.

A linesman's opinion is based on his agreement or disagreement with the referee's call. If a linesman is uncertain he should abstain from making an opinion.

2. Procedure

The linesman's judgment is conveyed by a visual signal of "thumbs up" if in agreement with the referee's call, "thumbs down" if in disagreement. If abstaining, a horizontal extension of the open hand, palm down, is given.

If one or both linesmen agree with the referee's call, the call stands. If both linesmen abstain from an opinion the referee's call stands. In case of a tie (one linesman disagrees and one abstains), the referee has the final decision. He may either make his call stand, call for a replay, or reverse his call. If both linesmen disagree with the referee, the call is reversed or replayed, depending on the situation.

The referee may appeal to the linesmen himself if he is uncertain of his own call, and either reverse or nullify his own call.

E. SCORERS

The scorer, when utilized, shall keep a record of the progress of the game in the manner prescribed by the committee or chairman. As a minimum, the progress record shall include the order of serves, outs, and points.

F. FLOOR MANAGER

The floor manager readies players for their court assignments, times, and their readiness to play.

PART IV. PLAY REGULATIONS

A. SERVE

1. General

a. *Order*

The player or side winning the toss of a coin becomes the first server and starts the first game.

b. *Start*

Games are started by the referee calling "play ball" and announcing the score.

c. *Place*

The server may serve from any place in the service zone. No part of either foot may extend beyond either line of the service zone. Stepping on the line (but not beyond it) is permitted. Server must remain in the service zone until the served ball passes the short line. Violations are called "foot faults." (See Rule IV.A.3.b.i.)

d. *Manner*

A serve is commenced by bouncing the ball to the floor in the service zone. After the serve is commenced, on the first bounce, the ball must be struck by the server's hand or fist so that it hits the front wall and on the rebound hits the floor behind the short line, either with or without touching one of the side walls.

e. *Time*

A serve shall not be made until the referee has announced the score. The referee shall call "point" or "side out" as soon as rally ends. The receiver then has up to 10 seconds to assume a receiving position. When the receiver has assumed a receiving position or 10 seconds has elapsed, whichever occurs first, the referee shall announce the score and the server must serve within 10 seconds.

If the first serve results in a fault, the referee shall give the defensive player a reasonable time to take a receiving position and then the referee shall announce "second serve," after which the server must serve within 10 seconds.

2. Doubles

a. *Server*

At the beginning of each game in doubles, each side informs the referee of the order of service, the order must be followed throughout the game. Only the first server may serve the first time up and continues to serve first throughout the game. When the first server is out, the side is out. Thereafter, both players on each side shall serve until an out for each occurs. It is not necessary for the server to alternate serves to his team's opponents.

b. *Partner's Position*

On each serve, the server's partner shall stand erect with his back to the side wall and with both feet on the floor within the service box until the served ball passes the short line. Violations are called "foot faults."

3. Defective Serves

Defective serves are of three types resulting in penalties as follows:

a. *Dead Ball Serves*

A dead ball serve results in no penalty and the server is given another serve without cancelling a prior illegal serve. They occur when an otherwise legal serve:

i. *Hits Partner*

Hits the server's partner on the fly on the rebound from the front wall while the server's partner is in the service box. Any serve that touches the floor before hitting the partner in the box is a fault. (See Rule IV.E.1.d.)

ii. *Screen Balls*

The ball passes so close to the server or the server's partner that the view of the returning side is obstructed. Any serve passing behind the server's partner, between the partner and the side wall, is an automatic hinder. (See Rule IV.E.1.d.)

iii. *Straddle Balls*

A legally served ball between the legs of the server is an automatic hinder.

iv. *Court Hinders*

Hits any part of the court that under local rules is a dead ball. (See Rule IV.E.1.a.)

b. *Fault Serve*

Two consecutive fault serves result in an out. The following serves are faults and any two in succession result in an out:

i. *Foot Faults*

(a). *Leaving the Service Zone*

When the server leaves the service zone before the served ball passes the short line.

(b). *Partner Leaves the Service Zone*

When the server's partner leaves the service box before the served ball passes the short line.

ii. *Short Serve*

A short serve is any served ball that first hits the front wall and on the rebound hits the floor in front of the back edge of the short line either with or without touching one side wall.

iii. *Three-wall Serve*

A three-wall serve is any served ball that first hits the front wall and then hits any two other walls before hitting the floor.

iv. *Ceiling Serve*

A ceiling serve is any served ball that touches the ceiling after hitting the front wall either with or without touching one side wall.

v. *Long Serve*

A long serve is any served ball that first hits the front wall and rebounds to the back wall before touching the floor.

vi. *Out-of-Court Serve*

Any serve which first strikes the front wall and then rebounds out of the court without touching the floor. (See Rule IV.D.6.)

c. *Out Serves*

An out serve results in an out if:

i. *Missed Ball*

Any attempt to strike the ball on the first bounce results either in a total miss or in striking the ball with any part of the server's body other than his serving hand or fist.

ii. *Non-Front Wall Serve*

Any served ball strikes the server's partner, the ceiling, floor, or side wall, before striking the front wall.

iii. *Touched Serve*

Any served ball on the rebound from the front wall that touches the server, or touches the server's partner when the partner's foot is outside of the service box. This includes the ball that is intentionally caught. When the partner is hit by the serve when he is outside the service box, the "out serve" penalty supercedes the partner's foot fault. (See rule IV.A.3.a.i.)

iv. *Out-of-Order Serve*

In doubles, either partner serves out of order or one player serves both serves. The violation must be detected before the next team serves. The result of any rally which leads to an out-of-order serve penalty is nullified.

v. *Crotch Serve*

Any served ball that hits a crotch in the front wall is an out. All balls hitting the crotch of the floor shall be considered to have hit the floor first. A serve which rebounds on the fly from the front wall into the crotch of the back wall and the floor is a legal serve, as is a three-wall crotch serve.

vi. *Delay*

A server fails to serve the ball within 10 seconds after the referee has announced the score.

B. RETURN OF SERVE

1. Receiving Position

The receiver or receivers must stand at least five feet back of the short line, as indicated by the six-inch restraining line, until the ball is struck by the server. Any infraction of this rule results in a point for the server.

2. Fly Return

In making a fly return, the receiver must play the ball after it passes over the short line and no part of his foot may extend on or over the short line. A violation results in a point for the server. After contact the receiver may step on or over the short line without penalty.

3. Legal Return

After the ball is legally served, one of the players on the receiving side must strike the ball either on the fly or after the first bounce, and before the ball touches the floor the second time, to return the ball to the front wall either directly or after it has touched one or both side walls, the back wall, or the ceiling, or any combination of those surfaces. A returned ball may not touch the floor before touching the front wall. A ball may be played off the back wall as well as the front wall provided the ball does not touch the floor a second time. Failure to make a legal return results in a point for the server.

C. CHANGES OF SERVE

A server is entitled to continue serving until he or his side makes an out. When the server or the side loses the serve, the server or serving side becomes the receiver, and the receiving side, the server; and so alternately in all subsequent services of the game. Outs are made by:

1. Out Serve

The server makes an out serve under Rule IV.A.3.c.

2. Fault Serves

The server makes two fault serves in succession under Rule IV.A.3.b.

3. Hits Partner

The server hits his partner with an attempted return before the ball touches the floor the second time.

4. Return Failure

The server or his partner fails to keep the ball in play by returning it as required by Rule IV.B.3.

5. Avoidable Hinder

The server or his partner commits an avoidable hinder. (See Rule IV.E.2.).

6. Second Out

In doubles, the side is retired when both partners have been put out, except on the first serve as provided in Rule IV.A.2.a.

D. RALLY

Each legal return after the serve is called a rally. Play during rallies must accord with the following Rules (each violation results in an out or point):

1. One Hand

Only the front or back of one hand may be used at any one time to return the ball. Using two hands together to hit a ball is an out. The use of the foot or any portion of the body, other than the hand or fist, is an out.

2. Wrist Ball

The use of any other part of the body to return the ball, including the wrist or arm above the player's hand, is prohibited, even though the wrist or arm is covered by a glove.

3. One Touch

In attempting returns, the ball may be touched only once by one player. In doubles, both partners may swing at the ball, but only one may actually hit it.

4. Return Attempts

a. *Singles*

In singles, if a player swings at but misses the ball in play, the player may repeat his attempts to return the ball until it touches the floor the second time.

b. *Doubles*

In doubles, if one player swings at but misses the ball, both he and his partner may make further attempts to return the ball until it touches the floor the second time. Both partners on a side are entitled to attempt to return the ball.

c. *Hinders*

In singles or doubles, if a player swings at but misses the ball in play, and, in his or his partner's continuing attempt to play the ball before it touches the floor a second time, there is an unintentional interference by an opponent, a hinder is called. (See Rule IV.E.)

5. Touching the Ball

Except as provided in Rule IV.E.1.b., any touching of a ball before it touches the floor the second time by a player other than one making a return is a point or out against the offending player.

6. Out-of-Court Ball

a. *After Return*

Any ball returned to the front wall that on the rebound or on the first bounce goes into the gallery or through any opening in a side wall is declared dead and the serve replayed.

b. *No Return*

Any ball not returned to the front wall but which caroms off a player's hand or fist into the gallery or into any opening in a side wall either with or without touching the ceiling, side, or back wall, shall be an out or point against the player failing to make the return.

7. Dry Ball and Gloves

During the game, and particularly on service, every effort must be made to keep the ball dry. Deliberately wetting the ball results in an out or point. The ball may be inspected by the referee at any time during a game. If a player's gloves are wet to the extent that they leave wet marks on the ball, the player must change to dry gloves on a referee's time out. This is strictly a referee's judgment. If a player wishes to change to dry gloves, he must hold the palms of his hands up to the referee and obtain the referee's permission to change. He may not leave the court without the referee's permission. Two minutes are allowed for glove changes. The referee should give a one-minute warning, but the player is still responsible to be back in the court within two minutes. Deliberately wetting the gloves results in an out or point.

8. Broken Ball

If there is any suspicion that a ball has broken on the serve or during a rally, play continues until the end of the rally. The referee or any player may request that the ball be examined. If the referee decides the ball is broken, a new ball must be put into play and the point replayed. Once the succeeding serve is begun (attempted), the previous rally stands.

9. Play Stoppage

If a player accidently loses a shoe or other equipment, or a foreign object enters the court, or any other outside interference occurs, the referee must stop the play immediately if such interference affects the play or poses an immediate danger.

E. HINDERS

Hinders are of two types: "dead ball" and "avoidable."

1. Dead Ball Hinders

Dead ball hinders as described in this rule result in the point being replayed. When called by the referee, the following are dead ball hinders:

a. *Court Hinders*

If, in the referee's opinion, an erratic bounce caused by a court obstruction affected play, it should be called a "court hinder." The player should not stop play at any time in anticipation of a call.

Included in court hinders is the unplayable, wet, skidding ball that hits a wet spot on the floor, walls, or ceiling. This is the referee's call, not the player's.

b. *Hitting Opponent*

When a returned ball touches an opponent on the fly before it returns to the front wall, and the shot obviously would not have reached the front wall on the fly, the player who is hit by the shot will be awarded the rally. If there is any doubt in the official's mind as to whether or not the ball would have reached the front wall, a dead ball hinder will be called.

c. *Body Contact*

When any body contact with an opponent interferes with seeing or returning the ball.

A player may not stop play, except on any physical contact during his backswing. He may immediately call "contact" if he wants the contact hinder. If he elects to shoot, no contact call will be permitted. At no other time should the players stop on physical contact. The defensive player may not stop play if contact occurs during his opponent's backswing.

Except for the offensive player stopping play during his backswing, physical contact is not an automatic hinder. It is the judgment of the referee as to whether or not the physical contact impeded the play.

d. *Screen Ball*

When any ball rebounds from the front wall close to the body of a player on the side that has just returned the ball in such a way as to interfere with or prevent the returning side from seeing the ball. (See Rule IV.A.3.a.ii.)

e. *Straddle Ball*

When a ball passes between the legs of a player on the side that just returned the ball, if there is no fair chance for the opposing player to see or return the ball. This is not automatic.

f. *Avoidance*

While making an attempt to return the ball, a player is entitled to a fair chance to see and return the ball. It is the duty of the side that has just served or returned the ball to move so that the receiving side may go straight to the ball and not be required to go around an opponent. On the other hand, the receiver must make a reasonable effort to move towards the ball. The referee should be liberal in calling hinders to discourage any practice of playing the ball in such a way that an opponent cannot see it until it is too late. When a player attempts a killshot in front of himself, and his position interferes with his opponent's attempt to retrieve the ball, the referee should give the benefit of any doubt as to whether or not the ball was retrievable to the defensive player. Hinders must be called without a claim by a player. It is not a hinder when one player hinders his partner.

g. *Doubles*

In doubles, both players on a side are entitled to a fair and unobstructed chance at the ball. Either one is entitled to a hinder even though it naturally would be his partner's ball and even though his partner may have attempted to play the ball and has already missed it.

h. *Effect*

A call by the referee of a "hinder" stops the play and usually voids any situation that follows, such as the ball hitting a player who stopped playing because of the call. However, if, in the opinion of the referee, his call of "hinder" was not responsible for the player being hit by the ball, the referee may overrule the hinder call and declare either a point or side out. No player is authorized to call a hinder, except the shooting player during his backswing and such call must be made immediately.

2. *Avoidable Hinders*

An avoidable hinder results in an out or a point depending upon whether the offender was serving or receiving. Player intent does not have any bearing on an avoidable call. An avoidable hinder should be called only when a hinder could have been avoided with reasonable effort. Avoidable hinders are called when:

a. *Failure to Move*

A player does not move sufficiently to allow his opponent his shot.

b. *Blocking*

A player moves into a position that effects a block or crowds his opponent about to return the ball; or in doubles, one partner moves in front of an opponent as his partner is returning the ball.

c. *Moving Into Ball*

A player moves into the path of and is struck by the ball just played by this opponent.

d. *Pushing*

A player forcibly pushes or shoves an opponent during a rally.

e. *View Obstruction*

Deliberately moving across a player's line of vision just before he strikes the ball.

f. *Distraction*

Any avoidable intimidation or distraction that would interfere with the player playing the ball such as stomping feet, shouting, whistling, or loud noise.

F. REST PERIODS

1. Time Outs

During a game each player in singles, or each side in doubles, either while serving or receiving may request a time out. Each time out must not exceed one minute. No more than three time outs in a game may be granted each singles player or to each team in doubles. Two one-minute time outs are allowed during the tie breaker.

A player may not call a time out after the referee has announced the score or called "second serve" after a fault.

A player may leave the court during a time out. Time outs may be called consecutively.

2. Equipment Time Outs

At the discretion of the referee, equipment time outs may be granted for lost shoes, broken shoelaces, torn equipment, wet shirts, wet floors, etc. A player is not charged for this time out.

3. Injury

No time out shall be charged to a player who is injured during play. An injured player shall not be allowed more than a total of 15 minutes of rest. If the injured player is not able to resume play after a period totalling 15 minutes per match, the match shall be awarded to the opponent or opponents.

Injury time outs may be allowed only for injuries which occur accidentally during the match. Pre-existing illnesses, fatigue or cramps are not injuries.

For any injury, the tournament director, if present, or committee, after considering any available medical opinion, must determine whether the injured player may be allowed to continue.

4. Between Games

Five-minute time outs are allowed between the first and second game, and before the tie breaker. Players may leave the court.

GOVERNING BODY

United States Handball Association, 930 North Benton Ave., Tucson, AZ 85711

The U.S. Handball Association (USHA) is the official regulatory agency for the game of handball and is dedicated not only to the growth and development of handball, but also to stimulating active participation in competitive sports and physical fitness programs by all age groups. The Association's network is administered through 50 state associations, 11 area commissioners, and the national office. Each year it sanctions 50 statewide tournaments, 9 regional tournaments and 7 separate national championships with competition for male and females in categories ranging in age from 13-and-under to 70-plus. Competition is also held in numerous ability classes including A, B, C, and novice. The USHA has held national championships at the collegiate level since 1953.

MAGAZINES

Handball, USHA, 930 N. Benton Ave., Tucson, AZ 85711.

HORSESHOE
• PITCHING •

OFFICIAL RULES FOR HORSESHOE PITCHING

(Reproduced by permission of National Horseshoe Pitchers' Association of America.*)

HORSESHOE COURT LAYOUT

RULE 1. Section a: Layout of Court. A court shall consist of two pitchers' boxes—an area of clay, dirt, or sand in which the shoes land—with a stake in the center of each; and shall cover a level area, overall, of 10 feet in width and 50 feet in length.

Section b: When a number of courts are constructed, as required in tournament play, the stakes shall be at least 10 feet—and 12 feet is better—apart between courts; and the foul lines at the front of the pitching boxes shall be in a straight line across the entire layout. Construction shall permit north-and-south pitching.

RULE 2. Pitching Distance. The pitching distance shall be 40 feet, between the bottoms of the stakes, where they emerge from the ground. Women's pitching distance shall be 30 feet.

RULE 3. Indoor Pitching. When indoor courts are constructed, the height of pitching boxes shall not be over 6 inches above floor level. Ceiling height shall be at least 12 feet.

RULE 4. The area of clay, dirt, or sand, in which the shoes land, shall be at least 43 inches long in the direction that the pitcher throws; and shall be at least 31 inches wide. The area may, however, be as much as 60 inches long and 36 inches wide. The stakes shall be set 3 feet back from the foul line, and in the center of the width of the area in which the shoes land. The foul lines, preferably of wood or concrete, are to be 2 inches wide, and extend up approximately an inch above the level of the pitching platform on which the pitcher stands. The pitching platform, preferably of concrete, shall be at least 2 feet wide and as long as the area in which the shoes land.

RULE 5. Stakes shall be one inch in diameter—no larger. They may be of cold rolled steel, mild iron, or soft steel. The top of each stake shall extend 14 inches above the level of the pitcher's platform on each side of the stake, with a 2-inch incline toward each other.

RULE 6. The area in which the shoes land shall be filled to a depth of 6 to 10 inches with potter's clay, or a substitute of like nature, and kept in a moist and putty-like condition. (When the pitcher's platforms are hard surfaces, the opening around the stake shall be filled with clay.)

Section a: When the pitchers' platforms are hard surfaced, the area with dimensions as given in Rule 4 must be left about the stake as a clay area.

Section b: Foul lines shall be clearly defined.

---

*See page 340 for additional information.

Section c: Official Shoe. A shoe shall not exceed 7 1/4 inches in width, 7 5/8 inches in length, and shall not weigh over 2 1/2 pounds. On a parallel line 3/4 inch from a straight edge touching the points of the open end of a shoe, the opening shall not exceed 3 1/2 inches

HORSESHOE COURT LAYOUT

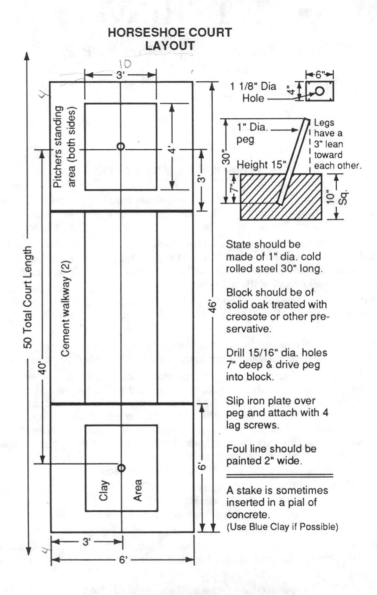

1 1/8" Dia Hole

1" Dia. peg

Height 15"

Legs have a 3" lean toward each other.

30"

7"

10" Sq.

6"

State should be made of 1" dia. cold rolled steel 30" long.

Block should be of solid oak treated with creosote or other preservative.

Drill 15/16" dia. holes 7" deep & drive peg into block.

Slip iron plate over peg and attach with 4 lag screws.

Foul line should be painted 2" wide.

A stake is sometimes inserted in a pial of concrete.
(Use Blue Clay if Possible)

50 Total Court Length

Pitchers standing area (both sides)

Cement walkway (2)

Clay Area

3'

4'

3'

46'

40'

6'

3'

6'

PLAYING RULES

RULE 7. Section a: Conduct of players and members: No contestant while opponent is in pitching position, shall make any remark, nor utter any sounds within the hearing of opponent, nor make any movement that does or might interfere with the opponent's playing.

Penalty: First offense, a warning by referee—second offense, warning by referee, and upon third offense that game will automatically be forfeited.

Section b: Any member of the N.H.P.A., who indulges in heckling or unfair rooting against any opponent in a tournament, whether with malicious intent or otherwise, shall be expelled from the grounds, and from the N.H.P.A.

Section c: No contestant shall move his own or opponent's shoe or shoes, until winner of point or points has been agreed upon by contestants, or decision rendered by the referee. Referee shall declare foul shoes thrown by a contestant failing to comply with this rule, and award points to the opponent, according to the position of his or her shoes.

Section d: No contestant shall walk to the opposite stake, or be informed of the position of shoes, prior to the completion of an inning.

Section e: A player, while not pitching, must remain on the opposite side of the stake to the player who is pitching, and on the rear one-fourth of the pitcher's platform, back of the stake. If standing back of the pitching platform the toe of one foot must remain on the rear one-fourth of the platform.

Section f: Any player repeatedly violating rules, or guilty of unsportsmanlike conduct, may be barred from further competition in the contest.

Section g: Drinking of alcoholic beverages, tobacco chewing, or smoking on the courts is prohibited at the World Tournament.

Section h: Between games pitchers shall be limited to four (4) practice shoes once the scorekeeper and both pitchers are on the court ready to proceed with the next game.

RULE 8. Section a: Foul Lines: Any shoe pitched while the pitcher's foot extends on or over the foul line, shall be declared foul, and removed from the counting distance.

Section b: In pitching the shoe, the pitcher shall stand on the pitcher's platform, at one side or other of the stake.

RULE 9. In delivering a shoe, the pitcher must remain behind the foul line until the shoe has left his hand.

RULE 10. Choice of Pitch: Choice of first pitch, or follow, shall be determined by the toss of a coin or a flipped-up shoe. In successive games between the same players, the loser shall have choice.

RULE 11. Broken Shoes: When a shoe lands in fair territory and is broken into separate parts it shall be removed and the contestant allowed to pitch another shoe in its stead.

RULE 12. Section a: Foul Shoes: Any shoe pitched by a contestant which lands outside the clay area of the opposite pitching box is a foul shoe. Any shoe that lands in fair territory but hits the backstop or other objects and comes back into the pitching area shall be called a foul shoe.

Section b: Foul shoes shall be removed from the opposite pitcher's box.

Section c: A foul shoe shall not be scored or credited except in the scoresheet column headed "shoes pitched."

Section d: When a foul shoe disrupts the position of a shoe in fair territory, the foul shoe is to be removed from the pitching area at the request of the opponent, and all other shoes are to remain as they are.

RULE 13. Measurements: Measurements to determine points shall be made with calipers and straight edge. Where all measurements are specified as maximum, there is no minimum.

SCORING RULES

There are two official methods of scoring: the cancellation method and count-all method.

CANCELLATION SCORING

RULE 14. Section a: A regulation game shall consist of forty (40) points in all contests where a National title is involved. Any other contest may be decided in any manner acceptable if National Rules, Constitution and By-Laws are not violated.

Section b: Game points in other tournaments, leagues or contests may be determined by local authorities to fit their conditions.

Section c: A game is divided into innings and each inning constitutes the pitching of two shoes by each contestant.

Section d: Score Calling Method:

No score 4 shoes—Called as no score

1 Point—Called as one point

2 Points—Called as two points

1 Ringer—Called as one ringer 3 points

1 Ringer 1 Point—Called as one ringer 4 points

2 Ringers 6 Points—Called as two ringers 6 points

1 Ringer Each No Score—Called as one ringer each no score

1 Ringer Each 1 Point—Called as one ringer each one point

3 Ringers 3 Points—Called as three ringers 3 points

2 Ringers Each No Score—Called as two ringers each no score

In each instance the player calling the score must call his name and must be the one scoring. In a no score situation the player pitching last shall be the one to call the score.

RULE 15. Section a: A shoe must be within six (6) inches of the stake to score.

Section b: Closest shoe to stake scores 1 point

Section c: Two shoes closer than opponent's scores 2 points

Section d: One (1) ringer scores 3 points

Section e: Two (2) ringers scores 6 points

Section f: One (1) ringer and closest shoe of same player scores 4 points

Section g: Party having two (2) ringers against one for opponent scores 3 points.

Section h: All equals count as ties. If each contestant has a shoe touching the stake or each has a shoe equal distance from the stake, then the closer of the other two shoes will be scored as a point, if within six (6) inches of the stake.

Section i: In case each contestant has a ringer, the next closest shoe, if within six (6) inches, shall score 1 point.

Section j: In case of tie, such as four (4) ringers, or contestants' shoes are equal distance from the stake, causing no score for either, party pitching last in the inning will start the next inning.

Section k: A leaning shoe has no value over one touching the stake.

RULE 16. Section a: The points shall be scored according to the position of the shoes at the inning's end, that is, after the contestants have each thrown two shoes.

Section b: Ringer credits shall be given on the same basis.

Section c: The winner of points shall call the result. In case of a tie, the party pitching last shall call.

RULE 17. Definition of a Ringer: A ringer is declared when a shoe encircles the stake far enough to allow the touching of both heel caulks simultaneously with a straight edge, and permit a clearance of the stake.

COUNT-ALL SCORING

RULE 18. Section a: Count-All Scoring: A game shall consist of fifty shoes pitched by each player (25 innings).

Section b: Each player shall receive credit for all points according to the position of the shoes at the end of each inning, regardless of what his opponent throws. Thus it is possible for each player to score six points in any one inning. Ringers count three points and shoes within six inches of the stake count one point each.

Section c: Players shall alternate first pitch, one player having first pitch in the even innings and the other player in the odd number innings.

Section d: Ties shall be broken by pitching an extra inning or as many extra innings as are necessary to break the tie.

RULE 19. Double Games: Two players are partners and pitch from opposite ends of the court against a similar combination of opponents. Partners' points are added together, but the individual records of ringers and shoes pitched should be kept. Otherwise the game is the same as the conventional singles or walking game.

RULE 20. Three-handed Games: In three-handed games, when two of the players each have a ringer and a third player no ringer, the party without a ringer is out of the scoring and other scores according to conditions pertaining if only two were in the game. Otherwise, the regulation rules apply.

RULE 21. Section a: Recording of Results: The recording of results shall be as follows: W—Games Won; L—Games Lost; P—Points; R—Ringers; DR—Double Ringers; SP—Shoes Pitched; OP—Opponent Points; PR—Percentage of Ringers.

Section b: All past and future World Tournament Play-Offs in any Championship division are to be included in total World Tournament Statistics.

JURISDICTION

RULE 22. Section a: A tournament committee, satisfactory to the Executive Council shall supervise National contests.

Section b: A referee appointed by the committee shall decide points when contestants are in doubt. He shall also see that rules are complied with.

All foul shoes shall be called by the referee. First a warning will be given and a second offense will be declared foul and taken out of court.

Section c: Appeal may be made to the committee if a ruling of the referee is not considered proper. Decision of the committee shall be final.

Section d: All protests shall be made immediately when the occasion arises. Protests covering shoes or conditions of play can only be made before the start of each game.

Section e: If rain or other elements interfere, players must stop play and not resume until officials authorize. On resuming play, score at time of interference will be in effect, also the same courts will be used by contestants unless they agree otherwise.

Section f: The interpretation of the tournament committee covering technical points and their rulings on matters uncovered by these rules shall be final.

Section g: An official scorer shall cover each game. When open scorers are also maintained, the official scorer shall watch closely the open score and correct immediately any error. The scoresheet kept by the official scorer shall be the official score, not the scoring device.

Corrections can be made at any time if the scorekeeper records the score incorrectly on the official scoresheet and/or scoreboard. The players are responsible for ensuring their scores are correct.

Section h: Any record set in a Sanctioned Tournament shall be called a World Record. Any record set in a World Tournament shall be called a World Tournament record. The statistics shall be kept in two different sets of records and recorded as such. The Executive Council shall decide on the authenticity of the records.

RULE 23: An official contest between two players shall consist of best six (6) out of eleven (11) games.

GOVERNING BODY

National Horseshoe Pitchers' Association, Box 278, Munroe Falls, OH 44262.

The National Horseshoe Pitchers' Association (N.H.P.A.) is an incorporated nonprofit organization, which serves as a federation of 45 state associations in the United States and Canada. The purpose of the NHPA is to promote and foster the sport; standardize the rules, equipment, and playing procedures; and serve as the unifying agent between state associations, local clubs, and individual players. Competitive championships are sponsored by the NHPA at all levels from local leagues and tournaments to the annual World Tournament. The Association provides a complete array of game-related items, technique instructional materials, and information for the organization of local clubs and the conduct of competition.

MAGAZINES

The Horseshoe Pitcher's News Digest, NHPA, Box 278, Munroe Falls, OH 44262.

• ICE HOCKEY •

ABRIDGMENT OF AHAUS
OFFICIAL PLAYING RULES 1987-89

(By permission of the Amateur Hockey Association of the United States*)

☐

Note: The abridgment of the official rules presented here provides coverage of the major elements of the game but does not include all standards and contingencies found in the official rules. The masculine gender is used throughout the rules for covenience and clarity.

A. THE RINK

1. RINK

The game of "Ice Hockey" shall be played on an ice surface known as a "RINK".

2. DIMENSIONS OF RINK

As nearly as possible, the dimensions of the rink shall be 200 feet long and 85 feet wide. The rink shall be surrounded by a wooden or fiberglass wall or fence, known as the "BOARDS", which shall extend not less than forty inches and not more than forty-eight inches above the level of the ice surface. The ideal height of the boards above the ice surface shall be forty-two inches.

It is recommended that the entire rink, including players' and penalty benches, be enclosed by protective safety glass, wire and/or other protective screens of sufficient height designed to separate players from spectators.

3. GOAL POSTS AND NETS

a. The goal posts shall be anchored in such a manner as to permit a goal post to be dislodged when hit by a degree of force such as would be provided by a player sliding into or being checked into it.

b. The goal posts shall be of approved design and material, extending vertically four feet above the surface of the ice and set six feet apart measured from the inside of the posts. A crossbar of the same material as the goal posts shall extend from the top of one post to the top of the other.

c. There shall be attached to each goal frame a net of approved design.

d. The goal posts and cross bars shall be painted in red and all other exterior surfaces shall be painted in white.

---

*See page 362 for additional information.

e. The red line, two inches wide, between the goal posts on the ice and extended completely across the rink, shall be known as the "GOAL LINE".

f. The Goal area, enclosed by the goal line and the base of the goal, shall be painted white.

4. GOAL CREASE AND GOALKEEPER'S PRIVILEGED AREA

a. In front of each goal a "GOAL CREASE" area shall be marked by a red line two inches in width.

b. The goal crease area shall include all the space outlined by the semicircular crease lines (including crease lines) and extending vertically four feet to the level of the top of the goal frame.

c. The goalkeeper's "PRIVILEGED AREA" is an area bounded in the rear by the goal line, in front by an imaginary line connecting the end zone face-off spots and on the sides by imaginary lines extending perpendicular from the goal line to the end zone face-off spots.

5. DIVISION OF ICE SURFACE

a. The ice area between the two goals shall be divided into three parts by lines, twelve inches in width, and blue in color.

b. That portion of the ice surface in which the goal is situated shall be called the "DEFENDING ZONE" of the team defending that goal; the central portion shall be known as the "NEUTRAL ZONE" and the portion farthest from the defended goal as the "ATTACKING ZONE". The zone line shall be considered part of the zone that the puck is in.

c. There shall also be a line, twelve inches in width, and red in color, drawn completely across the rink in center ice, parallel with the goal lines and continued vertically up the side of the boards, known as the "CENTER LINE".

6. CENTER ICE SPOT AND CIRCLE

A circular blue spot, twelve inches in diameter, shall be marked exactly in the center of the rink with this spot as the center of a fifteen foot radius circle. On both sides of the circle there shall be two lines two feet long, two inches wide and four feet apart.

7. FACE-OFF SPOTS IN NEUTRAL ZONE

Two red spots two feet in diameter shall be marked on the ice in the Neutral Zone five feet from each blue line.

8. END ZONE FACE-OFF SPOTS AND CIRCLES

In both end zones and on both sides of each goal, red face-off spots and circles shall be marked on the ice.

9. PLAYERS' BENCH

Each rink shall be provided with seats or benches for the use of players placed immediately alongside the ice, in the Neutral Zone, as near to the center of the rink as possible with doors opening in the Neutral Zone. The players' benches should be on the same side of the playing surface opposite the penalty bench and should be separated by a substantial distance.

10. PENALTY BENCH

Each rink must be provided with benches or seats to be known as the "PENALTY BENCH". It is preferable to have separate penalty benches for each team to be separated from each other and substantially separated from either players' bench. The penalty bench(es) must be situated in the Neutral Zone.

11. REFEREE'S CREASE

Immediately in front of the Penalty Timekeeper's seat there shall be marked in red on the ice a semicircle of ten feet radius and two inches in width which shall be known as the "REFEREE'S CREASE".

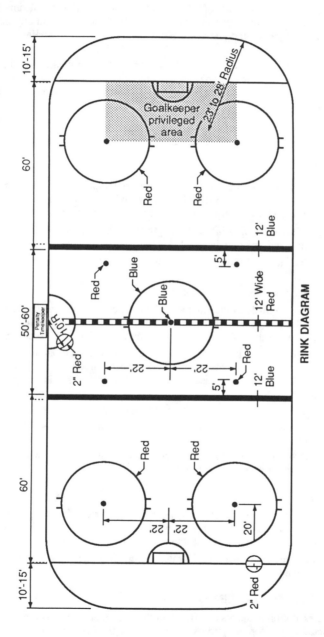

RINK DIAGRAM

12. SIGNAL AND TIMING DEVICES

a. Each rink shall be provided with a siren, or other suitable sound device, for the use of Timekeepers.

b. Each rink shall be provided with some form of electrical clock for the purpose of keeping the spectators, players and game officials accurately informed as to all time elements at all stages of the game, including the time remaining to be played in any period. Time recording for both game time and penalty time shall show time remaining to be played or served.

c. Behind each goal electric lights shall be set up for the use of the Goal Judges. A red light will signify the scoring of a goal. Where automatic lights are available, a green light will signify the end of a period or a game. (Note) A goal cannot be scored when a green light is showing.

B. EQUIPMENT

1. STICKS

a. The sticks shall be made of wood or other material approved by the Rules Committee and must not have any projections. Adhesive tape of any color may be wrapped around the stick at any place for the purpose of reinforcement or to improve control of the puck.

b. No stick shall exceed sixty inches in length from the heel to the end of the shaft nor more than twelve and one-half inches from the heel to the end of the blade.

The blade of the stick shall not be more than three inches in width at any point nor less than two inches.

All edges of the blade shall be bevelled.

The curvature of the blade of the stick shall be restricted in such a way that the distance of a perpendicular line measured from a straight line drawn from the base of the heel to the base of the toe to the point of maximum curvature shall not exceed one-half inch.

c. The blade of the goalkeeper's stick shall not exceed three and one-half inches in width at any point except at the heel where it must not exceed four and one-half inches in width; nor shall the goalkeeper's stick exceed fifteen and one-half inches in length from the heel to the end of the blade.

The widened portion of the goalkeeper's stick extending up the shaft from the blade shall not extend more than twenty-six inches from the heel and shall not exceed three and one-half inches in width.

d. A minor penalty shall be imposed on any player or goalkeepeer who uses a stick not conforming to the provisions of this rule.

2. SKATES

a. All players and on-ice Officials must wear hockey skates of a design approved by the Rules Committee. All skates worn by players (but not goalkeepers) and by the Referee and Linesmen shall be equipped with approved safety heel tips.

b. The use of speed skates or fancy skates or any skate so designed that it may cause injury is prohibited.

3. GOALKEEPER'S EQUIPMENT

a. With the exception of skates and stick, all the equipment worn by the goalkeeper must be constructed solely for the purpose of protecting the head or body, and he must not wear any garment or use any contrivance which would give him undue assistance in keeping goal.

b. The leg guards worn by goalkeepers shall not exceed eleven inches in extreme width when on the leg of the player.

c. It is compulsory for all goalkeepers to wear helmets and full face masks. No form fitted face masks shall be permitted.

d. A minor penalty shall be imposed on any goalkeeper using illegal equipment in a game.

4. PROTECTIVE EQUIPMENT

a. In Boys Junior and below and all Girls age classifications, each player is personally responsible to wear protective equipment for all games and practices. Such equipment should include shin pads, shoulder pads, elbow pads, hip pads or padded hockey pants, protective cup, tendon pads plus all head protective equipment as required by AHAUS rules. It is recommended that all protective equipment be designed specifically for ice hockey.

All protective equipment, except gloves, helmet/face mask and goalkeeper's leg guards, must be worn under the uniform. For violation of this rule after a warning by the Referee a minor penalty shall be imposed.

(Note) Players, including goalkeepers, violating this rule shall not be permitted to participate in the game until such equipment has been corrected or removed.

A player, excluding the goalkeeper, whose helmet/face mask has come off his head during play may not resume play until his helmet/face mask has been properly replaced. A player not conforming to this rule shall be assessed a minor penalty.

If the goalkeeper's helmet/face mask comes off during play, the Referee shall stop play immediately. A minor penalty shall be assessed a goalkeeper who deliberately removes his helmet/face mask during play.

b. It is compulsory for all players in all classifications to wear a hockey helmet, with chinstraps properly fastened.

It is recommended that all Referees and Linesmen wear a black hockey helmet.

c. All players, including goalkeepers, in the PeeWee through Junior (Girls: PeeWee through Senior) classifications are required to wear an internal mouthpiece, which covers all the remaining teeth of one jaw, customarily the upper.

For a violation of this rule a misconduct penalty shall be imposed.

d. All players, including goalkeepers, in Boys Junior and below and all Girls age classifications, are required to wear a face mask certified by the Hockey Equipment Certification Council (H.E.C.C.) plus any chin protection that accompanies the face mask.

5. DANGEROUS EQUIPMENT

a. The use of pads or protectors made of metal, or of any other material likely to cause injury to a player, is prohibited.

(Note) All elbow pads which do not have a soft protective outer covering of sponge rubber or similar material at least 1/2 inch thick shall be considered dangerous equipment.

b. A glove from which all or part of the palm has been removed or cut to permit the use of the bare hand shall be considered illegal equipment. A minor penalty shall be imposed on any player wearing such a glove in play.

6. PUCK

The puck shall be made of vulcanized rubber, or other approved material, one inch thick and three inches in diameter and shall weigh between five and one-half ounces and six ounces.

C. THE GAME

1. DESCRIPTION

The game is played on an ice surface between two teams of six players each. All players wear skates and are equipped with a long curved stick which is used to propel a hard rubber disk (puck) over the ice and to hit it into the opponent's goal. The team scoring the greater number of goals is the winner. The puck must be kept in continuous motion as it is controlled and passed among teammates. The game is not slowed or stopped by out-of-bounds plays since the puck is played as it rebounds from the walls surrounding the rink. The liberal substitution policy employed allows players to be substituted while the game is in progress. The body contact, within limits, allowed by the rules and the restrictions on player position when playing the puck are the source of most rules violations.

2. AGE CLASSIFICATIONS

The following age classifications have been established for all teams registered with AHAUS.

	Boys	Girls
Mites	9 or under	
Squirts	10-11	8-12
PeeWees	12-13	13-15
Bantams	14-15	
Midgets	16-17	11-19
Juniors	17-19	
Seniors	20<<	Any Age

3. TERMINOLOGY

a. Altercation. Any physical interaction between two or more opposing players resulting in a penalty or penalties being assessed.

b. Breakaway. A condition whereby a player·is in control of the puck with no opposition between the player and the opposing goal, with a reasonable scoring opportunity.

c. Butt Ending. The condition whereby a player uses the shaft of the stick above the upper hand to jab or attempt to jab an opposing player.

d. Creases. Goalkeeper's: Areas marked on the ice in front of each goal designed to protect the goalkeepers from interference by attacking players.

Referee's: Areas marked on the ice in front of the Penalty Timekeeper's seat for the use of the Referee.

e. Cross Checking. When a player, holding his stick with both hands, checks an opponent by using the shaft of the stick with no part of the stick on the ice.

f. Delayed Off-Side. A situation where an attacking player has preceded the puck across the attacking blue line, but the defending team has gained possession of the puck and is in a position to bring the puck out of their Defending Zone without any delay or contact with an attacking player.

g. Deflecting the Puck. The action of the puck contacting any person or object causing it to change direction.

h. Directing the Puck. The act of intentionally moving or positioning the body, skate or stick so as to change the course of the puck in a desired direction.

i. Face-Off. The action of an official dropping the puck between the sticks of two opposing players to start play. A face-off begins when the Referee indicates its location and the officials take their appropriate positions and ends when the puck has been legally dropped.

j. Game Suspension(s). When a player, Coach, or Manager receives a game suspension(s), he shall not be eligible to participate in the next game(s) that were already on the schedule of that team before the incident occurred.

k. Goalkeeper. A goalkeeper is a person designated as such by a team who is permitted special equipment and privileges to prevent the puck from entering the goal.

l. Heel of the Stick. The point where the shaft of the stick and the bottom of the blade meet.

m. Hooking. The action of applying the blade of the stick to any part of an opponent's body or stick and impeding his progress by a pulling or tugging motion with the stick.

n. Last play face-off. The location at which the puck was last legally played by a player or goalkeeper immediately prior to a stoppage of play.

o. Off-Ice (Minor) Official. Officials appointed to assist in the conduct of the game including the Official Scorer, Game Timekeeper, Penalty Timekeeper and the two Goal Judges. The Referee has general supervision of the game and full control of all game officials, and in case of any dispute the Referee's decision shall be final.

p. Penalty. A penalty is the result or an infraction or the rules by a player or team official. It usually involves the removal from the game of the offending player or team official for a specified period of time. In some cases the penalty may be the awarding of a clear shot on goal or the actual awarding of a goal.

q. Possession of the Puck. The last player or goalkeeper to make contact with the puck. This includes a puck that is deflected off a player or any part of his equipment.

r. Possession and Control of the Puck. The last player or goalkeeper to make contact with the puck and who also propels the puck in a desired direction.

s. Protective Equipment. Equipment worn by players for the sole purpose of protection from injury.

t. Shorthanded. Shorthanded means that a team is below the numerical strength of its opponents on the ice. When a goal is scored against a shorthanded team the minor or bench minor penalty which terminates automatically is the one which causes the team scored against to be "shorthanded". Thus, if an equal number of players from each team is each serving a penalty(s) (minor, bench minor, major or match only), neither team is "shorthanded".

u. Slashing. The action of striking or attempting to strike an opponent with a stick or of swinging a stick at an opponent with no contact being made. Tapping an opponent's stick is not considered slashing.

v. Spearing. The action of poking or attempting to poke an opponent with the top of the blade of the stick while holding the stick with one or both hands.

w. Substitute Goalkeeper. A designated goalkeeper on the Official Score Sheet who is not then participating in the game.

x. Team Official. A person responsible in any degree for the operation of a team, such as a Team Executive, Coach, Manager or Trainer.

y. Temporary Goalkeeper. A player not designated as a goalkeeper on the Score Sheet who assumes that position when no designated goalkeeper is able to participate in the game. He is governed by a goalkeeper's privileges and limitations, and must return as a "player" when a designated goalkeeper becomes available to participate in the game.

4. TIME OF MATCH

The maximum time allowed for a game is three 20-minute periods of actual play with a rest intermission of 15 minutes between periods.

5. CHOICE OF GOALS

The home team has the choice of goals to defend at the start of the game except where both players' benches are on the same side of the rink, in which case the home team starts the game defending the goal nearest its own bench. The teams change ends for each succeeding regular or overtime period.

6. BEGINNING PLAY

The game begins with a face-off at the center ice face-off spot and is renewed at the start of each succeeding period.

a. The puck is faced-off by the Referee or the Linesman dropping the puck on the ice between the sticks of the players facing-off. Players facing-off must stand squarely facing their opponents' end of the rink approximately one stick length apart with the blades of their sticks touching the ice. No other players shall be allowed to enter the face-off circle or come within 15 feet of the players facing-off the puck and must stand onside on all face-offs.

b. In the conduct of a face-off, no player facing-off shall make any physical contact with his opponent's body by means of his own body or by his stick except in the course of playing the puck after the face-off has been completed.

7. PUCK MUST BE KEPT IN MOTION

Except to carry the puck behind its goal once, a team in possession of the puck in its own Defending Zone must always advance the puck toward the opposing goal, except if it is prevented from so doing by players of the opposing side.

a. A minor penalty shall be imposed on any player including the goalkeeper who holds, freezes or plays the puck with his stick, skates or body along the boards in such a manner as to cause a stoppage of play unless he is actually being checked by an opponent.

b. A player beyond his Defending Zone shall not pass nor carry the puck backward into his Defending Zone for the purpose of delaying the game except when his team is below the numerical strength of the opponents'.

8. PASSES

a. (For Boys Junior and below and all Girls games)

The puck may be passed by any player to a player of the same team within any of the three zones into which the ice is divided and may be passed forward by a player in his own Defending Zone to a player of the same team anywhere in the Neutral Zone.

(For games above Junior)

The puck may be passed by any player to a player of the same side within any one of the three zones into which the ice is divided, but may not be passed forward from a player in one zone to a player of the same side in another zone, except by a player on the defending team, who may make and take forward passes from their own Defending Zone to the center line without incurring an offside violation. This pass, however, must be completed by a receiving player who is legally onside at the center line, or by a receiving player who is preceded by the puck across the center line, otherwise play shall be stopped and the face-off shall be at the spot from which the pass originated.

(Note 1) The position of the puck (not the player's skates) shall be the determining factor in deciding from which zone the pass was made.

(Note 2) Passes may be completed legally at the center red line in exactly the same manner as passes at the attacking blue line.

b. (For games above Junior)

The player last touched by the puck shall be deemed to be in possession.

Rebounds off goalkeeper's pad or other equipment shall not be considered as a change of possession or the completion of the play by the team.

c. (For Boys Junior and below and all Girls games)

If the puck precedes all players of the attacking team into their Attacking Zone, any player is eligible to play the puck except when "Icing the Puck" applies.

(For games above Junior)

If the player in the Neutral Zone is preceded into the Attacking Zone by the puck passed from the Neutral Zone he shall be eligible to take possession of the puck anywhere in the Attacking Zone except when the "Icing the Puck" rule applies.

d. If a player in the same zone from which a pass is made is preceded by the puck into succeeding zones, he shall be eligible to take possession of the puck in that zone except where the "Icing the Puck" rule applies.

e. (For games above Junior)

If an attacking player passes the puck backward toward his own goal from the Attacking Zone, an opponent may play the puck anywhere regardless of whether he (the opponent) was in the same zone at the time the puck was passed or not. (No "slow whistle".)

f. (For games above Junior)

If the Linesman shall have erred in calling an offside pass infraction (regardless of whether either team is shorthanded), the puck shall be faced-off on the center ice face-off spot.

9. PUCK OUT OF BOUNDS OR UNPLAYABLE

a. When the puck goes outside the playing area or strikes any obstacles above the playing surface other than the boards, glass or wire, or deflects off an Official out of the playing area, it shall be faced-off from where it was shot or deflected by a player, unless otherwise expressly provided in these rules.

b. When the puck becomes lodged in the netting on the outside of either goal so as to make it unplayable, or if it is frozen between opposing players intentionally or otherwise, the Referee shall stop the play and face-off the puck at either of the adjacent face-off spots unless in the opinion of the Referee the stoppage was caused by a player of the attacking team, in which case the resulting face-off shall be conducted in the Neutral Zone.

(Note) This includes a stoppage of play caused by a player of the attacking team shooting the puck onto the back of the defending team's goal without any intervening action by the defending team.

The defending team and/or the attacking team may play the puck off the net at any time. However, should the puck remain on the net for longer than three seconds, play shall be stopped and the face-off shall take place on an end zone face-off spot except when the stoppage is caused by the attacking team, in which case the face-off shall take place on a face-off spot in the Neutral Zone.

c. A minor penalty shall be imposed on a goalkeeper who deliberately drops the puck on the goal netting to cause a stoppage of play.

d. If the puck comes to rest on top of the boards surrounding the playing area, it shall be considered to be in play and may be played legally by the hand or stick.

10. PUCK OUT OF SIGHT

Should a scramble take place, or a player accidentally fall on the puck, and the puck be out of sight of the Referee, he shall immediately blow his whistle and stop the play. The puck shall then be faced-off at the point where the play was stopped, unless otherwise provided for in the rules.

11. PUCK STRIKING OFFICIAL

a. Play shall not be stopped because the puck touches an Official anywhere on the rink, regardless of whether a team is shorthanded or not.

12. GOALS AND ASSISTS

(Note) It is the responsibility of the Referee to award goals and assists, and his decision in this respect is final.

a. A goal shall be scored when the puck shall have been put between the goal posts by the stick of a player of the attacking team, from in front, and below the crossbar, and entirely across the goal line.

b. A goal shall be scored if the puck is put into the goal in any way by a player of the defending team. The player of the attacking team who last played the puck shall be credited with the goal but no assist shall be awarded.

c. If an attacking player kicks the puck and the puck goes directly into the goal or is deflected into the goal by any player, including the goalkeeper, a goal shall not be allowed.

d. If the puck shall have been deflected into the goal from the shot of an attacking player by striking any part of a player of the same team, a goal shall be allowed. The player who deflected the puck shall be credited with the goal. The goal shall not be allowed if the puck has been kicked, thrown or otherwise deliberately directed into the goal by any means other than a stick.

e. If a goal is scored as a result of a puck being deflected directly into the goal from an Official the goal shall not be allowed.

f. Should a player legally propel a puck into the goal crease of the opposing team and the puck should become loose and available to another player of the attacking team, a goal scored on the play shall be valid.

g. Any goal scored, other than as covered by the official rules, shall not be allowed.

h. A "goal" shall be credited in the scoring records to a player who shall have propelled the puck into the opponents' goal. Each "goal" shall count one point in the player's record.

i. When a player scores a goal, an "assist" shall be credited to the player or players taking part in the play immediately preceding the goal, but not more than two assists can be given on any goal. Each "assist" so credited shall count one point in the player's record.

j. Only one point can be credited to any one player on a goal.

13. TIED GAMES

If at the end of the three periods the scored is tied, the following procedures are invoked:

a. A five-minute rest period will be allowed.

b. The teams shall change ends.

c. A ten-minute period is played.

d. The game terminates upon a goal being scored and the team scoring declared the winner. If no goal is scored, the same procedure is repeated.

Any overtime period is considered part of the game and all unexpired penalties remain in force.

14. ADJUSTMENTS TO CLOTHING AND EQUIPMENT

Play shall not be stopped, nor the game delayed by reason of adjustment to clothing, equipment, skates or sticks. If adjustments are required, the player shall retire from the ice and play shall continue uninterruptedly with a substitute. This ruling also applies to the goalkeeper.

15. BROKEN STICK

a. A player without a stick may participate in the game. A player whose stick is broken may participate in the game provided he drops the broken portion. A minor penalty shall be imposed for an infraction of this rule.

(Note) A broken stick is one which, in the opinion of the Referee, is unfit for normal play.

b. A goalkeeper may continue to play with a broken stick until stoppage of play or until he has been legally provided with a stick.

c. A replacement for a stick which is either broken or no longer in possession of a player or goalkeeper may only be obtained from the player's bench or a teammate on the ice.

The team, a member of which throws a replacement stick into the playing area, must be penalized.

d. A goalkeeper whose stick is broken may not go to the players' bench for a replacement during a stoppage of play, but must receive his stick from a teammate.

For an infraction of this rule a minor penalty shall be imposed on the goalkeeper.

16. ICING THE PUCK

a. For the purpose of this rule, the center line will divide the ice into halves. Should any player of a team, equal or superior in numerical strength to the opposing team, shoot, bat with the hand or stick, kick or deflect the puck from his own half of the ice, beyond the goal line of the opposing team, play shall be stopped and the puck faced-off at the end face-off spot of the offending team. If the puck shall have entered the goal of the opposing team, after being legally shot, batted with the stick or deflected, the goal shall be allowed.

For the purpose of this rule, the point of last contact with the puck by the team in possession shall be used to determine whether icing has occured or not.

b. If the puck was so shot by a player of a team below the numerical strength of the opposing team, play shall continue and the face-off shall not take place.

c. If, however, the puck shall go beyond the goal line in the opposite half of the ice directly from either of the players while facing-off, it shall not be considered a violation of this rule.

d. If, in the opinion of the Linesman, a player of the opposing team excepting the goalkeeper is able to play the puck before it passes the goal line, but has not done so, icing shall not be called and play shall continue.

e. If any player of the opposing team (or goalkeeper) should touch the puck in any manner before it has reached his goal line, or the puck passes through any portion of the goal crease before crossing the goal line, it shall not be considered as "icing the puck".

17. INTERFERENCE

a. It is a violation of the rules to interfere with or impede the progress of an opponent who is not in possession of the puck.

(Note) The last player to touch the puck—other than a goalkeeper—shall be considered the player in possession. In interpreting this rule the Referee should make sure which of the players is the one creating the interference—often it is the action and movement of the attacking player which causes the interference since the defending players are entitled to "stand their ground" or "shadow" the attacking players. Players of the side in possession shall not be allowed to "run" deliberate interference for the puck carrier.

b. When the puck is in the Attacking Zone and not in the goal crease, a player of the attacking team may not stand on the goal crease line or in the goal crease, hold his stick in the goal crease or skate through the goal crease. If the puck should enter the goal while such a condition prevails, a goal shall not be allowed. For violation of this rule, while the attacking team has possession of the puck, play shall be stopped and a face-off held at the nearest Neutral Zone face-off spot.

c. If a player of the attacking team has been physically interfered with by the action of any defending player so as to cause him to be in the goal crease, and the puck should enter the goal while the player so interfered with is still within the goal crease, the "goal" shall be allowed.

d. If, when the goalkeeper has been removed from the ice, any member of his team (including the goalkeeper) not legally on the ice, including any Team Official, interferes by means of his body or stick or any other object with the movements of the puck or an opposing player, the Referee shall immediately award a goal to the non-offending team.

e. When a player in control of the puck on the opponent's side of the center red line, and having no opponent to pass other than the goalkeeper, is interfered with by a stick or part thereof of any other object thrown or shot by any member of the defending team including any Team Official, a penalty shot/optional minor shall be awarded to the non-offending team.

(Note) The attention of Referees is directed particularly to three types of offensive interference which should be penalized:

(1) When the defending team secures possession of the puck in its own end and the other players of that team run interference for the puck carrier by forming a protective screen against forecheckers;

(2) When a player facing-off obstructs his opponent after the face-off when the opponent is not in possession of the puck;

(3) When the puck carrier makes a drop pass and follows through so as to make bodily contact with an opposing player.

Defensive interference consists of bodily contact with an opposing player who is not in possession of the puck.

18. KICKING PUCK

Kicking the puck shall be permitted in all zones; however, a goal shall not be allowed if the puck was kicked by an attacking player and entered the goal either directly or after deflecting off any player including the goalkeeper.

19. LEAVING THE PLAYERS' BENCH OR PENALTY BENCH

a. No player may leave the players' bench or penalty bench at any time during an altercation or for the purpose of starting an altercation.

20. OFF-SIDES

a. Players of an attacking team may not precede the puck into the Attacking Zone.

b. For a violation of this Rule, play shall be stopped and a face-off conducted.

If the puck was carried over the blue line at the time of the violation, the face-off shall take place at the nearest Neutral Zone face-off spot to where the puck crossed the line. If the puck was passed or shot over the blue line, the face-off shall take place where the pass or shot originated.

(Note) A player actually propelling and in possession and control of the puck who shall cross the line ahead of the puck shall not be considered "off-side".

c. The position of the player's skates and not that of his stick shall be the determining factor in deciding an "off-side" violation. A player is off-side when both skates are completely over the outer edge of the blue line into his Attacking Zone. The question of "off-side" never arises until the puck has completely crossed the line into the Attacking Zone, at which time the decision is to be made.

d. If an attacking player precedes the puck, which is shot, passed or deflected, into the Attacking Zone, but a defending player is able to play the puck, the Linesman shall signal a delayed off-side (except that if the puck is shot on goal, play shall be stopped immediately for the off-side violation). The Linesman shall drop his arm to nullify the off-side violation and allow play to continue if:

1) The defending team passes or carries the puck into the Neutral Zone, or

2) All attacking players in the Attacking Zone clear the Attacking Zone by making skate contact with the blue line.

If the attacking team does not clear the Attacking Zone, the Linesmen shall stop play for the off-side violation if ANY attacking player touches the puck or attempts to gain possession of a loose puck while the puck is still in the Attacking Zone or forces the defending puck carrier farther back in the Attacking Zone.

(Note) The Attacking Zone must be completely clear of attacking players before a delayed off-side can be nullified with the puck still in the Attacking Zone.

e. If a player legally carries or passes the puck back into his own Defending Zone while a player of the opposing team is in such Defending Zone, the "off-side" shall be waived and play permitted to continue. (No "delayed whistle.")

f. If, in the opinion of the Linesman, a player has intentionally caused an off-side play, the Linesman shall stop play immediately and the puck shall be faced-off at the nearest end face-off spot in the Defending Zone of the offending team.

(Note) An intentional off-side is one which is made for the purpose of securing a stoppage of play, regardless of the reason, or where an offside play is made under conditions where there is no possibility of completing a legal play.

D. TEAMS

1. COMPOSITION OF TEAM

A team shall be composed of six players on the ice. A maximum of eighteen players, plus not more than two goalkeepers, shall be permitted to play in a game.

2. CAPTAIN OF TEAM

One Captain shall be appointed by each team, and he alone shall have the privilege of discussing with the Referee any questions relating to interpretation of rules which may arise during the progress of a game. He should wear the letter "C", approximately three inches in height and in contrasting color, in a conspicuous position on the front of his sweater.

If the Captain is not available due to injury or an imposed penalty, another player may be designated to act as Captain.

3. PLAYERS IN UNIFORM

a. At the beginning of each game the Manager or Coach of each team shall list the players and goalkeepers who shall be eligible to play in the game.

b. A list of names and numbers of all eligible players and goalkeepers must be handed to the Referee or Official Scorer before the game, and no change shall be permitted in the list or addition thereto shall be permitted after commencement of the game.

c. Each team shall be allowed one goalkeeper on the ice at one time. The goalkeeper may be removed and another "player" substituted. Such substitute shall not be permitted the privileges of the goalkeeper.

d. Each player and each goalkeeper listed in the lineup of each team shall wear an individual identifying number at least ten inches high on the back of his sweater.

The number may be eight inches in the Midget and Bantam classifications and six inches in height in the Squirt, PeeWee and Mite classifications.

All players of each team shall be dressed uniformly.

e. It is recommended that each team have on its bench a substitute goalkeeper. For State, District or Regional Play-offs, and National Championships, each team shall have on its bench a substitute goalkeeper who shall at all times be fully dressed and equipped to play.

When the substitute goalkeeper enters the game he will take his position without delay and no warm-up will be permitted.

f. Except when both goalkeepers are incapacitated, no player on the playing roster in that game shall be permitted to wear the equipment of the goalkeeper. If a team's goalkeeper(s) is unavailable to continue a team must immediately appoint a temporary goalkeeper (See Terminology) or place an additional skater on the ice with none of the goalkeeper's privileges.

4. CHANGE OF PLAYERS

a. Players may be changed at any time from the players' bench, provided that the player or players leaving the ice shall always be at the players' bench and out of the play before any change is made.

(Note) If, in the course of making a substitution, either the player entering or leaving the game deliberately plays the puck with the stick, skates or hands or checks or makes any physical contact with an opposing player while the retiring player is actually on the ice, then the infraction of "too many players on the ice" will be called.

If, in the course of a substitution, either the player entering the play or the player retiring is struck by the puck accidentally, the play will not be stopped and no penalty will be called.

b. A goalkeeper may be changed for another player at any time under conditions set out in this section.

(Note) When a goalkeeper leaves his goal area and proceeds to his players' bench for the purpose of substituting another player, the substitution made is not legal if there is premature departure of the substitute from the bench (before the goalkeeper is within ten feet of the bench).

c. If there are less than two minutes remaining in either regulation time or in the last permitted overtime and a minor or bench minor penalty is imposed for deliberate illegal substitution (too many players on the ice or leaving the penalty bench too soon), a penalty shot/optional bench minor shall be awarded against the offending team in lieu of the minor or bench minor penalty.

d. A player serving a penalty on the penalty bench, who is to be changed after the penalty has been served, must proceed at once by way of the ice and be at his own players' bench before any change can be made.

5. INJURED PLAYERS

a. When a player, other than a goalkeeper, is injured or compelled to leave the ice during a game, he may retire from the game and be replaced by a substitute, but play must continue without the teams leaving the ice.

b. If a goalkeeper sustains an injury or becomes ill he must be ready to resume play immediately or be replaced by a substitute goalkeeper and NO additional time shall be allowed by the Referee for the purpose of enabling the injured or ill goalkeeper to resume his position.

c. The substitute goalkeeper shall be subject to the regular rules governing goalkeepers and shall be entitled to the same privileges.

d. If a penalized player has been injured he may proceed to the dressing room without the necessity of taking a seat on the penalty bench. If the injured player receives a minor penalty the penalized team shall immediately put a substitute player on the penalty bench who shall serve the penalty without change. If the injured player receives a major penalty, the penalized team shall place a substitute on the penalty bench.

e. When a player is injured so that he cannot continue play or go to his bench, the play shall not be stopped until the injured player's team has secured possession of the puck; if the player's team is in possession of the puck at the time of injury, play shall be stopped immediately, unless his team is in a scoring position.

(Note) In the case where it is obvious that a player has sustained a serious injury the Referee and/or Linesman may stop the play immediately.

f. A player other than a goalkeeper, whose injury appears serious enough to warrant the stoppage of play, may not participate further in the game until the completion of the ensuing face-off.

E. OFFICIALS

1. REFEREE SYSTEM

The official method of refereeing AHAUS hockey games is with a Referee and two Linesmen. However, Districts or Regions are authorized to use two Referees for games under their jurisdiction.

2. REFEREE

a. The REFEREE shall have general supervision of the game and shall have full control of all game officials and players during the game, including stoppages; and in case of any dispute, his decision shall be final.

b. The Referee shall, before starting a game, see that the appointed Game Timekeeper, Penalty Timekeeper, Official Scorer and Goal Judges are in their respective places and satisfy himself that the timing and signaling equipment is in order.

c. The Referee shall announce to the Official Scorer or Penalty Timekeeper all goals and assists legally scored as well as penalties, and for what infractions such penalties are imposed. He shall report the name or number of the goal scorer and any players entitled to assists.

3. LINESMAN

The duties of the LINESMAN are to determine any infractions of the rules concerning off-side play at the blue lines, or center line, or any violation of the "Icing the Puck" rule.

4. GOAL JUDGE

a. There shall be one GOAL JUDGE at each goal.

b. Goal Judges shall be stationed behind the goals, during the progress of play, in properly screened cages, so that there can be no interference with their activities; and they shall not change goals during the game.

c. In the event of a goal being claimed, the Goal Judge of that goal shall decide whether or not the puck has passed between the goal posts, under the crossbar and entirely over the goal line. His decision is simply "goal" or "no goal".

5. PENALTY TIMEKEEPER

a. The PENALTY TIMEKEEPER shall keep record of all penalties imposed by the officials including the names of the players penalized, the infractions penalized, the duration of each penalty and the time at which each penalty was imposed. He shall report in the Penalty Record each penalty shot awarded, the name of the player taking the shot and the result of the shot.

b. The Penalty Timekeeper shall check and ensure that the time served by all penalized players is correct.

6. OFFICIAL SCORER

a. Before the start of the game, the OFFICIAL SCORER shall obtain from the Manager or Coach of both teams a list of all eligible players and the starting lineup of each team.

The Official Scorer shall secure the names of the Captain and Designated Alternate from the Manager or Coach at the time the lineups are collected and will so indicate by placing the letter "C" or "A" opposite their names on the score sheet.

b. The Official Scorer shall keep a record of the goals scored, the scorers, and players to whom assists have been credited, and shall indicate those players on the lists who have actually taken part in the game.

7. GAME TIMEKEEPER

The Game Timekeeper is responsible for monitoring the actual playing time and signaling the beginning and end of each period.

F. PENALTIES

1. PENALTIES

Penalties shall be actual playing time and shall be divided into the following classes:

(1) Minor Penalties

(2) Bench Minor Penalties

(3) Major Penalties

(4) Misconduct Penalties

(5) Match Penalties

(6) Penalty Shot

Where coincident penalties are imposed on players or both teams the penalized players of the visiting team shall take their positions on the penalty bench first in the place designated for visiting players, or where there is no special designation, then on the bench farthest from the gate.

2. MINOR PENALTIES

a. For a "MINOR PENALTY", any player, other than a goalkeeper, shall be ruled off the ice for two minutes during which time no substitute shall be permitted.

b. For a "BENCH MINOR" penalty one player of the team against which the penalty is imposed shall be ruled off the ice for a period of two minutes, during which time no substitute shall be permitted. Any non-penalized player except a goalkeeper of the team may be designated to serve the penalty by the Manager or Coach through the playing Captain and such player shall take his place on the penalty bench promptly and serve the penalty as if it was a minor penalty imposed on that player.

c. If the opposing team scores a goal while a team is shorthanded by one or more minor or bench minor penalties, the shorthanded team shall be permitted to immediately replace on the ice the first player whose penalty caused his team to be shorthanded.

(Note) "Shorthanded" means that the team must be below the numerical strength of its opponents on the ice at the time the goal is scored.

d. When a player receives a major penalty and a minor penalty at the same time the major penalty shall be served first by the penalized player.

e. A number of violations for which a minor penalty or a bench minor penalty (and in some instances additional penalties) may be imposed are:

(1) Unsportsmanlike conduct:

Challenging or disputing the rulings of any officials

Creating a disturbance

Shooting puck after whistle has blown

Delaying game by deliberately throwing or shooting puck outside playing area; deliberately displacing goal post; uses of obscene, profane or abusive language in vicinity of players' bench

Interfering in any way with a game official

Interference with play from the players' bench

Making physical contact with opponent after the whistle has blown

Abuse of officials

Not immediately following directions of officials following a penalty

Banging on boards with stick or other instruments

Throwing anything into the playing area

(2) Excessive violence:

Violent board-checking

Running, jumping into, or charging an opponent

Cross checking (See Terminology)

Unnecessary roughness

(Note) In Boys Squirt and below, and in all Girls classifications, body-checking is prohibited and shall be penalized.

Use of forearm or hands to check an opponent above the opponent's shoulders

(3) Injury or attempts to injure:

Slashing (See Terminology) or attempts to slash an opponent

Butt-ending or attempts to butt-end an opponent

(4) Altercations:

Retaliation with a blow after having been struck

Leaving players' bench or penalty bench during an altercation

(5) Obstructions:

Body checking or charging the goalkeeper while he is within his goal crease or privileged area

Use of elbow or knee in such a manner as to in any way foul an opponent

Holding opponent with hands or stick or in any other way impeding (or attempting to impede) his progress

Use of stick, foot, arm, knee or hand in such a manner as to cause his opponent to trip or fall

Leaving feet and making contact with any part of body causing opponent to trip or fall

Defending player, other than goalkeeper, falling on puck, holding or gathering puck into body or hands when the puck is within the goal crease

Goalkeeper deliberately falling on or gathering puck into his body when he is entirely outside the goal crease or outside his privileged area

Impeding the progress of an opponent who is not in possession of the puck or deliberately knocking a stick out of an opponent's hand or preventing an opponent from regaining possession of his stick or other equipment

Interfering with or impeding the movements of the goalkeeper by actual physical contact while he is in his goal crease unless the puck is already in the crease

(6) Technical violations:

Use of stick not conforming to rules

Leaving players' bench or penalty bench

Throwing stick in direction of puck

(7) Delaying game:

Failing to maintain proper position for face-off

Deliberately holding the puck against the boards, goal, or ice for the purpose of delaying the game.

Not having correct number of players on the ice

Persisting in having players off-side to delay game

3. MAJOR PENALTIES

a. For the first "MAJOR PENALTY" in any one game, the offender, except the goalkeeper, shall be ruled off the ice for five minutes, during which time no substitute shall be permitted.

b. For the second major penalty in the same game, to the same player or goalkeeper, that player shall be assessed a game misconduct penalty in addition to the major penalty and shall be suspended for the next two games of that team.

c. A number of violations for which a major penalty (and in some instances additional penalties) may be imposed are

(1) Injuring an opponent by cross checking or by hooking

(2) Injuring an opponent as result of foul committed by using elbow or knee

(3) Initiating fisticuffs

(4) Involved in fisticuffs off the playing surface before, during or after the game

(5) Grabbing or holding the face mask of an opponent

(6) Injuring an opponent by slashing

(Note) Any swinging of stick at opponent (whether in or out of range) without striking or a wild swing at puck with the object of intimidating an opponent is penalized as slashing.

4. MISCONDUCT PENALTIES

a. A "MISCONDUCT" penalty involves the removal of a player, other than a goalkeeper, from the game for a period of ten minutes but another player is permitted to immediately replace a player so removed. A player whose misconduct penalty has expired shall remain in the penalty bench until the next stoppage of play.

When a player receives a minor or a major penalty and a misconduct penalty at the same time, the penalized team shall immediately put an additional player on the penalty bench and he shall serve the minor or major penalty without change.

b. A "GAME MISCONDUCT" penalty involves the suspension of a player or Team Official for the balance of the game, but another player is permitted to immediately replace a player so removed.

c. A "GROSS MISCONDUCT" penalty involves the suspension of a player or Team Official for the balance of the game but another player is permitted to immediately replace a player so removed.

A player or Team Official incurring a gross misconduct penalty shall be suspended from participating in any further games until the case has been dealt with by the proper authorities.

d. A number of violations for which misconduct penalties (and in some instances additional penalties) may be imposed are:

(1) Abuse of officials

(2) Further dispute by same player following penalty

(3) Using obscene, profane or abusive language anywhere in the rink

(4) Intentionally knocking or shooting the puck out of reach of an official who is retrieving it

(5) Deliberately throwing a puck or any equipment out of playing area

(6) Entering Referee's Crease while Referee is consulting with other game officials

(7) Touching or holding any game official in any fashion

(8) Attempting to continue a fight after being ordered to stop

(9) Intentionally banging on the boards, protective glass, or goal with stick or other instrument

(10) Spearing or attempting to spear an opponent (attempt to spear shall include spearing gestures regardless of whether contact was made)

(11) Persisting in any course of conduct for which he has previously been assessed a misconduct penalty

(12) Persisting in using threatening or abusive language or gestures designed to incite an opponent into a penalty

(13) First to intervene in an altercation that is in progress

(14) A major penalty for fisticuffs will automatically also be assessed a game misconduct penalty

(15) Deliberately injure or attempt to injure a game official or team official

(16) Behaving in any manner which makes a travesty of, interferes with, or is detrimental to the conducting of the game

5. MATCH PENALTIES

a. A "MATCH" penalty involves the suspension of a player for the balance of the game, and the offender shall be ordered to the dressing room immediately. A substitute player is permitted to replace the penalized player after five minutes playing time has elapsed.

b. A number of violations for which a match penalty (and in some instances additional penalties) may be imposed are

(1) Attempts to injure an opponent

(2) Deliberately injuring an opponent in any manner (Note: No substitute will be permitted to replace the penalized player until 10 minutes actual playing time has elapsed)

(3) Kicking or attempting to kick another player (Note: Whether or not an injury occurs the Referee, at his discretion, may impose a 10-minute penalty)

6. PENALTY SHOT

a. Any infraction of the rules which calls for a "Penalty Shot" shall be taken as follows:

The Referee will place the puck on the center face-off spot and the player taking the shot will, on the instruction of the Referee, play the puck from there and shall attempt to score on the goalkeeper. The player taking the shot may carry the puck in any part of the Neutral Zone or his own Defending Zone but once the puck has crossed the attacking blue line it must be kept in motion towards the opponent's goal line and once it is shot the play shall be considered complete. No goal can be scored on a rebound of any kind and any time the puck crosses the goal line the shot shall be considered complete.

Only a player designated as a goalkeeper, substitute goalkeeper or temporary goalkeeper may defend against a penalty shot.

b. The goalkeeper must remain in his crease until the player taking the penalty shot has touched the puck and in the event of violation of this rule or any foul committed by a goalkeeper the Referee shall allow the shot to be taken and if the shot fails he shall permit the penalty shot to be taken again.

The goalkeeper may attempt to stop the shot in any manner except by throwing his stick or any object, in which case a goal shall be awarded.

c. While the penalty shot is being taken, players of both sides shall withdraw to the sides of the rink and beyond the center red line.

d. If a goal is scored from a penalty shot, the puck shall be faced at center ice in the usual way. If a goal is not scored, the puck shall be faced at either of the end face-off spots in the zone in which the penalty shot has been tried.

e. A number of violations for which a penalty shot may be assessed are:

(1) A defending player, except the goalkeeper, falling on the puck or holding the puck or gathering the puck into the body or hands when the puck is within the goal crease.

(2) Interference with an attacking player who is in possession and no opposition between him and the goalkeeper by a player who has illegally entered the game. If the goalkeeper has been removed under these circumstances and the player is interfered with or fouled from behind, being prevented from having a clear shot at the open goal, a goal shall be awarded.

(3) Throwing stick or any other object at the puck in his Defending Zone and goal is not scored (a goal shall be awarded if the player had a chance to score on an open goal).

7. GOALKEEPER'S PENALTIES

a. A goalkeeper shall not be sent to the penalty bench for an offense which incurs a minor, major or misconduct penalty, but instead any of these penalties shall be served by another member of his team who was on the ice when the offense was committed, such player to be designated by the Manager or Coach of the offending team through the Captain and such substitute shall not be changed.

b. Should a goalkeeper incur a game misconduct penalty, his place then will be taken by a member of his own team, or by a substitute goalkeeper who is available, and such player will be allowed the goalkeeper's full equipment. He shall also be suspended for the next game of that team.

c. Should a goalkeeper incur a match penalty, his place will be taken by a member of his own team, or by a substitute goalkeeper who is available, and such player will be allowed the goalkeeper's equipment. However, any additional penalties as specifically called for by the individual rules covering match penalties will apply, and the offending team shall be penalized accordingly; such additional penalty to be served by another member of the team on the ice at the time the offense was committed.

d. A minor penalty shall be imposed on a goalkeeper who leaves the immediate vicinity of his crease during an altercation.

e. If a goalkeeper deliberately participates in the play in any manner when he is beyond the center red line, a minor penalty shall be imposed upon him.

8. DELAYED PENALTIES

a. If a third player of any team shall be penalized while two players of the same team are serving penalties, the penalty time of the third player shall not commence until the penalty time of one of the two players already penalized shall have elapsed. Nevertheless, the third player penalized must at once proceed to the penalty bench but may be replaced by a substitute until such time as the penalty time of the penalized player shall commence.

b. When any team shall have three players serving penalties at the same time and because of the delayed penalty rule a substitute for the third offender is on the ice, none of the three penalized players on the penalty bench may return to the ice until play has been stopped. When play has been stopped, the player whose full penalty has expired may return to the play.

c. In the case of delayed penalties, the Referee shall instruct the Penalty Timekeeper that penalized players whose penalties have expired shall only be allowed to return to the ice when there is a stoppage of play.

9. CALLING OF PENALTIES

a. Should an infraction of the rules be committed by a player of the team in possession of the puck, the Referee shall immediately stop play and assess the penalty(s) to the deserving player(s).

The resulting face-off shall be made at the place where the play was stopped unless the stoppage occurs in the Attacking Zone of the player penalized in which case the face-off shall be made at the nearest face-off spot in the Neutral Zone.

b. Should an infraction of the rules be committed by a player of a team NOT in possession of the puck, the Referee shall signify the calling of a penalty by raising his arm and upon completion of the play by the team in possession will immediately stop play and assess the penalty to the deserving player.

The resulting face-off shall be made at the place where the play was stopped, unless during the period of a delayed whistle due to a foul by a player of the team NOT in possession, the team in possession ices the puck, shoots the puck from its defensive zone so that it goes out of bounds or is unplayable; then the face-off following the stoppage shall take place in the Neutral Zone near the defending blue line of the team shooting the puck.

c. If the Referee signals an additional minor penalty(s) against a team that is already short-handed because of one or more minor or bench minor penalties, and a goal is scored by the non-offending team before the whistle is blown, the goal shall be allowed, the delayed penalty(s) shall be assessed, and the minor penalty already being served which caused the team to be shorthanded shall terminate automatically.

d. Should the same offending player commit other fouls on the same play, either before or after the Referee has blown his whistle, the offending player shall serve such penalties consecutively.

10. SUPPLEMENTARY DISCIPLINE

a. In addition to the suspensions imposed under these rules, the proper disciplinary authority may, at the conclusion of the game, at its discretion, investigate any incident that occurs in connection with any game and may assess additional suspensions for any offense committed before, during the course of a game, or any aftermath thereof by a player or Team Official whether or not such offense has been penalized by the Referee.

b. Suspensions imposed during an AHAUS State, District, or Regional Play-Off, or National Championship, must be served during that same Play-Off or Championship.

GOVERNING BODY

Amateur Hockey Association of the United States, 2997 Broadmoor Valley Road, Colorado Springs, CO 80906

The Amateur Hockey Association of the United States (AHAUS), established in 1937, is the national governing body for ice hockey. A nonprofit organization, the AHAUS is committed to building a well-organized youth sports program for those interested in playing amateur hockey. Its goals are to educate players, parents, coaches, officials, and administrators with many varied programs. Each state has an "affiliate association," which is authorized by the AHAUS to govern and administer amateur hockey in its territory. The AHAUS is divided into 11 geographical registration districts. Each district has a Registrar to register teams, a Referee-In-Chief to register officials and conduct clinics, and a Coaching Program Director to administer an educational program. Four major councils—Youth, Junior, Senior, and International—plan and administer programs for their particular area of activity. The AHAUS provides an abundance of educational materials including guides, manuals, and films.

The AHAUS conducts National Championships in 12 age classifications. Hockey is a sport in the National Sports Festival, held in the summers of non-Olympic years, which is instrumental in the development and selection of Olympic team members. As the official and exclusive representative for the United States to the International Ice Hockey Federation (IIHF), the AHAUS has a responsibility to organize and enter teams in the World Championships each year.

MAGAZINES

American Hockey & Arena, AHAUS, 2997 Broadmoor Valley Road, Colorado Springs, CO 80906

• LAWN BOWLS •

LAWS OF THE GAME
REVISED TO 1984

(Reproduced by permission of the American Lawn Bowls Association*)

☐

LAW 1. DEFINITIONS OF GENERAL TERMS

(A) CONTROLLING BODY means the body having immediate control of the conditions under which a Match is played. The order shall be:

(1) The American Lawn Bowls Association Council.

(2) The Controlling A.L.B.A. Division Executive Board.

(3) The Controlling Tournament Committee.

(4) The Club on whose Green the Match is played.

(B) COMPETITION means the playing of one or more Matches (Law 5A) all under the supervision of one Controlling Body, generally a specific Committee, for the purpose of determining a winner in one or more events.

(C) CORRECT BIAS means that a Bowl in course is so delivered that it tends to return toward the center of the Rink from which it was delivered.

(D) HEAD means the Jack and such Bowls as have come to rest within the boundary of the Rink and which have not been declared Dead.

(E) MASTER BOWL means a Bowl which has been approved by the A.L.B.A. as having the minimum bias required as well as in all other respects complying with these Laws and is engraved with the words "Master Bowl." A replica of the Master Bowl shall be provided for the use of each official Licensed Tester.

(F) PACE OF THE GREEN means the length of time in seconds which it takes for a Bowl to travel from the point of delivery until the Bowl comes to rest at a point ninety (90) feet from the point of delivery. (A pace of not less than twelve seconds is recommended for National Open Tournaments and United States Championship play.)

LAW 2. THE PLAYING AREA

(A) GREEN

(1) The Green shall be a level square or rectangular area having an approved playing surface.

---

*See page 381 for additional information.

(2) Dimensions: To accommodate desired number of Rinks (Law 2D). When square, Max. 132 feet, Min. 120 feet.

(3) The top surface of the retaining wall of a Green on the inner side of the Ditch shall be level with the surface of the Green and shall be deemed for all purposes part of the Green.

(B) DITCH

(1) Each end of a Rink shall be bounded by an excavation called the Ditch.

(2) The ditch at the head end is called the Front Ditch, and that behind the mat the Rear Ditch.

(3) Depth: Maximum 8 inches, minimum 2 inches below the surface of the Green.

(4) The walls of the Ditch shall be perpendicular.

(C) BANK

(1) The continuation of the outer wall of the Ditch above the surface of the Green is called the Bank, and is the end boundary of the Rink.

(2) The top of the Bank shall be not less than 9 inches above the surface of the Green.

(3) The face of the Bank shall be constructed so that a Bowl or Jack striking it will not be damaged.

(4) The face of the Bank from the outer face of the Ditch may be either vertical or may slope inwards towards the Green so as to overhang the outer face of the Ditch no more than 2 inches at a point 9 inches above the surface of the Green. Where sod banks are used, they may slope outward from the green at an angle not to exceed 35 degrees from the perpendicular.

(D) RINK

(1) A rink is the basic playing surface used during play. It shall consist of all that portion of the Green and Front Ditch which is inside an imaginary straight line drawn between the centers of its boundary pegs or markers.

(2) Dimensions: Rectangular segment of Green: Length Max. 132 feet, Min. 120 feet; Width—Max. 19 feet, Min. 14 feet.

(3) The four corners of the Rink shall be marked by pegs or markings on the Bank clearly visible from the opposite end of the Rink.

(4) The prepared playing surface of the Green shall extend not less than 2 feet beyond the boundary pegs of a Rink.

(5) The center line of a Rink shall be indicated by a number plate located on the top of the Bank at each end of the Rink.

(6) Adjacent Rinks shall be numbered consecutively.

(7) Pegs, discs or other easily visible markings shall be fixed on the side Banks to indicate a clear distance of 81 feet from each Ditch on the line of play.

LAW 3. EQUIPMENT

(A) MAT

(1) Length: 24 inches.

(2) Width: 14 inches.

(3) Thickness: Maximum 1/4 inch.

Bowling Green

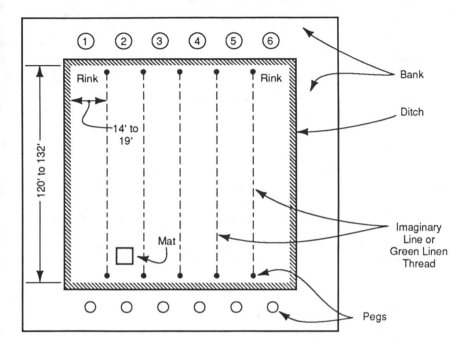

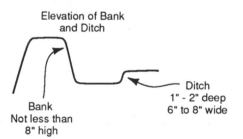

Elevation of Bank
and Ditch

Bank
Not less than
8" high

Ditch
1" - 2" deep
6" to 8" wide

(4) Material: Any suitable type.

(5) When groundsheets are in use, a Mat outline 24 inches long by 14 inches wide correctly and permanently marked at the rear center of a groundsheet shall be considered as the Mat to which all Laws shall apply.

(B) JACK

(1) Color: White.

(2) Diameter: Maximum 2-17/32 inches, Minimum 2-15/32 inches.

(3) Weight: Maximum 10 ounces, minimum 8 ounces.

(4) Material: Composition or Ceramic.

(5) Shape: Spherical.

(C) BOWL

(1) Bias: Not less than that of a Master Bowl.

(2) Diameter: Maximum 5 1/8 inches, Minimum 4 3/4 inches.

(3) Weight: Not more than 3 pounds, 8 ounces.

(4) Material: Wood, Rubber or Composition.

(5) Stamp: The imprint of a Licensed Tester's uncancelled A.L.B.A. or I.B.B. stamp shall be prima facie evidence of a bowl's conformity to these Laws.

(6) Duration of Stamp: Bowls carrying a valid, decipherable stamp shall be accepted for play at all A.L.B.A. sponsored tournaments.

(7) Reduced Validity of Stamp: Any division may require that Bowls used by members of that Division be retested at regular intervals and may adopt specific testing requirements which must be met for such approval provided the Division makes available to all members, at a reasonable charge, an approved bowls testing table operated by suitably trained personnel.

(8) Any Bowls acceptable for use in any Division may be used by a member of that Division when entered as a contestant in any sanctioned open tournament.

(D) MEASURING DEVICES

(1) A Standard Measure shall be any type of measure which accurately determines the result of an End.

(2) The following special measuring devices shall be provided by the Club on whose Green a Match is being played:

(a) A tape measure of not less than 75 feet.

(b) A length of cord sufficient to stretch between the boundary pegs at opposite ends of the Rink.

(c) A long flexible measure for use into the Ditch and for long measurements beyond the range of Standard Measures.

(d) Calipers for short, close measurements when the bowl and Jack being measured are on the same plane.

(e) One or more Standard Measures.

(E) FOOTWEAR

Players, Umpires, and Markers shall wear smooth-soled, heel-less footwear while playing on the Green or acting as Umpires or Markers.

(F) LAWS AND RULES

The Club upon whose Green a Match is being played shall have available for reference an up-to-date copy of these Laws and the Rules governing the Match.

LAW 4. THE TEAM

(A) TEAM

Any of the following combinations:

(1) FOUR or RINKS means a team of 4 players whose positions in order of play are called Lead, Scorer, Measurer, and Captain or Skip.

(2) TRIPLES means a team of 3 players whose position in order of play are called Lead, Scorer/Measurer and Captain or Skip.

(3) PAIRS or DOUBLES means a team of 2 players whose position in order of play are called Lead and Captain or Skip.

(B) SINGLES PLAYER

For the purposes of these Laws, a Singles player is the equivalent of a Team with each opponent responsible for the duties of the Lead, Scorer, Measurer and Captain or Skip. However, when a Marker (Law 15) is provided, the Marker usually takes over the duties of Scorer and Measurer for both opponents.

(C) DIRECTOR

The player who, for the time being is in charge of the Head on behalf of the Team.

(D) DUTIES OF TEAM MEMBERS

(1) CAPTAIN OR SKIP

(a) To act as Director except when playing.

(b) To decide, with his opponent, any dispute or to refer it to the Umpire.

(c) To sign both scorecards at the end of the Match.

(d) To act as Scorer in a Pairs Match.

(e) To have complete control of the Team and actions of Team members at all times.

(2) MEASURER

(a) To act as Director when his Captain is playing or absent.

(b) To advise his Captain of the result of each End.

(c) To direct his Captain only when so requested.

(d) To determine with his opponent the result of an End or to refer it to his Captain or Skip.

(e) To act as Scorer in a Triples Match.

(3) SCORER

(a) To enter the players' names on the scorecard.

(b) To record the score at each End and check the total with his opponent.

(c) To hand the scorecard, signed by both Captains, to the proper official at the end of the Match.

(d) To act as Measurer in a Triples Match.

(4) LEAD

(a) To place the mat as directed by the Captain.

(b) To deliver the Jack as directed by the Captain.

(c) To have the Jack aligned.

(d) To act as Measurer in a Pairs Match.

(5) DIRECTOR—In addition to his other duties as a Team member, the player acting as Director should:

(a) Prevent any disturbance of the head by an outside object or by a Dead bowl.

(b) Chalk his team's Touchers.

(c) Remove the chalk mark from an opponent's Bowl when it is not a Toucher.

(d) Have the Front Ditch guarded to prevent entry of a non-toucher Bowl whenever the Jack and/or one or more Toucher Bowls are in the Ditch.

(e) Have all Dead Bowls removed to the Bank at once.

(E) ELIGIBLE PLAYER

Eligibility of a player for Team membership in each case is determined by:

(1) The requirements set forth in these Laws.

(2) The Rules and ruling of the Controlling Body immediately responsible, as interpreted by their representative, provided such Rules and rulings do not conflict with these Laws.

(F) CONSTITUTED TEAM

(1) When the correct number of Eligible Players are assembled into a Team and each member of the Team has played his first Bowl, in turn, in a Match, the Team is considered "Constituted" and each member thereof is a "Constituted Team Member" for the remainder of the competition in which the Team is entered.

(2) After a Team is Constituted, no alterations in Team membership or order of play shall be permitted during the remainder of that Match except as required should a Substitute become necessary.

(3) A Constituted Team may change their playing positions between succeeding matches in the same competition, subject to the requirements of Law 4G8 should a Substitute become necessary.

(G) RULES GOVERNING SUBSTITUTION

(1) All Substitutes shall be specifically approved by the Controlling Body or their representative.

(2) Only one approved Substitute shall be permitted on any Team at any one time. If two Team members are absent or if an approved substitute is not available to replace a single absent Team member, the Match shall be forfeited.

(3) If, due to the conditions in Law 4G2 or for other reasons, a Team forfeits before the start of the first Match in a competition, any available members of the Team so forfeiting shall be considered as fully Eligible Players and may play as Substitutes in that competition.

(4) If an Eligible player, entered as a member of a Team in a competition, plans to transfer to another Team as a Substitute before play has started on the first game of the competition, he shall declare his intent to the controlling Body or their representative and have his transfer officially approved, otherwise he will normally be considered to be a Constituted member of the Team on which he was originally entered.

(5) All members of a Constituted Team shall be ineligible to act as Substitutes in the same competition even though the Team has been defeated and is no longer playing in that competition.

(6) If a Team is permitted a Substitute, the Substitute may be changed at any time during the Match or between succeeding Matches in the same competition, or he may continue the competition, if he remains Eligible. (See Law 4G1.)

(7) A Constituted member of a Team, for whom a Substitute was obtained, may, if still Eligible, join or rejoin the Team at any time in his correct position, at which time other Team members shall revert to their original positions.

(8) A substitute shall play in the second position in Fours and as Lead in Triples and Pairs. In the case of Triples and Fours, the Captain may arrange the positions of the rest of the Team as desired.

LAW 5. THE MATCH

(A) MATCH

A contest between two Singles players or Teams arranged to last until:

(1) A fixed number of shots has been scored.

(2) A fixed number of Ends has been played.

(3) A fixed period of time has elapsed. If an End has had at least one Bowl delivered at the time limit, then the End shall be continued, but not replayed if it becomes Dead.

(B) NUMBER OF BOWLS PLAYED

The number of Bowls used by each player shall be:

(1) Singles Match—4

(2) Pairs Match—4

(3) Triples Match—3

(4) Fours Match—2

(C) INSPECTION OF BOWLS

(1) The Umpire or his deputies shall inspect all Bowls before play commences.

(2) Any Bowl deemed by the Umpire as not complying with these Laws shall be disallowed. (See Law 3C.)

(D) DISALLOWED BOWLS

(1) While an Umpire may temporarily mark a disallowed Bowl to insure that it is not used in the remaining Matches of that competition, he shall NOT deface the Bowl or any markings on the Bowl in any manner.

(2) No player shall use or attempt to use a disallowed Bowl in any future Match unless the Bowl has been returned to and approved by an Official Bowls Tester after having been disallowed. When a disallowed Bowl is returned for testing, it shall be accompanied by a clear statement showing that it has been disallowed, the reasons given for disallowing and the name and address of the Controlling Body representative who made the decision.

(E) FORFEITED MATCH

A Match shall be forfeited to the opponents "for cause":

(1) When an ineligible player or a player who has been disqualified, in accordance with these laws, takes part in a Match.

(2) When an Umpire, upon request, has noted specific infractions of these laws and, after carefully warning the offending player or players, considers that the infractions are continuing and deliberate.

(3) If a player changes his Bowl(s) during a match unless such a change is specifically approved by the Controlling Body or its representative. Such approval shall not be given unless it is determined that at least one Bowl has been damaged during the Match sufficiently to affect play.

(4) If, prior to a Match, a player shall have practiced on the Rink assigned for the Match before starting time. Suspected infractions of this Law shall be referred to the Controlling Body and their decision shall be final.

(F) DELAYING PLAY

(1) No player shall delay the match by leaving the rink without the consent of his opponent.

(2) If such consent is granted, the maximum period of absence shall not exceed 10 minutes except in unusual cases, where a longer absence may be permitted by joint agreement of his opponent and a representative of the Controlling Body.

(3) Should the agreed upon absence period be exceeded and an approved Substitute is not available to complete the Team (see Law 4G), the opponent may request the Controlling Body to award him the Match.

(G) MATCH STOPPED

(1) If a Match is stopped "for cause" (inclement weather, darkness, etc.) either with the consent of or under orders from the Controlling Body, the resumed Match shall be continued with the scores and Ends played as they were when the Match was stopped.

(2) When a Match is stopped "for cause" with an End partially completed, that End shall be declared null and replayed later.

(H) LATE ARRIVAL

(1) The penalty for late arrival of a player at the posted location and time for any Match in a competition shall be specified and enforced by the Controlling Body, subject to the special conditions outlined in Law 5H2.

(2) If a player qualifies for more than one event in a competition and is instructed by the Controlling Body or its representative to play in a specific event, he shall not be penalized in any way because of his inability to appear at another event in the same competition for which he is also qualified but which has been assigned a conflicting starting time.

LAW 6. PLAY DURING AN END

(A) END

The playing of the Jack and of all Bowls of both opponents in the same direction on a Rink is called an End (see Law 7G2). Bowls which become or are declared "Dead" under those Laws are considered to have been played insofar as the End is concerned.

(1) Each End starts with delivering the Jack by the first player to play (Law 6H).

(2) Each End is completed when the score has been agreed upon by the opponents or decided by an Umpire (Law 11) or when the End becomes Dead (Law 6B).

(B) DEAD END

(1) An End is declared Dead whenever permitted or required by one of these Laws.

(2) If, after the Jack has been properly centered (Law 6H), action in the Head disturbs the Jack in a manner which causes it to come to rest beyond the boundaries of the Rink,

the End shall be declared Dead unless the Jack has been illegally disturbed and other of these Laws specifically permits the Jack to be replaced to its original position.

(3) A Dead End shall not be counted as an End played, even though all of the Bowls have been delivered, unless the specific, published conditions of the Match provide that it shall count.

(4) If a Dead End is not counted as an End play (Law 6B3), it shall be replayed in the same direction unless the opponents immediately agree to the contrary.

(C) ORDER OF PLAYING

The order of delivery shall alternate between the opponents with each Bowl played. Should a Bowl be delivered out of turn, apply Law 7J.

(D) STARTING AN END

(1) Prior to the commencement of play, the opponents shall toss and the winner shall have the right to decide who shall play first.

(2) Each succeeding End shall be started by the winner of the previous End at which a score was recorded.

(3) Succeeding Ends shall be played in opposite directions, subject to Law 6B4.

(4) The first to play at an End that results in a Dead End shall again play first at the next End. (For Tie Ends see Law 11F.)

(E) PLACING THE MAT

(1) The Mat shall always be centered on the center line of the Rink with the 24 inch length lengthwise of the Rink.

(2) The front end of the Mat (14 inches) which is closest to the Front Ditch is called the MAT LINE. All measurements from the Mat shall be made from the center of the Mat Line.

(3) At the first End of each Match, the Mat Line shall be 6 feet from Rear Ditch. Whenever ground sheets are in use, this Law shall apply to the first and all subsequent Ends.

(4) At all subsequent Ends, *including a tied or extra End*, subject to Law 6E3 as it relates to ground sheets, the Mat may be placed in any position along the center line of the Rink provided the Mat Line is not less than 6 feet from the Rear Ditch or less than 81 feet from the Front Ditch.

(5) The Mat shall be placed by the first to play for that End and shall not be moved during the remainder of the End except as permitted or required in Laws 6F and 6H.

(F) DISPLACEMENT OF MAT

(1) If the mat be displaced during the progress of an End, it shall be replaced as nearly as is practicable in the same position by the next to play.

(2) If the Mat be out of alignment with the center line of the rink, it may be straightened at any time during the End.

(G) REMOVAL OF MAT

The responsibility for the removal of the Mat at the conclusion of an End shall rest with the opponent of the last player.

(H) DELIVERING THE JACK

(1) The player whose turn it is to deliver the Jack shall take possession of the Rink. If any willful attempt be made by an opponent to divert his attention, the Jack may be delivered again.

(2) The Jack shall be delivered from the Mat by the first to play and it shall not be interfered with before it comes to rest while remaining within the boundary of the Rink. However, the Jack shall be returned and be delivered by the opponent who may relocate the Mat subject to Laws 6E3 and 6E4 if it comes to rest as follows:

(a) Wholly outside the Rink boundary.

(b) In the Front Ditch.

(c) With no portion at least 75 feet from the Mat Line before or after being aligned.

(3) After one improper delivery of the Jack by each player in any End, the Jack shall be placed 6 feet from the opposite Ditch and the Mat placed at the option of the first to play provided a 75 foot or more length of the Jack is maintained. The right of the player first delivering the Jack in that End to play the first Bowl shall not be affected.

(4) Any player on the Rink may challenge the length a Jack has been delivered before the first Bowl is delivered, subject in case of a Team, to the approval of his Captain.

(5) The Jack shall be placed on the center line of the Rink and as nearly as is practicable equal with the distance it was delivered, except that, when delivered to less than 6 feet from the Front Ditch, the Jack shall be placed 6 feet from the Front Ditch. If the length of the Jack is challenged before it is aligned, and all or a portion of the Jack is at least 75 feet from the Mat Line, it shall be aligned by swinging on an arc so that it remains the same distance from the center of the Mat Line.

(6) If the Jack is interfered with before coming to rest within the boundary of the Rink:

(a) By an opposing player or by the Marker, it shall be delivered again by the same player.

(b) By a teammate of the Lead delivering the Jack, it shall be delivered again by his opponent who may relocate the mat subject to Laws 6E3 and 6E4.

(J) DIRECTING A PLAYER

(1) The Director may assist a player by placing an object above the green for guidance but such object shall be withdrawn from the position indicated before the Bowl is delivered. At no time shall either the Jack or a Bowl be touched while directing a player.

(2) Each Director, while in possession of the Rink (Law 7A), may stand anywhere in the Head while directing his player but shall retire to a position behind the Jack as soon as the Bowl is delivered.

(K) LOCATION OF PLAYERS ON RINK

(1) All players at the Mat end of the Rink shall be not less than 5 feet behind the Mat Line, except the player in possession of the Rink.

(2) All players at the Head end of the Rink shall be not less than 6 feet behind the Jack, except the Director who is in possession of the Rink.

(3) All players at the Head end of the Rink on both Teams shall remain motionless from the time an opponent takes his stance on the Mat until the Bowl is delivered.

LAW 7. PLAYING THE BOWL

(A) POSSESSION OF THE RINK

The player whose next turn it is to deliver his Bowl and his Director shall have possession of the Rink immediately after the previously delivered Bowl has come to rest except for time allowed to mark a Toucher. The player in possession of the Rink shall be allowed to receive instructions and to deliver his Bowl without interference. Any conversation between the Head end and Mat end of the Rink by opponents during this period shall be deemed interference.

(B) DELIVERY

A Bowl is delivered when it leaves the hand of the player on the Mat while performing his normal delivery motion, provided it passes the Mat Line. A player may carry his Bowl beyond the Mat Line without penalty.

(C) BOWL IN COURSE

A Bowl from the time of its delivery until it comes completely to rest is referred to as a Bowl in course.

(D) FOOT FAULTING

A player shall take his stance on the Mat with one or both feet entirely within the confines of the Mat and, at the time of delivering his Bowl, one foot must be on or over the confines of the Mat. Any delivery not in accordance with this Law shall constitute Foot Faulting, in which case:

(1) If an Umpire is of the opinion that a player is foot faulting, he shall warn the player so offending. The Umpire may, after having given a warning, have the Bowl stopped and declared Dead.

(2) If such a Dead Bowl is not stopped and, while in course, touches any portion of the Head, the opponent shall immediately remove the Dead Bowl and decide whether the Head shall be reset, shall remain as disturbed or whether the End shall be Dead.

(E) PLAYING ANOTHER'S BOWL

If a player, in his turn, delivers a Bowl other than his own, it shall be allowed to complete its course. When the incorrect Bowl comes to rest it shall be replaced with a correct Bowl by the opponent or by the Marker, if so requested.

(F) PLAYING PREMATURELY

If a Bowl is delivered while the preceding Bowl is still in course, the first mentioned Bowl may be stopped by the opposing Director, or by the Marker on direction from the opponent, returned to the Mat and replayed. However, if it is not stopped, it shall be deemed to be a correctly delivered Bowl.

(G) OMITTING TO PLAY

(1) If the result of an End has been agreed upon or the head has been touched in the agreed process of scoring the End, then a player who has omitted to play a Bowl shall forfeit the right to play it.

(2) The Skip last to play in any End may decline to play his last Bowl by so stating to the opposing Skip and requesting that the Head be counted.

(H) DECLINING TO PLAY PROMPTLY

If a player, on request of his opponent, declines to deliver his Bowl within two minutes of the coming to rest of his opponent's previously delivered Bowl, he shall forfeit the right to play that Bowl during that End, and the Match shall proceed as though he had accepted his turn.

(J) PLAYING OUT OF TURN

(1) If a player delivers a Bowl out of his turn, it should be stopped by either Director or by the Marker (on the request of either player) and be replayed in its correct order.

(2) If it is not stopped, and comes to rest without having touched any portion of the Head, it shall be returned to the Mat and replayed in its correct order.

(3) If it is not stopped and, while in course, touches any portion of the Head, the opponent shall immediately decide whether the Head shall remain as disturbed, the opponent shall play two successive Bowls to restore the correct sequence.

(4) If, before the mistake is noticed, a Bowl has been delivered in the reversed order, the opponent shall then play two successive Bowls to restore the correct sequence.

(5) A player who has neglected to play a Bowl in the proper sequence shall forfeit the right to play such Bowl if a Bowl has been played by each Team or the End has been counted before such mistake was discovered.

(K) BOWL IN COURSE OUTSIDE THE RINK

(1) A Bowl in course, delivered on the WRONG BIAS, which leaves the Rink over a side boundary shall be Dead regardless of where it comes to rest.

(2) A Bowl in course, delivered on the CORRECT BIAS, which leaves the Rink over a side boundary shall:

(a) Continue in play, if it comes to rest on the Rink from which it was delivered without touching another object while in course.

(b) Be Dead, if it comes to rest wholly outside of the Rink from which it was delivered without touching another object while in course.

(c) Be replayable, if it collides with any person or object or be stopped to avoid such a collision while in course outside of the Rink from which it was delivered.

(L) BOWLS COLLIDING ON RINK

(1) If a Bowl or Jack delivered from or driven from an adjacent Rink collides with a Bowl in course on the Rink in play, the Bowl in course shall be returned to the Mat and replayed.

(M) DEAD BOWL

(1) A Bowl becomes Dead whenever any of these Laws specify that such a condition exists. A Bowl also becomes Dead under the following conditions not covered elsewhere in these Laws:

(a) If a Bowl in course comes to rest with the entire Bowl less than 45 feet from the center of the Mat Line.

(b) If, not being a Toucher, it rebounds from the face of the Bank back onto the Green.

(c) If, not being a Toucher, it falls into the Front Ditch.

(2) Directors shall agree as to whether a given Bowl is Dead and such agreement is final. Team members shall not remove a Bowl until notified of the Director's agreement.

LAW 8. TOUCHERS

(A) TOUCHER

This term describes a Bowl which, while in course (Law 7C), touches the Jack or falls over and touches the Jack before the next Bowl has been delivered while the Jack is on the playing surface of the Rink. No Bowl can be accounted a Toucher by playing onto or coming in contact with the Jack while the Jack is in the Front Ditch.

(B) CHALKING

(1) A Toucher is distinguished by a chalk mark placed on the Bowl, either by the Marker or the Director of the Team to which it belongs, before the next delivered Bowl has come to rest.

(2) If not so marked it shall not be regarded as a Toucher except that, if either Director feels that chalking a Toucher is likely to move the Bowl or alter the Head, such a Bowl may be "indicated a Toucher" and play continued on that basis. The same ruling also applies to removing an improper chalk mark from a non-toucher Bowl, which may be "indicated a non-toucher".

(C) REMOVAL OF CHALK MARK

If the chalk mark is not removed from a Bowl before it is delivered at the next End, such mark shall be removed by the opposing Director or the Marker as soon as the Bowl comes to rest except as specified in Law 8B2.

(D) MOVED WHEN CHALKING OR REMOVING CHALK MARK

(1) If a Toucher be moved when being chalked or when removing an improper chalk mark by the Marker, it shall be immediately replaced by him.

(2) If a Toucher be moved when being chalked or when removing an improper chalk mark by a Director, it shall be immediately replaced by his opposing Director.

(E) REBOUNDING FROM THE FACE OF THE BANK

If a Toucher rebounds from the face of the Bank back onto or touching the boundary of the Rink, it shall remain as part of the Head and continue in play. If the Head is disturbed by a rebounding Toucher, apply Law 10B3.

(F) IN THE DITCH

If a Toucher comes to rest in the Front Ditch and any portion is within or touching the boundary of the Rink, it shall remain as part of the Head and continue in play. If a ditched Jack and/or Toucher is disturbed by another Toucher entering the Front Ditch, apply Law 10B3. The position of a Toucher in the Ditch may be marked by placing a suitable object on the bank above it, never on the surface of the Rink.

(G) MOVEMENT OF TOUCHERS

A Toucher in play in the Ditch may be moved by the impact of a Jack in play or of another Toucher in play, and also by the impact of a non-toucher which remains in play after the impact and any movement of the Toucher by such incidents shall be valid. However, should the non-toucher enter the ditch after the impact, it shall be dead, and the Toucher shall be deemed to have been displaced by a Dead Bowl and the provisions of Law 10B shall apply.

LAW 9. JACK DISTURBED

(A) MOVED OR DITCHED JACK (Also see Law 6B2)

(1) If, by the effect of the play, the Jack is moved to a different location on the Rink or into the Front Ditch and any portion of the Jack remains within or touching the boundary of the Rink, it shall remain as part of the Head and continue in play.

(2) A Jack moved by a Bowl in play into the Front Ditch within the boundaries of the Rink shall be deemed to be Live. It may be moved by the impact of a Toucher in play and also by the impact of a non-toucher which remains in play after the impact; any movements of the Jack by such incidents shall be valid. However, should the non-toucher enter the Ditch after impact, it shall be Dead and the Jack shall be deemed to have been Displaced by a Dead Bowl and the provisions of Law 10B4 shall apply.

(3) The position of a ditched Jack still in play may be marked by placing any suitable object on the Bank above it, never on the playing surface of the Rink.

(B) REBOUNDING JACK

(1) If, by the effect of play, the Jack rebounds from the face of the Bank back onto or touching the boundary of the Rink, it shall remain as part of the Head and continue in play.

(2) If, by the effect of play, the Jack rebounds towards the Mat and all the Jack comes to rest less than 66 feet from the Mat Line, the end shall be Dead.

(C) JACK IMBEDDED IN THE BANK

(1) If, by the effect of play, the Jack becomes embedded in the face of the bank wholly above the level of the Green, the End shall be Dead.

(2) If, by the effect of play, the Jack becomes embedded in the face of the bank or the wall of the ditch so that any portion of the Jack is below the level of the Green and within the boundary of the Rink, it shall remain as part of the Head and continue in play.

(D) DAMAGED JACK

If, by the effect of play or other cause, the Jack is damaged sufficiently to affect the result of an End, the End shall be Dead.

LAW 10. HEAD DISTURBED

(A) DISTURBANCE BY A PLAYER

(1) If a Jack or Bowl is diverted from course or disturbed by any one of the players while it is in motion or at rest on the Green or in the Front Ditch, the opposing Captain shall have the option to:

(a) Have the disturbed Jack or Bowl replaced as nearly as practicable to its original position.

(b) Permit the Jack or Bowl to remain in the disturbed position and continue play.

(c) Declare a disturbed Bowl Dead, remove from Green and continue play.

(d) Declare the End Dead.

(2) The Chalking of or the removing of chalk mark on a Bowl shall NOT constitute a disturbance thereof (see Laws 8B2 and 8D).

(3) The lifting of a Bowl which is at rest and is likely to be disturbed by a Bowl in course on its correct bias from an adjoining Rink shall NOT be deemed to be deliberate disturbance.

(B) DISTURBANCE BY PLAY

(1) If the Head towards which the Bowl is delivered is disturbed by the Bowl in course, the Head shall remain as so disturbed except where Law 10B2 applies.

(2) If the Head is disturbed by a Bowl in course which has been deflected by outside influence (Law 7L), apply Law 10C2.

(3) If the Head is disturbed by the Jack or a Toucher Bowl entering the Front Ditch or rebounding from the face of the bank back onto the Green, the Head shall remain as so disturbed.

(4) If the Head is disturbed by a non-toucher Bowl entering the Front Ditch or rebounding from the face of the Bank back onto the Green the Jack and/or Bowl(s) so disturbed shall be immediately replaced by the opposing Director or Singles player, whose decision is final. In a Singles Match, the Marker may assist the opposing player in replacing the disturbed Jack and/or Bowl(s) but the final decision rests with the player.

(C) OUTSIDE DISTURBANCE

(1) If the Umpire or Marker, when measuring to determine the result of an End, moves either the Jack or Bowl being measured, he shall declare that particular measurement a tie.

(2) If any part of the Head is moved or interfered with by any neutral person or by any object from outside the Rink, the Jack or Bowl(s) shall be replaced by agreement between the opponents, or, failing an agreement, the End shall be Dead.

LAW 11. SCORING

(A) MEASURING ON COMPLETION OF AN END (See Law 16A)

Measurements shall be made to the nearest point of each object preferably using an approved measuring device which must be securely locked while measuring. Special conditions are:

(1) When measuring between a Jack or Bowl in the Front Ditch and a Jack or Bowl on the surface of the Green, a flexible tape or line must be used. Such measurements must be made directly over the edge of the Rink to the nearest points on the Jack and Bowl being measured.

(2) Calipers and other rigid measuring devices are permissible only when the Jack and all Bowls being measured are resting on the same plane.

(B) PREMATURE MEASURING

No measuring shall be allowed until the End has been completed. If a player deliberately measures by placing any object or part of his body between the Jack and the Bowl before the completion of an End, the opposing Captain shall have the option to:

(1) Continue play without penalty.

(2) Declare Dead all such improperly measured Bowls which belong to the player or Team making the measurement, remove such Dead Bowls from the Rink and continue play.

(3) Declare the End Dead.

(C) OBSTRUCTED MEASURE

If the determination as to whether any Bowl shall score as a shot is hindered or prevented by reason of its resting on another Bowl, the Bowl to be measured shall be suitably secured in its position and the obstructing Bowl removed.

(D) DETERMINING THE RESULT

(1) When the End is completed, or deemed to be completed, the opponents shall agree on the result, and such agreement shall be final.

(2) Neither the Jack nor Bowls shall be moved until each Director has agreed to the number of Shots, except as provided for by Law 11C. Either Director may request a delay of 30 seconds before counting the Head.

(3) If the opponents are unable to agree, the result shall be determined by the Umpire or, if requested by both opponents, by the Marker.

(E) SCORING

The player or Team having the nearest Bowl to the Jack shall score one shot and an additional one shot for every other Bowl that is nearer to the Jack than the nearest Bowl of the opponent.

(F) TIE ENDS

If the nearest Bowls of the opponents be equidistant from the Jack, no score shall be recorded for that End, but the End shall be counted as an End played in a Match of a fixed number of Ends, unless the specific, published conditions of the Match provide that it shall not count as an End played. In the event of a Tie End, the two Skips involved shall toss a coin to determine control of the Jack on the next End.

(G) TIE MATCH SCORES

(1) If the total number of shots scored by each opponent be equal at the conclusion of a Match, the Match shall result in a Tie, unless the conditions of the contest require a winner.

(2) If a winner is required, an additional End shall be played. The opponents shall toss a coin and the winner of the toss shall have the option to decide who shall play first.

LAW 12. CHALLENGED BOWL

(A) GROUNDS FOR

The challenge shall be based on the grounds that the Bowl does not comply with one or more of the requirements specified in Law 3C.

(B) PROCEDURE

(1) A challenge or any intimation thereof shall NOT be lodged with any opposing player during the progress of a Match. Penalty: Opponent may claim the Match.

(2) A challenge may be lodged directly with the Controlling Body for the competition, or through a neutral Umpire, at any time during a Match.

(3) If a challenge is lodged, it shall be made not later than ten minutes after the completion of the final End of the Match in which the Bowl was used.

(4) Once a challenge is lodged it cannot be withdrawn.

(C) DECISION OF THE UMPIRE

The Controlling Body for the competition shall immediately refer a challenge to a neutral Umpire who shall investigate and render a decision before the start of the next regularly scheduled Match. The decision of the Umpire shall be final for that competition.

(D) TESTING FOR BIAS

When the challenge is based on a claim of inadequate bias on a Bowl, the Judge (Law 12C) may resort to Green testing of the challenged Bowl versus a new or recently tested Bowl of the same or next adjacent size carrying an approved A.L.B.A. or I.B.B. stamp. Such testing shall be carried out by or in the presence of the Judge over a distance of not less than 75 feet on the most uniformly drawing green available.

LAW 13. APPEALS

(A) INITIAL APPEAL

The decision of an Umpire based on an interpretation of these Laws, or given upon a set of circumstances not herein provided for, may be called in question by an appeal to the Controlling Body of the competition, whose decision shall be final and binding with respect to the appeal submitted.

(B) REFERRAL TO RULES COMMITTEE

If the appellant requests, the Controlling Body involved shall submit the case up through the Division to the Rules Committee of the A.L.B.A. Council for a final decision which shall be binding in all future competitions but will not affect the results of the initial decision made under Law 13A.

LAW 14. DISQUALIFICATION OF A PLAYER

(A) GROUNDS FOR

The Controlling Body shall have the authority to disqualify a player from that competition if he is found guilty under any of the following conditions:

(1) If, upon challenge, the Umpire finds that Bowls used in a Match have been altered since last tested by an official Bowls tester.

(2) If a previously challenged Bowl which was ruled illegal is used in a Match, subject to the conditions in Law 5D2.

(3) If an unstamped Bowl or Bowl having only cancelled stamps is used in a Match without having been presented to the Controlling Body for approval before the start of competition.

(B) PENALTIES

(1) Under Law 14A—If a disqualified player takes part in a Match, that Match shall be forfeited to the opponent, provided that the only Match to be forfeited shall be the one for which a challenge was first entered or the Match in progress when a representative of the Controlling Body first became aware of the illegality.

(C) PLEA FOR CLEMENCY

(1) If a player has been disqualified under Laws 14A1, 14A2 or 14A3 only and wishes to enter another Match in the competition as a member of his original Team using approved Bowls, he may enter a plea for clemency with the Controlling Body. If the Controlling Body rules that extenuating circumstances justify granting clemency, they shall specify what Matches may be entered and what Bowls shall be used in these Matches.

(2) The decision of the Controlling Body hearing a plea for clemency under this Law shall be final for that competition.

LAW 15. DUTIES OF OFFICIALS

(A) MARKER

A Marker for a Singles Match shall be appointed by the Controlling Body and he shall carry out the following duties:

(1) He shall, before play commences, insure that the Bowls have been inspected for an I.B.B. or A.L.B.A. imprint, including a date stamp where required by the Controlling Body, and shall check to insure the Rink width is as specified for the event being played.

(2) He shall insure that the Jack is not less than 75 feet from the Mat Line before or after it has been centered.

(3) He shall center the Jack and shall place a full length Jack 6 feet from the Front Ditch.

(4) He shall stand at one side of the Rink and to the rear of the Jack.

(5) He shall answer "yes" or "no" a player's inquiry as to whether a Bowl is Jack high. If requested, he shall indicate the distance of any Bowl from the Jack or from any other Bowl. Also, if requested, he shall indicate which Bowl he thinks is Shot and/or the relative position of any other Bowl.

(6) He shall chalk all Touchers and mark the position of the Jack and any Touchers in the Front Ditch. He shall remove all "non-toucher" Bowls from the Front Ditch and place all Dead Bowls on the Bank.

(7) He shall NOT move or permit to be moved either the Jack or Bowls until each player has agreed to the number of shots.

(8) When requested by both players, he shall carefully measure all doubtful Shots (See Rule 7, above). If unable to come to a decision satisfactory to both players, he shall call an Umpire.

(9) He shall enter the score at each End and shall keep the players informed as to the state of the Match. When the Match is finished, he shall see that the scorecard is signed by the players and disposed of in accordance with the rules of the competition.

(B) UMPIRE

Each official Umpire shall be appointed by the Controlling Body for a specific period or competition and, during his appointment, shall act as a representative of the Controlling Body. These appointments shall be made from the roster of the National Umpires Club if members are available. Official Umpires shall have the authority to carry out the following duties:

(1) He shall, before play commences, examine all Bowls for an I.B.B. or A.L.B.A. imprint, including a date stamp where required by the Controlling Body, and shall check to insure that all Rink widths are as specified for each event to be played.

(2) He shall measure any shot or shots in dispute using a measure approved by these Laws. His decision shall be final.

(3) He shall decide all questions as to the distance of the Mat from the Back Ditch and of the Jack from the Mat Line.

(4) He shall decide as to whether or not the Jack and/or Bowls are in play.

(5) He shall enforce these Laws of the Game.

LAW 16. MISCELLANEOUS ITEMS

(A) LABELS ATTACHED TO BOWLS

The Controlling Body for any Match may furnish and require the contestants to use adhesive labels (preferably of very thin plastic material) on their Bowls for the purpose of improving identification of sides during the Match. When so required, such labels shall be considered to be a part of the Bowl for all requirements of these Laws, including measurements to determine shot.

(B) PLAYERS WITH DISABILITIES

A player suffering a disability shall be permitted to use a support and/or artificial limb when delivering his Bowl or walking on the Green. Such support shall be suitably shod with rubber, and may be placed on or adjacent to the Mat.

(C) ONLOOKERS

(1) Persons not engaged in a Match shall not be allowed on the Green or on the surrounding area within 3 feet of the face of the Bank, and shall preserve an attitude of strict neutrality.

(2) Any onlooker attempting to assist a player shall be asked by the Umpire to leave the vicinity.

GOVERNING BODY

American Lawn Bowls Association, 445 Surfview Drive, Pacific Palisades, CA 90272

The American Lawn Bowls Association (A.L.B.A.) is a member of the International Bowling Board (I.B.B.) and is the controlling body for the game of lawn bowls in the USA and its territories. The game is known around the world as Bowls, Lawn Bowls, or Bowling on the Green. The general object of the Association is to promote, foster, advance, and control the game through framing and revising the rules, assisting in the establishment of clubs, disseminating information regarding court construction and maintenance, publishing an informative periodical, authorizing national tournaments, and controlling international competition.

MAGAZINES

Bowls, William H. Todd, Circulation Manager, 26733 Winsome Circle, Newhall, CA 91321

Green, Lawn Bowls Canada, 333 River Rd., Vanier, ON K1L 8H9 Canada

• ORIENTEERING •

ABRIDGMENT OF RULES
FOR ORIENTEERING COMPETITION

(Reproduced by permission of the United States Orienteering Federation*)

□

Note: The rules for competitive orienteering included here are an abridgment of the USOF official rules. The complete rules and regulations required for USOF sanctioned meets may be obtained through the Federation.

A. GENERAL PROVISIONS

1. APPLICATION OF THE RULES

1.1 Competitions described as United States Orienteering Federation events and other orienteering events held in conjunction with USOF events shall be organized in accordance with these Rules.

1.2 These Rules shall be binding on all organizers, competitors, team officials and other persons connected with the organization or in contact with the competitors. The USOF Sanctioning Committee shall supervise the application of the Rules. The USOF Rules Committee shall interpret the Rules and any questions should be so addressed.

1.3 Event organizers, competitors and team officials must know these Rules and the Event Instructions. Ignorance of the Rules will not be accepted as a valid excuse for any infringement.

1.6 These Rules are supplemental to the "International Orienteering Federation (IOF) Rules for International Orienteering Events," and take precedence over them except:

a. IOF sanctioned meets hosted in the United States.

b. International meets when so agreed by the participating nations.

2. DEFINITION AND BASIC CHARACTERISTICS OF ORIENTEERING

2.1 Orienteering is a sport in which the competitor independently aided by map and compass must visit in a prescribed order a number of features marked in the terrain (by control flags) and on the map. In a regular orienteering competition the task is to run this course in the shortest possible time.

2.2 In orienteering both the running and navigating skill of the competitor shall be tested, but in such a way that the navigating skill is decisive.

2.3 Orienteering competitions shall be held primarily in forested terrain, which, ideally, is unfamiliar to the competitors.

---

*See page 400 for additional information.

2.4 It shall be possible to solve the orienteering problems with the map, aided by the control descriptions and a compass.

2.5 Sporting fairness shall be the primary consideration when organizing an event and when interpreting these Rules.

3. CLASSIFICATION OF USOF EVENTS

3.1 The term "USOF Orienteering Meet" shall refer only to meets sanctioned by the USOF.

3.2 Categories of events

3.2.1. The term "Orienteering 'A' meet" shall refer only to meets that are sanctioned by the USOF Sanctioning Committee and which comply with the provisions of these Rules.

3.2.1.1. When the term "A" Meet is used throughout these Rules and on Event Invitations without a qualifier, i.e., long "O," relay, night meet, etc. or when a meet is referred to as a regular "A" meet the Form shall be a day event (3.3.1.) and the type shall be an Individual Event (3.4.1.). If it is a regular multi-day event (3.4.3.) the number of days must be specified and the results shall be determined by adding each competitor's total time for each and every day. The winner in each class will be the individual with the lowest combined time. Any variations must be prominently placed on the Event Invitation.

3.2.2. Orienteering "B" meets shall refer only to the meets where the Meet Director and a Club Officer certify that the meet will comply with the provisions for "B" meets in Section E below.

3.2.3. Orienteering "C" meets are local meets, which are not bound by these Rules.

3.2.4. The Term "United States Championship Orienteering "A" Meet" shall refer only to meets that are sanctioned by the USOF Sanctioning Committee as "Orienteering "A" Meets" and are designated a U.S. Championship event by the USOF Board of Directors in one of the following categories:

a. United States Orienteering Championships

b. United States Intercollegiate Orienteering Championships

c. United States Long Orienteering Championships

d. United States Relay Orienteering Championships

3.3. Forms of events

3.3.1. Day event: The first start shall be at least 1 hour after sunrise, and the last at least the time limit plus 1 hour before sunset.

3.3.2. Night events: The course of a night event shall be run entirely in the dark. The first shall be at least 1 hour after sunset, and the last at least the time limit plus one hour before sunrise.

3.3.3. Combined day and night event: One course is run in the light, and another in darkness, or (only if a mass start is used) a course is begun in the dark and finished in daylight or vice versa.

3.4. Types of events

3.4.1. Individual: The participants compete separately and the results are based on each individual's performance. (Except as in 4.1.5. non-competitive)

3.4.2. Individual race with team assessment: The participants compete separately and the team result is the sum of the individual results (times or place number or points based thereon) of all the runners in a team. There must be individual results as well.

3.4.3. Multi-day event: In a multi-day event a competitor's results (times or place numbers or points based thereon) from at least half of the competition days shall be combined.

If the sum of the times for every competition day will not be used the organizer shall describe in the Invitation the precise procedures which will be used for the event.

3.4.4. Relay: A relay team has two or more runners. Each runner completes his/her course as in an individual event.

3.4.5. Group team event: The team has two or more runners, who together or partly separate complete the event.

4. CLASSES

4.1. Division by sex and age

4.1.1. The competitors are divided into the following classes by sex (M for male, and F for female), and age of December 31 of the current year. Eligibility (and ineligibility) for classes occurs at the beginning of the calendar year in which the competitor reaches a new age group.

4.1.2. The following classes are the minimum which a sanctioned "A" meet must offer, except as amended in Section 4.1.2. (Elite Meets) below. (Note: A description of the courses and course colors follows in section 24.4.)

4.1.2.1 USOF "A" Orienteering Elite Meets shall offer only championship or "A" category classes.

4.1.2.2. An Elite Meet may have as few or as many "A" classes as the Meet Director decides, but there shall be classes for both men and women.

4.1.2.3. Persons who might or might not be eligible for the stated classes may run on the course of their choice without competing in a class. They shall be started so as not to conflict with the competitive orienteers.

4.1.3. In USOF sanctioned meets this nomenclature shall be used to describe the classes and courses.

4.1.4. No competitor shall be entered in more than one class at a time.

4.1.4.1. Competitors may participate on a non-competitive course after finishing with their competitive course.

4.1.5. In an individual event, groups (more than one individual) shall be permitted only in non-competitive categories.

4.2. Division by other grounds

4.2.1. The age divisions are divided into classes by course difficulty and the competitor's skill. The last letter in the class notations are "A," most difficult, and "B," intermediate.

4.2.4. Classes for different age groups may be combined if they are on the same color course, and there are less than five pre-entries.

4.2.8. Non-competitive classes are classes that:

a. Are announced on the meet invitations as such.

b. Are open to any age individuals or groups.

c. The competition times are not posted.

d. Competitive awards are not given. (This does not prohibit awards for the successful completion of the course.)

4.2.9. The Map Hiker class is a non-competitive class for any age individuals or groups on a White or similar course.

4.3. Deviations from the division into classes by age

4.3.1. The dashes extend the age group beyond one year. If a dash is before an age then it means that anyone up to and including the age is eligible for the class. If the dash is between two ages then anyone between and including the ages is eligible, and if the dash is after the age, then anyone that age and older is eligible. The younger categories like

F-19-20 have two dashes and numbers. This indicates that the class is designed for 19-20 year olds, but that anyone younger than 19 who wishes to compete in it may do so.

4.4.1. Age is an automatic determinate in moving from one class to another. A competitor shall not compete in an age group in which he/she is not eligible as in Section 4.1.1. above.

USOF COURSE CLASS STRUCTURE

	COURSES					
AGE AS OF DEC. 31	WHITE	YELLOW	ORANGE	GREEN	RED	BLUE
-12	M-12A F-12A					
-13-14		M-13-14A F-13-14A				
-15-16			M-15-16A F-15-16A			
-17-18			M-17-18B F-17-18A	M-17-18A		
-19-20			M-19-20B F-19-20B	F-19-20A	M-19-20A	
-21-				F-21-B	M-21-B F-21-A	M-21-A
35-			F 35-B	M 35-B F 35-A	M 35-A	
40-				M 40-B F 40-A	M 40-A	
45-			F 45-B	M 45-B F 45-A	M 45-A	
50-			M 50-B	M 50-A F 50-A		
55-				M 55-A F 55-A		
60-				M 60-A		
OPEN	MAP HIKER	M OPEN F OPEN	M OPEN F OPEN	M OPEN		

4.4.2. Any age competitor may enter an Open class.

4.5. Championship Classes:

4.5.1. U.S. Champions shall be declared in all "A" classes represented at U.S. Orienteering Championships.

4.5.2. Intercollegiate U.S. Champions will be declared in the following classes at the U.S. Intercollegiate Championships.

a. Intercollegiate Senior Men's Champion (Blue course, M-21-A)

b. Intercollegiate Senior Women's Champion (Red course, F-21-A)

c. Intercollegiate Junior Men's Champion (Red course, M-19-20A and M-21-B)

d. Intercollegiate Junior Women's Champion (Green course, F-19-20A and F-21-B)

5. ELIGIBILITY

(*Note*: Section 5, deleted here, enumerates eligibility requirements for national championship meets including junior and senior intercollegiate championships.)

6. DUTIES OF THE MEET DIRECTOR

6.1. The Meet Director of a USOF "A" meet shall observe these Rules, and insure that all the officials and assistants know and abide by these Rules.

6.2. The Meet Director shall obtain all necessary permission from landowners, and forestry, state, and other pertinent officials.

6.3. To promote an acceptance of, and favorable attitude toward orienteering the Meet Director should aim for a good relationship with other users of the forest and forest officials.

7. APPLICATIONS TO HOLD USOF "A" ORIENTEERING MEETS

(*Note*: Section 7, deleted here, lists the stipulations for application and approval of USOF sanctioned meets.)

8. USOF ORIENTEERING EVENT CALENDAR

(*Note*: Section 8, deleted here, describes the event calendar which lists sanctioned meets for the following year.)

9. COMPETITION LEADERS

(*Note*: Section 9, deleted here, deals with the responsibilities of the hosting club in the appointment of officials.)

10. INVITATION

(*Note*: Section 10, deleted here, enumerates the requirements for meet invitations.)

11. ENTRIES

(*Note*: Section 11, deleted here, lists the requirements for entry forms.)

12. TRAINING

12.1. The organizer should when possible offer training areas for the competitors. The terrain, map, course and control descriptions should be as similar as possible to the competition area.

12.2. When maps are available it should be possible to order in advance maps of terrain similar to that of the event. If and only if the competition map has previously been used at a public meet it shall be made available for inspection and when possible advance purchase. (22.9. forbids the distribution of a new unused map prior to the event.)

12.3. The organizer may charge a reasonable fee for maps and training.

13. DRAW AND STARTING LIST

13.2. On U.S. Championship events, the starting order shall be designed such that top ranked competitors and those with the same interests (same college or club) start as far apart as possible.

13.5. The starting list of registered competitors shall be officially declared at least 15 hours before the first start time.

13.6. For individual starts the runners in each class start one by one. It is strongly recommended that they start at intervals of at least two minutes. Ideally all starting intervals on a course are equal.

14. EVENT INFORMATION

14.1. All information shall be supplied in writing in at least English.

14.2. In extenuating circumstances information may be supplied orally.

14.3. Event Information shall be given to the competitor in a timely manner, ideally upon arrival and check in at the event.

14.4. The Event Information shall contain details regarding:

a. Event officials.

b. Descriptions of the terrain, unusual map characteristics, control flag and marking device arrangement, refreshment controls, elements of risk, out of bounds areas, and dangerous areas.

c. Map scale, vertical interval.

d. Course lengths for the individual classes, leg lengths of the relay legs, and climb on the optimum route.

e. Safety bearings, instructions when one is lost.

f. Starting times.

g. Deviations from, and additions to the "Map symbols for International Orienteering Maps" of the IOF, overprinting that is not standard (not PMS Purple, or standard IOF symbols), and the colors of the streamers marking out of bounds and dangerous areas when not conforming to 23.9.

h. Dressing and washing facilities, toilets, first aid, housing and camping areas.

i. Travel time and distance between check in, parking, and the start location.

j. Time limit when other than three hours, finish closing time.

k. Location for results posting and the awards ceremony when not immediately at the finish, time of the awards ceremony, and the number of awards per class when different than three.

l. The procedure at the start and finish for distributing and collecting the maps, control descriptions, and control cards.

15. AWARDS

(*Note*: Section 15, deleted here, describes the USOF award policies.)

16. RESULTS AT AN EVENT

16.1. Within one hour of the close of the finish, provisional results shall be displayed in the vicinity of the finish or the announced location.

17. JURY

17.1. The Meet Director shall appoint a Jury of at least three people. One member must represent the organizers. The others should be from widely separated clubs, or foreign delegations as appropriate.

17.3. The duties of the Jury shall be to deal with infringements of the Rules and any other questions arising out of the competition.

17.5. Competitors for whom the preponderance of evidence shows that they have broken these Rules may be disqualified from the event by the Jury. (35. Fairness, 37. Conduct, 17.3.1. Appeal)

18. PROTESTS

(*Note*: Section 18, deleted here, deals with protest procedures.)

19. SECRECY

19.1. All those who are involved with the organizing of the event shall maintain the strictest secrecy regarding aspects of the venue, terrain and courses not officially publicized.

19.2. Team officials and spectators shall not influence the competition, and shall remain in the areas which are assigned to them.

19.3. The organizers shall put up notices and rope off areas or otherwise inform people to ensure that unauthorized people stay out of areas where they would interfere with the competition.

19.4. When the venue is placed on the USOF Event Calendar and publicly announced the area is closed to orienteering competitions, and training—either individually or in groups for those wishing to retain competition eligibility for the event.

20. REPORTS AND FEES TO USOF

(*Note*: Section 20, deleted here, deals with required reports and fees remitted to USOF for sanctioned meets.)

B. TECHNICAL REGULATIONS

21. COMPETITION AREA

21.1. The area shall be complex and varied enough to suit the requirements of the event. It shall offer adequate possibilities for setting the technically difficult as well as the novice courses represented at the event.

22. MAPS

22.1. "Drawing Specifications for International Orienteering Maps" shall be used. Deviant or additional symbols necessary because of local conditions are permissible, but they shall be published beforehand in the Event Information. (Section 14.4)

22.2. Maps for "A" meets shall conform to IOF map standards and shall be up-to-date in the opinion of the Map Committee.

22.4. The scale shall be 1:15,000 and the vertical interval 5m. A different scale or vertical interval may be used if permission is obtained from the USOF Map Committee.

22.5. Terrain conditions which are not visible on the map and map corrections or amendments that may influence the outcome of the event must be clearly communicated in writing to the competitors. Overprinting on the competition map is preferred, but simple corrections may be drawn on a sample map when displaying of the competition map is permitted. (22.9)

22.6. The map shall be printed on good quality and if possible waterproof paper. (80-120 g/sq.m)

22.7. When the quality of the map paper requires the use of a protective case this shall be provided by the organizer.

22.9. When the map for the event has not been used in competition it shall not be displayed, sold, or distributed prior to the event. (This does not prohibit display of sections of the map where the competition will not be held.)

22.9.1. When the competition map has been previously used in a competition or otherwise distributed to potential competitors it shall be posted in the competition center and shall be sold at a reasonable and customary price prior to and at the event. (12.2)

23. COMPETITION COURSES

23.1. The "Principles of Course Setting" published by the IOF shall be followed for setting the courses.

23.2. The characteristics of the courses—in particular the map reading and route choice requirements—shall be appropriate to the classes for which they are intended. The navigating ability and concentration of the competitors shall be tested.

23.2.1. The progression from White through Orange is one of increased length and technical difficulty; the technical difficulty of Green through Blue is to be equivalent, with only the length increasing.

23.3. The order of visiting the control locations shall be prescribed by the organizer and observed by the competitors. If visiting the control locations out of order is likely to be advantageous then the organizer shall check that they are visited in the proper order.

23.5. Any marked route or crossings included on a course shall be indicated on the map.

23.6. In connection with the course setting, the limitations mentioned in section 38.2 (areas to avoid) shall be especially observed.

23.7. When setting courses the following must be observed: a. There shall not be two control flags within 100m of each other on similar features.

23.8. Control locations shall be selected in such a manner that hazardous terrain is avoided.

23.9. Hazardous terrain features shall be marked with blue and yellow streamers (28.2) and competitors shall be routed around them by the use of orange and white streamers (28.1), or the use of special short legs if necessary. When it is not possible to use these colors different colored streamers may be used if the change is prominently included in the Event Information.

23.10. When legs cross deep water or dangerous gorges special control locations shall be located at safe crossing points. Courses shall be set so that swimming will not be necessary nor tempting as a route choice.

24. COURSE LENGTH AND CLIMB

24.1. When designing courses, besides factors affecting class such as sex, age, and the competitor's skill level, the difficulty of the terrain, the time of year, the possible effect of other competitions and the time of day must also be accounted for.

24.2. The course length shall be measured without regard for elevation change as the shortest possible route a runner could fairly take, i.e., around lakes and impassable and out-of-bounds areas as well as following any compulsory marked routes.

24.3. The closest possible approximation to the expected winning times given below shall be decisive in determining course lengths for these events.

24.4. The proper winning times and the approximate lengths for the various courses at multi-day events are:

Course	Optimum Winner's Time	Approximate Course Length
White	30 minutes	3 km or less
Yellow	40 minutes	3.5 - 4.5 km
Orange	50 minutes	4 - 5 km
Green	50 minutes	4 - 5 km
Red	60 minutes	5 - 7 km
Blue	60 - 80 minutes	7 - 12 km

24.5. Long "O" (long distance orienteering), for which the times and distances of the Green, Red, and Blue courses will be increased, may be organized.

24.5.1. The winning times of the following courses in Long "O" may be increased to these lengths.

Green	75 min.
Red	90-100 min.
Blue	120-135 min.

24.5.2. In addition to the normal refreshment controls, at approximately 2/3 of the way through the long "O" courses there shall be a manned aid station with clearly marked food, 2% sugar water, pure water, first aid supplies and evacuation facilities.

24.5.3. The time limit for Long "O" shall be 5 hours.

24.5.4. In addition to the procedures described in these USOF Rules the following "individual relay" format may be used for Long "O": There is a mass start for each class or the whole group. The courses consist of several loops through the start/finish area where a map exchange is set up. The competitors will run the loops in various sequences, but all competitors in the same class will run the same loops.

24.5.5. Mass starts are permitted at long "O" meets.

24.6. The winning time in relay events shall be about 20% shorter and in single-day individual events 20% longer than the specified winning times. (24.4)

24.7. Courses shall be so set that the total climb of the optimum route does not exceed 4% of the length of the optimum route.

25. COURSE MARKINGS ON THE MAP

25.1. The competition map shall be marked as follows:

a. The start or map issue point by an equilateral triangle 7mm per side.

b. The control features by circles 5-6mm in diameter.

c. The finish by two concentric circles 5 and 7mm in diameter.

d. Marked routes by dashed lines.

25.2. The center of any triangle or circle indicates the precise position of the feature, but it shall not be actually marked.

25.3. The control circles shall be numbered showing the required sequence (23.3). The numerals shall be printed with their tops oriented exactly toward North. The numbers shall be placed in such a way that they do not conceal important map features.

25.4. Except where there is a marked route, the triangle and circles shall be joined in numerical order by straight lines.

25.5. The control circles and their connection lines shall be interrupted or drawn thinner when they obscure important objects on the map.

25.6. Transparent waterproof PMS purple color shall be used for printing the courses.

25.6.1. When the courses are drawn and PMS purple is not available, then red may be used but this alteration must be included in the Meet Information.

25.6.1.1. Competitors who cannot properly see the red color used to mark their maps may have their courses redrawn in a color they can properly see by making their request to a registration official.

26. ADDITIONAL OVERPRINTING

26.1. Areas which are out of bounds because they are dangerous or for any other reason shall be surrounded by a line and cross hatched obliquely.

26.2. Forbidden routes (i.e., expressways) shall be overprinted with a chain of crosses.

26.3. Important crossing points or passages relevant to the course (i.e., a log over a stream, or a tunnel under a road) shall be indicated with reversed parentheses. '') (''

26.4. The color of additional overprinting shall be the same as that of the courses. (25.6)

27. CONTROL DESCRIPTIONS

27.1. The control description serves to clarify the picture of the control site as it appears on the map. It shall describe the control site accurately, but as briefly as possible.

27.2. The control descriptions shall correspond to the "Control Descriptions" of the IOF on all but the White and Yellow courses.

27.2.1. On the White and Yellow courses English words approximating the meanings and order of the IOF symbols shall be used. When possible they should be adjacent to the IOF symbols.

28. MARKINGS USED ON THE GROUND

28.1. Required routes (i.e., those that runners must follow) shall be marked by the use of both orange and white ribbons, except in night "O" where white shall be used. When not practical to use these colors others may be substituted provided the information is included in the Event Information.

28.2. Danger areas shall be marked with both blue and yellow ribbons. When those colors are not possible others may be substituted if the change is included in the Event Information.

29. CONTROL FLAGS AND EQUIPMENT

29.1. Every control feature shall be marked by a control flag.

29.2. The control flag consists of three squares arranged in triangular form. Each square is 30cm x 30cm and is divided diagonally, one half being white and the other half orange (ideally PMS 165). At least two of the white triangles shall be adjacent to the upper edge of the control flag.

29.2.1. In night "O" a light or reflecting device may be included with or may substitute for the control flag.

29.2.2. To allow the orderly phasing out of older red and white control flags they may be used when necessary until December 31, 1989.

29.3. The control flag shall be hung at the feature indicated on the map. The actual position shall be in accordance with the control description.

29.4. The control flag shall be visible by the competitor upon reaching the feature.

29.5. Ideally control flags shall be situated so that the presence or absence of competitors does not make them easier or more difficult to locate.

29.6. The physical arrangement of the control flag and marking devices shall be the same for all the control locations on a course. To minimize competitors waiting for a marker there shall be an ample number of marking devices at each control location.

29.7. Each control location shall be identified by a number (not less than 31), or up to two letters which will constitute the control code. The same code shall be included on the control description sheet. The figures shall be black, approximately 6-10cm high with a line width of approximately 6-10mm. Ideally the competitor will only be able to read the codes when immediately at the control flag.

29.7.1. There shall not be other confusing figures or marks on the control flag.

29.7.2. It is recommended that numbers or letters which can improperly be read upside down not be used (i.e., 86—98). If, however, they are used they shall have a line drawn beneath them to indicate the proper stance.

29.8. Any control location may be manned. When so manned, the number of each of the competitors visiting the control location and the time at which they punched may be recorded. The control official shall neither disturb nor retain any competitor nor supply any information as to time, position nor anything else. The official shall remain quiet, wear inconspicuous clothes and shall not help competitors approaching the control flag. These regulations apply also to all persons at media, communication, refreshment controls and spectator points.

29.9. On each course refreshments consisting of at least potable water shall be provided at least every 2.5 km. Refreshments shall be provided at the start and finish and at appropriate control flags and indicated on the description sheets as such. There shall be enough water for each competitor to have .25 liters (8 oz.) or more at each refreshment stop. In the event of hot weather additional refreshment locations are recommended. These additional locations need not be at control locations but must be indicated on the map.

29.9.1. Water must be offered in a sanitary manner such that it is not practical for competitors to drink from "community drinking jugs."

30. CONTROL CARD

30.1. The control card may be attached to or printed on the map (31.2). Alternately the control card may be handed out separately at least 10 minutes before a competitor's start time.

30.2. Competitors shall be responsible for marking the control cards provided by the organizers clearly and in the correct box at each control location using the marking equipment provided, and handing in their control card at the finish. When competitors mark an incorrect box they should continue the correct sequence beginning in the next box. Disqualifications will be decided on by the Jury. (33.4 & 33.5 disqualifications)

30.3. The organizer may have the control card checked and/or marked by officials at the control locations.

30.4. When competitors lose their control cards, or a control mark is missing, or it is established that the control locations were not visited in the prescribed order the competitor shall be disqualified unless an alternate proof is provided and accepted by the Jury.

30.5. The control card when not printed on the map shall not exceed 10cm x 21cm and shall be made of an adequately sturdy material.

31. START

31.2. The competitors take their competition maps at the starting time at the start location or after the starting time at the map issue point.

31.3. The start location and the map issue point shall be situated in such a way that before the starting time a competitor will not be able to see which route the previous runner takes. When possible the start location shall also be situated such that competitors arriving at the finish cannot communicate with those waiting to start.

31.4. The type of start for an individual event shall be either an individual or mass start. The use of a mass start shall be announced in the invitation and is to be used only when permitted elsewhere by these rules. (3.3.3, 31.6, 31.6.1)

31.6. The mass start shall be used when an event starts in the dark and ends in the daylight, or when an event starts in daylight and ends in twilight or darkness.

31.6.1. A mass start may be used in long "O" and relays.

31.8. If competitors are late for their start through their own fault they shall be started as soon as practically possible. The actual time of their start shall be noted on their map, or a start list at the start location. Their time will still be computed, however, from their original start time given in the official start list except as per (31.8.1).

31.8.1. At the discretion of the organizer late starters may have their actual start times substituted for their official start times when this can be done for all late starters within a class on the same day.

32. FINISH

32.1. The run-in to the finish shall be bounded by two suitable tapes or ropes and shall narrow on approaching the finish line. The finish at the finish line shall be approximately 3m wide, and shall be at right angles to the direction of the run-in.

32.3. After crossing the finish line the competitors shall hand in their control cards and when required by the organizer, their maps.

33. TIMING AND PLACING

33.1. The finishing time shall be measured at the finish line. The time shall be taken at the moment when the runner's chest crosses the finish line. Times will be truncated to full seconds, or hundredths of minutes. Times shall be given in minutes and seconds, or minutes and hundredths of minutes.

33.2. In the case of more than one competitor having the same running time, they shall be given the same finishing place, and the results should show the same place number for both. When practical they should be listed in the order in which they started.

33.3. In the relay the position of the team is determined by the last leg runner.

33.4. Competitors shall be disqualified for omitting a control mark, marking at an incorrect control location, or if it can be proved that they visited the control locations in the wrong order.

33.5. If the absence of a control mark is not the fault of the competitor (i.e., missing or broken punch) and the competitor states that he/she visited all the control locations in the proper sequence, in the absence of proof to the contrary the competitor will not be disqualified.

33.6. All competitors shall be given equal amounts of competition time to complete their courses. Unless a longer time is declared in the Meet Information the competition time shall be three hours for all events except Long "O." Without exception, in Long "O," the time limit shall be 5 hours.

33.7. Competitors completing a course in a time greater than the competition time will be recorded as overtime (OVT) and will not receive a time or place.

33.8. All competitors whether finished or not shall report to the finish by the announced closing time of the finish. (14.4.j Meet Information)

34. RELAY

(*Note*: Section 34, deleted here, deals with the particular rules for relay events.)

35. FAIRNESS

35.1. All persons who take part at an orienteering event (competitors, organizers, team managers and so on) shall demonstrate a high degree of fairness, a sporting attitude, a spirit of comradeship and honesty.

35.2. It is forbidden to obtain outside help or collaborate in running or navigation except in a non-competitive class.

35.3. A competitor shall not seek to obtain unfair advantage over fellow competitors, nor intentionally run with or behind other competitors during the event in order to profit from their skill.

35.4. Prior investigation of the competition area is forbidden.

35.5. Leaders of the event are obliged to bar entrants from competing (but not from participating in the event) when they are so well acquainted with the terrain that they would derive substantial advantage over others. In doubtful cases the matter is decided by the Jury.

35.6. A competitor wishing to retain eligibility shall not seek to obtain an unfair advantage by communicating with other competitors, team officials, event officials, journalists, spectators or others before or during the competition.

35.7. The competitor is obliged to show respect for other competitors, leaders, land owners or administrators, officials, journalists, spectators, and others as well as residents of the competition terrain and areas.

35.8. The use of drugs to obtain an advantage is forbidden. This does not prohibit the use of medically necessary drugs prescribed by a physician.

35.9. Competitors may be disqualified from current and future events as per section 17.5 and 17.6.

36. EQUIPMENT AND AIDS

36.1. So long as the particular conditions in the area (i.e., danger of infection) do not necessitate otherwise, choice of clothing shall be up to the individual. It is strongly recommended that the competitor's legs are completely covered. When particular clothing is required by the organizers it shall be announced by the Meet Invitation.

36.2. The organizers may require competitors to wear identifying numbers on a bib on the chest and/or the back. The competitor must not conceal any information on the bib. The bib shall not be larger than 20cm x 24cm. The numerals shall be at least 12cm high.

36.3. During the competition only a compass and the map provided by the organizer may be used for navigation.

36.3.1. Personal aids not used directly for navigation are permitted (e.g., magnifying glass, flashlight, cane, eyeglasses).

36.4. The use of any navigation aid other than a compass is prohibited (e.g., transport, electronic apparatus, radio, pedometer, altimeter).

37. CONDUCT DURING THE EVENT

37.1. The competitors take part at their own risk while traveling to the event, in the training event, and in the event itself.

37.2. The competitors shall move in the terrain as silently as possible and neither by shouting nor by sign give help or do harm to other competitors, nor intentionally draw their attention.

37.3. It is the duty of each competitor to help anyone who is injured.

37.4. Care will be taken when running along or crossing traffic routes.

37.5. Sections marked as required routes on the course must be followed by the competitor.

37.6. Once competitors cross the finish line their competition is over, and they shall not return to the competition area without permission from the organizer.

37.7. Competitors who do not finish (DNF) must report to the finish and return their control card and map. They shall in no way attempt to influence the competition or other competitors.

38. OUT OF BOUNDS AREA

38.1. It is forbidden to cause damage in the competition terrain. The competitors are solely responsible for their damage.

38.2. The competitor shall not enter the following areas except when specific permission is included in the Event Information:

a. Yards and gardens

b. Sown land and land with growing or standing crops

c. Limited access highways or fenced railways

d. Areas marked "out of bounds."

38.3. In consideration of nature conservation, the land owners and others, the crossing of fences and ditches, as well as passing across forest plantations, shall occur in such a way that no damage is done. Barriers and gates opened by the competitor shall be closed by same.

C. EVENT CONTROL AND US TEAMS

(*Note*: Division "C," deleted here, deals with the responsibilities of the meet organizers for USOF sanctioned meets, duties of officials, national ranking procedures, U.S. Orienteering team, and authorization for IOF competition.)

D. SPECIAL RULES FOR SKI-O

(*Note*: Division "D," deleted here, outlines the special rules for skiing orienteering events.)

E. SPECIAL RULES FOR USOF SANCTIONED "B" MEETS

1. APPLICATION OF THE RULES

1.1. Competitions described as "Club "B" Meets" where the club is chartered by USOF as a Regular or Associate Club shall be organized in accordance with these rules. It is only necessary to meet the provisions of this "B" meet Section, however, it is recommended that the complete set of "A" meet rules be used as a guideline, and followed where practical or needed.

4. CLASSES

4.1.2. Any division of classes may be used such that any competitor will be able to compete on the course of his/her choice. The minimum class structure shall be:

White Open, Yellow Open, Orange Open, Red Open

It is further recommended that the following be included:

Green Open, Blue Open

5. ELIGIBILITY

5.5. Anyone desiring to compete is eligible.

6. DUTIES OF THE MEET DIRECTOR

6.2. The club shall obtain all necessary permission from landowners, and forestry, state, and other pertinent officials.

7. APPLICATIONS TO HOLD USOF "B" ORIENTEERING MEETS

7.1. At the time the meet is first publicly announced, and at least two months prior to the meet the Meet Director together with a club official will send to the Sanctioning Committee a copy of the Event Invitation and a letter certifying that they understand the "B" meet rules and that the meet will conform to them.

10. INVITATION

10.1. An Invitation shall be published at least 2 months prior to the event in a way suitable for the event in question, and a copy will be sent to the USOF publications committee.

10.2. The Invitation shall contain the following information: a. Date, category, form and type of the event; b. Organizer, Mapper, and Course Setter; c. Classes; d. Courses and course lengths; e. Address and final date of entry; f. Fees; g. Location of the event, and time for arrival; h. Description of terrain and elements of risk, unique characteristics of the event; i. Map type and scale, and year of fieldchecking; j. First start, and type of start; k. Address and/or phone number where questions can be answered.

16. RESULTS AT AN EVENT

16.1. Results shall be posted in an announced place as soon as possible after the event.

22. MAPS

22.1. Maps will comply with IOF standards as far as possible.

22.1.1. A five color map, ideally conforming to IOF map standards, must be used.

22.4. Only scales between and including 1:5,000 and 1:20,000 may be used.

22.5. Corrections to the map in so much as they will significantly affect the competitors shall be posted.

24. COURSE LENGTH AND CLIMB

24.4. The proper winning times and the approximate course lengths for the various classes are:

Course	Winner's Time (Optimum)	Course Length (Approximate)
White	30 minutes	3 km or less
Yellow	40 minutes	3.5 - 4.5 km
Orange	50 minutes	4 - 5 km
Green	50 minutes	4 - 5 km
Red	60 minutes	5 - 7 km
Blue	60 - 80 minutes	7 - 12 km

24.5. Long distance orienteering for which the course lengths of the Green, Red, and Blue courses will be increased, can be organized.

24.5.1. In Long "O" events the winning times of the following courses may be increased to these lengths.

Green	75 min.
Red	90 - 100 min.
Blue	120 - 135 min.

24.8. The course length for the different classes will be posted along with an explanation of the classes and the time permitted for the competition. (33.6)

25. COURSE MARKINGS ON THE MAP

25.1. The competition map or master map shall be marked as follows:

a. Start location or map issue point by an equilateral triangle.

b. The control location by circles.

c. The finish location by two concentric circles.

d. Marked routes by dashed lines.

25.2. The center of any triangle or circle shows the precise position of the feature, but it shall not be actually marked.

25.3. The control circles shall be numbered showing the required sequence. The numerals shall be printed with their tops oriented exactly toward North. The numbers shall be placed in such a way that they do not conceal important map features.

25.4. Except where there is a marked route, the triangle and circles shall be joined in numerical order by straight lines.

25.5. The control circles and their connecting lines shall be interrupted or drawn thinner when they obscure important objects on the map.

25.7. When pre-marking of maps is not practical the following procedures for the use of Master Maps at "B" meets shall be used.

25.8. An official will observe all activity at the master map area and will prevent distracting noise and unnecessary talking.

25.9. Removal of a master map by a competitor is cause for disqualification.

25.10. Persons may observe the master map area provided they are approved by the Meet Director and do not distract the competitors. The Meet Director may assign someone to observe these persons.

25.11. Red waterproof pens or pencils will be provided for the competitors at the master map area. In addition a black waterproof pen or pencil will be available if requested.

25.12. The minimum number of master maps will be determined by the start interval of each course at the following ratio:

6 master maps for 1 minute interval

4 master maps for 2 minute interval

2 master maps for 3 minute interval

25.13. If a master map is found to be in error at least two meet officials will meet to determine the seriousness of the error. If the error is determined to be serious the course will be voided. All master maps will be available for review after the competition.

25.14. The master map area will be concealed from the view of all spectators and from all competitors who have not yet started.

29. CONTROL FLAGS AND EQUIPMENT

29.1. Every control feature shall be marked by a control flag.

29.2. If the usual control flags described in IOF Rule 29.2 are not being used a sample flag must be on display.

29.3. The flag shall be hung on the feature indicated on the map. The actual position shall be in accordance with the control description.

29.4. The control flags shall be visible to the competitors when they have reached the features.

29.5. Ideally control flags shall be situated so that the presence or absence of competitors does not make them easier or more difficult to locate.

29.9. On each course refreshments consisting of at least potable water shall be provided at least every 2.5 km. Refreshments shall be provided at the start and finish and at appropriate control flags and indicated on the description sheets as such. There shall be enough water for each competitor to have .25 liters (8 oz.) or more at each refreshment stop. In the event of hot weather additional refreshment locations are recommended. These additional locations need not be at control locations but must be indicated on the map, and the symbol used must be communicated to the competitors.

29.9.1. Water must be offered in a sanitary manner such that it is not practical for competitors to drink from "community drinking jugs."

33. TIMING AND PLACING

33.6. The time permitted for competition shall be posted when other than three hours, or five hours for long "O."

35. FAIRNESS

35.1. All persons which take part at an orienteering event, (competitors, organizers, team managers and so on) shall demonstrate a high degree of fairness, a sporting attitude, a spirit of comradeship and honesty.

37. CONDUCT DURING THE EVENT

37.3. It is the duty of each competitor to help anyone who is injured.

42. DUTIES OF THE COURSE CONSULTANT

42.5. There should be sufficient personnel involved in the meet organization to provide effective starting, finishing and timing procedures. It is recommended that at least 4 people are involved.

45. COURSE VETTER

45.1. A vetter, someone other than the course setter will be appointed. The vetter may be from the same club.

The duties of the vetter are to:

a. Check the suitability of the start, the map issue point, the controls and the finish as well as their correct position.

b. Check the correct marking of the control flags, and the situating and visibility of the control flags and punches.

c. Make sure that the control descriptions are appropriate and that they correctly describe the positions of the controls.

d. Make sure that the courses pre-printed on the maps, or the master maps are properly drawn.

APPENDIX 1
INSTRUCTIONS FOR CHOOSING COURSE DIFFICULTY
AND YOUR COMPETITIVE CLASS
AT USOF SANCTIONED "A" ORIENTEERING MEETS

At every "A" Meet sanctioned by the United States Orienteering Federation you will find at least six different courses varying in difficulty so that you—whether you have never tried Orienteering or are a seasoned expert—will have a course you can successfully finish yet still find challenging.

ORIENTEERING COURSES ARE DESIGNATED BY A COLOR

COLOR	LEVEL OF NAVIGATIONAL DIFFICULTY	PHYSICAL DIFFICULTY APPROXIMATE LENGTH IN KM	APPROXIMATE WINNING TIME
WHITE	BEGINNER	3 OR LESS	30 MINUTES
YELLOW	ADVANCED BEGINNER	3.5 - 4.5	40 MINUTES
ORANGE	INTERMEDIATE	4 - 5	50 MINUTES
GREEN	SHORT EXPERT	4 - 6	50 MINUTES
RED	MEDIUM EXPERT	6 - 8	60 MINUTES
BLUE	LONG EXPERT	8 - 12	60 - 80 MIN.

Use the above course descriptions to decide which color course is best for you. Then on the chart below look down the list of different age/sex classes under your course color to see which one you will fit into. Use your age as of the end of this year. So if your 19th birthday is December 31, you will use the age 19 class for the whole year. Notice the classes start with an "M" for male, and an "F" for female. Next are numbers and dashes, or the word "OPEN." If a dash precedes a number it means "UP TO" the age,

AGE, SEX, CLASS

WHITE	YELLOW	ORANGE	GREEN		RED	BLUE
F-12A	F-13-14A	F-15-16A	F-19-20A	M-17-18A	F-21-A	M-21-A
M-12A	F OPEN	F-17-18A	F-21-B	M 35-B	M-19-20A	
	M-13-14A	F-19-20B	F 35-A	M 40-B	M-21-B	
"MAP	M OPEN	F 35-B	F 40-A	M 45-B	M 35-A	
HIKER"		F 45-B	F 45-A	M 50-B	M 40-A	
		F OPEN	F 50-A	M 55-A	M 45-A	
		M-15-16A	F 55-A	M 60-A		
		M-17-18B		M OPEN		
		M-19-20B				
		M 50-B				
		M OPEN				

so -12 is for people up to and including age 12. If a dash is after a number it means "AND OLDER" so 35- is a class for people 35 and older, and if dashes are both before and between numbers they mean that the course is designed and recommended for the stated ages, but younger people are also eligible. Thus F-19-20 is specifically for 19 to 20 year olds but if younger women want to compete in this class they may do so. People of any age are eligible for the open class. Next is a letter. An "A" means the class is your Championship level class, and a "B" is your intermediate level. Finally, there is the MAP HIKER class for non-competitive people or groups. Within this system you can begin orienteering on an easy white course and advance one course at a time as you desire more challenge, finally reaching your championship class.

Be sure to keep in mind that if there are fewer than 5 people registered for your class it may be combined with an adjacent one, (except at US and Intercollegiate Championships) however you will still be running on the color course of your choice.

GOVERNING BODY

United States Orienteering Federation, P.O. Box 1444, Forest Park, GA 30051

The United States Orienteering Federation (USOF) was established in 1971 to promote orienteering in the United States. It is a nonprofit, tax-exempt organization supported by membership dues and donations. The USOF is composed of over 50 clubs and is affiliated with the worldwide International Orienteering Federation (IOF). Assistance in the formation of local clubs, developing maps, and course planning is provided by the USOF. Sources for instructional materials, supplies, equipment, films, and awards are also available through the Federation.

MAGAZINES

Orienteering USA, USOF, P.O. Box 1444, Forest Park, GA 30051

Orienteering North America, USOF, 23 Fayette St., Cambridge, MA 02139-1111

• PADDLEBALL •

NATIONAL PADDLEBALL ASSOCIATION
OFFICIAL FOUR WALL TOURNAMENT RULES

(Reproduced by permission of the National Paddleball Association*)

☐

RULE I THE GAME

Rule 1.1 Types of Games. Paddleball may be played by two players (singles), or four players (doubles).

1.2 Description. Paddleball is played with a paddle made of wood or some other composition material and an official paddleball.

1.3 Objective. The object is to win the rally by serving or returning the ball so the opponent is unable to return the ball to the front wall before it touches the floor twice.

1.4 Points. Points are scored only by the serving side when it serves an ace or wins a rally.

1.5 Game. A game is won by the first side scoring 21 points.

1.6 Match. A match is won by the side first winning two games.

1.7 Tie Breaker. In the event each side wins a game, the third game will be won by the side first scoring 11 points.

1.8 Championship Matches. All semi-final and final tournament matches will be 2 out of 3 games to 21 points.

RULE II THE COURT

Rule 2.1 The standard four-wall court is 40 feet long, 20 feet wide with front and side walls 20 feet high, a back wall at least 12 feet high and a ceiling. A line midway between and parallel with the front and back walls divides the court in the center and is called the short line. A line five feet in front of the short line and parallel to it is called the service line. The area between the service line and the short line is called the service zone. A line 18 inches from and parallel with the side wall at each end of the service zone is called the service box. Vertical lines 3 inches from the floor, marked on each side wall, five feet back of the short line are called receiving lines. All lines are 1 1/2 inches wide and are an appropriate distinguishing color. See handball court diagram on page 322.

RULE III EQUIPMENT

Rule 3.1 The Paddle. The paddle is made of wood or of a composition material and is approximately 16 inches long and weighs between 12-16 ounces. A safety thong is attached

---

*See page 405 for additional information.

to the handle and must be worn around the wrist during play. Paddles with metal rims are not permitted in tournament play.

3.2 The Ball. The official ball is the Penn ball manufactured by the General Tire-Pennsylvania Athletic products, Akron, Ohio. When dropped from a height of 6 feet it should rebound approximately 3 1/2 feet.

3.3 The Uniform. Shirt, shorts, and socks shall be clean white or pastel colors. Only team insignia, name of club, name of paddleball organization, name of tournament, name of sponsor or name of player may be on the uniform. Players may not play without shirts or shoes. Long pants are prohibited for tournament play.

RULE IV SERVE REGULATIONS

Rule 4.1 Serve. The serve shall be determined by a toss of a coin. In informal play contestants can rebound the ball from the front wall with the player landing closest to the short line winning the serve. The server of the first game also serves first in the third game, if any.

4.2 Position of Server. The server may serve from anywhere in the service zone with no part of either foot extending beyond either line of the service zone. The server must start and remain in the service zone until the served ball has passed the short line. Stepping on the line is allowed. Violations are called "foot faults." During the serve the server's partner is required to stand within the service box with his back against the wall and both feet on the floor until the ball passes the short line. Failure to take this position during a serve is a foot fault. If, while in legal position, a player is hit by a served ball on the fly it is a dead ball giving the server another serve. If hit by the serve when out of the box it is a serve-out. A ball passing behind a player legally in the box is a hinder. A dead ball serve does not eliminate a previous fault on that particular service.

4.3 Method of Serving. The ball must be dropped to the floor within the service zone and struck with the paddle on the first bounce, hitting the front wall first and rebounding back of the short line, either with or without touching one side wall.

4.4 Readiness for Serve. The ball shall not be served until the opponent is ready. The server is required to put the ball into play within 10 seconds after the referee calls the score. Failure to do so results in an out serve.

4.5 Illegal Serves. The serve is lost if two illegal serves are made in succession. An illegal serve cannot be played. The following are illegal serves:

(a) Short Serve—A served ball which hits the floor before crossing the short line.

(b) Long Serve—A served ball rebounding from the front wall to the back wall before hitting the floor.

(c) Ceiling Serve-A served ball rebounding from the front wall and hitting the ceiling before hitting the floor.

(d) Two-Side Serve-A served ball rebounding from the front wall and hitting both side walls before hitting the floor.

(e) Out of Court Serve—A served ball going out of the court.

(f) Foot Fault—The server stepping out of or leaving the service zone before the ball passes the short line. The server's partner in doubles, not staying in the service box until the ball has crossed the short line.

4.6 Service-out Serves. The following result in serve-outs:

(a) Bouncing the ball more than once before striking it when in the act of serving.

(b) Bouncing the ball and having it hit the side wall in the act of serving.

(c) Hitting a dropped ball before it has hit the floor.

(d) Striking at and missing the dropped serve.

(e) Touching the server's body or clothing with the ball in the act of serving.

(f) Any serve which strikes the floor, ceiling, or side wall before striking the front wall.

(g) Striking the server when rebounding from the front wall.

RULE V PLAYING REGULATIONS

Rule 5.1 Return of Service.

(a) The receiver(s) must remain behind the receiving lines (5 ft. behind the short line) until the ball is struck by the server.

(b) A legally served ball must be returned on the fly or after the first bounce to the front wall either directly or after touching the side wall(s), ceiling, or back wall. A return touching the front wall and floor simultaneously is not a good return.

(c) In returning a service on the fly, no part of the receiver's body may cross the short line before making the return.

(d) Failure to legally return the service results in a point for the server.

5.2 Playing the Ball. The following rules must be observed. Failure to do so results in a serve-out or point.

(a) The ball must be hit with the paddle in one or both hands. The safety thong must be around the wrist at all times.

(b) Hitting the ball with the arm, hand, or any part of the body is prohibited.

(c) In attempting a return the ball may be touched only once. If a player swings at the ball but misses it, the player or his/her partner in doubles, may make a further attempt to return it until it touches the floor a second time.

(d) In doubles, both partners may swing and simultaneously strike a ball.

(e) Any ball struck at in play which goes out of court, or which is returned to the front wall and then on the rebound or on the first bounce goes out of court, is a serve-out or point.

5.3 Dead Ball Hinders. Hinders are of two types—"dead ball" and "avoidable." Dead ball hinders result in the rally being replayed. A player is not entitled to a hinder unless the interference occurred before or simultaneously with his/her paddle's contact with the ball. Hinder calls shall be of sufficient volume so as to be heard by all players.

a. Situations of dead ball hinders:

(1) Court Hinders. If the ball hits any part of the court which under local rules is a dead ball.

(2) Hitting Opponent. Any returned ball that touches an opponent on the fly before it returns to the front wall.

(3) Body Contact. Any body contact with an opponent that interferes with seeing or returning the ball.

(4) Screen Ball. Any ball rebounding from the front wall close to the body of a player's opponent and interferes with or prevents the returning side from seeing the ball.

(5) Straddle Ball. A ball passing between the legs of a player's opponent in which there is no fair chance to see or return the ball.

(6) Back Swing Hinder. If there is body contact on the back swing, the player must call it immediately.

(7) Returning the Ball. While making an attempt to return the ball, a player is entitled to a fair chance to see and return the ball. It is the duty of the side that has just served or returned the ball to move so that the receiving side may go straight to the ball and not be required to go around an opponent. In doubles, both players on a side are entitled to

a fair and unobstructed chance at the ball. It is not a hinder when a player hinders his/her partner.

(8) Other Interference. Any other unintentional interference which prevents an opponent from having a fair chance to see or return the ball.

5.4 Avoidable Hinders. An avoidable hinder results in an "out" or a point depending upon whether the offender was serving or receiving.

(a) Failure to Move. Does not move sufficiently to allow opponent a shot.

(b) Blocking. A player moves into a position to block an opponent's shot.

(c) Moving into the Ball. Moves in the way and is struck by the ball just played by the opponent.

(d) Pushing. Deliberately pushing or shoving an opponent during a rally.

5.5 Wet Ball. On the service and during play the ball and the paddle must be dry.

5.6 Replay of Point. Play shall stop and the point shall be replayed when a) any foreign object enters the court or b) there is some other type of outside interference.

5.7 Broken Ball. If a ball breaks during play the rally is replayed. If a player breaks a paddle, loses a shoe, or other equipment, time should not be called until after the point has been decided, providing the paddle and/or equipment does not strike an opponent or interfere with ensuing play.

5.8 Rest Periods between Games. A two-minute rest period is allowed between games one and two. Players are not permitted to leave the court. A ten-minute period is allowed between the second and third game during which time players are allowed to leave the court.

5.9 Continuity of Play. Play shall be continuous from the first serve of each game until the game is concluded except that during a game each player in singles, or each side in doubles, either during serving or receiving may request a time-out not to exceed thirty seconds. No more than two time-outs per game shall be allowed each player in singles or each team in doubles. Deliberate delay shall result in a point or side-out against the offender.

5.10 Safety. The safety thong must be around the wrist at all times. The paddle may not be switched from one hand to the other. Both hands on the paddle together may be used in striking the ball.

5.11 Injuries. In a match, play may be suspended for up to 15 minutes for an injury. If the injured player is unable to continue the match is forfeited. If the match is resumed and must then be stopped again for the same player the match is forfeited.

5.12 Calling Score. Prior to each serve, the referee should call the score, giving the server's score first.

RULE VI OFFICIATING

Rule 6.1 Tournament Officials. All tournament matches shall be conducted with a referee. When possible, matches should also be conducted with a scorer.

6.2 The Referee. The referee's pre-game duties.

(a) Brief all players and officials on the rules and local playing regulations.

(b) Check the playing area for suitability for play.

(c) Check the playing equipment and uniform of players and approve of same.

(d) Check availability of other necessary equipment such as extra balls, towels, scorecards, pencils.

(e) Introduce players, toss coin for choice of serving or receiving.

6.3 Referee's Position. Whenever possible the referee shall take a position in center and above the back wall of the court.

6.4 Game Duties. During a game the referee shall decide on all questions that arise in accordance with the rules. The referee is responsible for the entire conduct of the game including:

(a) Legality of the serve and its return.

(b) Calling of dead ball hinders, avoidable hinders and faults.

(c) Preventing any unnecessary delay during match.

(d) Announcing when a point is made or server is out.

(e) Forfeiting or postponing a match at his/her discretion.

6.5 Match Forfeited. Matches may be forfeited when:

(a) A player refuses to abide by the referee's decision.

(b) A player fails to appear for a scheduled contest within 15 minutes.

(c) A player is unable to continue play for physical reasons.

6.6 Final Decisions. The decision of the referee is final.

6.7 Final Score. The referee shall approve the final score after announcing the name of the winner of the match and the scores of all games played.

6.8 The Scorer. The scorer's duties are to:

(a) Assist referee in prematch responsibilities.

(b) Obtain necessary equipment for scoring match including scorecard, pencils, extra balls, towels, etc.

(c) Assist the referee in any and all capacities at the referee's discretion.

(d) Keep a record of the progress of the game as prescribed by the tournament committee.

(e) Keep players and spectators informed on the progress of the game by announcing score after each exchange. The scorecard should then be given to the referee for his/her approval.

Note: Referee may assume the responsibility for announcing running game score.

GOVERNING BODY

National Paddleball Association, P.O. Box 712, Flint, MI 48501

In pursuit of its purpose to develop and promote the game of four-wall paddleball, the National Paddleball Association (NPA) establishes and distributes rules of the game, conducts tournaments (including national singles and doubles championships), and recommends equipment for play.

MAGAZINES

Paddleball Journal, National Paddleball Association, P.O. Box 712, Flint, MI 48501

• PADDLE TENNIS •

OFFICIAL PADDLE TENNIS RULES AS ADOPTED BY THE RULE COMMITTEE OF THE UNITED STATES PADDLE TENNIS ASSOCIATION, DATED OCTOBER 10, 1978

(Reproduced by permission of the United States Paddle Tennis Association*)

☐

1. DIMENSIONS OF COURT.

Fifty feet long x 20 feet wide. Same court for singles and doubles; there are no doubles alleys.

There are 4 service courts 22 feet long x 10 feet wide. (See Figure)

There shall be space behind each baseline of not less than 15 feet, and at the sides of not less than 10 feet wherever possible.

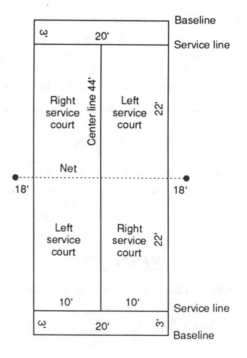

---

*See page 408 for additional information.

2. HEIGHT OF NET.

Thirty-one inches at net posts with cable pulled taut; not more than 1 inch allowable sag at center if there is no steel cable. Net post shall be 18 inches from sidelines.

3. OFFICIAL BALL.

A deadened tennis ball. A "deadened" tennis ball is a pressurized ball approved by the U.S.T.A. which has its internal pressure reduced by being punctured so that when dropped from a height of 6 feet to the court surface the bounce will be not less than 31 inches (the height of net) nor more than 33 inches. In other words, the punctured ball shall rebound 6 to 8 inches lower than a regular tennis ball. Puncturing with a safety pin or hypodermic needle is a simple method of achieving the required bounce.

4. THE PADDLE.

The paddle shall be not more than 17 1/2 inches long and 8 1/2 inches wide, and may be perforated or solid. No spongy or other extraneous material may be applied to paddle face; and no strung racket shall be used in any sanctioned tournament.

5. SERVICE.

Only one underhand serve is allowed. If serve is a fault the server loses that point. Before commencing to serve, the server shall stand with both feet at rest behind the baseline and within the imaginary extensions of the center and side lines. The server shall then project the ball by hand into the air and strike it with the paddle at a point not higher than 31 inches above the court surface at the instant of impact; or, the server may bounce or drop the ball to the court surface behind the baseline and strike it with the paddle upon its rebound at a point not higher than 31 inches above the court surface. Delivery shall be deemed complete at the instant of impact of paddle and ball. The server may choose either method of serving, that is, bouncing the ball or projecting it into the air before striking it with the paddle. However, whichever alternative he chooses, he must continue to serve in that manner for the entire set. In other words, he cannot switch from a bounce serve to the projecting serve at will, although he may change his manner of serving at the commencement of a new set.

The server shall throughout the delivery of the service not take 2 full steps (nor more) in the natural progression of making the serve. The server may take a step with either foot, with the other foot making the follow-through step. If either foot touches or swings over any area other than that behind the baseline before contact between ball and paddle it is a foot-fault.

Service shall begin in the right hand court at the start of every game. The ball served shall pass over the net and hit the ground within the 22 ft. x 10 ft. service court which is diagonally opposite, or upon any line bounding such court, and progress from there to the left hand court, alternating at each point until game is completed. If the ball is served from the wrong court, and is not detected, all points will stand as played, but the correct station shall be assumed as soon as the mistake is discovered.

One ball only shall be used during a set. Server may not substitute another ball during an unfinished set without consent of opponent or tournament official; nor may server hold another ball when serving.

6. BUCKET RULE (ALSO KNOWN AS RESTRAINT LINE RULE).

Although this rule is viewed as an unnecessary encumbrance by the U.S.P.T.A., it is still used in play on the West Coast. (The rule is a hold over from the era before the adoption of the 20 ft. x 50 ft. court.) The rule, which applies only in doubles play, restricts all four players to maintaining a position behind a restraint line, 12 feet from the net, until the served ball is contacted by the receiver's paddle.

7. "ONE BOUNCE" RULE (APPLIES TO SINGLES ONLY).

Each player must allow the ball to bounce once on his side before being permitted to volley; in other words the server must return the return of service as a ground stroke.

Except as noted above, the rules of play and scoring of the United States Tennis Association shall govern.

GOVERNING BODY

United States Paddle Tennis Association, 186 Seeley St., Brooklyn, NY 11218

The United States Paddle Tennis Association, Inc. (USPTA), organized in 1923, is a non-profit corporation made up of paddle tennis enthusiasts, clubs, and regional associations from all sections of the United States, with affiliates in Canada, Japan, Mexico, Peru, and Brazil. Its primary purposes are (a) extending the popularity of paddle tennis, (b) standardizing the court dimensions and rules of play, (c) organizing and conducting national tournaments in conjunction with regional associations, and (d) developing the recreational features of the game. Inquiries dealing with the interpretation of rules, history of the game, and related matters should be addressed to Murray Geller, Official Rules Interpreter, 189 Seeley St., Brooklyn, NY 11218.

MAGAZINES

Paddle Tennis News, USPTA, P.O. Box 30, Culver City, CA 90232

• POWERLIFTING •

ABRIDGMENT OF UNITED STATES
POWERLIFTING FEDERATION POWERLIFTING RULES

**(Reproduced by permission of the United States
Powerlifting Federation, Inc.*)**

☐

Note: The official USPF handbook contains extensive information including procedures for organizing and administering meets, qualifications and responsibilities of contest officials, loading charts, equipment specifications, official meet forms, USPF Constitution and By-Laws, etc. Only the technical rules of performance for the three required lifts are presented here.

I. GENERAL

1. COSTUME

A. Suit—There are no restrictions on color, combination of colors, emblems, logos, advertising, hem or seam design, except that no obscenity or profanity is allowed. Squatting and dead lifting suits must be 1-ply material, with the length of the suit leg not to exceed 15 mms measured from the middle of the crotch.

B. Shirt—There are no restrictions with regard to the type of shirt, except that it must be commercially available, be of 1-ply, and the sleeves must not extend beyond the elbow. The bench press shirt has been disallowed, as currently constructed, as of January 1, 1987.

C. Belt—The buckles may be up to 10 cms by 13 cms and the quick release type buckle is allowed, providing the underlap of the 2 ends of the belt doesn't exceed 10 cms. The limit of thickness is 13 cms.

D. Shoes—Any type of uncleated or unspiked shoe shall be worn, with no other restrictions.

E. Socks—There are no restrictions with regard to advertising emblems or logos, except no obscenity or profanity is allowed.

2. PLATFORM AND EQUIPMENT

Minimum measurement of 2.46 by 2.46 meters (8 x 8 feet) maximum measurement of 3.66 by 3.66 meters (12 x 12 feet), with non-slippery surface.

A. The seated judges' eye level should be at thigh level, for the squat.

---

*See page 416 for additional information.

B. There shall be no seams under the lifter, with the area upon which actual lifting occurs on a solid 4 x 8 sheet of plywood.

C. Bars—All meets shall use at least a 28 mm diameter bar, with good knurling, with a 30 mm bar to be used for squats over 275 kgs. The combination weight of a squat bar and collar may exceed 25 kgs.

(1) The central knurling should be 6" wide, with 5" of unknurled bar on either side, with the knurling to be 12-14 lines per inch, and the knurls to be pointed, not flattened and free of all paint, chrome, or other material.

(2) Plate opening clearance from the bar should allow rotation of the plates with the collars tightened at the discretion of the lifter.

(3) Judging lights at meets must be placed so that the audience and announcer may view the lights, in a position such that the judges cannot see the lights.

II. THE POWERLIFTS AND THE RULES OF PERFORMANCE

1. SQUAT

A. Rules of Performance

(1) The lifter shall assume an upright position with the top of the bar not more than 3 cms. (1 inch) below the top of the anterior deltoids. The bar shall be held horizontally across the shoulders with the hands in contact with bar or collars, and the feet flat on the platform with the knees locked. (See Figure.)

(2) After removing the bar from the racks, the lifter must move backwards to establish his position. The lifter shall wait in this position for the Chief Referee's signal. The signal will be given as soon as the lifter is motionless, erect with knees locked, and the bar properly positioned. If mechanical racks that withdraw are used, the lifter must remove the weights from the racks before they are withdrawn and wait motionless for the Chief Referee's signal. The Chief Referee's signal shall consist of a downward movement of the arm and the audible command "Squat" (See Figure). Before receiving the starting signal the lifter may make any adjustment within the rules without penalty.

(3) Upon receiving the Chief Referee's signal, the lifter must bend the knees and lower the body until the top surface of the legs at the hip joint are lower than the top of the knees (See Figures). Only one descent attempt is allowed. Locking and unlocking of the knees after the signal to squat is not defined as a descent. But the knees must be locked at the start and the completion of the lift.

(4) The lifter must recover at will, from the deepest point of his/her squat, without double bouncing or any downward movement (stopping is allowed) to an upright position with the knees locked. When the lifter is motionless, the referee will give the signal to replace the bar. This signal will be given when the lifter is in his apparent final position as best determined by the Chief Referee (even if the Chief Referee does not feel the lifter is in the correct final position, according to the USPF rules).

(5) The signal to replace the bar will consist of a backward motion of the hand and the audible command "Rack." The lifter must then make a bona fide attempt to return the bar to the racks. This is defined as one step towards the racks, then the lifter may request aid to rack the bar if needed.

(6) The lifter shall face the front of the platform.

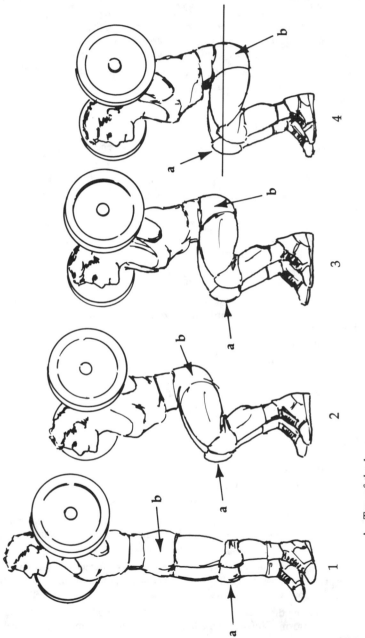

A. Top of the knees

B. The top surface of the legs at the hip joint

Diagram 4 shows a lifter just below parallel. Point "B" the surface of the legs at the hip joint is just below point "A" the top of the knees—a legal lift.

(7) Not more than five and not less than two spotter-loaders shall be on the platform at any time. Designated meet spotters may not be replaced unless approval is secured from the Head Referee in Charge.

(8) The lifter may enlist the help of the spotter-loaders in removing the bar from the racks; however, once the bar has cleared the racks, the spotter-loaders shall not assist the lifter any further with regards to proper positioning, foot placement, bar positioning, etc.

(9) The lifter may be given an additional attempt at the same weight at the Chief Referee's or the Jury's discretion if failure in an attempt was due to an error by one or more of the spotter-loaders.

B. Causes of Disqualification

(1) Failure to observe the Chief Referee's signals at the commencement or completion of a lift.

(2) Double bouncing or more than one recovery attempt at the bottom of the lift.

(3) Failure to assume an upright position with the knees locked at the commencement and completion of the lift.

(4) Any shifting of the feet laterally or stepping forwards or backwards, during the performance of the lift. The toes and/or heels may come up off the platform, but must go back down in approximately the same position.

(5) Failure to bend the knees and lower the body until the top surface of the legs at the hip joint are lower than the top of the knees. (Refer to Figures)

(6) Changing the position of the bar across the shoulders after the commencement of the lift. This applies to the intentional or unintentional rolling of the bar to aid the performance of the lift—not to a minute amount of position change that does not aid the lifter, and is done inadvertently.

(7) Contact with the bar by the spotter-loaders between the referee's signals.

(8) Contact of elbows or upper arms with the legs.

(9) Failure to make a bona fide attempt to return the bar to the racks.

(10) Any intentional dropping or dumping of the bar.

2. BENCH PRESS

A. Rules of Performance

(1) The front of the bench press bench must be placed on the platform facing the Chief Referee (racks holding the bar are closest to the Chief Referee).

(2) The lifter must lie on his back with head, shoulders, and buttocks in contact with the flat bench surface. His shoes must be reasonably flat on the floor or built up surface. This position shall be maintained to receive the starting signal.

(3) If the lifter's costume and the bench surface are not of a sufficient color contrast to enable the referees to detect possible raising movement at the points of contact, then the bench surface may be covered accordingly.

(4) To achieve firm footing the lifter may use plates or blocks or other materials to build up the surface of the platform. Whichever method is chosen, the foot must be reasonably flat on the surface to receive the starting signal.

(5) Not more than four and not less than two spotter-loaders shall be in attendance. The lifter may enlist the help of the spotter-loaders in removing the bar from the racks. The lift off must be to arms length and not down at the chest.

(6) The spacing of the hands shall not exceed 81 cms. (31 7/8 inches) measured between the forefingers. A reverse grip is permissible, provided that the distance between the little fingers does not exceed 81 cms. (31 7/8 inches).

(7) After receiving the bar at arms length, the lifter shall lower the bar to his chest and await the referee's signal. Before receiving the starting signal, the lifter may make any adjustments without penalty. This includes more than one partial descent to the chest.

(8) The signal shall be the audible command "Press" and will be given when the bar is motionless on the chest.

(9) After the signal to commence the lift has been given, the bar is pressed upward to straight arms length and held motionless until the audible command "Rack" is given.

(10) The bar is allowed to stop in its upward movement, but is not allowed any downward movement.

(11) The head may turn or raise and the feet may move in any direction and amount without penalty. The critical area here is if such foot movement may cause a change in the elected lifting position of the body on the bench during the lift.

B. Causes of Disqualification

(1) Failure to observe the referee's signals at the commencement or completion of the lift.

(2) Any change in the elected lifting position during the lift proper, i.e., any raising movement of the shoulders or buttocks from their original points of contact with the bench or lateral movement of the hands on the bar.

(3) Heaving or bouncing the bar off the chest. (Heaving or bouncing is defined as any downward movement of the bar after the signal to press is given, or a major change in the arch of the back.)

(4) Allowing the bar to sink into the chest after receiving the referee's signal.

(5) Any major uneven extension of the bar at the completion of the lift.

(6) Any downward movement of either hand that occurs as the bar is pressed upward.

(7) Contact with the bar by the spotter-loaders between the referee's signals.

(8) Any contact of the lifter's feet with the bench or its supports.

(9) Deliberate contact between the bar and the bar rest uprights during the lift to make the press easier.

3. DEADLIFT

A. Rules of Performance

(1) The bar must be laid horizontally in front of the lifter's feet, gripped with an optional grip in both hands and lifted upward until the lifter is standing erect and with knees locked. Stopping of the bar is allowed, but no downward movement is allowed.

(2) The lifter shall face the front of the platform.

(3) On completion of the lift, the knees shall be locked in a straight position and the shoulders held in an erect position (not forward or rounded). They do not have to be thrust back past an erect position, although if they are thrust back in that manner and all other criteria is acceptable, the lift would be good.

(4) The Chief Referee's signal shall consist of a downward movement of the hand and the audible command "Down." The signal will not be given until the bar is held motionless and the lifter is in the apparent finished position.

(5) Multiple attempt deadlift rule: A lifter may have any number of separate attempts (i.e., the hands must leave the bar between such attempts) as desired within each allowed deadlift

attempt until the one minute clock has expired signifying that he no longer has time to initiate a lift. (One minute begins when the lifter's name is called.) In order to utilize this multiple attempt provision, the lifter must remain on the platform between attempts. Leaving the platform surface at any time before his one minute expires means that all further attempts are forfeited. It must be a determined effort to leave the platform, not just standing at the edge.

B. Causes of Disqualification

(1) Any downward movement of the bar during the uplifting.

(2) Failure to stand erect with the shoulders held in an erect position.

(3) Failure to lock the knees straight at the completion of the lift.

(4) Supporting the bar on the thighs during the performance of the lift.

(5) Any lateral movement of the feet, or stepping backward or forward.

(6) Lowering the bar before receiving the Chief Referee's signal.

(7) Allowing the bar to return to the platform without maintaining control with both hands.

III. ADDITIONAL REGULATIONS

1. Rules of performance—The bar can stop its upward movement in the squat, deadlift, and bench press, but once started up, it cannot go back down.

2. Lifters may use blocks of any dimension under the feet for the bench press.

3. Final position in the deadlift is one of a normal erect standing position with the shoulders back and with the knees locked in a straight extended position.

4. In the deadlift, the lifter may have any number of separate attempts, each separate attempt determined by the hands leaving the bar between attempts, as desired, within the allotted time.

5. A lifter may choose any increase in weight from one attempt to another without penalty, and if 500 gram washers are utilized, the weight applied to the total must be the next lower multiple of 2.5 kgs. World record attempts may be requested on any of the lifts during any one of the 4 attempts available for the lifter to do so.

6. In the squat any grip is permissible so long as the hand touches the bar or collar.

7. No hand movement may be a cause for disqualification in the squat.

8. The command for the bench press is to be the clap of the hands.

9. No foot movement may be a cause for disqualification in the bench press.

10. Turning or raising of the head in the bench press after the signal to press is not a reason for an invalid lift.

11. If the head judge is asked, he must investigate with the other judges, and inform the lifter the reason why a lift was invalidated. Further discussion, if any, must be with the Chief Referee in charge, so that the meet will not be delayed.

12. Weigh-in—For all national meets, weigh-in shall occur within 24 hours of the beginning of competition, and shall end no sooner than 2 hours prior to the beginning of competition, for any particular category. This is optional for those meets other than national championships.

13. World Records—If a lifter is successful with an attempt that falls within 30 kgs of a current world record, he or she may, at the discretion of the jury, be granted a 4th attempt outside the competition. In no case can further additional attempts be granted. New records are valid provided they exceed the previous record by 200 grams, and fractions of 200 grams must be rounded downward to the nearest 1/5 of a kilogram.

The correct finished position in the deadlift is shown above. The lifter must be standing erect with the knees locked as indicated in the bottom diagram.

14. Referees—At national and international competition, only international referees may adjudicate.

15. Order of Competition—The rounds system, as currently espoused by the IPF, shall be utilized.

GOVERNING BODY

United States Powerlifting Federation, Inc., P.O. Box 18485, Pensacola, FL 32523

The United States Powerlifting Federation (USPF) (formerly the Powerlifting Committee of the Amateur Athletic Union) is affiliated with the International Powerlifting Federation. The primary purpose of the USPF is to regulate and promote the sport of powerlifting through sanctioned meets and a system of training state and international referees. The USPF sponsors clinics, seminars, and a sports medicine program, bestows awards, approves officials for international meets and championships, maintains a hall of fame, and compiles statistics.

MAGAZINES

Powerlifting—USA, USPF, P.O. Box 467, Camarillo, CA 93011

Ironsport, 2632 Great Hwy., San Francisco, CA 94116

• RACQUETBALL •

1988-89 AARA OFFICIAL RULES

**(Reproduced by permission of the American Amateur
Racquetball Association*)**

1—THE GAME

RULE 1.1. TYPES OF GAMES

Racquetball may be played by two, three, or four players. When played by two it is called
"singles," when played by three, "cut-throat," and when played by four, "doubles."

RULE 1.2. DESCRIPTION

Racquetball is a competitive game in which a racquet is used to serve and return the ball.

RULE 1.3. OBJECTIVE

The objective is to win each rally by serving or returning the ball so the opponent is unable to keep the ball in play. A rally is over when a player (or team in doubles) makes
an error, is unable to return the ball before it touches the floor twice, or when a hinder
is called.

RULE 1.4. POINTS AND OUTS

Points are scored only by the serving side when it serves an ace (an irretrievable serve)
or wins a rally. Losing the serve is called an out in singles. In doubles, when the first
server loses serve it is called a handout and when the second server loses the serve it is
a sideout.

RULE 1.5. MATCH, GAME, TIEBREAKER

A match is won by the first side winning two games. The first two games of a match
are played to 15 points. In the event each side wins one game, the tiebreaker game is
played to 11 points.

RULE 1.6. DOUBLES TEAM

A doubles team shall consist of two players who meet either the age requirements or player
classification requirements to participate in a particular division of play. A team with different skill levels must play in the division of the player with the highest level of ability.
When playing in age divisions, the team must play in the division of the youngest player.

---

*See page 432 for additional information.

(a) Change in Partners. A change in playing partners may be made so long as the first match of the posted team has not begun. For this purpose only, the match will be considered started once the teams have been called to the court. The team must notify the tournament director of the change prior to the beginning of the match.

RULE 1.7. CONSOLATION MATCHES

(a) Each entrant shall be entitled to participate in a minimum of two matches. Therefore, losers of their first match shall have the opportunity to compete in a consolation bracket of their own division. In draws of less than seven players, a round robin may be offered. See Rule 5.5 for determining round robin positioning.

(b) Consolation matches may be waived at the discretion of the tournament director, but this waiver must be in writing on the tournament application.

(c) Preliminary consolation matches will be two of three games to 11 points. Semifinal and final matches will follow the regular scoring format.

2—COURTS AND EQUIPMENT

RULE 2.1. COURTS

The specifications for the standard four wall racquetball court are:

(a) Dimensions. The dimensions shall be 20 feet wide, 20 feet high, and 40 feet long, with a back wall at least 12 feet high. All surfaces shall be in play with the exception of any gallery openings or surfaces designated as court hinders.

(b) Lines and Zones. Racquetball courts shall be divided and marked with lines 1 1/2 inches wide as follows:

1) Short Line. The back edge of the short line is midway between, and is parallel with the front and back walls.

2) Service Line. The front edge of the service line is parallel with, and five feet in front of the back edge of the short line.

3) Service Zone. The service zone is the 5-foot area between the outer edges of the short line and service line.

4) Service Boxes. The service boxes are located at each end of the service zone and are designated by lines parallel with the side walls. The inside edges of the lines are 18 inches from the side walls.

5) Drive Serve Lines. The drive serve lines, which form the drive serve zone, are parallel with the side wall and are within the service zone. The outside edge of the line is three feet from the side wall. Note: As a temporary measure, the lines may be designated by using plastic tape.

6) Receiving Lines. The receiving line is a broken line parallel to the short line. The back edge of the receiving line will be five feet from the back edge of the short line. The receiving line begins with a line 21 inches long that extends from each side wall: the two lines are connected by an alternate series of six-inch spaces and six-inch lines (17 six-inch spaces and 16 six-inch lines).

7) Safety Zone. The safety zone is the five-foot area bounded by the back edges of the short line and the receiving line. The zone is observed only during the serve. (See Rules 4.11.k and 4.12.)

RULE 2.2. BALL SPECIFICATIONS

(a) The standard racquetball shall be 2 1/4 inches in diameter; weigh approximately 1.4 ounces; have a hardness of 55-60 inches durometer; and bounce 68-72 inches from a 100-inch drop at a temperature of 70-74 degrees Fahrenheit.

Racquetball Court

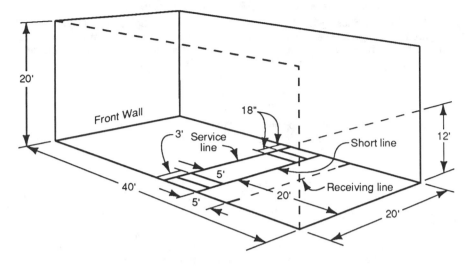

(b) Only a ball carrying the endorsement or approval of the AARA may be used in an AARA sanctioned event.

RULE 2.3. BALL SELECTION

(a) A ball shall be selected by the referee for use in each match. During the match the referee may, at his discretion or at the request of a player or team, replace the ball. Balls that are not round or which bounce erratically shall not be used.

(b) The referee and the players shall agree to an alternate ball, so that in the event of breakage the second ball can be put into play immediately.

RULE 2.4. RACQUET SPECIFICATIONS

(a) Dimensions. The racquet, including bumper guard and all solid parts of the handle, may not exceed 21 inches in length.

(b) The racquet frame may be of any material judged to be safe.

(c) The regulation racquet frame must include a thong that must be securely attached to the player's wrist.

(d) The string of the racquet should be gut, monofilament, nylon graphite, plastic, metal, or a combination thereof, providing the strings do not mark or deface the ball.

RULE 2.5. APPAREL

(a) Lensed Eyewear Required. Lensed eyewear designed for racquet sports is required apparel for all players. The protective eyewear must be worn as designed and may not be altered. Players who require corrective eyewear also must wear lensed eyewear designed for racquet sports. (Note: An updated list of lensed eyewear is available by writing the AARA national office. The AARA recommends that players select eyewear with polycarbonate plastic lenses with 3-mm center thickness.)

Failure to wear protective eyewear will result in a technical and the player will be charged with a time-out to secure eyewear. The second infraction in the same match will result in a forfeit. (See Rule 4.18.a.10.)

(b) Lensed Eyewear for Juniors. All players under the age of 19 and those participating in a Junior Division must adhere to the Rule 2.5.a currently.

(c) Clothing and Shoes. The clothing may be of any color; however, a player may be required to change extremely loose fitting or otherwise distracting garments. Insignias and writing on the clothing must be considered to be in good taste by the tournament director. The shoes must have soles which do not mark or damage the floor.

3—OFFICIATING

(Note: Rule 3, dealing with the appointment of tournament officials, their duties and signals, protests, forfeitures, and appeal procedures has been omitted here. The full text for Rule 3 will be found in the official rules publication.)

4—PLAY REGULATIONS

RULE 4.1. SERVE

(a) Order. The player or team winning the coin toss has the option to serve or receive for the start of the first game. The second game will begin in reverse order of the first game. The player or team scoring the highest total of points in Games 1 and 2 will have the option to serve or receive for the start of the tiebreaker. In the event that both players or teams score an equal number of points in the first two games, another coin toss will take place and the winner of the toss will have the option to serve or receive.

RULE 4.2. START

The serve is started from any place within the service zone. (For exceptions, see Drive Serve Rule 4.6.) Neither the ball nor any part of either foot may extend beyond the boundaries of the service zone. Stepping on, but not over the line is permitted. The server must remain in the service zone from the moment the service motion begins until the served ball passes the short line. See Rules 4.10.a, and 4.11.k for penalties for violation. The server may not start any service motion until the referee has called the score or second serve.

RULE 4.3. MANNER

After taking a position inside the service zone, a player may begin service motion and a non-interrupted, continuous movement. Once the service motion begins, the ball is bounced in the zone and after the first bounce is struck by the racquet so that the ball hits the front wall first and on rebound hits the floor behind the back edge of the short line, either with or without touching one side wall. A balk serve or fake swing at the ball is an out serve. Bouncing the ball outside the service zone is a fault serve.

RULE 4.4. READINESS

Serves shall not be made until the referee has called the score, or the second serve and the server has visually checked the receiver. The referee shall call the score as both server and receiver prepare to return to their respective positions, shortly after the previous point has ended.

RULE 4.5. DELAYS

Delays on the part of the server or receiver exceeding 10 seconds shall result in an out or point against the offender.

(a) This 10-second rule is applicable to both server and receiver simultaneously. Collectively, they are allowed up to 10 seconds after the score is called, to serve or be ready to receive. It is the server's responsibility to look and be certain that the receiver is ready. If the receiver is not ready, he must signal so by raising his racquet above his head or completely turning their back to the server (these are the only two acceptable signals).

(b) If the server serves the ball while the receiver is signaling not ready, the serve shall go over with no penalty and the server shall be warned by the referee to check the receiver. If the server continues to serve without checking the receiver, the referee may award a technical for delay of game.

(c) After the score is called, if the server looks at the receiver and the receiver is not signaling "not ready," the server may then serve. If the receiver attempts to signal not ready after that point, such signal shall not be acknowledged and the serve becomes legal.

RULE 4.6. DRIVE SERVICE ZONES

The drive serve rule lines will be three feet from each side wall in the service box, dividing the service area into two 17-foot service zones for drive serves only (see court diagram). The player may drive serve to the same side of the court on which he is standing so long as the start and finish of the service motion takes place outside the three-foot line. The call, or non-call, may be appealed.

(a) The drive serve zones are not observed for cross-court drive serves, the hard-Z, soft-Z, lob or half-lob serves.

(b) The racquet may not break the plane of the 17-foot zone while making contact with the ball.

(c) The three-foot line is not part of the 17-foot zone. Dropping the ball on the line or standing on the line while serving to the same side is an infraction.

RULE 4.7. SERVE IN DOUBLES

(a) Server. At the beginning of each game in doubles, each side shall inform the referee of the order of service which shall be followed throughout the game. When the first server is out the first time up, the side is out. Thereafter, both players on each side shall serve until the team receives a handout and a sideout.

(b) Partner's Position. On each serve, the server's partner shall stand erect with back to the side wall and with both feet on the floor within the service box from the moment the server begins his service motion until the served ball passes the short line. Violations are called foot faults. However, if the server's partner enters the safety zone before the ball passes the short line the server loses service.

RULE 4.8. DEFECTIVE SERVES

Defective serves are of three types resulting in penalties as follows:

(a) Dead-Ball Serve. A dead-ball serve results in no penalty and the server is given another serve (without cancelling a prior fault serve).

(b) Fault Serve. Two fault serves result in a handout.

(c) Out Serve. An out serve results in a handout.

RULE 4.9. DEAD-BALL SERVES

Dead-ball serves do not cancel any previous fault serve. The following are dead-ball serves:

(a) Ball Hits Partner. A serve which strikes the server's partner while in the doubles box is a dead-ball serve. A serve which touches the floor before touching the server's partner is a short serve. (See Rule 4.11.j.)

(b) Court Hinders. A serve that hits any part of the court, which under local rules is an obstruction, is a dead-ball serve.

(c) Broken Ball. If the ball is determined to have broken on the serve, a new ball shall be substituted and the serve shall be replayed, not cancelling any prior fault serve.

RULE 4.10. FAULT SERVES

The following serves are faults and any two in succession result in an out:

(a) Foot Faults. A foot fault results when:

1) The server does not begin the service motion with both feet in the service zone.

2) The server steps over the front service line before the served ball passes the short line.

3) In doubles, the server's partner is not in the service box with both feet on the floor and back to the wall from the time the server begins the service motion until the ball passes the short line. (See Rule 4.7.b.)

(b) Short Service. A short serve is any served ball that first hits the front wall and, on the rebound, hits the floor on or in front of the short line (with or without touching a side wall).

(c) Three-Wall Serve. A three-wall serve is any served ball that first hits the front wall and, on the rebound, strikes both side walls before touching the floor.

(d) Ceiling Serve. A ceiling serve is a served ball that first hits the front wall and then touches the ceiling (with or without touching a side wall).

(e) Long Serve. A long serve is a served ball that first hits the front wall and rebounds to the back wall before touching the floor (with or without touching a side wall).

(f) Out-of-Court Serve. An out-of-court serve is any served ball that first hits the front wall and, before striking the floor, goes out of the court.

(g) Bouncing Ball Outside Service Zone. Bouncing the ball outside the service zone as a part of the service motion is a fault serve.

(h) Illegal Drive Serve. A drive serve in which the player fails to observe the 17-foot service zone outlined in Rule 4.6.

(i) Screen Serve. A served ball that first hits the front wall and on the rebound passes so closely to the server, or server's partner in doubles, that it prevents the receiver from having a clear view of the ball. (The receiver is obligated to place himself in good court position, near center court, to obtain that view.) The screen serve is the only fault serve which may not be appealed.

RULE 4.11. OUT SERVES

Any of the following serves results in an out:

(a) Two Consecutive Fault Serves. See Rule 4.10.

(b) Failure to Serve Promptly. Failure of server to put the ball into play within ten (10) seconds of the calling of the score by the referee.

(c) Missed Serve Attempt. Any attempt to strike the ball that results in a total miss or in the ball touching any part of the server's body.

(d) Touched Serve. Any served ball that on the rebound from the front wall touches the server or server's racquet, or any ball intentionally stopped or caught by the server or server's partner.

(e) Fake or Balk Serve. Such a serve is defined as a non-continuous movement of the racquet towards the ball as the server drops the ball for the purpose of serving.

(f) Illegal Hit. An illegal hit includes contacting the ball twice, carrying the ball, or hitting the ball with the handle of the racquet or part of the body or uniform.

(g) Non-Front Wall Serve. Any served ball that does not strike the front wall first.

(h) Crotch Serve. Any served ball that hits the crotch of the front wall and floor, front wall and side wall, or front wall and ceiling, is an out serve (because it did not hit the front wall first). A serve into the crotch of the back wall and the floor is good and in play. A served ball hitting the crotch of the side wall and floor beyond the short line is in play.

(i) Out-of-Order Serve. In doubles, when either partner serves out of order, the points scored by that server will be subtracted and an out serve will be called: if the second server serves out-of-order, the out serve will be applied to the first server and the second server will resume serving. If the player designated as the first server serves out-of-order, a sideout will be called. In a match with line judges, the referee may enlist their aid to recall the number of points scored out-of-order.

(j) Ball Hits Partner. A served ball that hits the doubles partner while outside the doubles box results in loss of serve.

(k) Safety Zone Violation. If the server, or doubles partner, enters into the safety zone before the served ball passes the short line, it shall result in the loss of serve.

RULE 4.12. RETURN OF SERVE

(a) Receiving Position.

1) The receiver may not enter the safety zone until the ball bounces.

2) On the fly return attempt, the receiver may not strike the ball until the ball breaks the plane of the receiving (five-foot) line. The follow-through may carry the receiver or his racquet past the receiving line.

3) Neither the receiver nor his racquet may break the plane of the short line during the service return, except if the ball is struck after rebounding off the back wall. Any violation by the receiver results in a point for the server.

(b) Defective Serve. A player on the receiving side may not intentionally catch or touch a served ball (such as an apparently long or short serve) until the referee has made a call or the ball has touched the floor for a second time. Violation results in a point.

(c) Legal Return. After a legal serve, a player on the receiving team must strike the ball on the fly or after the first bounce, and before the ball touches the floor the second time; and return the ball to the front wall, either directly or after touching one or both side walls, the back wall or the ceiling, or any combination of those surfaces. A returned ball may not touch the floor before touching the front wall. (See Rule 4.11.f.)

(d) Failure to Return. The failure to return a serve results in a point for the server.

RULE 4.13. CHANGES OF SERVE

(a) Outs. A server is entitled to continue serving until:

1) Out Serve. See Rule 4.11.

2) Two Consecutive Fault Serves. See Rule 4.10.

3) Ball Hits Partner. Player hits partner with an attempted return.

4) Failure to Return Ball. Player, or partner, fails to keep the ball in play as required by Rule 4.12.c.

5) Point Hinder. Player or partner commits an avoidable hinder. (Rule 4.16.)

(b) Sideout. In singles, retiring the server is a sideout. In doubles the side is retired when both partners have lost service, except: the team which serves first at the beginning of each game loses serve when the first server is retired. (See Rule 4.7.)

(c) Effect of Sideout. When the server (or the serving team) receives a sideout, the server becomes the receiver and the receiver becomes the server.

RULE 4.14. RALLIES

Each legal return after the serve is called a rally. Play during rallies shall be according to the following rules:

(a) Legal Hits. Only the head of the racquet may be used at any time to return the ball. The racquet may be held in one or both hands. Switching hands to hit a ball, touching the ball with any part of the body or uniform, or removing the wrist thong results in loss of the rally.

(b) One Touch. In attempting returns, the ball may be touched or struck only once by a player or team, or the result is a loss of rally. The ball may not be carried. (A carried ball is one which rests on the racquet in such a way that the effect is more of a sling or throw than a hit.)

(c) Failure to Return. Any of the following constitutes a failure to make a legal return during a rally:

1) The ball bounces on the floor more than once before being hit.

2) The ball does not reach the front wall on the fly.

3) The ball caroms off a player's racquet into a gallery or wall opening without first hitting the front wall.

4) A ball which obviously did not have the velocity or direction to hit the front wall strikes another player on the court.

5) A ball struck by one player on a team hits that player or that player's partner.

6) Committing a point hinder. (Rule 4.16.)

7) Switching hands during a rally.

8) Failure to use wrist thong on racquet.

9) Touching the ball with the body or uniform.

10) Carry or sling the ball with the racquet.

(d) Effect of Failure to Return. Violations of Rule 4.14. a. b. c. result in a loss of rally. If the serving player or team loses the rally it is an out (handout or sideout). If the receiver loses the rally, it results in a point for the server.

(e) Return Attempts.

1) In singles, if a player swings at the ball and misses it, the player may continue to attempt to return the ball until it touches the floor for the second time.

2) In doubles, if one player swings at the ball and misses it, both partners may make further attempts to return the ball until it touches the floor the second time. Both partners on a side are entitled to return the ball.

(f) Out-of-Court Ball

1) After Return. Any ball returned to the front wall which, on the rebound or on the first bounce, goes into the gallery or through any opening in a side wall shall be declared dead and the server shall receive two serves.

2) No Return. Any ball not returned to the front wall, but which caroms off a player's racquet into the gallery or into any opening in a side wall either with or without touching the ceiling, side wall or back wall, shall be an out for the player failing to make the return, or a point for the opponent.

(g) Broken Ball. If there is any suspicion that a ball has broken on the serve, or during a rally, play shall continue until the end of the rally. The referee or any player may request the ball be examined. If the referee decides the ball is broken, the ball will be replaced and the rally replayed. The server will get two serves. The only proper way to check for a broken ball is to squeeze it by hand. (Checking the ball by striking it with a racquet will not be considered a valid check and shall work to the disadvantage of the player or team which struck the ball after the rally.)

(h) Play Stoppage.

1) If a foreign object enters the court, or any other outside interference occurs, the referee shall stop the play.

2) If a player loses a shoe or other properly worn equipment, the referee shall stop the play if the occurrence interferes with ensuing play or player's safety; however, safety permitting, the offensive player is entitled to one opportunity to hit a rally ending shot. (See Rule 14.16.i.)

(i) Replays. Whenever a rally is replayed for any reason, the server is awarded two serves. A previous fault serve is not considered.

RULE 4.15. DEAD-BALL HINDERS

A rally is replayed without penalty and the server receives two serves whenever a dead-ball hinder occurs.

(a) Situations.

1) Court Hinders. A ball that hits any part of the court which has been designated as a court hinder (such as a door handle); play also is stopped when the ball takes an irregular bounce off a rough or irregular surface which the referee determines affected the rally (such as a strange or dead bounce off a court light).

2) Ball Hits Opponent. When an opponent is hit by a return shot in flight, it is a dead-ball hinder. If the opponent is struck by a ball which obviously did not have the velocity or direction to reach the front wall, it is not a hinder, and the player that hit the ball will lose the rally. A player who has been hit by the ball can stop play and make the call, though the call must be made immediately and acknowledged by the referee.

3) Body Contact. If body contact occurs which the referee believes was sufficient to stop the rally, either for the purpose of preventing injury by further contact or because the contact prevented a player from being able to make a reasonable return, the referee shall call a hinder. Incidental body contact in which the offensive player clearly will have the advantage should not be called a hinder, unless the offensive player obviously stops play. Contact with the racquet on the follow-through normally is not considered a dead-ball hinder.

4) Screen Ball. Any ball rebounding from the front wall so close to the body of the defensive team that it interferes with, or prevents, the offensive player from having clear view of the ball. (The referee should be careful not to make the screen call so quickly that it takes away a good offensive opportunity.) A ball that passes between the legs of the side that just returned the ball is not automatically a screen. It depends on the proximity of the players. Again, the call should work to the advantage of the offensive player.

5) Back Swing Hinder. Any body or racquet contact, on the back swing or en route to or just prior to returning the ball, which impairs the hitter's ability to take a reasonable swing. This call can be made by the player attempting the return, though the call must be made immediately and is subject to the approval of the referee. Note: The interference may be considered a point (avoidable) hinder. (See Rule 4.16.b.)

6) Safety Holdup. Any player about to execute a return who believes he is likely to strike his opponent with the ball or racquet may immediately stop play and request a dead-ball hinder. This call must be made immediately and is subject to acceptance and approval of the referee. (The referee will grant a dead-ball hinder if he believes the holdup was reasonable and the player would have been able to return the shot, and the referee may also call a point hinder if warranted.)

7) Other Interference. Any other unintentional interference which prevents an opponent from having a fair chance to see or return the ball. Example: The ball obviously skids after striking a wet spot on the court floor or wall.

(b) Effect of Hinders. The referee's call of hinder stops play and voids any situation which follows, such as the ball hitting the player. The only hinders a player may call are specified in 14.15.a. 2,5,6, and are subject to the approval of the referee. A dead-ball hinder stops play and the rally is replayed. The server receives two serves.

(c) Avoidance. While making an attempt to return the ball, a player is entitled to a fair chance to see and return the ball. It is the responsibility of the side that has just hit the ball to move so the receiving side may go straight to the ball and have an unobstructed view of the ball. In the judgment of the referee however, the receiver must make a reasonable effort to move towards the ball and have a reasonable chance to return the ball in order for a hinder to be called.

RULE 4.16. POINT OR SIDEOUT HINDER (AVOIDABLE HINDERS)

A point or sideout hinder (avoidable) results in the loss of a rally. The hinder does not necessarily have to be an intentional act and is a result of any of the following:

(a) Failure to Move. A player does not move sufficiently to allow an opponent a shot; or a player moves in such a direction that it prevents an opponent from taking a shot.

(b) Stroke Interference. This occurs when a player moves, or fails to move, so that the opponent returning the ball does not have a free, unimpeded swing. This includes unintentionally moving the wrong direction which prevents an opponent from making an open offensive shot.

(c) Blocking. Moves into a position which blocks the opponent from getting to, or returning, the ball; or in doubles, a player moves in front of an opponent as the player's partner is returning the ball.

(d) Moving into the Ball. Moves in the way and is struck by the ball just played by the opponent.

(e) Pushing. Deliberately pushes or shoves opponent during a rally.

(f) Intentional Distractions. Deliberate shouting, stamping of feet, waving of racquet, or any manner of disrupting the player who is hitting the ball.

(g) View Obstruction. A player moves across an opponent's line of vision just before the opponent strikes the ball.

(h) Wetting the Ball. The players, particularly the server, have the responsibility to see that the ball is kept dry at all times. Any wetting of the ball either deliberate or by accident that is not corrected prior to the beginning of the rally shall result in a point hinder.

(i) Equipment. The loss of any improperly worn equipment, or equipment not required on court, which interferes with the play of the ball or safety of the players is a point/sideout hinder. Examples include improperly fastened eyewear, loss of hand towel, etc. (Rule 4.14.h.)

RULE 4.17. TIME-OUTS

(a) Rest Periods. Each player or team is allowed up to three 30-second time-outs in games to 15 and two 30-second time-outs in games to 11. Times-outs may not be called by either side after service motion has begun. Calling for time-out when none remain or after service motion has begun, or taking more than 30 seconds in a time-out, will result in the assessment of a technical for delay of game.

(b) Injury. If a player is injured during the course of a match as a result of contact with the ball, racquet, opponent, wall, or floor they shall be granted an injury time-out. An injured player shall not be allowed more than a total of 15 minutes of rest during the match. If the injured player is not able to resume play after total rest of 15 minutes, the match shall be awarded to the opponent. Muscle cramps and pulls, fatigue, and other ailments that are not caused by direct contact on the court will not be considered an injury.

(c) Equipment Time-Outs. Players are expected to keep all clothing and equipment in good, playable condition and are expected to use regular time-outs and time between games for adjustment and replacement of equipment. If a player or team is out of time-outs and the referee determines that an equipment change or adjustment is necessary for fair and safe continuation of the match, the referee may award an equipment time-out not to exceed two minutes.

(d) Between Games. The rest period between the first two games of a match is two minutes. If a tiebreaker is necessary, the rest period between the second and third game is five minutes.

(e) Postponed Games. Any games postponed by referees shall be resumed with the same score as when postponed.

RULE 4.18. TECHNICALS

(a) Technical Fouls. The referee is empowered to deduct one point from a player's or team's score when in the referee's sole judgment, the player is being overtly and deliberately abusive. The actual invoking of this penalty is called a Referee's Technical. If the player or team against whom the technical was assessed does not resume play immediately, the referee is empowered to forfeit the match in favor of the opponent. Some examples of actions which may result in technicals are:

1) Profanity. Profanity is an automatic technical and should be invoked by the referee whenever it occurs.

2) Excessive arguing.

3) Threat of any nature to opponent or referee.

4) Excessive or hard striking of the ball between rallies.

5) Slamming of the racquet against walls or floors, slamming the door, or any action which might result in injury to the court or other player.

6) Delay of the game, either in the form of taking too much time during time-outs and between games, in drying the court, in excessive questioning of the referee on the rules, or in excessive or unnecessary appeals.

7) Intentional front line foot faults to negate a bad lob serve.

8) Anything considered to be unsportsmanlike behavior.

9) Player under age of 19 who fails to wear eyeguards or wear them properly is an automatic technical on the first infraction. (See Rule 2.5.b.)

10) Failure to wear lensed eyewear designed for racquet sports is an automatic technical on the first infraction.

(b) Technical Warning. If a player's behavior is not so severe as to warrant a referee's technical, a technical warning may be issued without point deduction.

(c) Effect of Technical or Warning. If a referee issues a referee's technical, one point shall be removed from the offender's score. If a referee issues a technical warning, it shall not result in a loss of rally or point and shall be accompanied by a brief explanation of the reason for the warning. The awarding of the technical shall have no effect on service changes or sideouts. If the technical occurs either between games or when the offender has no points, the results will be that the offender's score will revert to a minus one (-1).

RULE 4.19. PROFESSIONAL

A professional shall be defined as any player (male, female, or junior) who has accepted prize money regardless of the amount in any tournaments including WPRA, RMA, and other events so deemed by the AARA Board of Directors.

(a) A player may participate in a tournament which awards cash prizes, but will not be considered a professional if NO prize money is accepted.

(b) The acceptance by a player of merchandise or travel expenses shall not be considered as prize money, and thus does not jeopardize a player's amateur status.

RULE 4.20. RETURN TO AMATEUR STATUS

Any player who has been classified as a professional can recover amateur status by requesting, in writing, this desire to be reclassified as an amateur. This application shall be tendered to the Executive Director of the American Amateur Racquetball Association (AARA), or his designated representative, and shall become effective immediately as long as the player making application for reinstatement of amateur status has received no money in any tournament, as defined in Rule 4.19, for the past 12 months.

RULE 4.21. AGE GROUP DIVISIONS

Age is determined as of the first day of the tournament:

(a) Men's And Women's Age Divisions: Open—All players other than pro; Junior Veterans—19+; Junior Veterans—25+; Veterans—30+; Seniors—35+; Veteran Seniors—40+; Masters—45+; Veteran Masters—50+; Golden Masters—55+; Senior Golden Masters—60+; Veteran Golden Masters—65+; Advanced Golden Masters—70+; and Super Golden Masters—75+.

(b) Other Divisions: Mixed Doubles; and Disabled.

(c) Junior Divisions. Age determined as of January 1st of each calendar year. Junior Boy's and Girl's Age Divisions: 18 & under; 16 & under; 14 & under; 12 & under; 10 & under; 8 & under; 8 & under Multi-Bounce; Doubles; and Mixed Doubles.

RULE 4.22. JUNIOR DIVISION EXCEPTIONS

(a) Eight & Under Multi-Bounce Modifications. After a legal serve, the ball remains in play as long as it is bouncing, though the player may swing only once at the ball. The ball is considered dead at the point it stops bouncing and begins to roll.

1) During the serve or rally, and after rebounding off the back wall, the ball must be struck before it touches the short line en route to the front wall. The one exception is explained in the Blast Rule.

2) Blast Rule. If the ball caroms from the front wall to the back wall on the fly, the receiver may retrieve the ball from any place on the court—including past the short line—so long as the ball is bouncing.

3) Front Wall Lines. Tape is placed across the front wall one foot from the floor and three feet from the floor. If the ball hits the front wall between the one-foot and three-foot lines during a rally, the ball must be returned before the third bounce. If the ball hits below the one-foot level, it must be returned before the second bounce.

4) Matches. All games in a match are to 11 points.

(b) Mandatory Lensed Eyewear. See Rule 2.5.b.

5—TOURNAMENTS

(Note: Rule 5, dealing with the organization and management of AARA local, state, and regional sanctioned tournaments has been omitted here.)

6—NATIONAL WHEELCHAIR RACQUETBALL ASSOCIATION OFFICIAL RULES

RULE 6.1 MODIFICATIONS OF STANDARD RULES

(a) Where the AARA Rule Book rules refer to server, person, body or other similar variations, for wheelchair play such reference shall include all parts of the wheelchair in addition to the person sitting on it.

(b) Where the rules refer to feet, standing or other similar variations, for wheelchair play it means where only the rear wheels are located.

(c) Where the rules mention body contact, for wheelchair play it shall mean any part of the wheelchair in addition to the player.

(d) Where the rules refer to double bounce or after the first bounce, it shall mean three bounces. All variations of the same phrases shall be revised accordingly.

RULE 6.2. DIVISIONS

(a) Novice Division. The Novice Division is for the beginning player who has never played racquetball or is just learning to play.

(b) Intermediate Division. The Intermediate Division is for the player who has played tournaments before or has a skill level to be competitive in the division.

(c) Open Division. The Open Division is the highest level of play and is for the advanced player.

(d) Multi-Bounce Division. The Multi-Bounce Division is for the individuals (men or women) whose mobility is such that wheelchair racquetball would be impossible if not for the Multi-Bounce Division.

(e) Junior Division. The Junior Division is for the player who is 18 years old or younger. The Junior Division will have both the two-bounce and multi-bounce rule as determined by the tournament director. Age divisions are 8-11, 12-15, 16-18.

RULE 6.3. RULES

(a) Two-Bounce Rule. Two bounces are used in wheelchair racquetball in all divisions except the Multi-Bounce Division. The ball may hit the floor twice before being returned.

(b) Out of Chair Rule. The player cannot intentionally jump out of his chair to hit or retrieve a ball. Nor can the player stand up in the chair to serve a ball. If a player unintentionally leaves the chair to make a play no penalty is assessed. If the referee determines a player intentionally left his chair to make a return it will result in the loss of serve for the offender or point for the opponent. Repeat offenders will be warned by the referee.

(c) Equipment Standards. In order to protect playing surfaces, the tournament officials may not allow a person to participate with black tires or anything which will mark or damage the court.

(d) Start. The serve is started from any place within the service zone. Front casters may extend beyond the short service line, but may not extend beyond the service line before the ball is served. At no time shall the rear wheels cross the front line or short line until the serve is completed.

(e) Maintenance Delay. A maintenance delay is a delay in the progress of a match due to a malfunction of a wheelchair, prosthesis, or assistive device. Such delay must be requested by the player, granted by the referee during the match, and shall not exceed five minutes. Only two such delays may be granted for each player for each match. After using both maintenance delays the player has the following options:

1) Continue play with the defective equipment.

2) Immediately substitute replacement equipment.

3) Postponement of game, with the approval of the referee and opponent.

RULE 6.4. DEAD-BALL HINDERS

(a) Hitting Opponent. Any returned ball that touches an opponent or an opponent's wheelchair on the fly before it returns to the front wall. (Refer to Rule 4.15.a.2.)

(b) Backswing Hinder. Any body or wheelchair contact whether on the back swing or en route to or just prior to returning the ball which impairs the hitter's ability to take a reasonable swing. (Refer to Rule 4.15.a.5.)

RULE 6.5. MULTI-BOUNCE RULE

(a) The ball may bounce as many times as the receiver wants though the player may swing only once to return the ball to the front wall.

(b) The ball must be hit before it crosses the short line on its way back to the front wall.

(c) The receiver cannot cross the short line after the ball contacts the back wall.

7—ONE-WALL AND THREE-WALL RULES

RULE 7.1. ONE-WALL AND THREE-WALL RULE MODIFICATIONS

The rules for one-wall and three-wall racquetball are very similar to the standard indoor four-wall game. The exceptions follow:

(a) One Wall. There are two playing surfaces, the front wall and the floor. The wall is 20 feet wide and 16 feet high. The floor is 20 feet wide and 34 feet to the back edge of the long line. To permit movement by players, there should be a minimum of three feet (six feet is recommended) beyond the long line and six feet outside each side line.

1) Short line. The back edge of the short line is 16 feet from the wall.

2) Service Markers. Lines at least six inches long which are parallel with, and midway between, the long and short lines. The extension of the service markers form the imaginary boundary of the service line.

3) Service Zone. It is the entire floor area in back of the short line, including the side lines and long line.

(b) Three Wall with Short Side Wall. The front wall is 20 feet wide and 20 feet high. The side walls are 20 feet long and 20 feet high, though the side wall tapers down to 12 feet high. The floor length and court markings are the same as four-wall.

(c) Three Wall with Long Side Wall. The court is 20 feet wide, 20 feet high and 40 feet long. The side walls may taper from 20 feet high at the front wall down to 12 feet high at the end of the court. All court markings are the same as four-wall.

(d) Service in Three-Wall Courts. A serve that goes beyond the side walls on the fly is considered long. A serve that goes beyond the long line on a fly, but within the side walls, is the same as a short.

8—HOW TO REFEREE WHEN THERE IS NO REFEREE

SAFETY IS THE RESPONSIBILITY OF EVERY PLAYER WHO ENTERS THE COURT.

At no time should the physical safety of the participants be compromised. Players are entitled, and expected to hold up their swing, without penalty, any time they believe there might be a risk of physical contact. Any time a player says he held up to avoid contact, even if he was overcautious, he is entitled to a hinder (rally replayed without penalty).

SCORE

Since there is no referee, or scorekeeper, it is important for the server to announce both the server's and the receiver's score before every first serve.

DURING RALLIES

During rallies, it is generally the hitter's responsibility to make the call. If there is a possibility of a skip ball, double-bounce, or illegal hit, play should continue until the hitter makes the call against himself. If the hitter does not make the call against himself and goes on to win the rally, and the player thought that one of the hitter's shots was not good, he may appeal to the hitter by pointing out which shot he thought was bad and request the hitter to reconsider. If the hitter is sure of his call, and the opponent is still sure the hitter is wrong, the rally is replayed. As a matter of etiquette, players are expected to make calls against themselves any time they are not sure. Unless the hitter is sure the shot was good, he should call it a skip.

SERVICE

(a) Fault Serves. The Receiver has the primary responsibility to make these calls, though either player may make the call. The receiver must make the call immediately, and not wait until he hits the ball and has the benefit of seeing how good a shot he can hit. It is not an option play. The receiver does not have the right to play a short serve just because he thinks it's a setup.

(b) Screen Serves. When there is no referee, the screen serve call is the sole responsibility of the receiver. If the receiver has taken the proper court position, near center court, and does not have clear view of the ball the screen should be called immediately. The receiver may not call a screen after attempting to hit the ball or, after taking himself out of proper court position by starting the wrong way. The server may not call a screen under any circumstances and must expect to play the rally unless he hears a call from the receiver.

(c) Other Situations. Foot faults, 10-second violations, receiving line violations, service zone infringement and other technical calls really require a referee. However, if either player believes his opponent is abusing any of these rules, be sure there is agreement on what the rule is, and to put each other on notice that the rules should be followed.

HINDERS

Generally, the hinder should work like the screen serve—as an option play for the hindered party. Only the person going for the shot can stop play by calling a hinder, and he must do so immediately—not wait until he has the benefit of seeing how good a shot he can hit. If the hindered party believes he can make an effective return in spite of some physical contact or screen that has occurred, he may continue to play.

POINT (AVOIDABLE) HINDERS

Since avoidable hinders are usually not intentional, they do occur even in the friendliest matches. The player who realizes he made such an error should simply award the rally to his opponent. If a player feels his opponent was guilty of an avoidable, and the player did not call it on himself, the offended player should appeal to his opponent by pointing out that he thought it was an avoidable. The player may then call it on himself, or disagree, but the call can only be made on yourself. Often, just pointing out what you think is an avoidable will put the player on notice for future rallies and prevent recurrence.

DISPUTES

If either player for any reason desires to have a referee, it is considered common courtesy for the other player to go along with the request, and a referee suitable to both sides should be found. If there is not a referee, and a question about a rule or rule interpretation comes up, seek out the club pro or a more experienced player. Then, after the match, contact your state racquetball association for the answer.

GOVERNING BODY

American Amateur Racquetball Association, 815 N. Weber, Suite 203, Colorado Springs, CO 80903

The American Amateur Racquetball Association (AARA) is a Group C (affiliated organization) member of the U.S. Olympic Committee and a member of the International Amateur Racquetball Federation. The paid national staff administers a network of volunteer organizations located in each of the 50 states and grouped into 16 regions. In pursuit of its primary goals to develop and advance the sport of racquetball, the AARA provides numerous programs, including (a) intercollegiate, high school, and court club programs; (b) over 44 categories of competition for players age 8 to 75+; (c) selecting players to represent the United States in international competition; (d) teaching, coaching, and referee certification; (e) national training camps; (f) disabled development programs; (g) junior development programs; and (h) national, regional, and state rankings in all categories.

MAGAZINES

National Racquetball, P.O. Drawer 6126, Clearwater, FL 33518

• SHUFFLEBOARD •

(Reproduced by permission of National Shuffleboard Association, Inc.*)

☐

A. GAME

1. The game of shuffleboard is played by either two (2) persons (called singles), or by four (4) persons (called doubles).

2. The object of the game is to propel discs by means of a cue onto scoring diagram at opposite end of court—to score, to prevent opponent from scoring, or both.

B. EQUIPMENT

1. Discs shall be made of composition not less than 9/16'' and not more than 1'' in thickness, 6'' in diameter, and not less than 11 1/2 ounces in weight. New discs shall weigh 15 ounces.

Four (4) discs shall be colored red, four (4) colored black. These eight (8) discs comprise a set. (Other color combinations may be used, as white or yellow, in place of red.) Care should be taken that all discs in a set shall be uniform in weight and thickness.

2. The cue shall not have an overall length of more than six feet, three inches (6'3''). No metal parts on cue shall touch playing surface of court.

3. Players shall not be required to play with discs, new or old, that are not in satisfactory condition. Defective discs will be replaced by good discs, if available. Any change of discs must be made before shooting for color choice. New discs are not to be used in tournament play, unless thoroughly broken in.

4. Official National Standard Court Dimensional Specifications (See Diagram, p. 434)

C. PLAYING RULES

1. Before practice rounds begin, each player may shoot two (2) discs only to check the speed of the court.

1a. Two full rounds of practice with each color are allowed for each player or team before play.

1b. In shooting for color choice, players must shoot from the head of the court.

To determine the color choice, two opposing players (one from each side), each shoot four discs to the far dead line. The players shoot alternately, first red (or substitute color), then black, then red, etc. The first three discs of each player are for practice and are removed progressively; the last disc of each player is left on the court. As between these last two discs, the disc nearer to the line determines who shall have color choice. The players then remain on the same color for the entire match. The measurement is from center of disc

---

*See page 440 for additional information.

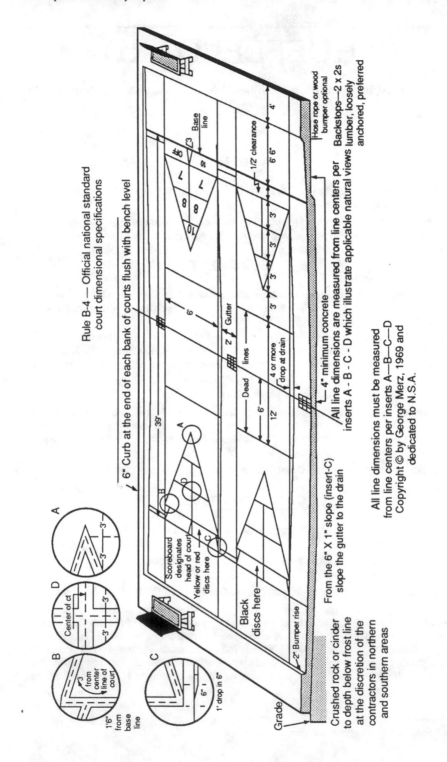

Rule B-4 — Official national standard court dimensional specifications

6" Curb at the end of each bank of courts flush with bench level

Hose rope or wood bumper optional

Backstops—2 x 2s lumber, loosely anchored, preferred

Base line

1/2" clearance

4'

6' 6"

3'

3'

3'

3'

3'

All line dimensions are measured from line centers per inserts A - B - C - D which illustrate applicable natural views

4" minimum concrete

From the 6" X 1" slope (insert-C) slope the gutter to the drain

6'

2' Gutter

Dead lines

6'

12 4 or more drop at drain

39'

Scoreboard designates head of court

Yellow or red discs here

Black discs here

2' Bumper rise

Grade

Crushed rock or cinder to depth below frost line at the discretion of the contractors in northern and southern areas

A

D Center of ct

3' 3'

3'

B

3' from center line of court

1'6" from base line

C

6' 1

1' drop in 6"

All line dimensions must be measured from line centers per inserts A—B—C—D
Copyright © by George Merz, 1969 and dedicated to N.S.A.

to center of line. If the last black disc shot touches or moves the last red disc, the color choice goes to the player of red.

1c. In Doubles, partners shall play on the same color at both ends of the court.

In doubles, each team may change ends of court ONCE immediately after color choice, but team winning color choice must make FIRST decision to change ends.

2. To start a game, the RED disc is shot first. Play alternates—red, then black—until all discs are shot. Red shall always be played from the right side of the head of court, and left side of foot of court.

ERROR IN COLOR LEAD: Error in color lead shall be corrected if discovered before half-round play is completed; otherwise, play continues in order started at beginning of game.

Correction means half round played over with correct color lead.

IN SINGLES, after all discs are played, constituting a HALF ROUND, the players walk to opposite end of court, or foot of court, and start play, with color lead changing to BLACK.

IN DOUBLES, after all discs are played at head of court, play starts at foot or opposite end—RED leading, BLACK following. Color lead does NOT change until both ends have been played (A ROUND).

The second game is started by the BLACK at the head of the court.

The third game is started by the RED at the head of the court.

3. All National Tournaments shall be 75 points, best two out of three games, main division. Consolation, one game of 100 points except final, which will be best two out of three 75 point games. Also games may be played in 8, 10, 12, or 16 frames.

4a. Players shall place their four (4) discs within and not touching lines of their respective half of 10-Off area. PENALTY—5 Off. Penalty not applied to a player until he has played a disc.

4b. Discs must be played from the clear from within the respective half of 10-OFF Area.

If disc played touches front or back lines—PENALTY—5 Off.

4c. If disc played touches side line, or triangle—PENALTY—10 Off; offender's disc removed, and opponent credited with any of his discs displaced.

All displaced discs shall be removed from the court immediately after scoring of opponent's displaced discs. Any 10-Offs the offender had on the court that were displaced will be removed before further play and also be deducted from the offender's score.

DISC TOUCHING LINES: It is common practice with players to jockey or slide the playing disc backward and forward to see if there is sand which might interfere with disc sliding evenly. NO PENALTY is to be called on this practice if lines are touched or crossed while jockeying. Disc in motion may cross out diagonal line.

A disc is played when it is completely in the seven area, but when a disc stops between the farthest dead line and seven area, it is a dead disc and shall be removed before further play. If a disc is touching farthest dead line, it is in play.

5. Players shall not step on or over base line of court, or extension of base line, except to gather and place their discs. PENALTY—5 Off for this offense when not in the act of executing a shot.

5a. Players must not touch a foot, hand, knee, or any other part of their body to the court on or over the base line or extension of the base line at any time while executing a shot. PENALTY—10 Off.

6. Players may stand behind base line extension in the alley between courts, before or while shooting, but not on adjoining court. PENALTY—5 Off.

6a. The area between the base line of the court and an imaginary line, even with the back of the bench, and bounded on the sides of the farthest line of each adjoining alley, should be considered part of the court.

7. In Doubles, players must remain seated when play is to their end of court until all discs are shot, score announced and official has called "Play" or signalled, or otherwise authorized them to do so. PENALTY—5 Off. In Singles, player must not cross the base line to proceed to the other end of the court until official has called "Play," or signalled, or otherwise authorized them to do so. PENALTY—5 Off.

8. Players must not leave court during a game without permission; EXCEPT to gather discs at end of half round. PENALTY—10 Off.

8a. No penalty if player leaves court between games. Player may not be gone more than ten minutes. PENALTY—10 Off. A game is concluded when the referee announces the score, the score is recorded on the scoreboard, and the scores are recorded on the player's card. The referee on the court shall start the time when the game is concluded. Additional penalties may be awarded for further infraction. See Rule C19.

9. Players shall not stand in the way of, or have a cue in the way of, or interfere with opponent while he is executing a play. PENALTY—5 Off.

10. Players shall not touch live discs at any time. PENALTY—10 Off, and that half round played over. An additional penalty may be invoked under C19 if necessary.

11. Players must not talk or make remarks to disconcert opponent's play. PENALTY—10 Off.

12. Any remark or motion to partner which indicates coaching his play is prohibited. PENALTY—10 Off.

13. Player shooting before opponent's disc comes to rest. PENALTY—10 Off, offender's disc removed, and opponent credited with any of his discs displaced. All displaced discs shall be removed from the court immediately after scoring of opponent's displaced discs. Any 10-Off the offender had on the court that was displaced will be removed before further play and also be deducted from offender's score.

14. For intentional delay or stalling: PENALTY—5 Off.

15. A cue slipping from a player's hand which touches or displaces any live disc, the player penalized 10 Off and opponent credited with any of his discs displaced, and that half round shall be played over unless game point has been reached by offender's opponent. If cue does not touch or displace any live disc, no penalty.

16. NO HESITATION SHOT ALLOWED. Forward motion of cue and disc must be continuous or accelerated. Any 10-Off(s) the offender had on the court that were displaced will be removed before further play and also be deducted from offender's score.

17. NO HOOK SHOT ALLOWED. The shot must be delivered in a straight line with continuous forward motion of cue and disc. PENALTY—10 Off, offender's disc removed and opponent credited with score of any of his discs displaced. All displaced discs shall be removed from the court immediately after scoring of opponent's displaced discs. Any 10-Off the offender had on the court that were displaced will be removed before further play and also be deducted from offender's score.

17a. Regarding a hook shot, hesitation shot, shooting off the line, there will be no appeal, as there is only one person who can tell if you have shot off the line or made a hook or hesitation shot, and that is the referee. That is strictly a judgment call by the referee, and once he has made that call, it will stand. The only time a divisional should be called is if the referee isn't sure of the penalty or gives wrong penalty—then the player will make an appeal.

18. Any player shooting two consecutive discs—PENALTY—10 Off, plus any 10 Offs offender may have on court. Other good discs of offender will not count. Opponent credited

with all good discs on court before second disc was played (except 10-Off), and that half round played over unless game point has been reached by offender's opponent.

19. In case of improper action of a player not specifically covered by the rules, the tournament director will ascertain the facts and may assess a penalty. He will also just insure that the offender gains no advantage from his improper action, and in addition, impose a penalty of 10 Off.

20. A disc or discs returning or remaining on the playing area of the court, after having struck any object outside the playing area, shall be removed before further play. It is called a dead disc.

20a. If a dead disc rebounds and touches a live disc, or causes another dead disc to touch a live disc, the half round shall be played over.

20b. EXCEPT, if it was the result of the last disc, which is the 8th disc, played in the half round; then, the half round is not replayed, and any score that was on the board immediately before the rebounding shall count.

20c. If a dead disc coming from another court moves or displaces a live disc, that half round shall be played over, with no score credited to any player.

Note: It shall be the responsibility of the host club to install proper backstops, preferably 2 X 2's loosely anchored, to prevent rebounds.

21. Any disc that clearly leaves the court beyond the farthest base line, or goes off the sides of the court is a dead disc.

22. A disc which stops less than eight inches beyond the farthest base line shall be removed.

23. A disc that is leaning over the edge of court and touching the alley shall be immediately removed.

24. A match will be forfeited after the third call of 5 minute intervals, total 15 minutes.

D. SCORING

1. Scoring Diagram—one 10-point area; two 8-point areas; two 7-point areas; one 10-off area.

2. After both players have shot their four (4) discs, SCORE ALL discs on diagram within and NOT touching lines; separation triangle in 10-off area not considered.

JUDGING DISC: When judging disc in relation to lines, the official shall sight DIRECTLY DOWN.

A MOUNTED DISC, or disc resting on top of disc, happens sometimes when players use excessive force in shooting. Each disc shall be judged separately according to scoring rules.

3. Play continues until all discs have been shot in that half round, even if game point has been reached.

4. If a tie game results at game point or over, play is continued in regular rotation of play, until two full rounds in doubles or one full round in singles are completed. At that time the side with the higher score wins, even if it has less than 75 points or the number of points specified as games points. If the score is tied again, play continues again as above outlined.

5. In tournament play, the winner of a match must sign the score card, thus approving the record entered thereon.

6. If an error occurs in the scoring of a score on the scoreboard at the end of a half round and it is discovered before the next half round is completed, the error must be corrected. Otherwise the score as scored on the scoreboard must stand, unless both sides are agreed on the correction.

E. OFFICIALS

1. Officials in Tournament Play shall be: Tournament Director, Assistant to the Tournament Director, Divisional Referees, Court Referees and Court Scorers.

2. THE TOURNAMENT DIRECTOR shall have complete charge of all arrangements of the tournament—namely, conduct the drawings, pairings, assign the courts, officials, set time for starting games and matches; inspect all courts and equipment, etc., and all other details which enter into tournament play.

3. An Assistant to the Tournament Director may be appointed as desired by the Tournament Director. He shall render final decision on any question of fact and no appeal from such decision may be made.

4. DIVISIONAL REFEREE—One or more Divisional Referees shall be appointed, number dependent on how many courts are in play.

The Divisional Referees are the aides of the Tournament Director, and shall carry out his orders regarding assigning officials and players to courts.

He shall see that discs, indicators, pointers, chalk, score cards, and other necessary equipment are at each court. He shall inform officials of any special rules and regulations which have been made for the conducting of the tournament. He shall collect all score cards at finish of matches and shall return them to Tournament Director.

He shall have jurisdiction only on the section of courts assigned to him. Divisional Referees shall be informed by Court Referees of all PLAYER APPEALS, and if decision made by Court Referee is not justified or not according to rules, may overrule him.

COURT REFEREE shall have complete charge of play on court assigned to him. He shall consult his Divisional Referee on APPEALS FROM PLAYERS.

He shall be sole authority on decisions and scores, except as above noted.

He shall determine and announce winner of color choice. He shall inform players of any rules and regulations made for the tournament.

He shall give signal for start of play, shall call disc good or no count, shall remove dead discs from play, shall announce score at end of each play, shall have charge of color indicator and announce color lead.

He shall announce any violation of rules to player and instruct scorer as to penalty of same.

He shall supervise the scoring and assure himself that it is correctly done.

He shall not touch live discs in determining whether they are good or no count. If he should disturb live discs, half round played over.

Except at end of half round, protested disc must be moved in order for the half round to be played over. He shall not gather discs for the players.

He shall sign score card at end of match and verify that scores are correct.

For any rule violation seen by the referee, a fine must be mandatory, with referee giving no warning at any time in all tournaments.

5. COURT SCORER shall tally clearly the score of game on scoreboard at end of court, tallying only score called by Court Referee after each half round. He shall also record on the official score card the final scores of each game of the match. Sign and return to the Divisional Referee.

F. APPEALS

1. Either player in singles, and either player in doubles at the end of the court to which the discs are played, may request permission from the referee to examine any close disc, as to good or no good.

1a. If a player wishes to make an appeal on any close disc, as to whether it is good or no count, it must be made before another disc is shot by either player, and the decision made shall be final and cannot be again appealed at the end of the half round, unless such disc or discs have been touched or moved by another disc after decision was made.

1b. If the referee and divisional agree, there will be no third call. If they disagree, there must be a third call by the Director or his representative.

1c. If there has been no request by either player to examine a close disc until AFTER the half round is completed, then the half round is played over if either player protests the referee's call, and the protest is sustained by the Tournament Director; UNLESS such disc or discs protested is the result of the last disc played. No live disc will be removed after a disc has been protested after the half round is completed, until the protested disc has been finalized. PENALTY—10 Off.

1d. Shooter may ask referee to have partner check close disc. Player shall not communicate with partner.

2. Player or players making appeal without sufficient reasons shall be PENALIZED 10 POINTS OFF SCORE.

3. Players may request officials to give them information concerning location of discs. Players shall not be permitted to examine these discs.

4. A player or team may protest any one or more officials assigned to their court, provided such protest is placed before the Divisional Referee or Tournament Director before shooting for color.

5. To refuse a referee, a player or team must have a good and valid stated reason.

Note: Tournament Director or Divisional Referee must appoint other officials to serve in place of those protested, whose appointment must stand.

G. SUBSTITUTES

Once a tournament starts there will be no substitutes allowed in any tournament. Tournament starts when the draw is completed.

H. WET COURTS

1. If it starts to rain during any unfinished half round of play, players will not be required to complete the half round. All discs will be removed from court to a dry place. In case of rain, score keeper will write on the back of the score card the scores, color lead, and at which end of the court play will resume. If the Tournament Director decides that the game is to continue after the rain ceases, play will then be resumed at score and color lead where play ceased. (If half round was not completed, then half round will be played over.)

2. If Tournament Director shall deem it necessary to discontinue play on account of weather conditions, any unfinished game or match shall be resumed later, at score and color lead where play ceased.

I. VIOLATIONS AND PENALTIES

C-4A	Discs not in starting area	5 OFF
C-4B	Discs touching front or back line	5 OFF
C-4C	Played disc touching sides or triangle (See Rule C-4)	10 OFF
C-5	Players stepping on or over base line or extension of base line while not in the act of shooting	5 OFF

C-5A	Players stepping on or over base line or extension of base line while in the act of shooting	10 OFF
C-6	Player may not stand or step on adjoining court while playing except to gather discs	5 OFF
C-7	Players not remaining seated	5 OFF
C-8	Player leaving court without permission during game	10 OFF
C-8A	Player leaving court between games and gone over 10 minutes	10 OFF
C-9	Standing in way of, or equipment in way of opponent	5 OFF
C-10	Touching live discs	10 OFF
C-11	Remarks disconcerting opponent	10 OFF
C-12	Any remark or motion to partner	10 OFF
C-13	Shooting disc while opponent's disc in motion (See Rule C-13)	10 OFF
C-14	For intentional stalling	5 OFF
C-15	Cue slipping from player's hand (See Rule C-15)	10 OFF
C-16	No hesitation shot allowed (See Rule C-16 & 17a)	10 OFF
C-17	No hook shot allowed (See Rule C-17 & 17a)	10 OFF
C-18	Player shooting two consecutive discs (See Rule C-18)	10 OFF
C-19	For improper action not otherwise covered, Tournament Director may impose penalty which prevents any advantage to the violator, plus PENALTY	10 OFF
F-1C	Moving disputed disc before inspection	10 OFF
F-2	Appealing without reason	10 OFF

GOVERNING BODY

National Shuffleboard Association, Trailer Estates, Box 6343, 2010 Iowa Ave., Bradenton, FL 33507

The National Shuffleboard Association (NSA), organized in 1931, is a nonprofit organization dedicated to the promotion of the game of shuffleboard throughout the United States and foreign countries. In addition to the adoption and distribution of the official national playing rules, the NSA (a) provides consultation and advice to shuffleboard clubs; (b) conducts national tournaments; and (c) distributes information materials regarding conduct of tournaments, location of clubs, club activities, equipment, and specifications for court design and construction.

MAGAZINES

National Shuffler, California Shuffleboard Association, 1100 Watt Ave., Sacramento, CA 95864

• SKIING •

THE INTERNATIONAL SKI COMPETITION RULES

(Reproduced by permission of the United States Ski Association*
in conjunction with the International Ski Federation)

☐

Note: The International Ski Federation (FIS) Competition Rules are recognized by the United States Ski Association (USSA) as the official rules for competitive skiing. Due to the lengthiness of the complete rules for the various disciplines of skiing, only a selected portion of the rules is presented here. Book III of the International Ski Competition Rules (ICR) includes the joint regulations for all ski competitions, ski jumping, ski flying, and nordic combined competitions. Book IV of the ICR includes the joint regulations for all ski competitions, downhill, slalom, giant slalom, parallel races, and combined alpine competitions. Only the particular rules for downhill, slalom, giant slalom and parallel events are presented here.

PARTICULAR RULES FOR EACH DISCIPLINE

700 DOWNHILL

701 THE COURSE

701.1 Joint Regulations for Men's and Ladies' Downhill Courses

Downhill courses for World Ski Championships, Olympic Winter Games and international competitions included in the Federation Internationale de Ski (FIS) Calendar must be approved by the FIS.

701.2 General Characteristics of the Course

It must be possible to slide on the downhill course continuously from start to finish without using ski poles. The terrain must be completely cleared of stones, stumps and such obstacles, in order to eliminate all objective danger for the competitors, even when the snow on the course is scarce. High speeds which may lead to the risk of dangerous falls must be eliminated by reducing the speed. This can be achieved by setting sufficient gates, which limit the average speed. The Technical Delegate (TD) must lay special stress on the observation of this rule.

701.3

It must be possible to take a means of transport right up to the start area.

---

*See page 458 for additional information.

701.4 Laying Out the Course

The course must not include any sharp, hard ridges. Above all, bumps which throw competitors far up into the air must be levelled out. The course must not include any steep ledges, which carry competitors through the air for long distances. This must be especially observed when the landing is flat, or onto a traverse or a counter-slope. The course must not include convex outward curves. Where medium or high speeds are involved, narrow sections must be avoided. The course must instead become wider with increasing speed. Such parts of the course and sections through wooded terrain must be at least 30 m wide. That does not mean that all parts of the course in wooded terrains must be more than 30 m wide, as sun and wind can often cause considerable damage to the snow of a course that is too wide. The inspector authorized to homologate the course decides whether this minimum width is adequate and if necessary can order it to be widened.

On the outside of medium or high speed curves there must be plenty of cleared space beside the course, so that a competitor who is falling and is thrown off the course cannot be injured by hitting obstacles (safety zone).

Obstacles, which a competitor might hit if he ran off the course, must be protected by snow, straw, safety nets or by other similar, suitable means.

On a natural course, no artificial obstacles may be built in to provide spectators with an acrobatic exhibition.

701.5 Men's Courses

701.5.1 For Olympic Winter Games, World Championships, World Cup and Continental Cups, the men's course must conform to the following technical data:

701.5.1.1 Minimum vertical drop: 800 m (in exceptional cases 750 m).

701.5.1.2 Maximum vertical drop: 1,000 m.

701.5.2 For other FIS races (junior and senior), the men's course must conform to the following technical data:

701.5.2.1 Minimum vertical drop: 500 m.

701.5.2.2 Maximum vertical drop: 1,000 m, junior 700 m.

701.5.3 Width of the gates: minimum 8 m.

701.5.4 At World Ski Championships and Olympic Winter Games, the best time of the men's downhill should not be less than two minutes.

701.6 Ladies' Courses

701.6.1 The ladies' downhill courses must have the following technical data for all competitions:

701.6.1.1 Minimum vertical drop: 500 m.

701.6.1.2 Maximum vertical drop: 700 m.

701.6.2 Width of the gates: minimum 8 m.

701.6.3 At World Ski Championships and Olympic Winter Games, the best time for the ladies' downhill should not be less than 1 min.40 secs.

701.6.4 Special Requirements for the Layout of Ladies' Courses

701.6.4.1 The downhill course for ladies should be a "controlled course" taking local conditions into account in setting it. It shall not include technical slalom figures, but must have sufficient gates on steep sections to eliminate excessive speed over difficult and bumpy terrain.

701.6.4.2 Ladies' downhill courses shall, if possible, be separated from the men's.

701.7 Exceptions

For the vertical drop of men's and ladies' courses, exceptions can be authorized by the FIS Council upon recommendation of the technical committees concerned.

702 MARKING AND GATES

702.1 Direction Flags

Enough red direction flags shall be placed down the left side of the course facing downhill, and green flags on the right, that competitors can recognize the course even in bad visibility.

The red and green flags may be replaced by twigs or branches approximately 30 cm high which are to be stuck into the snow. Both means of marking may be used on the same course. In addition enough pine needles and broken-up twigs should be strewn on the course to provide depth perception of bumps, dips and counter-slopes.

702.2 Size and Shape of the Gates

702.2.1 A downhill gate consists of 4 slalom poles, which must conform to the requirements of art. 802.2.1 and 2 flags.

702.2.2 For flags rectangular cloth panels are to be used, approximately 0.75 m wide by 1.0 m high. They are to be fastened on the poles so that they can be easily recognized by the competitors from a distance. Instead of red material a luminous orange color may be used.

702.2.3 The width of a gate must be at least 8 m.

702.3 Placement of the Gates

702.3.1 Gates shall be placed:

702.3.1.1 Always early enough before the dangerous section, so that the competitor can approach them in control and correctly positioned.

702.3.1.2 On extremely fast sections of the course, when it is considered necessary to check speed. In such places gates shall be set so that they may be properly anticipated without braking.

702.3.1.3 When the course changes suddenly from a steep face to a flat and bumpy section, to prevent dangerous falls on the flat. The gates shall always be placed sufficiently high on the steep face.

702.3.1.4 If in the judgement of the course setter, competitors should be directed onto a particular section of the slope, or if he thinks it desirable to indicate the direction of the course.

702.3.1.5 Where competitors could take dangerous short-cuts.

702.3.1.6 To keep competitors away from obstacles.

702.3.2 On traverses or a steep slope, the gates must be placed so that competitors are kept on the upper part of the slope.

702.3.3 On a bend, the gates must be placed always so that competitors are kept on the inner side of the curve (especially in wooded sections).

702.4 Numbering

The gates shall be numbered from top to bottom, not counting the start and finish.

702.5 Men's Gates

Men's downhill courses must be marked by red gates.

702.6 Ladies' Gates

Ladies' downhill courses must be marked with alternating red and blue gates or only red gates.

702.7 Marking the Gate's Position

The position of the gate's poles should be marked with ink or some other substance which remains visible throughout the entire race.

702.8 Preparation and Inspection of the Course

702.8.1 All downhill courses in the FIS Calendar must be completely prepared for racing and set with gates at least three days before the race, and must then be available for training.

702.8.2 Before the start of the first official training, the Jury is to make an inspection and final acceptance of the course setting with the FIS safety expert (if present) possibly in the presence of the team captains or coaches.

702.8.3 Before training begins on the first official training day, the competitors inspect the course wearing their training numbers easily visible. The time of inspection shall be determined by the Jury.

702.8.4 If the team captains' meeting so determines, the members of the Jury shall be available at the finish to receive from the competitors and trainers requests and suggestions regarding the course, training, etc.

703 OFFICIAL TRAINING

703.1 The official training for downhill races is an inseparable part of the competition. The competitors are required to participate according to the instructions of the Jury.

703.2 The official training shall encompass at least three training days: as an exception under extraordinary conditions, a minimum of three training runs.

703.2.1 In general a race shall be postponed or cancelled if the three days of training cannot be observed. An exception can be made in case of "force majeure", if nevertheless sufficient training runs can be carried out. The Jury can then decide to reduce the official training to two days.

703.2.2 The official training need not necessarily be on three consecutive days.

703.3 The entire facilities (start, course and finish area) must be completely prepared as for racing by the first official training day.

703.3.1 All safety measures and crowd control arrangements (fences, etc.) must be completed, so that the training may take place without danger to the competitors.

703.4 The first aid and medical services must be in complete operation during the time of training.

703.5 The organizers must arrange for the competitors to have priority on the lift facilities, and to use the training times without having to wait.

703.6 For all training runs during the official training, the competitors must wear their training numbers (bibs) in racing fashion. Training numbers shall be given to the competitor on the basis of their FIS points. Competitors without FIS points shall receive the last training numbers.

703.7 The start referee, or an official appointed by the Jury, must verify from a list that the competitors start their training in the order of their training numbers, and that in leaving the start a sufficiently safe interval of at least 30 seconds is maintained between competitors.

703.8 Timed Training

703.8.1 At the World Championships and Olympic Winter Games, times must be taken during the last two days of training.

703.8.2 At other FIS competitions, training times must be taken on at least one of the last two training days.

703.8.3 The registered times for the different runs of a training day will be given by loudspeaker. The information board can be used. They must be given to the team captains at the latest at the team captains' meeting.

703.8.4 A competitor must participate at least in one timed training run.

703.8.5 In case of a fall, or stopping, or being overtaken during a training run, the competitor must leave the race-course and leave it free. Continuation on the downhill race-course training is not permitted.

703.8.6 In case of atmospheric changes (snowfall, etc.) between the last training day and the day of the race, an inspection of the course will be organized for the competitors on the day of the race, accompanied by the members of the Jury.

703.8.7 At the time of the World Championships, Olympic Winter Games and all international races where substitutes are authorized, the designated substitutes must take part in the official training.

703.8.8 Whenever possible, one training should take place during the same hour as that scheduled for the race.

703.9 Closing and Modifications of the Course

Competitors are not allowed, under penalty of disqualification, to train on the course at times other than those announced by the race committee or the Jury, or to remove or rearrange gates, flags or visible hazards such as fences, bushes, overhanging branches, etc.

A competitor who discovers dangerous concealed hazards, such as rocks or horizontal fences thinly covered with snow, may, however, in case of urgency remove these hazards or render them visible, provided that he promptly reports the steps he has taken to a race official. A competitor may only use his skis and no other instrument for improvement of the course after the official training has begun. Marking the course, other than the official marking, is forbidden.

Marking any changes (such as short-cuts, for instance) on a closed course is also forbidden.

No competitor is allowed to go up or down a closed course with or without his skis.

The selection of those officials who are permitted to ski on a closed course shall be strictly limited by the Jury. The interdictions mentioned above apply also to the service personnel of the teams as well as those accompanying the teams.

704 YELLOW ZONES

If required, the Jury may establish "yellow zones" for the training and for the race. These must be equipped with clearly marked yellow or yellow/black flags which can be waved to alert the following competitor of danger. The competitor must stop when thus alerted.

705 START INTERVAL

The regular start interval shall be employed in all downhill races. As a rule competitors start at equal intervals of 60 seconds. The FIS or the Jury may order other intervals.

706 EXECUTION OF THE DOWNHILL

706.1 A competitor must complete the course on skis, but he may finish on only one ski (in accordance with art. 614.3).

706.2 A competitor must pass through all gates by crossing the gate lines with both feet. He has finished the race when both his feet have crossed the finish line (art. 614.3, 661.4.1, 661.4.1.3).

706.3 A competitor must wear the official start bib in the prescribed way.

707 CRASH HELMET

All competitors and forerunners in downhill races must wear crash helmets for the official training as well as for the race. If a competitor or forerunner fails to follow this regulation, he will not be allowed to start. The competitors are further required to wear helmets which have been approved by specialized testing organizations recognized by the FIS.

708 DOWNHILL IN TWO RUNS

708.1 If the topography of a country does not permit a downhill with the required vertical drop as stated in the International Competition Rules (ICR), a downhill in two runs can be organized.

708.2 The vertical drop must be at least 450 m.

708.3 The placing will be determined by the addition of the two runs. The rule for the start of the second run will be used (621.10).

708.4 All the prescriptions for the downhill are valid for the race in two runs. The Jury will rule in case of problems caused by the course, the training and the two runs.

708.5 The two runs should be run on the same day.

708.6 In World Cup and Continental Cups, it is normally not allowed to carry out downhill races in two runs. A special rule can be applied by the members of the respective committees.

708.7 Each national association may carry out two downhill races in two runs without calculating a special penalty (only minimum penalty).

800 SLALOM

801 THE COURSE

801.1 Vertical Drop

801.1.1 The vertical drop of a slalom course at World Championships and Olympic Winter Games should be 180 to 220 m for men; 130 to 180 m for ladies; at other international races 140 to 220 m for men; 120 to 180 m for ladies. In countries where courses with these vertical drops cannot easily be achieved, the vertical drop for a slalom may exceptionally be a minimum of 120 m.

Other exceptions can only be made in accordance with the FIS Council.

801.1.2 The course must be at least 40 m wide, if two runs are set on the same slope. In special cases the inspector can authorize exceptions for short parts of the course.

801.2 Characteristics of the Course

801.2.1 At World Championships and Olympic Winter Games the course must be set on slopes with a gradient of 20 to 27 new degrees (=33 to 45%). It may even be below 20, but may reach 30 degrees (=52%) only in very short parts of the course.

801.2.2 The ideal slalom course, taking into consideration the drop and the gradient specified above, must include a series of turns designed to allow the racers to combine maximum speed with neat execution and precision of turns.

801.2.3 The slalom should permit the rapid completion of all turns. The course should not require acrobatics incompatible with normal ski technique. It should be a technically clever composition of figures suited to the terrain, linked by single and multiple gates, allowing a fluent run, but testing the widest variety of ski technique, including changes of direction with very different radii. Gates should never be set only down the vertical fall-line of the slope, but so that some full turns are required, interspersed with traverses.

801.3 Preparation of the Course

Slalom competitions must be raced on snow that is as hard as possible. If snow falls during the race, the chief of course must ensure that it is stamped or, if possible, removed from the course.

802 SETTING THE COURSE

802.1 Course Setters

802.1.1 Inspection of the Slalom Slope

This must be carried out by the course setter with the TD, the referee and the course setter's assistant, so that the course setter can take into account the terrain, the snow conditions and the capability of the competitors before he sets the course, which should correspond to the average ability of the first 30 competitors.

802.1.2 Assistance must be provided for the course setter at the time fixed by the Jury for the setting of the course, so that he can concentrate on the actual setting and not be distracted by fetching poles, etc. The Chief of Course Equipment must provide enough of the following:

- Enough blue and red slalom poles.

- A corresponding number of flags, divided by colors.

- Sledge-hammers, crowbars or pneumatic drills.

- Number cards for numbering the gates.

- Coloring matter for marking the position of the poles.

802.2 Slalom Poles

802.2.1 A slalom gate consists of two solid, round, uniform poles of a diameter between a minimum of 20 mm and maximum of 32 mm. The poles must be of such a length that, when set, they project at least 1.80 m out of the snow. Slalom poles must be made of non-splintering material (plastic, plasticized bamboo or material with similar properties).

802.2.2 So-called "Colihue" slalom poles are allowed in Argentina and Chile.

802.2.3 Self-redressing slalom poles which meet the above standards are permitted.

802.2.4 Slalom poles are to be colored blue or red.

Consecutive gates must alternate color. Slalom poles must carry cloth flags of matching color. These may not be fastened in any way which might be a danger to the competitor.

802.3 Gates

802.3.1 The distance between two gates may not be less than 0.75 m. This distance must exist between the poles of different gates as well as between the gate line of one gate and the poles of another. The position of the poles must be marked on the snow with ink or some other substance which remains visible throughout the entire race, in case they are knocked out.

A gate must have a minimum width of 4 m and a maximum of 6 m. The distance from turning pole to turning pole of successive gates may not be less than 0.75 m nor more than 15 m.

802.3.2 A slalom must contain open and vertical gates as well as a minimum of two and, whenever possible, three vertical combinations (consisting of three to five gates) and at least four hairpin-combinations.

802.3.3 The most important types of gates and combinations of gates are:

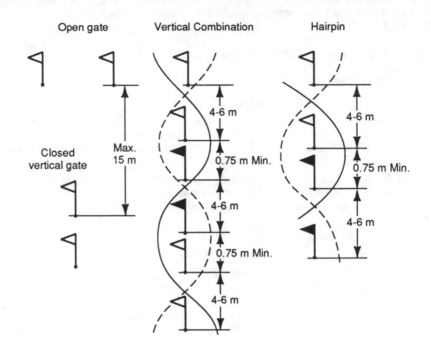

802.3.4 Number of Gates

Men	minimum	55 gates	−3)	
	maximum	75 gates	+3)	as exception
Ladies	minimum	45 gates	−3)	
	maximum	60 gates	+3)	

802.3.5 Numbering of Gates

The gates must be numbered from top to bottom and the numbers fixed preferably on the outside poles. The start and finish are not to be included.

802.4 Setting

In setting a slalom the following principles should be observed:

802.4.1 Avoidance of monotonous series of standardized combinations of gates.

802.4.2 Gates, which impose on competitors too sudden sharp braking, should be avoided, as they spoil fluency of the run without increasing the difficulties a modern slalom should have.

802.4.3 It is advisable before difficult combinations of gates to set at least one gate which allows the competitor to ski through the difficult combination under control.

802.4.4 It is not advisable to set difficult figures either right at the beginning or end of the course. The last gates should be rather fast, so that the competitor passes the finish at a good speed.

802.4.5 The last gate should not be too near the finish, to avoid the danger to competitors and timekeepers; it should direct competitors to the middle of the finish line. If the width of the slope necessitates it, the last gate can be common to both courses, provided the prescribed alternation of blue and red gates is maintained.

802.4.6 The finish must accord with art. 614 of Rules Common to Alpine Events.

802.4.7 Setting the course can be started at the top or bottom. The course setter can decide with which color to begin, taking into account the visibility.

802.4.8 The slalom poles should be rammed in by the chief of course or his assistants immediately after they have been set, so that the course setter can supervise the operation.

802.5 Reserve Poles

The chief of course is responsible for the correct placing and availability of enough reserve poles. They must be placed so that the competitors are not misled by them, and this must be checked by the Jury.

802.6 Checking the Slalom Course

The Jury must check that the course is ready for racing once the course setter has set it, paying special attention that:

- The slalom poles are firmly rammed in.

- The gates are in the right color order.

- The position of the poles is marked.

- The number tags are in the right order on the outside poles.

- The poles are high enough above the snow.

- The two slalom courses are far enough from each other to avoid misleading the competitors.

- The fencing of each course is far enough from the slalom poles.

- Obstacles at the edge of the course are either removed or neutralized.

- The last gate before the finish directs the competitors to the middle of the finish.

- The reserve poles are correctly placed not to mislead the competitors.

- Start and finish are in accordance with art. 613 and 614, of Rules Common to Alpine Events.

803 INSPECTION OF THE COURSE

803.1 The course must be in perfect racing condition from the time the competitors' inspection starts, and they must not be disturbed during it by workers on the course. The Jury decides the method of inspection. Competitors must wear their start numbers easily visible.

They may not ski down the prepared course or through the gates.

They are not permitted to enter the course on foot without skis.

803.2 It is absolutely essential to have a prepared practice slope near the start.

804 THE START

804.1 Start Intervals

The start takes place at irregular intervals in slalom. The chief of timing and calculation or his special assistant tells the starter when each competitor should start. The competitor on the way need not be over the finish before the next competitor starts.

804.2 Starting Order

804.2.1 In the first run according to the start numbers (art. 621.3).

804.2.2 For the second run see art. 621.10, of Rules Common to Alpine Events.

804.3 Start Signal

As soon as he has received the order for the next start, the starter gives the competitor the warning "Ready"—"Attention"—"Achtung," and a few seconds later the start signal "Go!"—"Partez!"—"Los!"

The competitor must start within 10 seconds of the start signal.

804.3.1 A competitor who has not appeared at the start 1 minute after being called by the official will be disqualified. Delays caused by the non-arrival of preceding competitors have to be taken into account. The start referee may, however, condone a delay which, in his opinion, is due to "force majeure". In doubtful cases he may allow the competitor a conditional start, inserted in the normal starting order. The start referee will make the necessary decisions. As soon as the race is ended, the start referee must report to the referee the start numbers and names of the competitors who:

804.3.1.1 Were not allowed to start, owing to their late appearance.

804.3.1.2 Were allowed to start in spite of their late appearance.

804.3.1.3 Were allowed to start conditionally.

804.4 Valid Start and False Start

Each competitor must start at the start signal, or he will be disqualified.

As soon as the race is over, the start referee must report to the referee the start numbers and names of the competitors who have made a false start or have infringed art. 613.3, of Rules Common to Alpine Events.

805 EXECUTION OF THE SLALOM

805.1 Dual Courses

A slalom must always be decided by two runs on two different courses. Both courses must be used one after the other, in the order decided by the Jury. Division of the competitors into two groups starting simultaneously on both courses is not allowed.

805.2 Limitations in the Second Run

The race committee has the right to reduce the number of competitors in the second run to half, provided that notice was given in the invitation or on the official notice board before the race started, and at the team captains' meeting before the draw.

805.3 A competitor must go through the gates according to art. 641.4.1, 641.4.1.2 and 641.4.1.3, of Rules Common to Alpine Events.

805.4 Interdiction to Continue after Clear Disqualification

A competitor who has been clearly disqualified for missing a gate may not continue through further gates. He cannot start in the second run, or be a forerunner.

By violation against this rule, the sanctions mentioned in art. 631.1 etc. will be valid.

805.5 Video Tape and Film Control

At World Championships and Olympic Winter Games, the race committee must arrange for recordings on video tape, so that the whole slalom can be reproduced.

At other international FIS Calendar races a video tape or film control is recommended.

900 GIANT SLALOM

901 THE COURSE

901.1 Vertical Drop

901.1.1 A course for men must have a vertical drop of between 250 and 400 m.

901.1.2 A course for ladies must have a vertical drop of between 250 and 350 m.

901.1.3 For World Cup the minimum vertical drop is 300 m (men and ladies).

901.1.4 The FIS Council may, however, authorize a competition on a course without the minimum vertical drop specified if the particular conditions in a country require it.

901.2 Terrain

The terrain should preferably be undulating and hilly. The course must be at least 30 m wide.

901.3 Preparation of the Course

The course must be prepared as for the downhill race. The parts of the course where gates are set and where competitors have to turn must be prepared as for a slalom.

902 SETTING THE COURSE, POLES AND FLAGS

902.1 Normal slalom poles are used, which must conform to the specifications of art. 902.2.1. For the turning pole of the gate flag a self-redressing pole may be used, provided self-redressing poles are used for all turning poles of the entire course.

The flags are at least about 75 cm wide and about 50 cm high. They are fixed between the poles so that the lower edge of the flag is at least 1 meter above the snow. The gates must be alternately red and blue, the blue flags preferably with a distinctive mark, ideally a diagonal white stripe. In bad visibility red direction flags should be placed down the left side of the course facing downhill, and green flags on the right (702.4.1).

The red and green flags may be replaced by twigs or branches approximately 30 cm high which are to be stuck into the snow. Both means of marking may be used on the same course. In addition enough pine needles and broken-up twigs should be strewn on the course to provide depth perception of bumps, dips and counter-slopes.

902.2 Placing the Gates

The gates must be at least 4 m and at most 8 m wide. The distance between the nearest poles of two successive gates must not be less than 10 m. The gates must be set so that the competitors can distinguish them clearly and quickly even at high speed. The two flags of a gate should be set at right angles to the racing line. For closed gates, the flags should be approximately 30 cm wide and 50 cm high.

902.3

Setting the course can be started from the top or bottom. The course setter can decide with which color to begin, taking into account the visibility.

902.4 Marking

The positions of the poles must be marked on the snow with ink or some other substance which remains visible throughout the entire race, in case they are knocked out.

902.5 Planning the Course

In planning the course the following principles must be followed:

902.5.1 The giant slalom has to be set as follows: 15% of the vertical drop equals the number of gates plus or minus 5 gates. The distance between the turning poles of two consecutive gates must be at least 10 m. The first run should be set the day before the race. Both runs can be set on the same piste but the second run must be re-set.

902.5.2 The skillful use of the ground when setting a giant slalom is, in most cases, even more important than for a slalom, since figures play a less important role owing to the prescribed width of the gates and the greater distances between them. It is therefore better to set mainly single gates, while exploiting the ground to the utmost. Figures can be set, but mainly on uninteresting terrain.

902.5.3 A giant slalom should present a variety of long, medium and small turns. The competitor should be free to choose his own line between the gates, which must not be set down the vertical line of the slope. The full width of a hill should be used wherever possible.

902.5.4 The finish must be prepared and equipped as in art. 614 of Rules Common to Alpine Events.

902.5.5 The course setter should set the two courses so that there is as little difference as possible between the best times of each run (art. 605.7.5).

902.5.6 The chief of course is responsible for the correct placing and availability of enough reserve poles. They must be placed so that the competitors are not misled by them and this must be checked by the Jury.

903 INSPECTION OF THE COURSE

The course will remain closed for training on the day of the race. The gates must be finally set at least one hour before the start. The competitors are allowed to study the course after its final setting, either by climbing on skis or by slowly skiing down alongside the course. Skiing through a gate, or practising turns parallel with those required by gates on the course, will lead to disqualification. Competitors must wear their start numbers easily visible.

904 START INTERVALS

904.1 As a rule, the competitors start at a constant interval of 60 seconds, according to their start numbers. The Jury or the FIS may order longer intervals (see art. 622).

904.2 Start order for the second run see art. 621.10 of Rules Common to Alpine Events.

905 EXECUTION OF THE GIANT SLALOM

A giant slalom must always be decided by two runs (men and ladies). The second run may be held on the same piste, but the gates must be re-set. Whenever possible, both runs should be held on the same day.

905.1 Interdiction to Continue after Clear Disqualification

A competitor who has been clearly disqualified for missing a gate may not continue through further gates, or start in the second run, or be a forerunner. By violation against these rules the sanctions mentioned in art. 631.9 etc. will be valid.

906 FURTHER RULES

Except where special exceptions are made above, the rules for downhill (art. 703.9 and 706) and slalom (art. 805.5 if possible) apply also to giant slaloms.

1100 PARALLEL EVENTS

1101 DEFINITION

The parallel is a race where two or more competitors race simultaneously side by side down two or more courses. The setting of the courses, the configuration of the ground and the preparation of the snow are to be as identical as possible.

1101.1 Normally (at World Cup level), parallel races count only for the Nation's Cup (see World Cup Rules). They may also be introduced in the World Cup circuit where World Cup points may be awarded for the first 15 finishers. Final decision in this matter rests with the World Cup Committee and is subject to the approval of the Alpine Ski Committee.

1102 VERTICAL DROP

The vertical drop of the course must be between 80 and 100 meters. There must be between 20 and 30 gates, not counting the start and finish. The run-time of each race should be between 20 and 25 seconds.

1103 CHOICE AND PREPARATION OF THE COURSE

1103.1 Choose a slope wide enough to permit two or more courses, preferably slightly concave (permitting a view of the whole course from any point). The terrain variations must be the same across the surface of the slope. The course layouts must have the same profile and the same difficulties.

1103.2 Over the full width of the chosen slope, the snow must be consistently hard, similar to course preparation for slalom, so that it is possible to offer equal race conditions on both courses.

1103.3 There must be a lift next to the course to ensure that the races are run smoothly and rapidly.

1103.4 The course must be entirely closed off by barriers. It is recommended to fence off reserved places intended for trainers, competitors and servicemen.

1104 COURSE LAYOUT

1104.1 Each course is designated by a series of gates, poles or curve markers; each gate marker is composed of two poles with a banner measuring 30 cm wide by 70 cm high, stretched between them.

1104.2 The slalom poles to be used must meet the requirements of art. 802.2.1. The use of self-redressing poles is not permitted.

1104.3 In the case of only two courses, poles and banners are red for the course on the left going down and blue for the other course. If there are more than two courses, the organizer must use different colors for the other course such as green or orange. The banners must be placed at least 1 m above the snow (the bottom of the banner).

1104.4 The same course setter establishes the courses and makes sure they are identical and parallel. He must ensure that the course flow is smooth and that there is variety in the curves (very pronounced curves) and that the course causes rhythm changes. In no case should this event resemble a long straight run from top to bottom. The gate poles must be set using a drill in order to avoid protests.

1104.5.1 The first gate in each course must be placed no less than 8 m from the start and no more than 10 m.

1104.5.2 Shortly before the finish line, after the last gate marker, the separation between the two tracks must be well designed so that they direct each competitor towards the finish line. The course setter must place the last gate in such a manner that the racers are guided towards the center of each finish line.

1105 DISTANCE BETWEEN THE TWO COURSES

The equidistance between two corresponding markers (from turning pole to turning pole) must be no less than 6 m and no more than 7 m. The distance between the starting gates must also be the same.

1106 START

1106.1 Start Device

Two hinged gates each 100 cm wide and 40 cm in height. The starting block (behind the skis) must be covered with teflon to protect the skis. The weight for each hinge gate is 30 kg.

Opening of the gate: Electric control (accu. 24v.). The bolt (lock) system should utilize an electromagnet so that the start gun opens simultaneously the hinge gates (outwardly). This start system could also be manually operated.

1106.2 The FIS Technical Delegate and the starter together will control the start. In order to co-ordinate their functions, the Technical Delegate should have a start platform set up between the hinge gates, either in front of or behind so that he can see the entire race course. The start signal can only be given after the Technical Delegate has given the competitors permission to start. Any starting system can be employed provided that the system guarantees a simultaneous start.

1106.3 False Starts

Disqualification will take place:

1106.3.1 If the competitor does not have at least one ski tip touching the hinge gate.

1106.3.2 If the competitor does not have both ski poles set on the visible and marked wood blocks.

1106.4 Start Command

Before the starter gives the command of either "Achtung bereit" or "Ready set" and the subsequent firing of the starting gun which opens the hinge gates, he must first ensure that the competitors are ready by asking the competitor starting in the red course "Red ready?" or "Rot fertig?" and then the competitor in the blue course "Blue ready?" or "Blau fertig?" Only after both competitors have answered "yes" or "ja", the starter can give the start command.

1107 FINISH

1107.1 The finish areas must be symmetrical. The line of the finish must be parallel with the line of the starts.

1107.2 Each finish line is marked by two poles connected by a banner which form the finish. Each of these must be at least 7 m wide. The inside poles of the areas are placed side by side.

1107.3 For safety reasons, it is necessary to set up visually separate finish approaches and exits.

1108 JURY AND COURSE SETTER

1108.1 In view of the special type of this competition, the Jury is set up as follows:
- the Technical Delegate
- the referee
- the assistant referee
- the chief of course
- two start referees, nominated by the organization, without voting right
- two finish referees, nominated by the organization, without voting right

1108.2 The course setter is designated by the Jury of the competition (if he is not chosen by the FIS). Before setting the course, he must conduct an inspection and study of the course in the presence of the Jury and those responsible for the course (the chief of race and the chief of course). If the Jury has designated an assistant course setter, he will assist in this inspection.

1109 TIMING

1109.1 As the start is simultaneous, only the difference in time between the competitors at the finsh will be registered. With several electric eyes and an automatic print-out, the first competitor that breaks one of the signals starts the chronometer and receives the time "zero", the following competitors stop successively the clocks (chronometers) and receive the time difference in 1/1000-seconds to the first competitor.

1110 RUNNING OF A PARALLEL ON TWO COURSES

Each match between two competitors consists of two runs; the two racers change courses for the second run.

1110.1 The finals of a competition should not include more than 32 competitors. These 32 competitors may either be entered directly or be the first 32 finishers from qualification competitions.

1110.2 Formation into Groups of Two

1110.2.1 Sixteen groups of two competitors are formed, either after the finish of the selected previous race or after their general classification in the World Cup at the time, or according to their value (FIS points), in the following manner:

Group together:		
	the 1st and the 32nd	the 9th and the 24th
	the 2nd and the 31st	the 10th and the 23rd
	the 3rd and the 30th	the 11th and the 22nd
	the 4th and the 29th	the 12th and the 21st
	the 5th and the 28th	the 13th and the 20th
	the 6th and the 27th	the 14th and the 19th
	the 7th and the 26th	the 15th and the 18th
	the 8th and the 25th	the 16th and the 17th

1110.2.2 The competitors receive the numbers from 1 to 32 in the order of their value and they keep them until the end of the races.

1110.2.3 Start order: following the order of the appended table, from top to bottom. All groups race in succession their first run and then their second.

The lower starting number goes down the red course first, the higher number the blue course. For the second run it is reversed. This same system is used for all elimination runs including the final.

1110.2.4 The competitors can examine the course once from top to bottom with skis on. Examination time 10 minutes.

1110.2.5 Sixteen winners remain as a result of the first elimination. In other words, those who, in their group, obtained the lower total for the two runs or possibly two times zero.

1110.3 Second Elimination Run

1110.3.1 The 16 qualified competitors start according to the start system in pairs from top to bottom.

1110.3.2 These races are also run in two runs. There are eight that qualify for the quarter-finals.

1110.3.3 If the results of a parallel event are to count towards overall standings such as the World Cup, then the finish positions for the 9th to 15th position will be obtained by using the results of the second elimination round. The competitors will be placed in order starting with the smallest losing time margin obtained in the second elimination round.

1110.4 Quarter-finals

1110.4.1 The eight qualified competitors start according to the start system in pairs from top to bottom.

1110.4.2 From the losing four competitors, positions 5, 6, 7 and 8 are determined by the time difference of each loser from the winner.

1110.5 Semi-finals

1110.5.1 The four qualified competitors start according to the start system from top to bottom.

1110.5.2 The losers of the semi-finals race their first run for the 3rd and 4th positions before the finalists race their first run; then the finalists race their first run, then the semi-finalists their second run and then the finalists their final race.

1111 CONTROL OF THE COURSE

The gate-keepers (course-judges) are situated on both exterior sides of the courses. Each gate-keeper (course-judge) is supplied with a flag which corresponds to the color of the course he is controlling (either blue or red). This flag is to be used immediately to notify the Jury of a disqualification in his section of the course. An official (judge) with a yellow flag is located approximately half way down the course where immediate judging of a gate-keeper's disqualification is done by raising the yellow flag in the direction of the course where the disqualification has been indicated. The raising of the yellow flag confirms the disqualification of the competitor.

1112 DISQUALIFICATIONS

1112.1 Causes for disqualification are the following:

- false start (art. 1106.3)
- changing from one course to another
- disturbing opponent, voluntarily or not
- passing one ski inside a gate or pole with the other ski outside
- turn not executed on the outside of a gate
- not finishing

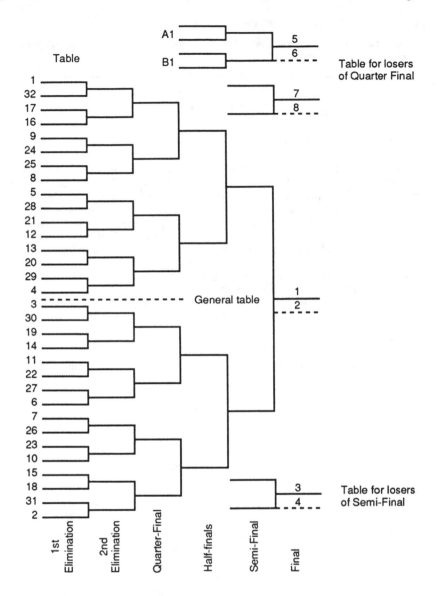

Table

Table for losers
of Quarter Final

General table

Table for losers
of Semi-Final

1st Elimination • 2nd Elimination • Quarter-Final • Half-finals • Semi-Final • Final

1112.2 If both competitors fall in either the first or second run of any round, the first competitor to reach the finish successfully will advance to the next round. If both competitors do not finish, the competitor who successfully skied the farthest distance will advance to the next round.

1112.3 The competitor that does not finish or is disqualified in the first run does not start in a second run.

1112.4 In every case the finalists start as last competitors for the second run (art. 1010.5.3) to finish the competition.

1113 SLALOM RULE EXTENSION

All slalom rules remain in effect, including the necessary homologation of the course as well as the competition rules.

GOVERNING BODY

United States Ski Association, 1750 E. Boulder St., Colorado Springs, CO 80909

As the national governing body of amateur skiing in the United States, the United States Ski Association (USSA) strives to develop programs to enrich the knowledge and skills of amateur athletes. Recognized by the U.S. Olympic Committee (USOC) and the Federation Internationale de Ski (FIS), USSA operates programs in alpine, nordic, freestyle, and recreational skiing. USSA programs on the local, regional, and national levels provide athletes the opportunity to reach their full athletic potential, whatever age or ability. The USSA administers numerous programs such as Junior Racing Teams; Youth Ski League; state, divisional, regional and national competition; officials' training clinics; and national rankings. A number of publications are available through the USSA, including Alpine Skiing Competition Guide, Nordic Skiing Competition Guide, Freestyle Skiing Competition Guide, Ski Racing for Children, and the USSA Directory.

MAGAZINES

Skiing Magazine, CBS Magazines, 1 Park Ave., New York, NY 10016

Ski Racing, United States Ski Association, 1750 E. Boulder St., Colorado Springs, CO 80909

• SOCCER •

LAWS OF THE GAME

(Reproduced by permission of the United States Soccer Federation*)

☐

Note: The rules of soccer have been commonly standardized worldwide through the international structure of the Federation Internationale de Football Association (FIFA) and its 160 affiliate national organizations. The Laws of the Game as presented here do not include the Decisions of the International Board (explanatory notes and interpretations) as contained in the official rules publication, Laws of the Game and Universal Guide for Referees, available through the USSF.

LAW I. THE FIELD OF PLAY

The Field of Play and appurtenances shall be as shown in the following plan:

(1) Dimensions. The field of play shall be rectangular, its length being not more than 130 yards nor less than 100 yards and its breadth not more than 100 yards nor less than 50 yards. (In International Matches the length shall not be more than 120 yards nor less than 110 yards and the breadth not more than 80 yards nor less than 70 yards.) The length shall in all cases exceed the breadth.

(2) Marking. The field of play shall be marked with distinctive lines, not more than 5 inches in width, not by a V-shaped rut, in accordance with the plan, the longer boundary lines being called the touch-lines and the shorter the goal-lines. A flag on a post not less than 5 ft. high and having a non-pointed top, shall be placed at each corner; a similar flag-post may be placed opposite the halfway line on each side of the field of play, not less than 1 yard outside the touch-line. A halfway-line shall be marked out across the field of play. The centre of the field of play shall be indicated by a suitable mark and a circle with a 10 yards radius shall be marked round it.

(3) The Goal Area. At each end of the field of play two lines shall be drawn at right-angles to the goal-line, 6 yards from each goal-post. These shall extend into the field of play for a distance of 6 yards and shall be joined by a line drawn parallel with the goal-line. Each of the spaces enclosed by these lines and the goal-line shall be called a goal area.

(4) The Penalty-Area. At each end of the field of play two lines shall be drawn at right-angles to the goal-line, 18 yards from each goal-post. These shall extend into the field of play for a distance of 18 yards and shall be joined by a line drawn parallel with the goal-line. Each of the spaces enclosed by these lines and the goal-line shall be called a penalty-area. A suitable mark shall be made within each penalty-area, 12 yards from the mid-point of the goal-line, measured along an undrawn line at right-angles thereto. These shall be the penalty-kick marks. From each penalty-kick mark an arc of a circle, having a radius of 10 yards, shall be drawn outside the penalty-area.

---

*See pages 469 and 470 for additional information.

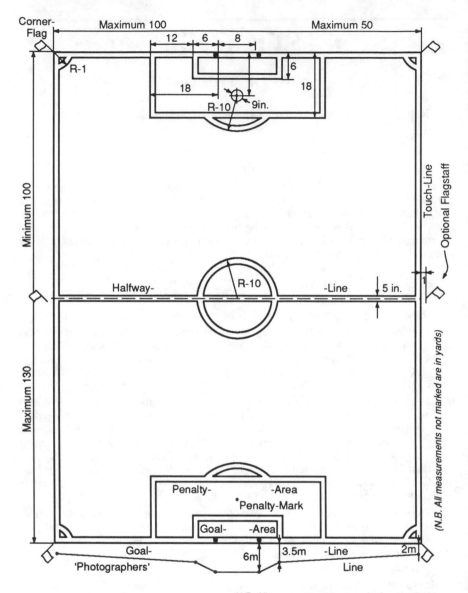

(N.B. All measurements not marked are in yards)

(5) The Corner-Area. From each corner-flag post a quarter circle, having a radius of 1 yard, shall be drawn inside the field of play.

(6) The Goals. The goals shall be placed on the centre of each goal-line and shall consist of two upright posts, equidistant from the corner-flags and 8 yards apart (inside measurement), joined by a horizontal cross-bar the lower edge of which shall be 8 ft. from the

ground. The width and depth of the goal-posts and the width and depth of the cross-bars shall not exceed 5 inches (12cm). The goal-posts and the cross-bars shall have the same width.

Nets may be attached to the posts, cross-bars and ground behind the goals. They should be appropriately supported and be so placed as to allow the goalkeeper ample room.

Editor's Note. Goal nets. The use of nets made of hemp, jute or nylon is permitted. The nylon strings may, however, not be thinner than those made of hemp or jute.

LAW II. THE BALL

The ball shall be spherical; the outer casing shall be of leather or other approved materials. No material shall be used in its construction which might prove dangerous to the players.

The circumference of the ball shall not be more than 28 in. and not less than 27 in. The weight of the ball at the start of the game shall be not more than 16 oz. nor less than 14 oz. The pressure shall be equal to 0.6-1.1 atmosphere ($=600$-$1,100$ gr/cm^2) at sea level. The ball shall not be changed during the game unless authorised by the Referee.

LAW III. NUMBER OF PLAYERS

(1) A match shall be played by two teams, each consisting of not more than eleven players, one of whom shall be the goalkeeper.

(2) Substitutes may be used in any match played under the rules of an official competition at FIFA, Confederation or National Association level, subject to the following conditions:

(a) that the authority of the international association(s) or national association(s) concerned, has been obtained,

(b) that, subject to the restriction contained in the following paragraph

(c) the rules of a competition shall state how many, if any, substitutes may be used, and

(d) that a team shall not be permitted to use more than two substitutes in any match.

(3) Substitutes may be used in any other match, provided that the two teams concerned reach agreement on a maximum number, not exceeding five, and that the terms of such agreement are intimated to the Referee, before the match. If the Referee is not informed, or if the teams fail to reach agreement, no more than two substitutes shall be permitted.

(4) Any of the other players may change places with the goalkeeper, provided that the Referee is informed before the change is made, and provided also, that the change is made during a stoppage of the game.

(5) When a goalkeeper or any other player is to be replaced by a substitute, the following conditions shall be observed:

(a) the Referee shall be informed of the proposed substitution, before it is made,

(b) the substitute shall not enter the field of play until the player he is replacing has left, and then only after having received a signal from the Referee,

(c) he shall enter the field during a stoppage in the game, and at the halfway-line.

(d) A player who has been replaced shall not take any further part in the game.

(e) A substitute shall be subject to the authority and jurisdiction of the Referee whether called upon to play or not.

Punishment:

(a) Play shall not be stopped for an infringement of paragraph 4. The players concerned shall be cautioned immediately the ball goes out of play.

(b) If a substitute enters the field of play without the authority of the Referee, play shall be stopped. The substitute shall be cautioned and removed from the field or sent off according to the circumstances. The game shall be restarted by the Referee dropping the ball at the place where it was when the play was stopped, unless it was within the goal area at that time, in which case it shall be dropped on that part of the goal area line which runs parallel to the goal-line, at the point nearest to where the ball was when play was stopped.

(c) For any other infringement of this law, the player concerned shall be cautioned, and if the game is stopped by the Referee, to administer the caution, it shall be re-started by an indirect free-kick, to be taken by a player of the opposing team, from the place where the ball was, when play was stopped. If the free-kick is awarded to a team within its own goal area, it may be taken from any point within that half of the goal area in which the ball was when play was stopped.

LAW IV. PLAYERS' EQUIPMENT

(1) A player shall not wear anything which is dangerous to another player.

(2) Footwear (boots or shoes) must conform to the following standard:

(a) Bars shall be made of leather or rubber and shall be transverse and flat, not less than half an inch in width and shall extend the total width of the sole and be rounded at the corners.

(b) Studs which are independently mounted on the sole and are replaceable shall be made of leather, rubber, aluminum, plastic or similar material and shall be solid. With the exception of that part of the stud forming the base, which shall not protrude from the sole more than one quarter of an inch, studs shall be round in plan and not less than half an inch in diameter. Where studs are tapered, the minimum diameter of any section of the stud must not be less than half an inch. Where metal seating for the screw type is used, this seating must be embedded in the sole of the footwear and any attachment screw shall be part of the stud. Other than the metal seating for the screw type of stud, no metal plates even though covered with leather or rubber shall be worn, neither studs which are threaded to allow them to be screwed on to a base screw that is fixed by nails or otherwise to the soles of footwear, nor studs which, apart from the base, have any form of protruding edge rim or relief marking or ornament, should be allowed.

(c) Studs which are moulded as an integral part of the sole and are not replaceable shall be made of rubber, plastic, polyurethane or similar soft materials. Provided that there are no fewer than ten studs on the sole, they shall have a minimum diameter of three eighths of an inch (10mm.). Additional supporting material to stabilise studs of soft materials, and ridges which shall not protrude more than 5mm. from the sole and moulded to strengthen it, shall be permitted provided that they are in no way dangerous to other players. In all other respects they shall conform to the general requirements of this Law.

(d) Combined bars and studs may be worn, provided the whole conforms to the general requirements of this Law. Neither bars nor studs on the soles shall project more than three-quarters of an inch. If nails are used, they shall be driven in flush with the surface.

(3) The goalkeeper shall wear colours which distinguish him from the other players and from the Referee.

Punishment: For any infringement of this Law, the player at fault shall be sent off the field of play to adjust his equipment and he shall not return without first reporting to the Referee, who shall satisfy himself that the player's equipment is in order; the player shall only re-enter the game at a moment when the ball has ceased to be in play.

LAW V. REFEREES

A Referee shall be appointed to officiate in each game. His authority and the exercise of the powers granted to him by the Laws of the Game commence as soon as he enters the field of play.

His power of penalising shall extend to offences committed when play has been temporarily suspended, or when the ball is out of play. His decision of points of fact connected with the play shall be final, so far as the result of the game is concerned. He shall:

(a) Enforce the Laws.

(b) Refrain from penalising in cases where he is satisfied that, by doing so, he would be giving an advantage to the offending team.

(c) Keep a record of the game; act as timekeeper and allow the full or agreed time, adding thereto all time lost through accident or other cause.

(d) Have discretionary power to stop the game for any infringement of the Laws and to suspend or terminate the game whenever, by reason of the elements, interference by spectators, or other cause, he deems such stoppage necessary. In such a case he shall submit a detailed report to the competent authority, within the stipulated time, and in accordance with the provisions set up by the National Association under whose jurisdiction the match was played. Reports will be deemed to be made when received in the ordinary course of post.

(e) From the time he enters the field of play, caution any player guilty of misconduct or ungentlemanly behavior and, if he persists, suspend him from further participation in the game. In such cases the Referee shall send the name of the offender to the competent authority, within the stipulated time, and in accordance with the provisions set up by the National Association under whose jurisdiction the match was played. Reports will be deemed to be made when received in the ordinary course of post.

(f) Allow no person other than the players and linesmen to enter the field of play without his permission.

(g) Stop the game if, in his opinion, a player has been seriously injured; have the player removed as soon as possible from the field of play, and immediately resume the game. If a player is slightly injured, the game shall not be stopped until the ball has ceased to be in play. A player who is able to go to the touch or goal-line for attention of any kind, shall not be treated on the field of play.

(h) Send off the field of play, any player who, in his opinion, is guilty of violent conduct, serious foul play, or the use of foul or abusive language.

(i) Signal for recommencement of the game after all stoppages.

(j) Decide that the ball provided for a match meets with the requirements of Law II.

LAW VI. LINESMEN

Two Linesmen shall be appointed, whose duty (subject to the decision of the Referee) shall be to indicate:

(a) when the ball is out of play,

(b) which side is entitled to a corner-kick, goal-kick or throw-in,

(c) when a substitution is desired.

They shall also assist the Referee to control the game in accordance with the Laws. In the event of undue interference or improper conduct by a Linesman, the Referee shall dispense with his services and arrange for a substitute to be appointed. (The matter shall be reported by the Referee to the competent authority.) The Linesmen should be equipped with flags by the Club on whose ground the match is played.

LAW VII. DURATION OF THE GAME

The duration of the game shall be two equal periods of 45 minutes, unless otherwise mutually agreed upon, subject to the following: (a) Allowance shall be made in either period for all time lost through accident or other cause, the amount of which shall be a matter for the discretion of the Referee; (b) Time shall be extended to permit a penalty-kick being taken at or after the expiration of the normal period in either half.

At half-time the interval shall not exceed five minutes except by consent of the Referee.

LAW VIII. THE START OF PLAY

(a) At the beginning of the game, choice of ends and the kick-off shall be decided by the toss of a coin. The team winning the toss shall have the option of choice of ends or the kick-off. The Referee having given a signal, the game shall be started by a player taking a place-kick (i.e., a kick at the ball while it is stationary on the ground in the centre of the field of play) into his opponents' half of the field of play. Every player shall be in his own half of the field and every player of the team opposing that of the kicker shall remain not less than 10 yards from the ball until it is kicked-off; it shall not be deemed in play until it has travelled the distance of its own circumference. The kicker shall not play the ball a second time until it has been touched or played by another player.

(b) After a goal has scored, the game shall be restarted in like manner by a player of the team losing the goal.

(c) After half-time; when restarting after half-time, ends shall be changed and the kick-off shall be taken by a player of the opposite team to that of the player who started the game.

Punishment. For any infringement of this Law, the kick-off shall be retaken, except in the case of the kicker playing the ball again before it has been touched or played by another player; for this offence, an indirect free-kick shall be taken by a player of the opposing team from the place where the infringement occurred, unless the offence is committed by a player in his opponents' goal area, in which case, the free-kick shall be taken from a point anywhere within that half of the goal area in which the offence occurred.

A goal shall not be scored direct from a kick-off.

(d) After any other temporary suspension; when restarting the game after a temporary suspension of play from any cause not mentioned elsewhere in these Laws, provided that immediately prior to the suspension the ball has not passed over the touch or goal-lines, the Referee shall drop the ball at the place where it was when play was suspended, unless it was within the goal area at that time, in which case it shall be dropped on that part of the goal area line which runs parallel to the goal-line, at the point nearest to where the ball was when play was stopped. It shall be deemed in play when it has touched the ground; if, however, it goes over the touch or goal-lines after it has been dropped by the Referee, but before it is touched by a player, the Referee shall again drop it. A player shall not play the ball until it has touched the ground. If this section of the Laws is not complied with, the Referee shall again drop the ball.

LAW IX. BALL IN AND OUT OF PLAY

The ball is out of play:

(a) When it has wholly crossed the goal-line or touch-line, whether on the ground or in the air.

(b) When the game has been stopped by the Referee.

The ball is in play at all other times from the start of the match to the finish including:

(a) If it rebounds from a goal-post, cross-bar or corner-flag post into the field of play.

(b) If it rebounds off either the Referee or Linesmen when they are in the field of play.

(c) In the event of a supposed infringement of the Laws, until a decision is given.

LAW X. METHOD OF SCORING

Except as otherwise provided by these Laws, a goal is scored when the whole of the ball has passed over the goal-line, between the goal-posts and under the cross-bar, provided it has not been thrown, carried or intentionally propelled by hand or arm, by a player of the attacking side, except in the case of a goalkeeper, who is within his own penalty-area.

The team scoring the greater number of goals during a game shall be the winner; if no goals, or an equal number of goals are scored, the game shall be termed a "draw."

LAW XI. OFF-SIDE

1. A player is in an off-side position if he is nearer to his opponents' goal-line than the ball, unless:

(a) he is in his own half of the field of play, or

(b) there are at least two of his opponents nearer their own goal-line than he is.

2. A player shall only be declared off-side and penalised for being in an off-side position, if, at the moment the ball touches, or is played by, one of his team, he is, in the opinion of the Referee

(a) interfering with play or with an opponent, or

(b) seeking to gain an advantage by being in that position.

3. A player shall not be declared off-side by the Referee

(a) merely because of his being in an off-side position, or

(b) if he receives the ball direct, from a goal-kick, a corner-kick, a throw-in, or when it has been dropped by the Referee.

4. If a player is declared off-side, the Referee shall award an indirect free-kick, which shall be taken by a player of the opposing team from the place where the infringement occurred, unless the offence is committed by a player in his opponents' goal area, in which case, the free-kick shall be taken from a point anywhere within that half of the goal area in which the offence occurred.

LAW XII. FOULS AND MISCONDUCT

A player who intentionally commits any of the following nine offences:

(a) Kicks or attempts to kick an opponent;

(b) Trips an opponent, i.e., throwing or attempting to throw him by the use of the legs or by stooping in front of or behind him;

(c) Jumps at an opponent;

(d) Charges an opponent in a violent or dangerous manner;

(e) Charges an opponent from behind unless the latter is obstructing;

(f) Strikes or attempts to strike an opponent or spits at him;

(g) Holds an opponent;

(h) Pushes an opponent;

(i) Handles the ball, i.e., carries, strikes or propels the ball with his hand or arm. (This does not apply to the goalkeeper within his own penalty-area);

shall be penalised by the award of a direct free-kick to be taken by the opposing team from the place where the offence occurred, unless the offence is committed by a player in his opponents' goal area, in which case, the free-kick shall be taken from a point anywhere within that half of the goal area in which the offence occurred.

Should a player of the defending team intentionally commit one of the above nine offences within the penalty-area he shall be penalised by a penalty-kick.

A penalty-kick can be awarded irrespective of the position of the ball, if in play, at the time an offence within the penalty-area is committed.

A player committing any of the five following offences:

1. Playing in a manner considered by the Referee to be dangerous, e.g., attempting to kick the ball while held by the goalkeeper;

2. Charging fairly, e.g., with the shoulder, when the ball is not within playing distance of the players concerned and they are definitely not trying to play it;

3. When not playing the ball, intentionally obstructing an opponent, i.e., running between the opponent and the ball, or interposing the body so as to form an obstacle to an opponent;

4. Charging the goalkeeper except when he

(a) is holding the ball;

(b) is obstructing an opponent;

(c) has passed outside his goal area.

5. When playing as a goalkeeper and within his own penalty-area:

(a) from the moment he takes control of the ball with his hands, he takes more than 4 steps in any direction whilst holding, bouncing or throwing the ball in the air and catching it again, without releasing it into play, or having released the ball into play before, during or after the 4 steps, he touches it again with his hands, before it has been touched or played by another player of the same team outside of the penalty-area, or by a player of the opposing team either inside or outside of the penalty-area.

(b) indulges in tactics which, in the opinion of the Referee, are designed merely to hold up the game and thus waste time and so give an unfair advantage to his own team.

shall be penalised by the award of an indirect free-kick to be taken by the opposing team from the place where the infringement occurred, unless the offence is committed by a player in his opponents' goal area, in which case, the free-kick shall be taken from a point anywhere within that half of the goal area in which the offence occurred.

A player shall be cautioned if:

(j) he enters or re-enters the field of play to join or rejoin his team after the game has commenced, or leaves the field of play during the progress of the game (except through accident) without, in either case, first having received a signal from the Referee showing him that he may do so. If the Referee stops the game to administer the caution the game shall be restarted by an indirect free-kick taken by a player of the opposing team from the place where the ball was when the Referee stopped the game. If the free-kick is awarded to a team within its own goal area it may be taken from any point within the half of the goal area in which the ball was when play was stopped. If, however, the offending player has committed a more serious offence he shall be penalised according to that section of the law he infringed;

(k) he persistently infringes the Laws of the Game;

(l) he shows by word or action, dissent from any decision given by the Referee;

(m) he is guilty of ungentlemanly conduct.

For any of these last three offences, in addition to the caution, an indirect free-kick shall also be awarded to the opposing team from the place where the offence occurred unless a more serious infringement of the Laws of the Game was committed. If the offence is committed by a player in his opponents' goal area, a free-kick shall be taken from a point anywhere within that half of the goal area in which the offence occurred.

A player shall be sent off the field of play, if, in the opinion of the Referee, he:

(n) is guilty of violent conduct or serious foul play;

(o) uses foul or abusive language;

(p) persists in misconduct after having received a caution.

If play be stopped by reason of a player being ordered from the field for an offence without a separate breach of the Law having been committed, the game shall be resumed by an indirect free-kick awarded to the opposing team from the place where the infringement occurred, unless the offence is committed by a player in his opponents' goal area, in which case, the free-kick shall be taken from a point anywhere within that half of the goal area in which the offence occurred.

LAW XIII. FREE-KICK

Free-kicks shall be classified under two headings: "Direct" (from which a goal can be scored direct against the offending side), and "Indirect" (from which a goal cannot be scored unless the ball has been played or touched by a player other than the kicker before passing through the goal).

When a player is taking a direct or an indirect free-kick inside his own penalty-area, all of the opposing players shall be at least ten yards (9.15m) from the ball and shall remain outside the penalty-area until the ball has been kicked out of the area. The ball shall be in play immediately it has travelled the distance of its own circumference and is beyond the penalty-area. The goalkeeper shall not receive the ball into his hands, in order that he may thereafter kick it into play. If the ball is not kicked direct into play, beyond the penalty-area, the kick shall be retaken.

When a player is taking a direct or an indirect free-kick outside his own penalty-area, all of the opposing players shall be at least ten yards from the ball, until it is in play, unless they are standing on their own goal-line, between the goal-posts. The ball shall be in play when it has travelled the distance of its own circumference. If a player of the opposing side encroaches into the penalty-area, or within ten yards of the ball, as the case may be, before a free-kick is taken, the Referee shall delay the taking of the kick, until the Law is complied with. The ball must be stationary when a free-kick is taken, and the kicker shall not play the ball a second time, until it has been touched or played by another player.

Notwithstanding any other reference in these Laws to the point from which a free-kick is to be taken:

1. Any free-kick awarded to the defending team, within its own goal area, may be taken from any point within that half of the goal area in which the free-kick has been awarded.

2. Any indirect free-kick awarded to the attacking team within its opponent's goal area shall be taken from the part of the goal area line which runs parallel to the goal-line, at the point nearest to where the offence was committed.

Punishment: If the kicker, after taking the free-kick, plays the ball a second time before it has been touched or played by another player, an indirect free-kick shall be taken by a player of the opposing team from the spot where the infringement occurred, unless the offence is committed by a player in his opponent's goal area, in which case, the free-kick shall be taken from a point anywhere within that half of the goal area in which the offence occurred.

LAW XIV. PENALTY-KICK

A penalty-kick shall be taken from the penalty-mark and, when it is being taken, all players with the exception of the player taking the kick, and the opposing goalkeeper, shall be within the field of play but outside the penalty-area, and at least 10 yards from the penalty-mark. The opposing goalkeeper must stand (without moving his feet) on his own goal-line, between the goal-posts, until the ball is kicked. The player taking the kick must kick the ball forward; he shall not play the ball a second time until it has been touched or played by another player. The ball shall be deemed in play directly it is kicked, i.e., when it has travelled the distance of its circumference, and a goal may be scored direct from such a penalty-kick. If the ball touches the goalkeeper before passing between the posts, when a penalty-kick is being taken at or after the expiration of half-time or full-time, it does not nullify a goal. If necessary, time of play shall be extended at half-time or full-time to allow a penalty-kick to be taken.

Punishment:

For any infringement of this Law:

(a) by the defending team, the kick shall be retaken if a goal has not resulted.

(b) by the attacking team other than by the player taking the kick, if a goal is scored it shall be disallowed and the kick retaken.

(c) by the player taking the penalty-kick, committed after the ball is in play, a player of the opposing team shall take an indirect free-kick from the spot where the infringement occurred.

If, in the case of paragraph (c), the offence is committed by the player in his opponents' goal area, the free-kick shall be taken from a point anywhere within that half of the goal area in which the offence occurred.

LAW XV. THROW-IN

When the whole of the ball passes over a touch-line, either on the ground or in the air, it shall be thrown in from the point where it crossed the line, in any direction, by a player of the team opposite to that of the player who last touched it. The thrower at the moment of delivering the ball must face the field of play and part of each foot shall be either on the touch-line or on the ground outside the touch-line. The thrower shall use both hands and shall deliver the ball from behind and over his head. The ball shall be in play immediately it enters the field of play, but the thrower shall not again play the ball until it has been touched or played by another player. A goal shall not be scored direct from a throw-in.

Punishment:

(a) If the ball is improperly thrown in the throw-in shall be taken by a player of the opposing team.

(b) If the thrower plays the ball a second time before it has been touched or played by another player, an indirect free-kick shall be taken by a player of the opposing team from the place where the infringement occurred, unless the offence is committed by a player in his opponents' goal area, in which case, the free-kick shall be taken from a point anywhere within that half of the goal area in which the offence occurred.

LAW XVI. GOAL-KICK

When the whole of the ball passes over the goal-line excluding that portion between the goal-posts, either in the air or on the ground, having last been played by one of the attacking team, it shall be kicked direct into play beyond the penalty-area from a point within that half of the goal area nearest to where it crossed the line, by a player of the defending team. A goalkeeper shall not receive the ball into his hands from a goal-kick in order that he may thereafter kick it into play. If the ball is not kicked beyond the penalty-area, i.e., direct into play, the kick shall be retaken. The kicker shall not play the ball a second time until it has touched—or been played by— another player. A goal shall not be scored direct from such a kick. Players of the team opposing that of the player taking the goal-kick shall remain outside the penalty-area until the ball has been kicked out of the penalty-area.

Punishment: If a player taking a goal-kick plays the ball a second time after it has passed beyond the penalty-area, but before it has touched or been played by another player, an indirect free-kick shall be awarded to the opposing team, to be taken from the place where the infringement occurred, unless the offence is committed by a player in his opponents' goal area, in which case, the free-kick shall be taken from a point anywhere within that half of the goal area in which the offence occurred.

LAW XVII. CORNER-KICK

When the whole of the ball passes over the goal-line, excluding that portion between the goal-posts, either in the air or on the ground, having last been played by one of the defending team, a member of the attacking team shall take a corner-kick, i.e., the whole of the ball shall be placed within the quarter circle at the nearest corner-flag-post, which must not be moved, and it shall be kicked from that position. A goal may be scored direct from such a kick. Players of the team opposing that of the player taking the corner-kick shall not approach within 10 yards of the ball until it is in play, i.e., it has travelled the distance of its own circumference, nor shall the kicker play the ball a second time until it has been touched or played by another player.

Punishment:

(a) If the player who takes the kick plays the ball a second time before it has been touched or played by another player, the Referee shall award an indirect free-kick to the opposing team, to be taken from the place where the infringement occurred, unless the offence is committed by a player in his opponents' goal area, in which case, the free-kick shall be taken from a point anywhere within that half of the goal area in which the offence occurred.

(b) For any other infringement the kick shall be retaken.

GOVERNING BODY

United States Soccer Federation, 1750 East Boulder St., Colorado Springs, CO 80909

The national governing body for all levels of soccer in the United States is the U.S. Soccer Federation (USSF). The USSF is affiliated with the Federation Internationale de Football Association (FIFA), the world governing body for soccer. The USSF is recognized by the U.S. Olympic Committee as the governing body for soccer for all U.S. international competition. The USSF structure includes (a) Youth Division (organized on a statewide basis for boys and girls at all age levels under 19 years of age), (b) Senior Division (organized on a statewide basis for men and women over the age of 19), and (c) Professional Division (includes both the indoor and outdoor versions of the game). Other affiliates include the armed forces, YMCA, AYSO, and high school/intercollegiate associations. In addition to supervising the growth and operations of its thousands of affiliates, the USSF also organizes cup competitions at all levels, structures programs for national teams that represent the United States, conducts clinics for coaches and referees, and offers a number of educational publications as well as a film library.

MAGAZINES

Soccer America, Berling Communications, Inc., Box 23704, Oakland, CA 94623

Soccer Digest, Box 10170, Des Moines, IA 50340

• SOFTBALL •

(Rules summary by author)

☐

Note: The game of softball is a modification of the game of baseball and the rules of play are much the same except for the equipment, field dimensions, pitching regulations and base running restrictions. Since the rules for baseball are also included in this book, only the major differences in the rules for softball are presented here. (See Baseball for rules not included in this section.)

FAST PITCH SOFTBALL
(RULE DIFFERENCES FROM BASEBALL)

A. THE GAME

1. The official game consists of 7 innings of play.

B. THE FIELD

1. The distance between bases is 60 feet.

2. The pitcher's plate is 46 feet (men) and 40 feet (women) from home plate.

3. The recommended distance to the outfield fence is 225 feet for men and 200 feet for women.

4. It is recommended that the backstop be located 25 feet behind home plate and that bleachers, dugouts, fences or other obstructions be 25 feet away from the foul lines.

5. See Figure on p. 472 for additional field dimensions.

C. EQUIPMENT

1. The official ball is 12 inches in circumference and weighs 6-1/4 to 7 ounces. The stitching of the outer cover panels is to be smooth-seamed making a flat surfaced ball.

2. The official bat shall not be more than 2 1/4 inches in diameter at the thickest part and no longer than 34 inches. Bats are marked "OFFICIAL SOFTBALL" by the manufacturers.

3. The fielder's glove shall not be more than 13-1/4 inches in length from the tip of the longest finger to the back edge of the glove. The width of the glove may not be more than 8 inches measured across the base of the fingers. The web space between the thumb and the first finger may not exceed 5 inches at the top of the opening.

4. The mitt type of glove (without fingers) which may be worn by the catcher and first baseman is restricted to the dimensions given for the fielder's glove.

5. The soles of shoes may be smooth or have hard rubber cleats.

6. The catchers must wear a mask with throat protector. A body protector is recommended but not required.

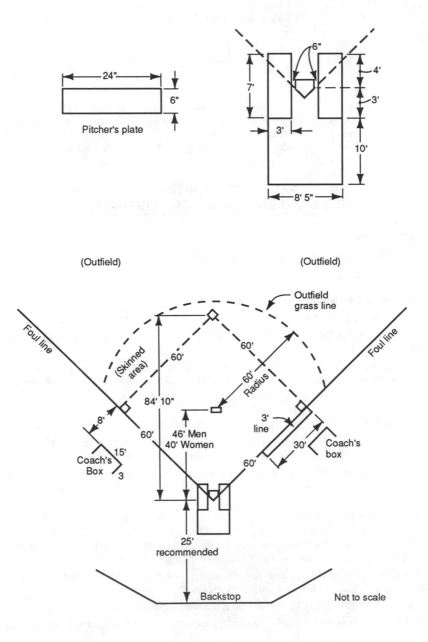

24"

6"

Pitcher's plate

6"

7'

4'

3'

3'

10'

8' 5"

(Outfield)

(Outfield)

Outfield
grass line

Foul line

(Skinned
area)

60'

60'

60'
Radius

84' 10"

60'

3'
line

30'

Coach's
box

8'

60'

46' Men
40' Women

15'

Coach's
Box   3

60'

25'
recommended

Backstop

Not to scale

D. PITCHING

1. A legal pitch must be delivered with:

a. an under hand motion;

b. the hand releasing the ball below the hip and the wrist no farther from the body than the elbow;

c. one step taken toward the batter;

d. the release of the ball and follow-through of the hand moving forward past the straight line of the body;

e. the pitcher facing the batter with shoulders in line with first and third bases;

f. pivot foot in contact with pitcher's plate and other foot on or behind the pitcher's plate;

g. pitcher holding ball in front of body with both hands (while in contact with pitcher's plate) for not less than 1 second nor more than 10 seconds before delivering the pitch.

2. The pitcher may use any type of windup but may not:

a. make any false motion as to pitch without immediately delivering the ball;

b. return the ball to both hands after beginning the pitching motion;

c. make more than one revolution with the arm;

d. stop during the pitching motion nor reverse forward motions;

e. continue a windup motion after taking the forward step;

f. make any rocker action.

3. The pitcher has 20 seconds to release the next pitch after the ball is returned to him or her by the catcher.

4. A ''no pitch'' is declared if a runner is called out for leaving a base before the pitcher releases the pitch or if the pitcher pitches before a baserunner has returned to his or her base after a foul ball.

a. An illegal pitch shall immediately be called by the umpire; however, the ball remains in play in case the batter hits the ball and baserunners advance. If the ball is not hit, a ball is called on the pitch.

E. BATTING

1. A fair ball hit into the stands or over a fence on the fly less than the prescribed fence distance from home plate is limited to two bases. (Prescribed distances: Men-225'; Women-200'; Youth play-175'.)

2. A fair ball that bounces over or through a fence is limited to two bases.

F. BASE RUNNING

1. Baserunners must remain in contact with the base occupied until the pitch leaves the pitcher's hand.

SLOW PITCH SOFTBALL
(RULE DIFFERENCES FROM FAST PITCH)

Slow pitch softball is a modification of the fast pitch game. The rules of slow pitch are the same as for fast pitch except for the following.

A. THE FIELD

1. The playing field dimensions differ slightly in that the distance between bases for men is 65 feet and the pitching distance for women is 46 feet.

B. THE PLAYERS

1. A team is made up of 10 players. (The additional player is designated as the short fielder and normally is positioned between the infielders and the outfielders.)

C. EQUIPMENT

1. It is recommended but not required that the catcher wear a mask in men's play. It is strongly recommended that women wear both a mask and body protector.

D. PITCHING

1. The pitch (underhand) must be at a moderate speed and with a perceptible arc reaching a height of not less than 6 feet from the ground nor more than 12 feet from the ground. To begin the pitching motion, the ball may be held in front with one hand or both hands. It is not necessary to take a step but, if a step is taken, it must be toward the batter.

E. BATTING

1. The strike zone extends from the shoulders to the knees.

2. An illegal pitch is counted as a ball on the batter. Baserunners do not advance on an illegal pitch.

3. Bunting or chopped ball is not permitted and batter will be called out.

F. BASE RUNNING

1. Stealing bases is not permitted.

2. Baserunners cannot leave their base until the pitched ball has reached home plate.

3. Batter is out on dropped third strike.

GOVERNING BODIES

Amateur Softball Association of America, 2801 N.E. 50th St., Oklahoma City, OK 73111

(Rules of Fast Pitch, Slow Pitch, Modified, and 16 Inch for Male, Female, and Youth Divisions)

United States Slo-Pitch Softball Association, P.O. Box 2047, Petersbury, VA 23804

(Rules of Slow Pitch, Mixed Team, 16 Inch, and One Pitch for Male, Female, and Youth Programs)

• SPEEDBALL •

OFFICIAL RULES OF SPEEDBALL

(Reproduced by permission of Dr. E.D. Mitchell,* originator of game.)

☐

RULE I. THE PLAYING FIELD

Section 1. (a) The entire field is a rectangle 160 x 360 feet (regulation football field). The two longer boundaries are called sidelines, and the two shorter boundaries the endlines. (It is expected that field dimensions will vary with age and conditioning of participants.)

(b) The entire field includes two end zones, each 10 yards in width, reaching from sideline to sideline. The outside length of the end zone is the endline of the field, and the inside length is the goal line. The accompanying diagram of the field shows the sideline, endline, goal line, and end zone.

Section 2. The field of play shall be that part of the playing field which is included between the goal lines and the two sidelines.

Section 3. The goal posts shall be placed on the endlines equidistant from the sidelines, and shall be 23 feet 4 inches apart, with a crossbar 10 feet from the ground (regulation football goal). The two uprights shall be 20 feet or more in height.

Section 4. A center line shall be drawn across the field connecting the middle points of the two sidelines. Ten yards on each side of the center line, restraining lines shall be drawn parallel with the center line.

Section 5. The penalty area is the space between the endline and the goal line, and also known as the end zone.

Section 6. The penalty mark is one foot in length, and is made at a point exactly in front of and exactly in the middle of the goal posts 12 yards from the endline.

Section 7. The goal that a team defends is its "own goal"; and the penalty area in front of it shall be termed its "own penalty area." A team also defends its own end zone.

RULE II. PLAYERS AND EQUIPMENT

Section 1. A team is made up of eleven players. The players shall be known by the names shown in the accompanying diagram.

Section 2. A player may be taken out of the game and resubstituted once during the game. A substitute shall first report to one of the Linesmen, who shall blow his whistle to allow the change. The Linesman shall wait until the ball is dead, and the substitute shall remain outside of the field of play in the meanwhile. (An unlimited substitution policy will prove satisfactory in most play.)

Section 3. The equipment of the players shall consist of jerseys, pants, and cleated shoes. For physical education classes it is well to insist that all players wear the ordinary gymnasium

---

*See page 483 for additional information.

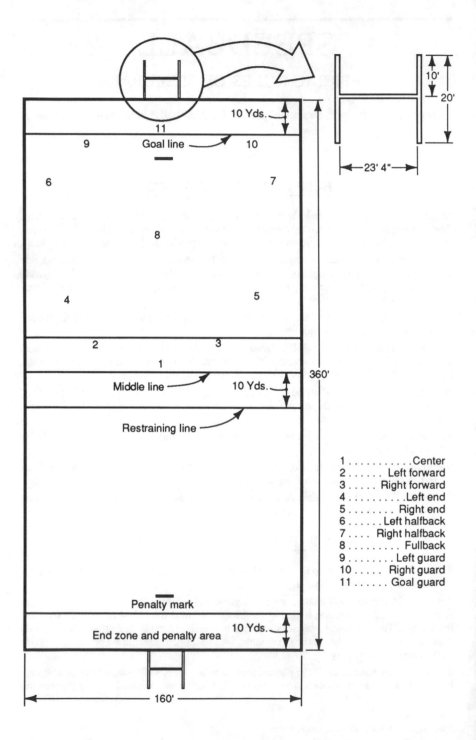

10 Yds.

11

9 Goal line 10

6 7

8

4 5

2 3

1

Middle line 10 Yds.

360'

Restraining line

1 . . . . .Center
2 . . . . . . Left forward
3 . . . . . Right forward
4 . . . . .Left end
5 . . . . Right end
6 . . . . . .Left halfback
7 . . . . Right halfback
8 . . . . Fullback
9 . . . . .Left guard
10 . . . . . Right guard
11 . . . . . . Goal guard

Penalty mark

End zone and penalty area 10 Yds.

160'

10'
20'

23' 4"

rubber-soled shoe. The jerseys and pants should be of uniform color and style. No shoes having metal spikes shall be permitted.

Section 4. Of balls presently being marketed, the official soccer ball is the most satisfactory.

RULE III. THE GAME

Section 1. The game shall consist of four quarters of 10 minutes each, with a 2-minute rest interval between the first and second, and third and fourth quarters, and a 10-minute rest interval between halves. The periods may be shortened by mutual consent of the two captains, and should be shortened for immature or untrained players. "Overtime" is a continuation of the second half in case of a tie score, and consists of one or more 5-minute periods until the tie shall be broken.

Time is up with the sounding of the Timer's signal, whereupon the Referee shall blow his whistle to terminate the play. A play which is started before time is up, may result in a score, provided that no further impetus is given to the ball by the attacking side after the whistle has sounded.

Section 2. The winner of the toss shall have the privilege of selecting: (a) to kick off, or (b) to receive at the goal of his choosing. The loser of the toss shall have the privilege of making the selection at the start of the second half.

Section 3. Goals shall be changed at quarters, and the side which received at the beginning of the half shall kick off to begin the next quarter.

Section 4. In case of overtime, teams shall continue their present goals for the first period, and thereafter shall alternate for each succeeding period. Each overtime period shall commence by a "tie ball" at the center of the field.

Section 5. The game shall be commenced by a place-kick from the center of the field of play in the direction of the opponents' goal line. The ball must be kicked forward more than its own circumference or it is a violation. The player who kicks off may not play the ball again until it has first been touched by another player in the game. All members of his side shall be behind the ball when it is kicked, and no opponent shall pass the restraining line until the ball has been kicked. No artificial tees are to be used in making the place-kick.

Section 6. Following a score, the side that has just been scored upon shall kick off.

Section 7. The ball is dead when out-of-bounds (either at sidelines or endline), following a score, after a foul, after a penalty-kick in which no follow-up play is allowed, during time-out, and on a tie ball. In the case of a score or time-out, the Referee's whistle is needed to start play again; but on out-of-bounds plays, free-kicks and penalty-kicks play can commence without the Referee's whistle.

Section 8. Time-outs may be taken by either captain three times during the game. The fourth and succeeding times shall constitute a technical foul for delaying the game. A time-out is not charged if requested for the purpose of substituting a player. The timekeepers shall take time-out after a score has been made, after a penalty-kick has been awarded, or whenever time-out is awarded by the Referee.

Time shall be resumed when the ball is actually kicked or passed on the next play, with the exception of a penalty-kick where no follow-up play is allowed in which case time shall be resumed at the commencement of the play following the penalty-kick.

The Referee may call time-out on an out-of-bounds, safety, or touchback whenever the ball has traveled such a distance that there will be delay in retrieving it. A time-out should not be granted while the ball is in play unless the team making the request is in possession of the ball.

Time-out is taken on a double foul, wherein both teams commit a foul simultaneously. No general play ensues until each team has attempted one penalty-kick, after which play is resumed by a tie ball at the center of the field. A requested time-out by a Captain shall not exceed two minutes.

RULE IV. SCORING

Section 1. Scoring shall count as follows:

Field goal . . . . .3 points

Touchdown . . . . 1 point

Penalty-kick . . . . .1 point

Drop-kick . . . . .2 points

Section 2. A field goal shall be scored when a ground ball is kicked or legally given impetus with the body so that it passes over the endline, between the posts and under the crossbar. If such a ball is touched by a defensive player, but goes under the crossbar without further impetus from the offensive side, the goal shall count. A field goal shall be scored whenever any ball passes under the crossbar as a result of impetus given by the defending side.

Interpretation. If the ball is legally touched by the hands of any player, no member of the attacking side may score a goal until the ball has touched the ground and then been played as a ground ball; consequently, a punt through the goal posts does not count.

Interpretation. A ball that is kicked or passed into the end zone and does not result in a score remains in play. For example, a forward pass which hits the ground in the end zone may still be kicked through the goal posts for a field goal. Such a ball, however, must be returned to the field of play outside the end zone before it can result in a forward pass or drop-kick score.

Interpretation. A drop-kick that is started from outside the end zone in the field of play shall not count as a field goal if it goes under the bar. It does, however, count as a field goal if started within the end zone.

A drop-kick started within the end zone does not count one point if it goes over the bar but, instead, becomes a touchback.

Section 3. A touchdown may be scored by the completion of a forward pass from the field of play which is between the two goal lines into the end zone. No part of the receiver's body shall touch the boundary lines of the end zone, or ground outside. If part of the receiver's body is in the end zone and part in the field of play when the ball is caught, no score shall result, but play continues.

Interpretation. A missed forward pass which hits the ground in the end zone will become a ground ball and will continue in play until a score is made or the ball goes out-of-bounds, or becomes otherwise dead. A forward pass which is intercepted by the opponents in the end zone likewise continues in play.

Note: Remember that no forward pass may score unless it is thrown from outside the end zone within the field of play and is caught by a teammate in the end zone.

Section 4. Penalty-kick. Following a personal or technical foul, the ball is placed by the Referee on the penalty mark and the kicker may then attempt to kick the ball between the goal posts under the crossbar. Only one member of the defending side is allowed to guard the goal at this time, and he must stand on the end line until the ball is kicked. On penalty-kicks where no follow-up is allowed (see Rule VIII, Sections 1, 2a, 3), only the kicker and opposing goal guard are concerned. The kicker may not play the ball a second time; if the goal is missed, the play shall be considered ended.

On penalty-kicks where a follow-up play is allowed (see Rule VIII, Sections 2, 4, 6), the teammates of the kicker and goaltender shall not encroach upon the end zone until the ball is actually kicked. The teammates of the kicker must be behind the ball when it is kicked. The teammates of the goaltender may be on the defending endline (except between the goal posts), or in the field of play (except in the defensive end zone, as already stated).

If the ball does not go over the endline it shall be considered a free ball and played with all the possibilities of scoring. The kicker may not play the ball a second time until it has been touched by another player. The kicker must make a bona fide attempt to kick the goal; otherwise, the Referee shall declare a touchback.

Section 5. Drop-kick. A ball that has been legally caught may be kicked over the crossbar from the ground by a drop-kick. If the ball passes over the bar between the posts it shall count one for the side making the kick. To count a score, however, the kick must be made from the field outside the defensive end zone.

See Interpretation, Rule IV, Section 2 for ruling on drop-kick that goes under the crossbar.

RULE V. BALL OUT-OF-BOUNDS

Section 1. Sidelines. If a ball goes over the sidelines it shall become the possession of the side opposite that which last touched it, and shall be put in play by a pass from the spot where it crosses the line. No score may be made on a direct pass from out-of-bounds; the ball must first be thrown into the field of play. The player who passes the ball inbounds is restricted from again touching the ball in any way until it has been played by someone other than himself.

A ball that goes over the sidelines between the goal line and endline shall be played as a touchback or safety, depending upon which team is given possession of the ball. The ball is put in play from the intersection of the sideline and the endline.

Section 2. Touchback. Whenever a ball that crosses the endline without resulting in a score has been touched by a player of the offensive team, a touchback shall be made. After a touchback the ball shall be put in play by the defensive team at the point where it crossed the endline by a punt, drop-kick, place-kick, or pass. The person putting the ball in play is not eligible to touch it again until it has been touched by another player in the game.

Section 3. Safety. If a ball that goes over the endline without scoring was last touched by a player of the defensive side, the ball shall be given to the offensive side and shall be put in play at the point where it crossed the endline by a punt, drop-kick, or pass.

No score may be made following a safety until the ball has been returned to the field of play outside the end zone.

Section 4. The ball is out-of-bounds when:

(a) It touches the ground on or outside the sidelines.

(b) When a player with the ball in his possession touches the sideline or ground outside with any part of his body.

(c) When it becomes dead over the endline without resulting in a score.

Section 5. A ball hitting the goal posts or crossbar is still in play. A touchdown, however, may not result from such a deflected ball.

Section 6. (a) On out-of-bounds plays the opponents of the player returning the ball are required to stand at least 3 feet inside the boundary line.

(b) The player returning the ball from out-of-bounds is allowed 5 seconds to make the play; otherwise, ball shall go to the opponents at the same spot.

(c) The player returning the ball from out-of-bounds must be outside the field of play when he puts the ball in play.

RULE VI. PLAYING PRIVILEGES

Section 1. The ball may be caught, or otherwise played with the hands, whenever it is clearly a fly ball; i.e., one that has been raised into the air directly from a kick by one or both feet. A ball thus raised into the air remains a fly ball until it again hits the ground. A fly ball that has been caught may be held, passed, punted, drop-kicked, or played as an overhead dribble, at option. A loose fly ball (not in the possession of a player) may not be kicked or kneed, but otherwise may be played in any manner by the hands or body. Kicking or kneeing a loose fly ball shall not be considered to include trapping it with the legs below the knees. An overhead dribble shall be considered a loose fly ball.

Section 2. A ground ball is one that is stationary, rolling, or bouncing. Even though it may be in the air as in the case when it is bouncing, the ball is ruled a ground ball until it is in the air from a direct kick. While the ball is a ground ball it may not be played with the hands or any part of the arms. Instead, it must be kicked or "headed," or bounced off the body.

Section 3. (a) A player may dribble the ball with his feet at will. He may bat or tip a fly ball or drop a caught ball to the ground and play it as a drop-kick or kicking dribble.

(b) A player may use one overhead dribble in advancing the ball without the aid of his teammates; that is, he may throw the ball in any direction and run and catch it before it touches the ground. He may not score a touchdown by this method.

Section 4. A player kicking a ball into the air is eligible to catch it himself before it hits the ground.

Interpretation. In order to be eligible for such a catch, the player must give some impetus to the ball. If he stands still and merely lets the ball hit his feet and bound upward, this would not be considered a kicked ball. The foot or feet must actually leave the ground as the ball is lifted upward and the ball must have left the foot before being touched by the hands.

Section 5. There is no distinction between the goaltender and the other players as regards privileges and restrictions in playing the ball.

Section 6. A player who is standing still when catching the ball from a kick or pass may take one step in any direction from the point at which he caught the ball, but must get rid of the ball before a second step is finished. If running with the ball, he is allowed two steps to make a play or come to a stop and if at full speed the Referee shall decide whether or not he stops as soon as possible. (The step the player is on when receiving the ball is not counted as one of the two steps permitted.) Violations of this rule shall be known as "carrying the ball." A player may not take a step over the goal line to score. He must be completely over the line when the ball is caught in order to score.

Section 7. A player may legally guard an opponent who has the ball. He must play to secure the ball, and in no way hold the opponent. If two opponents are running for the ball at the same time, each must play the ball and not the man. No obstruction shall be made to the progress of any player without the ball.

Section 8. Tie Ball. In case the ball is held by two opposing players simultaneously, or when the Referee is in doubt which side last played the ball out-of-bounds, the Referee shall declare a tie ball. The Referee or Linesman shall toss the ball up between the two contesting players, who attempt to bat or tip the ball to their teammates as in basketball. The players must not tap the ball before it reaches its highest point, and neither player may tap it more than twice until after it has hit the ground or some other player than either of the two jumpers. If the ball touches the ground before being tapped by either jumper, the official shall toss the ball up again at the same place. The two players must stay within an imaginary 4-foot circle until the ball is actually tapped.

No score may result from a tip-off that is caught in the end zone, although the ball is still in play (see Note, Rule IV, Section 3).

A tie ball at the center of the field shall be used to commence play after a double foul or at the beginning of an overtime period.

Section 9. Free-Kick. Whenever a free-kick is awarded a team, they shall have the privilege of putting the ball in play by a place-kick, the opposing team being required to stay 10 yards distant from the ball (any direction) until it is kicked. The ball may be kicked in any direction. The ball must travel its own circumference, and the kicker may not play it again until it has been touched by another player. The kicking side is free to take any positions on the field.

RULE VII. PLAYING RESTRICTIONS

Section 1. Personal fouls shall include:

(a) Kicking, tripping, charging, pushing, holding, or blocking an opponent. (Running into an opponent from behind is interpreted as a personal foul for charging in case bodily contact is made.)

(b) Unnecessary roughness of any description.

Section 2. Technical fouls shall include the following:

(a) Making an illegal substitution.

(b) Taking more than three time-outs in a game (see Rule III, Section 8).

(c) Unsportsmanlike conduct.

(d) Having more than eleven men on the field by one team at the same time.

(e) Unnecessarily delaying the game. This includes persistent interference on out-of-bounds plays and unreasonable delay in taking positions on free-kicks, penalty-kicks, etc.

Section 3. Violations shall include:

(a) Carrying the ball (also termed as "steps" or "traveling").

(b) Touching a ground ball with the hands or arms.

(c) Making two successive overhead dribbles.

(d) Violating the kick-off rule (see Rule III, Section 5).

(e) Violating the penalty-kick restrictions (see Rule IV, Section 4).

(f) Violating out-of-bounds rules by offensive player when returning the ball to field of play (see Rule V).

(g) Violating free-kick restrictions (see Rule VI, Section 9).

(h) Violating tie ball rule (see Rule VI, Section 8).

(i) Kicking or kneeing a fly ball by player unless he has first caught it. (If opposing player is kicked or kneed in such an attempt, a personal foul shall be charged against the offender.)

RULE VIII. PENALTIES

Section 1. In case of personal foul committed by a player outside his own penalty area, the opponents shall be awarded one penalty-kick to penalize the personal contact. The offended player shall attempt the kick. If missed, the ball shall be dead and a touchback be declared.

Section 2. In case a personal foul is committed by a player within his own penalty area or end zone, the opponents shall be awarded two penalty-kicks, one without a follow-up— to penalize the personal contact—and the second with a follow-up to afford a chance to recover the score that the foul may have prevented. The offended player must attempt the kicks.

(a) The ball shall be dead after the first attempt in all cases.

(b) The ball shall be in play after the second attempt if it is missed.

Section 3. In case a technical foul is committed by a player inside of his own penalty area, the opponents shall be awarded one penalty kick. Any member of the offended team may attempt the kick. The ball shall be dead on this play and no follow-up shall be allowed. If missed, a touchback shall be awarded.

Section 4. In case a technical foul is committed by a player inside of his own penalty area, the opponents shall be awarded one penalty kick. Any member of the offended team may attempt the kick. As soon as the ball is kicked, it shall be considered in play and a follow-up permitted.

Section 5. In case a violation is committed by a player outside his own penalty area, the opponents shall be awarded a free-kick at the spot where the violation occurred.

Section 6. In case a violation is committed by a player inside his own penalty area, the opponents shall be awarded a penalty-kick, with the opportunities of a follow-up if missed. Such a violation is considered as possibly depriving the attacking team of a chance to score and therefore will be penalized by a penalty-kick with a follow-up.

RULE IX. FORFEITURES AND SPECIAL RULINGS

Section 1. The Referee shall have jurisdiction to forfeit a game for refusal of one team to play, or for failure to appear on the field within 10 minutes of the scheduled time. The score of a forfeited game shall be 1 to 0.

Section 2. The Referee may suspend any player from the game for unsportsmanlike conduct.

Section 3. A player having four personal fouls charged against him is automatically suspended from the game.

Section 4. The Referee, on any case not specifically covered by the rules, may declare a technical foul which shall be governed by the penalty rules of Rule VIII.

Section 5. If, after a play has been started, the defense commits a personal or technical foul which does not, however, prevent a score from ensuing, the offended side shall be given the score and, in addition, be given one penalty-kick without a follow-up. This privilege assumes that no further impetus is given to the ball after the foul has been committed.

Section 6. If, after a play has been started, the defense commits a violation which does not, however, prevent a score from ensuing, the offended side shall have the option of refusing the penalty and accepting the score. This privilege assumes that no further impetus is given to the ball after the foul has been committed.

Section 7. If two fouls are to be shot successively (whether both by the same team, or one by each team) and one involves a follow-up play but the other does not, the latter penalty shot shall always be attempted first.

Section 8. In case fouls or violations are called successively on one team, so that more than one penalty with a follow-up is involved, then each penalty-kick except for the last one shall be attempted without a follow-up.

RULE X. OFFICIALS

Section 1. There shall be a Referee and two Linesmen. The Referee shall be in general charge of the game.

Section 2. It shall be the duty of the two Linesmen to assist the Referee. They shall decide when the ball is out-of-bounds, and shall blow their whistles to declare it so. The Referee shall then award the ball to the proper team or, in case the ball has gone over the endline, shall declare a score, touchback, or safety, as the case may be. The Linesmen have further jurisdiction in aiding the Referee to call any foul. The Referee shall decide all other questions unless he gives certain specific responsibilities to the Linesmen. He may ask their advice at any time he is in doubt on the proper decision to make. He may assign the duties of keeping time and of scoring to them.

Section 3. The Referee shall officiate within the field and follow the ball. The two Linesmen shall be stationed on opposite sides of the field and diagonally apart, so that each of them shall be near a goal line and in a position to judge on out-of-bounds for his respective side and end of the field.

GOVERNING BODY

Although there is not presently a recognized governing body for the game of speedball, the sport has been widely played by both men and women in physical education classes and intramural programs for over 60 years. The thoroughness of the game's founder, Dr. Elmer D. Mitchell of the University of Michigan, can be observed in the fact that speedball's current standardized rules vary little from the original rules. The National Association For Girls and Women In Sport (NAGWS) of the American Alliance for Health, Physical Education, Recreation and Dance (AAHPERD) has been the most instrumental organization in promoting the game over the years. Since the NAGWS recently ceased publishing its biannual speedball guide, the rules presented here are the only complete rules of speedball in current print.

• SPEED SKATING •

A.S.U. RACING RULES AND OFFICIALS

(Reproduced by permission of Amateur Skating Union of the United States*)

☐

I—APPLICABILITY OF RACING RULES

1. These Racing rules shall be utilized at all National and North American Indoor, and all National and North American Outdoor Championships sanctioned by this Union.

2. These Racing rules are intended to be utilized at all local and regional competitions sanctioned by members of the Union. The sanctioning member may alter or waive certain rules providing the change is published in advance of the start of competition.

II—OFFICIALS REQUIRED

1. THE OFFICIALS AT A MEET SHALL BE:

a. One Referee designated, and four Assistant Referees indoors and a minimum of six Assistant Referees outdoors, selected by the Referee.

b. One Starter similarly designated, and a maximum of four Assistants selected by the Chief Starter.

c. One Chief Clerk of Course similarly designated, and one or more Assistants selected by the Chief Clerk.

d. One Chief Judge and at least three Judges for each of the first five finish positions, plus eight Reserve Judges.

e. One Chief Timer, two Assistants, two Substitute Timers, and a Time Recorder.

f. One Chief Scorer, and one or more Assistants selected by the Chief Scorer.

g. One Lap Counter.

h. One Announcer.

i. Two Track Measurers or Surveyors.

j. One Physician.

k. No official may smoke while on the ice, at the finish line, or in the heat box.

l. It is mandatory that Referees and Corner Officials be on skates at indoor meets.

m. It is mandatory that Starters (appointed after 1979) and the Lap Counter be on skates at indoor meets if they are working on the ice surface.

2. INDOOR MEET OFFICIALS:

a. At all National and North American indoor meets, only 8 officials may be on the ice. These officials are: the Chief Starter, Assistant Starter, Lap Counter, Chief Referee, 2

---

*See page 498 for additional information.

Assistant Referees, and 2 Corner Officials. The sole responsibility of the Corner Officials shall be to replace the corner markers.

b. Relief officials may be provided at the direction of the Referee.

III—POWERS AND DUTIES OF OFFICIALS

1. THE REFEREE:

The Referee is the official representative of the A.S.U. at the meet and as such shall exercise authority at a meet when check-in of skaters begins and shall:

a. Assemble prior to the meet the Starter, Chief Judge, Chief Timer, Chief Clerk of Course, and all the other officials to review and summarize the rules to be followed in the meet. Coordination of effort and uniformity of application of the rules shall be stressed.

b. Approve or reject officials for the meet. He may remove any official at any time during the meet if he deems such removal advisable.

c. Hear and decide all disputes and protests; penalize infringements of these rules; uphold and enforce the A.S.U. Constitution, By-Laws and Racing Rules.

d. Change any heats he deems unfair to competitors.

e. Be sole judge as to whether the weather or ice conditions warrant the running of the meet; have the power to adjourn the meet.

f. Have authority to permit a skater to compete pending a decision on a protest against such skater.

g. Have authority to make decisions concerning all questions which arise during the meet; all decisions of the Referee shall be final unless reversed by the Board of Control.

h. Have the ability to skate with the contestants, a comparable track inside the corner markers while the race is in progress.

i. Inform the skater of the reason for disqualification as soon as possible after completion of the race.

2. THE ASSISTANT REFEREES:

The Assistant Referees shall perform all duties assigned to them by the Referee. Immediately after a race, they shall report any foul or irregularity they observe to the Referee.

3. THE CLERK OF COURSE:

The Clerk of Course shall name and assign duties to such Assistants as he may require. The Clerks shall:

a. Verify, check, and record competitors' names as they report prior to the meet and at the starting line before each race.

b. Fairly arrange and equitably distribute the competitors in the heats using the standardized A.S.U. Clerking procedure.

c. Advise the skaters of the distance of the race and, if a preliminary, the number to qualify.

d. The Clerk of Course shall have competitors draw for their position in races of 1000M and under and record their starting positions on the heat card.

4. TIMEKEEPERS:

a. The Chief Timer, two Assistants, and two Substitute Timers shall time each event. The time of one or more of the substitutes shall be used only when one or more of the three regular Timers fails to record the time of an event.

b. (1) If the time is recorded electronically, the electronic time is the official time.

(2) If an electronic time is not available, then the manual time is adjusted by the manual time error as determined by averaging the manual time error in the three prior races and adding the error to the manual time. Should any of the three manual time errors be more than one standard deviation from the average, then that manual time error will be discarded in making the computation.

c. If manual timing is used, then:

(1) If two of the watches agree and the third disagrees, the time indicated by the two is the official time.

(2) If all watches disagree, the time indicated by the watch showing the intermediate time is official.

d. Time starts with the firing of the pistol; flash type shells are to be used if any of the start lines are separate from the finish line. "Crimp" type shells are to be used if the starter is working in the timer-judge area. Thirty-two (.32) caliber shells are to be used for outdoor meets. Meets held in the United States shall be timed in hundredths.

e. Immediately after the finish of the event, each Timer must show the time to the Chief Timer who will record the individual time.

f. The Time Recorder shall assist the Chief Timer by recording each Timer's result in writing in order that all applications for records will note the exact time of each individual Timer. All such times must be included on each application for new records.

5. THE SCORER:

The Scorer shall name and assign duties to such Assistant Scorers as may be required. The Scorers shall:

a. Record the finish positions of the first four competitors as determined by the Judges.

b. Record the official time of each race as determined by the Timer and verify the time for record. The Scorer shall mark cards "Record" for all records set during the meet.

c. Keep a cumulative record of points scored by competitors.

d. Have the responsibility to forward the Record Application form properly entered and signed, together with the heat of final card, or a copy thereof, and the surveyor's certificate to the Chairman of the Records Committee within 15 days of the meet.

6. JUDGES:

a. The Chief Judge shall assign positions to the Judges.

b. Each Judge shall make a written note of the number only of the skater finishing in the position to which each is assigned, without referring to any selections made by any of the other Judges.

c. These individual decisions shall then be turned over to the Chief Judge who shall compute the standings, record the decision on the official judges card for that event, and note thereon the official time received from the Chief Timer.

d. In case of disagreement among the Judges, the Chief Judge shall hear each Judge involved and make the final decision as to the order of the finish, which shall be without appeal.

e. In determining the order of finish where there is disagreement in the results recorded by the individual Judges, the Chief Judge shall award the skater the finish position in which the most Judges recorded such skaters (i.e., if two first place Judges select No. 14 for that position and three second place Judges select No. 14 for that position, the skater No. 14 shall be awarded second position).

f. Determining the order of finish of a race under paragraph "e" above is called predominance of judging and without the required three Judges for each position this rule cannot apply. Following are some examples of predominance of judging.

"A"	Judge 1	Judge 2	Judge 3	
1st	11	11	21	= 11
2nd	11	32	21	= 32
3rd	21	21	44	= 21
4th	44	44	21	= 44

"B"	Judge 1	Judge 2	Judge 3	
1st	11	11	21	= 11-21
2nd	21	11	11	= (tie)
3rd	21	32	32	= 32
4th	44	44	44	= 44

"C"	Judge 1	Judge 2	Judge 3	
1st	44	44	11	= 44
2nd	21	21	11	= 21
3rd	32	32	44	= 32
4th	11	11	32	= 11

*"D"	Judge 1	Judge 2	Judge 3	
1st	11	11	32	= 11
2nd	11	11	44	= 21
3rd	32	32	11	= 32
4th	44	44	44	= 44

**"E"	Judge 1	Judge 2	Judge 3	
1st	11	21	44	= 11-21
2nd	11	21	44	= (tie)
3rd	44	32	32	= 32
4th	44	44	44	= 44

"F"	Judge 1	Judge 2	Judge 3	
1st	21	21	11	= 11-21
2nd	21	21	11	= (tie)
3rd	44	44	44	= 44
4th	44	44	32	= 32

Explanation:

*D In the scramble, 21 was missed completely. He is given 2nd because of predominance of 32 at 3rd and 44 at 4th, a judgment call based on the circumstances.

**E 11 and 21 tie, no predominance at either position. They split total of first and second place points.

7. THE LAP COUNTER:

The Lap Counter shall keep a tally of laps completed by each competitor in races with two or more laps and shall notify competitors by card or voice or both of the number of laps remaining to be skated. He shall, by the sound of a bell, pistol, or other distinctive noise, signal when the leading skater enters the last lap.

8. THE STARTER:

The Starter may name and assign duties to such Assistants as he may require. The Starter shall:

a. Have jurisdiction over skaters reporting to the starting line.

b. Be the judge of unfair starts.

c. Briefly announce any special rules of the meet or, in his discretion, remind the competitors concerning any standard racing rule.

d. Allow Assistant Starters to start some races.

9. THE ANNOUNCER:

The Announcer shall announce the results and any disqualifications in each event.

10. TRACK MEASURERS OR SURVEYORS:

The Track Measurers or Surveyors shall:

a. Insure that an official track pursuant to the A.S.U. diagrams contained in the official handbook has been laid out for the meet.

b. Deliver, prior to the meet, a certification that the track is correct and conforms to A.S.U. specifications and this rule.

11. MEDICAL SUPERVISION:

The Physician or First Aid facility shall be furnished by the sponsor of the meet and shall attend all competitors needing medical attention without compensation. An ambulance or emergency vehicle shall stand by during competitions and advance arrangements shall be made at a hospital to insure prompt admittance of an injured skater should such action be required.

12. It is recommended that Referees, Starters, Judges and Timers not officiate in any race in which their child is participating.

13. It is recommended that all timers, boxes, bells and other paraphernalia be banned from the rink during warmup periods when skaters are on the ice.

IV—CONDUCT OF RACES

1. ENTRIES:

a. Entries must be accompanied by a fee, as established by the Board of Control, for National Outdoor, National Indoor, North American Outdoor, and North American Indoor meets. The A.S.U. shall retain all fees for meets held in the United States. For meets held in Canada, the fees shall be paid to the Canadian Amateur Speed Skating Association.

b. All entries shall be made upon official A.S.U. entry blanks in the name of the competitor, with the age and address, name of club and Association, the registered or membership number of the competitor, and the ranking of the skater in his Association.

c. Entries for National and North American Championships shall be closed 48 hours prior to the opening of the meet.

d. A registration fee of $.25 shall be collected from each competitor at all open meets conducted by any member Association. The fees shall be forwarded to the A.S.U. treasurer within 30 days after the conduct of the meet and shall be earmarked for Growth and Development.

2. COMPETITORS SHALL:

a. Report immediately to the Registrar of the meet upon arrival at the meet and receive their competitor's number from the Registrar of the meet.

b. Obtain and wear on the lower back the specified number assigned for the meet.

c. Inform themselves of the times at which they must compete and report promptly to the heat area and starting line without waiting to be notified.

d. Not be accompanied by any person on the course or to the starting line.

e. Observe the following passing rules:

(1) In outdoor meets, upon gaining the inside or pole position, the skater has the right of way and may be passed on the right side; but should the skater stray from the pole position, any competitor has the privilege of passing such skater on the left providing there is ample room. When passing, the responsibility for collision or obstruction is upon the passing skater, provided that the skater being passed does not act improperly.

(2) In indoor races, any competitor is allowed to pass another skater on either the left or the right side. When passing, the responsibility for collision or obstruction is on the passing skater provided that the skater being passed does not act improperly.

f. Have no skates on ice inside of the blocks, poles, and markers which define the straight of way and corners of the track.

g. Not intentionally move the corner poles or flags.

h. Keep in their respective positions from start to finish on all races on straight-of-way tracks; and in all races with one or more turns, competitors shall not cross to the inner edge of the track except when they can do so without interfering with other competitors.

i. Upon entering the home stretch, competitors must stay in a straight line without deviation to the right or left until reaching the finish line. If the skater is far enough ahead so that his changing lanes will not interfere with the following skater, he may cross to another lane.

j. In a 1500 meter race or less, on an outdoor track, keep within one lap of the leader in the race; and when passed by the leader and lapped, competitors shall be declared distanced and shall be called out of the race by the Referee unless such competitor shall be finishing in a position for which a prize is offered.

k. Be deemed lapped when the leader has gained a lap on them but has not actually passed them, and if it appears that they are in any way impeding or attempting to set pace for the leader or leaders, they shall be called out of the race by the Referee.

l. In races over 1500 meters, not be considered lapped until they enter the last 1500 meters of the race and are then a lap behind the leader. Under such conditions, the competitors may be called out of the race by the Referee.

m. Be suspended for knowingly competing against an unregistered or suspended skater.

n. Not forsake an A.S.U. sanctioned meet for an unsanctioned meet.

o. Not enter an unsanctioned meet within the jurisdiction of another member Association.

p. Wear equipment when competing in any indoor meet consisting of a safety type helmet (which shall have a complete hard shell), gloves, and/or mittens and a long-sleeved jersey.

q. It is recommended that the front and rear tips of skate blades be rounded off to a 1/8 inch radius.

3. STARTING OF RACING EVENTS:

a. The Starter is responsible for:

(1) The Starter shall decide all disputes relating to the start.

(2) The Starter shall take his position behind or beside the skaters so that he has a clear view of all skaters starting in the heat.

b. The Start:

(1) On the command "Go to the Start" the skaters must take their position on the pre-start line (0.75 m behind the starting line) and on the command "Ready" they will position themselves at the start line and wait for the gun to be fired. There shall be a distinct interval between all skaters taking a motionless starting position and the firing of the gun. (The distinct interval should be about 1 to 1.5 seconds.)

(2) If a false start takes place, the Starter will recall the skaters with a second shot, or a blast with his whistle, and the skaters must return to their starting positions without delay.

(3) They will receive no more words of instruction from the Starter once the commands "Go to the Start" and "Ready" have been given. The skater who made the false start will be warned. The skaters must stand in their assumed starting position at the starting line. There shall be a distinct interval between all skaters becoming motionless and the starting shot.

(4) If a skater falls in the first 6 meters after the starting line, outdoors or before the first apex block of the turn after the starting line indoors the Starter may call the skaters back and make a new start.

(5) In the event of a false start or a fall, the skaters shall be recalled by a second shot or a whistle from the Starter. An Assistant to the Starter shall, on the order of the Starter, give a stop signal in front of the skaters from the inside of the track.

(6) The Starter shall warn a skater after the first false start. If in the event a skater has two false starts, he shall be disqualified only from the distance concerned.

(7) If more than one skater is responsible, they shall all be warned by the Starter. If one of the skaters breaks from his mark, thereby causing other skaters to follow him, the Starter shall warn the skater at fault only.

(8) Any skater that by his action, deliberately delays the start, shall be warned as if he has made a false start, and it will count as a false start.

(9) In the event of a misfire by the Starter's gun, or an official's delay in the start of a race, the complete starting procedure with all verbal commands shall be used. If the skaters have left the starting area, the Starter shall command their return to the starting line with a whistle. Skaters shall return without delay. All false starts or disqualifications shall remain in effect.

c. Assistant Starter

The Assistant Starter may, if directed by the Starter, recall the race if a false start or a fall occurs; this action will be taken by firing the pistol once or blowing the whistle once.

4. QUALIFYING FOR FINAL RACES:

a. Before each qualifying heat, the Clerk of Course shall announce to the competitors the number of competitors that may qualify in said heat for the final race.

b. Under normal conditions a competitor must finish in a qualifying position to be placed in the final event.

c. A competitor who does not finish in a qualifying position in a heat or subsequent event may be placed in the final event by the Referee; indoor, within the last 2 laps; outdoor, within the last 200 meters; if, in the judgment of the Referee, the competitor is the victim of a foul while in a qualifying position through no fault of his own, which thereby prevents the competitor from finishing in a qualifying position. In any event, the competitor, unless injured or temporarily disabled, must finish said race to the best of his ability in an attempt to qualify and the judgment of the Referee in respect thereto shall be final.

5. THE FINISH OF RACING EVENTS:

a. The competitor whose skate, or any part thereof, first crosses the finish line, shall be the winner of the race.

b. The position of subsequent finishers shall likewise be decided only upon the basis of the order of any part of a competitor's skate crossing the finish line, no matter what the position of the body of the competitor may be as he crosses the finish line.

6. DISQUALIFICATION:

a. The Referee and Assistant Referees shall signal all fouls by upraised arm and clenched fist.

b. The Referee may disqualify a competitor from an event if the competitor:

(1) Pushes against, impedes, crosses the course of, or in any way interferes with another competitor.

(2) Intentionally moves the corner poles or markers or fails to skate at all times outside the pole or corner markers.

(3) Willfully fails to wear his number in plain view, or is improperly clothed. Numbers shall be worn as issued, no folding or bending.

(4) Deliberately skates backward before crossing the finish line to ridicule other skaters in the race, or otherwise discredits the performance of other competitors, or delays the starting of the event.

c. The Referee may disqualify any competitor from the entire meet or any part of the meet if the competitor:

(1) At any time commits any acts unbecoming a gentleman or lady (such as use of profane language, engaging in fighting, causing undue disturbance), or commits any willful or deliberate act which results in damage, loss or injury to person or property, without regard to the location of the competitor's act from time for first check-in, during and until completion of presentation of awards.

(2) Loafs, competes to lose, coaches during the race, or uses unfair team work by blocking or impeding other competitors.

(3) Fails or refuses to compete in his first event on the meet program, or any subsequent event, after voluntarily entering, unless the competitor shows good cause for not competing.

d. The Referee may also disqualify an entire team for any unfair team work by any of the members thereof, such as boxing, pushing, blocking, etc.

e. The Referee may call out of a heat or race any competitors who are disqualified.

f. The Referee may in his discretion disqualify a competitor for the violation of any rule or regulation not specifically designated as grounds for disqualification.

7. CONDUCT OF THE RACE:

If in the event the field of competitors in qualifying heats or final events of championship races is deliberately slowing the pace to a speed not in keeping with the ability and caliber of the competitors, the Referee shall have the right to call the race no contest at any point and require such qualifying heat or final event to be re-skated. All false starts or disqualifications will remain in force on the re-skate.

8. SUSPENSION AND PERMANENT EXCLUSION:

a. Whenever a competitor shall have been disqualified from an entire meet, the Referee, within ten days from the termination of said meet, shall file a written report with the Secretary of the A.S.U., either personally or by certified or registered mail, which report shall contain the full facts and circumstances concerning the disqualification, the name of the competitor so disqualified, the names of any witnesses, and the Referee's recommendation with respect to what suspension, if any, should be imposed by the Board of Control.

b. Upon receiving such report and recommendation, the Secretary, after conferring with the Board of Control, shall serve a copy thereof, either personally or by registered or certified mail, upon the competitor named in the report together with notice of hearing to be held at a specific place designated therein and at a time not less than thirty nor more than sixty days from the date of the Secretary's receipt of the Referee's report.

c. The competitor disqualified by the Referee pursuant to the Racing rules shall have the right at such hearing to testify and present witnesses or any other evidence on his behalf.

d. In accordance with these rules of the A.S.U., at the conclusion of the hearing the Board of Control shall:

(1) Dismiss the charges against the competitor, or

(2) Suspend the competitor for a definite period of time, or

(3) Permanently exclude said competitor from all speed skating competition conducted by the A.S.U. and its members.

e. While suspended, a competitor may not compete in local, regional, National or North American meets or races. Any competitor entering a race with a skater known to him to be suspended shall himself be subject to suspension action.

V—PROTESTS

1. PROCEDURE:

a. Verbal protests may be made only by coach, appointed coach, or skater on behalf of any competitor, before or after any race against other competitors, or against any acts or any decisions of any official, including the Referee, or against any disqualifications by the Referee.

b. Competitors shall not enter the center of the track to present a protest in their own behalf.

c. Upon a verbal protest being made, the Referee shall make note of the same but shall not stop the races by reason of such verbal protest.

d. Verbal protests must be reduced to writing and filed with the Referee within one hour.

e. Written protest may be filed without previous verbal protest; provided, however, if no written protest shall be filed within one hour after the happening of the incident complained of by the competitor, the protest shall be deemed to have been waived.

f. The Referee, upon receiving written protests, shall promptly hold a hearing thereon, and after hearing all parties wishing to be heard, shall promptly render a decision. If the facts produced at said hearing warrant it, he may reverse previous decision or disqualifications made by him.

g. Upon written protest being filed, the Referee shall hold up all prizes until final decision has been rendered by him.

h. Written protests shall contain the following information and must be submitted on the official A.S.U. protest form.

(1) The date, time and event number of the incident.

(2) The person or persons involved, including skating numbers, whenever possible.

(3) The particular rule or rules alleged to have been infringed.

(4) A statement of the facts.

(5) Requested action of the Referee.

(6) Signature of protestor.

Failure to present the required information gives the Referee the authority to reject the protest if he/she sees fit to do so.

VI—CLASSIFICATIONS OF COMPETITORS

1. AGE CLASSIFICATIONS

a. The following definitions shall prevail to establish the age classification of skaters:

Master — Any skater who has passed his 40th birthday prior to July 1st. This class is open only to skaters who have passed their fortieth (40th) birthday prior to July 1st. (Classification at skater's option.)

Senior — Any skater who has passed his 18th birthday prior to July 1st.

Intermediate — Is a skater who has not reached the age of 18 by July 1, preceding the competition.

Junior — Is a skater who has not reached the age of 16 by July 1, preceding the competition.

Juvenile — Is a skater who has not reached the age of 14 by July 1, preceding the competition.

Midget — Is a skater who has not reached the age of 12 by July 1, preceding the competition.

b. At National and North American meets, a skater may compete in an advanced age class, except the Master class, but in the event a skater scores points, he shall be disqualified from competing in lower age group classes. This does not apply to open, local or exhibitional meets. In such non-national meets, a skater may compete in an advanced age class providing the skater has obtained the permission of the Referee or Clerk of Course of the meet. The Clerk of Course or Referee may combine classes if competitive conditions warrant without jeopardy to a skater's class status.

VII—REGISTRATION ELIGIBILITY AND RESIDENCE

(Note: The requirements for legal residence and membership in territory associations, deleted here, are detailed in the A.S.U. official rules publication.)

VIII—COMPETITIONS, SELECTIONS, EXPENSES AND PERMITS

(Note: Procedures for selection of skaters, expenses allowed and permits for meets outside of a territory are detailed in the A.S.U. official rules publication.)

IX—CHAMPIONSHIP EVENTS

1. OUTDOOR DISTANCES:

Distances to be skated in National Outdoor and North American Outdoor Championships, (All in Meters).

Masters Men	500	800	1000	1500	
Masters Women	500	800	1000	1500	
Senior Men	500	800	1000	1500	3000
Senior Women	500	800	1000	1500	3000
Intermediate Boys	500	800	1000	1500	3000
Intermediate Girls	500	800	1000	1500	3000
Junior Boys	300	500	800	1000	1500
Junior Girls	300	500	800	1000	1500
Juvenile Boys	300	500	800	1000	
Juvenile Girls	300	500	800	1000	
Midget Boys	300	400	500	600	
Midget Girls	300	400	500	600	

2. INDOOR DISTANCES:

Distances to be skated at National Indoor and North American Indoor Championships, (All in Meters).

Masters Men	500	800	1000	1500	
Masters Women	500	800	1000	1500	
Senior Men	500	800	1000	1500	3000
Senior Women	500	800	1000	1500	3000
Intermediate Boys	500	800	1000	1500	3000
Intermediate Girls	500	800	1000	1500	3000
Junior Boys	500	800	1000	1500	
Junior Girls	500	800	1000	1500	
Juvenile Boys	300	500	800	1000	
Juvenile Girls	300	500	800	1000	
Midget Boys	300	400	500	600	
Midget Girls	300	400	500	600	

Heats shall be run for the 3000 m, if more than 9 skaters are competing in the class. All skaters shall be permitted to skate in the 3000 m if 9 or fewer are competing in the class.

For the 111.12 meter track, all 200 M distances will be 222 M, and all 600 M distances shall be 611 M.

The above distances are mandatory for national competition and are subject to mutual agreement between A.S.U. and CASSA for the North American Competition.

Relaying racing consisting of teams from each Association is a part of North American Indoor Championships. Each Association may enter one (1) Male and one (1) Female team. Each team consists of four (4) competitors of any age division. Three (3) sets of four (4) medals will be presented to the top three (3) teams. Medals will be the official North American Design.

3. At least one final event per class shall be held on the first day of all National Championships and North American Championships held in the U.S.A.

4. At indoor competitions, the longest distance in Senior and Intermediate classes shall be skated the first day of a two day meet.

5. All championship events shall be determined by the greatest number of points won in all final events by one of the contestants; points shall be awarded in each final event as follows:

First place..5 points

Second place......................................3 points

Third place.......................................2 points

Fourth place......................................1 point

In the event of a tie for first place, the points for first and second places shall be added together and divided equally between the contestants so tying. In the event of a tie for second place, the points for second and third place shall be similarly added and divided. And in the event of a tie for third place, the points for third and fourth places shall be likewise added and divided. In case of a tie for the championship, the contestants so tying shall be known as co-champions and duplicate prizes shall be awarded.

6. CHAMPIONSHIP:

The contestant having the greatest number of points at the completion of the scheduled events shall be the champion and an award emblematic of the championship shall be awarded.

7. EVENT CANCELLATION:

In the event the meet is cancelled, the point standings at the time of cancellation shall determine the class champion, provided at least 50% of the class events have been held to completion.

8. COMPETITION REPORT:

The sponsoring Association of a National or North American meet shall submit a report of the competition to the A.S.U. Executive Secretary within five days after the conclusion of the meet. The report shall include the distances skated, time of the winner, full name of the competitors who placed in the final of each event, and the identity of his or her Association. A duplicate shall also be forwarded to the Editor of the Racing Blade.

X—PRIZES FOR CHAMPIONSHIP EVENTS

1. The medals for all A.S.U. Championships, outdoor and indoor, shall be provided by the A.S.U.

2. There must be four prizes for each event at a championship meet as follows:

First prize to be a gold medal.

Second prize to be a silver medal.

Third prize to be a bronze medal.

Fourth prize to be a green-bronze medal.

All shall be made from the standard Amateur Skating Union die.

3. No prizes shall be given except those approved by the Board of Control. A suitably engraved medallion shall be presented to each class champion. This medallion shall be made from the official A.S.U. or ASU/CASSA die. All medals and prizes shall be delivered to the winners as soon as possible after the events are finished.

XI—RECORDS

1. No records shall be listed or approved unless said times are made and recorded in one of the following sanctioned meets: National Outdoor, North American Outdoor, National Indoor and North American Indoor Championships.

2. Applications for records to be accepted as official shall be substantiated by a certificate signed by the Chief Judge, Chief Timer, and the Referee, certifying to the place, hour and date, the sponsor, the class, the distance, the time in which the race was skated, the competitor's name, address and Association, and in outdoor meets, the condition of the ice.

3. The applications for record to be accepted as official shall also contain a certification by at least one of the Track Measurers or Surveyors that the track used for the sanctioned meet where the record was broken complies with the measurements laid down by the Amateur Skating Union, and shall designate the track length in meters per lap.

4. Whenever a new record shall be established during the National or North American meets, outdoor or indoor, it shall be the duty and responsibility of the Chief Scorer of the meet to forward the Record Application form, properly entered and signed together with the heat or final card, or a copy thereof, and the Surveyor's certificate to the Chairman of the Records Committee within 15 days following the completion of the meet.

XII—AMATEUR STATUS IN SKATING

(Note: The regulations regarding amateur status in skating, deleted here, are detailed in the A.S.U. official rules publication.)

XIII—TRACK LAYOUT AND MEASUREMENTS

1. The two Track Measurers or Surveyors shall certify all track measurements consistent with the following:

a. Definitions

(1) Survey Lines — Those lines (or points) that define the track by positioning lines, marks or blocks on the ice.

(2) Skaters Path — 0.5 meter outside the survey line. This is to be used when calculating distances skated.

b. Tracks to be utilized are those approved by the Board of Control and published in the Handbook showing "Approved" on the diagram. Other tracks are published for local Association use but may be used in case of emergency upon the prior approval of the Chief Referee and an A.S.U. representative, for a National or North American meet.

c. For outdoor meets, the survey line may be marked by a snowline or by blocks set on the ice. If blocks are used, they shall be set so that their outside edge is on the survey line and shall be spaced 1.0 meter apart for the first 10 meters of the turn, 2.0 meters apart on the remainder of the turn, and 5.0 meters apart on the straight-of-ways.

d. Start and finish lines shall be a minimum of 0.02 meter (approximately 3/4 inch) to a maximum of 0.06 meter (approximately 2 inches) in width. The line shall have its upstream (approaching side) as the measured-to side. The starting line shall be divided into 6 equal spaces marked into the ice. These starting lanes shall be a minimum of 0.75 meter to a maximum of 1.0 meter to suit the ice dimensions.

e. "Fall-down" marks shall be used only on outdoor tracks and shall be 6 meters (19 feet, 8 1/4 inches) downstream of the starting line.

f. All marks in the ice shall be laid into the ice under the skating surface.

g. For indoor meets, the blocks consisting of rubber track markers shall be placed as indicated on the drawings; they shall consist of unweighted rubber toilet plungers, and they shall be placed with the outside edge on the marks on the ice.

h. For indoor meets, the spots marking the block location shall be a minimum of 0.02 meter (approximately 3/4 inch) in diameter with the outside edge marking the survey line.

i. A minimum of five tracks shall be set up for indoor championships. The intervals between marks shall not be less than 0.5 meter (19 3/4 inches), but the preferred distance shall be 0.75 meter (29 1/2 inches).

j. The tolerance for any individual measurement in track layout shall be (±3) mm or (±1/8) inch.

XIV—GLOSSARY

CHARGING:

1. Inside — Occurs when a competitor is on the inside attempting to pass a skater or skaters on a straight-of-way going into a turn, up to the apex of turn, and the passing skater makes strong physical contact with a competitor being passed.

2. Outside — Shall be when a skater leaves a position on the turn by skating wide and then attempts to regain the original position, thereby making strong, physical contact with another competitor skating a track to the left.

DRIFTING OR CHANGING LANES:

Skaters must stay in their respective positions from start to finish in all races on a straight-of-way track. However, if the lead skater is far enough ahead so that changing lanes will not interfere with the following skaters, the competitor may cross to another lane.

In all races with one or more turns, competitors shall not cross to the inner edge (or pole) of the track except when they are at least one skating length (approximately 1 meter) ahead and changing lanes will not interfere with other competitors.

FALSE START:

Occurs after skaters have been put on the mark, and one or more crosses the line before the gun signals the start of the race, or if a skater takes a starting position before the command "Ready".

However, if the "jump" is instigated by a skater due to a movement of the body (head, shoulders, arms), even though he does not complete the move by crossing the line, he shall receive the penalty.

INTERFERENCE:

When overtaking, the responsibility for any obstruction or collision shall be upon the skater passing, provided that the skater being overtaken does not act unfairly.

PUSHING:

Any skater who uses hands, forearms, elbows, shoulders, or hips on another skater, causing the latter to fall, trip, lose balance, skate wide of normal track, or lose position.

REFEREE HAND SIGNAL:

Notifies judges to pick extra places because a rule infraction has been committed and may change the order of finish.

TRIPPING:

Occurs when a skater, immediately after completing a pass, drags the rear foot, thereby knocking another skater's foot from under him.

GOVERNING BODY

Amateur Skating Union of the United States, 1033 Shady Lane, Glen Ellyn, IL 60137

The purpose of the Amateur Skating Union (A.S.U.) is to encourage, advance, and control amateur speed skating throughout the United States, and to develop excellence in national and international competition. The membership of the Union is composed of Associations that have jurisdiction over a specified allotted territory in the A.S.U. national structure. Associations in the Union are composed of amateur clubs and individuals interested in the promotion of amateur speed skating. The organizing and sanctioning of competition at the local, regional, national, and North American levels is a major function of the Union. Additional information regarding the A.S.U. and speed skating will be found in the A.S.U. Speed Skating Handbook.

MAGAZINES

The Racing Blade, Amateur Skating Union, 2504-17th St., Wyandotte, MI 48192

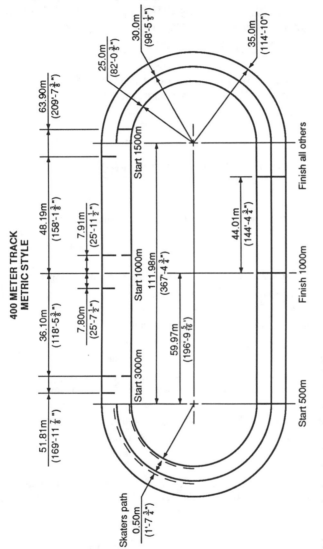

400 METER TRACK
METRIC STYLE

Note: Other standard tracks recognized by the A.S.U. and illustrated in the official rules publication are: a. 400—Mass Start; b. 384.18 Meter: c. 333.33Meter; d. 250 Meter; e. 200 Meter; f. 100 Meter Oval; g. 111.12 Meter Oval; and h. 100 Meter Twin Radius (Canadian Track).

• SQUASH RACQUETS •

SQUASH RACQUETS PLAYING RULES
OFFICIAL PLAYING RULES OF THE UNITED STATES
SQUASH RACQUETS ASSOCIATION.
REVISED FEBRUARY 1, 1981.

**(Reproduced by permission of the United States
Squash Racquets Association, Inc.*)**

☐

SINGLES PLAYING RULES

1. GAME

(a) The object of the game is to win by scoring points. Points are earned one at a time either by winning a rally or by being awarded. Each point won by or awarded to a player shall add one to his score. Each point taken away from a player shall subtract one from his score.

(b) The player who first scores fifteen points wins the game excepting that:

(1) At "thirteen all" the player who has first reached the score of thirteen must announce one of the following before the next serve:

(i) Set to five points—making the game eighteen points.

(ii) Set to three points—making the game sixteen points.

(iii) No set, in which event the game remains fifteen points.

(2) At "fourteen all," provided the score has not been "thirteen all," the player who has first reached the score of fourteen must announce one of the following before the next serve:

(i) Set to three points—making the game seventeen points.

(ii) No set, in which event the game remains fifteen points.

2. MATCH

(a) The player who first wins three games wins the match, except that a player may be awarded the match at any time upon the retirement, default or disqualification of an opponent.

3. SERVICE

(a) The service begins the play of each point and is the striking of the ball with the racquet in accordance with this entire Rule 3. At the start of a match the choice to serve or receive shall be decided by the spin of a racquet. The server retains the serve until he loses a point, in which event he loses the serve.

---

*See page 511 for additional information.

(b) The server, from the beginning of the service motion until the ball has left the racquet from the service,.must stand with at least one and the same foot touching the floor wholly within and not touching the line surrounding the service box and serve the ball onto the front wall above the service line and below the 16′ line before it touches any other part of the court, so that on its rebound (return) it first strikes the floor within, but not touching, the lines of the opposite service court, either before or after touching any other wall or walls within the court (see diagram). This player must be in control of and holding on to the racquet at the moment of contact. A ball so served is a good service, otherwise it is a Fault.

(c) If the first service is a Fault, the server shall serve again from the same side. If the server makes two consecutive Faults, he loses the point. A service Fault may not be played, but the receiver may volley any service which has struck the front wall in accordance with Rule 3(b).

(d) At the beginning of each game, and each time there is a new server, the ball shall be served by the winner of the previous point from whichever service box the server elects and thereafter alternately until the service is lost or until the end of the game. If the server serves from the incorrect box there shall be no penalty and the service shall count as if served from the correct box, except that if the receiver does not attempt to return the service, he may demand that it be served from the other box, or if, before the receiver attempts to return the service, there is a Let (See Rule 7), the service shall be made from the other box.

(e) A ball is in play from the moment at which it is struck with the racquet until (1) the point is decided; (2) a Fault, as defined in Rule 3(b), is made; or (3) a Let occurs (See Rules 6 and 7).

4. RETURN OF SERVICE AND SUBSEQUENT PLAY

(a) A return is deemed to be made at the instant the ball touches the racquet of the player making the return. This player must be in control of and holding on to the racquet at the moment of contact. To make a good return of a service or of a subsequent return the ball must be struck on the volley or before it has touched the floor twice, and reach the front wall on the fly above the tell-tale and below the 16′ line, and it may touch any wall or walls within the court before or after reaching the front wall. On any return the ball may be struck only once. It may not be "carried" or "double-hit."

(b) If the receiver fails to make a good return of a good service, the server wins the point. If the receiver makes a good return of service, the players shall alternate making returns until one player fails to make a good return. The player failing to make a good return loses the point.

(c) Until the ball has been touched or has hit the floor twice, it may be struck at any number of times.

(d) If at any time after a good service the ball hits outside the playing surfaces of the court (the tell-tale, the ceiling and/or lights, or on or above a line marking the perimeters of the playing surfaces of the court), the player so hitting the ball loses the point except as provided in Rule 7(c)(5).

5. RIGHT TO PLAY THE BALL

(a) Immediately after striking the ball a player must get out of an opponent's way and must:

(1) Give an opponent a fair view of the ball;

(2) Give an opponent a fair opportunity to get to and strike at the ball in and from any position on the court elected by the opponent. A player will be deemed to have failed to give his opponent a fair opportunity to get to and strike the ball when he has used an excessive follow through so that his opponent has to wait for an excessive swing;

(3) Allow an opponent to play the ball to any part of the front wall, either side wall or the back wall; and

(4) Refrain from creating a visual or audible distraction.

6. LET POINT

(a) A Let Point shall be awarded to a player:

(1) When an opponent, in violating Rule 5, deprives the player of a clear opportunity to attempt a winning shot; or

(2) When an opponent, in violating Rule 5, fails to make the effort within the scope of his normal ability to avoid the violation thereby depriving the player of an opportunity to attempt a shot; or

(3) When an opponent, in violating Rule 5, has caused repeated Lets, no one of which individually constitutes a Let Point.

(b) If a player refrains from striking at the ball because of a reasonable fear of injuring his opponent and he would have otherwise won the point under Rule 8(c)(2), the Referee shall award him the point.

(c) The Referee shall not award a Let Point as defined in this Rule 6 unless a Let Point or a Let (See Rule 7) is requested by a player.

7. LET

(a) A Let mandates the playing over of a point.

(b) On the replay of the point the server (1) is entitled to two serves even if a Fault occurred in the original point, (2) must serve from the correct box even if he served from the incorrect box on the original point, and (3) provided he is a new server, may serve from a service box other than the one selected on the original point.

(c) In addition to the Lets described elsewhere, the following are Lets if the player whose turn it is to strike the ball could otherwise have made a good return:

(1) When such player's opponent violates Rule 5 except for those violations described in Rule 6.

(2) When owing to the position of such player, his opponent is unable to avoid being touched by the ball.

(3) When such player refrains from striking at the ball because of a reasonable fear of injuring his opponent.

(4) When such player before or during the act of striking or striking at the ball is touched by his opponent, his racquet or anything he wears or carries.

(5) When on the first bounce from the floor the ball hits on or above the six and one half foot line on the back wall; and

(6) If a player thinks the ball has broken while play is in progress, he must nevertheless complete the point and then immediately request a Let, giving the ball promptly to the Referee for inspection. The Referee shall allow a Let only upon such prompt request if the ball in fact proves to be broken (See Rule 11(c)).

(d) A player may request a Let or a Let Point (See Rule 6). A request by a player for a Let shall automatically include a request for a Let Point. Upon such request, the Referee shall allow a Let, Let Point or No Let.

(e) No Let shall be allowed on any stroke a player makes unless he requests such before or during the act of striking or striking at the ball.

(f) The Referee shall not call or allow a Let as defined in this Rule 7 unless such Let is requested by a player; provided, however, the Referee may call a Let at any time (1) when there is interference with play caused by any factor beyond the control of the player, or (2) when he fears that a player is about to suffer severe physical injury.

8. BALL IN PLAY TOUCHING PLAYER

(a) If a ball in play, after hitting the front wall, but before being returned again, shall touch either player, or anything he wears or carries (other than the racquet of the player who makes the return) the player so touched loses the point, except as provided in Rule 7(c)(1) or 7(c)(2).

(b) If a ball in play touches the player who last returned it or anything he wears or carries before it hits the front wall, the player so touched loses the point, except as provided in Rule 7(c)(2).

(c) If a ball in play, after being struck by a player on a return, hits the player's opponent or anything the opponent wears or carries before reaching the front wall:

(1) The player who made the return shall lose the point if the return would not have been good.

(2) The player who made the return shall win the point if the ball, except for such interference, would have hit the front wall fairly; except that the point shall be a Let (see Rule 7) if:

(i) The ball would have touched some other wall before so hitting the front wall.

(ii) The ball has hit some other wall before hitting the player's opponent or anything he wears or carries.

(iii) The player who made the return shall have turned following the ball around prior to playing the ball.

(d) If a player strikes at and misses the ball, he may make further attempts to return it. If, after being missed, the ball touches his opponent or anything he wears or carries:

(1) If the player might otherwise have made a good return, the point shall be a Let.

(2) If the player could not have made a good return, he shall lose the point.

(e) If a player after striking at and missing the ball is successful in a further attempt but the ball, before reaching the front wall, touches his opponent or anything he wears or carries and under Rule 8(c)(2) the player would have won the point, the point shall nevertheless be a Let.

9. CONTINUITY OF PLAY

(a) Play shall be continuous from the first service of each game until the game is concluded. Play shall never be suspended solely to allow a player to recover his strength or wind. The provisions of this Rule 9 shall be strictly construed. If the Referee believes a player is violating this Rule during a game, the Referee may deduct one point from the offender's score for each violation or the Referee may default the offender.

(b) Between any two successive games play may be suspended by either player for a period not to exceed two minutes except that between the third and fourth games play may be suspended by either player for a period not to exceed five minutes. If a player is not on court ready to play at the expiration of the applicable time period, the Referee may deduct one point from the offender's score for each 30 seconds or fraction thereof he is late or the Referee may default the offender.

(c) Except as otherwise specified in this Rule 9, the Referee may suspend play for such reason and for such period of time as he may consider necessary.

(d) If play is suspended by the Referee because of an injury to one of the players, such player must resume play within one hour from the point and game score existing at the time play was suspended or default the match, provided, however, if a player suffers cramps or pulled muscles, play may be suspended by the Referee once during a match for such player for a period not to exceed five minutes after which time such player must resume play or default the match.

(e) In the event the Referee suspends play other than for injury to a player, play shall be resumed when the Referee determines the cause of such suspension of play has been eliminated, except that if such cause of delay cannot be rectified within one hour, the match shall be postponed to such time as the Tournament Committee determines. Any suspended match shall be resumed from the point and game score existing at the time the match was stopped.

10. ATTIRE AND EQUIPMENT

(a) A player's attire, including, but not restricted to, its color, design, insignia, advertisements, statements and slogans, shall be within the normal standards of good taste associated with the game of squash racquets.

(b) A standard singles ball as specified in the Court, Racquet and Ball Specifications of this Association shall be used.

(c) A racquet as specified in the Court, Racquet and Ball Specifications of this Association shall be used.

11. CONDITION OF BALL

(a) No ball, before or during a match, may be heated, chilled or otherwise artificially treated except by the mutual consent of the players or by decision of the Referee.

(b) At any time, when not in the actual play of a point, another ball may be substituted by the mutual consent of the players or by decision of the Referee.

(c) A ball shall be determined broken when it has a crack which extends through both its inner and outer surfaces. The ball may be squeezed only enough to determine the extent of the crack. A broken ball shall be replaced and the preceding point shall be a Let (See Rule 7(c)(6)).

(d) Upon determination of a cracked (but not broken) ball, the ball shall be replaced and the preceding point shall stand.

12. COURT

(a) The singles court shall be as specified in the Court, Racquet and Ball Specifications of this Association.

(b) No equipment of any sort shall be permitted to remain in the court during a match other than the ball used in play, the racquets being used by the players, and the clothes worn by them. All other equipment must be left outside the court. A player who requires a towel or cloth shall keep same in a pocket or in his waistband.

13. REFEREE

(a) A Referee shall control the game. This control shall be exercised from the time scheduled for the match and/or from the time that at least one player is on the court. The Referee may limit the time of the warm-up period to five minutes, or shall terminate a longer warm-up period so that the match commences at the scheduled time.

(b) The Referee's decision on all questions of play shall be final except as provided in Rule 13(c).

(c) Two judges may be appointed to act on any appeal by a player to a decision of the Referee. When such Judges are acting in a match, a player may appeal any decision of the Referee through the Referee to the Judges, except a decision under Rules 11 and 13(a).

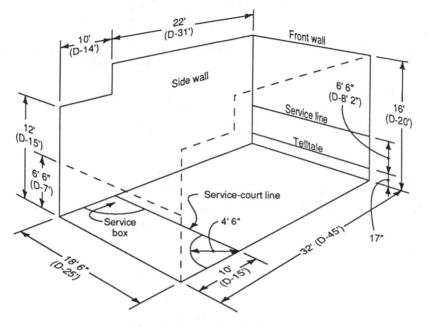

Squash Racquets Singles Court
(Doubles court dimensions indicated with (D-))

If one Judge agrees with the Referee, the Referee's decision stands. If both Judges disagree with the Referee, the Judges' decision is final. If the Referee is not overruled, his decision stands. The Judges shall make no ruling unless an appeal has been made. The decision of the Judges shall be announced promptly by the Referee.

(d) A player may not request the removal or replacement of the Referee or a Judge during a match. Any such request must be made by the player before or immediately upon entering the court.

(e) A player shall not state his reason for his request under Rule 7 for a Let or Let Point or for his appeal from any decision of the Referee except if the Referee permits the player to state his reasons.

(f) If a player uses speech or language unbecoming to the game of squash racquets, the Referee may deduct one point from the offender's score for each utterance or the Referee may default the offender.

(g) If a player's conduct is unbecoming to the game of squash racquets, the Referee may deduct one point from the offender's score for each such act or the Referee may default the offender.

14. PLAY WITHOUT A REFEREE

(a) When there is no Referee and the players are unable to agree with respect to the circumstances described in Rules 6,7, and 8 the point shall be a Let. No penalties described in Rules 9 and 13 shall apply.

DOUBLES PLAYING RULES

1. GAME

(a) The object of the game is to win by scoring points. Each side or team, consisting of two players, shall earn points either by winning a rally or by being awarded them. Each point won by or awarded to a side shall add one to its score. Each point taken away from a side shall subtract one from its score.

(b) The side which first scores fifteen points wins the game excepting that:

(1) At "thirteen all" the side which has first reached the score of thirteen must a. .iounce one of the following before the next serve:

(i) Set to five points—making the game eighteen points.

(ii) Set to three points—making the game sixteen points.

(iii) No set, in which event the game remains fifteen points.

(2) At "fourteen all," provided the score has not been "thirteen all," the side which has first reached the score of fourteen must announce one of the following before the next serve:

(i) Set to three points—making the game seventeen points.

(ii) No set, in which event the game remains fifteen points.

2. MATCH

(a) The side which first wins three games wins the match, except that a side may be awarded the match at any time upon the retirement, default or disqualification of the opposing side.

3. SERVICE

(a) The service begins the play of each point and is the striking of the ball with the racquet in accordance with this entire Rule 3. At the start of a match the choice to serve or receive shall be decided by the spin of a racquet. The two partners of a side shall serve in succession, the first retaining his serve until his side has lost a point. On the loss of a subsequent point the side shall be declared "out" and the serve revert to the opponents. On the first serve of every game, however, the "in" side shall be declared "out" after it has lost one point only. The order of serving within a side shall not be changed during the progress of a game. At the end of a game the side which has won the game shall have the choice of serving or receiving to commence the next game.

(b) The server, from the beginning of the service motion until the ball has left the racquet from the service, must stand with at least one and the same foot touching the floor wholly within and not touching the line surrounding the service box and serve the ball onto the front wall above the service line and below the 20' line before it touches any other part of the court, so that on its rebound (return) it first strikes the floor within, but not touching, the lines of the opposite service court, either before or after touching any other wall or walls within the court. This player must be in control of and holding on to the racquet at the moment of contact. A ball so served is a good service, otherwise it is a Fault.

(c) If the first service is a Fault, the server shall serve again from the same side. If the server makes two consecutive Faults, he loses the point. A service Fault may not be played, but the receiver may volley any service which has struck the front wall in accordance with Rule 3(b).

(d) At the beginning of each game and each time a side becomes "in" the ball shall be served from whichever service box the first server for the side elects, and thereafter alternately until the side is "out" or until the end of the game. If the server serves from the incorrect box there shall be no penalty and the service shall count and the play shall proceed as if the box served from was the correct box, except that if the receiver does not attempt to return the service, he may demand that it be served from the other box, or if, before the receiver attempts to return the service, there is a Let (See Rule 7), the service shall be made from the other box.

(e) A ball is in play from the moment at which it is struck with the racquet until (1) the point is decided; (2) a Fault, as defined in Rule 3(b), is made; or (3) a Let occurs (See Rules 6 and 7).

4. RETURN OF SERVICE AND SUBSEQUENT PLAY

(a) A return is deemed to be made at the instant the ball touches the racquet of the player making the return. This player must be in control of and holding on to the racquet at the moment of contact. To make a good return of a service or of a subsequent return the ball must be struck on the volley or before it has touched the floor twice, and reach the front wall on the fly above the tell-tale and below the 20' line, and it may touch any wall or walls within the court before or after reaching the front wall. On any return the ball may be struck only once. It may not be "carried" or "double-hit."

(b) At the beginning of each game each side shall designate one of its players to receive service in the right hand service court and the other to receive service in the left hand service court and throughout the course of such game the service must be received by the players so designated.

(c) If the designated receiver fails to make a good return of a good service, the serving side wins the point. If the designated receiver makes a good return of service the sides shall alternate making returns until one side fails to make a good return. The side failing to make a good return loses the point.

(d) Until the ball has been touched or has hit the floor twice, it may be struck at any number of times by either player on a side.

(e) If at any time after a service the ball hits outside the playing surfaces of the court (the ceiling and/or lights, or on or above a line marking the perimeters of the playing surfaces of the court), the side so hitting the ball loses the point except as provided in Rule 7(c)(5).

5. RIGHT TO PLAY THE BALL

(a) Immediately after he or his partner has struck the ball, each player must get out of his opponents' way and must:

(1) Give his opponents a fair view of the ball;

(2) Give his opponents a fair opportunity to get to and strike at the ball in and from any position on the court elected by an opponent. A player will be deemed to have failed to give his opponents a fair opportunity to get to and strike the ball when he has used an excessive follow through so that an opponent has to wait for an excessive swing;

(3) Allow either opponent to play the ball to any part of the front wall, either side wall or the back wall; and

(4) Refrain from creating a visual or audible distraction.

6. LET POINT

(a) A Let Point shall be awarded to a side:

(1) When an opponent, in violating Rule 5, deprives a player of a clear opportunity to attempt a winning shot; or

(2) When an opponent, in Violating Rule 5, fails to make the effort within the scope of his normal ability to avoid the violation thereby depriving a player of an opportunity to attempt a shot; or

(3) When an opponent, in violating Rule 5, has caused repeated Lets, no one of which individually constitutes a Let Point.

(b) The Referee shall not award a Let Point as defined in this Rule 6 unless a Let Point or a Let (See Rule 7) is requested by a player.

7. LET

(a) A let mandates the playing over of a point.

(b) On the replay of the point the server (1) is entitled to two serves even if a Fault occurred in the original point, (2) must serve from the correct box even if he served from the incorrect box on the original point, and (3) provided he is a new server, may serve from a service box other than the one selected on the original point.

(c) In addition to the Lets described elsewhere, the following are Lets if the player on the side whose turn it is to strike the ball could otherwise have made a good return:

(1) When an opponent of such player violates Rule 5 except for those violations described in Rule 6.

(2) When owing to the position of such player, either of his opponents is unable to avoid being touched by the ball.

(3) When such player refrains from striking at the ball because of a reasonable fear of injuring an opponent.

(4) When such player before or during the act of striking or striking at the ball is touched by either of his opponents, their racquets or anything either of them wears or carries.

(5) When on the first bounce from the floor the ball hits on or above the seven foot line on the back wall; and,

(6) If a player thinks the ball has broken while play is in progress, he must nevertheless complete the point and then immediately request a Let, giving the ball promptly to the Referee for inspection. The Referee shall allow a Let only upon such prompt request if the ball in fact proves to be broken (See Rule 11(c)).

(d) A player may request a Let or a Let Point (See Rule 6). A request by a player for a Let shall automatically include a request for a Let Point. Upon such request, the Referee shall allow a Let, Let Point or No Let.

(e) No Let shall be allowed on any stroke a player makes unless he requests such before or during the act of striking or striking at the ball.

(f) The Referee shall not call or allow a Let as defined in this Rule 7 unless such Let is requested by a player; provided, however, the Referee may call a Let at any time (1) when there is interference with play caused by any factor beyond the control of the player, or (2) when he fears that a player is about to suffer severe physical injury.

8. BALL IN PLAY TOUCHING PLAYER

(a) If a ball in play, after hitting the front wall, but before being returned again, shall touch any player, or anything he wears or carries (other than the racquet of the player who makes the return) the side of the player so touched loses the point, except as provided in Rule 7(c)(1) or 7(c)(2).

(b) If a ball in play touches the player who last returned it or his partner or anything either of them wears or carries before it hits the front wall, the side of the player so touched loses the point, except as provided in Rule 7(c)(2).

(c) If a ball in play, after being struck by a player on a return, hits either of the player's opponents or anything either of them wears or carries before reaching the front wall:

(1) The side of the player who made the return shall lose the point if the return would not have been good.

(2) The point shall be a Let (See Rule 7) if the return would have hit the front wall fairly except for such interference.

(d) If a player strikes at and misses the ball, he and his partner may make further attempts to return it. If, after being missed, the ball touches either of their opponents or anything they wear or carry:

(1) If the player or his partner would otherwise have made a good return, the point shall be a Let.

(2) If the player or his partner could not have made a good return, their side shall lose the point.

9. CONTINUITY OF PLAY

(a) Play shall be continuous from the first service of each game until the game is concluded. Play shall never be suspended solely to allow a player to recover his strength or wind. The provisions of this Rule 9 shall be strictly construed. If the Referee believes a player is violating this Rule during a game, the Referee may deduct one point from the offender's side's score for each such violation or the Referee may default the offender's side.

(b) Between any two successive games play may be suspended by either player for a period not to exceed two minutes except that between the third and fourth games play may be suspended by either player for a period not to exceed five minutes. If a player is not on court ready to play at the expiration of the applicable time period, the Referee may deduct one point from the offender's side's score for each 30 seconds or fraction thereof he is late or the Referee may default the offender's side.

(c) Except as otherwise specified in this Rule 9, the Referee may suspend play for such reason and for such period of time as he may consider necessary.

(d) If play is suspended by the Referee because of an injury to one of the players, such player must resume play within one hour from the point and game score existing at the time play was suspended or his side shall default the match, provided however, if a player suffers cramps or pulled muscles, play may be suspended by the Referee once during a match for each such player for a period not to exceed five minutes after which time such player must resume play or his side shall default the match.

(e) In the event the Referee suspends play other than for injury to a player, play shall be resumed when the Referee determines the cause of such suspension of play has been eliminated, except that if such cause of delay cannot be rectified within one hour, the match shall be postponed to such time as the Tournament Committee determines. Any suspended match shall be resumed from the point and game score existing at the time the match was stopped.

10. ATTIRE AND EQUIPMENT

(a) A player's attire, including, but not restricted to, its color, design, insignia, advertisements, statements and slogans, shall be within the normal standards of good taste associated with the game of squash racquets. A side shall have matching major items of attire.

(b) A standard doubles ball as specified in the Court, Racquet and Ball Specifications of this Association shall be used.

(c) A racquet as specified in the Court, Racquet and Ball Specifications of this Association shall be used.

11. CONDITION OF BALL

(a) No ball, before or during a match, may be heated, chilled or otherwise artificially treated except by the mutual consent of the sides or by decision of the Referee.

(b) At any time, when not in the actual play of a point, another ball may be substituted by the mutual consent of the sides or by decision of the Referee.

(c) A ball shall be determined broken when it has a crack which extends through both its inner and outer surfaces. The ball may be squeezed only enough to determine the extent of the crack. A broken ball shall be replaced and the preceding point shall be a Let (See Rule 7(c)(6)).

(d) Upon determination of a cracked (but not broken) ball, the ball shall be replaced and the preceding point shall stand.

12. COURT

(a) The doubles court shall be as specified in the Court, Racquet and Ball Specifications of this Association.

(b) No equipment of any sort shall be permitted to remain in the court during a match other than the ball used in play, the racquets being used by the players, and the clothes worn by them. All other equipment must be left outside the court. A player who requires a towel or cloth shall keep same in a pocket or in his waistband.

13. REFEREE

(a) A Referee shall control the game. This control shall be exercised from the time scheduled for the match and/or from the time that at least one player is on the court. The Referee may limit the time of the warm-up period to five minutes, or shall terminate a longer warm-up period so that the match commences at the scheduled time.

(b) The Referee's decision on all questions of play shall be final except as provided in Rule 13(c).

(c) Two judges may be appointed to act on any appeal by a player to a decision of the Referee. When such Judges are acting in a match, a player may appeal any decision of the Referee through the Referee to the Judges, except a decision under Rules 11 and 13(a). If one Judge agrees with the Referee, the Referee's decision stands. If both Judges disagree with the Referee, the Judges' decision is final. If the Referee is not overruled, his decision stands. The Judges shall make no ruling unless an appeal has been made. The decision of the Judges shall be announced promptly by the Referee.

(d) A player may not request the removal or replacement of the Referee or a Judge during a match. Any such request must be made by the player before or immediately upon entering the court.

(e) A player shall not state his reason for his request under Rule 7 for a Let or Let Point or for his appeal from any decision of the Referee except if the Referee permits the player to state his reasons.

(f) If a player uses speech or language unbecoming to the game of squash racquets, the Referee may deduct one point from the offender's side's score for each such utterance or the Referee may default the offender's side.

(g) If a player's conduct is unbecoming to the game of squash racquets, the Referee may deduct one point from the offender's side's score for each such act or the Referee may default the offender's side.

14. PLAY WITHOUT A REFEREE

(a) When there is no Referee and the players are unable to agree with respect to the circumstances described in Rules 6, 7, and 8 the point shall be a Let. No penalties described in Rules 9 and 13 shall apply.

GOVERNING BODY

United States Squash Racquets Association, Inc., 211 Ford Road, Bala-Cynwyd, PA 19004

The U.S. Squash Racquets Association (USSRA) is the governing body for squash in the United States and is a member of the International Squash Racquets Federation. The Association has 241 member clubs that make up the 29 member districts. In fulfilling the primary purposes of the Association—to promote the game of squash and to protect the mutual intents of the members—the activities of the organization include (a) conducting national championship tournaments by age level; (b) providing referee and player instructional films; (c) teaching clinics; (d) conducting a referee certification program; (e) establishing and enforcing uniformity in rules of the game; (f) providing junior development programs and clinics; and (g) studying the development of facilities and equipment.

MAGAZINES

Squash News, USSRA, 211 Ford Road, Bala-Cynwyd, PA 19004

• SWIMMING •

UNITED STATES SWIMMING RULES AND REGULATIONS 1989

(Reproduced by permission of United States Swimming, Inc.*)

☐

Note: The United States Swimming Rules and Regulations consist of eight parts including: (1) Technical Rules of Competition, (2) Administrative Regulations of Competition, (3) Athletes Rights, Registration and Eligibility, (4) Hearings and Appeals, (5) Governing Regulations of the Corporation, (6) Governing Regulations of the Local Swimming Committee, (7) United States Masters Swimming, (8) Long Distance Swimming. Only Part One, Technical Rules of Competition, is included here.

PART ONE
TECHNICAL RULES

ARTICLE 101
INDIVIDUAL STROKES AND RELAYS

101.1 BREASTSTROKE

.1 Start—The forward start shall be used.

.2 Stroke—From the beginning of the first armstroke after the start and after each turn, the body shall be kept on the breast and both shoulders shall be in line with the water surface. The arms shall move simultaneously and in the same horizontal plane without any alternating movement. The hands shall be pushed forward together from the breast, and shall be brought back on or under the surface of the water. The hands shall not be brought beyond the hipline, except during the first stroke after the start and each turn. Some part of the swimmer's head shall break the surface of the water at least once during each complete cycle of one arm stroke and one leg kick, in that order, except after the start and each turn the swimmer may take one arm stroke completely back to the legs and one leg kick while wholly submerged. The head must break the surface of the water before the hands turn inward at the widest part of the second stroke.

.3 Kick—All vertical and lateral movements of the legs shall be simultaneous. The feet must be turned outward during the propulsive part of the kick movement. A scissors, flut-

---

*See page 542 for additional information.

ter, or downward butterfly kick is not permitted. Breaking the surface with the feet shall not merit disqualification unless followed by a downward butterfly kick.

.4 Turns—At each turn, the touch shall be made with both hands simultaneously at, above, or below the water surface, and the shoulders shall be in line with the water surface. The head may be submerged after the last arm pull prior to the touch, provided it breaks the surface of the water at some point during any part of the last complete or incomplete cycle preceding the touch. Once a touch has been made, the swimmer may turn in any manner desired. The shoulders must be at or past the vertical toward the breast when the feet leave the wall and the form prescribed in .2 above must be attained from the beginning of the first arm stroke.

.5 Finish—At the finish the touch shall be made with both hands simultaneously at, above, or below the water surface. The body shall be on the breast and the shoulders in line with the water surface. The head may be submerged after the last arm pull prior to the touch, provided it breaks the surface of the water at some point during any part of the last complete or incomplete stroke cycle preceding the touch.

101.2 BUTTERFLY

.1 Start—The forward start shall be used.

.2 Stroke—After the start and after each turn the swimmer must remain on the breast and is permitted one or more leg kicks, but only one arm pull under water, which must bring him to the surface. Both arms must be brought forward over the water and pulled back simultaneously. The shoulders must be in line with the water surface from the beginning of the first arm stroke after the start and after each turn.

.3 Kick—All up and down movements of the legs and feet must be simultaneous. The position of the legs or the feet need not be on the same level, but they shall not alternate in relation to each other. A scissors or breaststroke kicking movement is not permitted.

.4 Turns—At each turn the body shall be on the breast and the shoulders in line with the water surface. The touch shall be made with both hands simultaneously at, above, or below the water surface. Once a touch has been made, the swimmer may turn in any manner desired.

.5 Finish—At the finish the touch shall be made with both hands simultaneously at, above, or below the water surface. The body shall be on the breast and the shoulders in line with the water surface.

101.3 BACKSTROKE

.1 Start

A The swimmers shall line up in the water facing the starting end, with both hands placed on the gutter or on the starting grips.

B Prior to the command "take your mark" and until the feet leave the wall at the starting signal, the swimmer's feet, including the toes, shall be placed under the surface of the water. Standing in or on the gutter or curling the toes over the lip of the gutter is not permitted at any time before or after the start. A backstroke starting block may not be used.

.2 Stroke—The swimmer shall push off on his back and continue swimming on the back throughout the race.

.3 Turns—The swimmer's head, shoulder, foremost hand or arm must touch the end of the course. The shoulders must not turn over beyond the vertical before the touch is made. It is permissible to turn the shoulders beyond the vertical after the touch, however, on the push off, the swimmer must return to a position where the shoulders are at or past the vertical toward the back before the feet leave the wall.

.4 Finish—The swimmer shall have finished the race when any part of the body touches the wall at the end of the course.

101.4 FREESTYLE

.1 Start—The forward start shall be used.

.2 Stroke—Freestyle means that in an event so designated the swimmer may swim any style; except that in a medley relay or individual medley event, freestyle means any style other than butterfly, breaststroke or backstroke.

.3 Turns—Upon completion of each length the swimmer must touch the solid wall or pad at the end of the course with some part of his body.

.4 Finish—The swimmer shall have finished the race when any part of his person touches the solid wall or pad at the end of the pool.

101.5 INDIVIDUAL MEDLEY

The swimmer shall swim the prescribed distance in the following order: the first one-fourth, butterfly; the second one-fourth, backstroke; the third one-fourth, breaststroke; and the last one-fourth, freestyle.

.1 The stroke and turns for each stroke shall follow the prescribed rules for each stroke.

.2 The turns from one stroke to another shall be considered turns, not finishes, and are as follows:

A. Butterfly to backstroke—Once a legal touch has been made, the swimmer may turn in any manner desired. The swimmer must have returned to a position where the shoulders are at or past the vertical toward the back before the feet have left the wall.

B. Backstroke to breaststroke—Once a legal touch has been made, the swimmer may turn in any manner desired. The shoulders must be at or past the vertical toward the breast when the feet leave the wall. The prescribed stroke form must be attained prior to the first arm stroke.

C. Breaststroke to freestyle—Once a legal touch has been made, the swimmer may turn in any manner desired.

.3 Finish—The swimmer shall have finished the race when any part of his person touches the solid wall or pad at the end of the pool.

101.6 RELAYS

.1 Freestyle Relay—Four swimmers on each team, each to swim one-fourth of the prescribed distance using any desired stroke(s). Freestyle finish rules apply.

.2 Medley Relay—Four swimmers on each team, each to swim one-fourth of the prescribed distance continuously in the following order: first, backstroke; second, breaststroke; third, butterfly; and fourth, freestyle. Rules pertaining to each stroke used shall govern where applicable. At the end of each leg, the finish rule for each stroke applies in each case.

.3 Rules Pertaining to Relay Races

A. No swimmer shall swim more than one leg in any relay event.

B. When automatic relay take-off judging is used, each swimmer must touch the touchplate or pad in his lane at the end of the course to have finished his leg of the relay race.

C. In relay races a swimmer other than the first swimmer shall not start until his teammate has concluded his leg.

D. Any relay team member and his relay team shall be disqualified from a race if a team member other than the swimmer designated to swim that leg shall jump into or enter the pool in the area where the race is being conducted before all swimmers of all teams have finished the race.

E. Each relay team member shall leave the water immediately upon finishing his leg, except the last member.

F. In relay races the team of a swimmer whose feet have lost touch with the starting platform (ground or deck) before his preceding teammate touches the wall shall be disqualified.

ARTICLE 102
CONDUCT AND OFFICIATING OF ALL SWIMMING COMPETITION

102.1 EVENTS

In planning any meet, careful consideration must be given the demands to be made upon swimmers, officials and spectators, in that order. Long, tiresome meets, with too many events and/or entries, often result in keeping small children up late at night. Meets should be planned to terminate within a maximum period of eight (8) hours of competitive events in any one day. Provide adequate meal and rest breaks and sheltered rest areas, properly supervised.

.1 Senior Events

The following events for National Championships are recommended for Local Swimming Committee (LSC) and other championship meets. Eligibility for these championships shall be determined by the LSCs involved.

Short Course Events

50 yd/mtr Freestyle	200 yd/mtr Butterfly
100 yd/mtr Freestyle	100 yd/mtr Breaststroke
200 yd/mtr Freestyle	200 yd/mtr Breaststroke
500 yd/400 mtr Freestyle	200 yd/mtr Individual Medley
1000 yd/800 mtr Freestyle	400 yd/mtr Individual Medley
1650 yd/1500 mtr Freestyle	400 yd/mtr Freestyle Relay
100 yd/mtr Backstroke	800 yd/mtr Freestyle Relay
200 yd/mtr Backstroke	400 yd/mtr Medley Relay
100 yd/mtr Butterfly	

Long Course Events

50 meters Freestyle	200 meters Butterfly
100 meters Freestyle	100 meters Breaststroke
200 meters Freestyle	200 meters Breaststroke
400 meters Freestyle	200 meters Individual Medley
800 meters Freestyle	400 meters Individual Medley
1500 meters Freestyle	400 meters Freestyle Relay
100 meters Backstroke	800 meters Freestyle Relay
200 meters Backstroke	400 meters Medley Relay
100 meters Butterfly	

.2 Age Group Events

10-and-Under	11-12 years
50-100-200 Freestyle	50-100-200-400/500 Freestyle
50-100 Backstroke	50-100 Backstroke
50-100 Breaststroke	50-100 Breaststroke
50-100 Butterfly	50-100 Butterfly
100-200 Individual Medley	100-200 Individual Medley
200 Medley Relay	200-400 Medley Relay
200 Freestyle Relay	200-400 Freestyle Relay

13-14, 15-16, 17-18, 15-18 Years

50-100-200-400/500, 800/1000, 1500/1650 Freestyle

100-200 Backstroke

100-200 Breaststroke

100-200 Butterfly

200-400 Individual Medley

200-400 Medley Relay

200-400-800 Freestyle Relay

102.2 ENTRIES—GENERAL RULES

.1 In any combination of aquatic events conducted on a single day at the same site and where preliminaries and finals are held, no swimmer shall be permitted to compete in more than three (3) events per day, exclusive of relays.

.2 The above restrictions are effective regardless of the classification mixture and/or that separate meets are being conducted and such limitations shall be clearly stated on the entry blanks.

.3 When timed finals are held, without preliminary heats, no swimmer shall be permitted to compete in more than 5 events per day exclusive of relays.

.4 In meets where a combination of preliminary and final events and timed finals are held, a swimmer may compete in only three (3) individual events per day, unless entered exclusively in timed final events on that day.

.5 If qualifying time standards are used they may be made in

A. A 25 yard or 25 meter course for short course events.

B. A 50 meter course for long course events.

.6 If a meet or event has no qualifying time standards, swimmers with no established time for an event may enter that event with no submitted time.

102.3 SCRATCH PROCEDURES

Each swimmer shall inform himself of the meet starting time and shall report to the proper meet authorities promptly upon call. Meet announcements and advance information shall specify check-in and scratch procedures for individual and relay events and penalties for violation of those procedures.

102.4 RELAYS

.1 Relay teams may not compete unattached. In all cases relay teams must be composed of USS members of the same club, school or organization which is a member of the Corporation.

.2 Relays may be conducted on a timed final basis or with preliminaries and finals.

.3 Timed final relays shall be swum in seeded heats, with not more than two heats (which shall be the fastest heats) conducted during the final session of meets holding preliminaries and finals, and the balance of relay heats will be conducted during the preliminaries.

.4 Relays conducted as preliminaries and finals shall be seeded and conducted in the same manner as individual events.

.5 Organizations entering two or more relay teams in an event shall designate them on the entry blank as Team A, Team B, etc.

.6 The best time of each relay team shall be entered on the entry blank for seeding purposes and no change in time will be permitted.

.7 First and last names of swimmers eligible to compete in relay events shall be entered on the entry blank according to the event in which they will be eligible to swim. There is no limit to the number of eligible swimmers who may be listed.

.8 First and last names of competing relay swimmers, their ages, and their order of swimming shall be declared to the clerk of course immediately prior to the start of the relay heat in which such team is entered, and no changes will be permitted thereafter.

.9 The competing teams, first and last names of members and their ages, must be listed in the meet results.

102.5 LANE ASSIGNMENTS—SEEDING—COUNTERS

.1 Preliminary Heats When Finals are Scheduled—In order to assure seeded positions, the best competitive times of all entries must be submitted. These times shall be assembled (listed) by the meet committee with the fastest swimmer first and the slowest swimmer last. Swimmers whose submitted times are identical should be assigned places in the list by draw. Swimmers with no submitted times shall be considered the slowest and shall be placed at the end of the list by draw. Swimmers shall be placed in lanes under procedure outlined for finals seeding in 102.5.3. Swimmers shall be placed in heats according to submitted times in the following manner:

A. Fewer than three heats

(1) If one heat, it may be seeded as a final heat and swum only during the final session, at the Referee's discretion.

(2) If two heats, the fastest swimmer shall be seeded in the second heat, next fastest in the first heat, next fastest in the second heat, next in the first heat, next in the second heat, next in the first heat, etc.

B. Three heats—The fastest swimmer shall be placed in the third heat, next fastest in the second, next in the first. The fourth fastest swimmer shall be placed in the third heat, the fifth in the second heat, and the sixth fastest in the first heat, the seventh fastest in the third heat, etc.

C. Four heats or more—The last three heats of an event shall be seeded in accordance with B above. The heat preceding the last three heats shall consist of the next fastest swimmers; the heat preceding the last four heats shall consist of the next fastest swimmers, etc. Lanes shall be assigned in descending order of submitted times within each heat, in accordance with the pattern outlined in 102.5.3.

D. Exception—When there are two or more heats in an event, there shall be a minimum of three swimmers seeded into any one preliminary heat, but subsequent scratches may reduce the number of swimmers in such heat to less than three.

.2 Swim-Offs—A swim-off is considered to be part of the total preliminary process of qualifying for the finals. In no case may a swimmer with a faster time displace another who placed ahead of him within a heat according to the ballot system. If this situation results in disputed qualifications, all swimmers having times tied or within the disputed times shall swim-off to qualify for the disputed place or places in the final. The swim-off will be swum with three watches and two judges on each of the swimmers' lanes and the ballot system or modified ballot system shall be used to determine the order of finish, except when automatic officiating equipment is used and is properly functioning. The official time for the swimmers involved shall be the time set in the original preliminary heat. This elimination may be held at any time set by the Referee, but not more than 45 minutes after the last heat of any event in which any one of these swimmers is competing in that session. In the case of a disqualification in a swim-off the swimmer so disqualified is relegated to the lowest qualifying position for which he is competing. Disqualification in a swim-off for a qualifying position in the championship finals shall not eliminate a swimmer from eligibility to compete in the accompanying consolation finals. If disqualification leaves a vacancy for the full complement of finalists, swim-offs shall be continued among the disqualified swimmers until a full complement of finalists is assured.

Note: It shall be the swimmer's responsibility to acquaint himself with all information pertaining to swim-offs, final events and the participants therein.

.3 Finals—In finals, the times to be considered are those times made in preliminary heats. If any qualifying swimmers have the same time their respective lanes shall be determined by draw. Lane assignments shall be made in descending order of qualifying times according to lanes as follows:

Pool											Number of lanes in the pool
					5	3	1	2	4		5
				6	4	2	1	3	5		6
			7	5	3	1	2	4	6		7
		8	6	4	2	1	3	5	7		8
	9	7	5	3	1	2	4	6	8		9
10	8	6	4	2	1	3	5	7	9		10
10	9	8	7	6	5	4	3	2	1		← Lane numbers

1 = Fastest time

.4 Time Finals

A. Heats—In order to assure seeded positions, the best competitive times of all entries must be submitted. The last heat shall be composed of the swimmers with the fastest submitted times, the next to last heat composed of the next fastest swimmers, etc. Lanes shall be assigned in descending order of submitted times within each heat, in accordance with the pattern outlined in .3 above. When there are two or more heats there shall be a minimum of three swimmers or relay teams seeded into the first heat. The last heat should be a full heat, but the requirement of seeding three swimmers or relay teams into the first heat may result in failure to fill the last heat.

B. Places—In timed finals, places shall be determined on a time basis, subject to the order of finish within each heat and based upon the ranking system used at the meet. Any ties resulting from the procedure used shall be declared officially tied for awards and points, with no further attempt at resolution.

.5 Seeding of 50 meter events in a 50 meter course—50 meter events swum in a 50 meter course shall be seeded as provided above. If the event is started at the turning end of the course no change in the lane assignments shall be made, i.e., the slowest swimmer in the heat will swim in the right outside lane.

.6 Counters

A. A swimmer in any individual swimming event of 400 yards or meters or more, except the individual medley, may appoint one counter to call lengths or indicate lengths by visual sign.

B. Verbal counters shall be limited to one per swimmer, shall be stationed at the end of the course opposite the starting end, and may not coach or aid the swimmer in any way except that they may use watches and signal intermediate times to the swimmer.

C. If visual counters are used, they may be stationed at the end of the course opposite the starting end. Visual counters may be lowered into the water at the end of the swimmer's lane, provided that, in the opinion of the Referee, they neither physically aid the swimmer nor interfere with another competitor or present any safety hazard.

D. The count may be in ascending or descending order.

E. In the event of official or counter error it is the responsibility of the swimmer to complete the prescribed distance.

.7 Distance Events—In 1000/1650 yard and 800/1500 meter freestyle events, the normal order of heats may be reversed by swimming the fastest heats first and alternating women's and men's heats. The meet announcement shall state the order of heats for these events.

102.6 AWARDS

When two or more swimmers tie for any place, duplicate awards shall be given to each of such tied swimmers. In such cases no awards shall be given for the place or places immediately following the tied positions. If two tie for 1st place, no award for 2nd place; if three tie for 1st place, no awards for 2nd, 3rd, and so on.

102.7 SCORING

.1 Dual meets

Individual events: 5-3-1-0

Relays: 7-0

.2 Triangular meets

Individual events: 6-4-3-2-1-0

Relays: 8-4-0

.3 All other meets

Individual events:

4-lane pools: 5-3-2-1

5-lane pools: 6-4-3-2-1

6-lane pools: 7-5-4-3-2-1

7-lane pools: 8-6-5-4-3-2-1

8-lane pools: 9-7-6-5-4-3-2-1

9-lane pools: 10-8-7-6-5-4-3-2-1

10-lane pools: 11-9-8-7-6-5-4-3-2-1

Individual point values shall be doubled for relays. When consolations and championship finals are swum, scoring shall be as follows:

Individual events:

6-lane pools (12 places):

final: 16-13-12-11-10-9

consolation: 7-5-4-3-2-1

7-lane pools (14 places):

final: 18-15-14-13-12-11-10

consolation: 8-6-5-4-3-2-1

8-lane pools (16 places):

final: 20-17-16-15-14-13-12-11

consolation: 9-7-6-5-4-3-2-1

9-lane pools (18 places):

final: 22-19-18-17-16-15-14-13-12

consolation: 10-8-7-6-5-4-3-2-1

10-lane pools (20 places):

final: 24-21-20-19-18-17-16-15-14-13

consolation: 11-9-8-7-6-5-4-3-2-1

Individual point values shall be doubled for relays, even when relays are swum as timed finals.

.4 Mixed Meets—When events of mixed classification, as Senior and Age Group, are included in the same meet, or if events do not meet standard distances, the LSC in charge shall establish the desired combination of values and publish it in the entry blank and meet information.

.5 Ties—Where two or more swimmers tie for any place in any event the points credited to such place or places, if any, next in order shall be equally divided between such swimmer, i.e., if two tie for first place, the points to be credited to first place and the points to be credited to second place shall be added and divided one-half and one-half. If three tie for first place, the points credited to first, second and third places shall be added and divided one-third, one-third and one-third, and so on for four or more tying first place. The same is true for those tying for second place, third place, and whatever places there may be.

.6 Disqualifications—When a relay team or individual swimmer is disqualified, the following places will move up accordingly and points awarded to conform to the new places. Consolation finalists may not receive championship final placing. Alternates may not receive consolation final placing.

102.8 CHANGE OF PROGRAM AND POSTPONEMENT

.1 The order of events, as laid down in the official program, shall not be changed. The announced arrangement of heats in any event shall not be added to or altered, except by the authority of the Referee, to the extent of consolidating the heats.

.2 At the Meet Referee's discretion, individual events 200 yards/meters or longer or any relay event may be combined by age, sex and/or distance provided there is at least one empty lane between any such combination. Strokes may not be combined.

.3 The entry provisions and starting time of any event, meet or portion thereof shall stand as stated on entry blank (except as permitted under 4. below) and may not be changed to an earlier time or date unless written notice of such change is delivered to each affected swimmer or his coach. If mailed, such notice must be postmarked no later than the entry deadline date stated on entry blank, and if lack of time prohibits mail notification, each affected swimmer must voluntarily agree in writing that he or she has been notified and is in accord with such change. Any affected swimmer or his coach may and should file a written protest with the Referee prior to running of event or meet if they do not agree to such change in time or date.

.4 Postponement or Cancellation

A. If, prior to its commencement, unusual or severe weather conditions preclude the possibility of safely and effectively conducting a meet, the meet committee may cancel or postpone it.

B. Should a meet have actually commenced, and in judgment of the Referee cannot safely and effectively continue because of unusual or severe weather conditions, or for some other compelling reason, the Referee, in his sole discretion, may suspend the meet or any particular event until conditions warrant continuance. If circumstances do not warrant continuance, the Referee may cancel the meet or postpone it to a future date or time, with the approval of the meet committee.

C. A decision to cancel or postpone shall be final.

D. Entry fees for teams or swimmers may be refunded, in whole or part, at the discretion of the meet committee, upon cancellation of a meet or particular event. The decision of the meet committee on refunding may be appealed to the LSC Review Section for hearing under the provisions of Article 401.

102.9 COSTUME

.1 Design—Swimmer's costume must be one-piece, non-transparent, and conform to the current concept of the appropriate. The Referee shall have authority to bar offenders from competition under this rule, until they appear properly costumed.

.2 Insignia—No swimmer shall be allowed to wear the insignia and/or name of any club or organization which he is not entitled to represent in open competition. He shall be permitted to wear the insignia and/or name of the organization he represents and he may wear the insignia of National Federation or Organizing Committees for Olympic, World, Continental or Regional Championships.

.3 Advertising

A. In the competition venue or complex of all events conducted by and under the control of the Corporation or any LSC or division thereof, no swimsuit shall carry any visible marque or insignia in the form of advertising or any words or numbers (except design or trademarks of members or Organizing Committees for Olympic, World, Continental and Regional Championships) other than the trademark on technical equipment or clothing, that is in excess of 16 sq. cm. (2.48 sq. in.) in area. A trademark may be repeated provided a name is used only once on a suit. Offenders may be barred from competition under this rule, until they appear properly costumed.

B. Products involving tobacco, alcohol or pharmaceuticals containing drugs banned under IOC or FINA rules may not be advertised under .3A above, but the advertiser's name only may be used.

102.10 DISQUALIFICATIONS

.1 A disqualification can be made only by the official within whose jurisdiction the infraction has been committed.

.2 The Referee or designated official making a disqualification shall make every reasonable effort to seek out the swimmer or his coach and inform him as to the reason for the disqualification.

.3 Any swimmer who acts in an unsportsmanlike manner may be considered for disciplinary action, at the discretion of the Referee.

.4 A swimmer must start and finish the race in his assigned lane.

.5 Standing on the bottom during a freestyle race shall not disqualify a swimmer, but he must not leave the pool, or walk, or spring from the bottom.

.6 Obstructing another swimmer by swimming across or otherwise interfering shall disqualify the offender, subject to the discretion of the Referee.

.7 Any swimmer not entered in a race who enters the pool or course in the area in which said race is being conducted before all swimmers therein have completed the race shall be barred from the next individual event in which he is entered on that day or the next meet day, whichever is first.

.8 Dipping goggles in the water or splashing water on the competitor's face or body prior to his next event shall not be considered as entering the pool unless the Referee finds that such action is interfering with the competition.

.9 Should a foul endanger the chance of success of a swimmer, the Referee may allow him to swim in the next round, or should the foul occur in the final he may order it re-swum. In case of collusion to foul another swimmer, the Referee may, at his discretion, disqualify the swimmer for whose aid the foul was committed, as well as the swimmer doing the fouling.

.10 Coaches having entrants in any event of the program shall not be allowed in the immediate starting area of swimming pools, which must be clearly marked, during the progress of any competition. Upon being apprised of a violation of this rule, it shall be the duty of the Referee to remove, or have such offender removed, immediately. Coaching of swimmers during the progress of an event shall not be permitted. It shall be permissible for coaches or others to signal intermediate times to a swimmer during competition, and this shall not be considered as "coaching."

.11 No swimmer is permitted to wear or use any device or substance to help his speed or buoyancy during a race. Goggles can be worn, and rubdown oil applied if not considered excessive by the Referee.

.12 For relay disqualifications, refer to 101.6.3.

.13 The time and/or place of any swimmer or relay team disqualified either during or following an event shall not be recorded in the results of that event. If awards have been made prior to the decision to disqualify they shall be returned and made to the proper recipient(s) and if points have been scored by those disqualified the event shall be rescored.

.14 Time and/or place officially recorded for a swimmer shall not be nullified for violations occurring subsequent to such performance.

102.11 PROTESTS

.1 Until final action is determined, results of any race conducted under protest, or of any protested race, shall not be announced, and no prizes for that race shall be awarded or scoring points allowed unless the protest is officially withdrawn.

.2 Protests affecting the eligibility of any swimmer to compete or to represent an organization in any race shall be made in writing to the meet director or Referee before the race is held, and if the meet committee deems it advisable, the swimmer may compete under protest and it shall be so announced before the race. The meet committee shall immediately refer such protest to review section having jurisdiction for adjudication at the earliest possible time.

.3 Protests against judgment decisions of starters, stroke, turn, place and relay take-off judges can only be considered by the Referee of the meet.

.4 Any other protest arising from the competition itself shall be made within 30 minutes after the race in which the alleged infraction took place. If the protest is not resolved immediately the protester shall at that time file a written protest with the chairman of the LSC, or his representative, having jurisdiction over the event. If the LSC does not satisfactorily resolve the protest within ten (10) days, the protester may appeal in writing to the National Rules Chairman, within the next five (5) days, for final adjudication which shall then be binding on all parties.

102.12 OFFICIALS

.1 All officials accepting an invitation to officiate at a swimming meet should arrive promptly and report immediately to the meet director.

.2 For all swimming meets or time trials except dual meets there should be not less than the following officiating positions filled or approved by the LSC in authority. Officials other than the Referee may act in more than one officiating capacity only when sufficient qualified officials are not available, but no one may simultaneously time and judge the finish (102.17).

1 Referee

1 Starter

3 Timers per lane

1 Clerk of Course

2 Lane Place Judges per lane or 2 Across-the-Board Place Judges

2 Stroke Judges and 2 Turn Judges or 2 Stroke & Turn Judges

Relay Take-off Judges

2 Recorders

2 Scorers

1 Recorder of Records

1 Announcer

Automatic Equipment Operators (as needed).

.3 When automatic officiating equipment is used in any competition, the placings and times so determined shall have precedence over the decisions of human judges and timers as outlined in 102.21.5. In case of malfunction, secondary information from a manual-electronic timing and judging device with one or more officials per lane or the prescribed ballot system of humans shall be used and integrated with primary information as outlined in 102.20.1.

.4 Minimum Number of Officials Required for Dual Meets

A. Referee, who may also act as a stroke and turn judge.

B. Starter.

C. One other stroke and turn judge (may be the Starter).

D. Two scorers—one from each team.

E. Announcer.

F. Three timers for each lane.

G. Relay take-off judges.

H. Two across-the-board judges, one on each side of the pool at the finish line whose independent decisions as to the order of finish may be used for balloting.

I. The visiting team may furnish officials as a courtesy, not a requirement.

.5 Officials For National Championships

A. Officials for national championship meets shall be assigned by the National Officials Chairman with the approval of the National Events Coordinator.

B. For all national championship competition the following officials shall be required and assigned but no more than those listed below shall be on the deck at one time.

1 Referee

1 Starter

1 Recall Starter

1 Chief Judge

1 Chief Timer

2 Stroke Judges—1 each side of pool

1 Timer/Turn Judge per lane

1 Timer/Take-Off Judge per lane

1 Timer/Split Taker per lane

4 Take-Off Judges—2 each side of pool

1 Turn Judge per lane (at opposite end of pool from starting blocks)

2 Clerks of Course

4 Marshals

2 Scorers

4 Recorders

1 Announcer

1 Recorder of Records

1 Press Steward

2 Automatic equipment operators.

C. In addition to officials listed above, assistant referees may be assigned.

D. All officials should be certified National Swimming Officials.

102.13 REFEREE

.1 Shall have full authority over all officials and shall assign and instruct them; shall enforce all applicable rules and shall decide all questions relating to the actual conduct of the meet, the final settlement of which is not otherwise assigned by said rules; can overrule any meet official on a point of rule interpretation, or on a judgment decision pertaining to an action which he has personally observed; shall also disqualify a swimmer(s) for any violations of the rules he personally observes and shall at the same time raise one hand overhead with open palm. If he does not make such a signal there shall be no penalty.

.2 Shall signal the starter that all officials are in position, that the course is clear, and that the competition can begin, before each race; shall assign marshals with specific instructions.

.3 Shall give a decision on any point where the opinions of the judges differ; shall have authority to intercede in a competition at any stage, to ensure that the racing conditions are observed.

.4 For LSC and local records only, may assign three (3) additional official timers on request to record a record attempt at initial distances in accordance with 104.2E.

.5 When automatic or manual-electronic officiating equipment is used and an apparent malfunction occurs it shall be his responsibility to make an immediate investigation to determine whether the swimmer finished in accordance with the rules and/or if there was an actual equipment malfunction.

.6 He may at his discretion prohibit the use of any bell, siren, horn or other artificial noisemaker during the meet.

.7 Starting rules may be modified by the Referee to adapt them for handicapped swimmers.

.8 When the meet sanction allows conducting the events by starting them from the alternate ends of a 50 meter course, the Referee shall establish the necessary administrative and officiating procedures to conform to Part One of the rules and local conditions.

.9 Refer to 102.11 concerning protests.

102.14 STARTER

.1 Preparation

A. Shall be provided with at least .22 caliber starting gun. An electronic starting horn with or without an underwater recall device may replace the gun start and recall herein.

B. Shall station himself within ten feet of starting end of pool at a point where gun flash is clearly visible to timers and gun report easily heard by starting swimmers.

C. Upon signal from Referee, assumes full control of swimmers until a fair start has been achieved.

D. Notifies swimmers of the distance, the event and for distances of 400 yards/meters or longer (except individual medley and relays), that "this is a gun/bell lap event."

E. Notifies relay swimmers that all but the last swimmer must leave the pool immediately upon completion of their leg.

F. Optional Instructions

Stroke(s) to be used and the order of swimming them. Number of pool lengths to be swum.

May advise heat when a swimmer is attempting a time at an initial distance.

.2 The Short Course Start

A. On receiving clearance from the Referee (for all events except backstroke and medley relay) directs swimmers to step onto the starting block or platform and assume a position with at least one foot at the front of the block before the command "take your mark." Refer to 101.3.1A for backstroke start.

B. Directs swimmers to "take your mark," to which they must respond at once by assuming a starting position. Sufficient time should follow the direction to "take your mark" to enable swimmers to assume a starting position, but no swimmer shall be in motion immediately before the starting signal is given.

C. When all swimmers are motionless in starting position, gives starting signal.

.3 The Long Course Start

A. On receiving clearance signal from the Referee (for all events except backstroke and medley relay) directs swimmers to step onto the back surface of the starting block or platform and remain there. Refer to 101.3.1B for backstroke start requirements.

B. Directs the swimmers to "take your mark," to which they must immediately respond by assuming a starting position with at least one foot at the front of the starting block. Sufficient time should follow "take your mark" to enable swimmers to assume starting positions, but no swimmer shall be in motion immediately before the starting signal is given.

C. When all swimmers are motionless in starting position, gives starting signal.

.4 Warning Signal—In all events 400 yards or meters or longer except the individual medley and relays, the starter shall sound a warning signal over the water at the finish end of the lane of the leading swimmer when that swimmer has two lengths plus five yards (or meters) to swim to finish.

.5 False Starts

A. When a swimmer does not respond promptly to the command "take your mark" or false starts before the starting signal is given, the Starter shall immediately release all swimmers with the command "Stand Up" upon which the swimmers may stand up to step off the blocks. Any swimmer who enters the water or backstroker who leaves the starting area shall be charged with a false start, except that a swimmer who would otherwise be charged with the false start may be relieved of the charge if the false start was caused by the swimmer's reaction to the command.

B. All swimmers leaving their marks before the starting signal is given shall be charged with a false start, except that a swimmer who has false started because of the action or movement of another competitor may be relieved of the responsibility for the false start and a false start may be charged only to the offender. (Note exception for deliberate delay or misconduct.)

C. In backstroke or medley relay events a false start may be charged to any swimmer who fails to maintain his feet and/or hands in a legal position after the first warning.

D. When the starting signal is given and one or more swimmers have obtained an unfair advantage, all swimmers shall be recalled at once by a second signal.

E. A swimmer can be charged with a false start by the starter or recall starter only if the Referee or an officially designated Assistant Referee has observed the violation and confirms that the violation occurred.

F. The Starter shall indicate the swimmer or swimmers, if any, who are charged with a false start.

G. Any swimmer who is charged with committing or causing a false start shall be disqualified and shall not be permitted to swim the event. This rule shall not apply to U.S. Swimming international events or to the Trials for Pan American, Pan Pacific, World Championships or Olympic teams, where current FINA false start rules shall apply except that all false starts shall be recalled.

H. A swimmer shall not be disqualified for an illegal starting position at the start or charged with a false start if the race is permitted to proceed without recall. Enforcement of the correct starting position is the responsibility of the Starter, who may impose the appropriate penalty for violation before the starting signal is given.

.6 Deliberate Delay or Misconduct

A. Any swimmer, who delays the start by entering water or by willfully or deliberately disobeying a Starter's command to step on the blocks or take a starting position, or for any other misconduct taking place at the start, can be disqualified from the event by the Starter with concurrence of the Referee.

B. A swimmer who fails to appear at the starting platform ready to swim in time for the initial start of his heat shall be disqualified.

C. Such disqualifications shall not be charged as a false start.

102.15 RECALL STARTER

A recall starter may be assigned to immediately discharge a gun or other sound device if the automatic equipment is not properly functioning on the starting signal or if a false start has been observed. The position of the recall starter shall be made known to the swimmers. He may also be assigned to assist the starter in any desired manner. A recall starter is mandatory in United States Swimming Championships.

102.16 JUDGES

Shall have jurisdiction over the swimmers immediately after the race has begun.

.1 Chief—An overall "Chief Judge" may assign and supervise the activities of all stroke, turn, place and take-off judges and may report their decisions, or if desired any judging category may have a designated "Chief." Any "Chief" may act as liaison for his judges and may himself serve simultaneously in one of the judging positions and he shall assign those judges within his category.

.2 Lane Place Judge

A. Two lane place judges shall be stationed at the finish of each lane. Each shall activate a separate switch recording the finish of their lane swimmer, and each recorded impulse shall constitute their placement ballot. If only one such recorded placement decision per lane is possible with the available equipment, either a visual judge shall be assigned to each lane or an across-the-board place judge shall be assigned to provide the second ballot decision.

B. It is not the responsibility of the lane place judge to determine if the finish touch meets the requirements of the appropriate stroke rule.

.3 Across-the-Board Place Judge—When limited personnel prevents assignment of lane place judges, two across-the-board judges, one on each side of the course, can be stationed near the finish and each shall judge the order of finish of all swimmers. Should both agree on all lanes, that shall be the official placement. If they disagree, the Modified Ballot System 102.20.2 shall prevail. An across-the-board judge may record a tie if a place distinction cannot be made. He shall award each swimmer the highest place that may have been attained.

.4 Stroke Judge—Shall operate on both sides of the pool, preferably walking abreast of the swimmers during all strokes except freestyle, during which events they may leave poolside, at the Referee's discretion; shall ensure that the rules relating to the style of swimming designated for the event are being observed; and shall report any violations to the Referee on signed slips detailing the event, the heat number, the lane number, the swimmer's name and infraction.

.5 Turn Judge—Shall operate on both ends of the pool; shall ensure that when turning or finishing the swimmer complies with the turning and finishing rules applicable to the stroke used; and shall report any violations to the Referee on signed slips detailing the event, the heat number, lane number, the swimmer's name and infraction observed.

.6 Jurisdiction of Stroke and Turn Judges—Before the competition begins the Referee shall determine the respective areas of stroke and turn responsibility and jurisdiction, which may include joint, concurrent, and coordinated responsibility and jurisdiction. The Referee shall insure that all swimmers shall have fair, equitable, and uniform conditions of judging.

.7 Relay Take-Off Judges

A. After the start of the race, relay take-off judges shall stand beside the starting block of each lane so that they can clearly see both the touch of the incoming swimmer and the feet of the departing swimmer as they leave the starting platform in that lane, and shall judge whether the swimmer is in contact with the platform when the incoming swimmer touches the end of the pool.

B. Additional relay take-off judges may be assigned to each side of the course to observe two assigned lanes each. In which case a relay will be disqualified only if the lane take-off judge has reported an infraction and the assigned poolside take-off judge has confirmed the same infraction. If dual relay take-off judging is used, the lane and poolside take-off judges shall independently report infractions in writing without the use of the infraction hand signal. If poolside relay take-off judges are used they shall be assigned for all relay races throughout the meet.

C. When automatic relay take-off judging equipment is available and in use, take-off judges will be assigned to each lane and stationed as described above. A team will only be disqualified when there is dual confirmation of an illegal take-off (i.e., visual and automatic equipment).

.8 Infraction Signal—Upon observing an infraction within his jurisdiction, the Referee, stroke, turn, or relay take-off judge shall immediately raise one hand overhead with open palm. If the official does not do so, there shall be no penalty.

Exception: Relay take-off judges as outlined in 102.16.7B.

102.17 TIMERS

In any race not timed with automatic or semiautomatic equipment (as provided in 102.21) the time for each competitor shall be taken by three timers stationed at or close to the finish. Each timer operates a manual watch (i.e., any hand-held mechanical or electronic timing device) that is both started and stopped by the timer as described below. These three timers are the official lane timers and their times must be individually recorded to determine the official time on the lane. Alternate or chief timers may substitute for an official lane timer only in the event of failure of a watch or its operator. No official lane timer may simultaneously determine time and place under any circumstances.

.1 Chief Timer

A. Assignment of official lane timers to their lanes shall be subject to the direction of the chief timer.

B. The chief timer shall be responsible for delivery to the recorders of all official times as recorded by the head lane timers, including the times of disqualified swimmers.

.2 Head Lane Timer—The chief timer designates one timer on each lane as the head lane timer. The head lane timer shall be responsible for the following:

A. Determination that the proper swimmer is in his lane and that relay swimmers are swimming in the order listed on the lane timer's card.

B. Determination of and recording of all manual watch times.

C. Assignment of one timer to take relay splits, and initial distance times.

D. Determination of and reporting if the swimmer has delayed in touching or has missed the finish touch pad of an automatic timing device.

.3 Official Lane Timers—The three timers shall be placed directly over their assigned lane at the finish.

A. Each timer shall look at the starter's gun and start his watch at the instant of the flash or smoke. If an electronic sounding device is used, the watch shall be started by the flash of a strobe light, when available, or by sound.

B. All watches shall be stopped when in the opinion of the timer any part of the swimmer's body touches the solid end of the pool or course.

C. It is not the responsibility of the lane timer to judge if the finish touch meets the requirements of the appropriate stroke finish rule, unless assigned additional responsibility as a turn judge.

D. All lane timers shall promptly report their times to the head lane timer or the designated recorder; present their watches for inspection, if requested, and shall not clear them until given the command to "clear watches."

E. The time of each watch is recorded on the lane timer's card, and the official time established as described below:

(1) If all manual watches on all lanes provide digital displays to a resolution of 0.01 seconds the times shall be recorded as displayed to the hundredths of a second.

(2) If dial watches are used, when the hand is not exactly centered on a mark, it shall be considered to be in the space between the marks and the reading shall be that of the following mark.

(3) If the manual timing in any lane is by a mixture of dial and digital watches, the dial watches shall be read as described above and the time on the digital watches in all lanes shall be rounded up to the next full tenth whenever there is one-hundredth or more. (Example: 51.11 is recorded as 51.20.)

F. Split times may be taken during a race by one of the lane timers upon request of the chief timer. The split hand (or function button) shall be stopped when any part of the swimmer's body touches the solid end of the pool or course. Split times shall be recorded on the lane timer's card.

.4 Alternate Timer—There shall be at least one alternate timer who shall start his watch on every race with the starting signal, and whose time shall be used only to substitute in the event of failure of an official lane timer's watch or its operator.

.5 Official Time Determination—Following proper watch reading and recording as described above for each lane:

A. If the times of two of the three watches agree, that time shall be the official time.

B. If all three watches disagree, the time of the intermediate watch shall be the official time.

C. If, because of the failure of a watch or its operator, times from only two watches are available, the official time shall be the average of those two watches. When dial watches are in use and the times rounded to the next slowest tenth as described in 102.17.3E(3), the official time shall be the average of those two watches in hundredths of a second. When the watches are read to the hundredth of a second, as described in 102.17.3E(1), any average resulting in thousandths of a second shall be rounded up to the next slowest hundredth of a second.

D. If the official time is registered in tenths of a second, a zero shall be added and the official time recorded in hundredths of a second (two decimal places) for all purposes. (Example: 56.4 is recorded 56.40.)

102.18 CLERK OF COURSE

.1 The clerk of course shall be provided with an area clearly marked "Clerk of Course" where all swimmers must report as soon as their event is called.

.2 He shall be provided with a list of the names of all swimmers in all events including relay swimmers in the order in which they will swim.

.3 All scratches which have occurred after the printing of the heat sheet shall be reported to the clerk of course and he shall notify the Referee and scoring desk in writing of the failure of any swimmer to report.

.4 He shall notify the swimmers to wait behind or adjacent to the starting position until the starter takes over control of the race and if they leave the area it will be their responsibility to return in time for their heat or event.

102.19 MARSHALS

Shall have full police charge of the immediate starting area, the sides of the course, and the finish. They shall maintain order among competitors, spectators, officials, and coaches and shall have authority to remove from the vicinity of the competition anyone using profane or abusive language, or whose actions are disrupting the orderly conduct of the meet.

102.20 SCORERS

Shall receive from the recorders the order of finish in timed finals, or consolation finals and championship finals for each event. They shall compile team and high-point scores as applicable.

.1 Ballot System

A. In any race not timed with automatic officiating equipment (as provided in 102.21), the combined duties of the lane place judges and the lane timers shall be to determine placement and official times of the swimmers. Two lane place judges and three timers shall be assigned to each lane.

B. The chief judge shall be responsible for delivery of the lane place judge's cards to the scoring table where the scorers record the appropriate ballot value, including the ballots of disqualified swimmers, on the basis of one for first place selection, two for second, three for third, four for fourth, five for fifth, six for sixth, seven for seventh, eight for eighth. There are two sets of lane place judges and thus two ballots per lane for place.

C. The chief timer shall be responsible for delivery of all the official times (including the times of disqualified swimmers) to the scorers who shall list them in numerical order beginning with the fastest official time per lane. This is for the purpose of assigning ballot values to each lane time. The fastest lane receives a ballot value of 1, the next fastest a value of 2, etc. For identical times, equal ballot values are recorded, with the same progressive numerical assignment; (i.e., swimmers A, B, C, record identical times of 58.47 while swimmer D records time 59.05. Swimmers A, B, C, receive ballot values of 1 and swimmer D a value of 2. Should swimmers E and F (same race) have identical times of 60.00 they would each be assigned ballot values of 3, and continuing in this manner.)

D. The scorers shall then eliminate disqualified swimmers and determine the order of finish of all swimmers in any heat or final event by adding the numerical value of three ballots for each lane. The lane (swimmer) having lowest numerical total shall be declared the winner, the second lowest shall be second, etc. If these totals result in a tie any place in a final race, no further attempt shall be made to resolve the tie.

E. In preliminary heats, in no case may a swimmer with a faster time displace another who places ahead of him within a heat according to the ballot system. If this situation results in disputed qualifications, the swimmers tied with or within the disputed times shall swim off the event within 45 minutes after the last heat or any event in which any one of the swimmers is competing in that session. The ballot system must be used to determine the qualifier(s) for the finals except when automatic officiating equipment is used and is properly functioning. The official time for the qualifier shall be the time set in the original preliminary heat.

.2 Modified Ballot System—When two across-the-board judges are used instead of lane place judges:

A. Value will be assigned to each time and place decision as prescribed under the ballot system.

B. If the two judges' ballots for a contestant agree, that shall be the official place for the contestant.

C. If all three ballots disagree, the Referee or his designate will evaluate all information and then determine the order of finish.

.3 Place Judging—The unanimous decision of the two (2) lane place judges as to placement takes precedence over official time in determining the order of finish in a race except where automatic equipment is used as outlined below.

102.21 AUTOMATIC OFFICIATING EQUIPMENT

No swimmer must ever be required to reswim a race due to equipment failure that results in unrecorded or inaccurate time or place results. Automatic and manual electronic equipment shall be backed up by any available equipment and/or human officials.

In any meet in which automatic equipment is used, the following practices and procedures shall apply. No time may be used unless it is the official time using the procedures of this section. Split times recorded to the hundredths of a second by automatic equipment shall be acceptable for all purposes including records and qualifying times, provided that the swimmer completes the full scheduled distance of the event.

.1 Description of Equipment

A. Automatic—Timing that is started automatically by a gun or horn start and is stopped at the finish of the race by the swimmer's touch.

B. Manual-Electronic—Timing that is started by a common start to all lanes (either manual or with a fixed-delay from the start signal, set to be equal to the manual delay at the finish). The finish is recorded by buttons pushed by timers at the finish touch of the swimmer. This timing may be a primary system if there are three (3) buttons per lane, each operated by a separate timer. A secondary system may use one (1), two (2), or three (3) buttons.

.2 Resolution (Timing Accuracy)—Timing is recorded to hundredths of a second. Any digits representing thousandths shall be dropped with no rounding-off. Identical times to the hundredth shall be ties, with swim-offs as required, to determine qualifiers or alternates for consolation or final heats.

.3 Equipment Location—The automatic equipment operators shall have an unobstructed view of the finish of the course.

.4 Secondary Requirements—It is required that the secondary system have a minimum of one (1) timer per lane. There must be at least one (1) manual watch per lane. If the secondary system is manual-electronic, the manual watches become a third system (a backup).

Note: An individual may simultaneously operate two dissimilar devices (one watch/one button), but not two similar devices (two watches or two buttons).

.5 Comparison and Ranking Procedures

A. Placement and Ranking—When completely automatic or three (3) button manual-electronic equipment is used as the primary timing, the placement and ranking of the swimmers shall be the integration of official times. The decision of human judges shall not be used for placement.

B. Primary—All primary times which are free of malfunctions shall be the official times.

C. Secondary—If there exists a time difference of .3 seconds or more (after correcting for a system timing error as described below, if required) between the primary and secondary (or backup) time in a given lane, a potential malfunction exists. If this potential malfunction is confirmed by other data such as; other watches or buttons in that lane; visual observation by equipment operators; or placement data by officials, the official lane time is the secondary time (after applying any required system timing errors).

D. Secondary System Timing Error—The secondary system timing error is the simple average of the valid time difference between the primary and secondary times of the individual swimmers in a given heat. Any digits past hundredths are dropped with no rounding-off. This average is used to add (or subtract if appropriate) from the secondary time of a swimmer not having a valid primary time, to find that swimmer's official time. This time is then used for ranking and placing. (See the following example of actual data.)

Example:
3-Button Manual Start Secondary

Lane	Primary	Fast	Middle	Slow	Official
1	52.21	52.07	52.12	52.14 ·	52.21
2	52.18	51.91	52.01	52.06	52.18
3	51.05	50.97	51.00	51.01	51.05
4	51.04	50.78	50.88	50.93	51.04
5	51.86	51.30	51.35	51.38	51.46
6	51.65	51.56	51.57	51.59	51.65
7	52.27	52.13	52.13	52.18	52.27
8	51.87	51.58	51.75	51.89	51.87

$$\text{secondary system error} = \frac{.09+.17+.05+.16+.08+.14+.12}{7} = .11 \text{ sec.}$$

Official Secondary Time (Lane 5) = 51.35+.11 = 51.46

E. Primary System Timing Error—When, through a start or other malfunction the primary system has a systemic error affecting the times of all lanes (but the relative order of finish is accurate) the determination of this error is made by comparison with accurate timing information (usually the lane manual watch times). This comparison and determination is done in the same manner as in the secondary system error calculations. The primary time for all swimmers is determined by adding (or subtracting if appropriate) this system error to the time of each swimmer in the heat. This preserves the order of finish, the relative time of each swimmer in the heat, and the accurate times of the full heat, so that integration and comparison with swimmers in other heats results in fair placement for all swimmers.

102.22 OFFICIAL TIME

.1 Official time may be achieved in a USS sanctioned meet or USS approved meet or by one of the following modes:

A. In a swim-off held to determine placement in a final event.

B. As lead-off leg in a relay race.

C. Split time recorded from the official start to the completion of an initial distance within a longer individual event.

D. In a time trial or record attempt.

.2 Official time for any swimming event can be achieved only in the relevant stroke/event; (i.e., backstroke time must be achieved in a backstroke event.) Times achieved in a freestyle event can only be recorded as a freestyle time regardless of the stroke used.

.3 The official time to establish records, times of record and qualifying time standards can be achieved only in accordance with the following timing methods:

TIMING METHOD	OFFICIAL TIME LEVEL
A Automatic timing	—World, American and U.S. Open records; —Initial splits and relay lead-off times for all purposes

TIMING METHOD	OFFICIAL TIME LEVEL
B Automatic timing or Manual-electronic with 3 buttons	—OVC's for 50 M distances in a 50 M pool; —Age group records and times of record for 50 M distances in a 50 M pool;
C Manual-electronic with 2 buttons or three watches	—Age group records and times of record, except 50 M distances in a 50 M pool; —OVC's, except 50 M distances in 50 M pool; —LSC/local records (unless prohibited by LSC); —Initial splits and relay lead-off times for age group times of record and age group time standards (A, B, C, times, etc.)
D Two watches or manual-electronic with 1 button or one watch	—Age group time standards (A, B, C times, etc.) —Zone, regional and LSC championship time standards.

.4 World records may be established only when timed by completely automatic timing equipment.

.5 It is the meet sponsors' or meet director's responsibility to provide a proper back-up timing system for all events so that swimmers are assured of achieving official times meeting the above requirements.

.6 A back-up time adjusted for system timing errors in accordance with the methods described in 102.21 may be used as an official time equal to the level of the timing system to which it has been adjusted.

102.23 ANNOUNCER

Before the start of each event he shall announce the number of heats and the method of qualifying. At the start of each heat he shall announce the lane, the name of each swimmer and club affiliation or if unattached. Promptly after the finish of each event he shall announce the results as given him by the recorders. He shall make any other announcements as requested by the Referee, the clerk, or the management.

102.24 RECORDER OF RECORDS

Shall obtain from the official recorders all times made in each event, including preliminaries and finals, shall have proper application forms and shall duly process all record claims as set forth in Article 104.

102.25 RECORDERS

There shall be two (2) recorders and the number of assistants deemed necessary to receive and record all times and all disqualifications for all preliminaries, consolation finals and finals of each event, and to furnish all pertinent information to the recorder of records, scorers, press, T.V., announcer and meet secretary.

102.26 PRESS STEWARD

Shall obtain from the clerk of course and the recorders the names of all swimmers in each event, the results of each finish with times or record performances, and keep the press and TV personnel thoroughly informed on all details of the competition during the meet.

102.27 MEET DIRECTOR

Is appointed by meet sponsor. Responsibilities include, but are not limited to: ordering awards; obtaining sanction; preparation of facility; arranging for personnel, equipment, and supplies necessary for meet operation; processing of entries; printing of programs; arranging for appropriate publicity and media coverage; preparing and distributing summary of results 14 days after meet; and filing of LSC report.

102.28 SMOKING

Smoking and use of other tobacco products is prohibited on the pool deck, in the locker rooms, in spectator seating or standing areas, and in all areas used by swimmers, during the meet or during the warm-up periods in connection with the meet.

102.29 ALCOHOLIC BEVERAGES

Sale and use of alcoholic beverages is prohibited in all areas of the venue, including, but not limited to, pool deck, locker rooms, spectators seating or standing areas, and in all areas used by swimmers.

ARTICLE 103
FACILITIES STANDARDS

IMPORTANT: Swimmers are advised that United States Swimming, Inc., accepts no responsibility or liability for injuries resulting from accidents occurring in facilities not owned by United States Swimming, Inc., and strongly urges that all safety precautions be observed during sanctioned events.

103.1 DEFINITIONS

.1 /M/ = Indicates mandatory requirement for all competition.

.2 /NC/ = Except as noted otherwise, indicates mandatory requirement for National Championships and International Competition.

.3 /LSC/ = Predicated on facility availability, LSC's may waive strict compliance with these requirements in sanctioning local competition.

.4 Where dimensions are given, the dimension listed first shall govern and dimensions given in parentheses are for reference only.

103.2 RACING COURSE DIMENSIONS

.1 /M/ Length

A. Long Course: 50.00 meters (164 feet and 1/2 inch).

B. Short Course: 25.00 yards or 25.00 meters (82 feet and 1/4 inch).

C. Dimensional Tolerance: Against the required length, a tolerance of plus (+) 0.03 meters (1 and 3/16ths of an inch) in a vertical plane extending 0.3 meters (12 inches) above and

0.8 meters (2 feet, 7 and 1/2 inches) below the surface of the water at all points of both end walls.

D. When automatic officiating equipment touch pads are used at one or both ends, the course shall be of such length that ensures the required distance between the two touch pads or between either pad and the opposite end of the course.

E. When the racing course is fixed by the use of movable bulkheads, such bulkheads shall be designed to resist lateral deflection due to tension exerted by the attachment of the lane dividers to ensure the required course distance in all lanes.

F. See Article 104, Rules for Swimming Records, for course measurements certification requirements.

.2 Width

A. /NC/ Eight lanes, 2.75 meters (9 feet) center line to center line in width, with approximately 0.43 meters (1 foot 6 inches) of additional open water outside lanes 1 and 8.

B. /M/ Minimum lane width for competitive swimming shall be 7 feet (2.13 meters). /LSC/

.3 Water Depth

A. /NC/ 2 meters (6 feet 7 inches) deep throughout the course. Based on facility availability, Program Operations may waive this requirement for National Championships.

B. /M/ Minimum water depth for competitive swimming shall be 4 feet (1.22 meters). /NC/LSC/

103.3 /M/ RACING COURSE WALLS

Walls enclosing the racing course shall be parallel and vertical. The end walls shall be at a right angle to the water surface and shall be constructed of solid material with non-slip surface that extends no less than 0.8m (2 feet 7 and 1/2 inches) below the water surface. It is recommended that a toe rest ledge be provided at approximately 4 foot depth in the walls of the deep water race course.

103.4 /M/ POOL AND BULKHEAD MARKINGS

.1 Pool bottom lane markers: Minimum 10 inch (25 centimeters) wide lines of a dark contrasting color (preferably black) shall be provided in the middle of each racing lane on the bottom of the pool. The lines shall, preferably, be uninterrupted the length of the course and shall terminate 2.0 meters (6 feet 7 inches) from each end wall with a distinctive cross line 1.0 meters (3 feet 4 inches) long and the same width as the bottom marker. /LSC/

.2 End wall targets: Flush, non-slip targets in a shape of a ''T'' or a cross and the same width as the lane bottom markers shall be provided in the center of each lane on each end wall of the course and shall extend at least 3 feet 4 inches (1.0 meters) below the level of the water surface. It is recommended that the top edge of the deck be of a contrasting color to provide a visual target above water at the end of the course. /LSC/

.3 The lanes shall be numbered from right to left as the swimmers stand facing the course. Lane numbers shall clearly identify the lanes to officials stationed on each side of the course.

103.5 /M/ OVERFLOW RECIRCULATION SYSTEM

The pool water recirculation and overflow system shall maintain water level in line with the overflow rim of the pool gutters without creating appreciable current or water turbulence and shall maintain smooth and calm water surface during competition. The pool recirculation system shall be turned off if, in the opinion of the Referee, the water movement interferes with the conduct of competition.

103.6 WATER AND AIR TEMPERATURE

.1 /M/ Water temperature between 78 and 80 degrees Fahrenheit shall be maintained for competition.

.2 Air temperature within 8 feet above deck level in indoor facilities shall be not lower than 76 degrees Fahrenheit, with relative humidity maintained at about 60% and air velocity at about 25 feet per minute.

103.7 /M/ LADDERS

All ladders, steps or stairs within the racing course shall be recessed in the pool side walls or shall be removed during competition.

103.8 OTHER DECK EQUIPMENT

.1 Use of portable lifeguard chair stands and other deck fixtures is recommended and they should be removed from the competition area to allow free passage and unobstructed view for competitors and officials along all sides of the course. /LSC/

.2 /M/ 1 meter diving boards which overhang the racing course shall be hinged out of the way or removed during competition.

103.9 /M/ LIGHTING

.1 A minimum of one hundred (100) foot candle illumination level is required at the water surface over the entire course. Overhead light fixtures shall be located to avoid the casting of shadows by the pool walls over the racing course. /LSC/

.2 /NC/ At National Championships the same type and level of illumination that will be used for finals must be provided and maintained during the warm-up period and preliminaries.

103.10 /M/ NO SMOKING SIGNS

No smoking indoors or outdoors shall be permitted in any area designated for swimmers and the facility shall be so posted.

103.11 /M/ STARTING PLATFORM

.1 Height

A. Long Course: The front edge of the starting platform shall be no less than 0.50 meters (1 foot 8 inches) nor more than 0.75 meters (2 feet 5 and 1/2 inches) above the surface of the water.

B. Short Course: The front edge of the starting platform shall be not higher than 2 feet 6 inches (0.762 meters) above the surface of the water.

.2 The front edge of the starting platform shall be flush with the face of the end walls.

.3 The top surface of the starting platform shall be not less than 0.50 by 0.50 meters (1 foot 8 inches square) and shall slope not more than 10 degrees from the horizontal. The entire surface of the platform shall be faced with permanent non-slip material.

.4 Backstroke starting grips: Starting platforms shall be equipped with firm starting grips located between 0.3 meters (12 inches) and 0.6 meters (24 inches) above water surface. The front edge of the grips shall be parallel to and flush with the face of the end wall.

.5 Starting platforms shall be clearly marked with lane numbers visible to competitors and officials.

103.12 /M/ FLOATING LANE DIVIDERS

.1 Floating lane dividers separating the racing lanes and on the outside of lanes 1 and 8, respectively, shall extend the full length of the course and shall be attached at each end wall with recessed anchors so located that the center line of the cable securing the dividers shall be at the surface of the water with bottom half of the floats uniformly submerged for the entire length of the divider.

.2 Dividers shall consist of contiguous floats having a minimum diameter of 5 centimeters (2 inches) to a maximum of 11 centimeters (4 and 1/4 inches). The color of the floats extending the distance of 5 meters for long course and 15 feet for short course shall be distinct from the rest of the floats.

.3 A single line of dividers between racing lanes shall be used in long course competition. Multiple lines may be installed for short course competition, provided the width of open water between dividers is not reduced to less than 7 feet. /LSC/

.4 /NC/ Minimum 11 centimeter diameter floats shall be required for National Championships.

103.13 /M/ BACKSTROKE FLAGS AND LINES

.1 Design: At least three triangular pennants six (6) to twelve (12) inches in width at the base and twelve (12) to eighteen (18) inches in vertical length, of two or more alternating and contrasting colors shall be suspended over each lane for all backstroke, individual medley and medley relay events.

.2 Location:

A. Long Course: 5 meters (16 feet 5 inches) from each end of the course, 1.8 meters (5 feet 11 inches) above the water surface.

B. Short Course: 15 feet (4.57 meters) from each end of the course, 7 feet (2.13 meters) above the water surface.

C. Height shall be measured to the horizontal line from which the pennants are suspended.

.3 For long course backstroke, individual medley, and medley relay events a firmly stretched 1/4 inch line without flags or pennants shall be suspended at midpoint of the course.

103.14 /NC/ LOUDSPEAKER START SYSTEM

An electronic sound generating device shall be provided to give the starting and recall signal. Loudspeakers may be mounted underneath or on the side of each starting platform, between every two platforms, on each side of the racing course, or positioned behind the starting platforms in such a manner that equitable dispersion of sound to all lanes is assured. The device shall also activate a strobe light, or similar optical signal, located on the starter's side of the course approximately 15 feet forward from the starting end, to indicate the start to manual timers and hearing impaired swimmers. The start system may include an underwater recall speaker and gun lap signal option.

103.15 /NC/ FALSE START RECALL ROPE

A recall rope to be dropped across the course in case of a false start shall be provided approximately 36 feet (11 meters) from the starting end in short course and 49 feet (15 meters) in long course competition. The rope shall be attached to vertical stanchions with quick release mechanism and shall be suspended at least 4 feet (1.22 meters) above the water surface at the lowest point.

103.16 /M/ PACE CLOCKS

There shall be at least two large accurate timing devices or clocks, preferably located one on each side of the course, clearly visible to all swimmers. Dial type clocks shall be at least 3 feet in diameter with a sweep second and minute hands. If digital readout clocks are provided, minimum size of the digits shall be 6 inches.

103.17 AUTOMATIC OFFICIATING EQUIPMENT

.1 /NC/ See Section 102.21 for Automatic and Manual-Electronic officiating equipment types and performance requirements. Equipment powered directly from the utility line electrical service shall have the capability to automatically switch to stand-by battery power source in case of line power failure without affecting the continuity and accuracy of the timing system.

.2 /M/ Installation and safety: Equipment shall be installed so that it will not interfere with swimmers' start, turns, or finish and the normal overflow functions of the pool water recirculation system. All deck-level wiring shall carry no more than 12 volts of current.

.3 /NC/ Touch Pads:

A. Size and thickness: Recommended pad size shall be 6 feet 6 inches (2 meters) wide and not less than 2 feet (0.60 meters) deep. Minimum width of pads shall be 5 feet (1.52 meters). Thickness shall not exceed 3/8 of an inch (1 centimeter).

B. Markings: Panel face markings shall conform and superimpose on pool end wall markings as closely as possible. Perimeter edges of the panel shall have a one inch wide black border.

C. Sensitivity: Panels shall stop the timing system instantaneously by a light hand touch anywhere on the flat surface facing the racing course and the upper edge but shall not be activated by water turbulence.

D. Panels shall be installed and firmly anchored in the center of each lane and shall have no sharp edges, corners, or other protrusions on any exposed surfaces.

.4 Optional Accessories: Automatic officiating equipment may provide relay judging capability, automatic lap counting, split times' read-outs for all lanes, correction of erroneous touch, and television equipment tie-in. Any corrections or impulses generated by the equipment operators shall be clearly identified on the results printout.

.5 Time display board:

A. An automatic display board visible to all swimmers shall give a digital time read-out to two decimal places, displaying split times, final times, and places for all lanes. In the event of a tie, the place shall be displayed as a tie.

B. /NC/ A separate line of display for each lane meeting the above requirements shall be provided for National Championships.

ARTICLE 104
RULES FOR SWIMMING RECORDS

104.1 WORLD RECORDS

.1 May be established only in 50 meter pools and shall conform to the recognized distance, stroke and other current effective governing regulations of the Federation Internationale de Natation Amateur (FINA).

.2 All claims shall be telegraphed immediately following performance to the national headquarters. Supporting evidence must be filed on official United States Swimming record application forms, which must be in the national headquarters within 21 days following performance, with copy also sent to the national director of records. Responsibility for this filing shall rest with the meet recorder of records, official scorer, or LSC records chairman.

104.2 UNITED STATES SWIMMING (INC.) RECORDS

.1 General Requirements and Conditions for Records

A. The official time for establishing specific records must be achieved and determined in accordance with Article 102.22.

B. A record can be made only in still water.

C. No record shall be considered which is applied for by or through a conference, league, LSC, allied member, or organizational member whose rules governing performance do not conform to these rules.

Exception: When such rules do not conform to these rules but performance by the swimmer is claimed to conform to them, application may be made to the Records Committee for consideration. Such application must be supported by documentary or other evidence of performance as may be requested by that committee.

D. Record times registered by automatic equipment shall be submitted in hundredths of a second (two decimal places). If first place times are tied to 100ths seconds, the results shall be declared to be a tie and records shared by each swimmer thus tied.

E. For LSC and local records only, unless prohibited by the LSC, the Referee, if requested, for the purposes of recording record attempts at an initial distance for an individual event or for the lead-off leg of a relay, may for any lane

(1) Permit the use of the split function button of digital manual watches where all three official lane timers on the lane are using digital watches with split function, or

(2) Assign three (3) additional official timers to the lane to time the record attempt.

Note: Performance in this category requires the swimmer(s) to complete the full distance of the scheduled event. No time recorded by a mechanical split hand can be used for records.

F. Should the first swimmer on a relay team complete his leg in a record time for that stroke/distance, his performance shall not be nullified by any disqualification of his team members.

G. A record set in a swim-off to decide placement or break a tie can be claimed if the ballot system or automatic equipment is used.

H. To be eligible for a record a swimmer must have won his race. Only the time of the winner is recognized for record purposes even though another swimmer may have a faster time but is displaced by judge's or ballot decision. If the judge's or ballot decision results in a tie, all tied swimmers shall share the faster time of such finish. The requirement to win the race does not apply when age or representation are conditions to setting LSC or Age Group records, or to a U.S. citizen setting an American record in competition with non-U.S. citizens.

I. Record Attempts Against Time

(1) Must be sanctioned by the LSC and conducted by the Local Swimming Chairman or his duly appointed representative in accordance with all pertinent rules, and all information relative to such attempt must be public and available to any interested person for at least three (3) days before the event. Programs, schedules, facility and other relevant fixtures may not be changed thereafter except as provided in 102.8.

(2) All times achieved in such attempts shall be duly certified and made matter of record by the LSC or Record Chairman or their representative.

(3) Record attempts against time are not acceptable for age group records.

.2 American and United States Open Records

A. Classification

(1) American—May be established only by United States citizens eligible to compete under and achieving an official time in accordance with U.S. Swimming rules.

(2) United States Open—May be established only within the geographical territory of the United States by any person eligible to compete under and achieving an official time in accordance with U.S. Swimming rules.

B. Recognized Distances and Strokes (Men and Women)

(1) Short Course—Made only over courses 25 yards or 25 meters long.

Freestyle	50, 100, 200, 500, 1000, and 1650 yards and 50, 100, 200, 400, 800, and 1500 meters
Backstroke	100-200 yards and 100-200 meters
Breaststroke	100-200 yards and 100-200 meters
Butterfly	100-200 yards and 100-200 meters
Individual Medley	200-400 yards and 200-400 meters
Medley Relay	200-400 yards and 200-400 meters
Freestyle Relay	200-400-800 yards and 200-400-800 meters

(2) Long Course—Made only over courses 55 yards or 50 meters long.

Freestyle	50-100-200-400-800-1500 meters
Backstroke	100-200 meters
Breaststroke	100-200 meters
Butterfly	100-200 meters
Individual Medley	200-400 meters
Medley Relay	200-400 meters
Freestyle Relay	200-400-800 meters

C. Special Requirements and Conditions

(1) Records established outside of the United States shall be applied for on official record application forms (this shall be the responsibility of the team leader), and are subject to all pertinent requirements of this Article 104. When an American record results from a world record performance outside the United States, it shall be accepted as such upon formal approval by the FINA without further certification.

(2) When a record is claimed, an official record application form shall be filled out, signed by the designated officials, and transmitted immediately following performance, with all supporting data, including official meet results and the primary printout tape from the automatic officiating equipment, to the national headquarters. Forms must be in the national headquarters ten (10) days prior to the next regular meeting of the Board of Directors and copies shall also be sent to the national records chairman. Responsibility for this lies either with the LSC records chairman, recorder of records, or the official scorer of the meet.

(3) Pool Certification

(a) Record applications will not be accepted unless certification of course length accompanies them or is on file with USS.

(b) Pool certification shall be reported on the standard form available from the Executive Director.

(c) Certification data need only be filed once unless structural changes have occurred since original certification.

(d) Certification forms must be filed with both the Executive Director and the National Records Chairman.

(4) Pool Measurement

(a) The exact length of the course, measured by a steel tape or other acceptable measuring device in feet and inches and fractions of an inch, or in meters and centimeters, must be attested to by an accredited surveyor or engineer.

(b) A statement of the conditions under which the course was measured must be included.

(c) Where a movable bulkhead is utilized, course measurement of each lane must be confirmed before each session of competition and at the conclusion of the meet. Confirmation of length before sessions, and at the conclusion of the meet may be attested to by that person designated or approved by the Referee or meet committee. (Certified benchmark may be used as reference in measurements.)

(5) Pending record claims properly documented and approved by the National Records Chairman may be approved and declared effective immediately prior to any national senior swimming championship with approval of two members of the Board of Directors.

(6) American and United States Open records established in the USS, NCAA Division I, or YMCA national championships, shall, upon proper completion of required forms, pool certification, and written approval by the National Records Chairman, be declared effective immediately unless a faster claim is pending. Approval thereof by the House of Delegates shall be automatic. Such pending record claims may also be approved and declared immediately effective by the Board of Directors at any time if properly documented and approved by the National Records Chairman.

(7) Record claims not previously accepted and declared effective under (5) or (6) above shall be considered by the National Records Committee for recommendation to the House of Delegates at its annual convention meeting. Applications ruled incomplete by said Records Committee may be reconsidered by them and final action recommended to the House of Delegates.

(8) Swimmers who establish a record shall be presented with a certificate signed by the President of United States Swimming and the National Records Chairman.

.3 National Age Group Records

A. Requirements

(1) Only U.S. citizen/USS-registered athletes are eligible to establish national Age Group records.

(2) Times submitted for Age Group records must comply with all the requirements for the 16 Best Times Tabulation as listed in 204.9.

B. Reporting—When a listed Age Group record is bettered, an official Age Group record application form (provided by the national Age Group Records Chairman to the LSC) shall be filled out, signed by the designated officials, and mailed to the national Age Group Records Chairman within thirty (30) days. Responsibility for this lies with the athlete, the meet director, recorder of records, or chief recorder of the meet at which the record is achieved.

C. Recognition—A certificate of record achievement will be issued to all Age Group record swimmers immediately upon receipt of the record application.

.4 Zone Age Group Records

A. Requirements—Zone records must be achieved in Zone Championship meets.

B. Reporting—Each Zone shall determine the means of reporting Zone records.

C. Recognition—Each Zone shall determine appropriate recognition for Zone records.

.5 All Star Records

A. Requirements—All Star Records or relay times achieved in USS competition by swimmers from more than one USS Club but representing the same LSC. These times may be achieved in inter-LSC competition such as LSC dual meets and Zone competition. These times are not eligible for Top 10 relay consideration.

B. Reporting—An appropriate record application form will be available from the National Age Group Records Chairman when requested. This form shall be filled out, signed by the designated officials, and mailed to the National Age Group Records Chairman. Responsibility for this lies with the athlete, the meet director, recorder of records, or chief recorder of the meet at which the record is achieved.

C. Recognition—If approved by the National Age Group Records Chairman a certificate of achievement will be sent to all relays whose time meets or betters the existing best time of record.

.6 LSC Records

A. Requirements

(1) LSC Records must be achieved by LSC member swimmers in USS or FINA sanctioned competition. This competition can be at any level including Senior and international competition.

(2) The LSC may choose to recognize times achieved by member swimmers in approved competition as in 204.9.2.

(3) The LSC may waive the requirement of fully automatic or semi-automatic timing for 50 meter distance events and/or split and lead-off timing where local LSC conditions warrant. This would apply to LSC records only and to LSC sanctioned competition.

(4) An LSC may establish All-Star records which would include All-Star relay performances achieved while representing the LSC in Zone, Regional, or dual meets involving All-Star teams. Individual times including lead-off splits should be recognized by the LSC with the swimmer's LSC club of record (or unattached if appropriate) for any LSC records, National records or Top 16 times of record.

B. Reporting—The LSC shall determine the method of reporting LSC records.

C. Recognition—The LSC shall determine appropriate recognition for LSC records.

GOVERNING BODY

United States Swimming, Inc., 1750 East Boulder St., Colorado Springs, CO 80909

United States Swimming, Inc. (a Corporation) is responsible for the conduct and administration of swimming in the United States and is affiliated with the Federation Internationale de Natation Amateur (FINA), the international federation for aquatics, through United States Aquatic Sports, Inc. (USAS). In the pursuit of the overall purposes of providing fair and open competition for its members, affording maximum opportunity for participation, providing an educational experience, enhancing physical and mental conditioning, developing a rich base of swimming talent, and developing a pool of talented athletes for international competition, the Corporation recognizes five competitive classifications. The classifications are Senior, Junior, Age Group/Junior Olympic, Masters, and Long Distance.

MAGAZINES

Swimming Technique, Swimming World Publications, 1130 W. Florence Ave., Inglewood, CA 90301

Swimming World, Swimming World Publications, 1130 W. Florence Ave., Inglewood, CA 90301

• TABLE TENNIS •

OFFICIAL RULES OF TABLE TENNIS

(Reproduced by permission of the United States Table Tennis Association*)

□

RULE 1
THE TABLE

1.1 The table shall be in surface rectangular, 274 cm. (9 ft.) in length, 152.5 cm. (5 ft.) in width; it shall be supported so that its upper surface, termed the "playing surface," shall lie in a horizontal plane 76 cm. (2 ft. 6 in.) above the floor.

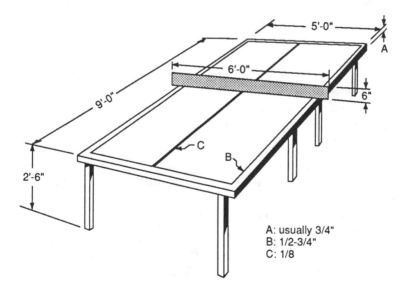

A: usually 3/4"
B: 1/2-3/4"
C: 1/8

1.2 It shall be made of any material and shall yield a uniform bounce of not less than 22 cm. (8 3/4 in.) and not more than 25 cm. (9 3/4 in.) when a standard ball is dropped from a height of 30.5 cm. (12 in.) above its surface.

1.3 The playing surface shall be dark colored, preferably dark green, and matt, with a white line 2 cm. (3/4 in. wide) broad along each edge.

---

*See pages 552 and 553 for additional information.

1.3.1 The lines along the 152.5 cm. (5 ft.) edges or ends shall be termed "end lines."

1.3.2 The lines along the 274 cm. (9 ft.) edges, or sides, shall be termed "side lines."

1.4 For doubles, the playing surface shall be divided into halves by a white line 3 mm. (1/8″) wide, running parallel with the side lines, termed the "center line." Permanent marking of the center line on the playing surface shall not invalidate the table for singles play.

1.5 The playing surface shall be considered to include the top edges of the table, but not the sides of the table top below the edges.

1.6 There shall be no lettering on the ends of the table.

RULE 2
THE NET

2.1 The playing surface shall be divided into two "courts" of equal size by a vertical net running parallel with the end lines.

2.2 The net shall be suspended by a cord attached at each end to an upright post 15.25 cm. (6 in.) high, the outside limits of the post being 15.25 cm. outside the side line.

2.3 The net, with its suspension, shall be 183 cm. (6 ft.) long and its top, along its whole length, shall be 15.25 cm. (6 in.) above the playing surface; the bottom of the net, along its whole length, shall be close to the playing surface and the ends of the net shall be close to the supporting posts.

RULE 3
THE BALL

3.1 The ball shall be spherical, with a diameter of 38 mm.

3.2 The ball shall weigh 2.5 gm.

3.3 The ball shall be made of celluloid or similar plastic material and shall be white or yellow, and matt.

3.4 The standard bounce required shall be not less than 23.5 cm. (9 7/32 in.) or more than 25.5 cm. (10 3/8 in.) when dropped from a height of 30.5 cm. (12 in.) on a specially designed steel block. These heights are measured from the bottom of the ball.

3.4.1 The standard bounce required, shall be not less than 22 cm. (8 3/4 in.) or more than 25 cm. (9 3/4 in.) when dropped from a height of 30.5 cm. (12 in.) on an approved table.

RULE 4
THE RACKET

4.1 The racket may be of any size, shape or weight.

4.2 The blade shall be of wood, continuous, of even thickness, flat and rigid.

4.2.1 At least 85% of the blade by thickness shall be of natural wood.

4.2.2 An adhesive layer within the blade may be reinforced with fibrous material such as carbon fibre, glass fibre or compressed paper, but shall not be thicker than 7.5% of the total thickness or 0.35 mm., whichever is the smaller.

4.3 The visible surface of each side of the blade, whether used for striking the ball or not, shall be uniformly dark colored and matt; any trimming or binding round the edge of the blade shall not be, either wholly or partly, white or brightly reflecting.

4.4 A side of the blade used for striking the ball shall be covered with either ordinary pimpled rubber with pimples outwards having a total thickness including adhesive of not more than 2 mm., or sandwich rubber with pimples inwards or outwards having a total thickness including adhesive of not more than 4 mm.

4.5.1 "Ordinary pimpled rubber" is a single layer of non-cellular rubber, natural or synthetic, with pimples evenly distributed over its surface at a density of not less than 10/sq. cm. and not more than 50/sq. cm.

4.5.2 "Sandwich rubber" is a single layer of cellular rubber covered with a single outer layer of ordinary pimpled rubber, the thickness of the pimpled rubber not being more than 2 mm.

4.6 The covering material shall extend up to but not beyond the limits of the blade, except that the part nearest the handle and gripped by the fingers may be left uncovered or covered with any material and may be considered part of the handle.

4.7 The blade, any layer within the blade and any layer of covering material or adhesive shall be continuous and of even thickness.

4.8 The two surfaces of the racket blade shall be of clearly different colors, whether or not both sides are used for striking the ball.

4.9 It is the responsibility of the player to ensure that the racket covering can be identified as an authorized brand and type and that the colors of the two surfaces of the blade are clearly distinguishable under normal playing conditions.

4.10 Subject to the requirements of 4.3, a side of the blade not intended for striking the ball may be painted or covered with any material, but if a player strikes the ball in play with a side of the blade whose surface does not comply with the requirements of 4.4-4.9 he shall lose a point.

4.11 Slight deviations from uniformity of color or continuity of covering due to fading, wear or accidental damage, may be ignored provided they do not significantly change the characteristics of the surface.

4.12 At the start of a match and whenever he changes his racket during a match, a player shall show his opponent and the umpire the racket he is about to use and shall allow them to examine it.

RULE 5
DEFINITIONS

5.1 A "rally" is the period during which the ball is in play.

5.2 A "let" is a rally of which the result is not scored.

5.3 A "point" is a rally of which the result is scored.

5.4 The "racket hand" is the hand carrying the racket.

5.5 The "free hand" is the hand not carrying the racket.

5.6 A player "strikes" the ball if he touches it with his racket, held in the hand, or with his racket-hand below the wrist.

5.7 A player "volleys" the ball if he strikes it in play when it has not touched his court since last being struck by his opponent.

5.8 A player "obstructs" the ball if he, or anything he wears or carries, touches it in play when it has not passed over his court or an imaginary extension of his end line, and when it has not touched his court since last being struck by his opponent.

5.9 The "server" is the player due to strike the ball first in a rally.

5.10 The "receiver" is the player due to strike the ball second in a rally.

5.11 The "umpire" is the person appointed to decide the result of each rally.

5.12 Anything that a player "wears or carries" includes anything that he was wearing or carrying at the start of the rally.

5.13 The ball shall be regarded as passing "over or around" the net if it passes under or outside the projection of the net assembly outside the table or if, in a return, it is struck after it has bounced back over the net.

5.14 The part of the playing surface nearest the server and to his right of the center line shall be called the server's right hand court, and to his left the server's left hand court. The part of the playing surface on the other side of the net from the server and to his left of the center line shall be called the receiver's right hand court, and on the server's right the receiver's left hand court.

RULE 6
THE ORDER OF PLAY

6.1 In singles, the server shall first make a good service, the receiver shall then make a good return and, thereafter, server and receiver alternately shall each make a good return.

6.2 In doubles, the server shall first make a good service, the receiver shall then make a good return, the partner of the server shall then make a good return, the partner of the receiver shall then make a good return and, thereafter, each player alternately in that sequence shall make a good return.

RULE 7
A GOOD SERVICE

7.1 Service shall begin with the ball resting on the palm of the free hand, which shall be stationary, open and flat, with the fingers together and the thumb free.

7.2 The free hand and the racket shall be above the level of the playing surface from the last moment at which the ball is stationary on the palm of the free hand until the ball is struck in service.

7.3 The server shall then project the ball upwards, by hand only and without imparting spin, so that it rises from the palm of the hand within 45 degrees of the vertical.

7.4 As the ball is then descending from the height of its trajectory, the server shall strike it so that it touches first his own court and then, passing directly over the net around or under the projection of the net and its supports outside the table, touches the receiver's court.

7.4.1 In doubles, the points of contact of the ball with the playing surface shall be the server's right half-court or center line and then the receiver's right half-court or center line.

7.4.2 If, in attempting to serve, a player fails to strike the ball while it is in play, he shall lose a point.

7.5 When the ball is struck in service, it shall be behind the end line of the server's court or an imaginary extension thereof, but not farther back than the part of the server's body, other than his arm, head or leg, which is farthest from the net.

7.6 It is the responsibility of the player to serve so that the umpire or assistant umpire can see that he complies with the requirements for a good service.

7.6.1 Except when an assistant umpire has been appointed, the umpire may, on the first occasion in a match at which he has a doubt about the correctness of a player's service, interrupt play and warn the server without awarding a point. On any subsequent occasion in the same match at which the same player's service action is of doubtful correctness, for the same or for any other reason, the player shall not be given the benefit of the doubt and shall lose a point.

7.6.2 Where, however, there is a clear failure to comply with the requirements for a good service no warning should be given and a point should be awarded against the server.

7.7 Exceptionally, strict observance of the prescribed method of service may be waived where the umpire is notified, before play begins, that compliance is prevented by physical disability.

RULE 8
A GOOD RETURN

8.1 The ball, having been served or returned in play, shall be struck so that it passes directly over or around the net and its supports and touches the opponent's court, except that:

8.1.1 if the ball, having been served or returned in play, returns with its own impetus over the net it may be struck so that it touches directly the opponent's court;

8.1.2 if the ball, in passing over or around the net, touches the net or its supports, it shall be considered to have passed directly.

RULE 9
BALL IN PLAY—UNTIL

9.1 The ball shall be in play from the last moment at which it is stationary before being projected in service until

9.1.1 it touches anything other than the playing surface, the net assembly, the racket held in the hand or the racket below the wrist, or

9.1.2 the rally is otherwise decided as a let or a point.

RULE 10
A LET

10.1 The rally is a let:

10.1.1 if the ball served, in passing over or around the net, touches it or its supports, provided the service is otherwise good or is volleyed or obstructed by the receiver or his partner;

10.1.2 if the service is delivered when, in the opinion of the umpire, the receiving player or pair is not ready, provided that neither the receiver nor his partner attempts to strike the ball;

10.1.3 if, in the opinion of the umpire, failure to make a good service or a good return or otherwise to comply with the Laws is due to a disturbance outside the control of the player;

10.1.4 if it is interrupted for correction of an error in playing order or ends;

10.1.5 if it is interrupted for introduction of the Expedite System;

10.1.6 if it is interrupted for warning a player for a service of doubtful correctness;

10.1.7 if the conditions of play are disturbed in a way which, in the opinion of the umpire, is likely to affect the outcome of the rally.

RULE 11
LOSS OF A POINT

11.1 Unless the rally is a let, a player shall lose a point:

11.1.1 if he fails to make a good service;

11.1.2 if he fails to make a good return;

11.1.3 if he volleys or obstructs the ball, except as provided in 10.1.1;

11.1.4 if he strikes the ball with a side of the racket blade having an illegal surface;

11.1.5 if, when he is serving, he or his partner stamps his foot;

11.1.6 if he, or anything he wears or carries, moves the playing surface while the ball is in play;

11.1.7 if his free hand touches the playing surface while the ball is in play;

11.1.8 if he, or anything he wears or carries, touches the net or its supports while the ball is in play;

11.1.9 if, in doubles, he strikes the ball out of proper sequence, except where there has been a genuine error in playing order;

11.1.10 if, under the Expedite System, his service and twelve successive good returns of the serving player or pair are each followed by good returns of the receiving player or pair;

11.1.11　if he strikes the ball twice successively;

11.1.12　if the ball touches his court twice successively.

RULE 12
A GAME

12.1 A game shall be won by the player or pair first scoring 21 points unless both players or pairs have scored 20 points, when the winner shall be the player or pair first scoring 2 points more than the opposing player or pair.

RULE 13
A MATCH

13.1 A match shall consist of the best of three games or the best of five games.

13.2 Play shall be continuous throughout, except that any player shall be entitled to claim an interval of not more than five minutes between the third and fourth games of a match and of not more than one minute between any other successive games of a match.

13.3 A player who breaks his racket shall immediately resume play with a spare racket kept close to the playing area, or one handed to him in the playing area.

RULE 14
THE CHOICE OF ENDS AND SERVICE

14.1 The choice of ends and the right to serve or receive first in a match shall be decided by toss.

14.2 The winner of the toss may:

14.2.1 choose to serve or receive first, when the loser shall have the choice of ends;

14.2.2 choose an end, when the loser shall have the right to choose to serve or receive first;

14.2.3 require the loser to make the first choice.

14.3 In doubles, the pair who have the right to serve first in any game shall decide which partner shall do so.

14.3.1 In the first game of a match, the opposing pair shall then decide which partner will receive first.

14.3.2 In subsequent games of a match, the serving pair will choose their first server and the first receiver will then be established automatically to correspond to the first server as provided in Rule 16.6.

RULE 15
THE CHANGE OF ENDS

15.1 The player or pair who started at one end in a game shall start at the other end in the immediately subsequent game, and so on, until the end of the match.

15.2 In the last possible game of a match, the players or pairs shall change ends when first either player or pair reaches the score 10.

RULE 16
THE CHANGE OF SERVICE

16.1 In singles: after five points, the receiver shall become the server, and so on, until the end of the game, or the score 20-20, or the introduction of the Expedite System.

16.2 In doubles:

16.2.1 the first five services shall be delivered by the selected partner of the pair who have the right to serve and shall be received by the appropriate partner of the opposing pair;

16.2.2 the second five services shall be delivered by the receiver of the first five services and shall be received by the partner of the first server;

16.2.3 the third five services shall be delivered by the partner of the first server and shall be received by the partner of the first receiver;

16.2.4 the fourth five services shall be delivered by the partner of the first receiver and shall be received by the first server;

16.2.5 the fifth five services shall be delivered and received as the first five, and so on, until the end of the game, or the score 20-20, or the introduction of the Expedite System.

16.3 From the score 20-20, or under the Expedite System, the sequence of serving and receiving shall be the same, but each player shall deliver only one service in turn until the end of the game.

16.4 The player or pair who served first in a game shall receive first in the immediately subsequent game, and so on, until the end of the match.

16.5 In the last possible game of a doubles match the receiving pair shall change the order of receiving when first either pair reaches the score 10.

16.6 In each game of a doubles match, the initial order of receiving shall be opposite to that in the immediately preceding game.

RULE 17
OUT OF ORDER OF SERVING,
RECEIVING OR ENDS

17.1 If by mistake, the players have not changed ends when ends should have been changed, play shall be interrupted as soon as the error is discovered and the players shall change ends.

17.2 If, by mistake, a player serves or receives out of his turn, play shall be interrupted and shall continue with that player serving or receiving who, according to the sequence established at the beginning of the match, should be server or receiver, respectively, at the score that has been reached.

17.3 In any circumstances, all points scored before the discovery of an error shall be reckoned.

RULE 18
THE EXPEDITE SYSTEM

18.1 If a game is unfinished after fifteen minutes of play, the game shall be interrupted and the rest of that game, and the remaining games of the match, shall be played under the Expedite System.

18.2 Under the Expedite System, if the service and twelve successive good returns of the serving player or pair are each followed by good returns of the receiving player or pair, the server shall lose a point.

18.2.1 If the ball is in play when the game is interrupted play shall restart with service by the player who served in the rally that was interrupted.

18.2.2 If the ball was not in play when the game was interrupted, play shall restart with service by the player who received in the immediately preceding rally.

18.3 The Expedite System may be introduced at any earlier time, from the beginning of the match up to the end of fifteen minutes of play in any game, at the request of both players or pairs.

18.4 Once introduced, the Expedite System shall remain in operation for the remainder of the match.

RULE 19
ADVICE TO PLAYERS DURING PLAY

19.1 A Player may receive advice from anyone between games or during other authorized suspension of play, but not at any other time, such as during a momentary break for towelling or at the change of ends in the last possible game of the match.

RULE 20
CLOTHING (DRESS CODE)

20.1 Playing clothing shall normally consist of a short-sleeved shirt and shorts or skirt, socks and playing shoes; other garments, such as part or all of a track suit, shall not be worn during play except with the permission of the referee.

20.2 A playing shirt, shorts or skirt shall be mainly of a uniform color other than white, but part or all of the collar and sleeves of a shirt and marking along the side seams of a garment may be of a contrasting color other than white.

20.3 A playing garment may carry:

20.3.1 the maker's normal trademark, symbol or name contained within a total area of 16 sq. cm.;

20.3.2 the ITTF logo, where the design has been authorized by the ITTF;

20.3.3 a badge or lettering on the front or side contained within a total area of 64 sq. cm.;

20.3.4 numbers or letters on the back of a playing shirt to identify a player or his Association or, in club matches, his club.

20.4 Any markings or trimming on the front or side of a playing garment and any objects such as jewelry worn by a player shall not be so conspicuous or brightly reflecting as to unsight an opponent.

20.5 Players must wear socks and soft sole shoes.

20.6 Absolutely . . . no playing without a shirt, no cutoffs, no jeans, no tank shirts but women may wear sleeveless blouses.

20.7 Any question of the legality or acceptability of playing clothing shall be decided by the referee, except that he may not rule illegal or unacceptable a design which has been authorized by the ITTF or USTTA.

20.8 Warm-up suits should not be worn during play unless with special permission of the Referee and it is his discretion of conformity to above requirements.

20.8.1 Anyone PRACTICING at three, four or five star tournaments must be dressed in accordance with the official dress code, with the exception that warm-up suits may be worn provided they are not white. (Referees at other tournaments may enforce this rule if prior notice is given to participant.)

20.9 Slacks may be worn but shorts are preferred. Default of a match for improper attire will be strictly enforced by the Referee at all USTTA sanctioned tournaments.

RULE 21
WHEELCHAIR COMPETITION

21.1 All rules in this section shall apply only to Wheelchair competition.

21.2 All competitors shall compete in wheelchairs.

21.2.1 Each wheelchair shall conform to the dimensions stated in Article III of the Constitution and Bylaws of the National Wheelchair Athletic Association (N.W.A.A.).

21.2.2 A cushion, of any size and made of any combination of foam rubber, may be used.

21.2.3 The wheelchair is not required to have a back support.

21.3 Wheelchair competitions may be divided into up to four divisions. These divisions shall be based on the N.W.A.A. classification system, as follows:

21.3.1 Division 1: all wheelchair players, classes I thru V

Division 2: classes I thru III

Division 3: classes IA, IB and IC

Division 4: class IA only

21.4 Each division shall have either 1) both a men's event and a women's event, or 2) an open event. If any division does not have a women's event, or if the women's event is cancelled the women entered in that division will be allowed to compete with the men in what becomes the open event for that division.

21.5 The table shall not have any physical barrier that can in any way hinder the normal and legal movement of the competitor's wheelchair.

21.6 In service, the receiver is required to make a good return. However, if the receiver does not strike or obstruct the service, and the served ball does not continue, under its own momentum, to leave the table by crossing the receiver's end line, the rally shall be a let.

21.6.1 In service, players classified as IA, IB or IC may project the ball upwards with either hand.

21.7 Players classified as IA, IB or IC may touch the playing surface with the free hand during play without losing the point; however, they may not use the free hand on the table for support while striking the ball.

21.8 In any match that includes at least one player classed as IA, IB or IC, all players may volley the ball after it has crossed the volleyer's end line or side line without losing the point.

21.9 The competitor's feet may not touch the floor during play.

21.10 Competitors may not rise noticeably off their cushions during play.

RULE 22
PLAYING CONDITIONS

22.1 Space. The minimum playing space for each table should be at least 12 m. (40 ft.) long, 6 m. (20 ft.) wide and 3.5 m. (11 1/2 ft.) high.

22.2 Light. Measured at table height, the light shall be at least 400 lux (38 foot candles) in strength uniformly over the table, and not less than half of the table strength over any other part of the playing area.

22.3 Flooring. The floor should be made of hard, non-slippery wood. Stone, linoleum, tile, etc. are not recommended.

22.4 The light source shall not be less than 3.5 m. above the floor.

22.5 The background shall be generally dark and shall not contain bright light sources nor daylight through uncovered windows.

22.6 The floor shall not be light-colored nor brightly reflecting.

RULE 23
ADVERTISEMENTS

23.1 Advertisements shall be displayed only on equipment or fittings which are normally present inside the playing area and there shall be no special, additional displays.

23.2 Fluorescent or luminescent colors shall not be used anywhere within the playing area and white shall not be used on the inside of surrounds.

23.3 Advertisements on the inside of surrounds shall be only on the longer sides of the playing area and any lettering shall not be more than 30 cm. in height.

23.4 Advertisements on tables shall be placed only on the longer sides of the table top and not on the legs or supporting structure.

23.5 There shall be no advertisements on tables, score indicators, umpires' tables or other furniture inside the playing area except for the maker's normal trademark, symbol or name contained within a total area on any face of 200 cm².

23.6 There shall be no advertisements on clothing or other equipment worn or carried in the playing area by players or officials except for the maker's normal trademark, symbol or name contained within a total area on any item of 16 cm².

GOVERNING BODY

United States Table Tennis Association, 1750 E. Boulder St., Colorado Springs, CO 80909-5769

The U.S. Table Tennis Association (USTTA) is the national governing body for both professional and amateur table tennis in the United States. The USTTA is affiliated with the International Table Tennis Federation (ITTF), and the AAU/USA Junior Olympics and is a Group A member of the U.S. Olympic Committee. Additionally, the USTTA supports the sanctioned table tennis activity of the Boy Scouts of America, Cub Scout Sports Awards Program, and Explorers. The Association sponsors a host of programs—including developing the sport and its athletes at the local and regional levels through coaching clinics, conducting national championships and international tournaments, and selecting teams for such international events as the Olympics, the World Championships, and the Pan American Games. Table tennis made its debut as a medal sport in the 1988 Olympic Games in Seoul, Korea. Information concerning club activities, tournaments, coaching, officiating, equipment, national ratings, publications, film/video, etc., is available through the USTTA.

MAGAZINES

Table Tennis Topics (formerly *Spin*), USTTA, 1750 E. Boulder St., Colorado Springs, CO 80909-5769

• TAEKWONDO •

ABRIDGMENT OF AMERICAN TAEKWONDO ASSOCIATION™ TOURNAMENT COMPETITION RULES

(Reproduced by permission of American Taekwondo Association*)

☐

Note: The rules included here are an abridgment of the ATA technical rules for Taekwondo. The complete official rules are available through the Association.

GENERAL ATA TOURNAMENT POLICY

TYPES OF TOURNAMENTS

ATA Tournaments are local ("C" rated), regional ("B" rated) or national ("A" rated) competitive events designed to provide several benefits:

1. Forum for students to display skills
2. Meeting ATA students from other schools
3. Opportunity for family and friends to participate as enthusiastic spectators
4. Opportunity for Instructor to evaluate effectiveness
5. Learning experience for students
6. Performing in the presence of strangers
7. Performing for judges other than own Instructor
8. Exercising martial arts courtesy, respect, and honor
9. Personal victory over fear and anxiety

ATA students across the nation learn the same forms and follow consistent rules of technique and courtesy. All rings are under direct supervision of Certified Instructors. Competition is designed to be exceptionally well-balanced compared to "open" tournaments.

Even beginning students should be encouraged to participate at their own level to supplement their training in the school.

OPEN TOURNAMENTS

ATA schools may not sponsor open or full-contact tournaments or contests. In the "early days" of the ATA, up to the mid-1970's, one major ATA goal was to have a major, meaningful "ATA Only" tournament circuit.

Why? One very good reason is that it is impossible for tennis, badminton, raquetball, paddleball and squash players to compete in a tournament to see who is best. Best at what?

---

*See page 559 for additional information.

Differences in martial art styles, goals, rules and teaching methods are not always obvious at open tournaments even to many junior Black Belts.

Also, safety is difficult in open competitions where "intimidation games" are part of sparring, along with groin kicks, takedowns and face punches.

There are a few reasons why most traditional martial arts groups, including the ATA, have closed competitions for their students. ATA tournament rules support ATA concepts.

Smaller organizational tournaments support their concepts. Open tournaments support whatever concepts individual judges and competitors bring...and that is obviously not ATA Taekwondo.

ATA NATIONAL CHAMPIONSHIPS:
BLACK BELT TOURNAMENT CIRCUIT

ATA officials introduced the "ATA Top Ten" national championship program to offer Black Belts an opportunity for an additional personal training goal. With ATA growth through the 1980's, more and more divisions were added to offer competition goals to men and women, boys and girls of all ages.

The program is open to Black Belts in good standing with the association. Competition points are awarded for placing in regional and national ATA sanctioned events. ("C" rated events do not award points.)

Points are compiled at ATA Grand Nationals each year to determine national championships.

ATA COMPETITION RULES

There are three major types of ATA competition at tournaments:

1. Forms
2. Sparring
3. One-step sparring for beginners and persons of advanced age.

Occasionally, large tournaments may have Black Belt board breaking competition, with a required "break". If the breaking competitor breaks his boards, he then is judged on points by the technical form demonstrated in the break. Forms are mandatory. Competitors may not spar unless they also compete in forms. This is to encourage a well-rounded martial artist.

Sparring, and one-step sparring for white and yellow belts, is a "head to head" competition.

Overall, however, one rule underlies all others:

Traditional martial arts values of courtesy, loyalty and self-control will be followed. There is no place for displays of ego.

SPECIAL ATA TOURNAMENT COURTESY

1. Each student will conduct himself in a manner that brings honor to himself, his school, and his organization.

2. Since all competitors are members of the ATA "family", courtesy and respect are part of tournaments. The ATA competitive spirit should be that of games at a family gathering. Students may encourage friends in a friendly, positive manner. Opponents are "family", too; negative cheering is not appropriate.

3. Regulation uniforms and belts are required. (White tennis shoes may be worn when student is not competing.) Sparring pads must be in good condition for safety. Red sparring pads of the ATA pattern are required for uniformity for all green belts and higher ranks. Mouthpieces and men's groin cups are required.

4. Students, in uniform or not, maintain ATA courtesy to other students, instructors, and guests. Courtesy is one reason why ATA events gain respect in the public eye. (There is often limited seating. Guests should be offered available chairs.)

5. Students and Instructors will bow to the flags whenever they enter and leave the tournament room, as they would in their school classroom.

6. Every ATA member, in uniform or not, whether competing or not, will stand at attention and recite the "Songahm Spirit" with the participants.

7. Students may change into "street clothes" and leave the tournament when their competition ring is dismissed, unless their instructor has given them other directions.

ATA FORMS RULES

ATA forms competition precedes sparring competition in an age-rank-sex division.

Judging is similar to that of a gymnastics floor exercise. Each ATA Taekwondo rank has a required form. This form is a pre-set combination of defense and countering movements which must be performed correctly in order. The required form for a rank is used in competition. This means every ATA competitor in a ring will execute the same form.

In smaller tournaments, the two ranks in a belt "color" may compete, using the proper form for their rank, resulting in two forms in a division.

Since all judges are familiar with, and have taught all the forms themselves, their judging is on quality of execution, correctness of movements, rhythm and "art" in the form. Judges, a "head judge" (who later will be "match referee" in sparring competition), and two or four judges sit at the front of the ring or spaced at the corners of the ring. Competitors are called into the ring individually to do their forms at random. At completion of the form, the head judge calls for points. All judges indicate points between 4 and 9 with their fingers simultaneously.

Since any individual competition takes personal courage (a goal of Taekwondo training), no score below "4" is allowed. Since people may approach, but never equal perfection of technique, no "10" may be awarded. No "fractional" points are awarded.

Competitors below Black Belt ranks may do their form a second time if they desire. (Usually if they forget moves.) In this event, a "6" is the highest score available. With this scoring system, ties are not only likely, but are expected. ATA senior instructors believe students are encouraged to improve more by running off ties than by winning or losing by a tenth of a point.

Again, there are four final placings, first, second and two thirds: The thirds are not differentiated regardless of points awarded.

The first three competitors called to perform are not scored until after the third has completed his form. All three are then recalled to the ring and each is scored successively. This gives judges a reference point to the days' division.

ATA TOURNAMENT "SPARRING" RULES

ATA tournament sparring rules are based on a concept similar to that of fencing, rather than boxing. This is not universal to all styles of "karate", "Taekwondo" or "Kung Fu"—but it has played a role in the American Taekwondo Association[tm] becoming the world's largest centrally administered martial arts association.

In boxing, the purpose is literally and physically to overcome the opponent.

In ATA Taekwondo sparring, as in fencing, the purpose is a simulation of combat, with safety and personal improvement of technique as common goals. Both fencing and ATA

Taekwondo rules require various equipment for the safety of competitors in what otherwise easily could be construed a duel rather than sport.

The equipment and rules in both "sportive" activities, along with recognition of potential dangers and respect for the opponent, make for outstanding excitement for competitors— even if it may appear less exciting to spectators.

Since there is no way for ATA Taekwondo to be "electrified" as in modern fencing, a match referee and two or four judges are used, similar to fencing before electrical scoring equipment was developed. A majority must agree a "point" has been scored.

The "ring" is approximately 20 feet square. The two-minute match time is kept running during point calls, which take about 5 seconds.

Time is halted for equipment problems, injury, or judges' conference on possible warnings or rules clarification. (Competitors are not allowed to question any judges' decision on penalty of disqualification and/or removal from the association.)

POINTS

"Points" may be called by the judges or the match referee. The match referee is to be in the ring controlling action only to the extent of maintaining safety. Judges may observe at a "proper" distance in or outside the ring, as necessary to closely observe but not obstruct action. A "point" is a controlled hand or foot technique landing on or near legal target areas. They are valued on a basis of difficulty—which leads competition away from a purely "combat simulation" orientation into an area of encouraging development of advanced technique.

Legal target areas for hand techniques—punch, knifehand strike, ridgehand strike, backfist strike—includes the front and sides of the torso from collar bones to the top of the hips.

Legal kicking target areas include that torso target and the head/face area. Legal kicks include front kick, round kick, side kick, hook kick, crescent kick and ax kicks and their variations in jumps and spins or turns.

The entire neck, back and "waist-down" areas are not legal target areas because of possible physical injury.

Scoring is 1 point for "successful" hand or foot techniques to the torso target; 2 points for successful foot techniques to the head or for jump kicks to legal torso areas; 3 points are awarded jump kicks to the head. A "successful" technique is one that approaches or touches the opponent, and is controlled so that if extended, would "stop" his opponent.

(Most ATA officials dislike any comparison of a "successful" point to actual damages to an opponent. Since a sparring match is not "combat" in any sense, it can not be honestly compared to combat. This means a sparring point is defined only in its own terms. A "point" is no more or less than a "point." Similar views are found among fencing masters.)

Five (5) points wins the match. If time is called before 5 points are reached, the competitor with more points wins. If the score is tied, a "sudden victory" overtime is held. The winner is the first competitor to score any point.

RULE INFRACTIONS

Rule infractions may bring three possible results. They may be given for: Striking to non-target areas, "running" from the opponent, feigning injury, falling to avoid point calls (rather than blocking or evading), excessive contact (a subjective call based on age, sex, rank of competitors), or other "sportsmanship" infractions. There is no appeal. If there is no illegal physical contact, the judges may give a warning for an infringement.

A more severe infraction, contact to illegal target areas, potentially dangerous "attitude" or a second "warning", brings a penalty point award to the innocent competitor.

A very severe infraction, a third "warning", one putting an opponent at risk of physical damage or damaging the martial arts attitude, brings disqualification. Again, there is no appeal.

Readers should consider that the rules stress:

1. Safety of competitors
2. Proper "martial arts attitude"
3. Development of technique
4. Fun competition for men, women and children of all walks of life

PROGRESSION OF MATCH

Match referee calls competitors into the ring after a single elimination "bracket" is set up, using a standard "bye" system. One has a red "flag" attached to the rear of his uniform belt. He is "red"; his opponent is "white". Competitors on match referee's command bow to judges and each other; then step back into ready positions. The match referee gives the order to begin.

If match referee or a judge sees a point, he calls "point"; and the match referee stops the action.

Referee calls out, "Point call." At that signal, he and the judges raise a colored flag noting whether "red" or "white" is given a point. If a judge believes the technique was blocked, or was not of quality to count as a point, he crosses his arms at belt level to signal "no point". A judge who was not positioned to be certain whether a point was scored or not signals by covering his eyes as "no see".

The match referee awards or does not award a point on a simple majority basis. "No See" is not counted for or against the point. (If two judges say "point", two say "no see", and one says "no point", there is a point.) If there is no majority, "point" or "no point" no point is scored. To note whether a technique is one, two or three points, judges hold up one, two or three fingers on the hand opposite the flag hand.

If, as the halt is called, a judge sees a rules infraction, he designates it by "stirring" his flag stick downwards. Usually time will be called to determine what, if any infraction was made. This precedes the scoring call since a competitor may not be both warned and awarded a point during the same phase of sparring.

If during the match a judge sees an infraction, he calls "warning"; the match is halted and judges discuss the possible infraction, with the result coming from concensus. This might be a warning, a penalty point award or disqualification.

As is obvious, the scoring system puts much pressure on judges. The Match Referee must be a Certified Instructor (at least 4 years personal training, plus instructor training and mandatory judging clinics). Judges, even in high Black Belt divisions, must be Black Belts senior to competitors and who have attended judging clinics.

ATA Taekwondo is unique in that there is no appeal in the ring; and that there may be no complaints or disputes of calls in the ring on penalty of disqualification.

Ring officials are monitored by yet more senior instructors and nationally appointed tournament officers. They may halt action, correct or remove ring staff, restart competition or do anything required in their opinion to best follow the overall aims of competition and the organization.

Ring officials may themselves be censured, placed on probation or removed from the organization for poor or improper judging practices.

In the final brackets, a first, second and two thirds are awarded. There is no runoff for third and fourth places.

ONE-STEP SPARRING

ATA tournament sparring aims at safety in competition. But beginning students, white and yellow belts with perhaps one to six months of training, do not have sparring as part of their curriculum.

Since they are not yet prepared, in understanding of technique or of skill, to spar, the best they could expect is a semi-controlled fight. Fear and lack of physical control would result in great risk to competitors of all ages.

In their classroom curriculum, they do "one-step sparring". This is an exercise, with required technical combinations in a stylized manner, which has a pair of students take turns as "attacker" and "defender". As they signal each other readiness, the attacker steps forward to punch at his opponent—who then does a prescribed defense.

At rank testings, these are judged similarly to forms. However, in tournaments, to give experience in "head to head" competition, judges simply signal a winner.

Competition brackets, the bye system and ring format are as close to "sparring" competition as practical to give competitors experience toward sparring as they gain Taekwondo rank.

GOVERNING BODY

American Taekwondo Association, 6210 Baseline Road, Little Rock, AR 72209

The American Taekwondo Association[tm] (ATA) was founded in 1969 in Omaha, NE, from Master H.U. Lee's earlier regional organization. The organization is designed to provide the most modern professional support services to Taekwondo instructors and students. The ATA has over 120,000 members in some 400 U.S. schools. Master Lee's international Songahm Taekwondo Federation, founded in 1985, offers similar services to Songahm-style Taekwondo schools outside the United States. The ATA provides its membership with numerous services, including educational materials, clinics, camps, testing and certification programs, national records on all students, supplies, regional and national tournaments, and a clearinghouse for distribution of information.

MAGAZINES

ATA Magazine, Martial Arts And Fitness, ATA Publications, P.O. Box 240835, Memphis, TN 38124-0835

• TEAM HANDBALL •

BASIC RULES OF TEAM HANDBALL

(Reproduced by permission of the United States Team Handball Federation*)

□

Note: The basic rules included here are an abridgment of the U.S.T.H.F. official rules of the game. The complete rules, including rule by rule comments and officiating signals are available through the U.S.T.H.F.

THE GAME

Team handball combines the skills of running, jumping, catching, and throwing into a fast-moving, exciting game. Elements of soccer, basketball, hockey and water polo all can be seen in team handball. The basic objective of the game is to outmaneuver the opponent by passing the ball quickly and then throwing the ball past the defense and goalie to score.

Team handball is essentially a simple game, easily played and enjoyed at first attempt by players of any age. The rapid continuous play, spectacular leaps and dives into the air by players attempting to score and the quick reactions of the goalie make the game equally enjoyable for spectators as well as players.

1. PLAYING COURT:

All court lines in team handball are referred to by their measurement in meters. The most significant line on the court is the 6 meter line, or goal area line. The area enclosed by the 6 meter line is called the goal area or the "circle." Only the goalie is allowed to stand inside the goal area. However, an offensive or defensive player may be in the air over the circle as long as their take off was from outside of the goal area line. The player cannot interfere with play in any way after landing in the goal area and must exit in the shortest route possible. The 9 meter line, or the free throw line, is used for minor penalties in the game. The 7 meter line, or penalty line, is used for a major penalty.

A regulation court is 20 x 40 meters (65′ x 131′), but the game can be easily adapted to a smaller area. The width of the court is more important than the length.

The goal area is made by marking a straight line 3 meters long at a distance of 6 meters from the goal line. The ends of this line are connected to the goal line by making a quarter circle with a radius of 6 meters from the back inside corners of the goal posts. The free throw line is done in the same manner except the line is dashed and uses a radius of 9 meters. It is recommended that floor markings be made with 2 inch wide floor tape.

The goals are 2 x 3 meters (6′7″ x 10′). Goals can be purchased or can be made. The goal is provided with a net to prevent the rebound of the ball. The goal should be secured to the floor if possible.

---

*See page 565 for additional information.

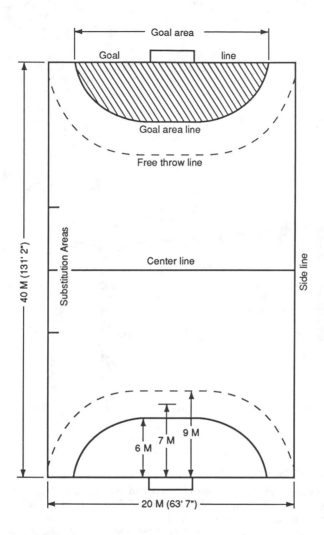

The ball varies in size and weight for the group participating. The men's ball is 58-60 cm. (23″) in circumference, and weighs about 425-475 g. (16 oz.). Women, junior high and children use a smaller ball, about 54-56 cm. (21″) in circumference and weighing about 325-400 g. (13 oz.). There is also a smaller mini-handball for younger children. The ball looks like a small soccer ball and has a rubber bladder and a one-color leather cover.

2. DURATION OF THE GAME:

The game is played in two 30 minute halves with a 10 minute intermission. There are no time outs except for injuries or other major interruptions, as determined by the referees. Playing time can be modified for tournaments and young children.

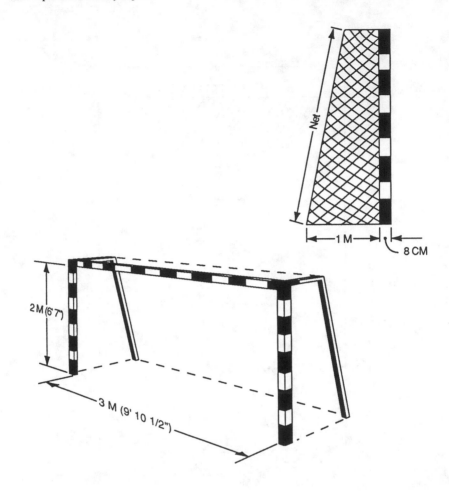

3. THE PLAYERS:

Each team has seven players, six court players and one goalie on the court. All players may play over the whole court. A team is allowed five substitute players for a total of twelve team members. Substitutions may take place at any time without notifying the timekeeper as long as the player replaced has already left the court. All players shall leave and enter the court within the boundaries of their team's substitution area. Players are designated by the position they play. The following diagram shows a basic offense and the names of each position.

4. BEGINNING THE GAME:

A coin is flipped to determine who will have possession of the ball. Following the official's whistle, the game is started at center court by a throw-off, a pass to a teammate. (See figure.) The same procedure is followed after each goal is scored with the team which conceded the goal executing the throw-off.

5. GOAL AREA:

Only the goalie is allowed to stand inside the goal area. If an offensive player is in the circle or on the line, with or without the ball, the ball is given to the opponent and a goal

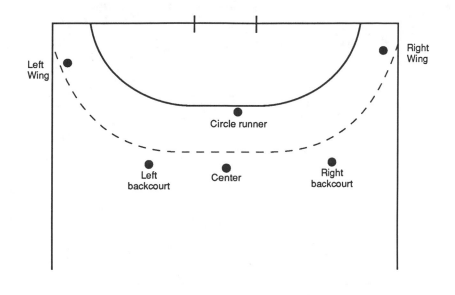

does not count. If the defense gains an advantage by being in the circle, a penalty throw is awarded. A ball inside the goal area belongs to the goalie. However, the ball is not considered to be in the goal area if it is in the air.

6. PLAYING THE BALL:

A player is allowed to run 3 steps with the ball or hold it for 3 seconds. A player is not allowed to the play the ball with the legs below the knee. There is no limit on dribbling the ball. However, a double dribble is not allowed and free throw is given to the opponents. A player may:

| take 3 steps | dribble (as many times desired) | take 3 steps | pass or shoot |

A player may not pass the ball in the air with the intention of catching it himself while advancing down the court. This is an air dribble and is not legal. Players are not allowed to dive to play the ball when it is on the floor.

7. DEFENDING THE OPPONENT:

A player is allowed to use the body to obstruct an opponent either with or without the ball. However, using the arms or legs to obstruct, push, hold, trip or hit is not allowed. The offensive player is not allowed to charge into a defensive player (a free throw is awarded).

8. THROW-IN:

A throw-in is taken if the ball goes out of bounds on the side line. The defense must be 3 meters (10') away when the ball is passed in bounds. The player taking the throw-in must have at least one foot on the side line. A throw-in is taken down in the area of the

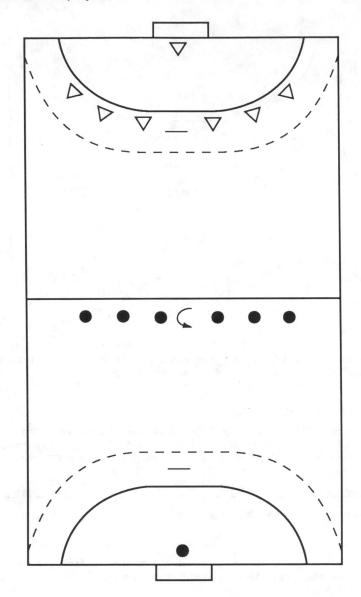

nearest corner when a defensive player (excluding the goalie) is the last to touch the ball as it goes out of bounds over the goal line.

9. REFEREE'S THROW:

A referee's throw is taken when the ball touches anything above the court (i.e., equipment on the ceiling), or the game has been interrupted with an infringement of the rules and neither team is in possession of the ball. The execution is basically a "jump ball" with any one player from each team standing next to the referee and all other players 3 meters away. With the toss, the two players may reach and grab the ball or direct it to a team-mate, but not until it has reached its apex and has started downward.

10. GOALS:

Goals may be scored from all formal throws (i.e., throw-in, throw-on, from center of court, and goal-throw by goalie out of his/her area onto the playing court).

11. PENALTY THROWS AND FREE THROWS:

a) A penalty throw is given when an offensive player is fouled and the referee feels that the offense had a sure chance to score when fouled. The officials follow the "advantage" rule: if a team fouled against is able to gain the advantage, play continues without a penalty.

b) A free throw is given for all other fouls and infringements of the rules, similar to a violation in basketball. The free throw is taken immediately, without the referee handling the ball, from the place the violation occurred. The defense must remain 3 meters away. The thrower must have one foot continuously in contact with the court and must make a throw or pass within 3 seconds. If the foul or infringement occurs between the goal line and the free throw line the free throw is taken just outside of the free throw line just opposite from where the foul took place. The "advantage" rule applies to free throws also.

12. PERSONAL PENALTIES:

Unsportsmanlike conduct or fouls such as pushing, hitting and holding result not just in a free throw (or penalty throw) for the opposing team, but also in a caution to the player by the referee. If the conduct or foul is repeated, the player is suspended for 2 minutes from the game and the team must play short. A third suspension of the same player results in a disqualification from the game.

GOVERNING BODY

United States Team Handball Federation, 1750 East Boulder St., Colorado Springs, CO 80909

The U.S. Team Handball Federation (U.S.T.H.F.) conducts the International Team Handball program of the USA and serves as the national governing body, directing the U.S. Team Handball program for the Olympic Games. It is also responsible for developing the national teams for women, men, and juniors and for administering the international regulations of the International Handball Federation (IHF). The U.S.T.H.F.'s goals revolve around the development of the game of team handball in the USA from the grass roots to the Olympic Games. Questions regarding equipment, instructional materials, rules, and so on, should be directed to the U.S.T.H.F. Although team handball was originated in Europe in the late 1920s, it has only been played in the United States since 1959. It is reported to be second only to soccer in popularity worldwide, being played in 72 nations.

MAGAZINES

Team Handball USA, U.S.T.H.F., 1750 East Boulder St., Colorado Springs, CO 80909

• TENNIS •

RULES OF TENNIS–1989

(Reproduced by permission of the United States Tennis Association*)

□

Note: The following Rules and Cases and Decisions are the official Code of the International Tennis Federation, of which the United States Tennis Association is a member. USTA Comments and USTA Cases and Decisions have the same weight and force in USTA tournaments as do ITF Cases and Decisions. When a match is played without officials the principles and guidelines set forth in the USTA Publication, The Code, shall apply in any situation not covered by the rules. Except where otherwise stated, every reference in these Rules to the masculine includes the feminine gender. The rules are amended annually and are available from the USTA.

THE SINGLES GAME

RULE 1 THE COURT

The court shall be a rectangle 78 feet (23.77m.) long and 27 feet (8.23m.) wide.

USTA Comment: See Rule 34 for a doubles court.

It shall be divided across the middle by a net suspended from a cord or metal cable of a maximum diameter of one-third of an inch (0.8cm.), the ends of which shall be attached to, or pass over, the tops of two posts, which shall be not more than 6 inches (15cm.) square or 6 inches (15cm.) in diameter. The centres of the posts shall be 3 feet (0.914m.) outside the court on each side and the height of the posts shall be such that the top of the cord or metal cable shall be 3 feet 6 inches (1.07m.) above the ground.

When a combined doubles (see Rule 34) and singles court with a doubles net is used for singles, the net must be supported to a height of 3 feet 6 inches (1.07m.) by means of two posts, called "singles sticks," which shall be not more than 3 inches (7.5cm.) square or 3 inches (7.5cm.) in diameter. The centres of the singles sticks shall be 3 feet (0.914m.) outside the singles court on each side.

The net shall be extended fully so that it fills completely the space between the two posts and shall be of sufficiently small mesh to prevent the ball passing through. The height of the net shall be 3 feet (0.914m.) at the centre, where it shall be held down taut by a strap not more than 2 inches (5cm.) wide and completely white in colour. There shall be a band covering the cord or metal cable and the top of the net of not less than 2 inches (5cm.) nor more than 2 1/2 inches (6.3cm.) in depth on each side and completely white in colour.

There shall be no advertisement on the net, strap, band or singles sticks.

The lines bounding the ends and sides of the Court shall respectively be called the base-lines and the side-lines. On each side of the net, at a distance of 21 feet (6.40m.) from it and

---

*See pages 585 and 586 for additional information.

parallel with it, shall be drawn the service-lines. The space on each side of the net between the service-line and the side-lines shall be divided into two equal parts called the service-courts by the centre service-line, which must be 2 inches (5cm.) in width, drawn half-way between, and parallel with, the side-lines. Each base-line shall be bisected by an imaginary continuation of the centre service-line to a line 4 inches (10cm.) in length and 2 inches (5cm.) in width called the centre mark drawn inside the Court, at right angles to and in contact with such base-lines. All other lines shall be not less than 1 inch (2.5cm.) nor more than 2 inches (5cm.) in width, except the base-line, which may be 4 inches (10cm.) in width, and all measurements shall be made to the outside of the lines. All lines shall be of uniform colour.

If advertising or any other material is placed at the back of the court, it may not contain white or yellow. A light colour may only be used if this does not interfere with the vision of the players.

If advertisements are placed on the chairs of the Linesmen sitting at the back of the court, they may not contain white or yellow. A light color may only be used if this does not interfere with the vision of the players.

Note: In the case of the International Tennis Championship (Davis Cup) or other Official Championships of the International Tennis Federation, there shall be a space behind each base-line of not less than 21 feet (6.4m.), and at the sides of not less than 12 feet (3.66m.). The chairs of the linesman may be placed at the back of the court within 21 feet or at the side of the court within 12 feet, provided they do not protrude into that area more than 3 feet (.914m).

USTA Comment: An approved method for obtaining proper net tautness is this: Loosen the center strap; tighten the net cord until it is approximately 40 inches above the ground, being careful not to overtighten the net; tighten the center strap until the center of the net is 36 inches above the ground. These measurements should always be made before the first match of the day. For a plan of the court see the accompanying figure.

USTA Comment: It is important to have a stick 3 feet, 6 inches long, with a notch cut in at the 3-foot mark for the purpose of measuring the height of the net at the posts and in the center. These measurements always should be made before starting to play a match.

RULE 2 PERMANENT FIXTURES

The permanent fixtures of the Court shall include not only the net, posts, singles sticks, cord or metal cable, strap and band, but also, where there are any such, the back and side stops, the stands, fixed or movable seats and chairs around the Court, and their occupants, all other fixtures around and above the Court, and the Umpire, Net-cord Judge, Foot-fault Judge, Linesmen and Ball Boys when in their respective places.

Note: For the purpose of this Rule, the word "Umpire" comprehends the Umpire, the persons entitled to a seat on the Court, and all those persons designated to assist the Umpire in the conduct of a match.

RULE 3 THE BALL

The ball shall have a uniform outer surface and shall be white or yellow in colour. If there are any seams, they shall be stitchless.

The ball shall be more than two and a half inches (6.35cm.) and less than two and five-eighths inches (6.67cm.) in diameter, and more than two ounces (56.7 grams) and less than two and one-sixteenth ounces (58.5 grams) in weight. The ball shall have a bound of more than 53 inches (135cm.) and less than 58 inches (147cm.) when dropped 100 inches (254cm.) upon a concrete base.

The ball shall have a forward deformation of more than .220 of an inch (.56cm.) and less than .290 of an inch (.74cm.) and a return deformation of more than .350 of an inch

PLAN OF THE COURTS
(See Rules 1 and 34)

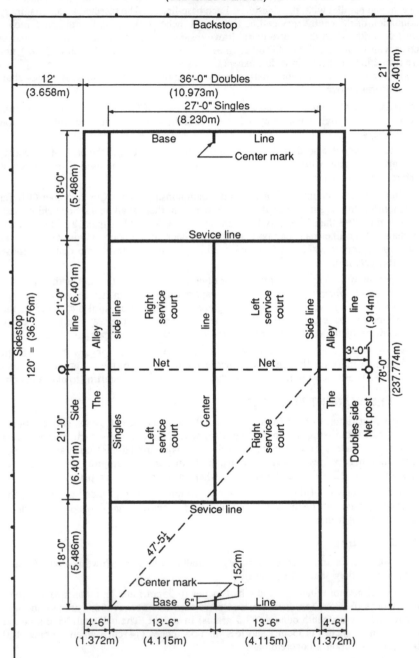

(.89cm.) and less than .425 of an inch (1.08cm.) at 18 lb. (8.165kg.) load. The two deformation figures shall be the averages of three individual readings along three axes of the ball and no two individual readings shall differ by more than .030 of an inch (.08cm.) in each case.

For play exceeding 4,000 feet (1219m) in altitude above sea level, two additional types of ball may be used. The first type is identical to those described above, except that the bound shall be more than 48 inches (121.92cm) and less than 53 inches (135cm), and the ball shall have an internal pressure that is greater than the external pressure. This type of tennis ball is commonly known as a pressurized ball. The second type is identical to those described above, except they shall have a bound of more than 53 inches (135cm) and less than 58 inches (147cm), and the ball shall have an internal pressure that is approximately equal to the external pressure and have been acclimatized at the altitude of the specific tournament for 60 days. This type of tennis ball is commonly known as a zero-pressure or non-pressurized ball.

RULE 4 THE RACKET

Rackets failing to comply with the following specifications are not approved for play under the Rules of Tennis:

(a) The hitting surface of the racket shall be flat and consist of a pattern of crossed strings connected to a frame and alternately interlaced or bonded where they cross; and the stringing pattern shall be generally uniform, and in particular not less dense in the centre than in any other area. The strings shall be free of attached objects and protrusions other than those utilized solely and specifically to limit or prevent wear and tear or vibration and which are reasonable in size and placement for such purposes.

(b) The frame of the racket shall not exceed 32 inches (81.28cm.) in overall length, including the handle and 12 1/2 inches (31.75cm.) in overall width. The strung surface shall not exceed 15 1/2 inches (39.37cm.) in overall length, and 11 1/2 inches (29.21cm.) in overall width.

(c) The frame, including the handle, shall be free of attached objects and devices other than those utilized solely and specifically to limit or prevent wear and tear or vibration, or to distribute weight. Any objects and devices must be reasonable in size and placement for such purposes.

(d) The frame, including the handle and the strings, shall be free of any device which makes it possible to change materially the shape of the racket, or to change the weight distribution, during the playing of a point.

The International Tennis Federation shall rule on the question of whether any racket or prototype complies with the above specifications or is otherwise approved, or not approved, for play. Such ruling may be undertaken on its own initiative, or upon application by any party with a bona fide interest therein, including any player, equipment manufacturer or National Association or members thereof. Such rulings and applications shall be made in accordance with the applicable Review and Hearing Procedures of the International Tennis Federation, copies of which may be obtained from the office of the Secretary.

Case 1. Can there be more than one set of strings on the hitting surface of a racket?

Decision. No. The rule clearly mentions a pattern, and not patterns, of crossed strings.

Case 2. Is the stringing pattern of a racket considered to be generally uniform and flat if the strings are on more than one plane?

Decision. No.

Case 3. Can a vibration dampening device be placed on the strings of a racket, and if so, where can it be placed?

Decision. Yes, but such devices may only be placed outside the pattern of crossed strings.

RULE 5 SERVER AND RECEIVER

The players shall stand on opposite sides of the net; the player who first delivers the ball shall be called the Server, and the other the Receiver.

Case 1. Does a player, attempting a stroke, lose the point if he crosses an imaginary line in the extension of the net?

(a) before striking the ball,

(b) after striking the ball?

Decision. He does not lose the point in either case by crossing the imaginary line and provided he does not enter the lines bounding his opponent's Court (Rule 20 (e)). In regard to hindrance, his opponent may ask for the decision of the Umpire under Rules 21 and 25.

Case 2. The Server claims that the Receiver must stand within the lines bounding his Court. Is this necessary?

Decision. No. The Receiver may stand wherever he pleases on his own side of the net.

RULE 6 CHOICE OF ENDS AND SERVICE

The choice of ends and the right to be Server or Receiver in the first game shall be decided by toss. The player winning the toss may choose or require his opponent to choose:

(a) The right to be Server or Receiver, in which case the other player shall choose the end; or

(b) The end, in which case the other player shall choose the right to be Server or Receiver.

USTA Comment: These choices should be made promptly and are irrevocable, except that if the match is postponed or suspended before the start of the match, then the toss stands, but now choices with respect to the service end may be made.

RULE 7 THE SERVICE

The service shall be delivered in the following manner. Immediately before commencing to serve, the Server shall stand with both feet at rest behind (i.e., further from the net than) the base-line, and within the imaginary continuations of the centre-mark and side-line. The Server shall then project the ball by hand into the air in any direction and before it hits the ground strike it with his racket, and the delivery shall be deemed to have been completed at the moment of the impact of the racket and the ball. A player with the use of only one arm may utilize his racket for the projection.

USTA Comment: The service begins when the Server takes a ready position and ends when his racket makes contact with the ball, or when he misses the ball in attempting to serve it. A match officially begins when the first serve is struck or when the first toss is swung at and missed.

Case 1. May the Server in a singles game take his stand behind the portion of the base-line between the side-lines of the Singles Court and the Doubles Court?

Decision. No.

USTA Comment: The server may stand anywhere in back of the baseline between the imaginary extensions of the center mark and the singles sideline.

Case 2. If a player, when serving, throws up two or more balls instead of one, does he lose that service?

Decision. No. A let should be called, but if the Umpire regards the action as deliberate he may take action under Rule 21.

USTA Case 3. May a player serve underhand?

Decision. Yes. There is no restriction regarding the kind of service which may be used; that is, the player may use an underhand or overhand service at his discretion.

RULE 8 FOOT FAULT

(a) The Server shall throughout the delivery of the service:

(i) Not change his position by walking or running. The Server shall not by slight movements of the feet which do not materially affect the location originally taken up by him, be deemed "to change his position by walking or running."

(ii) Not touch, with either foot, any area other than that behind the base-line within the imaginary extensions of the centre mark and side-lines.

(b) The word "foot" means the extremity of the leg below the ankle.

USTA Comment: This rule covers the most decisive stroke in the game, and there is no justification for its not being obeyed by players and enforced by officials. No official has the right to instruct any umpire to disregard violations of it. In a non-officiated match, it is the prerogative of the Receiver, or his partner, to call foot faults, but only after all efforts (appeal to the server, requests for an umpire, etc.) have failed and the foot faulting is so flagrant as to be clearly perceptible from the Receiver's side.

It is improper for any official to warn a player that he is in danger of having a foot fault called on him. On the other hand, if a player, in all sincerity, asks for an explanation of how he foot faulted, either the Line Umpire or the Chair Umpire should give him that information.

RULE 9 DELIVERY OF SERVICE

(a) In delivering the service, the Server shall stand alternately behind the right and left Courts beginning from the right in every game. If service from a wrong half of the Court occurs and is undetected, all play resulting from such wrong service or services shall stand, but the inaccuracy of station shall be corrected immediately it is discovered.

(b) The ball served shall pass over the net and hit the ground within the Service Court which is diagonally opposite, or upon any line bounding such Court, before the Receiver returns it.

RULE 10 SERVICE FAULT

The Service is a fault:

(a) If the Server commits any breach of Rules 7, 8 or 9;

(b) If he misses the ball in attempting to strike it;

(c) If the ball served touches a permanent fixture (other than the net, strap or band) before it hits the ground.

Case 1. After throwing a ball up preparatory to serving, the Server decides not to strike at it and catches it instead. Is it a fault?

Decision. No.

USTA Comment: As long as the Server makes no attempt to strike the ball, it is immaterial whether he catches it in his hand or on his racket or lets it drop to the ground.

Case 2. In serving in a singles game played on a Doubles Court with doubles posts and singles sticks, the ball hits a singles stick and then hits the ground within the lines of the correct Service Court. Is this a fault or a let?

Decision. In serving it is a fault, because the singles stick, the doubles post, and that portion of the net, or band between them are permanent fixtures. (Rules 2 and 10, and note to Rule 24.)

USTA Comment: The significant point governing Case 2 is that the part of the net and band "outside" the singles sticks is not part of the net over which this singles match is being played. Thus such a serve is a fault under the provisions of Article (c) above . . .

By the same token, this would be a fault also if it were a singles game played with permanent posts in the singles position. (See Case 1 under Rule 24 for difference between "service" and "good return" with respect to a ball's hitting a net post.)

USTA Comment: In a non-officiated singles match, each player makes calls for all balls hit to his side of the net. In doubles, normally the Receiver's partner makes the calls with respect to the service line, with the Receiver calling the side and center lines, but either partner may make the call on any ball he clearly sees out.

RULE 11 SECOND SERVICE

After a fault (if it is the first fault) the Server shall serve again from behind the same half of the Court from which he served that fault, unless the service was from the wrong half, when, in accordance with Rule 9, the Server shall be entitled to one service only from behind the other half.

Case 1. A player serves from a wrong Court. He loses the point and then claims it was a fault because of his wrong station.

Decision. The point stands as played and the next service should be from the correct station according to the score.

Case 2. The point score being 15 all, the Server, by mistake, serves from the left-hand Court. He wins the point. He then serves again from the right-hand Court, delivering a fault. This mistake in station is then discovered. Is he entitled to the previous point? From which Court should he next serve?

Decision. The previous point stands. The next service should be from the left-hand Court, the score being 30/15, and the Server has served one fault.

RULE 12 WHEN TO SERVE

The Server shall not serve until the Receiver is ready. If the latter attempts to return the service, he shall be deemed ready. If, however, the Receiver signifies that he is not ready, he may not claim a fault because the ball does not hit the ground within the limits fixed for the service.

USTA Comment: The Server must wait until the Receiver is ready for the second service as well as the first, and if the Receiver claims to be not ready and does not make any effort to return a service, the Server may not claim the point, even though the service was good. However, the Receiver, having indicated he is ready, may not become unready unless some outside interference takes place.

RULE 13 THE LET

In all cases where a let has to be called under the rules, or to provide for an interruption to play, it shall have the following interpretations:

(a) When called solely in respect of a service that one service only shall be replayed.

(b) When called under any other circumstance, the point shall be replayed.

Case 1. A service is interrupted by some cause outside those defined in Rule 14. Should the service only be replayed?

Decision. No, the whole point must be replayed.

USTA Comment: If a delay between first and second serves is caused by the Receiver, by an official, or by an outside interference, the whole point shall be replayed; if the delay is caused by the Server, the Server has one serve to come. A spectator's outcry (of "out," "fault" or other) is not a valid basis for replay of a point, but action should be taken to prevent a recurrence.

USTA Comment: Case 1 refers to a second serve, and the decision means that if the interruption occurs during delivery of the second service, the Server gets two serves. Example: On a second service a Linesman calls "fault" and immediately corrects it (the Receiver meanwhile having let the ball go by). The Server is entitled to two serves, on this ground: The corrected call means that the Server has put the ball into play with a good service, and once the ball is in play and a let is called, the point must be replayed . . . Note, however, that if the serve is an unmistakable ace—that is, the Umpire is sure the erroneous call had no part in the Receiver's inability to play the ball—the point should be declared for the Server.

Case 2. If a ball in play becomes broken, should a let be called?

Decision. Yes.

USTA Comment: A ball shall be regarded as having become "broken" if, in the opinion of the Chair Umpire, it is found to have lost compression to the point of being unfit for further play, or unfit for any reason, and it is clear the defective ball was the one in play.

RULE 14 THE "LET" IN SERVICE

The service is a let:

(a) If the ball served touches the net, strap or band, and is otherwise good, or, after touching the net, strap or band, touches the Receiver or anything which he wears or carries before hitting the ground.

(b) If a service or a fault is delivered when the Receiver is not ready (see Rule 12).

In case of a let, that particular service shall not count, and the Server shall serve again, but a service let does not annul a previous fault.

RULE 15 ORDER OF SERVICE

At the end of the first game the Receiver shall become Server, and the Server Receiver; and so on alternately in all the subsequent games of a match. If a player serves out of turn, the player who ought to have served shall serve as soon as the mistake is discovered, but all points scored before such discovery shall be reckoned. If a game shall have been completed before such discovery, the order of service remains as altered. A fault served before such discovery shall not be reckoned.

RULE 16 WHEN PLAYERS CHANGE ENDS

The players shall change ends at the end of the first, third and every subsequent alternate game of each set, and at the end of each set unless the total number of games in such set is even, in which case the change is not made until the end of the first game of the next set.

If a mistake is made and the correct sequence is not followed the players must take up their correct station as soon as the discovery is made and follow their original sequence.

RULE 17 THE BALL IN PLAY

A ball is in play from the moment at which it is delivered in service. Unless a fault or a let is called it remains in play until the point is decided.

USTA Comment: A point is not decided simply when, or because, a good shot has clearly passed a player, or when an apparently bad shot passes over a baseline or sideline. An outgoing ball is still definitely in play until it actually strikes the ground, backstop or a permanent fixture (other than the net, posts, singles sticks, cord or metal cable, strap or band), or a player. The same applies to a good ball, bounding after it has landed in the proper court. A ball that becomes imbedded in the net is out of play.

Case 1. A player fails to make a good return. No call is made and the ball remains in play. May his opponent later claim the point after the rally has ended?

Decision. No. The point may not be claimed if the players continue to play after the error has been made, provided the opponent was not hindered.

USTA Comment: To be valid, an out call on A's shot to B's court, that B plays, must be made before B's shot has either gone out of play or has been hit by A. See Case 3 under Rule 29.

USTA Case 2. A ball is played into the net; the player on the other side, thinking that the ball is coming over, strikes at it and hits the net. Who loses the point?

Decision. If the player touched the net while the ball was still in play, he loses the point.

RULE 18 SERVER WINS POINT

The Server wins the point:

(a) If the ball served, not being a let under Rule 14, touches the Receiver or anything which he wears or carries, before it hits the ground;

(b) If the Receiver otherwise loses the point as provided by Rule 20.

RULE 19 RECEIVER WINS POINT

The Receiver wins the point:

(a) If the Server serves two consecutive faults;

(b) If the Server otherwise loses the point as provided by Rule 20.

RULE 20 PLAYER LOSES POINT

A player loses the point if:

(a) He fails, before the ball in play has hit the ground twice consecutively, to return it directly over the net (except as provided in Rule 24(a) or (c)); or

(b) He returns the ball in play so that it hits the ground, a permanent fixture, or other object, outside any of the lines which bound his opponent's Court (except as provided in Rule 24(a) or (c)); or

USTA Comment: A ball hitting a scoring device or other object attached to a net post results in loss of point to the striker.

(c) He volleys the ball and fails to make a good return even when standing outside the Court; or

(d) In playing the ball he deliberately carries or catches it on his racket or deliberately touches it with his racket more than once; or

USTA Comment: Only when there is a definite "second push" by the player does his shot become illegal, with consequent loss of point. It should be noted that the word "deliberately" is the key word in this Rule and that two hits occurring in the course of a single continuous stroke would not be deemed a double hit.

(e) He or his racket (in his hand or otherwise) or anything which he wears or carries touches the net, posts, singles sticks, cord or metal cable, strap or band, or the ground within his opponent's Court at any time while the ball is in play; or

USTA Comment: Touching a pipe support that runs across the court at the bottom of the net is interpreted as touching the net; See USTA Comment under Rule 23.

(f) He volleys the ball before it has passed the net; or

(g) The ball in play touches him or anything that he wears or carries, except his racket in his hand or hands; or

USTA Comment: This loss of point occurs regardless of whether the player is inside or outside the bounds of his court when the ball touches him.

(h) He throws his racket at and hits the ball; or

(i) He deliberately and materially changes the shape of his racket during the playing of the point.

Case 1. In serving, the racket flies from the Server's hand and touches the net before the ball has touched the ground. Is this a fault, or does the player lose the point?

Decision. The Server loses the point because his racket touches the net whilst the ball is in play (Rule 20(e)).

Case 2. In serving, the racket flies from the Server's hand and touches the net after the ball has touched the ground outside the proper court. Is this a fault, or does the player lose the point?

Decision. This is a fault because the ball was out of play when the racket touched the net.

Case 3. A and B are playing against C and D. A is serving to D, C touches the net before the ball touches the ground. A fault is then called because the service falls outside the Service Court. Do C and D lose the point?

Decision. The call "fault" is an erroneous one. C and D had already lost the point before "fault" could be called, because C touched the net whilst the ball was in play (Rule 20(e)).

Case 4. May a player jump over the net into his opponent's Court while the ball is in play and not suffer penalty?

Decision. No. He loses the point (Rule 20(e)).

Case 5. A cuts the ball just over the net, and it returns to A's side. B, unable to reach the ball, throws his racket and hits the ball. Both racket and ball fall over the net on A's Court. A returns the ball outside of B's Court. Does B win or lose the point?

Decision. B loses the point (Rule 20(e) and (h)).

Case 6. A player standing outside the service Court is struck by a service ball before it has touched the ground. Does he win or lose the point?

Decision. The player struck loses the point (Rule 20(g)), except as provided under Rule 14(a).

Case 7. A player standing outside the Court volleys the ball or catches it in his hand and claims the point because the ball was certainly going out of court.

Decision. In no circumstances can he claim the point:

(1) If he catches the ball he loses the point under Rule 20(g).

(2) If he volleys it and makes a bad return he loses the point under Rule 20(c).

(3) If he volleys it and makes a good return, the rally continues.

RULE 21 PLAYER HINDERS OPPONENT

If a player commits any act which hinders his opponent in making a stroke, then, if this is deliberate, he shall lose the point or if involuntary, the point shall be replayed.

USTA Comment: 'Deliberate' means a player did what he intended to do, although the resulting effect on his opponent might or might not have been what he intended. Example: a player, after his return is in the air, gives advice to his partner in such a loud voice that his opponent is hindered. 'Involuntary' means a non-intentional act such as a hat blowing off or a scream resulting from a sudden wasp sting.

Case 1. Is a player liable to a penalty if in making a stroke he touches his opponent?

Decision. No, unless the Umpire deems it necessary to take action under Rule 21.

Case 2. When a ball bounds back over the net, the player concerned may reach over the net in order to play the ball.

What is the ruling if the player is hindered from doing this by his opponent?

Decision. In accordance with Rule 21, the Umpire may either award the point to the player hindered, or order the point to be replayed. (See also Rule 25.)

Case 3. Does an involuntary double hit constitute an act which hinders an opponent within Rule 21?

Decision. No.

USTA Comment: Upon appeal by a competitor that a server's action in discarding a "second ball" after a rally has started constitutes a distraction (hindrance), the Umpire, if he deems the claim valid, shall require the server to make some other and satisfactory disposition of the ball. Failure to comply with this instruction may result in loss of point(s) or disqualification.

RULE 22 BALL FALLS ON LINE

A ball falling on a line is regarded as falling in the Court bounded by that line.

USTA Comment: In matches played without officials, it is customary for each player to make the calls on all balls hit to his side of the net, and if a player cannot call a ball out with surety he should regard it as good. See The Code.

RULE 23 BALL TOUCHES PERMANENT FIXTURES

If the ball in play touches a permanent fixture (other than the net, posts, singles sticks, cord or metal cable, strap or band) after it has hit the ground, the player who struck it wins the point; if before it hits the ground, his opponent wins the point.

Case 1. A return hits the Umpire or his chair or stand. The player claims that the ball was going into Court.

Decision. He loses the point.

USTA Comment: A ball in play that after passing the net strikes a pipe support running across the court at the base of the net is regarded the same as a ball landing on clear ground. See also Rule 20(e).

RULE 24 A GOOD RETURN

It is a good return:

(a) If the ball touches the net, posts, singles sticks, cord or metal cable, strap or band, provided that it passes over any of them and hits the ground within the Court; or

(b) If the ball, served or returned, hits the ground within the proper Court and rebounds or is blown back over the net, and the player whose turn it is to strike reaches over the net and plays the ball, provided that neither he nor any part of his clothes or racket touches the net, posts, singles sticks, cord or metal cable, strap or band or the ground within his opponent's Court, and that the stroke is otherwise good; or

(c) If the ball is returned outside the posts, or singles sticks, either above or below the level of the top of the net, even though it touches the posts or singles sticks, provided that it hits the ground within the proper Court; or

(d) If a player's racket passes over the net after he has returned the ball, provided the ball passes the net before being played and is properly returned; or

(e) If a player succeeds in returning the ball, served or in play, which strikes a ball lying in the Court.

USTA Comment: i.e., on his court when the point is started, or lying on his court as a result of a first service fault. If a ball in play strikes a ball, rolling or stationary, that has come from elsewhere after the point started, a let should be played. If the ball in play strikes a ball dropped by a player while play was underway, that player loses the point, regardless of whether that striking occurred inside or outside the court. See the USTA Comment under Rule 20g and Case 7 under Rule 25.

Note: In a singles match, if, for the sake of convenience, a doubles Court is equipped with singles sticks for the purpose of a singles game, then the doubles posts and those portions of the net, cord or metal cable and the band outside such singles sticks shall at all times be permanent fixtures, and are not regarded as posts or parts of the net of a singles game.

A return that passes under the net cord between the singles stick and adjacent doubles post without touching either net cord, net or doubles post and falls within the area of play, is a good return.

USTA Comment: But in doubles this would be a "through"—loss of point.

Case 1. A ball going out of Court hits a net post or singles stick and falls within the lines of the opponent's Court. Is the stroke good?

Decision. If a service: no, under Rule 10(c). If other than a service: yes, under Rule 24(a).

Case 2. Is it a good return if a player returns the ball holding his racket in both hands?

Decision. Yes.

Case 3. The service, or ball in play, strikes a ball lying in the Court. Is the point won or lost thereby?

USTA Comment: A ball that is touching a boundary line is considered to be "lying in the court."

Decision. No. Play must continue. If it is not clear to the Umpire that the right ball is returned a let should be called.

Case 4. May a player use more than one racket at any time during play?

Decision. No; the whole implication of the Rules is singular.

Case 5. May a player request that a ball or balls lying in his opponent's Court be removed?

Decision. Yes, but not while a ball is in play.

USTA Comment: The request must be honored.

RULE 25 HINDRANCE OF A PLAYER

In case a player is hindered in making a stroke by anything not within his control, except a permanent fixture of the Court, or except as provided for in Rule 21, a let shall be called.

Case 1. A spectator gets into the way of a player, who fails to return the ball. May the player then claim a let?

Decision. Yes, if in the Umpire's opinion he was obstructed by circumstances beyond his control, but not if due to permanent fixtures of the Court or the arrangements of the ground.

Case 2. A player is interfered with as in Case No. 1, and the Umpire calls a let. The Server had previously served a fault. Has he the right to two services?

Decision. Yes: as the ball is in play, the point, not merely the stroke, must be replayed as the Rule provides.

Case 3. May a player claim a let under Rule 25 because he thought his opponent was being hindered, and consequently did not expect the ball to be returned?

Decision. No.

Case 4. Is a stroke good when a ball in play hits another ball in the air?

Decision. A let should be called unless the other ball is in the air by the act of one of the players, in which case the Umpire will decide under Rule 21.

Case 5. If an Umpire or other judge erroneously calls "fault" or "out," and then corrects himself, which of the calls shall prevail?

Decision. A let must be called unless, in the opinion of the Umpire, neither player is hindered in his game, in which case the corrected call shall prevail.

Case 6. If the first ball served—a fault—rebounds, interfering with the Receiver at the time of the second service, may the Receiver claim a let?

Decision. Yes. But if he had an opportunity to remove the ball from the Court and negligently failed to do so, he may not claim a let.

Case 7. Is it a good stroke if the ball touches a stationary or moving object on the Court?

Decision. It is a good stroke unless the stationary object came into Court after the ball was put into play in which case a let must be called. If the ball in play strikes an object moving along or above the surface of the Court a let must be called.

Case 8. What is the ruling if the first service is a fault, the second service correct, and it becomes necessary to call a let either under the provision of Rule 25 or if the Umpire is unable to decide the point?

Decision. The fault shall be annulled and the whole point replayed.

USTA Comment: See Rule 13 with its USTA Comments.

RULE 26 SCORE IN A GAME

If a player wins his first point, the score is called 15 for that player; on winning his second point, the score is called 30 for that player; on winning his third point, the score is called 40 for that player, and the fourth point won by a player is scored game for that player except as below: If both players have won three points, the score is called deuce; and the next point won by a player is scored advantage for that player. If the same player wins the next point, he wins the game; if the other player wins the next point the score is again called deuce; and so on, until a player wins the two points immediately following the score at deuce, when the game is scored for that player.

USTA Comment: In a non-officiated match, the Server should announce, in a voice audible to his opponent and spectators, the set score at the beginning of each game, and point scores as the game goes on. Misunderstandings will be avoided if this practice is followed.

RULE 27 SCORE IN A SET

(a) A player (or players) who first wins six games wins a set; except that he must win by a margin of two games over his opponent and where necessary a set is extended until this margin is achieved.

(b) The tie-break system of scoring may be adopted as an alternative to the advantage set system in paragraph (a) of this Rule provided the decision is announced in advance of the match. See the Tie-Break System following Rule 40.

In this case, the following Rules shall be effective:

The tie-break shall operate when the score reaches six games all in any set except in the third or fifth set of a three set or five set match, respectively, when an ordinary advantage set shall be played, unless otherwise decided and announced in advance of the match.

The following system shall be used in a tie-break game.

Singles

(i) A player who first wins seven points shall win the game and the set provided he leads by a margin of two points. If the score reaches six points all the game shall be extended until this margin has been achieved. Numerical scoring shall be used throughout the tie-break game.

(ii) The player whose turn it is to serve shall be the server for the first point. His opponent shall be the server for the second and third points and thereafter each player shall serve alternately for two consecutive points until the winner of the game and set has been decided.

(iii) From the first point, each service shall be delivered alternately from the right and left courts, beginning from the right court. If service from a wrong half of the court occurs and is undetected, all play resulting from such wrong service or services shall stand, but the inaccuracy of station shall be corrected immediately it is discovered.

(iv) Players shall change ends after every six points and at the conclusion of the tie-break game.

(v) The tie-break game shall count as one game for the ball change, except that, if the balls are due to be changed at the beginning of the tie-break, the change shall be delayed until the second game of the following set.

Doubles

In doubles the procedure for singles shall apply. The player whose turn it is to serve shall be the server for the first point. Thereafter each player shall serve in rotation for two points, in the same order as previously in that set, until the winners of the game and set have been decided.

Rotation of Service

The player (or pair in the case of doubles) who served first in the tie-break game shall receive service in the first game of the following set.

Case 1. At six all the tie-break is played, although it has been decided and announced in advance of the match that an advantage set will be played. Are the points already played counted?

Decision. If the error is discovered before the ball is put in play for the second point, the first point shall count but the error shall be corrected immediately. If the error is discovered after the ball is put in play for the second point the game shall continue as a tie-break game.

Case 2. At six all, an advantage game is played, although it has been decided and announced in advance of the match that a tie-break will be played. Are the points already played counted?

Decision. If the error is discovered before the ball is put in play for the second point, the first point shall be counted but the error shall be corrected immediately. If the error is discovered after the ball is put in play for the second point an advantage set shall be continued. If the score thereafter reaches eight games all or a higher even number, a tie-break shall be played.

Case 3. If during a tie-break in a singles or doubles game, a player serves out of turn, shall the order of service remain as altered until the end of the game?

Decision. If a player has completed his turn of service, the order of service shall remain as altered. If the error is discovered before the player has completed his turn of service, the order of service shall be corrected immediately, and any points already played shall count.

RULE 28 MAXIMUM NUMBER OF SETS

The maximum number of sets in a match shall be 5, or, where women take part, 3.

RULE 29 ROLE OF COURT OFFICIALS

In matches where an Umpire is appointed, his decision shall be final; but where a Referee is appointed, an appeal shall lie to him from the decision of an Umpire on a question of law, and in all such cases the decision of the Referee shall be final.

In matches where assistants to the Umpire are appointed (Linesmen, Net-cord Judges, Foot-fault Judges) their decisions shall be final on questions of fact except that if in the opinion of an Umpire a clear mistake has been made he shall have the right to change the decision of an assistant or order a let to be played. When such an assistant is unable to give a decision he shall indicate this immediately to the Umpire who shall give a decision. When an Umpire is unable to give a decision on a question of fact he shall order a let to be played.

In Davis Cup matches or other team competitions where a Referee is on Court, any decision can be changed by the Referee, who may also instruct an Umpire to order a let to be played.

USTA Comment: See second USTA Comment under Rule 30.

The Referee, in his discretion, may at any time postpone a match on account of darkness or the condition of the ground or the weather. In any case of postponement the previous score and previous occupancy of Courts shall hold good, unless the Referee and the players unanimously agree otherwise.

Case 1. The Umpire orders a let, but a player claims that the point should not be replayed. May the Referee be requested to give a decision?

Decision. Yes. A question of tennis law, that is, an issue relating to the application of specific facts, shall first be determined by the Umpire. However, if the Umpire is uncertain or if a player appeals from his determination, then the Referee shall be requested to give a decision, and his decision is final.

Case 2. A ball is called out, but a player claims that the ball was good. May the Referee give a ruling?

Decision. No. This is a question of fact, that is, an issue relating to what actually occurred during a specific incident, and the decision of the on-court officials is therefore final.

Case 3. May an Umpire overrule a Linesman at the end of a rally if, in his opinion, a clear mistake has been made during the course of a rally?

Decision. No, unless in his opinion the opponent was hindered. Otherwise an Umpire may only overrule a Linesman if he does so immediately after the mistake has been made.

USTA Comment: See Rule 17, Case 1.

Case 4. A Linesman calls a ball out. The Umpire was unable to see clearly, although he thought the ball was in. May he overrule the Linesman?

Decision. No. An Umpire may only overrule if he considers that a call was incorrect beyond all reasonable doubt. He may only overrule a ball determined good by a Linesman if he has been able to see a space between the ball and the line; and he may only overrule a ball determined out, or a fault, by a Linesman if he has seen the ball hit the line, or fall inside the line.

Case 5. May a Linesman change his call after the Umpire has given the score?

Decision. Yes. If a Linesman realizes he has made an error, he may make a correction provided he does so immediately.

Case 6. A player claims his return shot was good after a Linesman called "out." May the Umpire overrule the Linesman?

Decision. No. An Umpire may never overrule as a result of a protest or an appeal by a player.

RULE 30 CONTINUOUS PLAY AND REST PERIODS

Play shall be continuous from the first service until the match is concluded, in accordance with the following provisions:

(a) If the first service is a fault, the second service must be struck by the Server without delay.

The Receiver must play to the reasonable pace of the Server and must be ready to receive when the Server is ready to serve.

When changing ends a maximum of one minute thirty seconds shall elapse from the moment the ball goes out of play at the end of the game to the time the ball is struck for the first point of the next game.

The Umpire shall use his discretion when there is interference which makes it impractical for play to be continuous.

The organisers of international circuits and team events recognised by the ITF may determine the time allowed between points, which shall not at any time exceed 30 seconds.

(b) Play shall never be suspended, delayed or interfered with for the purpose of enabling a player to recover his strength, breath, or physical condition.

However, in the case of accidental injury, the Umpire may allow a one-time three minute suspension for that injury. The organisers of international circuits and team events recognised by the ITF may extend the one-time suspension period from three minutes to five minutes.

USTA Case 1. Although play has not been suspended, a player wearing glasses says that the heavy mist over the courts makes it almost impossible for him to see, and he requests a delay. Should his request be granted?

Decision. No. All players must follow the same rules with respect to suspending play, even though one who wears glasses may be handicapped in doing so.

(c) If, through circumstances outside the control of the player, his clothing, footwear or equipment (excluding racket) becomes out of adjustment in such a way that it is impossible or undesirable for him to play on, the Umpire may suspend play while the maladjustment is rectified.

USTA Comment: Loss of or damage to a contact lens or glasses shall be treated as equipment maladjustment.

(d) The Umpire may suspend or delay play at any time as may be necessary and appropriate.

USTA Comment: When a match is resumed after a suspension of more than ten minutes, it is permissible for the players to engage in a re-warm-up that may be of the same duration as that at the start of the match. The preferred method is to warm up with other balls, and then insert the match balls when play starts. If the match balls are used in the re-warm-up, then the next ball change will be two games sooner. There shall be no re-warm-up after an authorized intermission or after a suspension of ten minutes or less.

(e) After the third set, or when women take part the second set, either player is entitled to a rest, which shall not exceed 10 minutes, or in countries situated between latitude 15 degrees north and latitude 15 degrees south, 45 minutes and furthermore, when necessitated by circumstances not within the control of the players, the Umpire may suspend play for such a period as he may consider necessary. If play is suspended and is not resumed until a later day the rest may be taken only after the third set (or when women take part the second set) of play on such a later day, completion of an unfinished set being counted as one set. If play is suspended and is not resumed until 10 minutes have elapsed in the same day the rest may be taken only after three consecutive sets have been played without interruption (or when women take part two sets), completion of an unfinished set being counted as one set.

Any nation and/or committee organising a tournament, match or competition, other than the International Tennis Championships (Davis Cup and Federation Cup), is at liberty to modify this provision or omit it from its regulations provided this is announced before the event commences.

(f) A tournament committee has the discretion to decide the time allowed for a warm-up period prior to a match but this may not exceed five minutes and must be announced before the event commences.

USTA Comment: When there are no ball persons, this time may be extended to ten minutes.

(g) When approved point penalty and non-accumulative point penalty systems are in operation, the Umpire shall make his decisions within the terms of those systems.

(h) Upon violation of the principle that play shall be continuous the Umpire may, after giving due warning, disqualify the offender.

RULE 31 COACHING

During the playing of a match in a team competition, a player may receive coaching from a captain who is sitting on the court only when he changes ends at the end of a game, but not when he changes ends during a tie-break game. A player may not receive coaching during the playing of any other match.

After due warning an offending player may be disqualified. When an approved point penalty system is in operation, the Umpire shall impose penalties according to that system.

Case 1. Should a warning be given, or the player be disqualified, if the coaching is given by signals in an unobtrusive manner?

Decision. The Umpire must take action as soon as he becomes aware that coaching is being given verbally or by signals. If the Umpire is unaware that coaching is being given, a player may draw his attention to the fact that advice is being given.

Case 2. Can a player receive coaching during the ten-minute rest in a five set match, or when play is interrupted and he leaves the court?

Decision. Yes. In these circumstances, when the player is not on the court, there is no restriction on coaching.

Note: The word ''coaching'' includes any advice or instruction.

RULE 32 CHANGING BALLS

In cases where balls are to be changed after a specified number of games, if the balls are not changed in the correct sequence, the mistake shall be corrected when the player, or pair in the case of doubles, who should have served with new balls is next due to serve. Thereafter the balls shall be changed so that the number of games between changes shall be that originally agreed.

THE DOUBLES GAME

RULE 33

The above Rules shall apply to the Doubles Game except as below.

RULE 34 THE DOUBLES COURT

For the Doubles Game, the Court shall be 36 feet (10.97m.) in width, i.e., 4 1/2 feet (1.37m.) wider on each side than the Court for the Singles Game, and those portions of the singles side-lines which lie between the two service-lines shall be called the service side-lines. In other respects, the Court shall be similar to that described in Rule 1, but the portions of the singles side-lines between the base-line and service-line on each side of the net may be omitted if desired.

USTA Case 1. In doubles the Server claims the right to stand at the corner of the court as marked by the doubles side-line. Is the foregoing correct or is it necessary that the Server stand within the limits of the centre mark and the singles side-line?

Decision. The Server has the right to stand anywhere back of the base-line between the center mark imaginary extension and the doubles side line imaginary extension.

RULE 35 ORDER OF SERVICE IN DOUBLES

The order of serving shall be decided at the beginning of each set as follows:

The pair who have to serve in the first game of each set shall decide which partner shall do so and the opposing pair shall decide similarly for the second game. The partner of the player who served in the first game shall serve in the third; the partner of the player who served in the second game shall serve in the fourth, and so on in the same order in all the subsequent games of a set.

Case 1. In doubles, one player does not appear in time to play, and his partner claims to be allowed to play single-handed against the opposing players. May he do so?

Decision. No.

RULE 36 ORDER OF RECEIVING IN DOUBLES

The order of receiving the service shall be decided at the beginning of each set as follows:

The pair who have to receive the service in the first game shall decide which partner shall receive the first service, and that partner shall continue to receive the first service in every odd game throughout that set. The opposing pair shall likewise decide which partner shall receive the first service in the second game and that partner shall continue to receive the first service in every even game throughout that set. Partners shall receive the service alternately throughout each game.

Case 1. Is it allowable in doubles for the Server's partner or the Receiver's partner to stand in a position that obstructs the view of the Receiver?

Decision. Yes. The Server's partner or the Receiver's partner may take any position on his side of the net in or out of the Court that he wishes.

RULE 37 SERVICE OUT OF TURN IN DOUBLES

If a partner serves out of his turn, the partner who ought to have served shall serve as soon as the mistake is discovered, but all points scored, and any faults served before such discovery, shall be reckoned. If a game shall have been completed before such discovery, the order of service remains as altered.

USTA Comment: For an exception to Rule 37 see Case 3 under Rule 27.

RULE 38 ERROR IN ORDER OF RECEIVING IN DOUBLES

If during a game the order of receiving the service is changed by the Receivers it shall remain as altered until the end of the game in which the mistake is discovered, but the partners shall resume their original order of receiving in the next game of that set in which they are Receivers of the service.

RULE 39 SERVICE FAULT IN DOUBLES

The service is a fault as provided for by Rule 10, or if the ball touches the Server's partner or anything which he wears or carries; but if the ball served touches the partner of the

Receiver, or anything which he wears or carries, not being a let under Rule 14(a) before it hits the ground, the Server wins the point.

RULE 40 PLAYING THE BALL IN DOUBLES

The ball shall be struck alternately by one or other player of the opposing pairs, and if a player touches the ball in play with his racket in contravention of this Rule, his opponents win the point.

USTA Comment: This means that, in the course of making one return, only one member of a doubles team may hit the ball.

If both of them hit the ball, either simultaneously or consecutively, it is an illegal return. The partners themselves do not have to "alternate" in making returns. Mere clashing of rackets does not make a return illegal, if it is clear that only one racket touched the ball.

THE TIE-BREAK SYSTEM

A tournament committee must announce before the start of its tournament the details concerning its use of tie-breaks. A tournament that has been authorized by the USTA or by a USTA Section to use VASSS No-Ad scoring may use the 9-point tie-break in any set played under No-Ad; it may change to the 12-point tie-break in its later rounds. No-Ad scoring is authorized for tournaments held at the Sectional Championship level and below, and for consolation matches in any tournament (excluding any USTA National Junior Championship). Other than the foregoing exceptions, all sanctioned tournaments using tie-breaks will use the 12-point tie-break. Rule 27 establishes the procedure for the 12-point tie-break game. For a more detailed explanation see below.

If a ball change is due on a tie-break game it will be deferred until the second game of the next set. A tie-break game counts as one game in reckoning ball changes. The score of the tie-break set will be written 7-6 (x) or 6-7 (x), with the score of the winner of the match entered first followed by the score of the tie-break game in parentheses, such as (10-8) or (8-10), with the score of the winner of the match again entered first. Changes of ends during a tie-break game are to be made within the normal time allowed between points.

THE 12-POINT TIE-BREAK

Singles: A, having served the first game of the set, serves the first point from the right court; B serves 2 and 3 (left and right), A serves points 4 and 5 (left and right); B serves point 6 (left) and after they change ends, point 7 (right); A serves points 8 and 9 (left and right); B serves points 10 and 11 (left and right), and A serves point 12 (left). A player who reaches 7 points during these first 12 points wins the game and set. If the score has reached 6 points all, the players change ends and continue in the same pattern until one player establishes a margin of two points, which gives him the game and set. Note that the players change ends every six points, and that the player who serves the last point of one of these 6-point segments also serves the first point of the next one (from right court). For a following set the players change ends, and B serves the first game.

Doubles follows the same pattern, with partners preserving their serving sequence. Assuming A-B versus C-D, with A having served the first game of the set: A serves the first point (right); C serves points 2 and 3 (left and right); B serves points 4 and 5 (left and right); D serves point 6 (left) and the teams change ends. D serves point 7 (right); A serves points 8 and 9 (left and right); C serves points 10 and 11 (left and right); B serves point 12 (left). A team that wins 7 points during these first 12 points wins the game and set. If the score has reached 6 points all, the teams change ends. B then serves point 13 (right) and they continue until one team establishes a two-point margin and thus wins the game and set. As in singles, they change ends for one game to start a following set, with team C-D to serve first.

THE 9-POINT TIE-BREAK

Singles: With A having served the first game of the set, he serves points 1 and 2, right court and left; then B serves points 3 and 4, right and left. Players change ends. A serves points 5 and 6, right and left, and B serves points 7 and 8, right and left. If the score reaches 4 points all B serves point 9, right or left at the election of A. The first player to win 5 points wins the game and set. The players stay for one game to start the next set, and B is the first server.

Doubles: The same format as in singles applies, with each player serving from the same end of the court in the tie-break game that he served from during the set. (Note that this operates to alter the sequence of serving by the partners on the *second*-serving team. With A-B versus C-D, if the serving sequence during the set was A-C-B-D the sequence becomes A-D-B-C in the tie-break.)

VASSS NO AD SCORING

The No-Ad procedure is simply what the name implies: the first player to win four points wins the game, the 7th point of a game becoming a game point for each player. The receiver has the choice of advantage court or deuce court to which the service is to be delivered on the 7th point. If a No-Ad set reaches 6-games all a tie-break shall be used, which is normally the 9-point tie-break.

Note: The score-calling may be either in the conventional terms or in simple numbers, i.e., "zero, one, two, three, game" at the option of the tournament management.

CAUTIONARY NOTE

Any ITF-sponsored tournament should get special authorization from ITF before using No-Ad.

If you have a rules problem, send full details, enclosing a stamped self-addressed envelope, to Nick Powel, USTA Tennis Rules Committee, 3147 South 14th St., Arlington, VA, 22204, and you will be sent a prompt explanation.

GOVERNING BODY

United States Tennis Association, Inc., 51 East 42nd St., New York, NY 10017

Note: The national administration of the United States Tennis Association (USTA) is effected by four national offices, each with its distinct functions. Requests for information concerning various tennis publications, film libraries, clinics and workshops, school programs, etc., as well as the annual rules publication should be directed to USTA Center for Education and Recreational Tennis, 729 Alexander Road, Princeton, NJ 08540.

As the national governing body for tennis recognized by the U.S. Olympic Committee, the USTA is represented in the world's governing body for tennis, the International Tennis Federation (ITF). The ITF sets the rules for tennis throughout the world and advances the interests of tennis from an international point of view. The USTA is one of the largest volunteer organizations in the United States, with an estimated 10,000 individuals working at the district, sectional, and national levels. The national organization is divided geographically into 17 sections and 60 districts for administration of tennis affairs. The scope of activities directed by the USTA extends from assisting local communities in setting up beginners' programs to conducting the U.S. Open Tennis Championships. Leagues, tournaments, and clinics are conducted for all ages and for disabled players. The USTA works closely with tennis clubs, public facilities, educational institutions, recreation departments, youth organizations, camps, and resorts to promote the development of recreational and competitive tennis.

MAGAZINES

Tennis USA, 3 Park Avenue, New York, NY 10016

World Tennis Magazine, 3 Park Avenue, New York, NY 10016

• TRACK AND FIELD •

(Rules summary by author)

☐

Note: The standards as identified herein for Track and Field follow those adopted by the International Amateur Athletic Federation (I.A.A.F.). The numerous events and the varying specifications to be found at the different levels of competition, as illustrated in the accompanying table, are much too extensive for inclusion here.

Track and Field, or Athletics as commonly termed internationally, consists of many forms of athletic performance involving running, jumping and throwing. These activities or events may be viewed as separate sports in themselves or they may be viewed collectively as the sport. While the common practice is to refer to Track and Field (Athletics) as a team sport, most participants actually concentrate on one or two events and consider the event(s) as their sport.

Although Track and Field competition is concerned with basic running, jumping and throwing contests, the rules and adopted procedures are extremely lengthy and complex due to the numerous recognized events, the large number of participants in a single meet, the standardization of equipment and facilities required, the particular requirements of each event and the transposing of individual scoring to team scoring.

A Track and Field meet is normally conducted and scored on a team basis but it is actually a series of individual contests in which the results are summed to produce a team total. Some special meets are conducted as individual meets in which a single athlete may enter and may choose to only compete in a single event.

Track and Field meets are subject to considerable variation regarding the events to be contested and the number of participants to take part. Unless a meet is a recognized conference, state, national or international competition, the meet organizers will determine the events to be included and the number of participants to take part.

As indicated in the accompanying table there are some 60 recognized track and field events which are commonly grouped into 12 major areas of competition. Since the recognized events at the various levels of competition far exceed the number that can be included in a single meet, the selection of events is normally based on age, sex, facilities, interest, variety from major events, number of participants and time available. Cross Country is normally conducted as a special meet and Road Races and Race Walking are frequently conducted as special meets.

TRACK AND LANES

1. The standard outdoor track is an oval measuring 400 meters in total length and 7.32 meters in width.

2. The surface is normally composed of finely crushed cinders or one of the modern all-weather synthetic compositions.

3. The track is marked off in at least 6 lanes or preferably 8 lanes 1.25m in width. The lines are 50mm in width.

Table T.9   Track and Field Events

M—Men
W—Women

Events	International		College		High School		Outdoor	Indoor
	M	W	M	W	M	W		
Sprints/Dashes								
55m (60 yd.)	X	X	X	X	X	X		X
100m (100 yd.)	X	X	X	X	X	X	X	
200m (220 yd.)	X	X	X	X	X	X	X	X
300m			X	X				X
400m (440 yd.)	X	X	X	X	X	X	X	X
500m (500 yd.)			X	X	X	X		X
600m (600 yd.)			X	X	X	X		X
Middle Distances								
800m (880 yd.)	X	X	X	X	X	X	X	X
1000m	X	X					X	X
1500m	X	X	X	X			X	X
Distance								
1600m (1-mile)	X	X	X	X	X	X	X	X
2000m	X	X					X	X
3000m	X	X	X	X			X	X
3200m (2-miles)					X	X	X	X
5000m (3-miles)	X	X					X	X
10000m (6-miles)	X	X					X	X
Steeplechase								
2000m			X				X	
3000m	X		X				X	
Road Races								
5000m (5km)	X	X					X	
10000m (10km)	X	X					X	
15000m (15km)	X	X					X	
20000m (20km)	X	X					X	
1-Hour	X	X					X	
Half Marathon								
25000m (25km)	X	X					X	
30000m (30km)	X	X					X	
Marathon								
42.195km	X	X	X	X			X	
Cross Country	X	X	X	X	X	X	X	
Hurdles								
55m (60yd.) 39"/36"	X	X	X	X	X	X		X
55m (60 yd.) 33"		X		X		X		X
75 or 100m (80 or 110 yd.) 33"						X	X	

Events	International		College		High School		Outdoor	Indoor
	M	W	M	W	M	W		
100m 33″		X		X		X	X	
110m (120yd.) High	X		X		X		X	
300m (330yd.) Low or Intermediate					X	X	X	
400m (440 yd.) Low		X		X			X	
or Intermediate		X		X			X	
Relays								
4×100 (400m)	X	X		X	X	X	X	
4×200 (800m)	X	X	X	X	X	X	X	X
Sprint Medley			X	X	X	X	X	X
4×400 (1600m)	X	X	X	X	X	X	X	X
Shuttle Hurdle (4×110)			X	X			X	
4×800m (3200m)			X	X			X	X
4×1500m (6000m)			X	X			X	X
Distance Medley			X	X			X	X
Jumping								
High Jump	X	X	X	X	X	X	X	X
Long Jump	X	X	X	X	X	X	X	X
Pole Vault	X		X		X		X	X
Triple Jump	X	X	X	X	X	X	X	X
Throwing								
Discus	X	X	X	X	X	X	X	
Hammer	X		X				X	
Javelin	X	X	X	X	X	X	X	
Shot	X	X	X	X	X	X	X	X
35 lb. Weight	X		X					X
Combined Competition								
Decathlon	X		X		X		X	
Heptathlon		X		X		X	X	
Pentathlon	X	X	X	X	X	X	X	X
Walking								
5000m	X	X	X	X	X	X	X	
10000m	X	X	X	X			X	
20km	X	X					X	
Two Hour	X	X					X	
30km	X	X					X	
50km	X	X					X	

a. An extended straightaway section is provided at one end of the oval to provide for the 100m dash to be run on a straightaway.

4. The direction of the running shall be left hand inside.

GENERAL RULES

1. Clothing. Competitors must wear clean clothing that is designed and worn so as not to be objectionable.

2. Shoes. Competitors may wear footwear on one or both feet or may compete in bare feet. The sole and heel of shoes may have spikes not to exceed more than 25mm in length. The length of spikes for all-weather synthetic tracks is restricted to 9mm. The sole and/or heel may have grooves, ridges or protuberances provided construction is the same or similar to that of the sole. The total thickness may not exceed 13mm.

3. Competitors' Numbers. Each competitor must be provided with two numbers to be worn on the breast and back.

4. Simultaneous Entries. A competitor entered in more than one event taking place simultaneously may be permitted to take his or her trials in an order different from that decided previous to the meet.

TRACK EVENTS

1. Start.

a. The start and finish shall be indicated by a line 0.05m in width. In all races not run in lanes the starting line shall be curved so that all runners start the same distance from the finish.

b. The starting for all races will be the report of a pistol.

c. For all races up to and including 400m (including relays) the words of the starter shall be "On your marks", "Set", and when all competitors are steady, the pistol shall be fired. In races longer than 400m, the words shall be "On your marks" and when all competitors are steady, the pistol shall be fired.

d. If, for any reason, the starter is not satisfied that all is ready he or she shall order the competitors to stand up.

(1) In all races up to and including 400m where a crouch start must be used, both hands must be in contact with the ground when the competitor is in the "Set" position.

(2) Competitors must not touch either the start line or the ground in front of it with their hands or feet when on their marks.

(3) On the command "On your marks" or "Set", as the case may be, all competitors shall at once and without delay assume their full and final "Set" position. Failure to comply with this command after a reasonable time shall constitute a false start.

(4) If a competitor, after the command "On your marks", disturbs the other competitors in the race through sound or otherwise, it may be considered a false start.

(5) If a competitor leaves his or her marks with hand or foot after the words "On your marks" or "Set", as the case may be, and before the report of the pistol it shall be considered a false start.

(6) Any competitor making a false start must be warned and will be disqualified if he or she is responsible for a second false start.

(7) If in the opinion of the Starter, the start was not fair, he or she shall recall the competitors by firing a pistol.

e. Starting blocks must be used for all races up to and including 400 meters (including the first leg of the 4x200m and 4x400m Relays) but may not be used for any other race.

2. Finish.

a. Two white posts (1.4m in height, 80mm in width, 20mm in thickness) shall be positioned 30cm from the edge of the track to denote the extremities of the finish line.

b. Competitors shall be placed in the order in which their "torso" (as distinguished from head, neck, arms, legs, hands or feet) reaches the vertical plane of the nearer edge of the finish line.

c. In races decided on the basis of the distance covered in a fixed period of time, the Starter shall fire the pistol exactly one minute before the end of the race to alert competitors and judges that the race is nearing its end. As the pistol is then fired at the exact time to end the race, the judge (one for each competitor) must mark the spot of the last footprint of the competitor at the report of the pistol.

3. Scoring. Unless otherwise agreed upon by the competing teams, the number of team points allotted for place finish is as follows:

a. Two teams with 2 competitors in each event: 5, 3, 2, 1

b. Three teams with 2 competitors in each event: 7, 5, 4, 3, 2, 1

Two teams with 3 competitors in each event: 7, 5, 4, 3, 2, 1

Six teams with 1 competitor in each event: 7, 5, 4, 3, 2, 1

c. Relay races with 2 teams: 5, 2

Relay races with 3 teams: 7, 4, 2

Relay races with 6 teams: 7, 5, 4, 3, 2, 1

4. Obstructions. Any competitor jostling or obstructing another competitor is subject to disqualification. If any act of disqualification affects the performance of another competitor, the Referee may order the race re-held excluding the violator or may permit the offended competitor to compete in a subsequent round of the race.

5. Running in Lanes. In all races run in lanes, competitors must stay within their assigned lane from start to finish. If a competitor is forced outside his or her lane by another competitor and no material advantage is gained, the competitor shall not be disqualified.

6. Check Marks. Except for relay races, the use of check marks or placing objects alongside the track for assistance is prohibited.

7. Rounds and Heats. Preliminary rounds (heats) shall be held in track events in which the number of competitors exceeds the number that can be accommodated in a single round. Members of the same team shall be disbursed, as far as possible, in different heats. Heats should be arranged to insure not less than six competitors qualify for the final. It is also expected that previous performance of competitors will be considered in the placement in order to insure that the best performers will reach the final. It is recommended that at least three, whenever possible, in each heat should qualify for the next round. At least first and second in each heat should qualify for the next round.

In any event where all competitors cannot be placed in the first row, the draw for stations will allow for each team to have one competitor in the first row with additional starters from the same team placed behind in the same order.

8. Draw for Lanes. When it is necessary to hold successive rounds of a race for events between 100m to 800m inclusive, lanes should be drawn as follows:

a. In the first round, each competitor will draw for lane order.

b. In the following rounds, two draws are made:

(1) one for the athletes or teams with the four best times to determine the placings in lanes 3, 4, 5 and 6.

(2) the second draw will be for the athletes or teams with the four slowest times to determine the placing in lanes 1, 2, 7 and 8.

9. Time Between Rounds. The recommended minimum time lapse between rounds for various events is:

Up to 200 meters . . . . .45 minutes

Over 200 meters to 1000 meters . . . . .90 minutes

Over 1000 meters . . . . .Not on the same day

10. Assistance to Athletes. Except in Road Races and Walking events, no assistance conveyed by any means including technical devices may be given contestants. Assistance also includes pacing in running events by persons not participating in the races or lapped competitors.

FIELD EVENTS

1. Competing Order. The competitors shall compete in the order drawn by lot.

2. Delay. Competitors are expected to take their trials without unreasonable delay. Once the official indicates to the competitor that all is ready for the trial to begin, the time allowed begins and the competitor must begin the trial before the allowed time elapses. A delay will result in the trial being disallowed and recorded as a fault. A second delay will result in the competitor being debarred from taking further trials. Although not imperative, the following times should not be exceeded:

a. Preliminary trials in all field events except the Pole Vault—1-1/2 minutes.

b. Preliminary trials in Pole Vault—2 minutes. (Time begins when uprights have been adjusted according to previous wishes of the competitor. Further adjustments must be done during the 2 minutes.)

c. In the final stages of the competition when only 2 or 3 competitors remain in the competition the time is extended to 3 minutes in the High Jump and 4 minutes in the Pole Vault.

3. Qualifying Competition. If necessary in field events, qualifying competition may be held to decide who shall compete in the competition proper. Performance accomplished shall not be considered part of the competition proper.

4. Wind Information. A wind sock should be placed near the take-off ground in all jumping events to indicate to competitors the force and direction of the wind.

5. In jumping events, the minimum length of the runway should not be less than 40m while the maximum length is unlimited. The minimum width of the runway should not be less than 1.22m.

6. No marks may be placed on the runways but may be placed alongside the runways.

7. Once competition has begun in an event, practice is not permitted in the area.

8. A competitor will be credited with the best of all his or her jumps or throws including those taken to break a first place tie.

9. Where there are more than eight competitors, each competitor shall be allowed three trials and the eight competitors with the best performances shall be allowed three additional trials.

HURDLE RACES

1. Ten flights of hurdles are set out in each lane at the distances indicated in the following table:

Distance of race	Height of hurdle	Distance from start line to first hurdle	Distance between hurdles	Distance from last hurdle to finish line
(men)				
110m	1.067	13.72	9.14	14.02
400m	0.914	45	35	40
(women)				
100m	0.840	13	8.5	10.5
400m	0.762	45	35	40

2. All races shall be run in lanes with each competitor keeping to his or her own lane throughout.

3. The knocking down of hurdles does not disqualify a competitor nor prevent a record from being made.

4. A competitor may not trail a foot or leg alongside any hurdle or jump any hurdle not in his or her own lane or, in the opinion of the Referee, deliberately knock down any hurdle by foot or hand. Violations will result in disqualification.

RELAY RACES

1. The course for Relay Races should be marked with lines 50mm wide to designate the distances of the four stages of the race and to denote the scratch line.

2. Lines 50mm wide should also be drawn 10m before and after the scratch line to denote the take-over (exchange) zone. The baton must be passed within the exchange zone. The lines are included within the zone.

a. In races up to 4x200m, the runners (other than the first runner) may start their run not more than 10m outside the exchange zone. A mark should be made in each lane to denote this extended limit.

b. All relay races are not restricted to lanes from start to finish, but rather, at varying distances, only portions of the race must be in designated lanes.

3. It is permissible in relay races for a competitor to make a check mark within his or her own lane.

4. The baton must be carried in the hand throughout the race and must be passed (not thrown) within the exchange zone.

a. If the baton is dropped, it must be recovered by the competitor who dropped it.

b. The baton is considered passed when it is in the hand of the receiving runner. In regard to the exchange zone, it is the position of the baton which is decisive, and not the position of the body or limbs of the competitors.

5. After lanes have ceased to be used, waiting runners are free to move to an inner position as incoming teammates arrive, provided this can be done without fouling.

6. After passing the baton, the competitor should remain in his or her lane to avoid obstructing other competitors.

7. Any assistance such as pushing-off will result in disqualification.

STEEPLECHASE

1. The standard distances are: 3000m and 2000m (Junior events only).

2. There are 28 hurdle jumps and 7 water jumps included in the 3000m event and 18 hurdle jumps and 5 water jumps in the 2000m event.

3. The water jump shall be the fourth jump in each lap.

4. The exact length of laps or the precise position of the water jump cannot be specified since the water jump must be constructed inside or, preferably outside the track which will lessen or lengthen the standard distance of the laps. The two essential guidelines to be followed are: 1) there must be enough distance from the starting line to the first hurdle to prevent overcrowding and 2) there should be approximately 68m from the last hurdle to the finish line.

5. The distance from the start to the beginning of the first lap should not include any jumps, the hurdles being removed until competitors have entered the first lap.

6. The competitor may jump or vault over each hurdle or place a foot on the hurdles.

7. The hurdles shall be 0.914m high and at least 3.96m in width. The top bar shall be 127mm square. The weight of the hurdle and supporting base should be adequate to provide stability for runners to step on top of the hurdle.

8. The water jump should be 3.66m in length and width.

a. The water should be level with the track surface and 0.70m deep at the hurdle end and slope upward to the level of the track at the farther end.

b. Each competitor must go over or through the water.

ROAD RACES

1. The standard distances for men and women shall be 15km, 20km, Half Marathon, 25km, 30km and Marathon Race (42.195km).

2. The race may be run over a variety of surfaces such as regular streets and roads or, if duly marked, bicycle or foot paths but not on soft ground. Care must be taken to insure the safety of the competitors and, where possible, provisions should be made to close roads to traffic.

3. The distance in kilometers on the route shall be displayed to all competitors.

4. Refreshments shall be provided by the organizers of races over 20km at approximately every 5km.

a. In addition to the refreshment stations, sponging points, where only water is supplied, shall be provided midway between refreshment stations.

b. Refreshments which may be provided by the competitors themselves or by the organizers at the designated stations shall be easily accessible for the competitors or they may actually be put into the hands of the competitor.

c. Refreshments are not to be taken any place other than the points designated.

CROSS-COUNTRY RACES

Due to the nature and varying circumstances of cross-country running, it is not practical to establish rigid regulations for standardization of the sport. The following rules serve as guidelines for the accepted practice in the conduct of the sport.

1. The season normally extends throughout the winter months after the close of the track and field season.

2. The race should be run over a course of open country, fields and grasslands. The course must be clearly marked. It is recommended that the left side of the course be marked with red flags and the right side with white flags. Flags should be visible from a distance of 125 meters. Extremely high obstacles, deep ditches, dangerous ascents or descents, thick undergrowth and, in general, any obstacle which constitutes a difficulty beyond the aim of the competition should be avoided.

3. Distances:

a. Seniors: not less than 7km, nor more than 14km;

b. Juniors: not less than 5km, nor more than 10km;

c. Women: not less than 2km, nor more than 5km;

d. International races: Seniors approximately 12km; Juniors approximately 8km; and Women approximately 4km.

4. Regulations for number of entries and number of runners to score are subject to differ from one competition to another. The I.A.A.F. rulings in this regard are as follows:

a. In Senior races, not more than 12 competitors can be entered of which not less than 6 nor more than 9 of these shall be permitted to start the race of whom 6 will score.

b. For Women's and Junior races, teams of not less than 4 nor more than 8 competitors may be entered of which not more than 6 shall be permitted to start the race and only 4 will score.

c. In some races, it may be possible to permit individuals to enter on their own or to permit the entry of members of a depleted team (inadequate scoring number) to compete on an individual basis.

5. Positions for the start shall be drawn and members of each team shall be lined up behind each other.

6. No assistance, nor refreshments may be provided competitors during the progress of the race.

7. Scoring.

a. The finishing places of each eligible scoring competitor for each team are added together and the team with the lowest aggregate is declared the winner.

b. In case of a tie score, it will be resolved in favor of the team whose last scoring member finishes nearer first place.

WALKING

1. Definition.

a. Race walking is a progression of steps so taken that unbroken contact with the ground is maintained.

(1) During each step, the advancing foot must make contact with the ground before the rear foot leaves the ground.

(2) The supporting leg must be straightened (i.e., not bent at the knee) for at least one moment when in the vertical upright position.

2. Warning. Competitors must be warned by a Judge when they are in danger of failing to comply with the definition of race walking and the Judge must inform the Chief Judge of his action. Competitors are not entitled to a second warning from the same Judge for the same offense.

3. Disqualification.

a. Normally, a competitor is entitled a warning before a disqualification is given.

b. When, in the opinion of three Judges, a competitor fails to comply with the definition of race walking during any part of the competition, he or she shall be disqualified.

c. A white sign with the symbol of the offense on each side, must be shown to the competitor, when a warning is given. A red sign is used to indicate disqualification. Only the Chief Judge may employ the red sign.

4. Refreshment and Sponging Stations.

a. Sponging and drinking water stations should be provided at suitable intervals (considering weather conditions) for walking events of 10km or more.

b. In races of more than 20km refreshment stations should be provided every 5kms. Refreshments, which may be provided by the competitor or the race organizers, shall be available at the station assigned by the competitor. The refreshment shall be placed in a manner to be easily accessible to the competitors or may be put into the hands of the competitor. Refreshments are not to be taken any place other than the assigned stations.

5. Course. The circuit for the 20km walk should be a maximum of 2500m. The circuit for the 50km should be 2500m with a maximum of 5000m if held on an "out and back" course.

HIGH JUMP

1. Rules that apply to more than one event, as included in the General Rules section, are not repeated here.

2. A competitor is disqualified from further jumping after three consecutive failures at any height. (A competitor may forgo his second or third attempt at a particular height [after failing] and still jump at a subsequent height.)

3. The jump must be made with a take-off from one foot.

4. It is a failed attempt if the bar is knocked off the supports or if the jumper touches the ground beyond the plane of the uprights with any part of the body, without first clearing the bar.

5. No practice is permitted on the runway or take-off area once the competition has begun.

6. Following each round, the bar will be raised not less than 2cm until only one competitor remains or there is a tie.

7. A competitor may commence jumping at any height previously announced by the Chief Judge and may jump at his or her own discretion at any subsequent height.

8. Care must be taken by the Judges to insure that the underside and front of the cross-bar are distinguishable, and the bar is always replaced in the exact same fashion.

9. A single remaining competitor is entitled to continue jumping until disqualified.

10. The uprights shall not be moved during the competition unless the Referee decides the take-off or landing area is unsuitable. (Such change will only be made at the end of a round.)

11. The competitor may place marks for assistance in his or her run-up and take-off and may place an object such as a small handkerchief on the cross-bar for sighting.

12. The minimum length of the runway shall be 15m and the maximum length unlimited.

13. The cross-bar may be of wood, metal, or other suitable material, circular in cross-section. The bar shall be between 3.98m and 4.02m in length and weigh a maximum of 2.0kg. The diameter shall be at least 25mm but not more than 30mm.

14. The supports for the cross-bars shall be flat and rectangular, 40mm wide and 60mm long.

15. The landing area should measure 5m in width and 3m in depth.

POLE VAULT

1. Rules that apply to more than one event, as included in the General Rules section, are not repeated here.

2. Competitors may have the uprights moved in either direction, but not more than 0.4m in the direction of the runway, and not more than 0.8m to the landing area from the inside edge of the box. It is the responsibility of the competitor, before the competition begins, to inform the official of the position of the uprights he or she desires.

3. It is permissible to use substances on the hands or pole which will provide for a better grip. Tape may not be used on the hands except to cover an open wound.

4. The attempted vault is a failure if the competitor: a. knocks the bar off the supports; b. touches the ground beyond the vertical plane through the upper part of the stopboard with any part of the body or with the pole, without first clearing the bar; c. after leaving the ground, moving the lower hand above the upper hand or moving the upper hand higher on the pole.

5. An attempt will not be counted as a failure should the competitor's pole break.

6. No one shall be allowed to touch the pole unless it is falling away from the bar or uprights. Should the pole be touched and in the opinion of the Referee, but for the intervention, the bar would have been knocked off, the vault will be judged a failure.

7. The pole may be of any material or combination of materials and of any length or diameter but the surface must be smooth. Competitors may use their own poles.

8. The pole vault box shall be constructed of some suitable rigid material, sunk level with the ground. If constructed of wood, the bottom shall be lined with sheet metal for a distance of 800mm from the front of the box. The box shall be 1m in length and 600mm in width at the front end tapering to 150mm in width at the bottom of the stopboard.

LONG JUMP

1. Rules that apply to more than one event, as included in the General Rules section, are not repeated here.

2. An attempt shall be scored as a failure if the competitor:

a. touches the ground beyond the take-off line with any part of the body, whether running up without jumping or in the act of jumping;

b. takes off from outside either end of the board, whether beyond or behind the take-off line extended;

c. in the course of landing, touches the ground outside the landing area nearer to the take-off than the nearest break in the landing area made by the jump;

d. after a completed jump, walks back through the landing area;

e. employs any form of somersaulting.

3. If the competitor takes off before reaching the board it shall not for that reason be counted as a failure.

4. The take-off point shall be a board sunk level with the runway and the landing area. The precise take-off line is the edge of the board nearest the landing area.

a. It is recommended that a board of plasticine be installed immediately beyond the take-off line in order to record the competitor's footspring when he has foot-faulted.

b. If it is not possible to install a board of plasticine, it is recommended that soft earth or sand be sprinkled immediately beyond the take-off line over a width of 100mm.

5. The distance between the take-off board and the end of the landing area shall be at least 10 meters. The take-off board shall not be less than 1m from the edge of the landing area.

6. The take-off board shall be made of wood or other suitable rigid material measuring 1.21m to 1.22m in length and 198mm to 202mm in width. It shall be painted white.

7. The width of the landing area shall be a minimum of 2.75m.

8. All measurements shall be taken from the nearest break in the sand of the landing area, made by any part of the body or limbs, to the take-off line. It is essential that the surface of the sand be accurately controlled to keep it level with the top of the take-off board.

TRIPLE JUMP

1. Rules that apply to more than one event, as included in the General Rules section, are not repeated here.

2. The hop (of the hop, step and jump) shall be made so that the competitor lands first upon the same foot as that from which he has taken off; in the step he or she shall land on the other foot from which the jump is taken.

3. A jump will be judged a failure if the "sleeping" (non-jump) leg touches the ground.

4. Except for No. 2 and 3 above, the rules of failure for the Long Jump apply.

5. The take-off board installation, landing area and measuring for the Long Jump apply except the distance between the take-off board and the end of the landing area shall be at least 21 meters and the take-off board shall be not less than 13m from the edge of the landing area.

SHOT PUT

1. The official shot for men's competition shall be 120mm ($\pm$10mm) in diameter and weigh 7.27kg ($\pm$.01kg). The shot for women's competitions shall be 102.5mm ($\pm$7.5mm) in diameter and weigh 4.015kg ($\pm$.010kg).

2. Putting the shot shall be made from a circle 2.135m in diameter.

a. The circle may be made of band iron, steel or other suitable material 6mm in thickness and shall be painted white.

b. A stopboard, securely fastened to the ground, shall be located on the edge of the front half of the circle. The board shall be shaped in an arc so that the inner edge coincides with the inner edge of the circle. The board shall measure 112mm to 300mm wide, 1.21m to 1.23m long on the inside and 98mm to 102mm high.

c. The interior surface of the circle may be concrete, asphalt or other firm nonslippery material. The competitor may not spray or spread any substance in the circle nor on his shoes.

d. The putting area shall consist of cinders or grass or other suitable material on which the shot will make an imprint.

3. The competitor must commence the put from a stationary position inside the circle. The put must be from the shoulder with hand only. The shot shall touch or be in close proximity to the chin and the hand must not be dropped below this position during the putting motion. The shot must not be taken behind the line of the shoulders.

4. It is permissible to touch the inside of the iron band or the stopboard but touching the top of the iron band or stopboard will be judged as a foul throw.

a. The competitor may interrupt a trial once started provided there has been no infringement of the rules.

b. The competitor must not leave the circle until the shot has touched the ground.

5. The shot must fall within an area marked by a sector of 40 degrees set out on the ground so that the radii lines cross at the center of the circle. The distance between the two sector lines 20m from the center of the circle should be exactly 13.68m.

6. The measurement of each put shall be made immediately after the put from the nearest mark made by the shot to the inside circumference of the circle along a line from the mark made by the shot to the center of the circle.

7. No device of any kind which in any way may assist the competitor's performance is allowed. Gloves are not allowed, nor is the taping of two or more fingers together. Suitable substance on the hand to improve the grip is permitted. The competitor may wear a leather belt or other suitable material to protect the spine from injury.

8. Following a completed put, the shot must be carried back to the circle and never thrown.

DISCUS

1. The weight of the discus for men's competition shall be 2.015kg ($\pm$.010kg); women's competition—1.015kg ($\pm$.010kg).

2. The rules for throwing the Shot apply except:

a. the discus circle is 2.50m ($\pm$5mm) in diameter and the stopboard is eliminated.

3. Discus throws shall be made from an enclosure or cage to insure the safety of spectators, officials and competitors. The recommended specifications for cages depend upon the nature of the total facility including spectator accommodations. Basically, the cage should be U-shaped consisting of 6 panels of netting 3.17m wide. The width of the mouth should be 6m, positioned 5m in front of the center of the throwing circle. The minimum height of the netting panels should be at least 4m. The netting may be made from suitable natural or synthetic fiber cord or, from high tensile steel wire.

HAMMER

1. The hammer shall consist of three parts: a metal head, a wire and a grip.

a. The head shall be of solid iron or other metal not softer than brass and spherical in shape with a 120mm ($\pm$10mm) diameter.

b. The wire shall be a single straight length of steel wire not less than 3mm in diameter or No. 11 Standard Wire Gauge. The attachment of the wire to the head shall be by means of either a plain or ball bearing swivel.

c. The grip may be either of single or double loop construction but must be rigid and without any kind of hinging joints. The grip must be attached to the wire to increase the overall length of the hammer but a swivel may not be used.

2. The hammer must have a length of 1195mm ($\pm$20mm) and weigh 7.275kg ($\pm$.010kg).

3. The rules for throwing the discus apply to the hammer throw except:

a. gloves are permitted for protection of the hands.

b. taping of individual fingers is permitted.

c. prior to the preliminary swings or turns, the competitor is permitted to put the head of the hammer on the ground inside or outside the circle.

d. it is not a foul throw if the head of the hammer touches the ground during preliminary swings or turns, but having done so a foul will be charged if the competitor should stop the throw to begin again.

e. should the hammer break during the throw or while in flight it will not count as a throw.

JAVELIN

1. The javelin for men's competition shall weigh 815gm ($\pm$10gm) and be 2.65m in length; the weight for women's competition is 612.5gm ($\pm$7.5gm) and the length 2.25m ($\pm$.05).

2. The rules for throwing the shot apply to the javelin throw except:

a. the javelin must be held at the grip and thrown over the shoulder or upper part of the throwing arm (overhand throw) and must not be slung or hurled.

b. the tip of the metal head must strike the ground before any other part of the javelin for the throw to be counted as valid.

c. the competitor must not cross either of the parallel lines.

d. at no time after preparing to throw, until the javelin has been discharged into the air, may the competitor turn completely around, so that his or her back is towards the throwing arc.

e. if the javelin breaks at any time during the course of the throw, it shall not count as a trial provided the throw was made in accordance to the rules.

f. the length of the runway shall not be more than 36.5m but not less than 30m.

COMBINED COMPETITIONS

1. The Decathlon and Pentathlon are recognized as men's events.

a. The Decathlon consists of ten events which are held on two consecutive days in the following order: First-day—100m, long jump, putting the shot, high jump and 400m; Second-day—110m hurdles, throwing the discus, pole vault, throwing the javelin, and 1500m.

b. The Pentathlon consists of five events which are held on one day in the following order: long jump, throwing the javelin, 200m, throwing the discus, and 1500m.

2. The Heptathlon is recognized as a women's event.

a. The Heptathlon consists of seven events which are held on two consecutive days in the following order: First-day—100m hurdles, high jump, putting the shot, and 200m; Second-day—long jump, javelin throw and 800m.

3. Whenever possible, there should be an interval of at least 30 minutes between events for each individual competitor. The order of competing may be drawn before each separate event. Competitors are placed in groups of 5 or more, as decided by the Referee, and never less than four in each group.

4. In the last event of Combined Event Competition, the heats should be arranged so that one group contains the leading competitors after the previous events.

5. The standard rules for each event shall apply except for the following:

a. Only three trials will be allowed in the long jump and each of the throwing events.

b. In the running trials and the hurdles, a competitor will be disqualified in any event in which he or she makes three false starts.

c. Any competitor failing to start or make a trial in one of the events shall be disqualified from the remaining events and shall not be considered in the final classification.

6. The scores separately and combined should be announced to the competitors after the completion of each event.

7. The winner shall be the competitor who scored the highest number of points in the total number of events as awarded on the basis of the Scoring Tables.

GOVERNING BODIES

National Collegiate Athletic Association, P.O. Box 1906, Nall Ave. at 63rd, Mission, KS 66201

National Federation of State High School Associations, P.O. Box 20626, 11724 Plaza Circle, Kansas City, MO 64195

The Athletic Congress, P.O. Box 120, Indianapolis, IN 46206

MAGAZINES

Track & Field News, Track & Field News, Inc., Box 296, Los Altos, CA 94022

Track Technique: Official Technical Publication, (The Athletic Congress—USA) Track & Field News, Inc., Box 296, Los Altos, CA 94022

• TRAMPOLINING •

F.I.T. COMPETITION RULES FOR TRAMPOLINING
VALID FROM 1.1.1987

(Reproduced by permission of the United States Acrogymnastics Federation*
in affiliation with the Federation of International Trampoline)

☐

These Competition Rules are binding for all competitions and championships of the International Trampoline Federation (F.I.T.) and its members.

The following documents should be read in conjunction with these Rules:

Championship Regulations—Regulations for World, Intercontinental and Continental Championships

F.I.T. Norms—Dimensions and Tolerances for International Competition Equipment

F.I.T. Guide to Judging—Judges' Guide and Interpretations to current Rules.

A. GENERAL RULES

1. INDIVIDUAL COMPETITION

1.1 Trampoline competitions consist of one Compulsory and two Voluntary routines.

1.2 Preliminaries

1.2.1 Compulsory routine

The starting order for the compulsory routine is decided by a draw as detailed in the Championship Regulations.

1.2.2 Voluntary routine

The starting order for the Voluntary routines will be in order of merit, the competitor with the lowest Compulsory score going first. In the event of ties, the starting order will be decided by a draw.

1.3 Finals

1.3.1 The competitors with the ten best scores from the Preliminaries will go forward to the final.

1.3.2 The starting order for the Final will be order of merit, the competitor with the lowest Preliminary score going first. In the event of ties, the starting order will be decided by a draw.

---

*See page 612 for additional information.

2. Team Competition

2.1 A Trampoline team consists of a minimum of three ladies or three men and a maximum of four ladies or four men.

2.2 Every member of the team will perform one Compulsory and two Voluntary routines.

2.3 System of Scoring

The Team score for each round (Compulsory, first Voluntary, second Voluntary) will be the sum of the three highest scores obtained by the members of the team in each round.

2.3.1 At World, Intercontinental and Continental Championships only the Compulsory routine and the first Voluntary routine will be counted; otherwise the team results will be calculated as per Rule 2.3.

3. SYNCHRONISED COMPETITION

3.1 A Synchronised pair consists of two ladies or two men.

3.2 A competitor may only compete in one Synchronised pairing.

3.3 Synchronised competitions will consist of one Compulsory routine and two Voluntary routines in exactly the same way as the Individual competition. (See Rules 1.2.1, 1.2.2, 1.3.1 and 1.3.2.)

3.4 The compulsory skills set for the Individual competition are also the compulsory skills for the Synchronised competition.

3.5 Partners must do the same movement at the same time in the same rhythm and must start facing in the same direction. They need not twist in the same direction.

4. WINNERS

4.1 The winner is the competitor, pair or team with the highest overall number of points.

4.2 Competitors, pairs or teams with the same scores will be given the same place.

4.3 Medals will be awarded according to the Championship Regulations.

5. ROUTINES

5.1 Compulsory and Voluntary routines each consist of ten skills.

5.2 Second attempts at routines are not allowed.

5.2.1 If a competitor is obviously disturbed in a routine (faulty equipment or substantial external influence), the Superior Judge may allow another attempt.

5.2.2 Spectator noise, applause and the like would not normally constitute a disturbance.

6. DRESS FOR COMPETITORS AND SPOTTERS

6.1 Male Competitors:

Uniform leotard.

White gym trousers.

White trampoline shoes and/or white foot covering.

6.2 Female Competitors:

Uniform leotard.

White trampoline shoes and/or white foot covering of no more than ankle length.

6.3 Spotters:

Track suit and gym shoes.

6.4 The wearing of jewelry or watches is not permitted during the competition. Rings without gemstones may be worn if they are taped.

6.5 Any violation of Rules 6.1, 6.2 and 6.4 may result in disqualification from the round in which the offence occurs. The decision is made by the Superior Judge.

7. COMPETITION CARDS

7.1 The Compulsory routine, with each compulsory skill marked with an asterisk (*) and the Voluntary routine with Difficulty value, must be written down on the competition card.

7.1.1 Only the official terminology or the F.I.T. numeric system may be used to describe the skills written on the competition card.

7.2 The competition card must be handed in at the time and place specified by the Organising Committee. The Chief Recorder is responsible for ensuring that they are given to the Difficulty Judges at least two hours before the competition starts.

7.3 In the Compulsory routine, the competitor must execute the skills as written on the competition card otherwise the routine will be interrupted as per Rule 18.1.1.

7.4 In Voluntary routines, changes to the skills and the order in which they are written on the competition card are permitted.

8. TRAMPOLINES

8.1 The specifications must adhere to the F.I.T. Norms.

8.2 During Synchronised competitions the trampolines must be parallel and not staggered. The distance between them, measured from the outer edges of the frame, must be 2 metres.

9. HEIGHT OF THE HALL

9.1 The interior height of the hall, in which trampoline competitions are to take place, must be at least 8 metres.

10. SAFETY

10.1 The organiser of the competition must appoint a Floor Manager and at least eight experienced spotters for the warming up period and the competition.

10.2 Four spotters must be positioned around a trampoline while it is in use.

10.3 The Superior Judge and the Floor Manager are responsible for supervising the spotters.

10.4 The competitors must execute their routines without any external help. The Superior Judge will decide whether or not any assistance given by a spotter was necessary.

10.5 Gym mats must cover the floor around the trampoline.

10.6 Safety platforms or landing mats must be used on the ends of the trampoline. Their dimensions must adhere to the F.I.T. Norms.

10.7 A Spotter Mat may only be used by the competitor's own spotter. The dimensions of this mat must adhere to the F.I.T. Norms.

11. RECORDERS & SECRETARIAT

11.1 At World, Intercontinental and Continental Championships either the official score sheets of the F.I.T. or an approved computer program, for recording and printing the results, must be used as per 9.2.6 of the Championship Regulations.

11.2 A complete copy of the results must be sent to the President of the Technical Committee.

11.3 Duties of the Chief Recorder:

11.3.1 Collect and distribute the competition cards as per Rule 7.2.

11.3.2 Supply secretaries for the Judges.

11.3.3 Supervise the recorders.

11.3.4 Record the starting order for the Voluntary routines and determine the warm up groups.

11.3.5 Record the scores for Execution, Synchronisation and Difficulty.

11.3.6 Scrutinise and control the calculations on the competition cards and score sheets.

11.3.7 Display each competitor's total score for the round.

11.3.8 Produce a complete list of the results giving the total mark for each round, position and overall total.

12. ARBITRATION JURY

12.1 Composition:

12.1.1 Member of the Presidium or Organising Committee	1
12.1.2 Member of the Technical Committee or Organising Committee	1
12.1.3 Superior Judge	1
12.1.4 Judges	2
	—
12.1.5 Total	5

12.2 The Superior Judge is President of the Arbitration Jury and has a casting vote in the event of ties.

12.3 The Superior Judge and two other members of the Arbitration Jury will supervise the draw for the starting order for the Compulsories (see Rule 1.2.1).

12.4 The Arbitration Jury must announce the protest fee before the start of the competition and deal with any protests.

12.5 The Arbitration Jury will decide about the replacement of a Judge as per Rule 21.5.

13. PROTESTS

13.1 A protest can only be handed in by an official representative of a Federation (team manager, competitor or coach).

13.2 The written protest, with the protest fee, must be handed to the Superior Judge prior to the start of the next round. In the case of a protest concerning the final round, the protest must be submitted immediately after the end of the round.

13.3 Protests concerning the Execution and Synchronised scores can only be made in respect of a numerical error.

13.4 Protests must be dealt with by the Arbitration Jury prior to the start of the next round and their decision announced immediately.

13.5 The decision of the Arbitration Jury is final and must be abided by.

13.6 If the protest is sustained the fee will be returned. If the protest is overruled, the fee will be sent to the F.I.T. Treasurer.

B. COMPETITION PROCEDURE

14. WARMING UP

14.1 The equipment selected for the competition must be placed in the competition hall at least two hours prior to the start of the competition to enable competitors to warm up on the competition apparatus.

14.2 The competitors in each round will be divided into groups approximating 10 per group. They will be allowed one practice of 30 seconds each, prior to competing in the round.

15. START OF A ROUTINE

15.1 Each competitor will start on a signal given by the Superior Judge.

15.2 After the signal has been given (as per Rule 15.1), the competitor must initiate the first skill within one minute, otherwise there will be a deduction of 0.1 by each of the execution judges as per rule 23.4.4. If this time limit is exceeded as a result of faulty equipment or other substantial cause, the deduction of 0.1 will not apply. This decision is made by the Superior Judge.

16. REQUIRED POSITIONS DURING A ROUTINE

16.1 In all positions except straddle jumps, the feet and legs should be kept together and the feet and toes pointed.

16.2 Depending on the requirements of the movement, the body should be either tucked, piked or straight.

16.3 In the tucked and piked positions the thighs should be close to the upper body except in the twisting phase of multiple somersaults as per Rule 16.7.

16.4 In the tucked position the hands should touch the legs below the knees except in the twisting phase of multiple somersaults as per Rule 16.7.

16.5 The arms should be straight and held close to the body whenever possible.

16.6 The following defines the minimum requirements for a particular body shape:

16.6.1 Straight Position:

The angle between the upper body and thighs must be greater than 135 degrees.

16.6.2 Pike Position:

The angle between the upper body and thighs must be equal to or less than 135 degrees and the angle between the thighs and the lower legs must be greater than 135 degrees.

16.6.3 Tuck Position:

The angle between the upper body and thighs must be less than 135 degrees and the angle between the thigh and the lower leg must be less than 135 degrees.

16.7 In multiple somersaults with twists, the tuck and pike position may be modified during the twisting phase as shown in the Guide to Judging (Tuck & Pike twisting positions).

17. REPETITION OF THE SAME SKILLS

17.1 During a Voluntary routine the same skill may not be repeated otherwise the Difficulty of the repeated skill will not be counted.

17.2 Skills having the same amount of rotation but performed in the tucked, piked and straight positions are considered to be different skills and not repetitions.

17.2.1 The tucked and pucked positions are considered to be the same position.

17.3 Multiple somersaults (of more than 360 degrees) having the same number of twists and somersaults will not be considered a repetition if the twist is located in different phases of the skill.

18. INTERRUPTION TO A ROUTINE

18.1 A routine will be considered interrupted if a competitor:

18.1.1 Does not perform the Compulsory routine using the prescribed skills and in the sequence written on his competition card.

18.1.2 Obviously does not land simultaneously on both feet on the trampoline bed.

18.1.3 Does not use the elasticity of the bed after landing for the immediate continuation of the next skill.

18.1.4 Touches anything other than the trampoline bed with any part of the body.

18.1.5 Is touched by a spotter.

18.1.6 Leaves the trampoline due to insecurity.

18.1.7 Performs a different skill from that of his partner in a Synchronised routine.

18.1.7.1 If one of the competitors is more than half a skill ahead of their partner they will be deemed to have performed different skills.

18.2 No credit will be given for the skill in which the interruption occurs in respect of Rules 18.1.1, 18.1.3, 18.1.4, 18.1.5, 18.1.6 and 18.1.7.

18.3 A competitor will be judged only on the number of skills completed on the trampoline bed.

18.4 The Superior Judge will determine the maximum mark.

19. TERMINATION OF THE ROUTINE

19.1 The routine must end under control in an upright position, with both feet on the trampoline bed otherwise there will be a deduction as per Rule 23.3.2.

19.2 After the last skill in Individual competitions, the competitor is allowed to do one more jump in a stretched position (out-bounce) using the elasticity of the bed.

19.3 In Synchronised competition both competitors must either do a stretched jump, or they must both stand still, otherwise there will be a deduction as per Rule 25.3.3.

19.4 If a competitor executes more than 10 skills, a deduction of 1.0 point will be made as per Rule 23.4.3.

19.5 In the case of an interrupted routine, if the last bounce is a straight jump it will be considered an out-bounce not an intermediate jump.

19.6 After the final landing on the bed, competitors must stand upright for at least three seconds, otherwise they will receive a deduction for lack of stability as per Rule 23.3.2.2.

19.7 A routine is deemed to have ended after the three seconds, as per Rule 19.6, has elapsed.

20. SCORING

20.1 Degree of Difficulty

20.1.1 The Difficulty of each skill is calculated on the basis of the amount of twist and somersault rotation.

20.1.1.1 1/4 somersault (90 degrees)	0.1pts
20.1.1.2 1/1 somersault (360 degrees)	0.4pts
20.1.1.3 1/2 twist (180 degrees)	0.1pts
20.1.1.4 1/1 twist (360 degrees)	0.2pts

20.1.2 Skills without twist or rotation have no Difficulty value.

20.1.3 In skills combining somersault and twist, the Difficulty values of the somersault and twist are added together.

20.1.4 Somersaults executed in the straight or pike position will be awarded an extra 0.1 points provided that there is at least 1/1 somersault rotation without twist.

20.1.5 2/1 somersaults, or more, with twists, will be awarded an extra 0.1 points when executed in the piked or straight position.

20.2 Method of Scoring

20.2.1 The evaluation of Execution (form, consistency of height and control), Difficulty and Synchronisation is done in 10ths of a point.

20.2.2 Judges must write their deductions independently of each other.

20.2.3 Secretaries will be assigned to the judges. Any calculations made by the secretaries must be verified by the Judges.

20.2.4 When signalled by the Superior Judge the marks of the Judges for Execution and Synchronisation must be shown simultaneously.

20.2.5 If any of the Judges for Execution or Synchronisation fail to show their marks when signalled by the Superior Judge, the average of the other marks will be taken for the missing mark. The decision is made by the Superior Judge.

20.2.6 Evaluation of the score for Execution:

20.2.6.1 The deductions for poor Execution are subtracted from the maximum mark (see Rule 18.4).

20.2.6.2 In the Individual competition:

The highest and lowest marks of the Execution Judges are deleted. The total of the three remaining marks is the score for Execution, provided the difference between the three marks is not too great as per Rule 20.3.

20.2.6.3 In the Synchronised competition:

The highest and lowest marks of the Execution Judges for trampoline no. 1 and highest and lowest marks of the Execution Judges for trampoline no. 2 are deleted. The two remaining middle marks are added together by the recorder to give the score for Execution.

20.2.7 Evaluation of the score for Difficulty:

20.2.7.1 The Difficulty Judges (nos. 7 & 8) calculate the Difficulty of the Voluntary routine as per Rule 20.1 and enter it on the competition card.

20.2.8 Evaluation of the score for Synchronisation:

20.2.8.1 The evaluation of the Synchronised mark should be done electronically. The Superior Judge is responsible for controlling the electronic scores.

20.2.8.2 The deductions for lack of Synchronisation are subtracted from the maximum mark (see Rule 18.4) and this mark is doubled by the recorder and taken as the valid score for Synchronisation.

20.2.8.3 In the event of a breakdown or the non-availability of an electronic scoring system, the middle mark of the Judges for Synchronisation (nos. 9, 10 & 11) will be doubled by the recorder and taken as the valid score for Synchronisation.

20.2.8.3.1 If the breakdown occurs during a round, all the scores for that round will be recalculated using the marks of the Judges for Synchronisation (nos. 9, 10 & 11).

20.2.9 Evaluation of the competitor's total score for the round:

20.2.9.1 In Individual competition the Difficulty score is added to the Execution score.

20.2.9.2 In Synchronised competition the Synchronised score is added to the Execution and the Difficulty score.

20.2.9.3 The recorders will calculate the total score (Execution + Difficulty + Synchronisation) and enter it on the score sheet and the competition card.

20.2.10 All scores will be rounded to 2 decimal places. Such rounding will only be made in respect of the competitor's total score for a routine.

20.2.11 The Chief Recorder must verify the total score on the score sheets and the competiton cards.

20.2.12 The Superior Judge is responsible for determining the validity of the final scores.

20.3 Differences in Evaluation of Execution

20.3.1 In Individual competition, the permissible difference between the middle mark and either of the two remaining scores (as per Rule 20.2.6.2) is as follows:

20.3.1.1 1/10pts for middle marks equal to or greater than 9.0pts.

20.3.1.2 2/10pts for middle marks equal to or greater than 8.5 and less than 9.0pts.

20.3.1.3 3/10pts for middle marks of less than 8.5pts.

20.3.2 If either or both of the marks are not within the permissible difference then the middle mark will be multiplied by three to give the valid score for Execution.

C. COMPETITION JURY

21. COMPETITION JURY

21.1 Composition:

21.1.1 Superior Judge	1
21.1.2 Judges for Execution	6

21.1.2.1 for Individual competition (nos. 1-5)

21.1.2.2 for Synchronised competition:

Trampoline No. 1 (nos. 1, 2 & 3)

Trampoline No. 2 (nos. 4, 5 & 6)

21.1.3 Judges for Difficulty (nos. 7 & 8)	2
21.1.4 Judges for Synchronisation (nos. 9, 10 & 11)	3
21.1.5 Assistant Superior Judge	1
21.1.6 Total	13

21.2 In Synchronised competition the Assistant Superior Judge will stand beside Trampoline No. 2.

21.3 Judges nos. 1-8 must sit on the judges' platform 5 to 7 metres from Trampoline No. 1 and raised by a minimum of 1 metre.

21.4 Judges nos. 9-11 will be placed either on, or alongside, the judges' platform, so that the Trampoline bed is at eye level.

21.5 If a Judge fails to carry out his duties in a satisfactory manner he must be replaced. This decision will be made by the Arbitration Jury upon the recommendation of the Superior Judge.

21.5.1 If a Judge, who is the subject of the Arbitration Jury's discussion, is also a member of the Arbitration Jury, he may not vote on the decision.

21.5.2 If an Execution or Synchronised Judge is replaced, the Arbitration Jury may decide that his previous marks will be replaced by the average of the remaining marks (see Rule 20.2.5).

22. DUTIES OF THE SUPERIOR JUDGE

22.1 Control of facilities.

22.2 Organise the Judges' conference and the trial scoring.

22.3 Place and supervise all Judges, Spotters and Recorders.

22.4 Direct the competition.

22.5 Convene the Competition Jury.

22.6 Convene and Preside over the Arbitration Jury.

22.7 Supervise a draw for the starting order in the event of ties (see Rule 1.2.2 & 1.3.2).

22.8 Decide if a second attempt should be allowed (see Rule 5.2.1).

22.9 Decide about a competitor's dress (see Rule 6).

22.10 Decide whether any assistance given by a spotter was necessary (see Rule 10.4).

22.11 Declare the maximum mark in the case of an interrupted routine (see Rule 18).

22.12 Supervise and control all scores, calculations and the final results.

22.13 Decide if a Judge fails to show his mark immediately (see Rule 20.2.4).

22.14 Control the marks of the electronic apparatus for Synchronisation (see Rule 20.2.8.1).

22.15 Inform the Execution Judges of additional deductions (see Rule 23.4).

23. DUTIES OF THE JUDGES FOR EXECUTION (NOS. 1-6)

23.1 Evaluate the Execution (form, consistency of height and control) as per Rule 23.3 and write down their deductions so that their secretaries can copy them onto their respective deduction sheets.

23.2 Subtract their deductions from the maximum mark indicated by the Superior Judge (see Rule 18.4).

23.3 Deductions for faulty Execution:

23.3.1 lack of form, individual constant height and lack of control in each skill	0.1-0.5 pts
23.3.2 lack of stability on or after the last skill:	
23.3.2.1 landing on one foot only	0.3 pts
23.3.2.2 landing on both feet but lacking stability and not standing still for 3 seconds	0.1-0.3 pts
23.3.2.3 touching the bed with one hand	0.4 pts
23.3.2.4 touching the bed with both hands	0.5 pts
23.3.2.5 touching the bed with the knees or hands & knees	0.6 pts
23.3.2.6 touching the bed with the seat	0.7 pts
23.3.2.7 falling to the stomach or back	0.8 pts
23.3.2.8 touching or landing on the suspension system, pads, frame or Spotter Mat	0.9 pts
23.3.2.9 landing or falling outside the area of the trampoline	1.0 pts
23.4 Make the following deductions on the instruction of the Superior Judge:	
23.4.1 Talking to or giving any form of signal to a competitor by their own spotters or coach during the routine, for each occurrence	0.3 pts

23.4.2 Intermediate (straight) jumps in a
Voluntary routine, for each jump   1.0 pts

23.4.3 Additional skills as per Rule 19.4   1.0 pts

23.4.4 For exceeding the time limit as per
Rule 15.2   0.1 pts

23.5 During Synchronised competitions Judges nos. 1, 2 & 3 evaluate the Execution of the routine on trampoline no. 1, Judges nos. 4, 5 & 6 evaluate the Execution on trampoline no. 2.

23.6 The evaluation of Execution in the Synchronised competition will be done in the same manner as in the Individual competition.

(See F.I.T. Guide to Judging for a fuller explanation.)

24. DUTIES OF THE JUDGES FOR DIFFICULTY (NOS. 7 & 8)

24.1 Collect the competition cards from the Chief Recorder at least two hours prior to the start of the competition.

24.2 Check the compulsory skills and Difficulty values entered on the competition cards.

24.3 Check the compulsory in the Individual and Synchronised competitions as per Rule 7.3.

24.4 Determine the Difficulty score of the Voluntary routines as per Rule 20.1 and enter it on the competition cards.

24.5 Determine whether or not any of the skills were intermediate (straight) jumps and advise the Superior Judge accordingly.

24.6 Determine if the competitors in Synchronised competition perform the same skills at the same time as per Rule 18.1.7.

24.7 Display the Difficulty score.

25. DUTIES OF THE JUDGES FOR SYNCHRONISATION (NOS. 9, 10, 11)

25.1 Evaluate the Synchronised performance as per Rule 25.3 and write down their marks so that their secretaries can copy them on to their respective deduction sheets.

25.2 Subtract their deductions from the maximum mark indicated by the Superior Judge (see Rule 18.4).

25.3 Make and record the following deductions for each unsynchronised landing:

25.3.1 landing differences under 50cm in
height   0.1-0.3 pts

25.3.2 landing differences of 50cm or more in
height   0.4-0.5 pts

25.3.3 After the 10th skill, not making
the same movement (out-bounce or standing still)   0.2 pts

(See F.I.T. Guide to Judging for a fuller explanation.)

26. DUTIES OF THE ASSISTANT SUPERIOR JUDGE

26.1 Assist the Superior Judge during the Trial Scoring.

26.2 Advise the Superior Judge if the competitor touches anything other than the trampoline bed during the Individual competition.

26.3 Supervise trampoline No. 2 during the Synchronised competition.

GOVERNING BODY

United States Acrogymnastics Federation (in conjunction with the Federation of International Trampoline), c/o Jeff T. Hennessy, 102 Westmoreland Drive, Lafayette, LA 70506.

Through its affiliation with the Federation of International Trampoline (F.I.T.), the U.S. Acrogymnastics Federation (USAF) is recognized as the governing body for trampolining, tumbling, and double mini-tramp in the United States. The USAF and the F.I.T. have as their primary objectives fostering, developing, and promoting competitive trampolining, tumbling, and double mini-tramp from the local level through international competition. The documents noted in preface to the rules (page 587) are available along with other materials from the F.I.T.

• TRAPSHOOTING •

ABRIDGMENT OF OFFICIAL TRAPSHOOTING RULES

(Reproduced by permission of the Amateur Trapshooting Association*)

□

Note: The official trapshooting rules publication issued by the A.T.A. includes five sections as follows: (1) Organization of the A.T.A., (2) Information for New Shooters, (3) Official Rules of A.T.A. Tournaments, (4) The A.T.A. Handicap System, (5) Requirements and Recommendations for Conducting a Registered Shoot. Only that part of section three, Official Rules of A.T.A. Tournaments, dealing with actual range shooting and section four, The A.T.A. Handicap System, are included here. The complete rules covering all aspects of amateur trapshooting are available through the association.

III

OFFICIAL RULES OF A.T.A. TOURNAMENTS

In these rules the word "State" is intended to include province or other similar territory having an affiliated association.

A. REGISTERED SHOOTS

The A.T.A. governs the conduct of all shoots registered with it. Only clubs affiliated with their state association will be permitted to hold registered shoots.

To constitute a registered shoot at least five (5) or more persons must compete and complete each event, and provided that they first become members of A.T.A. and pay the registration fee of $1.00 for each day of competition at each shooting location, and such other state association fees and dues as may be charged.

No daily fee charges shall be permitted except those assessed by the A.T.A., the Zone, or the State in which the tournament is being held.

B. WHO MAY PARTICIPATE

Only Members in good standing who have paid their annual dues or Life Members may participate in a registered A.T.A. Shoot.

---

*See page 629 for additional information.

C. EVENTS AND HOW SHOT

In official A.T.A. usage a sub-event is any number of targets shot on any one field at one time, with one full rotation on all five stations by each shooter, such as 25 singles or handicap targets or in doubles 25 pairs, 15 pairs or 10 pairs. An event is the total targets of a specific type (16 yard, handicap, or doubles) such as 200 16-yard targets, 100 handicap targets, etc. for which separate entry is made. Therefore, an "event" consists of two or more "sub-events." It is not necessary to change traps after each sub-event. Events of less than 50 targets may not be registered.

1. 16 YARD SINGLES

This event must be shot 5 shots at each post from 16 yards (14.6m) with each shooter in order shooting at one target until all have shot five times, and then rotating in a clockwise manner to the next station.

2. HANDICAP TARGETS

This event must be shot 5 shots at each post from 17 to 27 yards (15.5-24.7m) with each shooter in order shooting at one target until all have shot five times, then rotating in a clockwise manner to the next station.

A contestant must stand on the highest whole yardage punched on his or her card. For example, if a card is punched at 20.5 yards, the shooter will stand on 20.0 yards. However, if one half yard is then earned, the card must be punched to 21.0 yards and the shooter must stand on the 21.0 yard line.

A shooter may not stand on a higher yardage than he is punched, unless assigned penalty yardage by the shoot handicap committee.

If there is a 200 target race, the second 100 handicap event must not begin prior to the awarding of earned yardage based on the first 100 target event.

It is not permitted to have more than one 50 and/or 75 target handicap event in a registered tournament in any one day.

3. DOUBLES

This event must be shot from 16 yards (14.6m), with each shooter in order shooting at two targets thrown simultaneously from the trap house until all have shot the specified number of times, then rotating in a clockwise manner to the next station. (A doubles event will be shot by having each squad shoot successive alternating 15 pair and 10 pair sub-events on the trap or traps being utilized, or a club may elect to throw Doubles in sub-events of 25 pairs.)

D. CLASSIFICATION, HANDICAPPING, AND SPECIAL DESIGNATION

1. CLASSIFICATION

For 16 yard targets and Doubles, shooters should be placed in 3 or more classes, according to their known ability.

a. To arrive at 'known ability' the following should be taken into account as far as such information can be made available.

(1) Official registered targets (abnormally low scores should be disregarded). Averages of all registered shooters are compiled and published annually.

(2) Non-registered scores including shootoff scores, non-registered events, practice scores, etc.

(3) Any other information bearing on a shooter's ability to shoot and break targets.

b. For 16-yard events the following systems are suggested:

FIVE CLASSES

97% and over	AA
94% and under 97%	A
91% and under 94%	B
88% and under 91%	C
Under 88%	D

FOUR CLASSES

95% and over	A
92% and under 95%	B
89% and under 92%	C
Under 89%	D

THREE CLASSES

95% and over	A
91% and under 95%	B
Under 91%	C

c. For Doubles events the following systems are suggested:

FIVE CLASSES

93% and up	AA
89% and under 93%	A
85% and under 89%	B
78% and under 85%	C
Under 78%	D

FOUR CLASSES

90% and up	A
85% and under 90%	B
78% and under 85%	C
Under 78%	D

THREE CLASSES

89% and up	A
83% and under 89%	B
Under 83%	C

d. Any club desiring to use a different classification may do so by printing the desired classification in the program of the shoot.

e. For better classification of shooters it is suggested that the following method be used

(1) If the shooter has less than 500 targets on current year's score card, then use the previous year average and known ability.

(2) If the shooter has between 500 and 1,000 targets (inclusive) on his current year's score card, use the current average and known ability or the previous year's average and known ability, whichever is the higher.

2. RECOMMENDED 16 YARD PUNCH SYSTEM

a. This system is to be utilized for classification at only the Grand American, A.T.A. Zone Championships, State Championships, Golden West Grand, Spring Grand, Midwestern Grand, and Southern Grand tournaments. Cards shall not be punched at any other than the above shoots.

b. Classification at all other shoots shall be decided by the club shoot classification and handicap committee.

c. All scores equaling or exceeding those of champions, runnerups, and the respective class winners will receive one punch. This will apply only to the singles championships when at the above mentioned shoots.

d. The shooter's average card will be printed providing for two punches in each of the five A.T.A. classes. When a shooter has one punch it indicates he has won that class at one of the above shoots. A shooter with two punches in a class should be advanced.

e. It will be the shooter's responsibility to see that his card is properly punched prior to entering any of the above listed tournaments.

f. The intent of the system is to inform classification and handicap committees of prior wins. Punches indicating these wins may be disregarded by the classification committee if they so choose.

3. HANDICAP YARDAGE

A shooter will be handicapped between 17 and 27 yards at the highest yardage punched on this card, unless he is required to shoot Penalty yardage. (Section 5.)

4. PENALTY CLASSIFICATION

The management of registered shoots may establish penalty yardage, and penalty classification for 16 yard targets and doubles, if said conditions are printed in the program. In no event shall any shooter be assigned a handicap of less than the minimum yardage appearing on his handicap card.

5. SPECIAL CATEGORIES

Ladies, Juniors, Sub-Juniors, Veterans, Sr. Veterans and Industry shooters shall be so designated.

a. All female shooters shall be designated as Ladies, though because of age they may also be designated as Juniors, Sub-Juniors, Veterans or Sr. Veterans.

b. A shooter who has not reached his or her 15th birthday will be designated as a Sub-Junior.

c. A male shooter upon reaching age 15 must shoot from a minimum handicap yardage of 19 yards unless he has already earned greater yardage.

d. A shooter who is 15 but has not reached his or her 18th birthday will be designated as a Junior.

e. A male shooter upon reaching age 18 must shoot from a minimum handicap yardage of 20 yards unless he has already earned greater yardage.

f. A male or female shooter who is 65 years or older will be designated as a Veteran.

g. A male or female shooter who is 70 years or older will be designated as a Sr. Veteran.

h. Industry personnel shall be so designated and may shoot for only those championships and trophies so designated.

i. All ladies, juniors, sub-juniors, veterans, senior veterans and industry shooters must declare their special category **at the time of their entry** in any registered event. Without such declaration **at the time of their entry,** the shooter will not be allowed to compete for the applicable special category trophies. No exceptions to this rule are to be allowed.

E. SQUADDING

1. In all A.T.A. events contestants shall shoot in squads of five except:

a. When there are less than five contestants available for the last squad of any program.

b. When yardage differences in handicap events make it impossible or unsafe.

c. When there are withdrawals from a squad after the competition has begun and squads scheduled.

d. When in the opinion of shoot management, the harmony of the shoot may be enhanced by squadding less than five contestants.

2. It is illegal for more than five shooters to be in a squad.

3. The squadding of practice shooters with those shooting registered events shall not be allowed, nor shall anyone be allowed to shoot registered events on a non-registered basis.

4. The shooter in position 1 is the SQUAD LEADER and should:

a. ascertain that all members of the squad are ready before commencing the event or sub-event.

b. initial the score sheet at the end of each sub-event.

c. the Squad leader ONLY may call for one target before starting his squad to shoot in a regular or shootoff event.

5. If a broken or irregular target is thrown, the Squad leader may ask to see another target; if there is a delay due to trap or gun trouble the contestant in turn, may ask to see another target. If during a sub-event a contestant is consecutively thrown two illegal or broken targets, the contestant shall have the right to see a legal target before he resumes shooting.

F. OFFICIAL SCORING

1. PROCEDURE

a. The official score is the record kept by the scorer on the sheet furnished him by the management for said purpose and shall show in detail the scores made in the event or sub-event for which furnished. It is recommended that the score sheet shall not be smaller than 10 inches by 28 inches and the box provided for each score not smaller than 3/4 by 3/4 of an inch. Score sheets on which more than one sub-event is recorded may be carried from trap to trap by the squad leader. Such score sheets must be left at the last trap to be handled by club personnel from that point.

b. The scorer shall keep an accurate record of each score of each contestant. If he calls dead or lost, the scorer shall promptly mark 1 for dead and zero for lost. His record of the competition shall be official and shall govern all awards and records of the competition to which it relates.

c. The scorer shall call all targets, or only the lost targets, as directed by the management.

d. Should more targets be fired in a sub-event than the event calls for, then the excess targets of the sub-event will not be scored.

e. It is the duty of the referee to see that the shooters change firing points at the proper time; however, any targets shot after failure to move at the proper time shall be scored.

f. The official score must be kept on a score sheet in plain view of the contestant. If contestant's view of the score sheet is obstructed for any reason, he may refuse to shoot until he has an unobstructed view of the score sheet.

g. It is an error if the scorer fails to properly mark the results of any shot in the section of the score sheet where the results should have been recorded. In such cases it is the duty of that contestant to have any error corrected before he has fired the first shot at the succeeding position or in the case of his last post before he leaves the trap. Failing to do so he shall be held to the score as recorded (see Rule C.3).

h. Every contestant in a squad shall be permitted to examine his score before the sheet is sent to the bulletin board or to the cashier's office. The score sheet should be initialed by the squad leader.

i. Errors in the details of the official score can only be corrected in strict accordance with the aforementioned rules, but an error made in totaling said details shall be corrected whenever same is discovered.

j. The referee shall distinctly announce "lost" when the target is missed and "no target" when a target is thrown broken.

2. BROKEN OR DEAD TARGET

A broken target (called dead) is one that has a visible broken piece from it; or one that is completely reduced to dust. The referee shall declare such target dead when it is so broken in the air. A "Dusted Target," is a target from which there is a puff of dust, but no perceptible piece is seen; it is not a broken target.

3. LOST TARGET

The referee shall call "lost"

a. When the contestant shoots and fails to break the target whether missed completely or when only dust falls from it.

b. When the contestant flinches and does not shoot.

c. When the shell is defective but no part of the over powder wads or shot remains in the barrel.

d. When a whole target appears promptly after a contestant's recognizable command and is within the legal limits of flight and the contestant does not shoot.

e. When the contestant after calling "pull" fails to shoot because his gun was unloaded, uncocked, not properly closed, because the safety was on, or was faulty, or jarred back, whether from his oversight or not, EXCEPT that some vital part of the gun has suddenly broken so that it cannot possibly be made to function without repairs, or that he has an allowable misfire.

f. When an illegal target, or freak target is shot at and missed. Contestant may refuse illegal targets, but if he shoots, the results must be scored.

g. If a contestant has more than 2 misfires in any sub-event of 25 targets (or other number in case of doubles) and did not change guns or change to the other barrel of double barrel gun, or change shells as outlined. If these changes are not made, any misfires shall be called lost.

h. When a contestant voluntarily withdraws from, or is disqualified, and takes no further part in a sub-event after having shot at one or more targets called for by said sub-event and thereby does not shoot at the total number of targets called for by such sub-event, the referee shall declare all targets which the contestant did not shoot at in the sub-event to be lost targets and they shall be scored accordingly.

i. When a score sheet shall come into the office with one or more targets that are not scored at all, they shall be scored as lost targets by the management.

j. If a contestant uses a shell after it has misfired, he shall abide by the result obtained through the use of that shell.

k. If after an apparent dud shell or misfire the contestant opens his gun before the referee comes to him to make a decision, the target shall be called "lost."

4. NO TARGET

a. To better apply the following rules, these definitions are given:

(1) Misfire (Dud Shell): failure of a shell to fire when the primer is struck with the firing pin or when evidence is present that the hammer did fall even though the primer shows no indentation, or a shell which lacks a live primer or one in which the primer fires, but through failure of the shell or lack of components, and which consequently leaves part of or all of the charge of shot or wad in the gun. A soft load, in which the shot and wad leave the barrel, is not a misfire.

(2) Malfunction of a gun; failure of the gun to function, or work as it was designed to do. Malfunction of a gun applies only to a second shot of doubles.

(3) Broken gun; a gun in which some vital part has broken so that the gun cannot be made to fire without repairs.

b. It is a "no target" and the referee shall allow another target under the following conditions:

(1) When the target is thrown broken, regardless of the results of any shots fired.

(2) When a contestant shoots out of turn.

(3) When two contestants, or a contestant and non-contestant shoot at the same target.

(4) When the trap is sprung without any call of pull, or when it is sprung at any material interval of time, before or after the call of the shooter, provided the contestant does not shoot. If the shooter shoots, the result must be scored, unless the shot is fired after the target has struck the ground.

(5) When in single shooting two targets are thrown at the same time, regardless of whether the shooter fires.

(6) When an "illegal" target is thrown, a target that is more than twenty-five degrees outside of the prescribed limits of the angles in single-target shooting, or what is known as a "flipper" or "freak" target that may have slipped out of the carrier of the trap or one not properly placed on the trap provided the contestant does not shoot at it. If he shoots, the result must be scored.

(7) When a target, whose color is markedly different from that of the others, is thrown and the contestant does not shoot. If he shoots, the result must be scored.

(8) When firing, the contestant's feet must be behind the firing mark assigned to him. He must stand with at least one foot on the imaginary line drawn through the trap and firing point, or have one foot on each side of the line. Exceptions to the rule contained in the second sentence of this paragraph may be granted by the referee due to inequalities in the shooting platform. Should a shooter fail to observe this rule the referee shall call any target shot at and broken a "no target," but if shot at and missed, the result shall be scored accordingly.

c. When the contestant has a misfire shell or apparent misfire he, without opening his gun or removing the shell or shells, must forthwith allow the referee to inspect his gun before making his decision. If the shooter opens his gun before the referee comes to him to make a decision, the target shall be called "lost." The referees shall not be required to handle firearms in any manner whatsoever in the performance of their duties.

d. If a contestant has a second misfire in the same sub-event of 25 targets (or other number in case of doubles) he shall be warned by the referee. The shooter must at that time demonstrate to the referee that he is either (1) changing guns or changing to the other barrel of a double barreled gun, or (2) that he is changing shells. If he fails to do one of these things, all succeeding misfires in that sub-event will be called "lost."

e. If, after the change of guns or of shells, the shooter has another misfire in the same sub-event, he must make the other change of the option for the remainder of the sub-event or be disqualified for interfering with the harmony of the shoot. Management shall also disqualify him on the same grounds for interference if he persists in using the same gun or guns, or shells on succeeding sub-events with resultant misfires. To avoid disqualification he may withdraw from the sub-event, have the gun repaired or shells replaced, and finish the sub-events as directed by the management.

f. In addition, in Doubles shooting, the referee shall declare "no target" under the following conditions:

(1) When only one target is thrown.

(2) When more than two targets are thrown.

(3) When both targets are broken by one shot.

(4) When there is an allowable misfire on either shot.

(5) When the gun breaks down so either shot cannot be fired.

(6) When there is a maximum of one (1) gun malfunction for the second shot on any one trap per sub-event, whether the sub-event consists of 10 or 15 pairs. In sub-events of 25 pairs two (2) gun malfunctions are allowed. If the shooter changes guns, he will be allowed another malfunction per sub-event. However, if the shooter does not change guns, any subsequent malfunction shall be called "lost." Misfires are not considered malfunction.

(7) When one or both targets are thrown broken even though the shooter fires at one or both targets.

(8) If one or both targets are not within the prescribed angle or height limits and the shooter does not fire either shot. If the shooter shoots at an illegal first target and the second target is legal, he must also shoot at the second target. However, a shooter is not required to shoot an illegal second target even though he shot at the first target which may have been either legal or illegal target.

(9) Both targets shall be called "lost" if the shooter deliberately shoots at the same target twice. This rule is not applicable to a gun "doubling" or "machinegunning," these are malfunctions and are not deliberate second shots.

G. SHOOT OFFS

The management of a tournament may rule that ties shall be carried over to the first (or more if needed) sub-event of the next like event. However, when there are ties in a handicap event and any tying shooter earns yardage and consequently will be shooting farther back in the subsequent handicap event, all tying shooters must agree to the carry over. All ties whenever possible shall be shot off and in such a manner as the management of the competition shall designate. Unless otherwise specified by the management, ties on singles events shall be shot off in 25 target events and doubles in 10 pair events.

Ties for All-Around championships shall be shot off on 20 singles, 10 handicap, and 5 pair of doubles. Ties for High-Overall shall be shot off in such a manner that the shoot off represents as closely as possible the same proportion of singles, handicap and doubles targets as the High-Overall program contains but keeping the shoot off to 50 targets or less. The singles, handicap and doubles portion of the shoot off shall be in order that the event occurred in the program.

When squadding shooters for shoot offs for High-Overall and All-Around the shooting order shall be in the order in which they shot in the last event involved except where such order would be inadvisable or dangerous because of yardage differences, and this order shall remain through subsequent shoot offs. In subsequent shoot offs the position shall be rotated in a clockwise manner, with the shooter from position 1 advancing to position 2 and the shooter from position 5 rotating to position 1 or the position dictated by the number of shooters remaining, but always in clockwise rotation.

The following method shall be used for rotation of shooters:

Starting firing points to be used shall be as follows, except where handicap yardage makes it unsafe.

If one shooter—firing points numbers 2.

If two shooters—firing points number 2 and 4.

If three shooters—firing points numbers 2, 3, and 4.

If four shooters—firing points numbers 2, 3, 4, and 5.

If five shooters—firing points numbers 1, 2, 3, 4, and 5.

If more than five shooters are involved in the tie, they shall be divided as equally as possible into two or more squads as directed by the management.

H. SAFETY

1. It is the shooter's responsibility and the shoot management's responsibility to conduct a shoot in a safe manner.

2. It is the shoot management's responsibility to remove any competitor who is conducting himself in an unsafe manner (repeat violators should be reported to the Executive Committee for further action).

3. It is the shoot management's responsibility to instruct the trap help in the proper and safe conduct of their respective duties.

4. All trap help must have a flag or other warning device to warn of the trap boy's exit from the traphouse.

5. Trap personnel should be totally instructed in the potential danger of the trap (particularly the target throwing arm).

6. Movement and exposure on adjacent traps should be kept to the minimum.

7. The practice of tracking targets behind a shooting squad is unsafe, disconcerting to the shooter and is not permitted.

8. Alcohol impairs judgment and the A.T.A. rules pertaining to alcohol must be enforced by club management. This rule shall be strictly complied with and shall apply to practice shooting as well as regular events.

9. In singles and handicap shooting, only one shell may be inserted in the gun at one time; in doubles only two shells may be inserted in a gun at anytime.

10. In handicap there shall be no more than two (2) yards difference between adjacent shooters in the squad, AND NO MORE THAN A TOTAL DIFFERENCE OF THREE (3) YARDS IN A SQUAD. When squadding 17, 18 and 19 yardages, there shall be no more than one yard difference between adjacent shooters in the squad, and no more than a total difference of two yards in a squad.

11. In case of failure to fire, where referee is needed, shooters must remain in position with the gun pointed toward the target area and the referee must go to the shooter.

12. A gun may be loaded only when the shooter is on the firing station and the gun must be empty when shooter is moving from station to station.

13. All guns must be unloaded with the action open at all times except on the firing line or in a gun rack. Violators subject themselves to immediate disqualification, without

recourse, with dismissal from the grounds. Repeat violators will be notified of a 30 day suspension upon second violation, third violation will receive a 90 day suspension and continuing violators will be reviewed by the Executive Committee for further disciplinary action.

14. As a safety precaution test shots will not be permitted.

15. A contestant shall load his gun only when at firing point facing THE TRAPS. IN SINGLES SHOOTING HE MAY PLACE ONLY ONE SHELL IN HIS GUN AT A TIME AND MUST REMOVE IT OR THE EMPTY CASE BEFORE MOVING FROM ONE POSITION TO ANOTHER. IN CHANGING FROM ONE POST TO ANOTHER, THE SHOOTER SHOULD NOT WALK IN FRONT OF THE OTHER COMPETITORS. All guns used by contestants must be so equipped and so used as not to eject empty shells in a manner to substantially disturb or interfere with other contestants. The management may disqualify a contestant for violation of these rules.

I. GUNS AND AMMUNITION

A contestant cannot use:

1. A gun whose chamber is larger than 12 gauge. Only 12 gauge shotguns and ammunition may be used at the Grand American Tournament; guns of smaller gauges are permissible in other registered shooting, but no consideration shall be given to that fact in handicap and classification.

2. Any load other than lead shot. This includes tracers, copper, and nickel coated shot.

3. Any load heavier than 3 drams equivalent of powder or 1 1/8 ounces of shot by standard measure struck, or any load containing shot larger than number 7 1/2.

4. Any shell loaded with black powder.

Any shooter violating any of these rules shall be barred from competition. Any such violator shall be referred to the Executive Committee for possible further disciplinary action.

J. FIRING POSITION AND SHOOTING ORDER

1. There shall be 5 firing points, numbered 1 to 5, left to right, spaced 3 yards apart, sixteen yards from B (Diagram II). At all positions the contestant's feet must be behind the firing mark assigned to him, and he must stand with at least one foot on the imaginary line drawn through the trap and the firing point or have one foot on each side of the line.

The 16 yard (14.6m) position shall be 16 yards behind the center of the trap in the traphouse. The distance that the target shall be thrown shall also be measured from this point.

2. All contestants must shoot in regular order or sequence according to his or her position in the squad. A contestant who does not shoot in regular order is "out of turn" and the results are not scored.

3. When the referee calls no target for any contestant, the next contestant is not in order until the preceding shooter has shot and the referee has ruled dead or lost.

4. The referee shall not throw a target unless all contestants are in the correct positions.

5. To preserve the harmony of the competition, no member of a squad shall move toward the next firing point until the last shot of the inning has been fired.

6. In any registered trapshooting competition, no person shall be permitted to "shoot up" that is, enter and take a part in any completed or partially completed event or events after Squad no. 1 shall have completed sub-event no. 1 of any new event to be shot on Trap no. 1.

7. At tournaments which are shot "section system" with several squads, starting at the same time on several traps, such procedure shall be construed for purpose of this rule to be the same as if all squads started on Trap no. 1.

K. TRAP MACHINE

An automatic trap machine which throws targets at an unknown angle shall be used. All trap machines used to throw A.T.A. registered targets shall be so manufactured, modified, or equipped as to interrupt irregularly the oscillation of the trap or otherwise assure the unpredictability of flight of substantially all targets thrown.

L. TRAPHOUSES

Traphouses must adequately protect the trap loaders and shall not be higher than necessary for the purpose. Traphouses constructed after January 1, 1956 shall conform to the following specifications:

Length not less than 7 feet, 6 inches (2.3m), nor more than 8 feet, 6 inches (2.6m).

Width not less than 7 feet, 6 inches (2.3m), nor more than 8 feet, 6 inches (2.6m).

Height not less than 2 feet, 2 inches (.7m), nor more than 2 feet, 10 inches (.9m), the height to be measured from the plane of the number 3 shooting position.

Firing Points. The firing points shall be three yards (2.7m) apart on the circumference of a circle whose radius is 16 yards (14.6m).

M. TARGETS

No target shall measure more than four and five-sixteenths (4-5/16) inches (10.94cm) in diameter, not more than one and one-eighth (1-1/8) inches (28.58mm) in height, and shall weigh 3.5 ounces (99.23g) with an allowable variation of 5 percent from this figure.

N. FLIGHTS AND ANGLES

Targets whether single or doubles, shall be thrown not less than 48 yards (44m) measured on level ground in still air. The recommended distances for the throwing of any target shall be 50 yards (46m).

Targets, whether single or double, shall be between 8 (2.4m) and 12 feet (3.7m) high, when ten yards from the trap. THE RECOMMENDED HEIGHT IS NINE FEET. The height at a point ten yards (9m) from the trap is to be understood to mean height above an imaginary horizontal straight line drawn through the firing point and the trap. (See Diagram II.)

In singles shooting the trap shall be so adjusted that within the normal distribution of angles as thrown by the trap, the right angle shall not be less than a straightaway from firing point 1 and the left angle shall not be less than a straightaway from firing point 5. To help in determining legal angles, stakes should be placed on the arc of a circle whose radius is 50 yards (46m) and whose center is the trap. One stake should be placed where a line drawn through firing point 1 and the base of the trap intersects this arc and another stake placed where a line drawn through firing point 5 and the base of the trap intersects the arc. These lines and stakes will assist in determining the required angles, but it is to be understood that the angle specifications apply when the target is from 15 to 20 yards (14-18m) from the trap rather than where the target strikes the ground. However, no target is to be declared illegal unless it is more than 25 degrees outside the angles prescribed.

In doubles target shooting the recommended method of throwing targets shall be such that the right hand target shall be an approximate straightaway from firing point number 1 and the left hand target shall be an approximate straightaway from firing point number 5. However, no target shall be declared illegal unless it varies more than 25 degrees from these recommended angles.

Distance Handicaps. The distance handicaps when used shall be prolongations of the lines given in Diagram I, commonly known as fan shaped. The distance between firing points at 16 yards (14.6m) shall then be 3 yards (2.7m).

A common misconception is that once the first squad of an event has shot over a trap the trap cannot be reset unless it is throwing illegal targets. This is not true. Should, for some reason, a trap be throwing targets that, though not necessarily illegal, are so poorly thrown that it will appreciably affect the shooter's score, any shooter may request that the management reset the trap. It will be the management's responsibility to decide if the trap(s) should be reset.

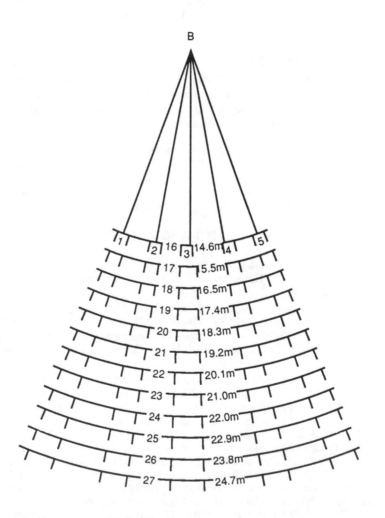

B - TRAP   YARDS (METERS) FROM B

Diagram 1
Trap and Firing Positions

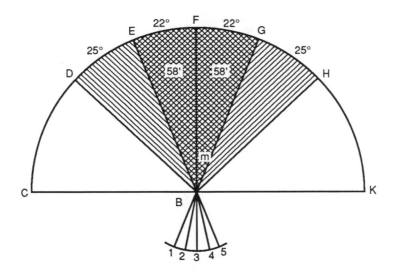

Diagram II
Legal Target Flight Area for 16 Yards and Handicap Shooting

1 to 5 Firing Points spaced 3 yards (2.7m) apart.

B-Trap

CDEFGHK—Fifty yards (46m) from Trap.

BDEFGHB Shaded—Area of Legitimate Target.

BEFGB—Cross Hatched-Most desirable area in which to throw target.

3BF—Imaginary straight line through trap and No. 3 firing position.

CBK—Imaginary straight line through trap at right angles to No. 3BF.

EF, FG—The distance between these points shall be a straight line 58 feet (17.7m) long.

Target elevation 8 to 12 feet (2.4 to 3.7m) above number 3 firing point at point M 30 feet (9m) in front of trap.

Target distance 48 to 52 yards (44 to 48m).

Double Target Shooting

1 to 5 Firing Points spaced 3 yards (2.7m) apart.

B-Trap, 16 yards (14.6m) from Firing Points.

CDEFGHK-Fifty yards (46m) from Trap.

3BF-Imaginary straight line through Trap and No. 3 Firing Position.

CBK-Imaginary straight line through Trap at right angles at 3BF.

Arrows indicate recommended flight of target.

Distance of Targets' Flight-48 to 52 yards (44 to 48m).

EF, FG- The distance between these points shall be a straight line 58 feet (17.7m) long.

Elevation of target 8 to 12 feet (2.4 to 3.7m) above number three firing point at a distance of 30 feet (9m) in front of the trap.

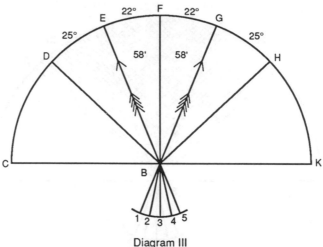

Diagram III
Double Target Shooting

THE A.T.A. HANDICAP SYSTEM

The A.T.A. Handicap system is the method whereby shooters whose ability to win has been demonstrated and shooters whose ability is unknown are handicapped by shooting a greater distance from the traphouse. The minimum handicap is 17.0 yards and the maximum is 27.0 yards. A shooter's yardage is determined by rules governing new shooters, by yardage earned, or by his established handicap yardage which is based on known ability and 1000 target reviews. At each State or Provincial shoot the handicapping and classifying shall be the responsibility of a committee appointed by the state association with the A.T.A. delegate as chairman.

A. CENTRAL HANDICAP COMMITTEE

1. The Central Handicap Committee, made up of a chairman and 5 or more members, is appointed by the Executive Committee.

2. It is the responsibility of the Central Handicap Committee to control yardage of all members of the A.T.A. Any Central Handicap Committee member may increase a shooter's yardage at his discretion when applying the known ability rule. The only others authorized to increase a shooter's yardage are members of the Executive Committee.

B. KNOWN ABILITY

Handicap and 16 yard averages and/or scores in both registered and non-registered shoots may be used as the basis for determining known ability. Scores abnormally low in relation to the remainder of the scores shot may be disregarded at the discretion of the handicap committee.

C. EARNED YARDAGE

1. Yardage will be automatically earned by shooters of high scores in all A.T.A. registered events, according to the table following. This additional yardage is indicated by punches on the shooter's handicap card.

EARNED YARDAGE TABLE

High Scores (and all ties)

Number of shooters	1st	2nd	3rd	4th	5th
15-24	1/2 yd				
25-49	1 yd	1/2 yd			
50-124	1 yd	1/2 yd	1/2 yd		
125-249	1 yd	1 yd	1/2 yd		
250-499	1 1/2 yd	1 yd	1/2 yd	1/2 yd	
500-1499	2 yd	1 1/2 yd	1 yd	1/2 yd	
1500-and up	2 1/2 yd	2 yd	1 1/2 yd	1 yd	1/2 yd

2. Any score of 96 will automatically earn 1/2 yard provided it does not earn at least that much under the earned yardage table. Any score of 50 x 50 or 75 x 75 in events of that length will automatically earn 1/2 yard provided it does not earn at least that much under the earned yardage table.

3. The State Handicap Champion will automatically earn 1 yard.

4. Any score of 97, 98 and 99 will automatically earn 1 yard, a score of 100 will automatically earn 1 1/2 yards provided these scores do not earn at least that much under the earned yardage table.

5. The earned yardage table applies to events of 50, 75, or 100 targets.

6. In case of handicap events of more than 100 targets, each 100 targets (or remaining part of 100 targets) shall constitute a separate event for earned yardage purposes and shall be reported as a separate event on the shoot report form.

7. A shooter's card will be punched from the yardage actually shot. IT IS THE SHOOTER'S RESPONSIBILITY TO SEE THAT THIS HANDICAP CARD IS PROPERLY PUNCHED BEFORE SHOOTING ANOTHER HANDICAP EVENT. FAILURE TO DO SO WILL MAKE HIM SUBJECT TO DISQUALIFICATION OR SUSPENSION.

8. Industry shooters or their scores shall not be counted when determining the number of shooters in an event for earned yardage purposes or in applying the earned yardage table. The number of amateurs starting the event will be the number used for the earned yardage table.

9. Any industry shooter whose score equals or exceeds that of an amateur earning yardage under the earned yardage table shall earn a like increase in yardage.

D. PENALTY YARDAGE

The management of registered shoots may establish penalty yardage, if said conditions are printed in the program. In no event shall any shooter be assigned a handicap of less than the minimum yardage appearing on his handicap card.

E. SPECIAL HANDICAP RULES

1. A shooter must continue to shoot from the last yardage assigned or earned until he receives a target review, regardless of the length of time that has elapsed since that yardage was assigned or earned.

2. A shooter's handicap yardage may be reduced only as a result of a 1000 target review or a special review. No reduction may be made in the field.

3. A shooter's handicap yardage may be increased at any time during the year including immediately before and during the Grand American Tournament.

a. because of earned yardage or

b. as a result of a review or

c. at the discretion of a member of the Central Handicap or Executive Committee.

4. A shooter at all times shall have the right to appeal any committee action to the Executive Committee.

5. Yardage earned for the high score and ties in any Grand American handicap event in the regular program (does not include preliminary events) may not be removed in part or whole by any committee action prior to the end of the Grand American Tournament in the following year.

6. If a shooter earns increased yardage while a reduction is in process the reduction shall automatically be void.

7. When multiple 100 target handicap events (marathon) are shot in the same day, only two 100 target events may be considered as a maximum per day towards reduction. The two events considered out of the marathon must be those in which the two highest scores are registered.

F. REVIEWS

1. 1000 TARGET REVIEW

The shooting record of each member will be automatically reviewed for possible yardage changes after each successive 1000 registered handicap targets shot in the current and previous year if no yardage was earned.

a. A shooter with a low purified handicap average accompanied by a relative 16 yard average will, with the approval of his state delegate, receive a one yard reduction, EXCEPT

(1) No shooter will be reduced more than two yards in any target year.

(2) No male shooter eighteen (18) years of age or older will be handicapped below 20 yards without a special review; exceptions to this policy may be Sub-Juniors, Juniors, Veterans, Senior Veterans, and ladies.

(3) The known ability rule will be used in assessing a shooter's record.

b. A shooter with a high purified handicap average will receive a "Special Review" for possible yardage increase.

c. If a yardage change is made, the shooter will receive by mail a new membership card with the new assigned yardage.

2. SPECIAL REVIEW

A "Special Review" is an evaluation by the Central Handicap Committee generated by high purified average on a 1000 target review or initiated by a shooter through his state delegate or the Central Handicap Committeeman. The results of a Special Review shall be agreed upon by the Central Handicap Committee and the shooter's state delegate. If after a reasonable communication, a disagreement in yardage assignment exists between the state delegate and the Central Handicap Committee, the matter may be directed to the Executive Committee. A Special Review may be used.

a. To determine possible yardage increases for shooters showing high purified handicap averages on a 1000 target review.

b. To determine possible yardage reduction for a shooter because of advancing age or physical disability. The review may be initiated by a shooter through his state delegate.

3. ASSIGNED YARDAGE INCREASE

a. To consider appeals from increased yardage by assignment, a member may appeal an assigned yardage increase by writing to the A.T.A. office after having shot 500 targets at the assigned yardage. However, for any further reduction, 1000 additional handicap targets must be shot.

b. There will be no yardage increase by shooter request.

c. THE ONLY PERSONS AUTHORIZED TO DECREASE OR INCREASE A MEMBER'S HANDICAP YARDAGE ARE THE MEMBERS OF THE CENTRAL HANDICAP COMMITTEE AND THE EXECUTIVE COMMITTEE.

GOVERNING BODY

Amateur Trapshooting Association, 601 W. National Road, Vandalia, OH 45377

The purpose of the Amateur Trapshooting Association (A.T.A.) is to promote and govern the sport of amateur trapshooting throughout the world. Membership is divided into two classes, Life and Annual, both of which have full shooting rights and privileges. Shooters in the various states and provinces are organized into associations that control shooting in their own territories and conduct state and provincial championship tournaments. Such associations receive aid from the A.T.A. in the form of trophies and cash refunds. Complete details of the organization of the A.T.A. are contained in the Articles of Incorporation and the Bylaws of the corporation.

MAGAZINES

Trap & Field, 1000 Waterway Blvd., Indianapolis, IN 46202

• TUMBLING •

F.I.T. COMPETITION RULES FOR TUMBLING
VALID FROM 1.1.1987

(Reproduced by permission of the United States Acrogymnastics Federation* in affiliation with the Federation of International Trampoline)

☐

These Competition Rules are binding for all competitions and championships of the International Trampoline Federation (F.I.T.) and its members.

The following documents should be read in conjunction with these Rules:

Championship Regulations—Regulations for World, Intercontinental and Continental Championships

F.I.T. Norms—Dimensions and Tolerances for International Competition Equipment

F.I.T. Guide to Judging—Judges' Guide and Interpretations to current Rules.

A. GENERAL RULES

1. INDIVIDUAL COMPETITION

1.1 Tumbling competitions consist of one compulsory and four optional passes.

1.1.1 Tumbling shall be characterised by continuous speedy, rhythmic hands to feet, and feet to feet rotational jumping skills without hesitation or intermediate steps.

1.1.2 A tumbling pass shall be planned to demonstrate a variety of forward, backward and sideward skills. The pass should show good control, form, execution, maintenance of height and tempo.

1.2 Preliminaries

1.2.1 One compulsory pass.

1.2.2 Two optional passes (1 of 5 elements and 1 of 10 elements).

1.2.3 The starting order for the Preliminaries is decided by a draw as detailed in the Championship Regulations.

1.3 Finals

1.3.1 There shall be two optional passes in the finals (1 of 5 elements and 1 of 10 elements).

1.3.2 The competitors with the ten best scores from the Preliminaries will take part in the Finals.

---

*See page 638 for additional information.

1.3.3 The starting order for the Finals will be in order of merit, the competitor with the lowest preliminary score going first in both passes. In the event of ties, the starting order will be decided by a draw.

2. TEAM COMPETITION

2.1 A Tumbling team consists of a minimum of three ladies or three men and a maximum of four ladies or four men.

2.2 Every member of the team will perform one compulsory and four optional passes.

2.3 System of Scoring

The Team score for each pass (compulsory, and four optional) will be the sum of the three highest scores obtained by the members of the team in each round.

2.3.1 At World, Intercontinental and Continental Championships only the preliminary passes (one compulsory and two optional) will be counted; otherwise the team results will be calculated as per Rule 2.3

4. WINNERS

4.1 The winner is the competitor or the team with the highest overall number of points.

4.2 Competitors with the same scores will be given the same place and medals will be awarded according to the Championship Regulations.

5. PASSES

5.1 The compulsory pass will consist of 10 elements.

5.2 The first optional pass will consist of 5 elements and the second optional pass will consist of 10 elements. In the final passes the competitor may repeat the optional passes performed in the Preliminaries.

5.3 A Tumbling pass must move in one direction only; however, a single skill in the reverse direction is allowed at the end of the pass.

5.4 All completed passes must end with a somersault otherwise there will be a deduction of 0.5 pts by the Execution Judges as per Rule 23.4.2.

5.5 Second attempts at passes are not allowed.

5.5.1 If a competitor is obviously disturbed in a pass (faulty equipment or substantial external influence), the Superior Judge may allow another attempt.

5.5.2 Spectator noise, applause and the like would not normally constitute a disturbance.

6. DRESS FOR COMPETITORS AND SPOTTERS

6.1 Male Competitors:

Uniform leotard.

Uniform gym shorts.

White shoes and/or white foot covering may be worn.

6.2 Female Competitors:

Uniform leotard.

White shoes and/or white foot covering of no more than ankle length may be worn.

6.3 Spotters:

Track suit and gym shoes.

6.4 The wearing of jewelry or watches is not permitted during the competition. Rings without gemstones may be worn if they are taped.

6.5 Any violation of Rules 6.1, 6.2 and 6.4 may result in disqualification from the round in which the offence occurs. The decision is made by the Superior Judge.

7. COMPETITION CARDS

7.1 Each pass with difficulty rating must be written on the competition card. Only the preliminary passes are handed in. Finalists will complete the last two (2) passes on their card prior to the finals.

7.2 The competition card must be handed in at the time and place specified by the Organising Committee. The Chief Recorder is responsible for ensuring that they are given to the Difficulty Judges at least two hours before the competition starts. (Finalists must hand in their final passes at least 30 minutes before the start of the finals.)

7.3 Changes to the skills and the order in which they are written on the competition card are permitted during a pass. (They must be written down on the competition card by the Difficulty Judges.)

8. TUMBLING EQUIPMENT

8.1 The specifications must adhere to the F.I.T. Norms.

9. HEIGHT OF HALL

9.1 The interior height of the hall in which tumbling competitions are to take place must be at least 5 meters.

10. SAFETY

10.1 The competitor may have a spotter, who must be dressed in terms of Rule 6.3.

10.2 The Superior Judge is responsible for controlling the actions of the spotter.

10.3 The competitors must execute their passes without external help. If a spotter touches the competitor, the pass will terminate at that point, and no credit shall be given for the assisted skill.

11. RECORDERS & SECRETARIAT

11.1 At World, Intercontinental and Continental Championships either the official score sheets of the F.I.T. or an approved computer program, for recording and printing the results, must be used as per 9.2.6 of the Championship Regulations.

11.2 A complete copy of the results must be sent to the President of the Technical Committee.

11.3 Duties of the Chief Recorder:

11.3.1 Collect and distribute the competition cards as per Rule 7.2.

11.3.2 Supply secretaries for the Judges.

11.3.3 Supervise the recorders.

11.3.4 Record the starting order for the final passes and determine the warm-up groups.

11.3.5 Record the scores for Execution and Difficulty.

11.3.6 Scrutinise and control the calculations on the competition cards and score sheets.

11.3.7 Display each competitor's total score for the round.

11.3.8 Produce a complete list of the results giving the total mark for each round, position and overall total.

12. ARBITRATION JURY

12.1 Composition:

12.1.1 Member of the Presidium or Organising Committee	1
12.1.2 Member of the Technical Committee or Organising Committee	1
12.1.3 Superior Judge	1
12.1.4 Judges	2
12.1.5 Total	5

12.2 The Superior Judge is President of the Arbitration Jury and has a casting vote in the event of ties.

12.2.2 The Superior Judge and two other members of the Arbitration Jury will supervise the draw for the starting order for the compulsories (see Rule 1.2.3).

12.3 The Arbitration Jury must announce the protest fee before the start of the competition and deal with any protests.

12.4 The Arbitration Jury will decide about the replacement of a Judge as per Rule 21.5.

13. PROTESTS

13.1 A protest can only be handed in by an official representative of a Federation (team manager, competitor or coach).

13.2 The written protest, with the protest fee, must be handed to the Superior Judge prior to the start of the next round. In the case of a protest concerning the final round, the protest must be submitted immediately after the end of the round.

13.3 Protests concerning the Execution scores can only be made in respect of a numerical error.

13.4 Protests must be dealt with by the Arbitration Jury prior to the start of the next round and their decision announced immediately.

13.5 The decision of the Arbitration Jury is final and must be abided by.

13.6 If the protest is sustained the fee will be returned. If the protest is overruled, the fee will be sent to the F.I.T. Treasurer.

B. COMPETITION PROCEDURE

14. WARMING UP

14.1 The equipment selected for the competition must be placed in the competition hall at least two hours prior to the start of the competition to enable competitors to warm up on the competition apparatus.

14.2 The competitors in each pass will be divided into groups approximating to 10 per group. They will be allowed one practice pass before each pass.

15. START OF A PASS

15.1 Each competitor will start on the signal given by the Superior Judge.

15.2 A competitor's pass shall be considered started once the first element is initiated. Prior to that, if there is a faulty start, the competitor may re-start without penalty on a signal from the Superior Judge.

16. REQUIRED POSITIONS DURING A PASS

16.1 In all positions, the feet and legs should be kept together and the feet and toes pointed.

16.2 Depending on the requirements of the movement, the body should be either tucked, piked or straight.

16.3 In the tucked and piked positions the thighs should be close to the upper body except in the twisting phase of multiple somersaults as per Rule 16.7.

16.4 In the tucked position the hands should touch the legs below the knees except in the twisting phase of multiple somersaults as per Rule 16.7.

16.5 The arms should be straight and held close to the body whenever possible.

16.6 The following defines the minimum requirements for a particular body shape:

16.6.1 Straight Position:

The angle between the upper body and thighs must be greater than 135 degrees.

16.6.2 Pike Position:

The angle between the upper body and thighs must be equal to or less than 135 degrees and the angle between the thighs and the lower legs must be greater than 135 degrees.

16.6.3 Tuck Position:

The angle between the upper body and thighs must be less than 135 degrees and the angle between the thigh and the lower leg must be less than 135 degrees.

16.7 In multiple somersaults with twists, the tuck and pike position may be modified during the twisting phase as shown in the Guide to Judging (Puck & Pike twisting positions).

16.8 A Whipback is defined as any single somersault executed in the middle of a pass in a layout position.

16.9 Single backward somersaults executed at the end of a pass must be above shoulder height otherwise there will be a deduction as per Rule 23.3.1.

17. REPETITION OF THE SAME SKILLS

17.1 With the exception of flic-flacs and round-offs no skill may be repeated in an optional pass, otherwise the Difficulty of the repeated skill will not be counted.

17.2 Skills having the same amount of rotation but performed in the tucked, piked and straight positions are considered to be different skills and not repetitions.

17.2.1 The tucked and pucked positions are considered to be the same position.

17.3 Multiple somersaults (of more than 360 degrees) having the same number of twists and somersaults will not be considered a repetition if the twist is located in different phases of the skill.

17.4 A somersault shall not be considered a repetition if preceded by a different element.

18. INTERRUPTIONS OF THE PASS

18.1 A pass will be considered interrupted if the competitor:

18.1.1 Does not perform the compulsory pass as prescribed. The pass terminates at the point of change.

18.1.2 Takes intermediate steps or stops.

18.1.3 Falls to the mat during a pass.

18.1.4 Touches any part of the floor or mats other than the tumbling track with any part of the body.

18.1.5 Touches the tumbling track with any part of the body other than hands or feet.

18.1.6 Performs movements without rotation.

18.1.7 Is touched by a spotter.

18.2 No credit will be given for the skill in which the interruption occurs in respect of Rules 18.1.1-18.1.7.

18.3 A competitor will be judged only on the number of skills completed on the track.

18.4 The Superior Judge will determine the maximum mark.

19. TERMINATION OF THE PASS

19.1 All completed optional passes must end with a somersault.

19.2 The pass must end on the track or landing zone.

19.3 For additional skills a deduction of a total of 1.0 pts will be made by the Execution Judges.

19.4 After the last skill, competitors must stand upright for at least three seconds, otherwise they will receive a deduction for lack of stability as per Rule 23.3.2.2.

19.5 A pass is deemed to have ended after the three seconds, as per rule 19.4, has elapsed.

20. SCORING

20.1 Degree of Difficulty

20.1.1 The Difficulty value of each skill is calculated on the following basis:

20.1.2 Only skills terminating on the feet will be evaluated.

20.1.3 Cartwheels have no Difficulty value.

20.1.4 Single Somersaults or less.

20.1.4.1 Aerials, flic-flacs, round-offs and front hand-springs.	0.2pts
20.1.4.2 Tuck back somersaults and whipbacks.	0.4pts
20.1.4.3 Tuck front somersaults.	0.5pts
20.1.4.4 Side Somersaults.	0.5pts
20.1.4.5 Somersaults done in the piked or straight position, without twist will receive a bonus of	0.1 pts
20.1.4.6 Each 1/4 twist up through two full twists.	0.1pts
20.1.4.6 Each 1/4 twist beyond two twists.	0.2pts

20.1.5 Multiple Somersaults—with or without twist:

20.1.5.1 Each somersault performed in the pike position will receive a bonus of	0.1pts
20.1.5.2 Each somersault performed in the layout position will receive a bonus of	0.2pts

20.1.5.3 The Difficulty value of the first and second somersault, including any twist, shall be doubled.

20.1.5.4 The Difficulty value of the third somersault, including any twist, shall be tripled.

20.1.6 Single or multiple somersaults, whether twisting or not,

which are executed from a previous somersault, if performed in the same direction will receive a bonus of	0.1pts.
If performed in the reverse direction, the bonus will be	0.2pts.

20.1.7 A skill is only considered valid if, after the skill, the competitor lands on the track or landing area on his feet or simultaneously on his hands and feet.

20.1.8 The Difficulty Judges will evaluate the difficulty of a skill according to the position of the feet upon landing.

20.1.9 The Difficulty Judges make all decisions regarding Rule 20.1.

20.2 Method of Scoring

20.2.1 The evaluation of Execution (form, consistency of height, control and rhythm), and Difficulty is done in 10ths of a point.

20.2.2 Judges must write their deductions independently of each other.

20.2.3 Secretaries will be assigned to the Judges. Any calculations made by the secretaries must be verified by the Judges.

20.2.4 When signalled by the Superior Judge the marks of the Judges for Execution must be shown simultaneously.

20.2.5 If any of the Judges for Execution fail to show their marks when signalled by the Superior Judge, the average of the other marks will be taken for the missing mark. The decision is made by the Superior Judge.

20.2.6 Evaluation of the score for Execution:

20.2.6.1 The deductions for poor Execution are subtracted from the maximum mark (see Rule 18.4).

20.2.6.2 In a five skill pass the Execution Judges will double the Execution score before making any other deductions as defined in Rules 23.3.2 and 23.4.

20.2.6.3 The highest and lowest marks of the Execution Judges are deleted and the three middle marks are averaged and doubled to give the valid score for Execution.

20.2.7 Evaluation of the score for Difficulty:

20.2.7.1 The Difficulty Judges (nos. 6 & 7) calculate the difficulty of the optional passes as per Rule 20.1 and enter it on the competition card.

20.2.8 Evaluation of the competitor's total score for a pass:

20.2.8.1 Each pass is scored separately and a total of Execution plus Difficulty is calculated for each optional pass. (No Difficulty is calculated for the compulsory pass.)

20.2.8.2 The recorders will calculate the total score (Execution + Difficulty) and enter it on the score sheet and the competition card.

20.2.9 All scores will be rounded to 2 decimal places. Such rounding will only be made in respect of the competitor's total score for a pass.

20.2.10 The Chief Recorder must verify the total score on the score sheets and the competition cards.

20.2.11 The Superior Judge is responsible for determining the validity of the final scores.

C. COMPETITION JURY

21. COMPETITION JURY

21.1 Composition:

21.1.1 Superior Judge	1
21.1.2 Judges for Execution (nos. 1-5)	5
21.1.3 Judges for Difficulty (nos. 6 & 7)	2
21.1.4 Total	8

21.2 The Judges must sit separately at least 5 meters from the side of the tumbling track.

21.3 If a Judge fails to carry out his duties in a satisfactory manner he must be replaced. This decision will be made by the Arbitration Jury upon the recommendation of the Superior Judge.

21.5.1 If a Judge, who is the subject of the Arbitration Jury's discussion, is also a member of the Arbitration Jury, he may not vote on the decision.

21.5.2 If an Execution Judge is replaced, the Arbitration Jury may decide that his previous marks will be replaced by the average of the remaining marks (see Rule 20.2.5).

22. DUTIES OF THE SUPERIOR JUDGE

22.1 Control of facilities.

22.2 Organise the Judges conference and the trial scoring.

22.3 Place and supervise all Judges and Recorders.

22.4 Direct the competition.

22.5 Convene the Competition Jury.

22.6 Convene and preside over the Arbitration Jury.

22.7 Supervise a draw for the starting order in the event of ties (see Rule 1.3.3).

22.8 Inform Judges nos. 1-5 of deductions for the optional passes (see Rule 5.4).

22.9 Decide on the competitors' dress (see Rule 6).

22.10 Decide whether the spotter touched the competitor (see Rules 10.3 and 18.1.7).

22.11 Decide when the competitor's pass has begun (see Rule 15.2).

22.12 Declare the maximum mark in the case of an interrupted pass (see Rule 18.4).

22.13 Inform the Execution Judges no. 1-5 of additional deductions (see Rule 23.4).

22.14 Decide if a Judge fails to show his score immediately (see Rule 20.2.5).

22.15 Supervise and control all scores, calculations and final results.

23. DUTIES OF THE JUDGES FOR EXECUTION (NOS. 1-5)

23.1 Evaluate the Execution (form, consistency of height, control and rhythm) as per Rule 23.3 and write down their deductions so that their secretaries can copy them onto their respective deduction sheets.

23.2 Subtract their deductions from the maximum mark indicated by the Superior Judge as per Rule 18.4.

23.3 Deductions for faulty Execution:

23.3.1 lack of form, constant height and lack of control, in each skill	0.1-0.5 pts
23.3.2 lack of stability on or after the last skill:	
23.3.2.1 landing on both feet but lacking stability and/or not standing still for 3 seconds	0.1-0.3 pts
23.3.2.2 touching the floor with one hand	0.4 pts
23.3.2.3 touching the floor with both hands	0.5 pts
23.3.2.4 falling to knees/hands & knees	0.6 pts
23.3.2.5 falling to seat	0.7 pts
23.3.2.6 falling to front or back	0.8 pts

23.3.2.7 After landing in the landing zone
or track, touching outside the landing zone
or track with any part of the body   0.9 pts

23.3.2.8 Landing out of the landing zone or
track with any part of the body   1.0 pts

23.4 Make the following deductions on the instruction of the Superior Judge:

23.4.1 Talking to or giving any form of
signal to a competitor by their own spotter,
for each occurrence   0.3 pts

23.4.2 Failing to end a completed pass with
a somersault, as per Rule 5.4   0.5 pts

23.4.3 Additional skills as per Rule 19.4   1.0 pts

24. DUTIES OF THE JUDGES FOR DIFFICULTY (NOS. 6 & 7)

24.1 Collect the competition cards from the Chief Recorder at least two hours prior to the competition.

24.2 Check the compulsory pass.

24.3 Determine the difficulty of each optional pass as per Rule 20.1, enter it on the competition card and write down any changes which occur as per Rule 7.3.

24.4 Display the Difficulty score.

GOVERNING BODY

United States Acrogymnastics Federation, c/o Jeff T. Hennessy, 102 Westmoreland Drive, Lafayette, LA 70506

Through its affiliation with the Federation of International Trampoline (F.I.T.), the U.S. Acrogymnastics Federation (USAF) is recognized as the governing body for trampolining, tumbling, and double mini-tramp in the United States. The USAF and the F.I.T. have as their primary objectives fostering, developing and promoting competitive trampolining, tumbling, and double mini-tramp from the local level through international competition. The documents noted in preface to the rules (p. 630) are available along with other materials from the F.I.T.

• VOLLEYBALL •

OFFICIAL 1988-89
UNITED STATES VOLLEYBALL RULES
AS APPROVED BY
THE UNITED STATES VOLLEYBALL ASSOCIATION

(Reproduced by permission of The United States Volleyball Association*)

☐

Note: The official USVBA rules publication includes extensive commentary (interpretation) on the rules of play as well as recommended standard procedure in game conduct, official hand signals, and instructions for official scoring procedures. Due to space limitations, only the technical rules of play are reproduced here. The rules printed here may not be copied. Current copies of rules can be purchased from the USVBA.

CHAPTER I

FACILITIES, PLAYING AREA AND EQUIPMENT

RULE 1. PLAYING AREA AND MARKINGS

Article 1. COURT—The playing court shall be 18 m. long by 9 m. wide (59' x 29'6"). A clear area of 2 m. (6'6") should surround an indoor court. A clear area of 3 m. (9'10") should surround an outdoor court.

Article 2. COURT MARKINGS—The court shall be marked by lines 5 cm. (2") wide. Areas being defined by court markings shall be measured from the outside edge of the lines defining such areas.

Article 3. CENTER LINE—A line 5 cm. (2") wide shall be drawn across the court beneath the net from sideline to sideline dividing the court into two equal team areas.

Article 4. ATTACK LINE—In each team area a line 5 cm. (2") wide shall be drawn between the sidelines parallel to the center line and 3 m. (9'10") from the middle of the center line to the rearmost edge of the attack line. The attack area, limited by the center line and the attack line, extends indefinitely beyond the sidelines.

Article 5. SERVICE AREA—At a point 20 cm. (8") behind and perpendicular to each end line, two lines, each 15 cm. (6") in length and 5 cm. (2") in width, shall be drawn to mark the service area for each team. One line is an extension of the right sideline and the other is drawn so that its farther edge is 3 m. (9'10") from the extension of the outside edge of the right sideline. The service area shall have a minimum depth of 2 m. (6'6").

---

*See page 657 for additional information.

Article 6. OVERHEAD CLEARANCE—For the Olympic Games there must be a clear space of 12 m. 50 cm. (41') above the court. For the final rounds of the World Championships, or similar competitions, the same clearance is required unless the Executive Committee of the International Volleyball Federation makes a special concession. For all other competitions, there should be an overhead clearance free from obstructions to a height of 7 m. (23') measured from the playing surface.

Article 7. SUBSTITUTION ZONE—The substitution zone is an area extending from the imaginary extension of the attack line to the imaginary extension of the center line between the court boundary and the scorer's table.

Article 8. MINIMUM TEMPERATURE—The minimum temperature shall not be below 10 degrees centigrade (50 degrees Fahrenheit).

Volleyball

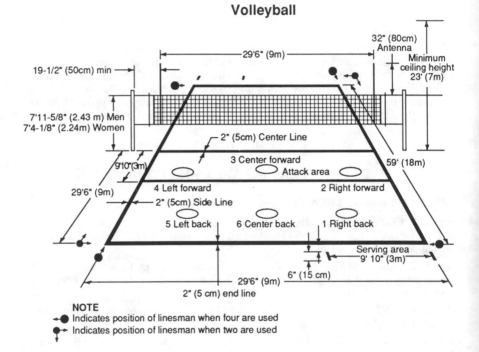

NOTE
Indicates position of linesman when four are used
Indicates position of linesman when two are used

RULE 2. THE NET

Article 1. SIZE AND CONSTRUCTION—The net shall be not less than 9.50 m. (32') in length and 1 m. (39") in width throughout the full length when stretched. A double thickness of white canvas or vinyl 5 cm. (2") wide shall be sewn along the full length of the top of the net. The net must be constructed of 10 cm. (4") square dark mesh only. A flexible cable shall be stretched through the upper and lower edges of the net. The ends of the net should be capable of receiving a wooden dowel to keep the ends of the net in straight lines when tight.

Article 2. NET HEIGHT—The height of the net measured from the center of the court shall be 2.43 m. (7'11 5/8") for men and 2.24 m. (7'4 1/8") for women. The two ends of the net must be at the same height from the playing surface and cannot exceed the regulation height by more than 2 cm. (3/4").

Article 3. VERTICAL TAPE MARKERS—Two tapes of white material 5 cm. (2″) wide and 1 m. (39″) in length shall be fastened to the net, one at each end, over and perpendicular to each sideline and the center line. The vertical tape side markers are considered to be a part of the net.

Article 4. NET ANTENNAS—Coinciding with the outside edge of each vertical tape marker, an antenna shall be fastened to the net at a distance of 9 m. (29′6″) from each other. The net antennas shall be 1.80 m. (6′) in length and made of safe and moderately flexible material with a uniform diameter of 10 mm. (3/8″). The upper half of each antenna shall be marked with alternating white and red or orange bands not less than 10 cm. (4″) and not more than 15 cm. (6″) in width. The antennas will be affixed to the net with fasteners that provide for quick and easy adjustment of the antenna. The fasteners shall be smooth surfaced and free of any sharp edges that might be considered hazardous to players.

Article 5. NET SUPPORTS—Where possible, the posts, uprights, or stands, including their bases, which support the net should be at least 50 cm. (19 1/2″) from the side lines and placed in such a manner as to not interfere with the officials in the performance of their duties.

Current Practices for Rule 2

1) NET HEIGHTS FOR AGE GROUPS SCHOLASTIC COMPETITION—The following net heights are currently in practice for the below indicated age groups and scholastic levels of competition:

HEIGHT OF NET

AGE GROUPS	GIRLS	BOYS/COED
17 years and under	2.24 m. (7′4 1/8″)	2.43 m. (7′11 5/8″)
15 years and under	2.24 m. (7′4 1/8″)	2.43 m. (7′11 5/8″)
13 years and under	2.24 m. (7′4 1/8″)	2.24 m. (7′4 1/8′)

SCHOLASTIC LEVELS	GIRLS	BOYS/COED
Grades 1 thru 6 (Elementary School):	1.85 m. (6′1″)	1.85 m. (6′1″)
Grades 7 and 8 (Middle School):	2.24 m. (7′4 1/8″)	2.24 m. (7′4 1/8″)
Grades 7 thru 9 (Junior High School):	2.24m. (7′4 1/8″)	2.43m. (7′11 5/8″)
Grades 9/10 thru 12 (Senior High School):	2.24 m. (7′4 1/8″)	2.43 m. (7′11 5/8″)

In the interest of safety for age group and scholastic competition, the height of the net shall be that specified for male competition. This height requirement shall not be modified.

2) USA YOUTH VOLLEYBALL NET HEIGHTS—Where competition is being conducted under rules for USA Youth Volleyball, the following net heights are recommended:

Ages 7 thru 9	2.3m.	(7′6 1/2″)
Ages 10 thru 12	2.15 m.	(7′1″)

A higher net has been recommended for the younger age groups in an effort to have them refrain from attempting to spike the ball and to concentrate on the basics of using three hits to return the ball to the opponents. The lower net height for the older age group will provide an opportunity for them to spike the ball as a natural progression in the overall skills of volleyball.

3) COLOR OF THE NET—When reference is made to the requirement for the net to be constructed of dark mesh, it is currently a suggestion with a requirement for dark mesh to be instituted after a reasonable period of time to be determined by the Committee on Equipment and Supplies.

RULE 3. THE BALL

Article 1. SIZE AND CONSTRUCTION—The ball shall be spherical with a laceless leather or leatherlike cover of 12 or more pieces of uniform light color with or without a separate bladder; it shall not be less than 62 cm. nor more than 68 cm. (25″ to 27″) in circumference; and it shall weigh not less than 260 grams nor more than 280 grams (9 to 10 ozs.)

CHAPTER II

PARTICIPANTS IN COMPETITION

RULE 4. RIGHTS AND DUTIES OF PLAYERS AND TEAM PERSONNEL

Article 1. RULES OF THE GAME—All coaches and players are required to know the rules of the game and abide by them.

Article 2. DISCIPLINE OF TEAM—The coaches, managers and captains are responsible for discipline and proper conduct of their team personnel.

Article 3. SPOKESMAN OF THE TEAM—The playing captain is the only player who may address the first referee and shall be the spokesman of the team. The captains may also address the second referee, but only on matters concerning the second referee's duties. The designated head coach may address the referees only for the purpose of requesting a time-out or substitution.

Article 4. TIME-OUT REQUESTS—Requests for time-out may be made by the designated head coach and/or by the playing captain when the ball is dead.

a) Each team is allowed two time-outs in each game. Consecutive time-outs may be requested by either team without the resumption of play between time-outs. The length of a time-out is limited to 30 seconds.

b) If a team captain or head coach inadvertently requests a third time-out, it shall be refused and the team warned. If, in the judgment of the first referee, a team requests a third time-out as means of attempting to gain an advantage, the offending team will be penalized (red card—point or side out).

c) During a time-out, players may move to the sideline or to the vicinity of the team bench. All players and bench personnel may participate in discussions, provided bench personnel do not enter the court.

1) Water and/or other liquids may only be administered in the vicinity of the team bench. Where possible, this area should be at least 2m (6′6″) from the court.

Article 5. TEAM BENCHES—Benches are to be placed on the right and left of the scorer's table. Team members shall occupy the bench located on the side of the net adjacent to their playing area. Only the coaches, a trainer, managers, statisticians and the reserve players can be seated on such benches. Coaches shall be seated on the end of the bench nearest the scorer's table.

Article 6. INDIVIDUAL SANCTIONS—The following acts of coaches, players, substitutes and other team members are subject to sanction by the referee:

a) Addressing of officials concerning their decisions.

b) Making profane or vulgar remarks or acts to officials, players or spectators.

c) Committing actions tending to influence decisions of officials.

d) Disruptive coaching during the game by any team member from outside the court.

e) Crossing the vertical plane of the net with any part of the body with the purpose of distracting an opponent while the ball is in play.

f) Shouting, yelling, or stamping feet in such a manner as to distract an opponent who is playing, or attempting to play, a ball.

g) It is forbidden for teammates to clap hands at the instant of contact with the ball by a player, particularly during the reception of service.

h) Shouting or taking any action conducive to distracting the first referee's judgment concerning handling of the ball.

Article 7. DEGREES OF INDIVIDUAL SANCTIONS—Offences committed by coaches, players and/or other team members may result in the following warning, penalty, expulsion from the game or disqualification from the match by the first referee:

a) WARNING: For minor unsporting offenses, such as talking to opponents, spectators or officials, shouting or unintentional acts that cause a delay in the game, a warning (yellow card) is issued and is recorded on the scoresheet. A second minor offense must result in a penalty.

b) PENALTY: For rude behavior or a second minor offense, or other serious offenses, a penalty (red card) is issued by the first referee and is recorded on the scoresheet. A penalty automatically entails the loss of service by the offending team if serving, or if not serving, the awarding of a point to the opponents. A second act warranting the issue of a penalty by the first referee results in the expulsion of a player(s) or team member(s).

c) EXPULSION: Extremely offensive conduct (such as obscene or insulting words or gestures) towards officials, spectators or opponents, results in expulsion of a player from the game (red and yellow cards together). A second expulsion during a match must result in the disqualification of a player or team member. No further penalty is assessed.

d) DISQUALIFICATION: A second expulsion during a match of any attempted or actual physical aggression towards an official, spectator or opponent results in the disqualification of a player or team member for the remainder of a match (red and yellow cards apart). Disqualified persons must leave the area (including spectator area) of the match. No further penalty is assessed.

Article 8. MISCONDUCT BETWEEN GAMES—Any sanctions for misconduct between games will be administered in the game following such misconduct.

Article 9. TEAM SANCTIONS—Penalties assessed against a team are indicated by the first referee showing the appropriate signal or penalty card (yellow or red) and notifying the coach or captain of the reason for the sanction. Such sanctions must be noted in the comments section of the scoresheet. Sanctions assessed teams are not accumulative during a game or match (two warnings against a team does not result in a red card, etc., regardless of the accumulative total). Team sanctions include:

(a) Illegal substitution requests (charged time-out)

(b) Delay in completing a substitution (charged time-out)

(c) A delay by a team in returning to play after a time-out or period between games (charged time-out)

(d) An illegal request for time-out by other than the captain or coach (team warning—yellow card)

(e) A third request for a time-out (team warning—yellow card)

(f) Illegal substitute or disqualified player attempting to enter the game (charged time-out)

(g) Failure to submit a lineup 2 minutes prior to the start of a match or prior to the expiration of the intermission between games (charged time-out)

(h) A charged third time-out (team penalty—red card—point or side out)

(i) A fourth request for time-out (team penalty—red card—point or side out)

(j) Administering water and/or other liquids at the sideline (first time in game, team warning—yellow card; second time, team penalty—red card)

RULE 5. THE TEAMS

Article 1. PLAYERS' UNIFORMS—The playing uniform shall consist of jersey, shorts and light and pliable shoes (rubber or leather soles without heels).

a) It is forbidden to wear head gear or jewelry (including taped earrings, string bracelets, etc), with the exception of medical medallions, religious medallions, or flat wedding bands. If worn, medical and religious medallions must be taped under the uniform. If a ring, other than a flat wedding band, cannot be removed, it must be taped in such a manner as to not create a safety hazard for other personnel. If requested by a team captain before the match commences, the first referee may grant permission for one or more players to play without shoes.

  1) It is forbidden for Junior Olympic age players to wear jewelry.

b) Players' jerseys must be marked with numbers not less than 8 cm. (3″) in height on the chest and not less than 15 cm. (6″) in height on the back. Numbers shall be located on the jersey in such a position that they are clearly visible. Numbers shall be in a color clearly contrasting to that of the jersey. For United States competition, shirts may be numbered from 1 to 99 inclusive.

c) Members of a team must appear on the court dressed in clean presentable uniforms (jerseys and shorts, pants or culottes) of the same color, style, cut and trim. If tights, leotards, body suits, bicycle shorts, etc., are worn in such a manner that they are exposed, they will be considered to be a part of the uniform and must be worn by all team members and must be identical. For the purpose of identical uniforms, shoes, and socks are not considered a part of the uniform and are not required to be identical for team members. During cold weather, it is permissible for teams to wear identical training suits provided they are numbered in accordance with the specifications of paragraph b) above and are of the same color, style, cut and trim.

Article 2. COMPOSITION OF TEAMS AND SUBSTITUTIONS—A team shall consist of six players regardless of circumstances. The composition of a complete team, including substitutes, may not exceed twelve players.

a) Before the start of a match, including during tournament play, teams shall submit a roster listing all players, including substitutes, and the uniform number each player will wear. Rosters shall also indicate the designated head coach. Once the roster has been submitted to the second referee or scorer, no changes may be made.

b) At least two minutes before the start of a match and prior to the expiration of the intermission between games, the head coach or captain shall submit to the scorer a lineup of players who will be starting the game and the position in the service order each will play. Lineups will be submitted on the official lineup sheets provided by the scorer. Players shall be listed on the lineup sheet in the floor position they shall occupy at the start of the game. After the lineup sheets have been received by the scorer, no changes may be made. Errors in line-ups entered on the score sheet may be corrected if necessitated due to a scorer error or omission. Players listed on the lineup sheets may be replaced prior to the start of play through a substitution request by the team coach or captain under the provisions of paragraph e) below. One of the players on the lineup sheet must be designated as the playing captain. Prior to the start of play, opponents will not be permitted to see the lineup submitted by the opposing team.

c) Substitutes, coaches and non-playing members of the team shall be on the side of the court opposite the first referee.

d) Substitution of players may be made on the request of either the playing captain on the court or the designated head coach off the court when the ball is dead and when recognized by either referee. A team is allowed a maximum of six (6) team substitutions in any one game. Before entering the game, a substitute must report to the second referee in proper playing uniform ready to enter upon the floor when authorization is given. If the requested substitution is not completed immediately, the team will be charged with a time-out and shall be allowed to use such time-out unless it has already used the allowable number of time-outs. In case the team has already exhausted the allowable two time-outs, the team shall be penalized by point or side out and may not use the time.

e) The captain or coach requesting a substitution(s) shall indicate the number of substitutions desired and shall report to the second referee the numbers of players involved in the substitution. If the coach or captain fails to indicate that more than one substitution is desired, the first or second referee shall refuse any additional substitute(s) until the next legal opportunity. Following a completed substitution, a team may not request a new substitution until play has resumed and the ball is dead again or until a time-out has been requested and granted to either team. During a legal charged time-out, any number of requests for substitutions may be made by either team. Immediately following a time-out, an additional request for substitution may be made.

f) A player starting a game may be replaced only once by a substitute and may subsequently enter the game once, but in the original position in the serving order in relation to other teammates. Only the original starter may replace a substitute during the same game. There may be a maximum of two players participating in any one position in the service order (except in case of accident or injury requiring abnormal substitution under the provision of paragraph h) below). If an illegal substitution request is made (i.e., excess player entry, excess team substitution, wrong position entry, etc.) the request will be refused and the team charged a time-out. At the expiration of the time-out period, if a substitution is still desired, a new request must be made.

g) If a player becomes injured and cannot continue playing within 15 seconds, such player must be replaced. After that brief period, if the team desires to have the player remain in the game, and if the player cannot continue to play immediately, the team must use a charged time-out. If the player is replaced, regardless of time required to safely remove the player from the court, no time-out shall be charged.

h) If through accident or injury a player is unable to play and substitution cannot be made under the provision of paragraph f), or if the team has used its allowable six (6) team substitutions, such player may be replaced in the following priority without penalty:

(1) By any substitute who has not participated in the game.

(2) By the player who played in the position of the injured player.

(3) By any substitute, regardless of position previously played.

Players removed from the game under the abnormal substitution provisions of paragraph h), or substitutes whose injuries create an abnormal substitution due to their inability to enter the game to replace an injured player, will not be permitted to participate in the remainder of the game.

i) If through injury or accident a player is unable to play and substitution cannot be made under the provisions of paragraph f) and h), the referee may grant a special time-out of up to three (3) minutes. Play will be resumed as soon as the injured player is able to continue. In no case shall the special injury time-out exceed three minutes. At the end of the special time-out, a team may request a normal time-out provided they have not already used their allowable two (2) time-outs. If, after three minutes, or at the expiration of time-outs granted subsequent to the special time-out, the injured player cannot continue to play, the team loses the game by default, keeping the points acquired.

j) If a team becomes incomplete through expulsion or disqualification of a player, and substitution cannot be made under the provisions of paragraph f) above, the team loses the game by default, keeping the points acquired.

Article 3. MODIFIED SUBSTITUTION RULES—For USVBA Senior/Junior Divisions, USVBA BB Divisions or lower, NCAA Women's competition, Recreation or other levels of competition where the capability of players would require a more liberal substitution rule to permit teams to be competitive, the following modified substitution rules may be used.

a) A player shall not enter the game for a fourth time (starting shall count as an entry). A team shall be allowed a maximum of twelve (12) substitutions in any one game. Players starting a game may be replaced by a substitute and may subsequently re-enter the game twice. Each substitute may enter the game three times. Players re-entering the game must assume the original position in the serving order in relation to other teammates. No change shall be made in the order of rotation unless required due to injury requiring abnormal substitution under the provisions of paragraph b) below. Any number of players may enter the game in each position in the service order.

b) If through accident or injury a player is unable to play, and substitution cannot be made under the provisions of paragraph a), or if the team has used its allowable twelve (12) team substitutions, such player may be replaced in the following priority without penalty:

(1) By the starter or substitute who has played in the position of the injured player, if such starter or substitute has not already been in the game the allowable three times, or by any player who has not already participated in the game.

(2) By any player on the bench who has not been in the game three times, regardless of position previously played.

(3) If all players have been in the game the allowable three times, by the substitute who previously played in the position of the injured player.

(4) By any substitute, even though all substitutes have been in the game the three allowable times.

Note: If a substitute is injured to the extent that entry is not possible under the provisions of 2)b)(1) or (3), the substitute will not be permitted to participate for the remainder of the game.

c) If through injury or accident a player is unable to play and substitution cannot be made under the provision of paragraph a) or b), the first referee may grant a special time-out under the provisions of Rule 5, Article 2h).

d) If a team becomes incomplete through disqualification or expulsion of a player and substitution cannot be made under the provision of paragraph a) above, the team loses the game by default, keeping the points acquired.

Article 4. WRONG POSITION ENTRY OR ILLEGAL PLAYER IN GAME—If a player participates in the game and is then found to be illegally in the game or has entered in a wrong position in the service order, play must be stopped, the player(s) removed from the game and the following corrective action taken:

a) If discovered before a service by the opponents, all points scored during that term of service while any player(s) was illegally in the game or in a wrong position in the service order shall be cancelled. If the team at fault is serving at the time of discovery of the error, a side out will be declared.

b) If the team at fault is not serving at the time of discovery of the error, all points scored by the opponents will be retained. The serving team shall be awarded a point unless discovery of the error is immediately following a play in which the serving team scored a point. In such case, no additional point will be awarded. The wrong position will be corrected and play continued without further penalty.

c) If it is not possible to determine when the error first occurred, the player(s) at fault and the team in error shall resume the correct position(s). If the offending team is serving, a side out shall be declared and only the last point in that term of service removed. If the other team is serving, it shall be awarded a point unless the play immediately preceding discovery of the error in position or player illegally in the game resulted in a point.

d) If correction of the error requires a substitution due to an illegal or wrong position entry of a player(s), neither the team or player(s) will be charged with a substitution. In addition, any player or team substitutions charged at the time of the wrong entry shall be removed from the scoresheet as though they have never occurred.

CHAPTER III

RULES OF PLAY

RULE 6. TEAM AREAS, DURATION OF MATCHES AND INTERRUPTIONS OF PLAY

Article 1. NUMBER OF GAMES—Matches shall consist of the best of two out of three games or the best of three out of five games.

Article 2. CHOICE OF PLAYING AREA AND SERVE—The captains will call the toss of a coin for choice of team area or the service. The winner of the toss chooses: 1. first serve, or; 2. choice of team area for the first game. The loser of the toss receives the remaining option.

Article 3. CHOICE OF PLAYING AREA FOR DECIDING GAME—Before the beginning of the deciding game of a match, the first referee makes a new toss of the coin with the options described in Article 2. The captain of the team not calling the toss of the coin for the first game shall call the toss of the coin for the deciding game.

Article 4. CHANGE OF PLAYING AREAS BETWEEN GAMES—After each game of a match, except when a deciding game is required, teams and team members will change playing area and benches.

Article 5. CHANGE OF PLAYING AREA IN DECIDING GAME OF MATCH—When teams are tied in number of games won in a match, and one of the teams reaches eight (8) points (or when four minutes have elapsed in a timed game) in a deciding game, the teams will be directed to change playing areas. After change of areas the serving will continue by the player whose turn it is to serve. In case the change is not made at the proper time, it will take place as soon as it is brought to the attention of the first referee. The score remains unchanged and is not a grounds for protest.

Article 6. TIME BETWEEN GAMES OF A MATCH—A maximum interval of two (2) minutes is allowed between games of a match. Between the fourth and fifth games of a match, the interval shall be five (5) minutes. The interval between games includes the time required for change of playing areas and submitting of lineups for the next game.

Article 7. INTERRUPTIONS OF PLAY—As soon as the referees notice an injured player, or a foreign object on the court that could create a hazard to a player(s), play will be stopped and the first referee will direct a play-over when play is resumed.

Article 8. INTERRUPTIONS OF THE MATCH—If any circumstances, or series of circumstances, prevent the completion of a match (such as bad weather, failure of equipment, etc.), the following shall apply:

a) If the game is resumed on the same court after one or several periods, not exceeding four hours, the results of the interrupted game will remain the same and the game resumes under the same conditions as existed before the interruption.

b) If the match is resumed on another court or in another facility, results of the interrupted game will be cancelled. The results of any completed game of the match will be counted. The cancelled game shall be played under the same conditions as existed before the interruption.

c) If the delay exceeds four hours, the match shall be replayed, regardless of where played.

Article 9. DELAYING THE GAME—Any act which, in the judgment of the first referee, unnecessarily delays the game may be sanctioned. (Rule 4, Article 7)

Current Practices for Rule 6

1) ONE GAME PLAYOFF—A one game playoff shall be considered as a deciding game of a match and the teams shall change sides when one team has scored eight points or 4 minutes have elapsed in timed games.

2) MATCHES WITHOUT DECIDING GAMES—In the interest of consistency, a toss of the coin should be held prior to a third or fifth game of a match in which such games will be played regardless of outcome of preceding games of the match.

a) In the final game of a three or five game match where all games are played, regardless of outcome, teams will change playing areas when one team has scored its eighth point or 4 minutes have elapsed in timed games.

3) TIMED GAME—In circumstances where the efficient management of a tournament or series of matches requires adherence to a time schedule in order to complete the competitions, the time game may be employed. Such timed games may be played on the basis of 8 minutes ball-in-play time or 15 points, whichever occurs first. Such basis must be established before the first game where round robins, a specific number of games, etc., are indicated as the format.

RULE 7. COMMENCEMENT OF PLAY AND THE SERVICE

Article 1. THE SERVICE—The service is the act of putting the ball into play by the player in the right back position who hits the ball with the hand (open or closed) or any part of one arm in an effort to direct the ball into the opponent's area.

a) The server shall have five seconds after the first referee's readiness to serve whistle in which to release or toss the ball for service.

b) After being clearly released or thrown from the hand(s) of the server, the ball shall be cleanly hit for service. (EXCEPTION: If, after releasing or throwing the ball for service, the server allows the ball to fall to the floor (ground) without being hit or contacted, the service effort shall be cancelled and a re-serve directed. However, the referee will not allow the game to be delayed in this manner more than one time during any service.)

c) At the instant the ball is hit for the service, the server shall not have any portion of the body in contact with the end line, the court or the floor (ground) outside the lines marking the service area. At the instant of service, the server may stand on or between the two lines, or their extensions which mark the service area.

d) The service is considered good if the ball passes over the net between the antennas or their indefinite extensions without touching the net or other objects.

e) If the ball is served before the first referee's whistle, the serve shall be cancelled and a re-serve directed. The first referee will not allow a player to delay the game in this manner more than one time.

Article 2. SERVING FAULTS—The referee will signal side out and direct a change of service to the other team when one of the following serving faults occurs:

a) The ball touches the net.

b) The ball passes under the net.

c) The ball touches an antenna or does not pass over the net completely between the antennas or their indefinite extensions.

d) The ball touches a player of the serving team or any object before entering the opponent's playing area.

e) The ball lands outside the limits of the opponent's playing area.

Article 3. DURATION OF SERVICE—A player continues to serve until a fault is committed by the serving team.

Article 4. SERVING OUT OF ORDER—If a team has served out of order, the team loses the service and any points gained during such out of order service. The players of the team at fault must immediately resume their correct positions on the court.

Article 5. SERVICE IN SUBSEQUENT GAMES—The team not serving first in the preceding game of a match shall serve first in the next game of the match, except in the deciding game of a match (Rule 6, Article 3).

Article 6. CHANGE OF SERVICE—The team which receives the ball for service shall rotate one position clockwise before serving.

Article 7. SCREENING—The players of the serving team must not, through screening, prevent the receiving player from watching the server or the trajectory of the ball. Screening is illegal and a fault.

a) A team makes a group screen when the server is hidden behind a group of two or more teammates and the ball is served over a member(s) of the group.

b) A player who jumps or moves in a distracting manner at the moment of service shall be guilty of screening.

c) A player with hands extended clearly above the height of the head at service shall be considered to be screening if the ball passes over the player.

Article 8. POSITIONS OF PLAYERS AT SERVICE—At the time the ball is contacted for the serve, the placement of players on the court must conform to the service order recorded on the scoresheet as follows (the server is exempt from this requirement):

a) In the front line, the center forward (3) may not be as near the right sideline as the right forward (2) nor as near the left sideline as the left forward (4). In the back line, the center back (6) may not be as near the right sideline as the right back (1) nor as near the left sideline as the left back (5). No back line player may be as near the net as the corresponding front line player. After the ball is contacted for the serve, players may move from their respective positions.

b) The serving order as recorded on the official scoresheet must remain the same until the game is completed.

c) Before the start of a new game, the serving order may be changed and such changes must be recorded on the scoresheet. It is the responsibility of the head coach or team captain to submit a lineup to the scorer prior to the expiration of the authorized rest period between games of a match.

Current Practices for Rule 7

1) PRELIMINARY SERVICE ACTION—Preliminary actions, such as bouncing the ball on the floor or lightly tossing the ball from one hand to the other, shall be allowed, but shall be counted as part of the five seconds allowed for the server to initiate service release or toss the ball preparatory for the service.

2) SERVICE FOR ELEMENTARY GRADE PLAYERS—Where elementary grade age players are in a competition, it can be considered legal service if the ball is hit directly from the hand of the server, not necessarily dropped or tossed. Where this serve is acceptable, it should be established in advance or otherwise agreed upon mutually before competition starts and the officials notified. In such levels of team play, players should be

encouraged to develop ability and skills necessary for a serve which does satisfy the requirements of the official rule.

3) REQUESTING LINEUP CHECK—Team captains may request verification of the service order of their team if done on an infrequent basis. Requests for lineup checks for opponents will be limited to determining whether or not the players are in a correct service order. No information will be provided to disclose which opposing players are front line or back line players.

RULE 8. PLAYING THE BALL

Article 1. MAXIMUM OF THREE TEAM CONTACTS—Each team is allowed a maximum of three (3) successive contacts of the ball in order to return the ball to the opponent's area. (EXCEPTION: Rule 8, Article 11)

Article 2. CONTACTED BALL—A player who contacts the ball, or is contacted by the ball, shall be considered as having played the ball.

Article 3. CONTACT OF BALL WITH THE BODY—The ball may be hit with any part of the body on or above the waist.

Article 4. SIMULTANEOUS CONTACTS WITH THE BODY—The ball can contact any number of parts of the body down to and including the waist providing such contacts are simultaneous and that the ball rebounds immediately and cleanly after such contact.

Article 5. SUCCESSIVE CONTACTS—Players may have successive contacts of the ball during blocking (Rule 8, Article 11) and during a single attempt to make the first team hit of a ball coming from the opponents, even if the ball is blocked, provided there is no finger action used during the effort and the ball is not held or thrown. Any other player contacting the ball more than once, with whatever part of the body, without any other player having touched it between these contacts, will be considered as having committed a double hit fault.

Article 6. HELD BALL—When the ball visibly comes to rest momentarily in the hands or arms of a player, it is considered as having been held. The ball must be hit in such a manner that it rebounds cleanly after contact with a player. Scooping, lifting, pushing or allowing the ball to roll on the body shall be considered to be a form of holding. A ball clearly hit with one or both hands from a position below the ball is considered a good play.

Article 7. SIMULTANEOUS CONTACTS BY OPPONENTS—If the ball visibly comes to rest by two opposing players, it is a double fault and the first referee will direct a play-over.

a) If the ball is contacted simultaneously by opponents and is not held, play shall continue.

b) After simultaneous contact by opponents, the team on whose side the ball falls shall have the right to play the ball three times.

c) If, after simultaneous contact by opponents, the ball falls out of bounds, the team on the opposite side shall be deemed as having provided the impetus necessary to cause the ball to be out of bounds.

Article 8. BALL PLAYED BY TEAMMATES—When two players of the same team contact the ball simultaneously, this is considered as two team contacts and neither of the players may make the next play on the ball. (EXCEPTION: Rule 8, Article 11)

Article 9. ATTACKING OVER OPPONENT'S COURT—A player is not allowed to attack the ball on the opposite side of the net. If the ball is hit above the spiker's side of the net and then the follow-through causes the spiker's hand and arm to cross the net without contacting an opponent, such action does not constitute a fault.

Article 10. ASSISTING A TEAMMATE—No player shall assist a teammate by holding such player while the player is making a play on the ball. It shall be legal for a player to hold a teammate not making a play on the ball in order to prevent a fault.

Article 11. BLOCKING—Blocking is the action close to the net which intercepts the ball coming from the opponent's side by making contact with the ball before it crosses the net, as it crosses the net or immediately after it has crossed the net. An attempt to block does not constitute a block unless the ball is contacted during the effort. A blocked ball is considered to have crossed the net.

a) Blocking may be legally accomplished by only the players who are in the front line at the time of service.

b) Multiple contacts of the ball by a player(s) participating in a block shall be legal provided it is during one attempt to intercept the ball.

(1) Multiple contacts of the ball during a block shall be counted as a single contact, even though the ball may make multiple contacts with one or more players of the block.

c) Any player participating in a block shall have the right to make the next contact, such contact counting as the first of three hits allowed the team.

d) The team which effected a block shall have the right to three additional contacts after the block in order to return the ball to the opponent's area.

e) Back line players may not block or participate in a block, but may play the ball in any other position near or away from the block.

f) Blocking or attacking a served ball is prohibited.

g) Blocking of the ball across the net above the opponent's court shall be legal provided that such block is:

(1) After a player of the attacking team has spiked the ball, or, in the first referee's judgment, intentionally directed the ball into the opponent's court; or,

(2) After the opponents have completed their allowable three hits; or,

(3) After the opponents have hit the ball in such a manner that the ball would, in the first referee's judgment, clearly cross the net if not touched by a player, provided no member of the attacking team is in a position to make a legal play on the ball; or,

(4) If the ball is falling near the net and no member of the attacking team could reasonably make a play on the ball.

Article 12. BALL CONTACTING TOP OF NET AND BLOCK—If the ball touches the top of the net and a player(s) participating in a block and the ball returns to the attacker's side of the net, this team shall then have the right of three more contacts to return the ball to the opponent's area.

Article 13. BACK LINE ATTACKER—A back line player returning the ball to the opponent's side while forward of the attack line must contact the ball when at least part of the ball is below the level of the top of the net over the attacking team's area. The restriction does not apply if the back line player jumps from clearly behind the attack line and, after contacting the ball, lands on or in front of the line.

a) It is a fault when a back line player in the attack zone or contacting the attack line, or its imaginary extension, hits the ball while the bottom of the ball is completely above the height of the net and causes the ball to cross directly and completely the plane of the net or intentionally directs the ball towards the opponent's area so that it is contacted by an opponent before fully passing the plane of the net.

RULE 9. PLAY AT THE NET

Article 1. BALL IN NET BETWEEN ANTENNAS—A ball, other than a served ball, hitting the net between the antennas may be played again. If the ball touches the net after a team's allowable three contacts and does not cross the net, the referee should not stop the play until the ball is contacted for the fourth time or has touched the playing surface.

Article 2. BALL CROSSING THE NET—To be good, the ball must cross the net entirely between the antennas or their assumed indefinite extension.

Article 3. PLAYER CONTACT WITH NET—If a player's action causes the player to contact the net during play, whether accidentally or not, with any part of the player's body or uniform, that player shall be charged with a fault. If the ball is driven into the net with such force that it causes the net to contact a player, such contact shall not be considered a fault.

Article 4. SIMULTANEOUS CONTACT BY OPPONENTS—If opponents contact the net simultaneously, it shall constitute a double fault and the first referee shall direct a replay.

Article 5. CONTACT BY PLAYER OUTSIDE THE NET—If a player accidentally contacts any part of the net supports (e.g. a post, cable), the referee's stand, etc., such contact should not be counted as a fault provided that it has no effect on the sequence of play. Intentional contact or grabbing of such objects shall be penalized as a fault.

Article 6. CROSSING THE CENTER LINE—Contacting the opponent's playing area with any part of the body except the feet is a fault. Touching the opponent's area with a foot or feet is not a fault providing that some part of the encroaching foot or feet remain on or above the center line.

a) It is not a fault to enter the opponent's side of the court after the ball has been declared dead by the first referee.

b) It is not a fault to cross the assumed extension of the center line outside the playing area.

(1) While across the extension of the center line outside the court, a player of the attacking team may play a ball that has not fully passed beyond the plane of the net. Opponents may not interfere with a player making a play on the ball.

(2) A player who has crossed the extension of the center line and is not making a play on the ball may not interfere with an opponent.

Article 7. BALL PENETRATING OR CROSSING THE VERTICAL PLANE—A ball penetrating the vertical plane of the net over or below the net, whether over or outside the court, may be returned to the attacking team's side by a player of the attacking team provided the ball has not yet completely passed beyond the vertical plane of the net when such contact is made. A ball which has penetrated the vertical plane above the net may be played by either team.

RULE 10. LIVE BALL/DEAD BALL

Article 1. WHEN BALL BECOMES ALIVE—The ball becomes alive when legally contacted for service.

Article 2. WHEN BALL BECOMES DEAD—A live ball becomes dead when:

a) The ball touches an antenna or the net outside an antenna.

b) The ball does not cross the net completely between the antennas.

c) The ball strikes the floor, floor obstructions or wall.

d) The ball contacts the ceiling or overhead object at a height of 7 m. (23′) or more above a playable surface, or any object above an unplayable area.

e) A player(s) commits a fault.

f) A served ball contacts the net or other object.

g) The first or second referee blows a whistle, even though inadvertently.

h) A player causes the ball to come to rest on a rafter or other overhead object that is less than 7 m. above the height of the playing surface.

i) The ball contacts an object that is less than 15' above playable surface.

RULE 11. TEAM AND PLAYER FAULTS

Article 1. DOUBLE FAULT—A double fault occurs when players of opposing teams simultaneously commit faults. In such cases, the first referee will direct a play-over.

Article 2. FAULTS AT APPROXIMATELY THE SAME TIME—If faults by opponents occur at approximately the same time, the first referee shall determine which fault occurred first and shall penalize only that fault. If it cannot be determined which fault occurred first, a double fault shall be declared.

Article 3. PENALTY FOR COMMITTING FAULTS—If the serving team, or a player of the serving team, commits a fault, a side out shall be declared. If the receiving team, or a player of the receiving team, commits a fault, the serving team shall be awarded a point.

Article 4. TEAM AND PLAYER FAULTS—A fault shall be declared against a team or player when:

a) The ball touches the floor (R. 10 A. 1)

b) The ball is held, thrown or pushed (R. 8 A. 6)

c) A team has played the ball more than three times consecutively (R. 8 A. 1) (EXCEPTION: R. 8 A. 11)

d) The ball touches a player below the waist (R. 8 A. 3)

e) A player touches the ball twice consecutively (R. 8 A. 5) (EXCEPTION: R. 8 A. 5 and A. 11)

f) A team is out of position at service ((R. 7 A. 9)

g) A player touches the net or antenna (R. 9 A. 3)

h) A player completely crosses the center line and contacts the opponent's playing area (R. 8 A. 9)

i) A player attacks the ball above the opponent's playing area (R. 8 A. 9)

j) A back line player while in the attack area hits the ball into the opponent's court from above the height of the net (R. 8 A. 13)

k) A ball does not cross the net entirely between the antennas (R. 9 A. 2)

l) A ball lands outside the court or touches an object outside the court (R. 10 A. 1)

m) The ball is played by a player being assisted by a teammate as a means of support (R 8 A. 10)

n) A player reaches under the net and touches the ball or an opponent while the ball is being played by the opposite team (R. 9 C. 1)

o) Blocking is performed in an illegal manner (R. 8 A. 11)

p) Illegally served ball or service fault (R. 7 A. 2; R. 7 C. 1f)

RULE 12. SCORING AND RESULT OF THE GAME

Article 1. WHEN POINT IS SCORED—When a fault is committed by the receiving team, a point is awarded to the serving team.

Article 2. WINNING SCORE—A game is won when a team scores 15 points and has at least a two point advantage over the opponents. If the score is tied at 14-14, the play continues until one team has a lead of two points (e.g., 16-14,17-15,18-16, etc.).

Article 3. SCORE OF DEFAULTED GAME—If a team does not have sufficient players to start a game, or fails to play after the first referee requests play to begin, that team shall lose the game by default. Score of each defaulted game will be 15-0.

Article 4. SCORE OF DEFAULTED GAME DUE TO INJURY—If a game is defaulted due to a team being reduced to less than six players because of an injury, the defaulting team shall retain any points earned. The winning team shall be credited with at least 15 points or will be awarded sufficient points to reflect a two point advantage over the opponents.

Article 5. SCORE OF DEFAULTED GAME DUE TO EXPULSION OF A PLAYER— If a game is defaulted due to expulsion or disqualification of a player, the defaulting team shall retain any points earned. The offended team shall be credited with at least 15 points or a sufficient number of points to indicate a two point winning advantage over the opponents.

Article 6. REFUSAL TO PLAY—If, after receiving a warning from the first referee, a team refuses to play, the entire match is defaulted. The score for each defaulted game is 15-0 and the score of the match is 2-0 or 3-0, depending upon the number of games scheduled for the match.

Article 7. INCOMPLETE TEAM DURING MATCH—If a team is reduced to less than six players and cannot complete the remainder of a match, the opponents shall be awarded sufficient points to reflect a winning score of 15 points, or more if 15 points do not provide a winning margin of at least 2 points, for the incomplete game and sufficient games necessary to win the match. The defaulting team keeps its points and games won.

RULE 13. DECISIONS AND PROTESTS

Article 1. AUTHORITY OF THE REFEREE—Decisions based on the judgment of the referee or other officials are final and not subject to protest.

Article 2. INTERPRETATION OF THE RULES—Disagreements with interpretations of the rules must be brought to the attention of the first referee prior to the first service following the play in which the disagreement occurred. The captain of the protesting team may be the only one to bring the protest to the attention of the first referee.

Article 3. APPEAL OF DECISION OF THE REFEREE—If the explanation of the first referee following a protest lodged by the team captain is not satisfactory, the captain may appeal to a higher authority. If the protest cannot be resolved, the first referee shall proceed to the scorer's table and shall record, or cause to be recorded, on the scoresheet all pertinent facts of the protest. After the facts of the protest have been recorded, the first referee will continue to direct the game and will forward a report later on the protest in question.

Article 4. DISAGREEMENT WITH THE REFEREE'S DECISION—If a team captain is in disagreement with a first referee's decision in the assessment of a sanction, such decision is not protestable, but the team captain may state such disagreement in writing on the back of the official scoresheet after completion of the match.

CHAPTER IV

OFFICIALS AND THEIR DUTIES

Note: Chapter IV is included as a guideline for officials and shall not be construed to be a part of the official playing rules subject to protest by teams.

RULE 14. THE FIRST REFEREE

Article 1. AUTHORITY OF THE FIRST REFEREE—The first referee is in full control of the match and any judgment decisions rendered by the first referee are final. The first referee has authority over all players and officials from the coin toss prior to the first game of a match until the conclusion of the match, to include any periods during which the match may be temporarily interrupted, for whatever reason.

Article 2. QUESTIONS NOT COVERED BY RULE—The first referee has the power to settle all questions, including those not specifically covered in the rules.

Article 3. POWER TO OVERRULE—The first referee has the power to overrule decisions of other officials when, in the first referee's opinion, they have made errors.

Article 4. POSITION OF FIRST REFEREE DURING MATCH—The first referee shall be located at one end of the net in a position that will allow a clear view of the play. The referee's head should be approximately 50 cm. (19 1/2″) above the top of the net.

Article 5. PENALIZING VIOLATIONS—In accordance with Rule 4 the first referee penalizes violations made by players, coaches and other team members.

Article 6. USE OF SIGNALS—Immediately after giving a signal to stop play, the first referee shall indicate with the use of hand signals the nature of the violation, if a player fault, the player committing the fault and the team which shall make the next service.

RULE 15. THE SECOND REFEREE

Article 1. POSITION DURING MATCH—The second referee shall take a position on the side of the court opposite and facing the first referee.

Article 2. ASSISTING THE FIRST REFEREE—The second referee shall assist the first referee by making calls such as:

a) Violations of the center line and attack line.

b) Contact with the net by a player.

c) Contact of the ball with an antenna or ball not crossing the net entirely inside the antenna on the second referee's side of the court.

d) Foreign objects entering the court and presenting a hazard to the safety of the players.

e) Calling back court attacker/blocker violations.

f) Performing duties in addition to those outlined when instructed to do so by the first referee.

Article 3. KEEPING OFFICIAL TIME—The second referee shall be responsible for keeping official time of time-outs and rest periods between games of match.

Article 4. CONDUCT OF PARTICIPANTS—The second referee shall supervise the conduct of coaches and substitutes on the bench and shall call to the attention of the first referee any unsportsmanlike actions of players or other team members.

Article 5. SUPERVISION OF SUBSTITUTIONS—The second referee shall authorize substitutions requested by captains or the head coach of the teams.

Article 6. SERVICE ORDER OF TEAMS—The second referee shall verify at the beginning of each game that players of both teams are on the court in positions corresponding with lineups submitted to the scorer. The second referee shall supervise the rotation order and positions of the receiving team at the time of service.

Article 7. GIVING OPINIONS—The second referee shall give opinions on all matters when so requested by the first referee.

Article 8. ENDING PLAY—The play is considered as ended when the second referee blows a whistle.

RULE 16. THE SCORER

Article 1. POSITION DURING MATCH—The scorer's position is on the side of the court opposite the first referee and behind the second referee.

Article 2. RECORDING INFORMATION—Prior to the start of a match the scorer will clearly print the names of the 1st referee, and 2nd referee, and scorer on the scoresheet. The scorer obtains the team rosters and lineup sheets and records the numbers of the starting players on the scoresheet. Once a lineup and team roster have been received by the scorer, no changes may be made. Between games of the match, the scorer reminds the second referee to obtain new lineups from the captains or coaches in order to properly record any changes in the lineups. In addition, the scorer:

a) verifies the team rosters prior to the start of the match.

b) records the scores as the match progresses.

c) makes sure that the serving order and rotation of players is followed correctly.

d) carefully checks the eligibility of substitutes before authorizing their entry into a game

e) records substitution information on the scoresheet.

f) records time-outs and notifies the second referee and the first referee of the number of time-outs which have been charged to each team.

Article 3. DURING DECIDING GAME OF MATCH—During the deciding game of a match the scorer signals the referees when one of the team has scored an eighth point and indicates that the teams should change playing areas.

Article 4. VERIFICATION OF FINAL SCORE—At the conclusion of a game, the scorer verifies the final results of the game by signing the appropriate block of the scoresheet.

RULE 17. THE LINE JUDGES

Article 1. POSITION DURING MATCH—During the match, the line judges will be stationed:

a) With two line judges, they must be placed diagonally opposite each other, one at each end of the court at the corner away from the service area near the intersection of the end line and side boundary line.

b) With four line judges, one line judge shall be placed opposite each service area with the sideline extended approximately 2 m. behind the end line. One line judge shall be placed approximately 2 m. outside the sideline nearest the service area in line with the end line extended. Each line judge watches the line to which assigned.

Article 2. DUTIES—Line judges shall signal the first referee when:

a) Ball lands inbounds (Signal 3 or Signal 2)

b) Ball lands out of bounds (Signal 5 or Signal 4)

c) Foot fault by server or other player (Signal 8 or Signal 2)

d) Ball touches, passes over or outside an antenna (Signal 8 or Signal 4)

e) Ball contacts player before going out of bounds (Signal 7 or Signal 6)

f) Ball contacts overhead object (Signal 25)

Article 3. USE OF SIGNAL FLAGS—Each line judge shall be responsible for signaling to the first referee when a ball is "OUT" by raising the flag above the head, and when a ball is "IN" by pointing the flag towards the floor (ground) of the playing area.

GOVERNING BODY

United States Volleyball Association, 1750 E. Boulder Street, Colorado Springs, CO 80909-5766

The U.S. Volleyball Association (USVBA) is the leading organization for volleyball in the USA and is recognized by the U.S. Olympic Committee as the national governing body for the sport. It is the exclusive representative of the nation to the Federation Internationale de Volleyball. The USVBA is concerned with the promotion of volleyball at all levels throughout the nation and with the representation of the sport nationally and internationally. The organization conducts men's and women's open national championship tournaments as well as various age group tournaments. The organizational structure of the USVBA has the nation divided into some 25 regions through which a number of programs are conducted, including competition by age and/or ability, summer instructional camps, and clinics for development of coaches, players, and referees. All major national sports organizations that are concerned with promoting the sport of volleyball are associated with the USVBA.

MAGAZINES

Volleyball USA, USVBA, 1750 E. Boulder St., Colorado Springs, CO 80909-5766

Volleyball Monthly, Straight Down, Inc., Box 3137, San Luis Obispo, CA 93403

• WATER POLO •

ABRIDGMENT OF OFFICIAL WATER POLO RULES

(Reproduced by permission of United States Water Polo, Inc.*)

□

Note: The official Corporate Code of Regulations and Playing Rules for Water Polo issued by USWP consists of six parts as follows: 1) Conduct of Championship; 2) Athlete Registration and Bill of Rights; 3) Corporate Code of Regulations; 4) Rules of Competition; 5) U.S. Water Polo Hall of Fame; 6) U.S. Aquatic Sports, Inc. Only Part Four, Rules of Competition (with abridgment as indicated in text) is included here.

RULES OF COMPETITION

RULE 1. ORGANIZATION

WP1. The promoting club or organization shall be responsible for correct measurements and markings of the field of play and must provide all stipulated fixtures and equipment.

RULE 2. FIELD OF PLAY

DIAGRAM AND MEASUREMENTS

WP2. Diagram

WP3. The uniform distance between the respective goal lines is 30 meters. The uniform width of the field of play is 20 meters. The depth of the water must nowhere be less than 1.80 meters (preferably 2.00 meters). For matches in Olympic Games, World Championships, International competitions, and Men's Senior National Outdoor Championships (including the Zone and Pre-Zone Qualifying Tournaments leading to the Men's Senior National Outdoor Championships), the field of play shall be full measurements as above. For FINA events, the water temperature will be at least 24 degrees centigrade as a mandatory requirement and preferably will be a maximum of 26 degrees centigrade. These temperatures are recommended for other international competitions. The light intensity must not be less than 100 foot candles, and fresh water is to be used in all FINA events.

(USWP) For all JO competitions, the maximum length of the field of play shall be twenty-five (25) meters.

WP4. For matches played by women, the maximum measurements are 25 meters by 17 meters.

(USWP) For Senior Women's National Championships conducted jointly with men in the same pool, maximum dimensions shall be as described in WP3.

---

*See page 676 for additional information.

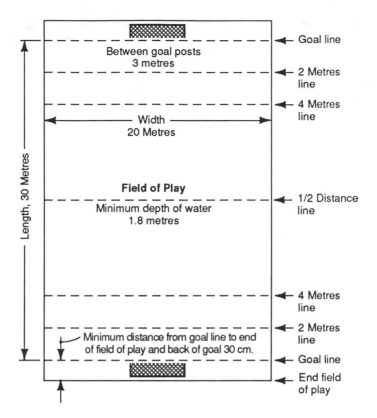

WP5. Distinctive marks must be provided on both sides of the field of play to denote the goal line, lines two meters and four meters from that line, and half distance between the goal lines. These markings must be clearly visible throughout the game. As uniform colors, the following are recommended for these markings: goal lines and half-distance line, white; two meters from goal line, red; four meters from goal line, yellow. A red or other visible colored sign shall be placed on the end of the field of play two meters from the corner of the field of play on the side of the goal judge (or on the side opposite the timekeeper if there are no goal judges). The boundary of the field of play at both ends is 0.30 meters behind the goal line.

WP6. Sufficient space must be provided to enable the referees to have free way from end to end of the field of play. Space must also be provided at the goal lines for the goal judges.

(USWP) Goal judges will be located on each side of the pool to the referee's left.

RULE 3. GOALS

WP7. The goal posts and crossbar must be of wood, metal, or synthetic (plastic) material, with rectangular sections of 0.075 meters, square with the goal line and painted white. The goal posts must be fixed, rigid, and perpendicular at each end of the playing space, equal distance from the sides and at least 0.30 meters in front of the ends of the field of play or of any obstruction. Any standing or resting place for the goalkeeper, other than the floor of the pool is not permitted.

WP8. The inner sides of the goal post must be 3 meters apart.

WP9. The underside of the crossbar must be 0.90 meters above water surface when the water is 1.50 meters or more in depth, and 2.40 meters from the bottom of the pool when the depth of the water is less than 1.50 meters.

WP10. Limp nets must be attached to the goal fixtures to enclose the entire goal space, securely fastened to the goal posts and crossbar and allowing not less than 0.30 meters clear space behind the goal line everywhere within the goal area.

RULE 4. THE BALL

WP11. The ball must be round and fully inflated and with an air chamber with a self-closing valve. The pressure in the ball shall be 13-14 pounds atmospheric.

WP12. The circumference must not be less than 0.68 meters (27 inches) nor more than 0.71 meters (28 inches).

WP13. It must be waterproof without external strappings and without a covering of grease or similar substance.

WP14. The weight of the ball must be not less than 400 grams (15 ounces) nor more than 450 grams (17 ounces).

RULE 5. FLAGS

WP15. The referees must be provided with a stick 70 cm long, fitted with a white flag on one end and a blue flag on the other end, each flag to be 35 cm x 20 cm.

WP16. Each goal judge must be provided with a red flag and a white flag, each measuring 35 cm x 20 cm, mounted upon separate sticks which shall be 50 cm long. One of the secretaries must be provided with a white flag and a blue flag to signal the re-entrance of excluded players, and the other with a red flag with which to signal third personal fouls (WP116). These flags also shall be of the dimensions prescribed above.

RULE 6. CAPS

WP17. One team must wear dark blue and the other white caps, except goalkeepers, who must wear red caps. Caps must be tied with tapes under the chin. If a player loses his cap, it must be replaced at the next stoppage of the game. For Olympic Games and World Championships, and other FINA events, caps must be fitted with malleable ear protectors, and it is recommended that they be used for all other competitions. The malleable ear protectors of the goalkeepers must be of the same color as those of the teams' field players' caps.

(USWP) Caps used in all USWP competitions must contain malleable ear protectors.

WP18. Caps must be numbered on both sides, the numbers to be 0.10 meters in height.

WP19. The goalkeeper shall wear cap No. 1, and the other caps shall be numbered from 2 to 13. A substitute goalkeeper shall wear the goalkeeper's cap. No player is allowed to change his cap number without the referee's permission.

(USWP) The above rule concerning hat numbers governs Senior National Championships, including Zone and Pre-Zone Tournaments. In all other USWP competitions the caps may be numbered 1-14, or higher, as appropriate.

(USWP) When bathing caps are worn, they must be of the same color as the cap the player is wearing.

(USWP) The use of NCAA caps is acceptable for other than Senior National, including Zone and Pre-Zone Tournaments and International play.

RULE 7. TEAMS

WP20. Each team shall consist of seven (7) players, one of whom will be the goalkeeper and wear the goalkeeper's cap, and no more than six (6) reserves, who may be used as substitutes. Prior to taking part in a match the players must discard all articles likely to cause injury. The referee shall satisfy himself that the players observe this condition. A player failing to comply must be dismissed from the game. Players must wear swimsuits with separate drawers or slips underneath. NOTE: When a player is dismissed from the game in accordance with this paragraph, a reserve player may immediately take his place.

(USWP) Women's swimsuits must be of one-piece construction.

(USWP) For the purposes of this rule, safety sport glasses are not to be considered as an article likely to cause injury.

(USWP) At the start of a game, a team must consist of seven players, one of whom must be the goalkeeper.

(USWP) For tournament play, each team may consist of a maximum of fourteen (14) players, except for Senior Men's National Championships, including Pre-Zone and Zone Qualification Tournaments, where a maximum of thirteen (13) players is allowed.

(USWP) For games or tournaments involving men's teams, unless the entry blank specifically limits team members to USWP registered male athletes, the teams may be comprised of USWP registered male or female athletes.

(USWP) It is strongly recommended by U.S. Water Polo, that for all sanctioned tournaments and games, players should wear a protective mouth piece.

WP21. Players shall not be allowed to have grease, oil, or any similar composition on the body. If the referee ascertains before starting the game that such substance has been used, he must order the offending substance to be removed immediately. Should this offense be detected after the game has started, the player concerned must be ordered from the water for the whole game. A substitute may enter immediately within 2 meters from the corner of the field of play at his own goal line at the point nearest the goal judge (or on the side opposite the timekeeper if there are no goal judges).

WP22. The captains must be playing members and are responsible for the good conduct and discipline of their respective teams.

WP23. Prior to the commencement of the game the captains must, in the presence of the referees, toss for the choice of ends or colors, the winner to have the choice of ends or colors.

(USWP) The team bench is to be located at the defensive end of the pool at the start of the game, and is to remain at this location throughout the course of the game.

RULE 8. OFFICIALS

WP24.1 For Olympic Games and World Championships, the officials shall consist of two referees, two goal judges, timekeepers and secretaries.

WP24.2 For all other competitions there must be at least a secretary, a timekeeper and either (a) two referees or (b) one referee and two goal judges. However, it is recommended that two referees be used for all competitions. Each timekeeper and secretary may have assistants as needed.

WP24.3 The officials shall have the powers and duties as specified below except that if a competition is held with two referees without goal judges, the referees shall assume the duties specified for the goal judges in WP38 through WP41 inclusive, except that it shall not be necessary for them to make any of the flag signals specified in those rules.

Referees

WP25. The referees are in absolute control of the game. Their authority over the players is effective during the time that they and the players are within the precincts of the pool.

INSTRUCTIONS to WP25. The referee is not to make any presumptions as to the facts but to interpret what he observes to the best of his ability.

WP26. Each referee must use a shrill whistle with which to start and restart the game and to declare goals, goal throws, corner throws (whether signaled by the goal judge or not), and infringements of the rules.

(USWP) For signals by the referee, see WP141 and WP142.

WP27. All decisions of the referees on questions of fact are final and their interpretation of the rules must be obeyed during the game.

WP28.1 A referee may refrain from declaring a foul if, in his opinion, such declaration would be an advantage to the offender's team.

WP28.2 NOTE: It is important that referees apply this principle to the full extent. Example: To declare a foul in favor of a player who is in possession of the ball and making progress toward his opponent's goal, or whose team is in possession of the ball, is considered to give an advantage to the offender's team.

WP29. He may alter his decision providing he does so before the ball is again in play.

WP30. He has the power to order any player from the water in accordance with the appropriate rules. If a player refuses to leave the water when so ordered, the game must be stopped.

WP31. He may stop the game at any time if, in his opinion, the behavior of the players or spectators or other circumstances prevent it from being brought to a proper conclusion.

WP32. If the game has to be stopped, the referee must report his actions to the competent authority.

(USWP) The competent authority to whom the referee reports is the Tournament Officials Committee.

Timekeepers

WP33. The timekeepers must be fully acquainted with the rules of water polo and each must be provided with a water polo stop watch and a shrill whistle.

WP34.1 The duties of the timekeepers shall be (a) to record on the watch the exact periods of actual play and the intervals between periods as provided by these rules, (b) to record the respective periods of exclusion of any player or players who may be ordered from the water in accordance with these rules, and (c) to record the periods of continuous possession of the ball by each team (WP89).

WP34.2 The timekeeper recording the 35 seconds of continuous possession shall reset the clock only when the ball is put into play.

WP35. All signals to stop play must be made by whistle. Play is resumed when the ball leaves the hand of the player taking a free throw, goal throw, corner throw or penalty throw or when one player touches the ball after a neutral throw.

WP36. A timekeeper must signal by whistle the end of each period of play, independently of the referee. His signal takes immediate effect with the exceptions stated in WP89.5 and WP127. The last minute of any game, and of any extra time, shall be audibly announced.

NOTE to WP36. It is acceptable for the timekeeper to give this signal other than by whistle, provided that his signal shall be distinctive, acoustically efficient, and readily understood.

(USWP) It is recommended that a gun be used.

WP37. The timekeepers must be near a referee.

Goal Judges

WP38. The goal judges must take up a position opposite a referee and they must mutually agree upon ends. They must stand directly level with the goal line and stay there for the whole game.

COMMENT to WP38. Where a game is officiated by two referees and two goal judges, the goal judges shall be on opposite sides from each other, each at the end of the field of play to his left.

WP39. Their duties are to signal with the white flag for a goal throw (see WP13), with a red flag for a corner throw (see WP14), with both flags for a goal (see WP12), and with a red flag for an improper re-entry of an excluded player (see WP114.2 and WP115.2.1).

Their further duty is to throw in a new ball when the original ball goes outside the field of play. Goal judges shall each have a supply of balls (see WP4). When the original ball goes out of the field of play in a manner resulting in a goal throw or corner throw, the goal judge shall give a new ball immediately to the goalkeeper for each goal throw or to the nearest member of the attacking team for each corner throw.

(USWP) For signals by the goal judge see WP141 and WP142.

WP40. Goal judges shall be responsible to the referee for the correct score of each team at their respective ends.

WP41. Goal judges should exhibit the red flag to indicate to the referee that players are correctly positioned on their respective goal lines, according to WP51, but the referee's whistle to start or re-start the game takes immediate effect.

(USWP) If the players are incorrectly positioned in respect to WP41, WP76, or WP77, the goal judge should exhibit a white flag until they are in conformance, at which time he should exhibit the red flag. If, after the goal judge has exhibited the red flag to show conformance, the team becomes in violation of the rules, he should immediately exhibit the white flag to the referee.

Secretaries

WP42. The duties of the secretaries shall be:

WP42.1 To maintain a record of all players, the score, all major fouls (time, color, and cap number) and to signal the award of a third personal foul (WP116) to any player by one of the following means:

(1) with only a red flag if the third personal foul is an exclusion under WP115.1,

(2) with a red flag and a whistle if the third personal foul is incurred as a result of the award of a penalty throw, or

(3) with a red flag and a distinctive sound if the third personal foul is incurred as a result of a violation of WP104.1.

INSTRUCTIONS to WP42.1 The secretary must signal the award of a third personal foul in the appropriate manner of WP42.1 very quickly.

WP42.2 To control the periods of exclusion of players and to signal permission for re-entry upon expiration of their respective periods of exclusion by raising the flag corresponding with the color of the player's cap.

WP42.3 To signal any improper entry (including after a flag signal by a goal judge of an improper re-entry), which signal stops play immediately.

(USWP) In USWP competition, an air horn may be used for this signal.

(USWP) The secretary must signal the award of the third personal fault to any individual with the red flag and whistle immediately upon such award if the third personal foul is an offensive foul or a foul requiring the award of a penalty throw. If the third personal foul is an ejection foul, wave the red flag throughout the ejection period, or until acknowledged by the ejected player's coach.

COMMENT to Rule 8 Officials: (Detailed explanation of duties of each official is given in the official rules publication.)

RULE 9. TIME

WP43. The duration of the game shall be four periods of seven (7) minutes each of actual play. The teams shall change ends before commencing a new period. There shall be a two-minute interval between periods. Time starts when a player touches the ball at the start of any period of the game. At all signals for stoppages the recording watch must be stopped until play is resumed.

Comment to WP43. Any visible clocks should show time in a descending manner (that is, the clock should indicate time remaining in a period). This is applicable to a clock indicating the time remaining under WP89 (the 35-second rule), as well as the time remaining in the period.

RULE 10. GOALKEEPERS

WP44. While within the four meter area the goalkeeper is exempt from the following clauses of Rule 16 (WP76-WP105), viz.:

- standing and walking;
- striking at the ball with clenched fist;
- jumping from the floor;
- touching the ball with both hands at the same time.

WP45. He must not go or touch the ball beyond the half-distance line. The penalty for his doing so is a free throw awarded to the nearest opponent to be taken from where the offense occurred.

WP46. The goalkeeper may shoot at his opponents' goal as long as he is still within his half of the field of play. Refer to WP57.

WP47. When a goalkeeper is penalized for holding or pushing off from the bar, rail, or gutter at the end of the pool, the free throw must be taken from the two-meter line opposite the point at which the foul occurred.

WP48. If a goalkeeper taking a free throw or goal throw releases the ball and before any other player has touched it regains possession and allows it to pass through his own goal, a corner throw must be awarded. If in the same circumstances, he releases the ball and after another player has touched it regains possession and allows it to pass through his own goal, a goal must be awarded.

WP49. Should a goalkeeper retire from a game because of accident, illness, or injury, WP133 shall apply.

WP50. A goalkeeper who has been replaced by a substitute may, if he returns to the game, play anywhere.

INSTRUCTIONS to Rule 10. If, when a goal throw is awarded, the goalkeeper is out of the water, the nearest defending player must take the throw. In this case, for the purpose of the throw, the limitations and privileges of a goalkeeper will apply. In any other circumstances a player defending the goal shall not be subject to a goalkeeper's limitations and privileges. See WP69 and WP124.

RULE 11. STARTING

WP51. At the commencement of each period of play, the players must take up positions on their respective goal lines, about one meter apart and at least one meter from either goal post. More than two players are not allowed between the goal posts. When he has ascertained that the teams are ready, the referee shall give the starting signal by a blast of his whistle and immediately afterwards release or throw the ball into the center of the field of play.

NOTE to WP51. If the ball is thrown giving one team a definite advantage, the referee shall call for the ball and declare a neutral throw between the two players. Time shall commence when one player touches the ball.

(USWP) At the start or restart, if it is not possible for the players to position themselves on their respective goal lines, both teams will start on their respective two-meter lines.

(USWP) If the referee starts or re-starts the game, or starts play after a goal, and one team has more than seven players in the water, this is not to be interpreted as an illegal player. The referee should stop play, remove the extra players, re-set the time, and re-commence the game in the normal manner.

After a Goal

WP52. After a goal has been scored, players must take up positions anywhere within their respective halves of the field of play, behind the half-distance line. A player of the team not having last scored shall re-start the game from the center of the field of play. Upon the referee's signaling by one blast of the whistle the ball must be put into play, promptly, by passing it to another player on his team who must be behind the half-distance line when he receives it.

(USWP) If the referee starts or re-starts the game, or starts play after a goal, and one team has more than seven players in the water, this is not to be interpreted as an illegal player. The referee should stop play, remove the extra players, re-set the time and re-commence the game in the normal manner.

WP53. RULING: Actual play is resumed when the ball leaves the hand of the player making the re-start.

WP54. A re-start made improperly must be re-taken.

WP55. RULING: When the start or re-start is from the goal line, no portion of a player's body, at water level, may be beyond the goal line and when the re-start is from the center, no part of a player's body may be beyond the half-distance line.

RULE 12. SCORING

WP56. A goal is scored by the ball passing fully over the goal line, between the goal posts and subject to the following conditions:

WP57. A goal may be scored by any part of the body, except the clenched fist, provided that at the start or re-start of the game the ball has been played by two or more players. The team to which they belong or the place in the field of play from where the goal is scored is immaterial.

WP58. Any attempt by the goalkeeper to stop the ball before it has been played in this way does not constitute "playing," and should the ball cross the goal line or hit the goal post or goalkeeper, the goalkeeper must be awarded a goal throw.

WP59. Dribbling the ball through the goal posts is permissible.

WP60. Should a foul occur before the above conditions have been complied with, Rules 16 through 21 (WP76 through WP129) operate.

(USWP) In order for a goal to be scored at the end of a period when the timekeeper signals to the referee the end of the period, the ball must have passed fully over the goal line, between the goal posts, prior to the signal ending the period.

(USWP) If a shot is taken and while the ball is in the air a foul is called, the play stops. If the ball goes into the goal, the goal is not scored. The referee must be careful to avoid taking the advantage away.

RULE 13. GOAL THROW

WP61. The referee must signal by whistle immediately when the ball crosses the goal line.

WP62. When the entire ball passes over the goal line, excluding that portion between the goal posts, having last been touched by one of the attacking team, a goal throw is awarded to the defending goalkeeper, to be taken from any place within the two-meter area. See also WP90 and WP103.

(USWP) This means last having been "touched" by the attacking team. If the ball floats or is splashed over the goal line without being "touched" by the defending team, it becomes a goal throw.

WP63. A goal throw taken improperly must be re-taken, except as provided by WP89.

WP64. RULING: In the event of a goalkeeper's being out of the water, another player must take the goal throw from any place within the two-meter area.

RULE 14. CORNER THROW

WP65. The referee must signal by whistle immediately when the ball crosses the goal line.

WP66. When the entire ball passes over the goal line, excluding that portion between the goal posts, having last been touched by one of the defending team, a corner throw is awarded to the opposing team, to be taken at the two-meter mark on the side of the field of play where the ball goes out.

(USWP) This means last having been "touched" by the defending team. If the ball floats or is splashed over the goal line without being "touched" by the attacking team, it becomes a corner throw.

INSTRUCTIONS to WP66. A corner throw is to be taken as expeditiously as possible but not necessarily by the closest player.

WP67. The throw is to be taken from the two-meter mark.

WP68. When a corner throw is taken, no player (except the defending goalkeeper) may be within the two-meter line.

WP69. RULING: Should a defending goalkeeper be out of the water when a corner throw is awarded, another player on his team may take up a position on the goal line, but without the limitations and privileges of a goalkeeper.

WP70. If a goalkeeper, taking a free throw or a goal throw, releases the ball and before any other player has touched it, regains possession and allows it to pass through his own goal, a corner throw must be awarded.

WP71. A corner throw taken improperly must be re-taken.

WP72. RULING: If a corner throw is taken before the players have left the two-meter area, the throw must be re-taken.

WP73. If a player taking a free throw passes the ball toward his own goalkeeper and before any other player has touched it, the ball crosses the goal line or enters the net, a corner throw must be awarded. An attempt by the goalkeeper to stop the ball is not regarded as "touching" for the purposes of this rule.

RULE 15. NEUTRAL THROW

WP74.1 When one or more players of each team commit a foul at the same moment making it impossible for the referee to distinguish which player offended first, he must take the ball and throw it into the water in such a manner that the players of both teams have an equal opportunity to reach the ball after it has touched the water. WP101, WP102, and WP103 must be applied.

INSTRUCTIONS to WP74.1. The referee shall conduct the neutral throw at approximately the same lateral position as the fouls occurred.

WP74.2 All neutral throws awarded within the two-meter area are to be taken on the two-meter line opposite the point at which the incident took place.

(USWP) If one team has definite possession of the ball and the game is stopped because of accident or illness or other unforeseen reason, this team is awarded a free throw when play is resumed.

WP75. RULING: If from a neutral throw a referee is of the opinion that the ball has fallen in a position to the advantage of one team, he must make the throw again.

RULE 16. ORDINARY FOULS

It is a foul (for goalkeeper's exceptions see WP44):

WP76. To advance beyond the goal line at the start or re-start of the game, before the referee has given the signal.

WP77. To assist a player at the start or re-start or during a game.

WP78. To hold on to, or push off from, the goal posts or their fixtures. To hold on to the rails, except at the start or re-start. To hold on to, or push off from, the sides or ends of the pool during actual play.

WP79. To take any active part in the game when standing on the floor of the pool; to walk on the bottom of the pool when play is in progress.

WP80. To take or hold the ball under water when tackled.

COMMENT to WP80: (Diagram and annotated interpretation included in official publication.)

WP81. To strike at the ball with clenched fist.

WP82. To touch the ball before it reaches the water when thrown in by the referee.

WP83. To jump from the floor of the pool to play the ball or tackle an opponent.

WP84. Deliberately to impede, or prevent the free movement of an opponent unless he is holding the ball. Swimming on the shoulders, back, or legs of an opponent constitutes impeding. "Holding" is lifting, carrying, or touching the ball. Dribbling the ball is not considered to be "holding."

COMMENT to WP84: (Diagram and annotated interpretation included in official publication.)

WP85. To touch the ball with both hands at the same time.

WP86. To push, or push off from an opponent.

COMMENT to WP86: (Diagram and annotated interpretation included in official publication.)

WP87.1 To be within two meters of the opponents' goal line or to remain there except when behind the line of the ball.

WP87.2 RULING: It is not an offense if the player taking the ball into the two-meter area passes the ball to his associate who is behind the ball and who shoots at the goal immediately before the first player can leave the two-meter area.

INSTRUCTIONS to WP87.2. If the associate does not shoot, the passer of the ball must immediately leave the two-meter area.

WP88. To waste time.

INSTRUCTIONS to WP88. A player is not to be penalized for wasting time if he does not hear the whistle as a result of being under the water. The referee must determine if the actions of the player are deliberate. It is wasting time for the goalkeeper to receive a pass from his own team member who is in the other half of the field of play. The free throw will be taken on the halfway line.

WP89.1 For a team to retain possession of the ball for more than 35 seconds without shooting at their opponents' goal is deemed to be wasting time, and a free throw shall be awarded against the player last having touched the ball before this foul is signaled.

WP89.2 Should a team shoot at the goal as above and regain possession upon the ball's rebounding or being in any other manner kept in play, the measurement of 35 seconds shall immediately re-commence from 35.

WP89.3 Time re-commences from 35 seconds when the ball comes into the possession of the opposing team, or immediately the ball is put into play after a major foul. (Ruling: The ball does not leave the possession of the holding team merely by being touched in flight by an opponent player, provided that it is not deflected into the possession of the opponent team.)

(USWP) Time re-commences from 35 seconds when the ball comes into the possession of a team as a result of the ball going out of bounds, i.e.:

tipped out by offense—new 35 and possession turnover

tipped out by defense—new 35

tipped out by offense and defense simultaneously—new 35.

WP89.4 Time re-commences when the ball comes into the possession of a team as the result of a "neutral throw."

WP89.5 If at the expiration of the 35 seconds or at the end of the periods, the ball is in flight and crosses the goal line between the goal posts, the resultant goal shall be allowed.

WP89.6 At expiration of the 35 seconds the free throw shall be taken by the opposing player nearest the point at which the game is stopped, and undue delay by any member of the penalized team shall be punished as a major foul.

WP89.7 It is always permissible for the referee to penalize a foul under WP88 before the period of 35 seconds has expired.

WP89.8 There should be at least two 35-second clocks placed at diagonal corners of the field of play. They shall be at the corners beside the goal judges.

(USWP) The diagonal placement of the two 35-second clocks is a requirement for all national championships and international competitions. In all other competitions two 35-second clocks are required; however, it is recommended, but not required, that they be placed diagonally as described above.

WP90. For the goalkeeper to go or touch the ball outside his own half of the field of play.

WP91. To take a penalty throw otherwise than in the prescribed manner.

WP92. To delay unduly when taking a free throw, a goal throw, or a corner throw.

WP93. RULING: The time allowed for a player to take a free throw is left to the discre-
ion of the referee. It must be reasonable and without undue delay but does not have to be immediate.

(USWP) A reasonable length of time would be three (3) seconds from the time the referee determines that the player is ready to take the throw. The player must not delay unnecessarily in putting the ball in play.

WP94. Except as provided by WP47 or WP96 the punishment for an ordinary foul shall be a free throw to the opposing team to be taken by any one of its players.

RULE 17. FREE THROWS

WP95. The referee must blow his whistle to declare fouls and exhibit the flag corresponding in color to the caps worn by the team to which the free throw is awarded.

WP96. A free throw awarded for a foul committed within the two-meter area by defending player must be taken from the two-meter line opposite the point at which the foul occurred. With this exception, and the exception in WP128.2, free throws are to be taken from the point at which the foul occurred. Should the game be stopped through illness, or accident, or other unforeseen reason, the team in possession of the ball at the time is awarded a free throw at the point when time is resumed.

WP97. RULING: The responsibility for returning the ball to the player who is to take the free throw is primarily that of the team to which the free throw is awarded. The opponents have no duty to do this, but no player may deliberately throw the ball away to prevent the normal progress of the game. See also WP113.

WP98. RULING: A goalkeeper awarded a free throw must take the throw himself and the throw is subject to the limitations and privileges of a goalkeeper.

WP99. The throw must be made to enable other players to observe the ball leaving the hand of the thrower. It is permitted to dribble the ball before passing to another player.

COMMENT to WP92 and WP99: (Diagram and annotated interpretation included in official publication.)

WP100. As soon as the ball leaves the hand of a player taking a free throw it is in play. In the meantime all players are allowed to change position.

WP101. Except as provided by WP48, in all cases of a free throw, corner throw, or neutral throw at least two players (excluding the defending goalkeeper) must play or touch the ball before a goal can be scored.

WP102. RULING: To touch the ball means to touch intentionally.

WP103. Except as provided by WP48, an attempt by the goalkeeper to stop the ball, from an attacking player, before it has been touched or played by a second player, is not regarded as touching and should the ball cross the goal line or hit the goal posts or the goalkeeper, the goalkeeper must be awarded a goal throw.

WP104.1 If before a free throw, corner throw, goal throw, neutral throw, or penalty throw is taken, an offense against WP84, WP86, or Rule 18 (WP106 through WP115) is committed by a member of the team not in possession of the ball, the offender shall be ordered from the water for a period of 35 seconds actual play, when a goal is scored, or when the attacking team loses possession of the ball, whichever period is the shortest, and the original throw maintained. If a member of the team in possession of the ball commits such an offense, a free throw shall be awarded to the opponent team (except, where a penalty throw had been awarded it shall be maintained), and a personal foul shall be recorded against the player having committed the offense (see WP116).

WP104.2 NOTE: If simultaneous fouls, described in this rule, are committed by players from opposing teams, both players shall be evicted from the water for a period of 35 seconds actual play, when a goal is scored, or when the attacking team loses possession of the ball, whichever period is the shortest, and the original free throw shall be maintained.

WP104.3 RULING: In the special circumstances described in this paragraph, an offense committed by a player of either team against WP84, or WP86 shall be deemed to be a major foul and a personal foul shall be recorded against the player having committed the offense.

COMMENT to WP104: (Annotated interpretation included in official publication.)

WP105. A free throw taken improperly must be retaken, except as provided by WP92.

RULE 18. MAJOR FOULS

It is a major foul for a player:

WP106. To hold, sink, or pull back an opponent not holding the ball.

COMMENT to WP106: (Diagram and annotated interpretation included in official publication.)

WP107. To kick or strike an opponent or make disproportionate movements with that intent.

COMMENT to WP107: (Diagram and annotated interpretation included in official publication.)

WP108.1 To commit any foul within the four-meter area, but for which a goal would probably have resulted.

WP108.2 NOTE: In addition to other offenses, it is a major foul within the meaning of this paragraph to pull down the goal, or to play the ball with a clenched fist or with both hands in the four-meter area with the object of preventing a goal from being scored. A penalty throw must be awarded.

WP108.3 RULING: When the goalkeeper or any other player pulls over the goal completely with the object of preventing a goal, the player has shown disrespect and must be excluded from the remainder of the game (WP110). A substitute may enter the game within two meters from the corner of the field of play on the side of the goal judge (or on the side opposite the timekeeper if there are no goal judges), under his goal line, after the expiration of 35 seconds of actual play, when a goal has been scored, or when the attacking team loses possession of the ball, whichever period is shortest. The eviction of the offending player is in addition to awarding the penalty throw.

COMMENT to WP108: (Diagram and annotated interpretation included in official publication.)

WP109. To splash in the face of an opponent intentionally.

COMMENT to WP109: (Diagram and annotated interpretation included in official publication.)

WP110. To refuse obedience to, or show disrespect for, the referee. The offender shall be excluded from the remainder of the game, and a substitute may enter the game at his own goal line at the point nearest the goal judge at the earliest occurrence of the following:

(1) after expiration of 35 seconds actual play;

(2) when a goal is scored, or

(3) when the defending team re-takes possession of the ball or re-starts play after a stoppage of play.

It shall be deemed to be disobedience if a player excluded under WP115.1 (who is to re-enter in accordance with WP115.1) removes himself from the water (unless in accordance with WP132).

WP111.1 To commit an act of brutality against another player or an official. A free throw MUST be awarded to the opponent team and the offending player MUST be excluded from the remainder of the game and MUST NOT BE SUBSTITUTED.

WP111.2 NOTE: Brutality includes deliberately striking or kicking or attempting deliberately to strike or kick.

(USWP) In the event of a foul being committed under this section by a goalkeeper, the team shall play a man down for the remainder of the game, but after the next stoppage of play (a goal scored, or a period concluded), the team of the goalkeeper having committed the foul may substitute a goalkeeper for the excluded goalkeeper, who shall wear the goalkeeper's cap, and shall have the privileges and limitations of the goalkeeper. If they decide to play with six field players, a field player may play in the goal in defensive situations, but he shall not have the privileges of the goalkeeper.

WP112. To be guilty of misconduct. Misconduct is violence, the use of foul language, persistent foul play, etc. (This is deemed to be an offense against WP110.)

INSTRUCTIONS to WP112. Persistent foul play is totally different and unrelated to "persisting in an ordinary foul." Persisting in any ordinary foul is no longer a major foul.

WP113.1 To interfere with the taking of a free throw, goal throw, corner throw, or penalty throw.

WP113.2 NOTE: "Interference" includes:

(1) Deliberately to throw the ball away to prevent the normal progress of the game.

(2) Any attempt to play the ball before it leaves the hand of the thrower.

COMMENT to WP113: (Diagram and annotated interpretation included in official publication.)

WP114.1 For an excluded player to re-enter or a substitute to enter the water improperly.

WP114.2.1 Improper entry is to enter or re-enter:

(1) without permission of the Secretary at the expiration of the 35 seconds ejection time;

(2) without being waved in by the defensive referee in accordance with the provisions of WP115.1;

(3) by jumping or pushing off from the side or wall of the pool or field of play;

(4) from any place other than prescribed by WP115.2.1.

(USWP) If an excluded player enters early, he is charged with another personal foul and is excluded for another 35 seconds. Under (3) above, diving is also considered as improper entry. After a goal has been scored, an excluded player, or a substitute, may enter from anywhere and in any manner.

WP114.2.2 When this offense occurs during the last minute of the final quarter of any game, or during the last minute of any of the two periods of extra time (Rule 23, WP138 through WP140), the offender shall be excluded for the remainder of the game without substitution, and a penalty throw shall be awarded to the opposing team.

WP114.3 RULING: Entry at any time of a player not entitled under the rules to participate at that time (except for a player awaiting the passage of a 35 seconds exclusion period to be entitled to participate and except in the situation described in WP115.2.3) shall cause such player to be excluded from the remainder of the game with immediate substitution when appropriate, and one penalty throw will be awarded to the opposing team.

WP114.4 RULING: At any time when a player awaiting the passage of an expulsion period enters illegally with the object of preventing a goal, it is deemed to constitute a violation of WP108. After the player has left the water to complete the original exclusion period, a penalty throw shall be awarded to the opposing team. This penalty takes precedence over the penalty otherwise provided under WP114 (expulsion or penalty throw).

(USWP) In the case of the last minute of play and two excluded players, one from each team, enter the water illegally, a penalty throw is awarded each team. The first penalty throw shall be taken by the team in possession of the ball at the stoppage. After the second penalty throw, it shall be neutral ball.

Except as otherwise expressly provided in these rules, the punishment for a major foul is:

WP115.1 The offending player shall be excluded from the field of play until the earliest occurrence of the following:

(1) after expiration of 35 seconds actual play, or

(2) when a goal is scored, or

(3) when the defending team retakes possession of the ball or re-starts play after a stoppage of play.

A free throw is to be taken by a player of the opponent team after the excluded player has commenced to leave the field of play and the referee has signaled the free throw to be taken. The penalty period will start upon the taking of the free throw. If the player leaving the field of play intentionally interferes with the play, it shall constitute an additional major foul, and a penalty throw shall be awarded. Upon a change of possession, referred to above, all players excluded for 35 seconds re-enter immediately upon the signal of the defensive referee. A change of possession does not occur merely because of the end of a period. This depends on the result of the start in WP51 of the next period.

(USWP) Where an excluded player disobeys the referee or makes some disparaging or insulting gesture but does not interfere with the game, he is excluded for the rest of the game with substitution after 35 seconds and without a penalty throw.

COMMENT to WP115.1 (Interpretation included in official publication.)

INSTRUCTIONS to WP115.1. If a player who is excluded under WP115.1 does not commence to leave the water almost immediately, then the referee may deem this to be intentional interference under WP115.1.

WP115.2.1 After expiration of time the excluded player himself must re-enter within two (2) meters from the corner of the field of play on the side of the goal judge (or on the side opposite the timekeeper if there are no goal judges), under his goal line, and without affecting the alignment of the goals.

WP115.2.2 In case of simultaneous fouls by members of both teams, the offending players shall be excluded and a neutral throw shall be taken. Both excluded players will return at the earliest occurrence of the following:

(1) after expiration of 35 seconds actual play, or

(2) when a goal is scored, or

(3) when the defending team retakes possession of the ball or re-starts play after a stoppage of play.

WP115.2.3 If a player is excluded and there are not three personal faults recorded against him and at the end of his exclusion period a substitute player enters in his place, this is deemed to be an offense against WP110.

(USWP) The substitute player in WP115.2.3 is excluded from the remainder of the game and the original player must re-enter after the expiration of 35 seconds of actual play, when a goal is scored, or when the defending team retakes possession of the ball or restarts play after a stoppage of play, whichever period is the shortest. The original player is not charged with another personal foul.

(USWP) An excluded player cannot be substituted during an interval between periods.

INSTRUCTIONS to WP115.2. A change of possession does not occur just because one team gains possession from the neutral throw in the special circumstances of this rule.

INSTRUCTIONS to WP110, WP115.1, and WP115.2.2. When a player has been excluded from the field of play for committing a personal foul, the player will re-enter at the earliest occurrence of the following:

(1) after expiration of 35 seconds actual play when the secretary will raise the appropriate flag to permit the re-entry,

(2) after a goal is scored, or

(3) if that player's team regains possession of the ball or re-starts play after a stoppage of play. In this case, the defensive referee will give the player permission to enter the field of play by giving a wave-in signal with his free hand, not with his flag.

RULE 19. PERSONAL FOULS

WP116.1 A player committing a major foul anywhere in the field of play shall be awarded a personal foul and upon being awarded a third such personal foul in any one game he shall be excluded from the remainder of the game. A substitute may enter at his own goal line at the point nearest to the goal judge after expiration of the exclusion time under the rules.

(USWP) The player shall enter on the side opposite the timekeeper if there are no goal judges.

WP116.2 If such a third personal foul results from a foul requiring the award of a penalty throw, the entry of the substitute shall be immediate and before the penalty throw is taken. If such a third personal foul results from a violation of WP104 by a member of a team in possession of the ball, the player continues in the game until the next interruption by the referees or upon a loss of the ball by the opposite team of the player who has received the third personal foul. The entry of the substitute shall be after this interruption or loss of possession.

COMMENT to WP116.2 (Interpretation given in official publication.)

RULE 20. PENALTY THROW

WP117. Should a player be fouled within his opponents' four-meter area according to WP107 or WP111 or commit a foul according to WP108.1, WP114.2.2, or WP115.1, a penalty throw MUST be awarded against the offender's team. The referee must announce the offender's number to the secretary.

COMMENT to WP117: (Diagrams and annotated interpretation given in official publication.)

WP118. When a penalty throw is awarded, the offending player shall be ordered from the water only if the offense is so serious as to justify ordering from the water for the remainder of the game (WP111, WP114.2.2, and WP116).

WP119. A penalty throw may be executed by any player of the team to which it is awarded, except the goalkeeper. The player taking the throw may elect to do so from any point on his opponents' four-meter line.

WP120.1 The player taking the throw must await the referee's signal which shall be given by whistle and by simultaneously lowering the respective flag from a vertical to a horizontal position. The player must have possession of the ball and immediately throw it with an uninterrupted movement directly at the goal (see WP91). Should the ball rebound from the goal posts or crossbar, it remains in play. It is not necessary for the ball to be played by any other player before a goal can be scored.

WP120.2 RULING: A penalty throw may commence by lifting the ball from the water or with the ball held in the raised hand. It is permissible for the ball to be taken backwards from the direction of the goal in preparation for the forward throw at the goal, but the throw shall commence immediately upon the signal, and continuity of the movement shall not be broken before the ball leaves the thrower's hand.

WP121. All players except the defending goalkeeper, or the other player according to WP124, must leave the four-meter area until the throw is taken and no player may be within two meters of the player taking the penalty throw.

WP122. The goalkeeper must take a position anywhere on the goal line and the referee will withhold the signal to throw until satisfied on this point.

WP123. RULING: No portion of the goalkeeper's body, at water level, may be beyond the goal line.

WP124. RULING: Should the defending goalkeeper be ordered from the water before or after the award of a penalty throw, another player of his team may take a position on the goal line before the throw is taken, but without the privileges and limitations of a goalkeeper.

WP125. A player must take a penalty throw as described. The penalty for not complying shall be a free throw to the player's nearest opponent.

WP126. If the taking of a penalty throw is interfered with or WP121 and WP122 are not complied with, the offender or offenders must be punished in accordance with WP110, and the throw must be re-taken.

WP127. If, at precisely the same time as the referee awards a penalty throw or before a penalty throw is completed, the timekeeper whistles for an interval, or full time, the penalty throw must be allowed, and should the ball rebound into the field of play from the goal post, crossbar, or goalkeeper, it is dead. (Note: When a penalty throw is to be taken in accordance with this paragraph, all players except the defending goalkeeper and the player taking the penalty throw shall leave the water.)

RULE 21. OUT OF PLAY

WP128.1 Should a player send the ball out of the field of play at either side, a free throw is awarded to the opposing team, to be taken at the point where the ball left the field of play.

WP128.2 Should the ball go out of the field of play between the goal line and the two-meter line, the free throw must be taken from the two-meter mark on the side where the ball went out.

WP129. Should the ball strike or lodge in an overhead obstruction, it must be considered out of play, and the referee must stop the game and conduct a neutral throw. In that case the ball may not be played until it has touched the water. Should the ball rebound from the goal posts or crossbar or from the side of the field of play at water level, it remains in play except as provided by WP58 and WP103. If the ball rebounds from the side of the field of play above water level, it is considered to be out of play.

(USWP) A neutral throw is awarded if the ball strikes or lodges in an overhead obstruction.

RULE 22. LEAVING THE WATER AND SUBSTITUTES

WP130. A player must not leave the water or sit or stand on the steps or side of the pool during a game except:

(1) during an interval,

(2) in case of illness or accident, or

(3) by permission of the referee.

INSTRUCTIONS to WP130. The players not in the game at the time, the coaches, manager, medical personnel must all sit together on the team bench and are not to move away from there from the commencement to the end of each quarter of play.

WP131. A player infringing upon this rule must be deemed guilty of misconduct. A player having left the water legitimately may re-enter at his own goal line at the point nearest the goal judge by permission of the referee.

WP132. In the case of accident or illness, the referee may, at his discretion, suspend the game for not more than three (3) minutes. It shall be the duty of a referee to instruct the timekeeper when any three-minute stoppage for injury shall commence.

WP133. In the event of a player retiring from the game through accident or injury, the referee may permit his immediate substitution by a reserve. The referee shall refuse such permission only if he considers the request unjustified. The player so retiring shall not be allowed at any time to re-enter the game. Otherwise a player may be substituted only:

(1) in accordance with provisions of WP20, WP21, WP110, or WP116;

(2) during the interval between periods of play;

(3) after a goal has been scored; or

(4) prior to the commencement of extra time.

NOTE: During extra time the provisions (1), (2), and (3) above shall apply.

WP134. A substitute shall not be allowed for a player who has been ordered from the water according to WP111 and WP114.2.2.

WP135. A substitute must be ready to replace a player without delay; if he is not ready, the referee may re-start the game without him, in which case he may not take part in the match until the next stoppage.

INSTRUCTIONS to WP130 and WP135. In the special circumstances when any player has personally incurred two personal fouls, a potential substitute will be allowed to walk to the re-entry area provided that he does not walk on the referee's platform or in front of the desk area, or impede the goal judges' view of the pool. The designated waiting area will depend on the conditions of the pool. Where possible, the potential substitutes must wait in the water at least two meters behind the re-entry zone. If this water area is not available, the potential substitutes may wait behind the bench. If there is no bench, the potential substitute must wait out of the water behind the goal judge. Such potential substitute players must be very carefully observed by the referees for any breach of WP110 and WP112.

(USWP) After a goal a substitute wishing to enter must be recognized by the referee (he need not report to the secretary). He then may enter the water from anywhere and in any manner. If he does not get the recognition of the referee but enters anyway, he must be removed, and the original player must stay in the game. The opposing team gets the ball on the center line.

WP136. RULING: In case of accident, illness, or injury, a substitute takes his position in the water where the accident occurred and will take the free throw or corner throw which may have been awarded the injured player, but should there be no substitute, another player shall take the throw.

WP137. The captain, coach, or team manager must notify the referee of substitutions.

RULE 23. EXTRA TIME

WP138. Should there be level scores at full time (WP43) in any game for which a definite result is required, any continuation into extra time must be after an interval of five (5) minutes. There shall then be played two periods of three (3) minutes each actual play, with an interval of one minute for changing ends.

WP139. This system of extra time shall be continued until a decision has been reached.

WP140. A player who has been ordered from the water by the referee—but not for the rest of the game—shall resume with his team during extra time only when his penalty time has expired, a goal has been scored, or the defending team regains possession of the ball and puts it into play, whichever time is the shortest.

INSTRUCTIONS to WP140. A player who has been excluded by virtue of WP115.1 shall not be permitted to take part in extra time. All players carry forward into extra time their own personal fouls awarded against them earlier in the game.

RULE 24. ADDENDUM

INSTRUCTION FOR REFEREES

WP141. (This section of the official rules publication includes diagrams and detailed comments regarding officials' duties and signals.)

RULE 25. JUNIOR OLYMPIC WATER POLO

WP142-150. (This section of the official rules publication details the requirements for Junior Olympic competition.)

RULE 26. AGE GROUP WATER POLO

WP151-152. (This section of the official rules publication includes regulations regarding age group classification.)

GOVERNING BODY

United States Water Polo, Inc., 1750 East Boulder St., Colorado Springs, CO 80909-5765

United States Water Polo, Inc. (USWP), is recognized by and affiliated with the Federation Internationale de Natation Amateur (FINA) as a member of the United States Aquatic Sports, Inc. (USAS) and is the sole governing body controlling water polo in the United States. USWP is concerned with the promotion of water polo at all levels nationally and internationally. The organization conducts indoor and outdoor age group championships for men and women, lends assistance in the development of water polo clubs, conducts clinics for players, coaches, and officials, selects All-American teams, and makes arrangements for water polo participation in the U.S. Olympic festival, as well as the International Olympic Games. The organizational structure of USWP provides for 6 zones made up of 13 regions from 58 districts.

MAGAZINES

Water Polo in Canada, Canadian Water Polo Association, 333 River Rd., Tower C, 9th Fl., Ottawa, ON K1L 8B9 Canada

Water Polo Scoreboard, 5876 Los Pacos St., Buena Park, CA 90620

• WEIGHTLIFTING •

INTERNATIONAL WEIGHTLIFTING FEDERATION AND USWF RULES

(Reproduced by permission of the United States Weightlifting Federation*)

☐

Note: The Official USWF Rulebook contains five major divisions as follows: Part I—Federation By-Laws; Part II—Local Weightlifting Committee Structure; Part III—Provisions Relating To Athletes And Athletic Events; Part IV—International Weightlifting Federation And USWF Rules; Appendix. Only Part IV dealing with the technical rules of the competition is presented here.

INTERNATIONAL WEIGHTLIFTING FEDERATION AND USWF RULES

1. PROGRAMME OF THE COMPETITION

1.1 THE TWO LIFTOFFS

1.1.1 The IWF recognizes two lifts which must be executed in the following sequence in all competitions under IWF rules:

a) the snatch

b) the clean and jerk

1.1.2 Both lifts must be executed with two hands

1.1.3 Only three attempts are allowed in each lift

1.1.4 An extra attempt outside of the competition may be allowed in certain occasions (see relevent rules for World Records, 7.9)

1.2 PARTICIPANTS

1.2.1 In the sport of weightlifting, competitions are organized for men or women. The athletes shall compete within the categories established by the rules, according to their bodyweight.

1.2.2 In its activities, the IWF recognizes three (3) main age groups:

JUNIOR: Up to and including twenty (20) years of age.

SENIOR: *(Editor's Note*—no age restrictions except 12 years minimum)

VETERAN: Age 40 to 44; age 45 to 49; age 50 to 54; age 55 to 59; 60 years and over.

---

*See page 692 for additional information.

U.S. POLICY—In U.S. meets, the following additional age groups shall be recognized: 1) age 60 to 64; 2) age 65 to 69; 3) continues in 5-year increments to 85 to 89. Masters (Veterans) birthdates shall be actual age on day of competition.

Note 1: The minimum age for participation in the Junior World Championships is fifteen (15).

Note 2: The minimum age for participation in the Senior World Championships and the Olympic Games is seventeen (17).

Note 3: All the above-mentioned age groups are calculated in the calendar year of the athlete's anniversary.

Note 4: The minimum age for USWF registration is twelve (12) years.

1.3 CATEGORIES

1.3.1 There are ten (10) bodyweight categories for men. All competitions under IWF rules must be held in these categories:

1—up to 52.0 kg.	(up to 114 1/2 pounds)
2—52.01 kg. to 56.0 kg.	(up to 123 1/4 pounds)
3—56.01 kg. to 60.0 kg.	(up to 132 1/4 pounds)
4—60.01 kg. to 67.5 kg.	(up to 148 3/4 pounds)
5—67.51 kg. to 75.0 kg.	(up to 165 1/4 pounds)
6—75.01 kg. to 82.5 kg.	(up to 181 3/4 pounds)
7—82.51 kg. to 90.0 kg.	(up to 198 1/4 pounds)
8—90.01 kg. to 100.0 kg.	(up to 220 1/4 pounds)
9—100.01 kg. to 110.0 kg.	(up to 242 1/2 pounds)
10—110.01 kg. +	(over 242 1/2 pounds)

1.3.2 There are nine bodyweight categories for women:

1—Up to 44.0 kg.	(up to 97 pounds)
2—44.01 kg. to 48.0 kg.	(up to 105 3/4 pounds)
3—48.01 kg. to 52.0 kg.	(up to 114 1/2 pounds)
4—52.01 kg. to 56.0 kg.	(up to 123 1/4 pounds)
5—56.01 kg. to 60.0 kg.	(up to 132 1/4 pounds)
6—60.01 kg. to 67.5 kg.	(up to 148 3/4 pounds)
7—67.51 kg. to 75.0 kg.	(up to 165 1/4 pounds)
8—75.01 kg. to 82.5 kg.	(up to 181 3/4 pounds)
9—82.51 kg. +	(over 181 3/4 pounds)

1.3.3 At World and Continental Championships and Regional Games, each country may enter ten (10) athletes and three (3) reserves, at Olympic Games, ten (10) athletes and only two (2) reserves spread over the different categories with a maximum of two athletes per category. National championships or other international meetings may allow differently.

1.3.4 During any competition, an athlete cannot compete in more than one category.

2. THE TWO MOVEMENTS

2.1 SNATCH

2.1.1 The bar shall be placed horizontally in front of the lifter's legs. It shall be gripped, palms downwards, and pulled in a single movement from the ground to the full extent of both arms above the head, while either "splitting" or bending the legs. The bar shall pass with a continuous movement along the body.

No part other than the feet may touch the ground during the execution of the lift. The weight which has been lifted, must be maintained in the final motionless position, arms and legs extended, with the feet on the same line, until the referees give the signal to replace the bar on the platform. The turning over of the wrist must not take place until the bar has passed the top of the lifter's head. The lifter may recover in his own time, either from a "split" or a "squat" and have his feet on the same line, parallel to the plane of the trunk and the barbell. The referees shall give the signal as soon as the lifter becomes absolutely motionless in all parts of the body.

2.2 CLEAN AND JERK

2.2.1 The first part, the Clean:

The bar shall be placed horizontally in front of the lifter's legs. It shall be gripped, palms downwards and pulled in a single movement from the ground to the shoulders, while either "splitting" or bending the legs. During this continuous movement, the bar may slide along the thighs and the lap. The bar must not touch the chest before the final position. It shall then rest on the clavicles or on the chest above the nipples or on the arms fully bent. The feet shall be returned to the same line, legs straight, before performing the Jerk. The lifter may make this recovery in his own time and have his feet on the same line, parallel to the plane of his trunk and the barbell.

2.2.2 The second part, the Jerk:

The athlete bends the legs and extends them as well as the arms so as to bring the bar to the full stretch of the arms vertically extended. He returns the feet to the same line, arms and legs extended and waits for the referee's signal to replace the bar on the platform. The referees shall give the signal as soon as the lifter becomes absolutely motionless in all parts of the body.

IMPORTANT REMARK: After the Clean and before the Jerk, the lifter may assure the position of the bar. This must not lead to confusion. It cannot mean in any case, granting an additional jerk attempt to the lifter, but allowing him to: a) either withdraw his thumbs or "unhook" if he has used this method, b) lower the bar in order to let it rest on his shoulders if the bar is placed too high and impedes his breathing or causes pain, c) change the width of his grip.

2.3 GENERAL RULES FOR ALL LIFTS

2.3.1 The technique known as "hooking" is permitted. It consists of covering the last joint of the thumb with the other fingers of the same hand at the moment of gripping.

2.3.2 In all lifts, the referees must count as "no lift" any unfinished attempt in which the bar has reached the height of the knees.

2.3.3 After the referees' signal to replace the bar, the lifter must lower the bar in front of his body and not let it drop either deliberately or accidentally. He may release his grip on the barbell when it has passed the level of the waist.

U.S. POLICY—Releasing the bar after it passes the level of the waist may occur only when rubber bumper plates are used. The meet director shall decide whether or not the hands may be released at this level in U.S. meets.

2.3.4 If a competitor cannot fully stretch his arm resulting from anatomical deformation of his elbow, he must report this fact to the three referees and the Jury before the beginning of the competition.

2.3.5 When snatching or cleaning in the "squat" position, the lifter may help his recovery by a swinging and a rocking movement of his body. (More than one recovery attempt is allowed.)

2.3.6 The use of grease, oil, water, talcum or any similar lubricant on the thighs is forbidden. The lifter who uses lubricants will be ordered to remove it. The Jury will decide if during the removal, the clock shall go on or not. Note: No "slippery" substance is allowed, regardless of its composition.

2.4 INCORRECT MOVEMENTS AND POSITIONS FOR ALL LIFTS

2.4.1 Pulling from the hang.

2.4.2 Touching the ground with any part of the body other than the feet.

2.4.3 Uneven or incomplete extension of the arms at the finish of the lift.

2.4.4 Pause during the extension of the arms.

2.4.5 Finishing with a press out.

2.4.6 Bending and extending the arms during the recovery.

2.4.7 Leaving the platform during the execution of the lift, i.e., touching the area outside the platform with any part of the body.

U.S. POLICY—When tape is used to mark the proper dimensions of an oversized platform or on the floor, the outside edge of the tape marks the platform boundary. The lifter's toes may touch the tape, but not reach beyond the tape.

2.4.8 Replacing the bar on the platform before the referees' signal.

2.4.9 Dropping the bar after the referees' signal.

2.4.10 Failing to finish with the feet and the barbell in line and parallel to the plane of the trunk.

2.4.11 Failing to replace the complete barbell on the platform, i.e., the complete barbell has to touch the platform first.

2.5 INCORRECT MOVEMENTS FOR THE SNATCH

2.5.1 Pause during the lifting of the bar.

2.5.2 Touching the head of the lifter with the bar when finishing the lift.

2.6 INCORRECT MOVEMENTS FOR THE CLEAN

2.6.1 Placing the bar on the chest before raising the elbows.

2.6.2 Touching the thigh or the knee with the elbow or the upper arm.

2.7 INCORRECT MOVEMENTS FOR THE JERK

2.7.1 Any apparent effort of jerking which is not completed. This includes lowering the body or bending the knees.

2.7.2 Any deliberate oscillation of the bar to gain advantage. The athlete and the barbell have to become completely motionless before starting the jerk.

3. APPARATUS

3.1 BARBELL

3.1.1 Weightlifting competitions must be carried out with Olympic barbells that meet IWF specifications.

3.1.2 The barbell shall consist of the following parts: a) the bar; b) the discs; c) the collars.

A. The Bar

3.1.3 The Olympic bar must meet the following specifications:

a) its weight is 20 kgs

b) the length of the bar is 2,200 mm with a tolerance of ±1 mm

c) the diameter of the bar is 28 mm with a tolerance of ±0.03 mm on the smooth part of the bar

d) the diameter of the sleeve is 50 mm with a tolerance of -0.2 mm and +0.0 mm

e) the distance between the inside collars is 1,310 mm with a tolerance of ±0.5 mm

f) the width of the inside collar including the collar of the sleeve must be 30 mm with +0.1 mm tolerance

g) there shall be knurlings on the bar, according to the Figure in order to facilitate the grip

h) there shall be interruptings on the knurling, also according to the Figure to facilitate the orientation of the grip.

B. The Discs

3.1.4 The discs must meet the following specifications:

a) shall be of the following range: 25 kg—coloured red; 20 kg—coloured blue; 15 kg—coloured yellow; 10 kg—coloured black (if of a 450 mm diameter); 5 kg; 2.5 kg; 1.25 kg; 0.5 kg; 0.25 kg

b) the diameter of the largest discs is 450 mm with a tolerance of ±1 mm

c) the 450 mm diameter discs shall be covered with a rubber or plastic and coated with permanent colour or painted at least on the surface of the rims

d) 10 kg (if not of 450 mm diameter) and smaller discs can be of any colour depending on the manufacturer

e) the discs smaller than 10 kg can be made of metal

f) all the discs must have a clear indication of their weight.

U.S. POLICY—The use of 5 kg., 450 mm diameter discs, may be approved for all domestic U.S. Weightlifting competitions from LWC-level, Regional and State. In addition to the foregoing competitions, 5 kg., 450 mm diameter discs may be approved for use at U.S. Junior, U.S. Women's and U.S. Masters Championships. This provision only applies if the 5 kg., 450 mm diameter discs comply with the specifications set forth in the current IWF Technical Rules; such specifications being:

(1) Weight specification of +10 grammes and -0 gram

(2) Diameter specification of ±1 mm.

If the 5 kg., 450 mm diameter discs are brought to the competition by an athlete or coach for use at the competition, rather than supplied by the competition management, the discs shall be impounded for weighing and measuring by the Technical Controller and Meet Director and/or Competition Secretary. If the owner of such discs uses them in the competition, then those discs shall remain part of the competition until no other lifter will require their usage. When it is declared by the Officials that no lifter will require such discs, then the rightful owner may then repossess them and remove them from the competition area at the end of the competition.

In no case will the 5 kg., 450 mm diameter discs be refused for use of other lifters by the owner, or coach, without forfeiting all of her/his/team lifts made within the competition with such discs on the bar.

C. The Collars

3.1.5 Each bar must be equipped with two collars (fastening the discs to the bar), weighing 2.5 kg each.

3.1.6 The tolerance on the nominal weight of each component of the barbell weighing more than 5 kg. is +0.1% and -0.05%. On parts weighing 5 kg. or less the tolerance is +10 grammes and -0 gramme, per part.

3.1.7 The bar must be loaded with the largest discs inside and the smaller ones in descending order of weight towards the outside. They must be placed in such a way that the referees can read the numbers indicating the weight of each disc. They must be locked on the bar by means of the collars.

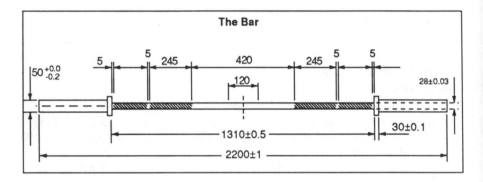

The Bar

3.2 PLATFORM

3.2.1 The lifts of a competition shall be executed on a platform.

3.2.2 The platform must be square, measuring four (4) meters on each side, the edges must be coloured. (13' 1 1/4" x 13' 1 1/4")

3.2.3 It may be made of wood, plastic or any solid material and may be covered with a non-slippery material.

3.2.4 The height must be between 50 and 150 mm.

3.3 ELECTRONIC REFEREE LIGHT SYSTEM

The electronic referee light system consists of the following components:

a) One control box for each of the three (3) referees. These control boxes are equipped with two (2) push buttons, one white and one red, and one signal device.

b) One apparatus giving a visual and audible "Down" signal, to be placed on a stand in front of the competition platform.

c) Two (2) or more "decision lights" displays, equipped with three (3) red and white lights, horizontally placed, showing the referees' decisions to the competitors and the audience.

d) One or more control panels, equipped with three (3) red and three (3) white lights that light up instantly when the referees press the appropriate button. These control panels, to be placed on the Jury table, are also equipped with a signaling device that can be used to call any or all the referees to the Jury table.

3.3.2 Operation of the system

During the course of the competition, as soon as the three (3) referees have judged a lift "Good lift," they shall press the white button on their control box. Immediately, the apparatus, located in front of the platform, shall give a simultaneous visual (white light) and audible "Down" signal to the competitor to lower the barbell.

When the three (3) referees judge that the athlete has committed a fault, during the execution of a lift, they shall give a "No lift" decision by pressing the red button on their control box. Immediately, the apparatus, in front of the platform, shall give a simultaneous visual (red light) and audible "Down" signal.

The "decision lights" will light up only after all the three (3) referees have given their decision.

To operate the visual and audible "Down" signal, two (2) out of the three (3) referees must have given identical decisions, "Good lift" or "No lift."

Should one of the referees press the white button and another press the red button while the third referee does not press any, the latter will hear a beep-beep signal from his control box, urging him to give his decision. Also, when two (2) white lights or two (2) red lights have been given by two (2) of the three (3) referees, and the "Down" signal has been seen and heard, then the third referee shall be reminded to give his decision by the beep-beep signal. After the visible and audible "Down" signal and before the "decision lights" operate, the referees have three (3) seconds to reverse their decision. E.g., if after a completed good lift, the athlete drops the barbell behind his back, the referees shall press the button and the red "decision lights" shall light up indicating "No lift."

U.S. POLICY—When the electronic judging system is not in use, the chief referee shall give both a visual and audible down signal consisting of lowering his hand from overhead while saying "Down."

3.3.3 Responsibilities of the referees

The three (3) referees have equal rights of decision and adjudication on a lift. Each of them must give the "Down" signal by pressing the white button for "Good lift" or the red button for "No lift," according to the relevant rules for all lifts. Should a referee see a mistake or fault during the execution of a lift, he must immediately press the red button.

3.3.4 Jury monitoring

During the competition, the Jury members may monitor the work of the referees by using the control panels. Every decision by the referees may be verified as the lights on the control panels light up instantly when the appropriate button is pressed by the referees. Slow, fast or no decision may be identified for immediate or further action.

Should the Jury President want to call one of the referees to the table, he may do so by pressing the appropriate button which shall give a beep-beep signal to the called referee.

3.4 SCALE

3.4.1 For weightlifting competitions scales (weighing machines) which are able to weigh up to 200 kg with a precision of 50 g minimum should be used.

3.4.2 When a scale is precise up to 10 g, the bodyweight indicated must be recorded as such for the competition.

3.4.3 At World Championships, Olympic Games and major international competitions there shall be an identical back-up scale which may be used by the competitors as control scale. *Note*: At National Championships a back-up scale should be provided.

3.4.4 The scale certificate accompanying the scales must not be older than one (1) year at the date of the competition.

3.5 TIMING CLOCK

3.5.1 At official IWF competitions, an electrical timing clock which can operate continuously up to three (3) minutes, minimum, and indicating periods of ten seconds, minimum, giving automatically an audible warning signal one minute before the end of the allocated time, shall be used.

3.5.2 The elapsed time shall be well displayed simultaneously in the competition area and in the warm-up area.

3.5.3 This electrical timing device shall be controlled by a qualified referee.

3.6 FORMS

3.6.1 The following forms are necessary for the good running of a weightlifting competition: a) weigh-in list; b) competitor's cards; c) competition protocol; d) certificate of the weight of the barbell; e) record protocol; f) passes for the warm-up area; g) cards for the Jury.

3.7 OTHER EQUIPMENT

3.7.1 The ATTEMPT BOARD: A well visible board on which must appear the name of the competitor, the weight to be attempted and the number of his attempt.

3.7.2 SCORE-BOARD: A score-board shall be set up at a prominent place in the competition area in order to record and display the results of a specific category. The score-board shall contain the following information: a) the start numbers; b) the name of the competitors in order of the lots drawn; c) their bodyweight; d) the name of their country; e) the three attempts in the Snatch; f) the three attempts in the Clean and Jerk; g) the Olympic Total; h) the final classification.

3.7.3 RECORD BOARD: A board shall be set up in the competition area to display the following information: a) the up-dated records of the category being contested; b) their weight; c) the name and the country of the record holders.

3.7.4 WARM-UP ROOM: The competitors must be provided with a warm-up area, close to the competition platform. This area shall be equipped with the appropriate number of platforms, barbells, chalk, etc., in relation with the number of competitors. There shall also be a loudspeaker linked with the microphone of the speaker and a score-board showing the names of the competitors in the order of the lots drawn, their respective bodyweight and the weights which they have requested before being called to the platform. There shall be a table for the doctor on duty.

3.7.5 At Olympic Games weightlifting competitions and in any other major international championships such as World and Continental Championships or regional Games, the organizers shall provide: a) electronic scales; b) electronic digital clock; c) electronic referee light system; d) electronic score-board and display board. On the display board, both the light system and the clock must operate simultaneously in the warm-up and the competition areas.

3.7.6 The use of any additional equipment or device which may improve the running of the competition may be allowed.

4. OUTFIT OF THE COMPETITORS

4.1 COSTUME

4.1.1 The athlete must wear a correct dress which consists of a full length, one piece costume (leotard type). The costume must cover the entire buttocks and shall have an aesthetic appearance. The next figure demonstrates what the aesthetic dress should look like. *Note*: Women must wear correct dress which consists of a full length, one piece costume, with or without trunks, with T-shirt. The top (T-shirt) must cover the entire bust and the suit or trunks must cover the entire buttocks. The costume must form a horizontal line across the thigh.

4.1.2 A T-shirt may be worn under the costume. The sleeves shall not extend farther than half way on the upper arms. The T-shirt must be collar-less.

4.1.3 Trunks may be worn over the costume.

4.1.4 A T-shirt and trunks cannot be worn instead of the costume.

4.1.5 The T-shirt and costume may be of any colour. Only the national emblem may be worn on the costume. On the T-shirt, the emblem of the competition may be worn but any advertising is forbidden.

U.S. POLICY—In domestic competitions, the T-shirt may be either plain, or show the official competition logo, the logo of the athlete's USWF registered club, or the athlete's LWC.

4.1.6 Stockings (Socks) may be worn, but they cannot go higher than below the knees and shall not cover other bandages.

Diagram 1—The costume

4.2 WEIGHTLIFTING SHOES

4.2.1 The athlete must wear sport shoes (weightlifting shoes) to protect his feet, give him stability and a firm stance on the platform.

4.2.2 The weightlifting shoes shall be made in such a way as not to give the athlete an unfair advantage or to give him additional support other than what has been specified in 4.2.1.

4.2.3 A strap over the instep is permitted.

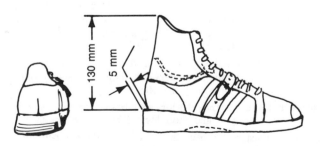

Diagram 2—The shoe

4.2.4 The part of the shoe that covers the heel may be reinforced.

4.2.5 The maximum height permitted on the upper part of the shoe, measured from the top of the sole, is 130 mm.

4.2.6 The sole cannot project from the shoe by more than 5 mm at any point.

4.2.7 The heel of the shoe must not be tapered.

4.2.8 The shoes may be made of any material or combination of materials.

4.2.9 There are no minimum or maximum heights for the soles.

4.2.10 There are no restrictions for the shape of the shoes.

4.3 BELT

4.3.1 The maximum width of the belt worn may be 120 mm at its widest part.

4.3.2 No belt can be worn under the vest or costume.

4.4 BANDAGES AND PLASTERS

4.4.1 Bandages may be worn on the wrist, the knees, the hands, the fingers and the thumbs.

4.4.2 The bandages may be made of gauze, medical crepe or leather. An elastic knee-cap may be worn on the knee.

4.4.3 The maximum width of skin that can be covered at the wrists, for all categories is 100 mm.

4.4.4 The maximum width of skin that can be covered at the knees, for all categories is 300 mm.

4.4.5 There is no limit for the length of the bandages.

4.4.6 The use of plasters and bandages on both the inner and outer surface of the hands is allowed. The plasters or bandages shall not be fastened to the wrist or the barbell.

4.4.7 Plasters on the fingers are allowed, but cannot cover the tip of the fingers.

4.4.8 No bandages or substitute for bandages are allowed on the following parts of the body: a) the elbows; b) the torso; c) the thighs; d) the shins.

5. COMPETITIONS

5.1 ENTRIES

5.1.1 Before each competition, a technical conference shall be held.

5.1.2 The maximum number of competitors entered in a competition is listed in part 1.3.3.

5.1.3 The final nomination of competitors is done at the Technical Conference. Information concerning the name, bodyweight, category, date of birth and best total achieved by each competitor must be given. After this nomination, the name of the competitors cannot be modified and the indicated bodyweight category may only be changed to the next higher category when the relevant rules apply. No athlete may compete in a lower category than the one in which he is entered.

5.1.4 In any category, during a competition, the athletes may be divided in two (2) or more groups by the Competition Secretary, the number in each group depending on the performance achieved previously by the lifter.

5.1.5 At the technical conference the Jury members, referees, technical controllers and doctors on duty will be appointed and allocated into the different categories.

5.1.6 Information must be given on the program of the competition.

5.2 DRAWING OF LOTS

5.2.1 Two hours and fifteen minutes before the start of the competition of each individual bodyweight category, in the weigh-in room, the competitors or their representative will draw a number. They will retain this number throughout the competition.

5.2.2 The drawing of lots shall be done under the supervision of the Competition Secretary, the Technical Controller and the three appointed referees. The lot number shall decide the order of the weigh-in and the order of lifting during the course of the competition. Should a competitor not be present when it is his turn to be weighed according to his lot number, he will be weighed next upon his return.

5.2.3 The drawing of lots shall take place within the fifteen (15) minutes prior to the weigh-in. Should any competitor, for any reason, be late for it, he shall get the number drawn by the Technical Controller. Any competitor who has drawn a number, must weigh-in for the category.

5.2.4 An athlete entered in a specific category may pass on to a heavier category, if himself or his representative announces his wish to do so, at the latest, at the drawing of lots of the category in which he was originally entered and if he meets the requirement of the relevant rule for weigh-in, (5.3.8).

5.2.5 When two (2) or more bodyweight categories compete as one (1) group, the drawing of lots shall take place separately for each category and different series of numbers shall be used.

Example: 14 competitors in B group:

8 in the 100 kg category

6 in the 110 kg category

Lots numbers 1 to 8 shall be drawn for the 100 kg and numbers 9 to 14 for the 110 kg category.

5.3 WEIGH-IN

5.3.1 The weigh-in of each bodyweight category shall begin two (2) hours before the start of the competition and will last one hour.

5.3.2 The official weigh-in shall take place in a room equipped with the following facilities: a) the official scale of the competition; b) a table and chairs for the Secretariat; c) all the necessary competition forms.

5.3.3 The Chief Referee shall operate the scale and the two (2) referees shall verify with him the bodyweight that the Competition Secretary will record.

5.3.4 Each competitor of a specific category must be weighed in the presence of the three (3) appointed referees, one official from his team and the Competition Secretary. During the weigh-in, the only other persons that can be also present are: the President and the General Secretary of the IWF, the President of the Medical Committee and the President of the Technical Committee.

U.S. POLICY—Women competitors shall be weighed in with or without costume, by women. *Note*: No weight allowance is made for costume.

5.3.5 The bodyweight list can only be published after all the competitors have been weighed.

5.3.6 Each competitor must prove his identity by presenting his passport or identity card to the Secretariat.

U.S. POLICY—In domestic competitions, the athlete shall present a valid USWF registration card at weigh-in, together with proof of age where applicable.

5.3.7 The competitors shall be weighed nude or in briefs.

5.3.8 When a competitor is within the weight of the category, he shall be weighed only once. During the time allocated for the weigh-in, only the competitors which are under or over the limits of the category may return as many times as required to make the weight.

After the allocated time is elapsed, these competitors shall be eliminated and only the competitors who are too heavy will be allowed to move up to the next higher category on the condition that no more than one athlete from their own country is entered and provided also that they have totalled the required minimum for that category.

5.3.9 During the weigh-in, the coach of each competitor must write the first attempts (Snatch and Clean and Jerk) on the competitor's card.

U.S. POLICY—During the weigh-in the athlete, coach, or team manager must enter first attempts on the competitor's card.

5.3.10 Before the weigh-in, one team official of each national federation shall give to the Competition Secretary the names of the team officials that will accompany the competitors taking part in this specific category. For one competitor this number shall not exceed four (4) officials.

For two competitors, this number shall not exceed five (5). The Competition Secretary shall issue passes to these team officials. The team officials that have been issued with passes will be the only ones permitted to enter the warming-up area. New passes will be issued for each category.

U.S. POLICY—One competitor allowed a maximum of two (2) officials, two competitors from the same team allowed a maximum of three (3) officials.

5.4 PRESENTATION

5.4.1 Before that start of the competition of each bodyweight category, there will be a presentation of the following persons: a) the competitors in the order of the lots drawn; b) the referees; c) the doctor on duty; d) The Technical Controller; e) The Competition Secretary.

5.4.2 All the above-mentioned persons must obligatorily appear at the presentation together and also leave the presentation together.

5.4.3 After the presentation, there will be a ten minute recess to permit the competitors to warm up.

5.5 COURSE OF THE COMPETITION

5.5.1 The necessary number of officials shall be appointed by the organizers. Their duty is to arrange, under the supervision of the Competition Secretary, the order and the progress of the attempts chosen by the competitors. For this purpose, they shall use the competitor's cards which have spaces for the three attempts in the two lifts.

5.5.2 The officials will ask each competitor or his coach to write on the card the weight required for each attempt. The card will then be brought immediately to the speaker who can make the proper announcement. After each attempt, the officials will ask the competitor or his coach to write the required weight for the next attempt.

5.5.3 One or more speakers shall be appointed and their duty is to make the appropriate announcements. This includes the name of the competitor called to the platform, the name of his country, the weight on the barbell and the number of his attempt. The speaker shall also warn the next competitor in advance that he will be next to lift.

5.5.4 The barbell shall be loaded progressively, the competitor taking the lowest weight-lifting first. In no case can the barbell be reduced to a lighter weight when a competitor has performed a lift with the weight announced. The competitors or their coaches must therefore observe the progress of the loading and be ready to make their attempt at the weight they have chosen.

5.5.5 The weight of the barbell must always be a multiple of 2.5 kg. The only exception to this shall be a record attempt where it must be a multiple of 500 grammes.

5.5.6 The progression between the first and second attempt must be a minimum of 5 kg. A request for 2.5 kg shall indicate a last (third) attempt.

5.5.7 Two minutes will be allowed to each competitor between the calling of his name and the beginning of the attempt. After one minute, there will be a warning signal. If, at the end of the two minutes, the competitor has not raised the barbell from the platform to make his attempt, this attempt shall be declared "No lift" by the referees. When a competitor attempts two lifts in succession, he will be allowed three (3) minutes for the succeeding attempt. After two (2) minutes there will be a warning signal. If at the end of the three (3) minutes, the competitor has not raised the barbell from the platform to make his attempt, this attempt shall be declared "No lift" by the referees.

5.5.8 The time limit for a fourth attempt at a record outside of the competition shall be of three (3) minutes. The warning signal shall be given after two (2) minutes.

5.5.9 When a competitor wishes to increase or decrease the weight which he originally selected, he or his coach must notify the officials before his final call. (The final call shall be with one minute remaining. No changes may occur after this time.)

5.5.10 Before the first attempt or between two attempts only two changes of weight are allowed. After the competitor has received his final call to the platform, he cannot have the weight on the barbell changed.

5.5.11 The final call is the same as in (5.5.7), the signal given by the time-keeper, one minute before the end of the allocated time. The coach may go directly to the speaker table and request this change verbally in order to save the time that would be taken to write the change on the competitor's card.

5.5.12 When a competitor asks for a change of weight and he himself must take the higher weight, the clock will be stopped while the weight is changed. After the change has been completed, the clock will continue to run until the end of his allocated time. When a competitor asks for a change and in doing so, follows another competitor, he shall receive the normal two minutes when he is called again for his attempt.

5.5.13 A competitor or his coach cannot change his decision about the decline of an attempt or the withdrawal from the competition, once it has been officially announced.

5.5.14 In an international match between two individuals or between two nations contested in separate categories, the competitors may lift alternately. The competitor taking the lighter weight will lift first and that order shall be maintained throughout this particular lift.

5.5.15 The weight announced by the speaker must be immediately written on the attempt board.

5.5.16 During any competition organized on a platform or stage, nobody other than the members of the Jury, the officiating referees, the speakers, the technical officials, the managers (one per country taking part) and the competitors of the specific category shall be allowed around the platform or stage.

5.6 ORDER OF CALLING

5.6.1 There are four (4) factors to take in consideration in the order of calling of the competitors: a) the weight of the barbell (kg. of the attempt); b) the number of the attempt (first, second or third); c) the number of lot drawn by the athlete; d) the progression (the difference in kg. between his previous attempt and the requested attempt).

5.6.2 In consideration of the above-mentioned factors, the order of calling shall be the following:

a) the competitor taking the lighter weight, shall lift first;

b) the competitor with the lower number of attempts shall lift before the one with the higher number, i.e., a first attempt is executed before a second attempt and a second attempt before a third;

c) when more than one competitor ask for the same weight and the number of their attempts is identical, the order of calling shall be decided by the lot number drawn before the weigh-in, done in a progressive way, i.e., the athlete with the lower lot number shall lift before the one with a higher number;

Exception: if the athlete with the higher number started earlier than the athlete with the smaller number (the progression between his previous attempt and the requested attempt is bigger than the one of the other athlete)

d) the order of call applies to both the Snatch and the Clean and Jerk. Example

	Snatch	Clean and Jerk
Competitor A	102.5 107.5 110.0	135.0 140.0 142.5
Competitor B	100.0 105.0 110.0	135.0 145.0 145.0
Competitor C	102.5 107.5 110.0	135.0 142.5 145.0

The order of calling shall be the following:

Snatch:	B-A-C, B-A-C, B-A-C
Clean and Jerk:	A-B-C, A-C-A, B-C-B

5.7 ANNOUNCEMENT OF WINNERS

5.7.1 After both the Snatch and the Clean and Jerk, the names of the competitors in the first six (6) places shall be announced (for Snatch, Clean and Jerk and Total).

5.7.2 The Snatch or the Victory Ceremony after the Snatch, must be followed by a ten minute break to allow the competitors to warm up for the Clean and Jerk.

5.8 CLASSIFICATION OF ATHLETES AND TEAMS

5.8.1 The title of champion shall be awarded for the individual lifts, Snatch, Clean and Jerk as well as for the Olympic Total (the aggregate of the best Snatch and the best Clean and Jerk results). The competitors who have won first, second, and third place in the two lifts and the Total in official competitions under IWF rules shall be awarded gold, silver and bronze medals, respectively.

U.S. POLICY—Medals for Snatch, Clean and Jerk and Total shall only be mandatory at USWF National Championships.

5.8.2 The final classification of the competitors shall be calculated in accordance with the total weight lifted by adding the best results in the Snatch and the Clean and Jerk of the lifts accepted by the referees.

5.8.3 Any extra attempt outside of the competition cannot be included in the Total.

5.8.4 In World and Continental Championships and Regional Games and where agreed by the countries participating in international tournaments, the classification by teams will be calculated according to the following schedule: allocating 16 points to the first competitor, 14 to the second, 13 to the third, 12 to the fourth, 11 to the fifth, 10 to the sixth, 9 to the seventh, 8 to the eighth, 7 to the ninth, 6 to the tenth, 5 to the eleventh, 4 to the twelfth, 3 to the thirteenth, 2 to the fourteenth, and 1 to the fifteenth.

At World Championships, team points for each lift (Snatch and Jerk) will be allocated to a team as well as for the Total.

U.S. POLICIES—Point scoring for all U.S. National Championships shall be ten places of finish in this order: 12 points to the first competitor, 9 to the second, 8 to the third, 7 to the fourth, 6 to the fifth, 5 to the sixth, 4 to the seventh, 3 to the eighth, 2 to the ninth, 1 to the tenth.

Point scoring for all other domestic meets shall be: 5 points for the first competitor, 3 points for the second, 1 point for third.

Only currently registered member clubs of an LWC of USWF are eligible to score points in sanctioned competitions. At National, Regional, State and LWC Championships, team competitors may only score points for actual placing in the category.

Example ''Unattached'' athlete places first in the category, the team athlete may only get second place points.

5.8.5 For the team classification, Snatch and Jerk points can be counted only when medals are awarded for these lifts.

5.8.6 In the case of a tie, the lighter competitor will be classified before the heavier one, to avoid supplementary attempts.

5.8.7 When two or more competitors obtain the same result in a competition where they registered at the same bodyweight, they will be classified equal and will receive the same type of medal, same place and points. The following medals and places, according to the number of equally classified competitors, shall not be awarded and the next best competitor will be classified according to the number of places left out.

Example: A, B and C competitors all weighed in at 51.95 kg and their total is 245 kg. Competitors A, B and C will be awarded each a gold medal, 1st place and 16 points. Competitor D will be awarded 4th place and 12 points.

5.8.8 In the case of a tie in the classification of teams, the team having the largest number of first places shall be classified first. In the case of two teams having the same number of first places, the one having the most second places shall be classified first and so on through the third places, etc.

5.8.9 Zero in the Snatch will not eliminate a competitor from the championship, he will be allowed to continue in the Jerk. He qualifies for a place in the Jerk but not in the Total and he shall receive points for the team classification.

5.8.10 Similarly, a competitor who has been successful in the Snatch but has a zero in the Jerk, is qualified for the Snatch but not in the Total. He shall receive points for the team classification.

6. OFFICIALS OF THE COMPETITION

(*Note*: Rule 6, omitted here, is primarily concerned with the selection and functions of the jury, competition secretary, technical controller and referees for National and International championships, including the Olympic Games.)

7. WORLD RECORDS

(*Note*: Rule 7, omitted here, is concerned with the regulations which must be met for recognition of world records.)

8. CEREMONIES

(*Note*: Rule 8, omitted here, is concerned with the procedures to be followed in the opening ceremony, victory ceremony, and closing ceremony at World Championships.)

GOVERNING BODY

United States Weightlifting Federation, Inc., 1750 E. Boulder St., Colorado Springs, CO 80909-5764

The U.S. Weightlifting Federation (USWF) has Group A membership status on the U.S. Olympic Committee and is affiliated with The International Weightlifting Federation. The USWF has jurisdiction and control over the administration, eligibility, sanctioning, authority, representation, and rules of competition for the sport of weightlifting in the United States. The purpose and objectives of the Federation are to encourage, improve, and promote amateur weightlifting at all levels in the United States. The administrative structure of the Federation divides the nation into seven regions that are made up of individual state Local Weightlifting Committees (LWC).

MAGAZINES

Weightlifting USA, USWF, 1750 E. Boulder St., Colorado Springs, CO 80909-5764

World Weightlifting, International Weightlifting Federation, 1374 Budapest, Pf, 614, Hungary

• WRESTLING •

INTERNATIONAL AMATEUR WRESTLING FEDERATION
RULES OF INTERNATIONAL WRESTLING
GRECO-ROMAN AND FREESTYLE
INCLUDING
AAU/USA JUNIOR OLYMPIC PROGRAM RULES

(Reproduced by permission of Amateur Athletic Union*)

☐

Note: The rules of wrestling included herein are an accurate translation of the rules promulgated by FILA (The International Amateur Wrestling Federation). Certain passages, as clearly indicated, have been inserted where the AAU Junior Olympic Program Rules differ from those of the International organization. These regulations apply to the styles recognized by modern wrestling, the Greco-Roman style and Freestyle. Basically, they differ as follows:

- In Greco-Roman wrestling, it is formally forbidden to grasp the opponent below the hips, to trip him or to actively use the legs in the execution of any action.

- In Freestyle wrestling, on the contrary, it is permissible to grasp the legs of the opponent, to trip him, and to use the legs actively in the execution of any action.

PREAMBLE

Article 1 OBJECT

The International rules of wrestling have as their specific objectives:

a) to define and specify the practical and technical conditions under which the bout must take place

b) to fix the values assignable to wrestling situations and holds

c) to list these situations and all prohibitions

d) to determine the methods of classification, penalization and elimination of competitors, etc.

Being subject to modifications in light of practical observations as to their application and their effectiveness, the international rules set forth herein constitute the framework within which the sport of wrestling takes place in the Greco-Roman and Freestyle forms.

---

*See page 726 for additional information.

Article 2 APPLICATION

These rules shall apply to the Olympic Games, World Championships, World Cups, Continental Cups, International and Regional Events, and at all International Meets. These rules are likewise mandatory for all events organized by National Governing Body affiliated with FILA.

Note: The International Wrestling Rules presented in this publication are the official rules of the Federation Internationale de Lutte Amateur (FILA) and are in effect for all competitions at the Open, Espoir, Elite and Cadet levels. Certain modifications have been adopted by the AAU Junior Olympics Program for use in the Schoolboy, Junior, Midget and Bantam levels.

Article 3 INTERPRETATION

The FILA Technical Committee is the sole authority empowered to clarify the exact meaning of the articles that follow in cases of disagreement. The French language shall be considered the authoritative text.

Note: During tournament competition, the Executive Committee of the AAU Wrestling Officials Organization, or their representative as Head Official will be responsible for the interpretation of the rules contained in this book.

Article 4 METHODS OF COMPETITION

International wrestling competitions consist of two parts, the preliminary rounds and the Finals. This rule applies to all individual competitions having four or more wrestlers in a weight class. If there are only three or two wrestlers, the system of "one against the other" (round robin) is applied and the preliminary rounds are omitted.

Article 5 COMPETITION PROCEDURE

The duration set for Tournaments is as follows:

a) OLYMPIC GAMES: Five days on three mats, per style.

b) SENIOR WORLD CHAMPIONSHIPS: Four days on three mats or three days on four mats.

c) ESPOIR CHAMPIONSHIPS: Three days on three mats.

d) CONTINENTAL CHAMPIONSHIPS: Three days on two or three mats depending on the number of participants.

In principle, no session should be longer than three hours, and each weight class should complete wrestling in a maximum of three days.

Note: Technical requirements for facilities, scheduling and personnel contained in this section are recommended for all AAU Junior Olympic Wrestling tournaments, but are subject to modification by the Tournament Committee to accommodate local conditions.

PART ONE—BASIC FRAMEWORK

Article 6 WEIGHT CLASSES-AGE CATEGORIES

WEIGHT CLASSES: Weight classes are as follows:

Note: Bantam, Midget, and Junior are AAU age division, not FILA.

Table T.10

A. BANTAM (7-8 years)	B. MIDGET (9-10 years)	C. JUNIOR (11-12 years)
1. up to 45 lbs.	1. up to 50 lbs.	1. up to 55 lbs.
2. up to 50 lbs.	2. up to 55 lbs.	2. up to 60 lbs.
3. up to 55 lbs.	3. up to 60 lbs.	3. up to 65 lbs.
4. up to 60 lbs.	4. up to 65 lbs.	4. up to 70 lbs.
5. up to 65 lbs.	5. up to 70 lbs.	5. up to 75 lbs.
6. up to 70 lbs.	6. up to 75 lbs.	6. up to 80 lbs.
7. Heavyweight	7. up to 80 lbs.	7. up to 85 lbs.
	8. up to 85 lbs.	8. up to 90 lbs.
	9. up to 92 lbs.	9. up to 95 lbs.
	10. up to 100 lbs.	10. up to 100 lbs.
	11. up to 112 lbs.	11. up to 108 lbs.
	12. Heavyweight	12. up to 119 lbs.
		13. up to 132 lbs.
		14. up to 148 lbs.
		15. Heavyweight

D. SCHOOLBOY (13-14 years)	E. CADET (15-16 years)
1. up to 66 lbs.	1. up to 83.5 lbs.
2. up to 70.5 lbs.	2. up to 88 lbs.
3. up to 75 lbs.	3. up to 92.5 lbs.
4. up to 80 lbs.	4. up to 99 lbs.
5. up to 85 lbs.	5. up to 105.5 lbs.
6. up to 90 lbs.	6. up to 112 lbs.
7. up to 95 lbs.	7. up to 121 lbs.
8. up to 100 lbs.	8. up to 130 lbs.
9. up to 105 lbs.	9. up to 138.5 lbs.
10. up to 112 lbs.	10. up to 149.5 lbs.
11. up to 119 lbs.	11. up to 160.5 lbs.
12. up to 126 lbs.	12. up to 171.5 lbs.
13. up to 133 lbs.	13. up to 192 lbs.
14. up to 140 lbs.	14. up to 242 lbs.
15. up to 148 lbs.	
16. up to 160 lbs.	
17. up to 185 lbs.	
18. Heavyweight	

(Cont.)

Table T.10 (Continued)

F. ELITE (17-18 years)	G. ESPOIR (19-20 years)	H. SENIOR (open)
1. up to 98 lbs.	1. up to 105.5 lbs.	1. up to 105.5 lbs.
2. up to 106 lbs.	2. up to 114.5 lbs.	2. up to 114.5 lbs.
3. up to 115 lbs.	3. up to 125.5 lbs.	3. up to 125.5 lbs.
4. up to 123 lbs.	4. up to 136.5 lbs.	4. up to 136.5 lbs.
5. up to 132 lbs.	5. up to 149.5 lbs.	5. up to 149.5 lbs.
6. up to 143 lbs.	6. up to 163 lbs.	6. up to 163 lbs.
7. up to 154 lbs.	7. up to 180.5 lbs.	7. up to 180.5 lbs.
8. up to 165 lbs.	8. up to 198 lbs.	8. up to 198 lbs.
9. up to 178 lbs.	9. up to 220 lbs.	9. up to 220 lbs.
10. up to 192 lbs.	10. up to 286 lbs.	10. up to 286 lbs.
11. up to 220 lbs.		
12. up to 275 lbs.		

All contestants are presumed to be participating of their own free will. They can only enter an event in one weight class—the one corresponding to their body weight at the time of the official weigh-in. However, they can opt for the weight class immediately above the one in which they were entered, except for the heavyweight class. For Espoirs and Seniors to enter the heavyweight class, they must weigh over 220 lbs. on the first day of weigh-ins.

Note: A competitor at any sanctioned AAU wrestling event WILL NOT be required to compete against any opponent weighing 12% (bodyweight) more at either the listed LOWEST weight or GREATEST weight in the Bantam, Midget, Junior, or Schoolboy age divisions, or at the listed LOWEST weight in the Cadet, Elite, Espoir, or Senior age divisions. Where this condition does exist, the event committee shall create additional weight class(es) to allow for those affected participants the opportunity to compete in that event.

AGE CATEGORIES:

The age categories are as follows:

Bantam	7 or 8 years of age
Midget	9 or 10 years of age
Junior	11 or 12 years of age
Schoolboy	13 or 14 years of age
Cadet	15 or 16 years of age
Elite	17 or 18 years of age
Espoir	19 or 20 years of age
Senior (open)	21 to 34 years of age
Masters	34 years of age and older

Note: A participant's age category is established by the wrestler's age on January 1 of that year.

Article 7 DURATION OF BOUTS

The duration of bouts is fixed as follows:

a) for Bantam, Midget and Junior Divisions, two 90-second periods with no rest between periods

Note: These are not FILA age categories.

b) for Schoolboy and Cadet Divisions, two 2-minute periods with a 30-second rest between periods

c) for Elite, Espoir and Senior Divisions, two 3-minute periods with a 60-second rest between periods

d) for Masters Division, two 2-minute periods with a 30-second rest between periods

Note: These time periods are mandatory at all AAU Regional and National Championships, but may be modified at local and Association competitions.

Article 8 COMPETITOR'S LICENSE

All wrestlers taking part in World Championships and World Festivals, World Cups, Continental Championships, Continental Cups and Continental Games, or Regional Games, must possess an international license. The license is not valid unless it bears a current FILA stamp.

Note: All competitors in AAU wrestling events must have a currently valid AAU card for presentation and weigh-ins.

Article 9 WEIGH-IN

A final list of competitors must be submitted by each team leader to the Organizing Committee before the weigh-ins are to take place. Competitors will be weighed nude and examined by officially designated doctors who will exclude any wrestler posing any danger whatsoever of contagious disease. Competitors should be in perfect physical condition. Fingernails should be cut short and will be checked at weigh-in. Wrestlers have the right, in turn, to step on the scale as many times as they wish up until the end of the weigh-ins. At tournaments lasting several days, the contestants shall be weighed in each day. This procedure was introduced at the FILA Congress in 1986. All tournament weigh-ins shall take place the night before each day of competition.

Article 10 DRESS

a) Competitors should show up to the mat in a single piece outfit in the color assigned to them (red or blue) with protective undergarments or supporter underneath. The outfits (singlets) should be tight-fitting, cover the body from the mid-thigh and should not be cut away more than the width of two palms around the neck and arms. Each competitor must have two complete outfits (one red and one blue) which comply with these provisions. Each competitor must also carry a handkerchief. The use of knee pads is permitted.

b) Nothing else may be added to this outfit, except in cases where the bout is interrupted because of injury. During such times wrestlers can cover themselves with warm-up garments.

c) Competitors should wear appropriately soft, lightweight sport shoes without soles which cover the ankle. The use of shoes with heels or spiked soles or shoes with buckles or metal parts is forbidden. Special attention should be given to the laces, the ends of which should be cut off if they are metallic or rigid.

d) It is also forbidden to:

1) wear bandages on wrists, arms or ankles except in case of injury or medical prescription

2) coat the body with greasy or sticky substances

3) present oneself in a sweaty state

4) wear any object which could injure the opponent such as rings, bracelets, etc.

e) At the weigh-in, each competitor must be closely shaven or have a beard of several month's growth.

Note: Reinforced headgear and hard helmets are forbidden in internationl competition. Headgear are permitted in AAU wrestling events, but they must be tight-fitting with an adjustable strap and provide no possibility of injury to the opponent.

Article 11 THE MAT

a) Mats approved by FILA measuring 9 meters (29.5 feet) in diameter with a protective area of equal thickness measuring 1.2 meters to 1.5 meters wide (3.9 to 4.9 feet) are required for all the following events: 1) World Championships and World Cups; 2) Continental Championships and Continental Games; and 3) All International Events.

b) The mat should have a 9 meter (29.5 foot) circle drawn on it along the interior. A one meter (3.3 foot) wide red ring should be added around the length of the circumference; the zone defined by this red ring is an integral part of the wrestling area. To designate the different parts of the mat, the following terminology should be employed: 1) PROTECTION AREA (SURFACE DE PROTECTION); 2) PASSIVITY ZONE (ZONE DE PASSIVITE); and 3) CENTRAL WRESTLING AREA (SURFACE CENTRALE DE LUTTE).

c) The portion of the mat inside the red ring is called the "CENTER" and is 7 meters or 22.9 feet wide. The red ring is called the PASSIVITY ZONE and is 1 meter or 3.3 feet wide. The outer area is called the PROTECTION AREA and is 1.2 meters to 1.5 meters or 3.9 to 4.9 feet wide.

d) Mats which are 10 meters wide may also be used. The dimensions of the Passivity Zone and Protection Area shall remain as above. Mats which are 8 meters wide may be used for tournaments other than those listed above.

e) In cases of poor visibility, the mat should be mounted on a raised platform. The height of the platform should not exceed 1.10 meters. Posts and ropes as used for boxing rings are prohibited. If the mat is installed on a platform, and the total margin of protection including the border and free space around the mat is less than two meters, the sides of the platform should be covered with panels slanted at 45 degrees. In either case the protective covering around the border should be in a contrasting color. The floor near the mat should be lined with a soft, neatly installed cover.

f) The mat should be covered with a canvas which should be cleaned and disinfected to avoid contamination. The ringlets should be hidden. When using modern mats with a uniformly smooth and unwrinkled surface, the same hygienic measures should be applied. Certain synthetic mats with a rigid outer layer may be used with a tarpaulin. Finally, the mat should be set up in such a way that a wide area can be cleared all around it to allow routine functions to take place.

g) The mat should be 4 to 6 centimeters (1.5 to 2.5) inches thick, depending on the density and elasticity of the mat.

Note: Mats used in AAU competition may meet the above criteria, but must have a circular wrestling area of 28 feet diameter or a rectangular area 24 feet on a side. All mats must have a five foot protection area of mat around the wrestling area proper.

Article 12 MEDICAL ATTENDANTS

a) All wrestlers must submit to a special medical examination in their own country three days before departing for all official FILA authorized tournaments, in accordance with Article 8 of the FILA statutes.

b) Tournament organizers are required to provide medical attendants to oversee the weigh-in and the bouts and detect possible drug use. The medical attendants shall include in their number an adequate number of doctors and medical assistants. The medical attendants will be called upon to work throughout the duration of the event. They are under the authority of the FILA Medical Commission.

c) Doctors will examine the competitors and determine the state of their health before weigh-ins. Competitors who are not considered to be medically in good health or who present any condition dangerous to themselves or their opponents will be forbidden from participating in the event. The medical examination will look for contagious diseases, in particular skin or venereal disease.

d) Medical attendants should be ready at all times to intervene in case of accident and determine whether the wrestler should continue or stop the bout. The doctors of the participating teams have the right to intervene in the care given to their injured wrestlers, but only the coach or team leader can assist the team doctors.

Note: Technical requirements for facilities, scheduling and personnel contained in this section are recommended for all AAU Junior Olympic Wrestling tournaments, but are subject to modification by the Tournament Committee to accommodate local conditions.

Article 13 INTERVENTION BY THE MEDICAL ATTENDANTS

a) The medical attendants described in Article 12 above have the right and duty to stop a bout at any time they consider that there is a danger to either competitor. Their intervention is through the Mat Chairman. They may end the match immediately by declaring one of the wrestlers unfit to continue.

b) Wrestlers should not leave the mat area during injuries or controversies, except in cases of severe injury which require they be withdrawn immediately.

c) Referees can stop the wrestling for up to three minutes per bout as injury time for nosebleeds or a fall to the head or because of any other acceptable incident beyond the control of the wrestlers, provided where the pause is approved by the FILA or Tournament Doctor.

d) An injured wrestler can be allowed to continue the competition in the next round at the advice of the doctor. This medical advice must be presented to the technical head of the competition by the Team Leader of the injured wrestler's team before the pairing chart of the next round is posted or before the weigh-in for the next day.

e) The delegate of the FILA Medical Commission will ask the officials to stop the bout in case of any dispute over a medical order, notwithstanding the right of the team doctor of the wrestler involved to intervene in any possible treatment or to form his own opinion concerning the intervention or decision of the medical attendants.

f) At international competitions where the FILA Medical Commission is not represented, the decision to interrupt the bout will be made by the FILA delegate after consultation with the tournament director and the team doctor of the injured wrestler.

Article 14 DRUG USE

a) Drug use is formally forbidden. To combat it, FILA reserves the right to subject wrestlers to examination or testing at all competitions it sanctions, in accordance with the provisions of Article 9 of the FILA statutes. Competitors or leaders cannot oppose such checks for any circumstances, under penalty of sanction.

b) The FILA Medical Commission will decide the timing, the number, and the frequency of these checks, which will be undertaken by any means deemed effective. The appropriate measures will be carried out by a doctor accredited by FILA, in the presence of a member of the Executive Bureau and one of the team leaders of the wrestler or wrestlers called upon to be tested.

c) In any case where the measures are not carried out in accordance with the conditions above, the results thereby obtained may be considered void.

PART TWO—RUNNING A TOURNAMENT

Article 15 DRAWING LOTS AND POOLING

(In AAU competition, annotations regularly published by the officials committee shall apply.)

The participants in an event should be pooled into two elimination groups and paired for each round according to a draw number assigned to each by the drawing of lots at the time of the weigh-in, prior to the beginning of the Tournament.

a) Drawing Lots

1) The drawing should be public.

2) Wrestlers will be placed in pools and paired according to draw numbers which they themselves draw upon leaving the scale.

3) This number should immediately be written down on the posting board, in full public view, as well as on the preliminary list.

IMPORTANT: If the person responsible for the weigh-in and the drawing of lots ascertains any error in the regulation procedure set forth above at the time of the drawing, THE DRAWING FOR THAT WEIGHT CLASS WILL BE NULLIFIED.

4) The drawing of lots for that weight class will start over.

b) Preliminary Classification

1) Immediately after the weigh-in is finished, wrestlers will be listed in order of classification, going from the smallest to the largest number.

c) Forming Pools

1) Wrestlers assigned odd draw numbers will form pool "A".

2) Wrestlers assigned even draw numbers will form pool "B".

3) Example: 14 wrestlers registered; 12 wrestlers weigh-in.

Draw Numbers:

Wrestler A—4	Wrestler G—12	Since two wrestlers did
Wrestler B—3	Wrestler H— 2	not show up for the
Wrestler C—6	Wrestler I—10	weigh-in, two numbers
Wrestler D—5	Wrestler J— 8	were not shown:
Wrestler E—1	Wrestler K—13	No. 7 and No. 11.
	Wrestler L— 9	

Preliminary Classification

No. 1—E	No. 5—D	No. 9—I	Wrestlers are then
No. 2—H	No. 6—C	No. 10—G	listed in order of
No. 3—B	No. 7—J	No. 11—K	increasing size.
No. 4—A	No. 8—L	No. 12—F	

FORMING POOLS

POOL "A"	POOL "B"
1—E	2—H
3—B	4—A
5—D	6—C
7—J	8—L
9—I	10—G
11—K	12—F

After the formation of pools, wrestlers are listed in order of increasing size.

Example:

POOL "A"	POOL "B"
E—1	H—1
B—2	A—2
D—3	C—3
J—4	L—4
I—5	G—5
K—6	F—6

Article 16 PAIRING

a) A prospectus setting forth the procedures and timetable for the event should be drawn up furnishing all necessary details on the planned running of the Tournament.

b) The pairings for each round and the results should be posted on charts for the benefit of the contestants, who should be able to check them at all times.

c) In each pool, if there is an odd number of contestants, the one who drew the largest number (exempt or bye) will advance to the next round without points and will be moved to the top of the pairing chart in the next round.

d) That wrestler will remain at the top until another competitor becomes the unmatched wrestler and is in turn moved to the top of the pairing chart.

e) A bye results in exemption from wrestling for one round. It is a right acquired through the drawing of lots.

f) This right may not be taken away except where having a bye makes it impossible to pair the other contestants that round, or where taking it away permits the pairing of a greater number of bouts in the round.

g) The pairing of the other rounds will be done in the following manner:

Begin with the name of the contestant at the top of the chart. Their opponent will be the contestant with the number closest to theirs whom they have not yet wrestled.

Examples: Pairing for a weight class with 19 wrestlers:

POOL "A" (10 WRESTLERS)

1st Round	2nd Round	3rd Round
1—2	1—3	1—5
3—4	2—4	2—3
5—6	5—7	7—10
7—8	6—9	8—9
9—10	8—10	

In the second round 4 and 6 were eliminated with two defeats.

POOL "B" (9 WRESTLERS)

1st round	2nd round	3rd Round
1—2	9—1	8—9
3—4	2—3	1—4
5—6	4—5	2—6
7—8	6—7	
9—Bye	8—Bye	

In the second round 3, 5, and 7 were eliminated with two defeats.

h) The pairings drawn up for the various rounds of the tournament shown above should be modified each time a wrestler who has not been eliminated due to injury or medically established illness withdraws from the event. It is the responsibility of the withdrawing wrestler (or the wrestler's team leader) to immediately make known the withdrawal. A new pairing must be drawn before the next round of the weight class involved.

i) In events where several wrestlers from the same country participate in the same weight class, they may be called upon to wrestle each other beginning with the first round, if so required by the pairings, and the pairings were drawn by lot.

Article 17 ELIMINATION ROUNDS

Elimination rounds will be conducted in two pools "A" and "B" for each weight class.

a) Duration

Elimination rounds will be conducted until all competitors are progressively eliminated. They will continue until the top three can be determined in each pool.

b) Standings in Pool "A" and "B"

1) The standings in each pool will be determined by the positive points acquired by each of the last three uneliminated competitors after wrestling the other two remaining competitors. The one who earned the most positive points in two bouts shall be first.

2) If only two wrestlers remain after the last round of eliminations, the one who wins the bout between them will be first. The other will be second. The wrestler who acquired the most points among the eliminated wrestlers in the next to last round will be third. If two wrestlers have an equal number of points, their standing is determined by the result of the bout between them, which will have to be wrestled if it did not occur previously.

3) If three undefeated or once-defeated remain in the final round, they must wrestle one another, unless they met in the preceding rounds. If so, the result of their earlier match will decide the standings.

4) Round Robin Finals in the elimination pools:

Will take place among undefeated wrestlers or wrestlers having no more than one (1) defeat.

If, due to circumstances, a wrestler with two defeats would be in the round robin for that pool, that wrestler will automatically be third in the pool without wrestling the other two contestants.

5) Pool standings will be determined by the points which each of the three contestants have acquired after meeting the other two contestants. The one with the most points will be first.

6) In cases where the positive points of several wrestlers are equal, the final standings will be determined by the successive application of the following criteria:

(a) the most points accumulated in the course of the entire tournament,

(b) the most victories,

(c) the most "falls" including the most wins by technical superiority (15 point margin),

(d) the most victories by 4:0 not counted as falls (default, forfeit, etc.),

(e) the most victories by superiority (12 to 14 points),

(f) the least defeats.

-If at this point the wrestlers are still equal, check the number of technical points scored by each contestant in the two matches which counted as part of the round robin, and the one who scored the most technical points will be ranked above the other,

-In cases where each of the three wrestlers won one bout by total victory against one other wrestler, the standings will be based on the fastest fall.

Article 18 FINALS

a) The contestants placing 1st, 2nd, and 3rd in each pool will participate in the finals.

b) The third place finishers in each pool "A" and "B" will wrestle for 5th and 6th place.

c) The second place finishers in each pool "A" and "B" will wrestle for 3rd and 4th place.

d) The first place finisher in each pool "A" and "B" will wrestle for 1st and 2nd place.

e) The results of these head-to-head bouts will determine the final standings.

Special Cases:

a) If wrestlers do not show up for the final when their names are called, they will be disqualified and will not place. Their opponent will win the bout.

Wrestlers acknowledged by the medical attendants to be injured and unable to continue the competition will receive the places they would otherwise obtain at the moment they ceased competition. They will not be disqualified.

b) PAIRING THE FINALS IN THE CASES WHERE COMPETITORS FAIL TO MAKE WEIGHT OR MISS THE WEIGH-IN WILL BE AS SHOWN BELOW:

If one or more of the competitors who qualified to wrestle off for 1st through 6th place fail to make weight or miss the weigh-in, the following procedure should apply:

1) Pair the finals in accordance with the procedures already set forth among those competitors who did weigh in that day of the tournament.

2) Re-do the standings for the pool from which the eliminated competitors came, replacing them with the wrestlers that immediately followed them in the pool standings.

3) Competitors with no opponents will place without wrestling.

4) Competitors classified in qualifying groups in place of wrestlers who failed to make weight will place without wrestling in the vacant positions down to 6th place in the standings. Where contestants from both pools fail to make weight, the wrestler who placed higher in the elimination pool will place higher. If they placed the same in their respective pools, apply the criteria of most positive points, victories, type of victory, etc.

Article 19 FINAL STANDINGS

a) Bouts which determine the final standings for 1st, 2nd, 3rd, 4th, 5th, and 6th place must end with one wrestler winning.

b) In any case, a fall, or a victory by technical superiority (15 point margin) will stop the bout and determine the winner.

Additional Details:

a) Wrestlers who do not show up for the weigh-in or who fail to appear when called to the mat and accordingly do not finish the tournament, will not place.

b) The same applies to wrestlers disqualified for unnecessary roughness or improper dress.

c) Wrestlers who are hurt, immobilized or hospitalized, and as a result cannot go on the mat according to FILA or tournament doctor, may forfeit or be declared beaten, but not disqualified.

d) Those wrestlers may place, or continue on in the competition if not eliminated.

e) Finally, wrestlers who otherwise place but are required by the official doctor to withdraw, may place according to where they would have ended up at the end of the event.

f) In cases where two wrestlers are eliminated for passivity in the final bout, they will both be classified 2nd or 4th or 6th, without the higher place being awarded (no 1st, 3rd, or 5th place).

Note: Warnings will not result in any technical points being awarded to the opponent. They cannot be counted in determining the winner.

Article 20 AWARD CEREMONY

a) The top eight place wrestlers in each weight class will participate in the award ceremony and receive a certificate.

b) The top three place wrestlers in each weight class will receive a medal according to how they finish: 1st: Gold; 2nd: Silver; 3rd: Bronze.

NOTE: TEAM SCORING — IN AAU COMPETITION, TEAM SCORING SHALL BE AS FOLLOWS:

FIRST PLACE (CHAMPION) ....10 POINTS

SECOND PLACE ....7 POINTS

THIRD PLACE ....5 POINTS

FOURTH PLACE ....3 POINTS

FIFTH PLACE..2 POINTS

SIXTH PLACE..1 POINT

—THE TOP TWO WRESTLERS (HIGHEST PLACE WINNERS) MAY SCORE TEAM POINTS FOR THEIR TEAM.

—NO PRE-TOURNAMENT DESIGNATION IS REQUIRED AS TO THOSE TWO WRESTLERS: IF A TEAM HAS MORE THAN TWO WRESTLERS IN THE WEIGHT CLASS, THE TOP TWO TEAMS WILL SCORE, REGARDLESS WHO THEY ARE.

—A COMPLETE, UNALTERABLE TEAM ROSTER MUST BE SUBMITTED AT THE END OF THE WEIGH-IN ON THE FIRST DAY.

—NO TEAM POINTS ARE SCORED FOR FALLS.

PART THREE—OFFICIALS

Article 21 COMPOSITION

(In AAU Junior Olympic competition, modifications to the requirements concerning officials may be made when necessary.)

a) At all tournaments, the officials for each bout shall consist of: 1 mat chairman + 1 referee + 1 judge + 1 controller = 4 officials, rated or qualified according to the rule on international officials.

b) Officials cannot be changed during the course of a match, except in the case of a severe medically confirmed problem.

c) Two officials of the same nationality cannot officiate the same bout simultaneously. In addition, officials cannot officiate matches contested by their countrymen.

d) The dress of the mat chairmen, the judges and the referees shall be white.

Article 22 GENERAL DUTIES

a) Officials carry out all functions provided for by the rules for organizing wrestling events and by whatever particular arrangements are set forth for the organization of the various events.

Their duty is to observe each bout with the greatest care, from beginning to end, and to evaluate moves, in order that the result appearing on the judge's bout sheet accurately reflects the countenance of the bout.

b) Mat chairmen, referees and judges assess holds individually in order to arrive at a correct consensus decision. They collaborate under the direction of the mat chairman, who coordinates the officials.

c) Officials should assume all functions of refereeing and judging, of scoring and or pronouncing sanctions provided for by the rules.

d) The bout sheets of the judge and the mat chairman record the points for all holds carried out by the two wrestlers.

e) If a bout does not end by fall, superiority, default, or disqualification, a decision should be given by the mat chairman based on the scoring for all moves made by each wrestler, as recorded from the start of the bout to the finish on the bout sheets of the judge and the mat chairman.

f) All of the judge's points should be made public as soon as awarded, by paddles, by light apparatus, or other appropriate method.

g) Officials should express themselves using the basic FILA vocabulary terms to conduct and fulfill their respective roles. However, they may not speak with anyone during the bout, except the other officials, where necessary to properly carry out their duties.

Article 23 REFEREES

a) Referees are responsible for the normal running of the bout, conducted in accordance with the rules.

b) Referees should command the respect of the competitors. They should exert authority over them, in order that all orders and instructions be immediately obeyed. Referees should conduct the bout without tolerating any irregular or inopportune outside interference.

c) Referees are to work in close collaboration with the judge, under the supervision of the mat chairman, and should follow the action of the bout without intervening in any thoughtless or inopportune way. The referee's whistle starts, stops and ends the match.

d) Referees alone return the wrestlers to the center of the mat when they go out.

e) Referees score points. They are required to have a red wrist band on their left arm and a blue wrist band on their right. After a hold is executed (if it is valid, if it was carried out within the bounds of mat, etc.) the referee should indicate with fingers the number of points scored, raising the right arm if the wrestler dressed in blue scored the points, and raising the left arm if the wrestler dressed in red scored them.

f) Referees, as circumstances require, should never hesitate to:

1) discipline passive wrestler,

2) stop the bout at required times, neither too soon nor too late,

3) indicate whether holds executed at the edge of the mat are in or out,

4) signal and declare TOUCHE (fall) after seeking confirmation from the judge or, alternatively, from the mat chairman. To determine that a wrestler was actually pinned to the mat with both shoulders touching simultaneously (see Article 45), the referees should say the word "tomber" (TOM-BAY), raise their hand for confirmation from the judge or mat chairman, slap the mat and then blow their whistles.

g) Referees should especially be careful not to get too near the wrestlers while they are standing, since their legs would be difficult to watch up close. They should stay close when the wrestling is on the ground, however.

h) Referees are also expected to:

1) in GRECO, closely observe the legs of the wrestlers,

2) require the wrestlers to remain on the mat until the result is announced,

3) ask for an opinion at any time from the judge who is situated at the edge of the mat facing the mat chairman,

4) vote for or against elimination or disqualification, along with the other officials,

5) declare the winner, with the concurrence of the mat chairman.

i) Referees can request sanctions for infractions of the rules or for unnecessary roughness.

j) Referees must stop the bout upon the intervention by the mat chairman to declare victory by technical superiority (15 point margin).

Article 24 JUDGES

a) Judges are to assure that all duties generally provided for in the rules of wrestling are carried out.

b) Judges should attentively observe the bout taking place without being distracted in any way, and record the points they score on their bout sheets. Judges give scores for all moves.

c) Following each move, judges should write down the number of points to be scored for that move based on the score given by the referee (which they should compare with their own assessment). They should indicate the result with scoreboards placed next to them, which should be equally visible to the spectators and wrestlers.

d) Judges can score points or signal passivity independent of the referee.

e) If judges see something they think should be brought to the attention of the referee during a bout, when the referee could not see or could not pay attention to it (such as an illegal hold or unfair position), they should bring the matter up by raising the paddle which is the color of the wrestler involved, even if the referee has not asked for an opinion. Judges should always draw the referee's attention to everything which seems abnormal to them or irregular as regards the running of the bout or the behavior of the wrestlers.

f) Judges should sign the bout sheet brought to them upon receipt and, at the end of the bout, clearly indicate the result of the bout, crossing out the name of the loser.

g) If the calls made by the judge and the referee agree, those calls alone decide the points scored without further recourse to the mat chairman, except for declaring victory by technical superiority.

h) The judge's bout sheet should clearly indicate the time elapsed in the bout when it is stopped, in case of total victory, technical superiority, withdrawal, or whatever.

i) In order to facilitate their view of the bout, particularly in close situations, judges are authorized to move about, but only along the edge of the mat where they are stationed.

j) Judges should indicate each instance where the wrestler is warned for passivity on their bout sheets, in the place provided.

Article 25 MAT CHAIRMEN

a) The mat chairman is the ultimate authority and should assume all duties provided for in the rules of wrestling.

b) Mat chairmen coordinate the work of the referees and the judges.

c) Mat chairmen should attentively observe the bout taking place without being distracted in any way and assess the comportment and work of the other officials, in accordance with the rules.

d) Mat chairmen may interrupt the bout and request reasons for the decisions of the referees and judges.

e) In cases of disagreement between referees and judges, the duty of the mat chairmen is to side with one or the other to determine the result, the number of points, or total victory. Mat chairmen cannot signal their score first.

f) In awarding a decision on points or by evident superiority, mat chairmen should take into account the notations recorded on the judge's bout sheet, where the various corrections and the scores for the bout involved were recorded after agreed upon by the officials. The chairmen can check the correctness of any notations using their own bout sheet.

g) In general, mat chairmen should live up to the technical competence and particulars set forth in Chapter V of the rules for international officials.

h) Where mat chairmen determine that a decision by the referee or the judge does not correctly reflect what occurred, they must immediately stop the bout. After consulting with the judge and the referee they may, by majority vote (2 to 1), immediately correct the decision.

Article 26 SANCTIONS AGAINST OFFICIALS

In addition to the measures provided for in Chapter Three of the FILA disciplinary rules, FILA shall have the right, on the advice of the Officials Commission, to undertake the following measures against officials who have made technical mistakes: a) Warn them; b) Remove them from the tournament; c) Demote them to a lesser category; d) Temporarily suspend them; e) Permanently expel them.

PART FOUR—POINTS FOR MOVES AND HOLDS

Article 27 RECORDING POINTS

a) Judges should write down points scored by the wrestlers for moves and holds on a special bout sheet.

b) They should write them down as they go along each period.

Article 28 "GRAND TECHNIQUE" HOLDS (GRECO AND FREESTYLE)

a) Definition: A move or hold is considered to be a "grand technique" if the move or hold:

1) forces the opponents to completely lose contact with the ground,

2) controls the opponent,

3) results in the opponent traveling through the air in a curve of great amplitude or height, and

4) returns the opponent to the ground directly into a position of immediate danger (back exposure).

b) Scoring: A "grand technique" move or hold which brings the opponent to the mat in a position of direct and immediate danger, as described above, scores 4 points. If the "grand technique" move or hold does not bring the opponent to the mat in a position of direct and immediate danger, it will score only 2 points.

c) Remark: If wrestlers executing "grand technique" holds touch their own shoulders in the process, they will receive 4 points and their opponents will receive 2 points because of the instant fall that occurred during the execution of the hold. If the "grand technique" is initiated from the "parterre" position an additional bonus point (total 5) may be given.

Article 29 SCORES GIVEN TO TECHNICAL MOVES

a) 1 point:

1) For the wrestler who brings an opponent to the mat and goes behind them, in which position the attacking wrestler holds the opponent down and controls them (takedown) with 3 points of contact: two arms and one knee, or two knees and one arm.

2) For the wrestler who correctly completes a hold (takedown) for standing or on the ground which does not place the opponent in danger of a fall (no back contact).

3) For the wrestler who escapes and goes behind the opponent, holding them down and controlling them (reversal).

4) For the wrestler who forces an opponent back onto one or two extended arms with the back exposed to, but not touching the mat (danger).

5) For the wrestler whose hold is illegally blocked by an opponent.

6) For the wrestler whose opponent flees the mat.

b) 2 points:

(In principle, back exposure (danger) generally scores 2 points in ground wrestling.)

1) For the wrestler who correctly completes a hold on the ground and places the opponent in a position of danger (back touching the mat) or into an instant (touch) fall.

2) For the attacking wrestler who rolls an opponent across the shoulders.

3) For the attacking wrestler whose opponent flees a hold and leaves the wrestling area touching both shoulders to the mat.

4) For the attacked wrestler if the attacker lands on both shoulders (touch fall) or rolls across the shoulders while executing a hold.

5) For the attacked wrestler if the attacker is blocked with back in contact with the mat.

6) For the wrestler who executes a "grand technique" which does not directly and immediately touch the opponent's back to danger.

7) For the attacking wrestler if the opponent blocks the move with an illegal hold.

c) 3 Points:

1) For the wrestler who executes a standing throw of small amplitude which directly takes the opponent's back to danger.

2) 3 Point holds include those where the opponent is lifted from the mat, with a throw of small amplitude, even if the attacker has one or two knees on the mat, provided the attacked wrestler's back is immediately placed in danger.

d) 4 Points:

1) For the wrestler who completes a "grand technique" throw from standing which brings the opponent directly into a position of immediate danger.

e) 5 Points:

1) The same as a 4 Point throw initiated from the ground (parterre).

Article 30 EVALUATING MOVES AND HOLDS

In order to force wrestlers to undertake a greater variety of holds in ground wrestling, the following rules should be applied:

a) The attacking wrestler can only execute two consecutive gut wrenches or gut wrench variations.

b) The number of times the hold scores and not the number of points scored should be considered (a maximum of two consequent times).

c) After having scored at most two gut wrenches in a row, the attacking wrestler should undertake the execution of another technique worth two or more points before scoring again with gut wrench. If not or if there is no immediate action, the referee will stand the wrestlers up.

d) The attacking wrestler subsequently attempts additional gut wrenches, under the same conditions as outlined above, as many times as desired.

e) Where the holds being used by the two wrestlers change from one position to another, points should be given for each separate hold.

f) The referees will score the points. If the judges agree, they should raise their paddles (if they disagree, the mat chairman should intervene to decide the points).

g) A move scores at the end of the period if it was begun before the bell. A counterattack by the wrestler underneath will not score if it takes place after the bell.

h) When a total victory occurs at the moment the bout ends, the bell (and not the referee's whistle) is determinative.

i) If there is a difference of opinion concerning the points scored for a move and all three officials disagree, the mat chairman will decide the points to be scored.

Article 31 DECISIONS AND VOTING

a) Referees signal the score by raising their arms in a well-defined manner. If the referee and the judge agree, the points are scored.

b) Where there is disagreement and a vote of the officials is required, the judge and the mat chairman should show their scores with paddles. There should be fifteen paddles per set in GRECO and FREESTYLE painted different colors (blue, red, and white) as follows: (Two sets per mat)

-one white

-seven red, six of which should be numbered 1, 2, 3 and 5 to indicate points scored, and one blank, to be used for warnings to get the attention of the wrestler concerned.

-seven blue, six of which should be marked like the red ones and one blank.

The paddles should be placed within reach of those using them. Judges and mat chairman cannot abstain from voting and should give their vote clearly, leaving no room for doubt. In general, the score is determined by the judge and the referee. Where there is a disagreement, the score is decided by the mat chairman. This tie-breaking vote should be decided between the contradictory scores given by the judge and the referee. This requires the mat chairman to choose one or the other of the scores already given.

c) If the bout goes to the end of the time allowed, the bout sheets of the judge and the mat chairman are used to determine the winner. If there is a difference of one or more points between the wrestlers, as shown on the bout sheets, the wrestler with the greater number of points will be the winner. If there is no difference in points on the bout sheets (tie bout), a sudden death overtime period is employed to determine a winner.

Article 32 DECISION TABLE

a) If a vote on the score by the officials concerns a single wrestler, the only paddle that can be raised is the one that is the same color as the wrestler concerned, provided the final decision favors that wrestler. If the decision is against, the white paddle. Mat chairmen signal their votes only when the judge and the referee disagree.

b) If a vote on the score by the officials concerns both wrestlers, any of the three colored paddles can be used, red, blue, or white. Only the red and the blue paddles can decide the score. If the judge and referee disagree, the mat chairman will decide the score, except where it consists of elimination or disqualification, which can only be decided by a majority vote of the officials, and the head official of the tournament or the head official representative. Unanimity is not required, but the majority (3-1) must include the mat chairman and the head official.

DECISION TABLE

Scoring Points

Points scored by judges and referee as shown in each case set forth below will result in the final official decision indicated in the chart. (R = red wrestler, B = blue wrestler, 0 = zero points.)

Vote of the:

Referee	Judge	Mat Chairman	Official Result	Remarks
1. R	1. R	—	1. R	In these examples,
2. B	2. B	—	2. B	the judges and
3. R	3. R	—	3. R	referees agreed
4. R	4. R	—	4. R	and the mat
				chairman did not
				intervene
1. R	0	0	0	In these examples,
1. B	1. R	1. R	1. R	the judges and
2. R	1. R	2. R	2. R	the referees dis-
2. B	0	2. B	2. B	agreed on points
2. R	2. B	0	0	scored. The mat
3. R	2. R	2. R	2. R	chairman intervened
3. B	0	3. B	3. B	and the result was
3. R	3. B	0	0	determined by
4. B	2. B	4. B	4. B	majority vote

PART FIVE—THE BOUTS

Article 33 THE CALL TO THE MAT

a) Competitors should be called to the mat in a loud, clear voice.

b) Competitors who do not show up after their names are called will be considered beaten and eliminated from the tournament.

c) However, a delay up to three minutes will be permitted to wrestlers who have acceptable excuses, but only for their first bout in the first round.

d) Beginning with the second round, competitors will be called three times, 30 seconds apart. If the wrestler called does not show up, that wrestler is disqualified, excluded from the tournament and not ranked.

e) Calls to the mat will be made in French and English.

Note: In AAU competition, calls to the mat in French are optional.

Article 34 STARTING THE BOUT

a) When their names are called for bouts, wrestlers should go to the positions assigned to them in their respective corners which are the same as the color assigned to them for their uniforms.

b) The referee in the circle at the middle of the mat will call the two wrestlers to the center, shake their hands, inspect their uniforms, check that they are not covered with any greasy or sticky material, that they are not sweating, that their hands are bare, that their fingernails are cut short and that they have a handkerchief in their possession.

c) The wrestlers should greet one another, shake hands and, at the referee's order return to their respective corners.

d) On the whistle, wrestlers should approach each other and start wrestling immediately. They will not shake hands again until the end of the bout.

Note: In AAU competition, sight-disabled wrestlers should be allowed the option of a touch start in the standing position, where the outstretched fingers and palms of one hand are over and one under the opponent's outstretched fingers and palm, as is done in US High School and collegiate styles.

Article 35 STOPPING THE BOUT

a) The timekeeper will signal the end of the first period and the end of the bout with a bell.

Note: In AAU competition, any appropriate device may be used to signal the end of the period or bout.

b) The referee should then immediately blow the whistle. The mat chairman should intervene and stop the bout if the bell was not heard.

c) Moves begun at the sound of the whistle will not count. Moves undertaken between the bell and the whistle will not score.

d) At the end of the first period, the two wrestlers should return to their respective corners for one minute to rest. Before one minute is up, the referee will call the wrestlers to the middle of the mat to determine if the wrestlers have been dried off. They should make sure that the coaches and masseurs have left the mat five seconds before the bell sounds to resume the bout.

e) At the end of the one minute rest period, the bout will resume with both wrestlers standing, regardless of the position they were in at the end of the previous period.

Article 36 TIME-OUTS AND INJURY TIME

a) If competitors have to stop wrestling because of a nosebleed, fall to the head or for some other legitimate reason beyond their control, the referee can stop the bout for up to three minutes per bout as injury time.

Note: In AAU competition, equipment alterations and contact lens problems will also be treated as injury time situations.

Injury time-outs may be granted one or more times, but if a wrestler used up more than three minutes of injury time in a single match, the bout cannot continue. The wrestler involved will be declared beaten. The injured wrestler and the wrestler's coach should be advised, minute by minute, of the injury time elapsed.

b) Injury time cannot exceed a total of three minutes per match for any other injuries and each minute elapsed should be announced. The medical attendants will decide whether the bout can continue after three minutes have passed. Wrestlers can continue to compete in the tournament the following round, if they have not been eliminated and the FILA doctor does not disapprove.

c) Mat chairmen can interrupt bouts if there has been a serious mistake made by the judge or the referee. They should consult with the judge and the referee, settle any differences, and start the bout again.

d) Contestants cannot interrupt a bout themselves and send opponents back to the middle of the mat from the edge.

Article 37 END OF THE BOUT

a) The bout ends when a fall or technical superiority (15 points) is established, when one of the two wrestlers is eliminated or disqualified, when there is an injury, or when the time allowed for wrestling expires, as signaled by the bell and the referee's whistle.

b) Once the bout has ended, referees should return to the middle of the mat, and face the officials' table. The wrestlers should shake hands and stand beside the referee to await the decision.

c) As soon as the decision is announced, wrestlers should shake hands with the referee.

d) Each wrestler should then shake hands with the opposing coach. Wrestlers who fail to comply with these requirements should be sanctioned.

e) THE FOLLOWING RULES APPLY IN THE EVENT OF A TIE IN ANY MATCH IN THE REGULATION TIME:

1) Overtime (Prolongation)-tie match

2) This overtime shall take place immediately following regulation time with no intervening rest period.

3) The order to continue the bout into overtime shall be made by the mat chairman and the head official of the tournament, who may consult the bout officials at the end of regulation time.

4) The first "sudden death" point scored in overtime will stop the bout and determine the winner.

Article 38 THE REST PERIOD

a) During the one-minute rest between the periods, the competitor's coach and a masseur can come to the edge of the mat to coach and attend to the competitor, but they must leave the mat five seconds before the bell, in accordance with Article "35". They must be wearing warm-up uniforms.

b) During the one-minute rest period, wrestlers may, as they wish, remain standing in their corner or sit down on a small stool situated no more than 50 centimeters (20 inches) from the mat. During this time period, the wrestlers may receive instructions from their coach.

c) Timekeepers and mat chairmen may throw rubber squares onto the mat if the officials and the wrestlers do not notice that the bout has ended.

d) Referees must maintain control over the activities of the masseur and the coach, since it is strictly forbidden to give wrestlers any solid substances or drugs to help them recover their strength.

e) Coaches should use completely dry towels to wipe off their wrestlers.

f) Wrestlers are permitted to drink water or to rinse their mouths during the one-minute rest period, provided the water does not contain any stimulants. The sanctions provided for violating this rule are:

The wrestler should be declared beaten.

The wrestler should be disqualified from the competition.

g) The bell following the referee's signal indicates the beginning of the second period of the bout.

Article 39 COACHES

a) During the match, coaches can remain at the base of the platform or at a distance of at least four meters (13 feet) from the edge of the mat.

b) Coaches are forbidden from insulting the judges and referees or trying to influence the bout in any way, except for the coaching activity specifically authorized during the one-minute rest period and for assistance with the medical care provided by the doctor.

c) If these prohibitions are disregarded, referees are required to give the coach a "yellow" card (warning). If the coach continues, the referees should give the coach a "red" card (elimination).

d) From that moment on, the coach will be eliminated from the tournament and cannot be replaced, subject to the approval of the mat chairman.

Note: In AAU competition, the coaches are required to be in a team warm-up or civilian clothes. If an official acts as a coach his white uniform shirt must be covered so as to avoid the appearance of possible bias by having a referee in one corner.

Article 40 OUT-OF-BOUNDS

The rules for starting and stopping the bout are as follows:

1. STANDING WRESTLING

The bout should be stopped and resumed STANDING in the middle of the mat in the following cases:

if one foot touches the protection area,

if the move ends in the protection area,

if a move in the zone is not executed in a continuous manner,

if wrestlers in a tie up or in open stances enter the zone with three or four feet without executing the hold,

if the wrestlers completely leave the mat.

2. GROUND WRESTLING

a) The bout should be stopped and resumed STANDING, in the middle of the mat, in the following cases:

if the wrestling in the zone is not continuous (any pause without moves or holds),

if a hold begun on the ground ends on the protection area,

if a wrestler in danger (back exposed) slides from the mat to the protection area or if the shoulder or neck of the wrestler touches the protection area.

Ground wrestling is required when the bout is returned to the center only where the attacked wrestler is truly dominated by the opponent when the two go out of bounds, through the zone and onto the protection area. Otherwise, the wrestling should resume standing in the middle of the mat.

b) The bout should be stopped and resumed on the ground, in the middle of the mat, in the following cases:

A wrestler touches the protection area with the head while flat on his back, on the mat, under control.

The active wrestler requests ground wrestling following a caution for passivity on the opponent.

PART SIX—CLASSIFICATION POINTS FOLLOWING A BOUT

Article 41 POSITIVE POINT

a) A bout cannot end without any technical points being scored (except in the case of disqualification or injury).

b) WRESTLERS GIVEN A BYE EARN NO POSITIVE POINTS but they advance to the next round without running the risk of losing a bout.

c) When a wrestler is disqualified for having wrestled in a manner contrary to the conception of total and dynamic wrestling, in other words, without action or points, he will be awarded 0 positive points.

d) To determine the standings in the pools, the following positive points are given:

1) 4 points to the winner and 0 points to the loser in the case of: a) Fall; b) Technical superiority (15 point margin); c) Injury; d) Withdrawal; e) Forfeit; f) Failure to appear when called to wrestle; and g) Disqualification of the opponent for unsportsmanlike conduct.

2) 3.5 points for the winner and 0.5 points for the loser when the bout ends with a difference of 12 to 14 points between the wrestlers and the loser scored at least one technical point.

3) 3.5 points for the winner and 0 points for the loser when the bout ends with a difference of 12 to 14 points in favor of the winner and the loser scored no technical points.

4) 3 points for the winner and 1 point for the loser when the bout ends with a margin of 1 to 11 points and the loser scored at least one technical point.

5) 3 points for the winner and 0 points for the loser when the bout ends with a margin of 1 to 11 points and the loser scored no technical points.

Points in Cases of Elimination for Passivity

6) 3.5 points for the winner and 0 points for the loser if, at the time of elimination, there is a difference of 12 points or more between the wrestlers.

7) 3 points for the winner and 0 points for the loser if, at the time of elimination, the winner has scored technical points (less than 12).

8) 2 points for the winner and 0 points for the loser if, at the time of elimination, the winner has scored no technical points.

e) Points in Cases of Disqualification

1) 0 points when one or both of the wrestlers are disqualified for serious unsportsmanlike conduct and offenses against the rules.

2) In such cases, the wrestler or wrestlers will not place.

3) The positive points earned by wrestlers determine their standing.

4) If two wrestlers are eliminated in the same round with the same number of points, they will be ranked the same. However, if they wrestled, the wrestler who beat the other will be ranked higher.

5) The odd wrestler (with the bye) who cannot be paired for a round, will receive no positive points and the list for the round will indicate "bye".

Article 42 DECIDING THE WINNER WHEN POINTS ARE EQUAL (BREAKING THE TIE)

If two wrestlers have the same number of points at the end of regulation time, the winner will be determined by the first wrestler to score in an immediate sudden death overtime period.

Article 43 ELIMINATION

a) Wrestlers who are defeated twice are eliminated.

b) Wrestlers who suffer their second defeat, in the elimination rounds, in a round robin final of their pool will not be eliminated. They must wrestle against the remaining wrestler whom they have not met.

c) If, after their second defeat, in the elimination rounds, it is necessary to list them to be able to rank the top three in their pool, they will automatically occupy third place.

d) If two wrestlers with the same number of points qualify for this third place, the result of the bout between them will determine who is ranked third. If there was no such bout, it must automatically take place.

e) The round in which wrestlers are eliminated should be indicated on the pairing sheet, as well as on the charts. Competitors eliminated in the same round will be considered as having gone out at the same time and will be ranked according to the positive points they acquired.

1) Wrestlers who do not show up for the weigh-in or fail to appear to wrestle when their names are called will be disqualified and not ranked, unless they have a medical excuse or some notice from the official Secretariat, as required by the rules.

2) Wrestlers who fail to make weight are eliminated and not ranked. (See Article 18 of these rules.)

Article 44 DANGER-BACK EXPOSURE

Wrestlers are considered to be in a "position of danger" whenever the line of their back (or the line of their shoulders) faces the mat vertically or parallel, forming an angle of less than 90 degrees, and accordingly, they resist the "fall" with the upper part of their bodies. (See the definition of "fall" in the next article.) Wrestlers may resist with their heads, elbows, or shoulders. A position of danger (back exposure) exists whenever:

a) The defense wrestler bridges to avoid a fall.

b) The defense wrestler is pressed against one or two elbows with back exposed while attempting to avoid touching the shoulders.

c) The wrestler has one shoulder in contact with the mat and breaks the vertical line of 90 degrees with the other shoulder (forming an acute angle) less than 90 degrees.

d) The wrestler is in instant or touch fall position, in other words, two shoulders touching for less than a second.

e) The wrestler rolls across both shoulders.

f) The wrestler escapes from an opponent's hold and then exposes the back.

Back exposure ("danger") ceases as soon as the wrestler breaks the vertical line of 90 degrees, with the chest and stomach turned towards the mat.

Article 45 THE FALL

a) A "Fall" (touch) occurs when one wrestler is held by the opponent with both shoulders touching the mat long enough to allow the referee to ascertain the total control needed for a pin (see Article 23f). For a fall to be recognized at the edge of the mat, both of the competitor's shoulders must touch the mat (as stated above). The head cannot be touching the protection surface.

b) If wrestlers touch both shoulders as a result of their own breach of the rules or else their own illegal hold, the fall will count.

c) A fall called by the referee will be deemed valid if the judge confirms. If the referee does not call the fall when it should have been, it can still be declared by the judge and mat chairman if both agree.

d) In order for the fall to be determined and confirmed, it is important that it be clearly held. In other words, the two shoulders of the pinned wrestler must lie flat against the mat simultaneously for the short period of time described in the first paragraph of this article, even in the case of a backward fall achieved by a standing rear body lock and lift. The referee should never slap the mat until after the judge confirms or, if the judge does not, the mat chairman. The referee should then whistle.

Article 46 TECHNICAL SUPERIORITY

a) Aside from falls elimination or disqualification, the bout should be stopped before the end of regulation time if there is a difference of 15 points between the wrestlers.

b) The match may not be stopped to pronounce technical superiority before the action is completed (attack and immediate counterattack).

c) The mat chairman will signal the referee when a difference of 15 points occurs. After confirmation by the other officials, the referee will declare the winner.

Article 47 ELIMINATION AND DISQUALIFICATION

A. ELIMINATION

a) The fundamental principle behind any wrestling match is that it cannot end without a technical point being scored.

b) In principle, elimination for passivity should only be applied to one wrestler.

c) In exceptional cases where it is impossible to determine which of the two wrestlers is the more active, both wrestlers can be eliminated only with the concurrence of the head official of the tournament.

Note: In cases of elimination for passivity, positive points will be awarded as specified in Article ''41''. The eliminated wrestler may continue in the tournament if the elimination for passivity is the wrestler's first defeat. If the elimination involves the second defeat, the wrestler will be eliminated from the competition and placed according to positive points earned.

B. DISQUALIFICATION

a) Wrestlers who commit an obvious breach of ''fair play'' or of the spirit and conception of FILA's total, dynamic wrestling, in a situation clearly involving cheating or the intentional execution of an illegal hold causing serious injury to the opponent, will be immediately disqualified from the tournament by majority vote of the officials and with the concurrence of the head official or his representative.

b) The wrestlers will then place according to where they stood at the time of their disqualification.

c) Wrestlers disqualified for serious fouls (brutality) will be disqualified from the tournament and will not place. Such a ruling requires unanimous consent of the officials.

PART SEVEN—PROHIBITIONS AND ILLEGAL HOLDS

Article 48 GENERAL PROHIBITIONS

a) It is forbidden to pull hair, ears, or genitals, to pinch skin, to bite, to twist fingers or toes, etc.

b) In general, it is forbidden to undertake any move, gesture or hold which is intended to hurt opponents or put them in pain so as to make them quit.

c) It is equally forbidden:

To punch, kick, butt with the head, strangle, push, apply holds that may endanger the lives of opponents, to fracture or dislocate arms and legs, walk on the feet of opponents, or touch their faces between the eyebrows and line of the mouth.

It is more strictly forbidden:

-to force elbows or knees into the chest or stomach of opponents,

-to do any twisting capable of hurting,

-to hold opponents by the trunks,

-to cling to or grab the mat,

-for contestants to speak to each other during the bout,

-to grab the sole of the opponent's foot (only holds above the foot and heel are permitted).

Article 49 ILLEGAL HOLDS

a) The following holds or moves are illegal and strictly forbidden: a) throat holds; b) bending arms behind the back (wrestling arm bar) more than 90 degrees; c) gathering arms from above by the forearm; d) headlock on the neck only with both hands; e) double headlock (full nelson) unless executed from the side without using legs on any part of the opponent's body; f) bringing the opponent's arm behind the back from above and applying pressure to it in a position where the forearm and upper arm form an angle less than 90 degrees (chicken wing); g) holds stretching the backbone of the opponent; and h) holds with a headlock on the head alone (with arms and hands locked).

b) In standing holds carried out from behind, where the opponent is turned upside down (reverse waist lock), the throw should only be executed to the side, and absolutely not downward from above (spike). In FREESTYLE and GRECO, some part of the body other than the feet of the wrestler executing the above must touch the mat before the upper part of the attacked wrestler's body.

c) The opponent's head or neck by itself can only be held with one arm when executing a hold.

d) Finally, it is forbidden to lift an opponent who is bridging and then throw them back to the mat (forceful Slam). In other words, a bridge can only be compressed.

e) In addition, it is forbidden to drive forward on a bridge in the direction of the head.

f) In general, if an attacking wrestler violates a rule at any point during the execution of a hold, from the beginning to the end, the hold in question is completely voided and the attacker penalized.

g) Points awarded for illegal holds:

Illegal holds (which do not adversely affect any move) 1 point.

Illegal holds (which do adversely affect a move) 2 points.

Article 50 SPECIAL PROHIBITIONS

a) In GRECO-ROMAN wrestling, the opponent may not be grabbed below the hips nor clenched with legs.

1) Any push, press or "lift" by leg contact with a part of the opponent's body is prohibited.

2) In GRECO-ROMAN wrestling, the opponent must be accompanied to the mat, but this is not required in FREESTYLE wrestling.

b) In FREESTYLE, leg scissors with locked legs, on the neck or the body, are forbidden (but they are permitted on limbs, arms, legs).

c) In FREESTYLE wrestling, scissor locks with crossed feet on the head, neck or body are forbidden (but they are permitted on arms and legs). However, leg trips, foot sweeps or leg sweeps are permitted.

Article 51 CONSEQUENCES

a) If the wrestler applying an illegal hold is disadvantaged as a result of the hold, the bout should continue without interruption until the action ends. The wrestler at fault will receive a caution and the opponent will receive one point additional to the points scored.

b) Any advantage gained by a wrestler from an illegal hold should be voided, even if the hold was released. The wrestler at fault will receive a caution and the opponent will receive one point.

c) Violations should be stopped by the referee without breaking the hold, if possible. Where the opponent is put in danger, the referee should allow the hold to continue and see what develops. After that, the referee is free to act, in other words accept the hold or void it and caution the wrestler at fault.

d) If hold begins correctly and then becomes illegal, points should be awarded up to the point where the hold became illegal.

e) For good cause, in cases of willful head butting or any other type of brutality, the wrestler at fault can be disqualified, according to the gravity of the case.

f) A wrestler who keeps an opponent from developing a hold by means of an illegal hold should be cautioned and the opponent given one or two points (see Article 49).

g) The wrestler at fault should be given a caution.

h) The duty of the referee towards the competitor committing an infraction involves the following procedure: a) stop the infraction; b) break the hold, if dangerous; c) give a caution; d) declare the wrestler at fault, beaten or disqualified; and e) award points (1 or 2 points).

PART EIGHT—PASSIVITY

Article 52 DEFINITION

a) In general, an attitude of one or both wrestlers which is contrary to the goals of total, dynamic universal wrestling, standing or on the ground, is considered passivity.

-not undertaking proper holds,

-being satisfied with efforts aimed at neutralizing the opponent,

-not giving the impression of genuinely attempting holds,

-continually obstructing the opponent's holds,

-voluntarily fleeing the mat, from standing or on the ground,

-continually lying flat on the chest in a closed position,

-wrapping both legs around one leg of the opponent and lying flat without attacking,

-pushing the opponent off the mat,

-pushing the opponent in the center of the mat,

-voluntarily placing oneself down on the mat.

b) Passivity and fleeing the mat will be treated in the following manner:

1) As soon as one wrestler leaves the mat, the referee should stop the bout by whistling, which stops the clock. As soon as the referee starts the bout again, also by whistling, the clock should start.

2) Cases of fleeing the mat should be penalized throughout the bout, from the first to the last minute, with a warning to the wrestler at fault. Actions aimed at avoiding wrestling are considered fleeing the mat. Cautions shall also be given against wrestlers pushing their opponents off the mat. The referee should be sure that the wrestler in question voluntarily left the mat and was not pushed by the opponent.

3) A caution should be given against the wrestler at fault after the first incident of fleeing the mat, standing or on the ground.

Article 53 FIGHTING PASSIVITY (STALLING)

a) Whenever the wrestler acts in a manner contrary to the FILA conception of total, dynamic wrestling. The referee, with the agreement of the judge or mat chairman, should stop the bout and caution the wrestler at fault, in order to fight against passivity (stalling).

b) The caution should be noted on the bout sheet of the judge and the mat chairman with a circle (O) as a reminder.

c) As soon as the officials agree (2/3) to give a caution, whatever the reason may be (passivity, fleeing the mat or illegal hold), the referee must stop the bout.

d) After the bout is stopped, the wrestlers should be brought back to the center of the mat, on either side of the referee. The referee should indicate with open hand, pointing up or down, that the wrestler not at fault may choose the starting position of the opponent (standing or on the ground). Wrestlers with the choice of position should immediately indicate their preference to the referee and the bout will resume in accordance with that stated preference.

e) The choice of position is given to the wrestler not at fault following the first and second warning.

Note: The rules requiring ground wrestling when a dominated wrestler goes out of bounds under control should be applied as often as required.

f) Whenever wrestling takes place on the ground, the referee should allow as much time as necessary to undertake and execute a hold and never interrupt a hold in progress.

g) The referee should use the standard vocabulary when cautioning a passive wrestler.

h) The referee should clearly indicate the wrestler at fault and indicate the nature of the infraction. Example: Red: Action; Blue: Contact; Red: Open.

i) When the referees want to signal passivity to the judge or mat chairman, they should do so using the arm with the sleeve that has the same color as the wrestler at fault, clearly indicating the reason why he feels there is passivity. Example: Red: Passive; or Blue: Passive. If the judge or referee confirms, the referee should stop the bout.

Article 54 CHOOSING GROUND WRESTLING

When ground wrestling has been chosen following a caution for passivity, wrestling will resume on the referee's whistle after the wrestlers have assumed the regulation "parterre" position on the ground, defined as follows:

a) Position:

1) The competitor on bottom must kneel and place both hands on the mat, hands and elbows apart 20 centimeters (8 inches) from the knees. Arms should be straight and feet not crossed.

b) Contact:

1) The wrestlers on top may start in any position they choose, after first making contact with the opponent by placing both hands parallel, flat on the opponent's back.

2) After checking and approving the position of the wrestlers, the referee will whistle to start the match.

3) At that point, the wrestler on top can attack the opponent. The wrestler on bottom is free to move from the starting position and can also attack or defend against the wrestler on top, as well as stand up.

4) If one of the wrestlers is taken down in the course of the bout, wrestling will continue on the ground. The bottom wrestler can defend against the attacks of the opponent or stand up.

5) A wrestler who takes an opponent to the mat must be aggressive. If the wrestler is passive in that situation, the referee can order the wrestlers back up and start the bout again standing. The passive wrestler will be given a caution.

6) The wrestler on top cannot start wrestling by jumping on the opponent. If the wrestler does, the referee should reprimand that wrestler and stand the down wrestler up.

7) The bottom wrestler does not have the right to interrupt the bout or to demand that wrestling be resumed standing.

8) If the bottom wrestler leaves the mat as the result of some move and is not controlled by the opponent, wrestling will resume standing.

Article 55 CAUTIONS AND PENALTIES

A. BASIC RULE

a) A caution for passivity does not result in technical points. By contrast, a caution for fleeing the mat and fleeing a hold will always result in awarding 1 or 2 technical points.

b) Cautions for illegal holds which do not interfere with the development of the action are penalized 1 point. By contrast, if they interfere with the development of the action, they are penalized 2 points.

c) The referee can make remarks to the wrestler at fault without confirmation from the judge or mat chairman. In GRECO and FREESTYLE, the choice of ground wrestling may be given to the above wrestler only with confirmation.

d) The mat chairman should decide between the referee and the judge in case of disagreement.

e) Stimulation of wrestling is the sole responsibility of the referee, who may do so as often as deemed necessary to compel moves or modify incorrect positions.

f) They may also insist on genuine wrestling at all times and intervene in the bout to comment on ineffective attempts.

g) They should distinguish between a wrestler who is being dominated and one who is passive.

h) A wrestler who is being dominated should not be disqualified.

B. LOOKING FOR AND APPLYING PENALTIES

a) It is important to observe and determine which of the two competitors is wrestling openly and which one is seeking to avoid wrestling, especially when no action is being undertaken by either wrestler.

b) This is all the more important in the final moments of the bout. Once the officials agree (2/3) that there is passivity, the referee must stop the bout, indicate the nature of the passivity to the wrestler at fault, and apply the procedure for choosing ground wrestling.

c) If the wrestler continues to be passive, the referee should stop the bout after confirmation, again indicate to the passive wrestler the nature of the passivity and especially note that this caution is the last before disqualification. In GRECO and FREESTYLE, the referee should then apply the procedure set forth in paragraph 2 of the section on choosing ground wrestling.

C. ELIMINATION FOR PASSIVITY

a) In wrestling, like all sports, athletes must take risks throughout the event.

b) A wrestler who continues to be passive or who executes an illegal hold after the second caution will be eliminated from the bout by majority vote of the officials, with the concurrence of the head official of the tournament.

c) Passivity also exists in ground wrestling. For this reason, the referee should insist that the wrestler on top, in a position of superiority, be active.

d) If wrestlers on top do not respond to the demands of the referee, the passivity procedures should be applied against them.

Note: In principle, only one wrestler should be eliminated for passivity. The positive points awarded in cases of passivity are indicated in the decision table chapter. To eliminate a wrestler for passivity, the following must agree: a) the mat chairman; b) the head official of the tournament or his designated representative; and c) the judge or the referee.

Article 56 THE PASSIVITY ZONE AND GROUND WRESTLING

A. GENERAL RULES

a) The passivity zone is designed to show which wrestler is passive, and to eliminate systematic wrestling at the end of the mat, including leaving the mat inadvertently.

b) All holds and moves begun in the central wrestling area and finished in the zone will score including back exposure (1, 2, 3, 4, 5 points), counterattacks, and fall.

c) Holds or counterattacks begun standing, in the central wrestling area of the mat (inside the passivity zone) will score, wherever they end up (wrestling area, passivity zone, or protection surface).

d) However, if they end in the protection surface, the wrestling will be stopped, the wrestlers returned to the center standing and points will be awarded (1, 2, 3, 4, 5 points).

e) In the case of a hold correctly begun on the mat which, due to great amplitude, finishes beyond the passivity zone in the protection surface, points will be awarded only for the value of the hold.

f) While executing a hold or move which began in the central wrestling area, wrestlers may enter the zone and, in a continuous motion, further develop the hold or move in any direction, provided there is no interruption in the execution (pushing-block-pull-scuffle).

g) A move or hold cannot be started standing in the passivity zone unless the wrestlers involved have only two feet in the zone. In such a case, the referee will allow the wrestlers to remain in the zone for a limited period of time awaiting the development of the hold.

h) Wrestlers can continue to develop their holds with 3 or 4 feet in the zone if they enter the zone in a continuous motion.

i) If the wrestlers stop their moves in the passivity zone and become inactive, or if they enter the zone with 2, 3, or 4 feet without any action, the referee should stop the bout and return the two wrestlers to the central wrestling area without applying the passivity procedure.

j) In all cases where one foot enters the protection surface while the wrestlers are standing, in other words beyond the passivity zone, the bout is automatically stopped.

k) The moment a wrestler puts one foot in the passivity zone, the referee should loudly call out "zone."

l) At this remark, the wrestlers themselves should return to the middle of the mat without necessarily stopping any wrestling in progress.

m) In ground wrestling, all holds or counterattacks effected at the edge or in the passivity zone are valid, even if they end on the protection surface.

n) The referee and judge should award points for all moves begun on the ground in the passivity zone and completed on the protection area, but the bout will be stopped and the wrestlers returned to the center of the mat standing.

o) In ground wrestling, attacking wrestlers can complete moves if, while executing the holds they go beyond the zone, provided the shoulders and the head of the opponent are still in the zone.

p) In such cases, even four legs can be off the mat.

B. CLARIFICATIONS AND DETAILS

a) Counterattacks on the protection surface are invalid. The passivity zone does not change the rules regarding penalties for passivity.

b) These rules should especially be applied:

c) When one wrestler enters and remains in the zone without effecting any moves.

d) When one wrestler pushes the opponent into the zone or keeps the opponent from returning to the central wrestling area.

e) When one wrestler pushes the opponent off the mat, onto the protection surface, etc.

C. FLEEING THE MAT AND FLEEING A HOLD

a) Whenever there is a case of fleeing the mat or fleeing a hold, standing or on the ground, a caution should be given immediately to the wrestler at fault.

b) The points shown below should be awarded to the attacking wrestler:

Fleeing the mat: 1 point + 1 caution

Fleeing a hold: 2 points + 1 caution

D. NATURE OF THE POINTS

All points awarded for an opponent's fleeing the mat, fleeing a hold, or applying an illegal hold are considered technical points.

PART NINE-PROTESTS AND MODIFICATIONS OF THE RULES

Article 57 WRITTEN PROTESTS

a) A written protest of any result involving an infraction of the rules of wrestling can be submitted to the President of the Officials Committee no later than 30 minutes after the bout.

b) The reason for the protest must be specified in one of the official languages of FILA.

c) The protest will be reviewed by the Jury of Appeals which will decide the matter.

Note: In AAU competition, all protests will be handled by a tournament committee as follows:

This committee will consist of:

1) the tournament director or his designee

2) chief official or his designee

3) chief pairing master or his designee

4) the chairman of the wrestling event being conducted or his designee

5) one at large member

e) Any three of the five can act on the protest. The protest filing procedure is as follows:

1) Protest must be of a technical (rule violation), not a judgment nature.

2) Protest must be submitted to the tournament technical committee within 30 minutes of the end of the bout in which the violation occurred.

3) Must have in writing the following:

(a) names of contesting athletes involved.

(b) mat number or identification thereof.

(c) names of any or all officials assigned to the bout in question.

(d) nature of protest (rule identification by code number if possible).

(e) desired settlement or adjustment.

4) Protest must have a $15.00 cash deposit for JO/Age group and $25.00 cash deposit for all others, which will be returned if the protest is denied. For all international competitions, FILA has set the protest fee at $25 for the younger age groups and $60 for the Espoir and Senior World divisions.

5) An unappealable final decision will be rendered by the tournament technical committee, as soon as possible, before the next round in that weight class can begin.

6) The match protest filing procedure and the names of those on the technical committee shall be posted with the pairings information at the start of the tournament.

7) All written materials pertaining to the protest, including the decision of the technical committee, shall be placed on file and recorded with the reports submitted to the National Officials Chairman.

Article 58 MODIFICATIONS AND UNFORESEEN ITEMS

Modifications of the preceding provisions deemed necessary for the improvement of the Technical Rules of Wrestling will be made only by the Executive Bureau, after consultation with the technical department. Such modifications will remain in force until the next congress, which will be called upon to consider them.

APPENDIX NO. 1

STANDARD VOCABULARY

All officials should know and apply the following vocabulary, which constitutes the official means of communication between them.

In addition, wrestlers should familiarize themselves with the use of this vocabulary.

1) START

Invitation to the wrestlers, standing at the corners of the mat to come to the center to be inspected and to shake hands, after which they will return to their respective corners and await the official's whistle which starts the bout.

2) TIME-OUT

The referee uses this expression to stop the clock when one wrestler stops wrestling, intentionally or as a result of injury, or for any other reason.

3) FAULT

Illegal hold or infraction of the technical rules.

4) ATTENTION DISQUALIFICATION OR ATTENTION ELIMINATION

The referee is putting the passive wrestler on notice before requesting disqualification or elimination.

5) DAWAI

The referee is encouraging the wrestlers to be more active.

6) CONSULTATION

The referee is consulting the judge, as necessary, before declaring a disqualification or making a decision of any other question.

7) REMARQUE

A referee's indication of passivity by one wrestler.

8) O.K.

The hold is valid (legal or correct). Used when the judge and the mat chairman are seated in a position where they cannot follow what happened on the opposite side of the mat. The referee should indicate with the arm whether a hold at the edge of the mat was inside or out of bounds.

9) OUT

The hold was out-of-bounds.

10) NO

Word used to indicate an invalid move which should be voided.

11) PLACE

Pronounced while slapping the mat with one hand to remind the wrestlers not to leave the mat.

12) DANGER

Put in danger.

13) TOTALE

Used to indicate that a wrestler has been beaten by total victory.

14) CONTINUER

Order given by the referee to resume wrestling. The referee also uses this word to continue wrestling if the wrestlers stop out of confusion and look as if they need an explanation. The same word is used each time the wrestlers stop for whatever reasons, while standing or on the ground.

15) CENTRE

Wrestlers should return to the center of the mat and resume wrestling.

16) UP

The bout will continue standing.

17) INTERVENTION

The judge, referee or mat chairman request intervention.

18) SALUS

Wrestlers should shake hands.

19) ZONE

Word loudly called out when wrestlers enter the passivity zone.

20) VICTORY

The referee declares the winner.

21) STOP

Used to stop the bout.

22) DEFAITE

The opponent is beaten.

23) DISQUALIFICATION

Disqualification is pronounced following an infraction.

24) ELIMINATION

Elimination of one or both passive wrestlers.

25) GONG

The sound of the gong indicates the beginning and end of the periods of a bout.

26) CHRONOMETRE

The timekeeper, by this order of the referee, stops or starts the clock.

27) JURY

The three officials.

28) ARBITRE

The official (referee) who runs the match.

29) JUDGE

An official who has passed a referee-judge's test, who assists the referee, and who records the points of the wrestlers during the bout. The judge should note, on the bout sheet, all moves successfully completed in the bout.

30) PROTEST

A protest of any type of decision.

31) PASSIF

Remark made to a wrestler who is too passive.

32) DOCTEUR

The official doctor of the bout.

33) CLINIC

A technical teaching clinic.

34) DECLARE BATTU

Decision taken at the end of a defeat by evident superiority.

35) OPEN

The wrestler should wrestle more openly.

36) ACTION

The wrestler should develop the hold undertaken.

37) CONTACT

Wrestlers should make contact.

GOVERNING BODY

Amateur Athletic Union, 3400 West 86th St., P.O. Box 68207, Indianapolis, IN 46268

The Amateur Athletic Union (AAU) is the largest nonprofit volunteer organization in the United States dedicated solely to the promotion and development of amateur sports and physical fitness programs. The AAU is the only sports organization in the country that provides a multisport program for all age groups.

The AAU sponsors and administers the AAU/USA Junior Olympics program consisting of some 20 Olympic sports and several age classifications. Youth (ages 8 to 18) are given the opportunity to compete regardless of skill, experience, or formal training. The AAU conducts the AAU/USA Junior Olympic Games, the largest annual multisport competition in the nation.

Additional programs sponsored or administered by the AAU are: a) AAU Senior Sports; b) Presidential Sports Award; c) Chrysler Fund/AAU Physical Fitness Program; d) AAU/James E. Sullivan Memorial Award; and e) AAU/Milky Way Bar All-American Award.

MAGAZINES

USA Wrestler, USA Wrestling, 405 West Hall of Fame, Stillwater, OK 74075

APPENDIX A

□

ORGANIZATIONS CONCERNED
WITH SPORTS FOR THE HANDICAPPED

American Alliance for Health, Physical Education, Recreation and Dance
1900 Association Dr.
Reston, VA 22091

American Athletic Association for the Deaf
10604 E. 95th St. Terrace
Kansas City, MO 64134

American Blind Bowling Association
3500 Terry Dr.
Norfolk, VA 23518

American Blind Skiing Foundation
610 S. William St.
Mt. Prospect, IL 60056

American Sailing Foundation
c/o American Sailing Association
13922 Marquesas Way
Marina Del Ray, CA 90292

American Wheelchair Bowling Association
N 54 W15858 Larkspur Ln.
Menomonee Falls, WI 53051

Amputee Sports Association
P.O. Box 60129
Savannah, GA 31420

Blind Outdoor Leisure Development
533 E. Main St.
Aspen, CO 81611

Blind Sports
1939 16th Ave.
San Francisco, CA 94116

Handicapped Scuba Association
1104 El Prado
San Clemente, CA 92672

International Foundation of Wheelchair Tennis
Peter Burdwah International
2203 Timberlock Place
The Woodlands, TX 77380

International Sports Organization for the Blind
Butler University
Indianapolis, IN 46208

International Wheelchair Road Racers Club
165 78th Ave. N.E.
St. Petersburg, FL 33702

National Amputee Golf Association
P.O. Box 1228
Amherst, NH 03031

National Association for Disabled Athletes
17 Lindley Ave.
Tenafly, NJ 07670

National Association of Sports for Cerebral Palsy
1522 K St. NW, Suite 1112
Washington, DC 20005

National Center for Therapeutic Riding
P.O. Box 42501
Washington, DC 20015

National Deaf Bowling Association
9244 E. Mansfield Ave.
Denver, CO 80237

National Deaf Women's Bowling Association
Meadow Lark Lane
Ervin, SD 57233

National Foundation of Wheelchair Tennis
15441 Red Hill Ave., Suite A
Tustin, CA 92680

National Handicapped Sports and Recreation Association
P.O. Box 33141, Farragut Station
Washington, DC 20033

National Wheelchair Athletic Association
3617 Betty Drive, Suite S
Colorado Springs, CO 80907

National Wheelchair Basketball Association
110 Seaton Building
University of Kentucky
Lexington, KY 40506

National Wheelchair Softball Association
P.O. Box 22478
Minneapolis, MN 55422

New York Road Runners Club
9 E. 89th St.
New York, NY 10128

North American Riding for the Handicapped Association
111 E. Wacker Dr.
Chicago, IL 60601

Ski for Light
1455 W. Lake St.
Minneapolis, MN 55408

Special Olympics
1350 New York Ave. NW, Suite 500
Washington, DC 20005

Tennis Association for Mentally Retarded
22704 Ventura Blvd., Suite 121
Woodland Hills, CA 91364

U.S. Amputee Athletic Association
Suite 149-A, Belle Forest Circle
Nashville, TN 37221

U.S. Association for Blind Athletes
55 W. California Ave.
Beach Haven Park, NJ 08008

United States Deaf Skiers Association
5053 Kenmore Dr.
Concord, CA 94521

APPENDIX B

□

ADDITIONAL RULES SOURCES

Sport	Source
Biathlon	U.S. Biathlon Association P.O. Box 5515 Essex Junction, VT 05453
Bobsled	U.S. Bobsled Association P.O. Box 828 Lake Placid, NY 12946
Duckpin bowling	National Duckpin Bowling Congress Fairview Ave. Baltimore-Linthicum, MD 21090
Equestrian	American Horse Shows Association 220 E. 42nd St., Rm. 409 New York, NY 10017-5806
	U.S. Equestrian Team c/o Bill Landsman/Associates 17 E. 45th St. New York, NY 10017
Figure skating	U.S. Figure Skating Association 20 First St. Colorado Springs, CO 80906
Gymnastics	U.S. Gymnastics Federation 1099 N. Meridian St., Suite 380 Indianapolis, IN 46204
	National Collegiate Athletic Association P.O. Box 1906 Mission, KS 66201
	National Federation of State High School Associations P.O. Box 20626 Kansas City, MO 64195
Judo	United States Judo Association 19 N. Union Blvd. Colorado Springs, CO 80909
	United States Judo Federation 2530 Taraval St. San Francisco, CA 94116
Karate	American Amateur Karate Federation 1930 Wilshire Blvd., Suite 1208 Los Angeles, CA 90057
	The USA Karate Federation 1300 Kenmore Blvd. Akron, OH 44314

Lacrosse (men)	National Collegiate Athletic Association P.O. Box 1906 Mission, KS 66201
(women)	United States Women's Lacrosse Association 20 E. Sunset Ave. Philadelphia, PA 19118
Luge	U.S. Luge Association P.O. Box 651 Lake Placid, NY 12946
Pentathlon	U.S. Modern Pentathlon Association, Inc. P.O. Box 8178 San Antonio, TX 78208
Polo	United States Polo Association 120 N. Mill St. Lexington, KY 40507
Roller skating	U.S. Amateur Confederation of Roller Skating P.O. Box 83067 Lincoln, NE 68501
Roque	American Roque League P.O. Box 261 Lapaz, IN 46537
Rowing	U.S. Rowing Association 251 N. Illinois St., Suite 980 Indianapolis, IN 46204
Rugby	Northern California Rugby Football Union Referee Society 67 Water St. San Francisco, CA 94133
Shooting	National Rifle Association 1600 Rhode Island Ave. NW Washington, DC 20036 (Rule books available: Smallbore Rifle, Highpower Rifle, Pistol, Action Pistol Shooting, Police Pistol Combat, Silhouette Pistol, International Rifle, International Pistol, International Shotgun, NRA Position Air Rifle)
Skeet shooting	National Skeet Shooting Association P.O. Box 68007 San Antonio, TX 78268
Snowshoeing	United States Snowshoe Association P.O. Box 170 Corinth, NY 12822
Synchronized swimming	U.S. Synchronized Swimming, Inc. 901 W. New York St. Indianapolis, IN 46223
Triathlon	Federation International Triathlon 2235 Encinitas Blvd. Encinitas, CA 92024 Triathlon Federation/USA P.O. Box 1963 Davis, CA 95617

Yachting (sailing)   U.S. Yacht Racing Union
                              P.O. Box 209
                              Newport, RI 02840

                              Inter-Collegiate Yacht Racing Association of North America
                              8893 Melinda Ct.
                              Milan, MI 48160

OLYMPOS

OLYMPOS

DAN SIMMONS

An Imprint of **HarperCollins***Publishers*

Sim

OLYMPOS. Copyright © 2005 by Dan Simmons. All rights reserved. Printed in the United States of America. No part of this book may be used or reproduced in any manner whatsoever without written permission except in the case of brief quotations embodied in critical articles and reviews. For information address HarperCollins Publishers, 10 East 53rd Street, New York, NY 10022.

HarperCollins books may be purchased for educational, business, or sales promotional use. For information please write: Special Markets Department, HarperCollins Publishers, 10 East 53rd Street, New York, NY 10022.

FIRST EDITION

Printed on acid-free paper

Library of Congress Cataloging-in-Publication Data

Simmons, Dan.
  Olympos / Dan Simmons.—1st ed.
    p. cm.
  ISBN 0-380-97894-6 (hardcover)
  1. Mars (Planet)—Fiction. 2. Imaginary wars and battles—Fiction.
3. Mythology, Greek—Fiction. 4. Gods, Greek—Fiction. I. Title.

PS3569.I47292O49 2005
813'.54—dc22   2005040024

05 06 07 08 09 JTC/QW 10 9 8 7 6 5 4 3 2 1